SAVARKAR AND THE MAKING OF HINDUTVA

Savarkar and the Making of Hindutva

JANAKI BAKHLE

PRINCETON UNIVERSITY PRESS
PRINCETON & OXFORD

Published by Princeton University Press
41 William Street, Princeton, New Jersey 08540
99 Banbury Road, Oxford OX2 6JX

press.princeton.edu

Library of Congress Cataloging-in-Publication Data

Names: Bakhle, Janaki, 1962– author.
Title: Savarkar and the making of Hindutva / Janaki Bakhle.
Description: Princeton : Princeton University Press, 2024. | Includes bibliographical references and index.
Identifiers: LCCN 2023030306 (print) | LCCN 2023030307 (ebook) | ISBN 9780691250366 (hardback) | ISBN 9780691251486 (ebook)
Subjects: LCSH: Savarkar, Vinayak Damodar, 1883–1966. | Nationalists—India—Biography. | Revolutionaries—India—Biography. | Intellectuals—India—Biography. | Hindutva. | Authors, Marathi—20th century—Biography. | BISAC: BIOGRAPHY & AUTOBIOGRAPHY / Political | RELIGION / Islam / History
Classification: LCC DS481.S36 B33 2024 (print) | LCC DS481.S36 (ebook) | DDC 320.540954092 [B]—dc23/eng/20230719
LC record available at https://lccn.loc.gov/2023030306
LC ebook record available at https://lccn.loc.gov/2023030307

British Library Cataloging-in-Publication Data is available

Editorial: Priya Nelson, Morgan Spehar, and Emma Wagh
Production Editorial: Natalie Baan
Jacket Design: Haley Chung
Production: Danielle Amatucci
Publicity: William Pagdatoon
Copyeditor: Kenny Hoffman

This book has been composed in Arno

Printed on acid-free paper. ∞

Printed in the United States of America

10 9 8 7 6 5 4 3 2 1

For Nick

CONTENTS

ACKNOWLEDGMENTS

THIS BOOK has been far too long in the making. Soon after finishing my first book *Two Men and Music*, two other men, Nick Dirks (husband) and Partha Chatterjee (former advisor) suggested that I write a *quick* book on Savarkar, because I read Marathi, and because I had punted on a question that I raised but didn't fully answer in *Two Men*. I did not expect that this book would take as long as it has. It is done, but it has not been quick, and the debts I have accumulated over the years of writing it, rewriting it, conducting research, arguing with fellow scholars about it, and changing my argument have been many.

Val Daniel has read many iterations of all chapters, and with each reading he has improved my prose, shown me how to read poetry and how not to dismiss the "poetic" as a form of historical writing. Partha Chatterjee read the manuscript literally as soon as I asked him, line-edited it, and gave me the kind of feedback I knew I would get from him—tough, skeptical, challenging—and all of it forced me to fine tune my argument and alter my rhetoric. Manan Ahmad did the same, commenting on everything from stylistic issues to substantive ones. While on sabbatical, he looked at second and third drafts of this manuscript, and helped me rewrite catalog copy. Abhishek Kaicker has been a colleague and champion, believing in this project and encouraging me when I no longer wanted to read anything ever again about or by Savarkar. He too has read the manuscript twice and commented on it with his characteristic incandescent intellect. Val, Partha, Manan, and Abhishek—I hope you will see your suggestions and criticisms addressed in this final version; the book is so much better for your careful reading.

Roger Grant, who I met while we were both at the Stanford Humanities Institute, has been the most generous of readers as well as an intellectual comrade. In addition to reading everything, from a chapter to the entire manuscript in rough draft, all on a subject he knew little about, he has also lent me his shoulder and helped me through some very tough times.

Prachi Deshpande gave me detailed feedback in the midst of correcting her own page proofs, for which I owe her a huge debt of gratitude. Polly O'Hanlon read every word in the manuscript with care, and I hope will see all the places in the manuscript where I have made changes as she advised. Thomas Hansen has been an early and constant supporter of this project, and I am very thankful to him for his encouraging and helpful feedback and for pushing me to note my own stakes in this project. Christian Novetzke too read very early and very rough drafts and has given generously of his time to help me shape a mammoth mess into a readable book. Faisal Devji gave me an enthusiastic thumbs up after reading it. Keya Ganguly has been my fellow traveler in so many ways for over two decades and a friend to whom I have turned in my lowest, and highest, moments. Keya read my manuscript at a busy time of the semester and helped me make my argument much clearer, providing enormously helpful perspectives on how to read Savarkar's politics. Tim Brennan gave this manuscript the same extraordinary close read as he did my first book, and his feedback came right at the moment when I was struggling to put some concluding notes to the book—I am grateful to him for his generous and thoughtful comments. Dorothea von Mucke's theoretical and precise formulations, along with our conversations in Riverside Park, allowed me to craft first an article on Savarkar's *Essentials of Hindutva* and subsequently a long chapter on history and memory.

This book has been written over many years and from two departments of history. At Columbia, I was fortunate to get feedback on parts of the chapters as I was writing or presenting them from Rashid Khalidi, Matt Connolly, Mamadou Diouf, Adam Kosto, Claudio Lomnitz, Mark Mazower, Brinkley Messick, Tim Mitchell, Lila Abu-Lughod, Mae Ngai, Susan Pederson, Alice Kessler Harris, Akeel Bilgrami, Philip Hamburger, and Sheldon Pollock. My colleagues at UC Berkeley read the entire manuscript and made suggestions on how to improve it, and I hope they will see their comments reflected in the final book. I have benefitted enormously from Ussama Makdisi's careful and critical reading. Christine Philliou, colleague and friend across two departments of history, has fielded endless questions about Mustafa Kemal, the CUP, and the abolition of the Caliphate, and helped me make sense of a very complex and complicated period in Turkish history, for which I cannot thank her enough. I am grateful to Carlos Norena, Emily Mackil, Wen-hsin Yeh, James Vernon, Jonathan Sheehan, Ethan Shagan, Susanna Elm, Asad Ahmad, Munis Faruqui, and John Connolly for their comments and feedback on the manuscript. Beyond the two departments I have worked in, I have had wonderful and helpful conversations about parts of this book with Judy Friedlander, Michael Hassett, Afiya Zia, and Akbar Zaidi (who in his characteristic manner simply told me he didn't like one of my chapters and that I had to fix it). I am also grateful to Saurabh Dube, Dipesh Chakrabarty, Elizabeth Kolsky (my friend and fellow dancer), Keith Nield, Gyanendra Pandey, Anupama Rao, Satadru Sen, Peter van der Veer, Stacey van Vleet, David Freedberg, Christophe Jaffrelot, Ira Bhaskar, Pradeep Chibber, Wang Hui, and Mahmood Mamdani.

I offer my thanks to the staff of the following institutions where I conducted research for this book: the India Office Library and Records, London; the National Archives of India, New Delhi; the Nehru Memorial Museum and Library, New Delhi; the Maharashtra State Archives, Mumbai: and the Swatantryaveer Savarkar Rashtriya Smarak, Mumbai. I am particularly grateful to Dhananjay Shinde, Librarian at the Savarkar Smarak in Bombay, for his kind help with bibliographic materials and to Satyaki Savarkar for graciously meeting with me and granting me permission to use Savarkar's words.

My research over the years has been supported by grants or fellowships from the National Endowment for the Humanities, the Stanford Humanities Center, the Italian Academy for Advanced Studies at Columbia, and the department of history at UC Berkeley. I have presented parts of this book at conferences, workshops, institutes, departments. My grateful thanks to Satya Mohanty for inviting me to Cornell; Roger Grant for inviting me to Wesleyan; Peter van der Veer for inviting me to speak in Utrecht and at the Max Planck institute; to Sudipta Sen for inviting me to UC Davis to present an early version of this book; to Dipesh Chakrabarty, Rochona Majumdar, and Andrew Ollett for inviting me to speak at SALC at the University of Chicago; and to Aamir Mufti for inviting me to UCLA. Karen Barkey, friend and colleague over two universities, has followed the progress of this book for years, and I am grateful to her for organizing a panel at Bard College so that I could get feedback and comments just before receiving the copyedited manuscript, and to Sudipta Kaviraj, Nabanjan Maitra and Rupali Warke for their incisive and thoughtful comments on the manuscript on that panel.

Martha Schulman was the best developmental editor, working with me over the past year to take an unruly manuscript and help me turn it into a book. Without her cheerful, ever-encouraging, and prompt responses, this would never have made it. She rolled with every punch I threw, considered every small and large argument I tried out, and consistently pushed me to clarify in clear prose what I meant. If this book reads well, it is in no small measure because of Martha.

Over the years I have taught a number of graduate students who have read Savarkar with me in one or another class. Nirvikar Jassal, Shaivya Mishra,

Brent Otto, Sourav Ghosh, Anurag Advani, Christian Gilberti, Pranav Kuttiah, Justin Grosnick, Adam Jadhav, Joanna Korey, Zainab Wani, Amar Zaidi, and Aparajita Das have all helped me hone my arguments. Shaivya and Sourav in particular were my research assistants for the Muslim chapter, corrected errors, and worked on transliteration with me, and I am grateful to them for both their careful reading and their many suggestions.

In the course of writing this book, I turned into Savarkar's research assistant. Savarkar's Marathi writings are liberally sprinkled with numerous Sanskrit *ślokas*. Often he quoted one line from a *śloka* without indicating where it came from or using the next line. He was writing for a particular Marathi audience that might not have needed the exact citation or the second line of the verse, an audience that knows Sanskrit literature well. But I do not. And in hunting down the second lines of *śloka*s he used, and translating them, I turned again and again to my two erudite and learned colleagues who, in effect, became my Sanskrit teachers: Madhav Deshpande and Robert Goldman. Madhav and Bob not only translated *śloka*s for me—they gave me the exegetical context and explained them to me. Madhav read my chapter on poetry within twenty-four hours, corrected my mistakes, and gave me detailed suggestions. Bob sent me PDFs of Sanskrit works (as did Madhav) at a moment's notice, and I am immensely grateful for their unfailing, prompt, and incredibly generous help. Just before I received the copyedited manuscript, I was fortunate enough to meet Nabanjan Maitra at a panel at Bard College where he volunteered to correct the mistakes I'd made in my transliterations of Sanskrit verses. How does one even say thank you to such a generous offer? Nabanjan, thank you for all your help. To Luther Obrock, likewise, my grateful thanks for cheerfully chasing down with me the last couple of Sanskrit phrases quoted by Savarkar that I had missed, and for correcting (again) my translations and transliterations, and for mulling with me the question of what Savarkar knew, what he made up, and what he put together.

I don't have the right words to express my gratitude to Vidyut Aklujkar. Vidyut helped me with most of the readings of the poetry in this book, and without her help, advice, and suggestions, I would have been lost given how Sanskritized Savarkar's poetry is. Ashok and Vidyut welcomed me into their home, and I sat with Vidyut working on translations of Savarkar's poetry which makes an appearance in four of six chapters. I am grateful as well to Mrs. Prabha Ganorkar for looking over my poetry chapter and correcting some of my mistakes. Shrikant Botre, who I met because I read his dissertation, has become a good friend, and as friends do, he pushed me to turn a few chapters from their original versions into a more focused investigation into Brahminism.

Alok Oak and Ajinkya Lele have been the most cheerful, knowledgeable, resourceful, indefatigable, and helpful research colleagues I could hope for. Ajinkya's persistence in chasing down sources and citations from all the Marathi libraries in Mumbai and Pune has meant that this book is a far better resource than it could have been otherwise. I am grateful as well to Ajinkya for his numerous suggestions that all began with the words "ताई, एक मिनिट, एकच मिनिट, एक सांगु का तुम्हाला?" (Tai, one minute, just one minute?) and ended with "हे पुस्तक तुम्ही नक्की वाचा" (You have to read this book), which resulted in my reading many more Marathi works on Savarkar than I had intended to! Alok read my chapters with care and—I have to note—brutal honesty. He found my last chapter a little boring, so I rewrote it. I hope he finds it less so now. From Alok's comprehensive dissertation on Tilak, I have learnt an enormous amount, as I have as well from his extraordinary knowledge of early twentieth-century Maharashtra. Rahul Sarwate has been supportive throughout the project and a continuous source of material and insight about early twentieth-century Maharashtra.

It has been a great pleasure to work with Princeton University Press. Priya Nelson has been the best of editors. I am grateful for her prompt attention to all my questions, for her reading of parts of the manuscript on which I needed her opinion, and for securing me reports that were more like review essays. To the two anonymous readers of my manuscript, you have my appreciative thanks and I hope you will see the final version reflecting my own attention to your critical feedback. At Princeton, Emma Wagh and Morgan Spehar shepherded the manuscript through production with remarkable efficiency. Kenny Hoffman copyedited the manuscript and allowed me to basically hijack months of his time during which I got in touch daily with some question or the other about track changes, formatting, and style—I am enormously grateful to him for his patience and willingness to answer all my questions.

Natalie Baan was without question the best production editor an author could ever hope to have assigned to her book. Not only did she give me great advice about all production matters, including how to set the poetry, Natalie all but copyedited the copyedited manuscript, proofed the proofs, copyedited and proofed the index, and did all of this not just once but a few times. She found errors in transliterations and inconsistencies of translation after I had gone through the copyedited manuscript and proofs, and gave me ample opportunities and time in which to correct them. In particular, when I was utterly sick of reading my prose and looking through yet another version, Natalie's always cheerful, encouraging, and meticulous attention kept me going. I cannot thank her enough. Any errors that remain in this book are mine and mine alone.

The year I finished my first book, my father was diagnosed with ALS. A good part of the next decade I conducted research in Bombay at the Savarkar Smarak in between doctor's visits, physical therapist visits, and neurological checkups. He is not alive to see this book come to an end, which is one of my single largest regrets. But my mother has patiently waited for me to be done, periodically asking me "कधी हे पुस्तक संपणार तुझं? झालं कि नाही अजून?" ["When is this book of yours going to be done? Isn't it done yet?"] and answering impromptu questions about her childhood, her knowledge of the RSS, Moropant, Samartha Ramdas, subhasitas, and so on. Bhaiya, Arti, and Diya have always been a source of strength and support for me, in ways I don't acknowledge enough. A shout out to Punekar International, for being the best tribe of cousins ever. Gauri (for her unflagging encouragement and support), Lacho, Pipsa, and Tanu—thank you for reading as much of this book as you have. Of my nieces and nephews who have heard about this book and talked to me about it, I would like to thank Latika, Malu, Avani, Kabir, Tahir, Tanvir, Swara, Abu, Nishad, Revati and Shiven. Diane Carty has been friend, sister and house companion these past few years and a steady source of encouragement, pushing me every day to just keep at it. Abhishek and Stacey, and Sandhya and Cameron, have brought feisty, tutu-dress-obsessed Ashapasha and warrior extraordinaire Zubinbabu into my life, which has now become richer and more joyous than I ever knew possible—thank you!

Over the decade it has taken me to write this book, my wonderful, beautiful son Ishan has grown up and moved fully into his own life as a scholar athlete and now dedicated teacher. But through it all he has waited patiently by my side as I have struggled with writing, sweetly nudging me to flip sand (he knows what I mean), as he is wont to do, and monitoring and altering my exercise routines throughout so that I stayed somewhat fit—what would I do without you?

And finally, I dedicate this book to Nick. Nick is not sentimental and would be embarrassed if I were to be so, particularly in praise of him. So this dedication will be restrained. He started me on this journey, and all through the years when I thought I could not complete this book, he has always steadfastly believed that I could and gently pushed me to finish it. His belief in me and this book is the one thing that has kept me going, through some particularly tumultuous and trying times. Would that I had the words to thank him for his unflagging, calm, consistent, and loving support, even through the period when he was Vice President for the Arts and Sciences at Columbia and Chancellor at Berkeley. I have discussed every line in this book with him. I have tried every last argument on him, large or small, argued with him when he pushed back only to both clarify what I meant and reformulate the argument anew. Nick has read every line in this book not once but many times. Cliched as this may sound, I simply could not have written this book without him.

Berkeley, California
January 23, 2022

Introduction

ON JULY 20, 1910, *The* (London) *Times* reported a daring escape by a young Indian law student being extradited to India to stand trial on charges of treason and abetment to murder. When the SS *Morea* docked near the port of Marseilles, the student squeezed himself out of a porthole in the ship's bathroom and swam to shore. He requested asylum as a political prisoner but was returned to the British detectives in charge of him. The *New York Times* reported that French socialists agitated on his behalf, claiming that he had been improperly returned to British authority; the case eventually went to the Hague Tribunal for arbitration.[1] Much to the relief of the British Secretary of State for India, Sir John Morley, the Permanent Court of Arbitration ruled that France could not hold him. The twenty-seven-year-old student was then brought to India, where he was tried and sentenced to an unprecedented two life terms of banishment to a penal colony. Indian students frequently ran into trouble with British police without it being covered by British and American national newspapers, but this was no ordinary student. His name was Vinayak Damodar Savarkar (1883–1966), an Indian revolutionary nationalist who believed uncompromisingly that armed struggle was the only way for India to free herself from British colonial rule, and he would become one of the most important figures associated with right-wing Hindu nationalism.[2]

Savarkar was born in Bhagura—a village in Bombay Presidency—into a lower middle-class Marathi Chitpavan Brahmin family on May 27, 1883, and

1. "Hindu Case at Hague: Question between France and England over Extradition of Student," *New York Times*.

2. The Marathi transliteration of Savarkar's full name, with the accent marks, is Vināyaka Dāmōdara Sāvarakara. However, since Savarkar wrote his name in English as "Savarkar," I am using the same.

his early life seemed to lead naturally to revolutionary nationalism. His childhood and adulthood were filled with tragedy: the death of his mother from cholera when he was nine years old, the subsequent death of his father and uncle from the plague, and the experience of bumbling and insensitive colonial efforts to alleviate a catastrophic plague that devastated the population of rural western India. During his adulthood, his four-year-old son died; just before Savarkar was released from prison, his beloved sister-in-law died; and while under house arrest in Ratnagiri, he lost another child.[3] During his adolescence, the plague became the proximate cause for anticolonial sentiment across western India, resulting in political assassinations, the glorification of revolutionary nationalists and anarchists from far away—particularly Italians and Russians—and tactics that the colonial government would quickly categorize as "terrorist."

In 1899, a teenage Savarkar and some friends founded a secret revolutionary society called Rāshtrabhakta Samuha (Devotees of the Nation Society), which in 1901 became the Mitra Mela (Friends Society).[4] In 1902 he entered Fergusson College in Pune, where he organized anticolonial protests. Like many other young educated Indian men, he went to London for postgraduate study, arriving in 1906, but spent most of his time engaged in political activities, some benign and some less so, including procuring Browning pistols to smuggle into India for political assassinations. He was a classic example of the early twentieth-century revolutionary Indian nationalist, enamored with guns and bombs. He went to London to study law only to have the Metropolitan Police decide he was breaking it.

His companions during the five years he spent there were a motley group of like-minded revolutionary Indian students—the British authorities labeled them all extremists—who idolized Irish nationalists, Russian bomb makers,

3. Karandikar, *Savarkar Charitra*, 105, 290, 468. Savarkar's son, Prabhakar, was born in 1905 but died of smallpox in 1909.

4. *Samagra Savarkar Vangmaya*, Svatantryaveer Savarkar Rashtriya Smarak Prakashan [SSRSP] 1: 122–25. I have used two major collections of Savarkar's Marathi works: *Samagra Savarkar Vangmaya*, vols. 1–8, published by the Maharashtra Prantik Hindusabha Samiti (hereafter identified as *SSV*, MPHS) and *Samagra Savarkar Vangmaya*, vols. 1–9, published by Svatantryaveer Savarkar Rashtriya Smarak Prakashan (hereafter identified as *SSV*, SSRSP). While the material collected in both is the same, the editor of the first was S. R. Date—a close associate of Savarkar's who consulted with him about the compilation. The second one was compiled by a committee put together by Savarkar's family members with a different set of prefatory remarks than the ones written by Date, so I found it worthwhile to use both.

and Italian thinkers. Within six months of his arrival, Savarkar translated Giuseppe Mazzini's biography into Marathi; by the end of the year, he started another secret revolutionary society called the Free India Society that was clearly modeled after Mazzini's Young Italy. In 1909 a housemate of his, Madanlal Dhingra, shot Sir William Hutt Curzon Wyllie—the political aide-de-camp to Sir John Morley—and in 1910 Savarkar was arrested in connection with not just that shooting but also for having supplied pistols for political assassinations back in India, after which he was repatriated to India to stand trial.[5]

The notoriety surrounding his trial made him a world-famous "terrorist" and captured the interest of the international press as well as figures like Maxim Gorky.[6] Savarkar was sentenced to two life terms in the notorious Cellular Jail on the Andaman Islands[7] but was brought back to India in May 1921.[8] He was placed under house arrest from 1924 to 1937 during which time he promised to cease all political activities—but nonetheless wrote history, poems, plays, speeches, and editorials as he became known as a serious political figure even while under police watch. In 1937, after his release, he became the president of the Hindu political party, the Hindu Mahasabha. By the time he stepped down from that position in 1943, his rhetoric had taken on a particularly strident and virulent tone, denouncing Gandhi and the main

5. Singh, "Trial and Martyrdom of Dhingra," 728–39.

6. There were interrelations and connections between Egyptian nationalists and Indian extremists that were strong enough to render Savarkar's early historical tome on the 1857 Rebellion as the chief source of Indian history for the Egyptian nationalist paper *al-Liwa*. Following the assassination of Curzon Wyllie by Madanlal Dhingra, what traveled was the image of an Indian nationalist martyr in Egypt, Ibrahim Nassif al-Wardani, who was well acquainted with the Dhingra case and shot the Egyptian prime minister Boutros Ghali, leading some British officials to focus on his connection to Indian extremism. See Khan, "The Enemy of My Enemy," 74–78.

7. The Andaman Islands are located in the Indian Ocean, about 600 km east of the southern coast of Myanmar, between the Bay of Bengal and the Andaman Sea, to the north of Sumatra. In the seventeenth century, Archibald Blair of the Royal Indian Navy founded a naval base, and soon after the 1857 Rebellion, the British Government of India started a penal colony named Port Blair. Construction of the Andaman Cellular Jail was completed by 1910. The jail was built in a circular pattern, with a total of 698 cells. Indian revolutionaries were sent from mainland India to Port Blair, and prisoners were used to clear the surrounding jungles until the settlement was abandoned.

8. Karandikar, *Savarkar Charitra*, 489–92. He was moved to a jail in Ratnagiri thereafter for a few years, where, according to Karandikar, he was despondent to the point of considering suicide.

voice of Indian nationalism, the Indian National Congress (INC), for taking too soft a line on Muslims.

In 1944, three years before independence, a veteran American war correspondent interviewed Savarkar. He was one of the very few political leaders not in jail because the Hindu Mahasabha had stayed aloof from the Quit India movement that had roiled most of British India in 1942. Tom Treanor describes Savarkar as unshaven and disheveled but intellectually engaged and eager to talk about how he perceived Indian Muslims. Asked by Treanor how he planned to treat the "Mohammedans," Savarkar said he would regard them "as a minority in the position of your Negroes." To Treanor's follow-up question about what might happen "if the Mohammedans secede and set up their own country," Savarkar, according to Treanor, "waggl[ed] a menacing finger" and promised that "as in your country there will be civil war."[9]

When British India was partitioned in 1947, Savarkar's promise of civil war seemed to come true in the paroxysm of Hindu-Muslim violence that midwifed the birth of Pakistan and India as two independent and mutually hostile new nations. At midnight, August 14, 1947, India's first prime minister Jawaharlal Nehru spoke to the new nation. "Long years ago," he said, "we made a tryst with destiny, and now the time comes when we shall redeem our pledge. . . . A moment comes . . . when an age ends, and when the soul of a nation, long suppressed, finds utterance." While his lofty words and ideals captured the ebullient spirit of independence, they also evoked the horrific possibility that the violence of partition was also an expression of the nation's soul, but of its dark side.

On January 30, 1948, Nathuram Godse, a former member of the right-wing cultural organization the Rashtriya Swayamsevak Sangh (RSS) and a close associate of Savarkar, pushed his way through the crowd assembled to greet Gandhi for his usual prayer meeting. He made a short bow to Gandhi, then shot him dead. Later it was discovered that Godse had not only met Savarkar before setting out on his mission but had received his blessing. As a result, Savarkar was arrested in connection with yet another political assassination, this time of the "Father of the Nation." Whether Savarkar was directly responsible or not, there is little doubt that his animus against Gandhi—indeed his complete rejection of Gandhi's idea of India—was a dominant factor in Nathuram Godse's decision to fire the gun. The police could not find concrete evidence of any complicity and released Savarkar. In an odd twist of fate, he

9. Treanor, *One Damn Thing after Another*, 84.

lived out the remainder of his life as if he were back in house arrest, in the Bombay neighborhood of Shivaji Park. He was disallowed by the newly independent Indian nation from participating in politics, though he remained influential in the Hindu Mahasabha and, in an echo of earlier colonial restrictions on him, remained under surveillance. He continued writing, publishing one tract after another until his death in 1966.[10]

One of the charges that landed Savarkar in jail in 1910 was sedition. Yet soon after his 1921 repatriation to an Indian prison, he wrote another potentially seditious work, even if it may not have been seditious in a legal sense since it made no critical mention of British rule in India, smuggling it out of his prison cell in Ratnagiri in 1923.[11] Titled *Essentials of Hindutva,* the tract was published the same year by a lawyer in Nagpur named Shri Vishwanathrao Kelkar. Savarkar wrote the work in English under the pseudonym "A Mahratta."[12] The extended essay was a passionately lyrical celebration of the Indian territorial nation. Some five decades after it was written, it has become the de facto bible of militant and exclusionary Hindu nationalism, which sees as its foremost enemy India's minority Muslim community.[13] The essay not only encapsulated this suspicion of Muslims—it also encapsulated Savarkar's entire oeuvre, dramatically influencing the course of modern Indian history.

One word—an abstract noun—from the essay's title, Hindutva, would come to stand as the exemplary expression of militant Hindu nationalism, while one couplet became the cornerstone of Hindutva ideology:

10. Savarkar's death in the Marathi literature is usually termed *ātmārpaṇa* or self-sacrifice. Upon falling ill, he began eating less and less and eventually refused all food and water, taking his last breath on February 26, 1966. For a firsthand description of his last months and weeks, see Savarkar's son's recollections, *Athavani Angaracya,* 21–26.

11. Karandikar writes that, from 1908 onward, Savarkar was playing with the idea of Hindutva, and during the war, while unwell and practically bed-bound in the Andaman Islands, he worked on the concept between 1915 and 1918. However, in prison in Ratnagiri, according to Karandikar, he was already concerned about the discourse of unity that was spreading; he was particularly concerned about the Mappila Rebellion and was eager to publish his book. Karandikar, *Savarkar Charitra,* 465–66, 493.

12. Karandikar, *Savarkar Charitra,* 465–66, 493. Karandikar also tells us Savarkar was moved from Alipur Jail in Calcutta to a jail in Ratnagiri for a few years, and then to Yerawada Jail in Pune, where following a meeting with the governor of Bombay, Sir George Lloyd, he was released into house arrest in Ratnagiri. He was released from prison once and for all on June 1, 1924.

13. For ease of access, I have used *Essentials of Hindutva* as published in volume 4 of the (English) *Selected Works of Veer Savarkar.*

Asindhu sindhu paryanta yasya bharata bhumika
Pitrabhu punyabhushchaiva sa vai hinduriti smritaha[14]

Translated literally, the couplet claims that India's geographical contours extend from the Sindhu River in the North (in present-day Pakistan) to the seas below in the South.[15] All people who claimed India as both *pitrabhumi* (the land of their ancestors) and *punyabhumi* (holy land) were its natural inhabitants. He clarified what he meant by *punyabhumi* ten years after publishing *Essentials* to ensure that he was not misunderstood.

> The land in which the founder of a religion appeared as a Rishi, an Avatar, or Prophet, and in which he preached that religion, and by his living in the land it acquired sacredness, that land can be considered the punyabhu of a religion. Like Palestine for the Jews and Christians, and Arabia for the Muslims. . . . It is not to be understood simply as sacred land.[16]

The modern boundaries of India contain the oldest shrines and sacred sites of its Hindu, Sikh, Jain, and Buddhist communities; they also contain sacred shrines of India's Christian, Jewish, and Muslim communities. But because Jerusalem, Mecca, and Medina were outside the territorial boundaries of modern India, by Savarkar's definition, Jews, Christians, and Muslims were neither natural nor national inhabitants of India. This territorial demarcation and its accompanying exclusionary ideology—the idea that India is primarily a Hindu country—are at the core of Hindutva. To call someone a Hindutvavadi in today's India is to either bestow upon her a great compliment or bruise her with a contumelious insult, depending upon that person's ideological persuasion. For these and other reasons Savarkar's *Essentials* has received its share of attention from Indian historians and political commentators, as has Savarkar himself.

There is, in fact, a large body of literature on and by Savarkar, and no conversation about Hindutva or Hindu nationalism, whether by historians, sociologists, political scientists, or anthropologists, takes place without naming him as the father of Hindu fascism, Hindu fundamentalism, and/or Hindu right-wing nationalism. His supporters think of him as an extraordinary patriot and the champion of Hindus. There is also an enormous biographical

14. Savarkar, *Essentials*, 537. I have copied the verse exactly as it appears in the work cited without correcting it or marking it with the appropriate diacritical marks.

15. I am grateful to Sheldon Pollock for the precise translation.

16. See *SSV*, MPHS, 3: 6, for Savarkar's essay titled "Hindutvace Pancha Prana," published in the Marathi magazine *Sahyadri* in May 1936.

body of literature on Savarkar published in his native language, Marathi, and even some works in Sanskrit. A few of these biographies are scholarly, but most are not, and all are adulatory. There are, additionally, Sanskrit plays, Sanskrit *mahākāvya* (courtly poetry), *povāḍās* (bardic poems), Marathi plays, *bakhars* (chronicles), Hindi plays, Marathi musicals, children's comic books, and graphic novels. There is also a specific regional reading public devoted to him and his memorialization along with a varied reading practice. Such practices date to the period following Savarkar's return to India, even as the process of memorialization continues to this day.[17] In addition, there is Savarkar's own literary production, mostly in Marathi. He was first and foremost a poet, though he was also a prolific polemicist, occasional playwright, and nationalist historian. His collected works in Marathi span ten volumes. While English-language scholarship on him focuses on *Essentials*, he has a much larger corpus—from poetry to prose, from music dramas to speeches, from jeremiads to historical writings—that is read only by Marathi readers. His patriotic poems set to music and songs such as "Shatajanma Shodhitana" from his music drama (*San'yasta Khaḍga* [Forsaken sword]), are routinely performed at commemorative events and on television. Yet the works of his that tend to have the largest circulation and have been translated into English and Hindi (and, on occasion, Gujarati, Tamil, Bengali, and Malayalam) are his historical works and political tracts. His writings on *Bhāśā Śud'dhi* (purification of the language) and *Lipisudhāraṇā* (reform of the script), his poetry, his essays on caste reform, his writings on the Manusmr̥ti, and, most importantly, the numerous articles he wrote in which he attacked the orthodox Hindu community and M. K Gandhi remain untranslated.[18] Savarkar has also had a very different afterlife in his home state of Maharashtra compared to the rest of India. To take just one example, in no part of Savarkar's writings do we see a recidivism, or a desire to return to the Vedas, or any support for Hindu ritual. Indeed, Savarkar is widely viewed in Maharashtra as a progressive and a caste reformer. But the Savarkar who is iconic all over India is not the progressive, let alone the caste reformer, but rather the

17. See most recently the two-volume biography of Savarkar by Vikram Sampath, *Savarkar: Echoes from a Forgotten Past, 1883–1924* and *Savarkar (Part 2): A Contested Legacy, 1924–1966*. See also my review of Sampath's biography in *India Today* and my statement about Sampath's plagiarism of my article, "'Vikram Sampath Is Claiming My Ideas, Words as His Own.'"

18. In 1982 Savarkar's writings were distributed across several small books and published in a format that did not require one to purchase his collected works. In the front matter of each of these small books, Savarkar's secretary Balarao Savarkar has published a list of Savarkar's works and the languages into which they have been translated. I get my information from this front matter.

revolutionary Hindu nationalist. In many current formulations, he has been severed from Maharashtra, and there are different afterlives of Savarkar in Maharashtra compared to all other regions of the country.

I am not writing a story of Savarkar's life, nor am I writing the first intellectual biography of Savarkar. I am, however, writing a book that brings both English and Marathi sources into conversation with one another to tell a story through Savarkar about the foundational political ideas that have become central in, and inexorably intertwined with, modern Indian political life. For the most part, the English and Marathi worlds have been completely bifurcated. *Essentials* and Savarkar's histories are frequently cited, not least because they link the present Hindu moment of Indian history to the pre-independence anticolonial period; not even Gandhi's texts from the 1920s can claim such an enduring influence. Savarkar's histories have the largest circulation of all his writings because, in them, he offers a history of the Hindu state. But the poetry upon which *Essentials* is based, with which Marathi writers are well acquainted, is rarely brought into the analytic frame. This bifurcation means that Savarkar, despite his iconic status, remains elusive; I argue here that his importance cannot be fully grasped until not just his writings but also his reception in English as well as Marathi are covered together in a single work. It is not possible to fully understand Savarkar in his own terms unless he is read in the language in which he couched those terms—a language deeply rooted in the regional formation of which he was so proud and over which he displayed an unmistakable mastery. To not read Savarkar in Marathi, in other words, is to reproduce a colonial dynamic in which the regional is assumed to be parochial, and only the national or international is taken to be of global significance.

There is an additional element to the bifurcation of historical treatments of Savarkar, related in fundamental ways as well to Savarkar's own sustained effort to reclaim and re-narrate the history of India. Savarkar fervently believed that the domination of historical literature by Muslims and the British had resulted in the denigration, if not downright suppression, of the glories of the Hindu past. Savarkar's reclamation project was nativist in the extreme, a part of his more general critique not just of earlier non-native historiography but even of what he saw as an accommodationist tendency on the part of nationalists such as Gandhi and Nehru. The English historical record, like the Muslim one before it, was contaminated by an outsider's perspective and was not engaged with so much as simply dismissed or ignored.

A similar nativism continues to dominate the writings of many of the Marathi historians writing about Savarkar, including Y. D. Phadke, S. N. Navalgundkar, Sheshrao More, Raja Dixit, and Sudhakar Bhalerao, among others, even when (as is usually the case) they are fluent in English. The English sources referenced tend to be the occasional primary source, such as the colonial Sedition Committee Report or police files, and only a few secondary sources at most. It is not as if a broader conception of history and sources was unknown either in Savarkar's time or now. Savarkar himself studied the works of Spencer, Comte, Mill, Darwin, Bentham, and Macaulay (in addition to studying the Upaniṣads and Vedanta).[19] Savarkar's contemporary, T. S. Shejwalkar, found much to learn from the stalwarts of Anglo-European history and engaged seriously with canonical European historians: Toynbee, Gibbon, Macaulay, Weber, Marx, Kant, Hegel, Croce. Historians writing in Marathi on Savarkar rarely do the same. On occasion, references to historiography appear in the form of an allusion to a distant English historian such as Carlyle or Gibbon, sometimes to Nietzsche, or, even more surprisingly, Arthur Schlesinger.[20] But by and large, Marathi historians writing on Savarkar entirely avoid the extraordinarily large corpus of Indian history written in English.

Just as the respective literatures are split, so too is the English scholarly literature on Savarkar. Nationalist histories have dominated the field for generations, and only nationalists and political parties on the so-called "correct" side of Indian history—which is to say on the Gandhi/Nehru side of history—receive sustained and serious historical inquiry and examination.[21] With a few notable exceptions, the almost obsessive focus in scholarship on Gandhi has been

19. See Wolf "Vinayak Damodar Savarkar's 'Strategic Agnosticism'" for a fine-grained and detailed analysis of Savarkar as a philosopher, examining the possible influences of European liberal thinkers on him. See also Visana, "Savarkar before Hindutva," 1–24. In "Majhi Janmathep" ("My transportation for life"), Savarkar provides an extraordinary list of materials that he and other political prisoners requested for the library at Cellular Jail in the Andaman Islands. It includes journals such as *Modern Review* and *Indian Review*; biographies of Swami Vivekanda, Michael Madhusudan Dutt, Raja Ram Mohan Roy, Tagore, and Vidyasagar in Bengali; Sanskrit copies of the Rāmāyaṇa, Mahābhārata, and Yogvasishtha; Marathi books such as the *Dnyaneshwari, Moropantanche Kavya,* and *Kramik Pustake* (textbooks). In English, the list includes the collected works of Spencer, Mill, Darwin, Huxley, Hegel, Emerson, Carlyle, Gibbon, Macaulay, Shakespeare, Milton, and Alexander Pope; biographies of Napoleon, Bismarck, and Garibaldi; the novels of Dickens and Tolstoy; the works of Kropotkin and Nietzsche on politics; Plato's *Republic*; the Qur'an in translation; Kalidas's plays; Hindi books on the 1857 Rebellion; and talks and lectures given by Tilak. For a full list, see https://www.savarkarsmarak.com/activityimages/Marathi%20-%20Mazi%20Janmathep.pdf, 163–73.

20. Y. D. Phadke, "Savarkaranchi Vicharsrushti," 156.

21. For instance, there is no good work on Madan Mohan Malaviya, the leader of the Hindu nationalist party, nor very much scholarship on the Hindu Mahasabha political party, or on nationalist figures like Tej Bahadur Sapru or K. M. Moonshi.

conspicuously absent for right-wing anticolonial nationalists such as Savarkar, who is written about almost exclusively by those who either see him as the founder of an Indian "fascism" and as a eugenicist interested in producing a master Hindu race, or by partisan apologists and eulogizers.[22] In the first instance, he is condemned as an extremist. In the second, he becomes the prescient oracle of all that has come to pass in modern India. Neither side subjects him to careful analysis, meaning that his role as a major (if not always original) contributor to modern Indian intellectual and political history has so far been little understood. This is true as well for the Marathi literature on Savarkar, with a few exceptions. Raosaheb Kasbe, Vasant Palshikar, and Ashok Chousalkar, all of whom are political scientists, have written works critical of Savarkar.[23] But for the most part, the literature both in Marathi and English takes partisan positions on him.[24]

In this book I will cite extensively from Savarkar's own words, as I have directly translated them from the original Marathi. I do so not just as a scholarly method—to bring Savarkar to the reader as much as possible unmediated by my own historical judgment—but also to bypass the partisanship that otherwise marks previous scholarship on Savarkar. A word of warning is in order. Savarkar's prose is often extraordinarily polemical. He seems to have intended to offend a good many people—whether those were liberal nationalists, Muslims, or orthodox (Sanātani) Hindus. The founding publisher of the leading Marathi publication, *Kirloskar*, recognized this both when editing Savarkar's essays on caste reform and when recounting his actions in his autobiography.[25]

22. One notable exception is Pincince's excellent dissertation "On the Verge of Hindutva."

23. In particular, see Kasbe, *Hindurashtravada*. Kasbe addresses Savarkar's social, political, and religious thought but does not see him as a serious thinker because he did not delve into philosophical questions. On the other hand, see Wolf's "Vinayak Damodar Savarkar's 'Strategic Agnosticism'" and Visana, "Savarkar before Hindutva," 1–24. Both of these scholars read Savarkar almost as an architectonic philosopher.

24. The corpus of writing on Gandhi is too voluminous to be easily cited. A simple keyword search for works on "Mahatma+Gandhi" yields over 1,700 citations, and I will not attempt to be comprehensive. I offer a tiny sample of the journalistic and scholarly writings on Gandhi: David Arnold, *Gandhi: Profiles in Power* (2001); William L. Shirer, *Gandhi: A Memoir* (1979); Louis Fischer, *The Life of Mahatma Gandhi* (1950); David Hardiman, *Gandhi in His Time and Ours: The Global Legacy of His Ideas* (2003). On Nehru, see Sarvepalli Gopal, *Jawaharlal Nehru: A Biography* (1989); M. J. Akbar, *Nehru: The Making of India* (2002); *Indian Foreign Policy: The Nehru Years*, edited by B. R. Nanda (1976). On Subhas Chandra Bose, see Leonard Gordon, *Brothers against the Raj* (1990). On Maulana Azad, see *Islam and Indian Nationalism*, edited by Mushirul Hasan (1992).

25. Kirloskar, *Shanavakiya*, 268.

Unlike Kirloskar I have not edited or censored Savarkar's prose. I have translated long passages, with the original Marathi provided in the appendix, precisely to show its force, its polemical character, and the ways in which he confronted—by being provocative and sometimes offensive—orthodox Hindu sensibilities one hundred years ago. His prose may well be seen as no less offensive today. My intention, however, is not to offend. It is to contextualize why Savarkar was considered progressive, even a social radical, in his time, and to represent him and his thought through his own rhetoric and language.

As critical a figure as he was, however, he was largely derivative in his actual views. Reading through the Marathi scholarly literature on Savarkar and his contemporaries, predecessors, and mentors makes clear that he did not inaugurate many of the conversations in which he participated upon his return to India, whether on eradicating untouchability, the writing of history, or the so-called Muslim Question. Even his poetry was not unique, except insofar as it was overtly patriotic. Moreover, every single one of his agendas, from his determination to purify Marathi to his demonization of Muslims, was challenged by intellectuals and scholars within his home state of Maharashtra. How then did he not just insert himself into the major debates of his time but co-opt them and fashion himself so often as their major spokesperson?

When we move beyond Maharashtra, this question becomes even more puzzling. The 1920s featured figures—Gandhi, Lenin, Ataturk, Mao—who were at the center of major national movements, claiming the world's attention. It was a strange and unsettling time for the British Empire, which, even as it spanned a vast territory ranging from India at one end to the spoils of the Ottoman Empire at the other, faced threats inside and out. Britain's imperial project was gnawed at by the Russian Revolution (1917), Turkish Republicanism, rising Arab nationalism, Irish nationalists and Sinn Féin, British communists working to foster labor unrest in India, and Italian anarchists who influenced the Indian "terrorists" who set off bombs in Parliament and assassinated British officials in London.

Even more important, the twenties and thirties saw the germination of a series of ethnonationalist movements in numerous places around the globe—what we might call global localisms. In 1892, Bengali literary critic and writer Chandranath Basu coined the term Hindutva, describing it as the best expression of the fundamental characteristics of "Hindu-ness."[26] A few years later,

26. Sen, "A Hindu Conservative Negotiates Modernity," 178.

Rabindranath Tagore wrote an essay called "Hindutva."[27] Around the same time, B. G. Tilak, Savarkar's hero and inspiration, also wrote an essay in Marathi on Hindutva—a term he used to refer to the Hindu community.[28] Some twenty years later, when Savarkar took the same term and injected it with steroidal rage against a Muslim other, he was part of a larger movement. In different parts of the world, charismatic men were defining the boundaries, both physical and cultural, of their lands. In the wake of the First World War, extreme right-wing pan-European revivalist movements and organizations challenged the basic premises of liberal democracies in favor of a fascist-tinged conservatism that usually started by defining who was and was not genuinely part of the nation.

Such concepts and movements were present in India too.[29] There was a perceptible global zeitgeist and striking resemblances between Savarkar's concept of Hindutva and the earlier German concept of Volkisch, the subsequent cult of Romanita in Italy, or even Ferenc Szalasi's Hungarism.[30] A little further afield, the academic Karelia Society advocated the purging of non-Finnish influences from Finnish life and culture, hoping to create a greater Finland whose boundaries went east as far as the Urals. All these groups romanticized a deep connection to native soil, privileged the country over the city, and advocated a palingenetic renewal of ethnic and, in some cases, racial purity alongside the removal of foreign influences.

From colonial India to Finland and beyond, in other words, the 1920s saw a global emergence of intense localisms.[31] Scholars have debated how to define

27. For an analysis of Tagore's essay on Hindutva, see Chatterjee, "Tagore's Non-Nation," in *Lineages of Political Society: Studies in Postcolonial Democracy*.

28. Tilak, "Hindutva ani Sudharna," 294–98. Bal Gangadhar Tilak (1856–1920) was the editor of *Kesari* (Marathi) and *Marhatta* (English). A Hindu nationalist politician and leader, he was known in his native Maharashtra as "Lokamanya" ("respected by the people") Tilak and as an "extremist" politician by the colonial government. See Oak, *Political Ideas of B. G. Tilak*, and Rao, *Foundations of Tilak's Nationalism*.

29. On fascism in Bengal, see Zachariah, "A Voluntary Gleichschaltung?" Zachariah documents the fascination with fascism in colonial Bengal and the active attempts to implement it in India. In particular, see 69–77.

30. Stanley Payne has argued that Hungary takes the prize for the single largest number of right-wing radical secret societies, all cultivating the spirit of national revival. See Payne, *A History of Fascism 1914–1945*, 267. The association called the Etelkoz Association (EKSZ) made new members swear unquestioning oaths of complete obedience and promise to court death before giving up on the idea of a racially pure and Christian Hungary. See Kallis, *The Fascism Reader*, 203.

31. See Hoffman, *The Fascist Effect*, on Shimoi Harukichi, who in the 1920s was the most aggressive promoter of the ideas of fascism as he had learned them from his association in Italy

and describe these movements and ideologies. Were they fascist or semi-fascist movements? Were they proto-fascist or fascist-tinged, or did they partake discriminatingly of a "fascist repertoire" of ideas?[32] Whatever the case, these movements and ideologies were bolstered by political and cultural organizations and cult-like secret societies.[33] In Romania in 1927, Corneliu Codreanu founded the Legion of the Archangel Michael, which aimed to regenerate Romania and create a new spirit—a cultural and religious revolution that would bring forth the *omul nou* (new man). India had the Tarun Hindu Sabha, founded in 1923 by Savarkar's older brother, and the RSS, founded in 1925. The Hitler Youth, Italian Youth, Hungarian Youth, Austrian Youth, Romanian Youth, and the RSS *swayamsevaks* (volunteer members) all imagined a new man who was young, militant, energetic, and forward-looking. This new man also aimed to forge a noncosmopolitan sense of identity and enact an identitarian and exclusionary politics.

In India during the same period, Gandhi began his slow but sure takeover of the anticolonial nationalist movement, though not without being challenged regarding his insistence on nonviolent noncooperation as a political strategy, his conservative and paternalistically reformist views on caste, his support for the Khilafat movement, or his idea that spinning was the best way to further the cause of Indian independence from colonial rule.

Savarkar entered all this political and social ferment from house arrest in Ratnagiri. Brought back to India in 1921, he set in motion in the Marathi language and milieu a starkly alternative process and set of assertions and ideas about Hindu primacy that a wide range of Hindu fundamentalists across India would later appropriate. This book is about that process, one that took place primarily in Maharashtra, in Marathi, in conversation with other Marathi intellectuals, nationalists, and poets, but also in the context of Savarkar's chief

---

with political figures such as Gabriel D'Annunzio. I am grateful to David Freedberg for his suggestion that what I was describing might more accurately be described as global localism.

32. Zachariah, "A Voluntary Gleichschaltung?"

33. See Griffin, *Fascism*, in particular part 3, "Abortive Fascisms 1922–1945" (213–14 on Finland, 219–21 on Romania, and 223–28 on Hungary). See also Kallis, *The Fascism Reader*, in particular part 2 for discussions about what Griffin has termed "the fascist minimum" and essays by Stanley Payne, Ernst Nolte, Zeev Sternhell. See 191–241 for variations on the fascist theme in Romania and Hungary. See also Payne's magisterial *A History of Fascism: 1914–1945*, 245–328, for non-European variants of fascism; Paxton's canonical *The Anatomy of Fascism*; and Blinkhorn, *Fascism and the Right in Europe: 1919–1945*. This is a tiny selection from the enormous body of literature on fascism.

nemesis, Gandhi, along with his other contemporary, B. R. Ambedkar, whom Savarkar admired even as they had major differences.

Savarkar never doubted that he was a legendary leader of global significance, and his hubris served him well in crafting for himself a near mythological persona for posterity. He did so through his writings, which ranged across the genres of history, biography, historical novels, and Marathi poetry. Always under surveillance, Savarkar threw himself into the political conversations about caste, minorities, and the nation with other nationalists inside and outside Maharashtra.

Savarkar is not especially well understood by modern Indians, who assume he was deeply devout and religious or a straightforward Hindu fundamentalist, neither of which is correct. Nor is he understandable outside of a colonial context, within which he was an adamant anticolonial nationalist even as his contempt for Muslims served colonial interests. He is even less understandable if we remove him from his native region of Maharashtra, where the reverence for his anticolonial revolutionary activities has been joined with admiration for him as a social reformer as well as a brilliant poet and writer. Savarkar the poet is also Savarkar the historian; Savarkar the caste reformer is Savarkar the anti-Muslim polemicist in a different guise. For all these reasons, along with the divided cultural and linguistic worlds already mentioned, it is difficult to produce a neat and tidy historical narrative about Savarkar because he either evades or escapes most of the hermeneutic boxes into which one might place him. As a consequence, I have envisioned this book as providing a kaleidoscopic view of Savarkar not just because he looks completely different depending on how the lens is turned but also because it is only by the constant turning of the lens that one can gain a more complete view of Savarkar.

Both his detractors and his fervent supporters see him narrowly, and selectively. Savarkar was a patriotic nationalist who in the eyes of the colonial (and subsequently Indian) police was also feared as a "terrorist." He was admired in the larger international and underground world of revolutionaries for his extreme anticolonial views, and at home for standing up for the Hindu community. In one view he was a rationalist and progressive voice on caste, even as he seemed ever more radical in the ways he challenged the orthodox (Sanātani) community. He was a pandit/śāstri, a poet, historian, playwright, novelist, biographer, and political leader. But while he was famous in his region as a poet and a progressive leader, he was also extreme in his anti-Muslim rhetoric, viewed as dangerous not just by the British but by many Hindu nationalists who took a more cosmopolitan view. Each one of these Savarkars was connected to the other. To understand how his ideas relate to each other, or are coherent, it is necessary, I believe, to look at a combination of contradictory ideas, none of which are clear without a kaleidoscopic gaze. One needs to keep turning the kaleidoscope to see how the pieces rearrange themselves and reveal new connections. No part of this can be accomplished without reading Savarkar both from within Maharashtra and from the outside.

I turn the kaleidoscope not just on Savarkar's work and life, but across three frames: regional, national, and global. The book's chapters do not move lockstep from region to nation to globe; rather, each examines the interplay among the three. Savarkar's poetry, for instance, was intensely nationalist and patriotic, but it was rooted in regional history. For all his travels, he maintained a deep and affective relationship with the language, people, poetry, politics, and landscape of the rural world of Bhagur and Nashik, where he grew up. Indeed, a large part of his reading audience—and his subsequent base—comes from places like Makhjan, Aamneshwar, Solapur, Kolhapur, Nagpur, Nashik, Amravati, Aurangabad, and Ratnagiri—the villages, towns, and small cities of Maharashtra. It is from here that his base reads Savarkar's works and the many commemorative books about him in Marathi. Beyond the hinterland, however, he is also revered in the two major cities of Maharashtra—Pune and Mumbai. He penned an homage poem to a Marathi poet named Moropant (also known as Mayurpandit) and to his village of Bhagur, in addition to praise poems to Generals Washington and Kruger.

There are two especially important moments in the history of nationalism, and around Gandhi's canonical role in that history, that offer a sharp portrait of Savarkar's developing nationalist thought and persona. The first has to do with Gandhi and his nonviolent movement. In March 1922, a group of angry villagers set fire to a police station, killing nineteen policemen while proclaiming "Gandhi Raj is here." Outraged by this violence, and without consulting anyone, Gandhi called off the noncooperation movement. Many noncooperators heard the news in jail and were incredulous that a relatively small act of violence made Gandhi call off a movement when success seemed within reach. But the Mahatma was resolute. India was not ready for independence, he argued, if her inhabitants resorted to violence—even in a good cause. This quixotic decision renewed the colonial regime's hold on power just when it had seemed most precarious. The colonial government rewarded Gandhi by arresting him in March 1922, rendering him absent from politics for the next six years. When Savarkar returned in 1921, his mentor and idol, B. G. Tilak—a fiery, charismatic, and immensely popular Hindu nationalist politician—had died, leaving a leadership vacuum that needed an equally charismatic figure to fill it. At the same time, Gandhi was about to disappoint many of his followers and depart from the political scene, which would give Savarkar the opportunity to reenter the public sphere through his publication of *Essentials of Hindutva*, along with a historical work glorifying in purple Victorian prose the legacy of Chhatrapati Shivaji and the Peshwas titled *Hindu-Pad-Padashahi*. Written in English, these books were in part intended to reassure the larger Hindu community that, even if Gandhi was gone, a finer, better, more authentic man was ready to lead, from a region (Maharashtra) with prior experience of having struck the first blow against three different foreign invaders: Muslims, the Portuguese, and the British. Maharashtra's history, he wrote, offered a better model for an ongoing nationalist struggle than what Gandhi was offering.

The second moment, also irrevocably linked to Gandhi's political leadership, was the Khilafat movement (1920–24). Led by brothers Mohammad Ali Jauhar and Shaukat Ali, the movement aimed to put pressure on the British government to maintain the territorial sovereignty of the Turkish Sultan despite Turkey's defeat in the First World War on the grounds that he still had spiritual sovereignty as the Khalifa of the Sunni *umma*. Since the defeated Ottoman Empire contained within it the Holy Lands and the cities of Mecca and Medina, the leaders of the Khilafat movement argued that any breakup of the territory of the Ottoman Empire would diminish the Khalifa's authority. Gandhi supported the movement, and even though it failed and the Allied powers divided the Ottoman territories into mandates, the movement brought unprecedented unity to India's Muslims for a cause outside the boundaries of territorial British India. This rendered it an irritant for some nationalists, none more so than for Savarkar.

As the movement petered out, there was escalating tension and violence for the rest of the decade between the Hindu and Muslim communities, brought on by hot-button issues like cow slaughter and the playing of music outside mosques. Even before being confined to house arrest, Savarkar loudly opposed the Khilafat movement in a conspicuous break with Gandhi that he thought could build a new kind of political constituency which, frustrated with Gandhi's apparent accommodationism, might see Savarkar as a welcome alternative.

I start chapter 1 with a counterintuitive premise: Savarkar's ascent to political prominence might not have happened had the British not released him from prison when they did. The release is odd, given that they were fully aware of his views and their dissonant relationship to dominant nationalist views. The background for this story begins long before Savarkar was born, in

1857, when British concern about an international Islamic conspiracy first began to overtly surface in police documents. British surveillance of anticolonial agitators began soon after the suppression of the 1857 Rebellion, when the colonial government completely reorganized the Indian police force. Some decades later, the British established the Criminal Investigation Department. Initially, ordinary Muslims bore the brunt of surveillance, as police documents reveal—a process that continued through the Indian Khilafat movement and beyond. The Khilafat movement appeared to the British as something they had both feared and anticipated for so long—an international Islamic movement that might rise up against the British on a global scale. While the British police were especially worried about Muslims making extraterritorial alliances with Turkey or Afghanistan, they were also concerned that Hindu nationalists might join the Islamic conspiracy.

Savarkar and his two brothers were clearly identified as revolutionary "terrorists" and were surveilled from an early age. The British police in India knew a great deal about Savarkar, including the full extent of his anti-Muslim sentiments. They viewed him as dangerous, seditious, and violent and monitored him before and during his imprisonment. And yet they released him from prison at a time of extreme colonial vigilance about the nationalist movement. Indeed, they not only released him but refrained from arresting him again when he continually violated the terms on which his release was based. I argue that, at a time when fears of global Islam were enhanced, Savarkar became a useful mouthpiece for the colonial government. A known firebrand Hindu polemicist, he, if free, could be counted upon to attack Gandhi, the waning Khilafat movement, and Muslims. In effect, Savarkar ventriloquized the colonial British fear of Muslims and did so eloquently, passionately, and constantly, focusing over and again on Muslims and Gandhi.

In chapter 2, I probe the "Muslim question." Savarkar's biographers often claim that he had no problem with Muslims as a group, just with individual bad and unpatriotic Muslims. In this chapter, I show that, for Savarkar, there were few to no "good" Muslims—that he saw Muslims in the language of race as genetically and characterologically untrustworthy, incapable of being true patriots of India. The demands of the Khilafatists proved for him that all Muslims were part of an international conspiracy to steal Hindu sovereignty. In fact, as I show, Khilafat meant a great deal to the Muslim community in India in large part because it revealed the community's deep feelings of insecurity about its place in the post-British India being imagined around them. While Gandhi recognized the affective hold of the idea of Khilafat and supported the movement, Savarkar was not only aghast at the idea of Muslim loyalty to a political idea based outside India but also at the role Gandhi played in fanning what in his view were anti-nationalist flames.

Savarkar was not an episodic or occasional anti-Muslim but rather a systemic one. I show that his obsession with Khilafat long outlasted the movement itself, becoming the foundational example for him of a Muslim internationalism in fundamental conflict with Indian nationalism. At the same time, unafraid of contradicting himself, he wrote constantly about how, despite their reputation for bravery, Muslims were actually cowards. On the flip side, he savaged Hindu pusillanimity and emasculation and celebrated the new Hindu man, usually an RSS *swayamsevak*, who knew how to take violent action. In all of these cases, Savarkar cherry-picked gruesome events that usually took place outside Maharashtra to scare his readers and draw attention to his views.

In this chapter, I have largely chosen to translate rather than paraphrase a good deal of Savarkar's anti-Muslim writings because doing so captures the passion of his language and the full force of his prejudice. To gain a complete view of Savarkar, it is critical to demonstrate that I have not taken his writings or opinions out of context. I also include the Marathi itself in the appendix to the chapter since Savarkar's Marathi—powered by sarcasm, mockery, puns, polemics, and alliteration—was powerful in large part because of its overwrought poetic form. Marathi readers who might be tempted to argue that my translations render him a disservice can encounter firsthand both his linguistic virtuosity and his arrogance; his wordplay and his vitriol; his deep well of knowledge and his willingness to invent history. Alternatively, readers—Marathi and non-Marathi alike—who might think I am making too much of his anti-Muslim sentiments are invited to read his words directly and decide for themselves. I have not transliterated with diacritics every word, proper name, place, book and article title, or phrase in Marathi, Hindi, Urdu, Turkish, Arabic, or Sanskrit. For ease of reading, I have only used transliterations with diacritics when I cite Savarkar's words, articles, essays, and poems and have left diacritical marks only where I thought they were useful or necessary (as in the chapter on Savarkar's poetry) and when I quote Savarkar's Sanskrit.

In chapter 3, I turn to how Savarkar viewed caste, and because of Savarkar's distinctive and strong views about caste, I quote him directly at some length. This too is deliberate on my part, knowing that such long quotations are not the norm, but I have deemed it particularly important for readers to encounter his actual words. Even by the standards of the 1920s, when India was rocked by what B. R. Ambedkar retrospectively called a civil war between Hindus and

Muslims, Savarkar's rhetoric was extreme. He did not hesitate to represent Muslim women as cannibals and Muslim men as rapists. But if he was reactionary and xenophobic about Muslims, on caste he articulated a progressive and at times aggressive reformist agenda. This allows his supporters to argue that, since his anticasteism was often couched in angry and deprecatory language, he criticized Hindu and Muslim communities equally, the former for its casteism, the latter for its fanaticism.

While it is true that Savarkar wrote as a rationalist and progressive (or *purōgāmī*), this equivalency is false. Savarkar's stance on caste was unquestionably radical. It was aimed, however, solely at the orthodox Hindu community and voiced from within it, using its own dearly held sacred literature (the Vedas, the purāṇas, the epics) to demonstrate the absurdity and illogicality of caste division. Savarkar was unwilling to concede leadership to anyone, so his caste reform was as much a Brahmin-led effort as it was securely anchored in his own upper-caste community. His critique was scathing to be sure, attacking as he did every part of Hindu ritual life, from the practice of cow worship to vegetarianism. Yet, for all that, his critique must be seen in relationship to his other political aims. Savarkar's challenge to caste and untouchability was primarily motivated by his desire to rebuild a lost Hindu sovereignty, while keeping Muslims—whom he imagined as always seeking to convert Hindus—from capitalizing on disaffected lower-caste Hindus or Dalits.

Savarkar fashioned himself first and foremost as a poet. For this reason, his poetry makes an appearance in virtually every chapter. Here again, the Marathi poetry is in the appendix, and transliterations and translations are in the main body of the chapter. To understand how Savarkar created such a large following, we must look especially carefully at his poetic writings. He wrote close to 100 poems, many of which are still performed at national events in Maharashtra, but, in another example of how the kaleidoscope's viewer is fixed in one place, his poetry is usually omitted in discussions of his influence in the English scholarship on him. Rooted in the Marathi literary tradition and the history of classical Sanskrit poetry, his poems were his first published works, and he turned to the genre at moments of crisis. Poetic language infused his most influential political essay—*Essentials of Hindutva*—and he insisted that history should be written like poetry.[34] As patriotic and ideological as his prose was, his poems directly addressed the political problems of his time such as child widowhood, the plague, or the need for an Indic civilizational malaise to be

34. Bakhle, "Country First?," 149–86.

enlivened with a hearty dose of modern medicine. Indeed, on every important issue, Savarkar wrote a poem.

Chapter 4 focuses on Savarkar's poetry in two parts. In the first, it surveys a small representative sample of his poetry, published and unpublished, translated and untranslated, well-known in his native Maharashtra and obscure. In the second, the focus shifts to Savarkar's recasting of one of the most beloved of Marathi ballads, from a genre called *povāḍā*. The genre itself is performative, didactic, historical, and elegiac, and the chapter examines how Savarkar nationalizes (and Brahminizes) one of the region's best-known and well-loved *povāḍās*, making it not just a local myth, but potentially a national one that resonates with the ideal Hindu nation he is building.

Savarkar was also a self-proclaimed historian, even as he used multiple genres for his historical narratives and arguments. In this fifth chapter I juxtapose four of Savarkar's representative historical works with those of the historical writings of one of his contemporaries, the eminent historian Tryambak Shankar Shejwalkar (1895–1963). I do so to show how Savarkar hijacked the writing of history as memory work, even as other historians in his native region—Shejwalkar most of all—were trying to ensure that historical writing was rooted in disciplinary rigor and the careful use of primary-source evidence.

Savarkar wrote as a popular historian, not an academic one. In other words, although his histories would not be recognized as such today by scholars in the discipline, they are widely read *as* histories, and he had a great deal to say about how history ought to be written and a good bit of contempt for how histories were being written. He wrote his four major works in 1909, 1922, 1925, and 1965–66, the last just before he died. The first, on the Rebellion of 1857, was written when he was a student in London; the second, *Essentials of Hindutva,* was published just after his return to India from the Andaman Islands; the third, *Hindu-Pad-Padashahi,* was written from Shirgaon; and the last, *Six Glorious Epochs,* from Mumbai. Despite consigning all of Indian history to memory (work), Savarkar repeatedly invoked the importance of history. The books were both calls for and examples of his argument that historical writing should serve the needs of agitprop; in each of them, he positioned himself as the model historian for others to follow.

I have picked Shejwalkar as a foil for two reasons. First, he was a contemporary of Savarkar's, a reader in Maratha history at Deccan College from 1939–55, and an eminent, if iconoclastic, scholar of Maratha history. Second, and more important, Savarkar and Shejwalkar represent two strands of history writing, one popular and the other more academic, both within a nationalist frame, both emerging at about the same time. While Shejwalker was by far the better academic historian, Savarkar's historical writings secured a much broader readership; even Jawaharlal Nehru, independent India's first prime minister, read them. This makes it a mode of historical writing to which we must pay careful attention, both because of its importance to his followers and its larger appeal during his own time and beyond.

The late nineteenth- and early twentieth-centuries in Maharashtra witnessed an explosion of histories written in Marathi. This burst of history writing produced empiricist and positivist works by historians like Shejwalkar to be sure, but it also enabled the writing of exuberant, if undisciplined, histories—a category that includes Savarkar's own historical writings. The academic discipline of history—what Dipesh Chakrabarty has termed the "cloistered" life of history—was still in its infancy, and only a few universities offered degree-granting programs in Indian history.[35] Research languages taught in these universities were ranked on the basis of an Orientalist colonial agenda with Sanskrit at the top followed by Pali, Prakrit, Persian, and Arabic, with the primary aim of separating the literary from the historical.[36] The curricular bent of regional languages such as Marathi, considered "vernaculars," was entirely literary in this first instance and not oriented toward source criticism or narrative history. Prachi Deshpande has argued that the emphasis of this early work was toward the *mulyamāpaṇa* (evaluation) of exemplary figures and epochs and dynastic chronologies.[37] Academic norms about how history should be written, and on the basis of what kinds of sources and orientation, were debated in institutions, such as the one founded by V. K. Rajwade—the Bharat Itihas Sanshodhan Mandal (1910)—on the fringes of the young academy.[38] This allowed enormous room for the "popular" yet authoritative historian who was not an academic professional to emerge.[39] It is against such a background that one can see Savarkar writing not just rhetorically powerful but also authoritative histories for his time and place.

35. Chakrabarty, *The Calling of History*, 6–8.

36. Deshpande, *Creative Pasts*, 86–88.

37. Deshpande, *Creative Pasts*, 88–79. See also Naregal, *Language Politics*, 101–37.

38. Deshpande, *Creative Pasts*. For a quick look at the Bharat Itihas Sanshodhan Mandal and the dispute in the 1920s and 1930s between Jadunath Sarkar and G. S. Sardesai on the one side and the "Poona School" of historians on the other, see 103–4. For a detailed look at the rise of academic history in India, see Chakrabarty, *The Calling of History*.

39. I am grateful to Prachi Deshpande for pointing this out to me and redirecting me to her book, *Creative Pasts*.

In the final chapter, I take up the manner in which Savarkar and others have used the story of his life. In Maharashtra, there is a near-mythological story about him that circulates widely. Reduced to its essentials, it goes like this: Savarkar was such a brilliant student, poet, writer, and historian that his genius generated resentment from lesser men. While in London, rising in reputation and stature while staying at Shyamji Krishnavarma's India House, he emerged as the mesmerizing leader of other young revolutionaries, writing fiery nationalist and patriotic tracts. He was then falsely arrested by the British, enduring unspeakable hardship in prison in the Andamans, where he was singled out for brutal and abusive treatment by an evil warder. The story then follows him back to India, describes his house arrest and his subsequent leadership of the Hindu Mahasabha, focusing on his stalwart defense of the rights of Hindus against the perfidious and untrustworthy Muslims on the one hand and the perfidious and untrustworthy Gandhi on the other. The story concludes with his false implication in Gandhi's assassination, which led to him spending the rest of his life in seclusion in Bombay, where, eventually, by a supreme act of will, he refused medication when ill and died of his own free will, taking *ātmārpan*.

This mythologized tale of a great revolutionary is replete with unidimensional figures that are household names in the parts of Maharashtra that revere Savarkar: Yesuvahini, the saintly sister-in-law; the evil warder; fanatical Afghans; generally untrustworthy Muslims (with a few exceptions here and there); Muslim-appeasing Gandhi; the cowardly INC party. It is also Savarkar's narrative about himself.

A cursory reading of Savarkar's writings reveals that he was not given to humility. In his memoirs, he matter-of-factly remarks on his own brilliance. While self-representations are inherently inaccurate, Savarkar's biographers follow his lead, never questioning his views, in ways that became critical factors in the making of his own legacy. Very few of Savarkar's Marathi biographers insert any genuine critical distance between themselves and their subject. What Savarkar wrote about himself became what Savarkar's acolytes claimed about him, only then to be used as straightforward evidence of the truth of what Savarkar claimed.

In this last chapter, I examine selections from three examples of this continuous Marathi memorialization. The first is Savarkar's biography—*Life of Barrister Savarkar*—and his memoirs, which spell out the core narrative of his life and function almost as a template-gospel. The second is a sampling of authorized biographies, beginning with Sadashiv Rajaram Ranade (1924) and followed by R. G. Bhope (1938), M. S. Gokhale (1940), and S. L. Karandikar (1943). Y. D.

Phadke, the renowned Marathi historian, eviscerated these books for their inattention to factual accuracy in his work *Śōdha Sāvarakarāñcā* (Search for Savarkar). I am not interested in repeating Phadke's work but in examining these biographies for their role in encouraging a steady stream of biographies in Marathi on Savarkar that continue to be written in the present. The third set of works I look at are what I am calling the *darśana-dakṣiṇā* (witness-homage) literature. These are books that are linked to the biographies, but they offer a humanization of the remote myth of Savarkar with an authorizing gloss: the moment of *darśana* (witness) or *pratyakṣa* (direct experience with one's own eyes) and the biography as prestation or homage—a gift offered to one's spiritual parent or teacher (*dakṣiṇā*). All this literature is central, I argue, in spreading the secular gospel of Savarkar, who remains widely known within Maharashtra in large measure because of this literature. Commemorative biographies of Savarkar continue to be written, even now. If we wish to understand how Savarkar was mythologized and by whom, this literature provides some of the answers.[40]

I began this project over ten years ago, initially hoping to write a quick and concise biography of a complicated man and thereby expand both the content and scope of our understanding of Hindu fundamentalism. The more I read, the more the complexities kept mounting. Savarkar's prose was incendiary, without a doubt—he verbally assaulted his interlocutors, threw ad hominem insults around, made assertions that were fanciful or worse—and yet he came to be venerated. If we do not understand the affective power of his poetry or the poetic resonance of his rage, we cannot understand his charisma and his influence. My recognition that he was precociously gifted or learned or knowledgeable about poetry is not meant as a gesture of support for his politics. At the same time, my critical attention to the rage of his anti-Muslim diatribes is not meant as a dismissal of his clearly copious intellect or anticolonial nationalist passion. Both are intended to explain the different features and facets of his appeal because it will not do, in my opinion, to assume that all those who support him and his politics are deluded, brainwashed, ignorant, simple-minded, or worse—fascists or fools.

In India today, Savarkar is a near-mythic figure, in large part because he has become the intellectual father for the political party currently in power, the Bharatiya Janata Party (BJP), and its leader, Prime Minister Narendra Modi,

40. I am grateful to my colleague Jonathan Sheehan for posing the question of genre and reception in pointed ways that allow me to make the argument that the genre of *darśana-dakṣiṇā* literature itself answers the reception question.

whose views are largely congruent with Savarkar's. Viewed from the perspective of the early years when Savarkar wrote his formative works and poems and established his nationalist persona, the story of his apotheosis was by no means inevitable. After reading this book, I suspect the reader will no longer find the apotheosis quite as surprising as it might once have seemed. I provide the background for understanding Savarkar's ascendancy, even though I conclude my history of Savarkar's life—as he was released from house arrest in 1937—when India was still ten years away from independence. I do not address Savarkar's writings or participation as President of the Hindu nationalist political party, the Hindu Mahasabha, in the major anticolonial events post-1937, which include the Viceroy, Lord Linlithgow, plunging India into a world war without consulting any elected Indian representatives, the Quit India movement (1942), the traumatic partitioning of British India, and Pakistani and Indian independence (August 14, 1947, and August 15, 1947, respectively). I leave it for others to explain why, and how, Savarkar has become the most important political thinker in contemporary India, displacing the architects of independence and India's early postcolonial history. Gandhi, Nehru, and Ambedkar had views of India that could not have been more different than those of Savarkar. And yet the history I tell here will both explain the conditions under which Savarkar developed his fundamental ideas about nationalism, about Muslims, about caste, about history, and ultimately about his own foundational role for the emergence of an independent India and why these ideas might have undergone a resurgence at a time of populist politics, backlash against the tolerant secularism of India's early history, and widespread geopolitical tension across Asia and the Middle East. Although I stop my account in 1937, I explicitly address how Savarkar fashioned an image for himself that was meant to be available for further mythologization and how it might be that the contradictory elements of his thought and life have not just survived but thrived in our current historical moment.

Let us begin with the first part of this story.

1

An Anticolonial Revolutionary

SAVARKAR AND THE COLONIAL POLICE

OUR STORY begins in 1857.[1] While this is a book about V. D. Savarkar and the connections in his writings between Muslims, caste, and his formulation of a peculiarly secular Hindu nationalism, his early life and views about India developed in relation to a much older hatred and fear—one that echoes that of the British for what they perceived as an international Muslim conspiracy against them. Indeed, while Savarkar's politics were defined by his own extreme nationalism, he shared a sense of the Muslim threat with the colonizing enemy he wished to force out of India.

Savarkar was born in 1883 and made his greatest impact between the 1920s and the 1940s. If we start there, however, we miss much that is crucial. Instead, we begin our story at the moment in March 1857 when a Hindu foot soldier named Mangal Pandey from the 34th Infantry of the East India Company army, convinced that the British were in India to take away his religion, fired at his Sergeant Major and inaugurated a rebellion. Pandey was apprehended and hanged, but two months later, in a different colonial garrison in the city of Meerut, eighty-five soldiers refused to touch cartridges they believed had been greased with pig and cow fat. When they were sentenced to ten years imprisonment, their fellow soldiers rose in protest, released them, and made for Delhi to establish Bahadur Shah Zafar, the eighty-two-year-old infirm poet and gentle Mughal emperor as their rightful leader. The revolt moved speedily across the northeast of India over the next two years, with news of a British

1. I am grateful to Val Daniel, Shrikant Botre, Alok Oak, Roger Grant, Abhishek Kaicker, Ajinkya Lele for their comments, suggestions, and corrections to an early draft of this chapter.

defeat spurring similar revolts in Aligarh, Lucknow, Indore, Gwalior, Jhansi Banaras, Allahabad, and Etawah.

The East India Company spent a great deal of money to recruit soldiers and successfully put down the rebellion between 1857 and 1859. It captured Bahadur Shah Zafar in September 1857 and, while the rebellion still raged, indicted him through a military commission on the charges of treason and of masterminding an international Muslim conspiracy against the British.[2] The British prosecutor Major Harriot asserted that

> the known restless spirit of *Mahommedan fanaticism* has been the first aggressor, the *vindictive intolerance* of that peculiar faith has been struggling for mastery, *seditious conspiracy* has been its means, the prisoner its active accomplice, and every possible crime the frightful result. . . . Thus the *bitter zeal of Mahommedanism* meets us everywhere. It is conspicuous in the papers, flagrant in the petitions, and *perfectly demoniac* in its actions [emphasis mine].

The British agreed that those who had participated in the rebellion were motivated by "Mahommedan fanaticism," and *intolerance, sedition, zealousness,* and *demonic actions* became the terms by which the British understood Muslims in India. As we will see, Savarkar reproduced much the same language in his own writings about 1857, as well as about much else.

How had an eighty-two-year-old Bahadur Shah organized such a massive conspiracy? Again, Major Harriot pointed to the fanaticism of the followers of Mohammed:

> . . . there was also a general unsettling of men's minds throughout the country and among the Mahommedans in particular. . . . Coupling this with the prophecy among the Mahommedans that English sovereignty in India was to cease 100 years after its first establishment by the battle of Plassey in 1757, we are able to form something more than conjecture as to the causes which have given to *Mahommedan fanaticism its delusive hope of recovering all its former prestige*. . . . I have endeavored to point out how intimately the prisoner as the head of the Mahommedan faith in India, has been connected with the *organization of that conspiracy either as its leader or its unscrupulous accomplice* (emphasis mine).[3]

2. See Bell, "1858 Trial of the Mughal Emperor," 10–11, for a legal analysis of how the trial of Bahadur Shah Zafar violated international law.

3. Dirks, *Autobiography of an Archive*, 220–21. Major Frederick Harriot was Deputy Judge Advocate General, and all through the trial he emphasized that Bahadur Shah was not to be recognized as a real sovereign or the King of Delhi but a criminal, indeed one of the greatest of

That he had organized such a large undertaking or had such influence would have come as a surprise to Bahadur Shah Zafar, who was more interested in composing melancholic poetry than in revolution. Still, he was exiled for life and saw his sons and heirs executed. Meanwhile, the narrative of the "fanatical Muslim" engaged in an unceasing conspiracy to restore Muslim sovereignty, and the concomitant need for constant vigilance entered the British Indian Police and administrative lexicon and stayed there for close to a century.

The Rebellion was comprehensively squashed by 1859; two years later an all-India police force was established.[4] Enter Charles Forjett. He began his police career in India two years before the Rebellion and rose speedily to the top, mainly because of his exemplary service in proactively arresting anyone in Bombay who spoke approvingly of the 1857 rebels.[5] Forjett wrote a book about his time in India in which he boasted of his "experience of 40 years of Indian official life, as topographical surveyor; as translator in Hindoostanee and Mharatta." His writing, he said, could be trusted because he had been "in close, constant, and familiar intercourse with all classes of natives of India . . ."[6] Forjett's goal was to impress on British high officials that India's Muslims were not just troublesome but were always monitoring international politics with

---

all criminals. For the trial documents and an analysis, see Bell, "1858 Trial of the Mughal Emperor," ch. 1.

4. IOR/Mss Eur/C/235/1; Tegart, *Charles Tegart*, 25. The undated memoir written by Charles Tegart's wife is only available as a typewritten sheet in the British Library's India Office Records (IOR). The Oriental and India Office Collections (OIOC) is where all IOR materials are housed.

5. Forjett, *Our Real Danger*, 32. Forjett writes proudly of his accomplishments during the Rebellion.

> Shortly after the outbreak there was some talk of introducing martial law into Bombay. . . . I considered it a fitting opportunity to impress upon the evil-disposed and disaffected, the danger of conduct in the least subversive of good order. I therefore put up a gibbet in the yard of the police office, and summoned the leading men among those who, in the event of a mutiny, would be foremost in the ranks of the lawless, and intimated to them, that if I should have the least reason to believe that any among them contemplated an outbreak in Bombay, they should be at once seized and hanged. What I stated was listened to in solemn silence, and every man, I felt assured, left the police office overawed, and under a thorough conviction that the game of rebellion would be a dangerous one. And if, during my presence at any place of rendezvous, the language of anyone bordered on the seditious I immediately threw off my disguise and seized him on the spot; and such was the fear inspired by the police, and such the opinion in regards to its ubiquity that though the number assembled was 100, or 200, or more they immediately hastened away, leaving the man who was taken into custody to his fate.

6. Forjett, *Our Real Danger*, 19.

an eye toward other nations that might help them. Forjett was particularly concerned about the ongoing Russo-Turkish conflict.

It was most urgent, he opined, that the Secretary of State for India understood that "from the earliest time that Russia ha[d] become a power her aim has been the acquisition of Constantinople."[7] While there was little reason to believe Russia would invade India, her actions "[p]roduced on the Turkoman hordes in the neighborhood, on the Afghans, on the Persians, and even on the thinking portion of the population of India, a deep impression that the power of Russia was such as prevented England from contending with her."[8] Forjett's concern was that England might be seen as weak relative to Russia, which was dangerous because, if Russia defeated Turkey,

> [t]he charm of England's prestige, which has enabled a handful of Europeans to hold in subjection the hundreds of millions of the populations of India, would be dispelled, and the Oriental mind, divested of the influences of the spell, would learn to invest Russia's power and irresistibility with highly exaggerated notions of superiority, and British supremacy, now standing on the pinnacle of their estimation would then be precipitated to the very lowest depth. The Mahomedans especially, so deeply interested in the fate of Turkey, would view us with contempt.[9]

If Russia were defeated, then, "[t]he success of the Turks, on the other hand, would lead the Mahomedan world of India and of Asia to view British power with a deeper contempt for having abandoned Turkey in the hour of her need. . . ."[10]

Either way, Muslims were likely to lose their faith in the British. Muslims had to be monitored to ensure the security of British India. By 1880 Muslim conspiracy was back in the police files, if it had ever left. Muslims writing letters to anyone in Turkey, Muslim associations, Muslim presses—even Muslim princely state rulers—along with the Turkish Consul and Vice Consul in Bombay, were under surveillance, as were Turkish visitors, dignitaries, and travelers.[11] By 1903, the

7. Forjett, *Our Real Danger*, 145.

8. Forjett, *Our Real Danger*, 149.

9. Forjett, *Our Real Danger*, 159.

10. Forjett, *Our Real Danger*, 162.

11. The police opened letters sent to the Turkish Sultan from Karachi Muslims, for instance, congratulating him for his victories in the campaign against the Greeks, annotating passages that British informants found objectionable. NAI [National Archives of India] FD/Sec/E Oct. 1897, 262–91. I am grateful to Faiz Ahmad for sharing his research on the policing of Turks

supposedly Turkophilic neighboring Afghan Amir was also being monitored.[12] The ghost of 1857 haunted policemen who feared that the "Mahomedans" of India, having followed Bahadur Shah Zafar into one rebellion, might follow the Sultan of Turkey or the Emir of Afghanistan into another.[13]

While Forjett focused on Muslims, Charles Tegart, his counterpart in Bengal many years later, was scrutinizing Hindus. Tegart joined the Indian Police Service in 1901 and served in Bengal for thirty-some years. In 1932, at the close of his Indian career, he gave an address on terrorism in India. Terrorism's history,

---

and Afghans by the British in the same period. Faiz generously shared his findings with me along with the actual files.

12. NAI FD/Sec/F Feb. 1904, 247–49 (re: Abdul Baki, an Afghan in Constantinople and Damascus). A memo from St. John Brodrick of the India Office in London to the Governor-General of India, dated January 8, 1904, "regarding an Afghan, named Abdul Baki, who was at that time residing at Constantinople, but has since moved to Damascus . . ." The following was included. N.R. O'Conor of the British Embassy in Istanbul writes on December 8, 1903, that he "received from His Majesty's Consul at Damascus, reporting certain statements made to him by one Abdul Baki respecting the Turcophil tendencies of the Amir of Afghanistan." The report from the British Consul at Damascus in a memo to O'Conor dated from Damascus on November 19, 1903:

> I have lately had several interviews with an Afghan of rank of the name of Abdul Baki, in the course of which he has made certain statements to me of a very interesting and confidential nature. . . . Abdul Baki Khan, who has been residing in Damascus, on and off, for the last six years, belongs to the Wazir Yar Muhammad Khan branch of the Elicozai-Durrani clan, and is the son-in-law of the late Sardar Ghulam Muhammad Khan, Terzi, a cousin of the late Amir Abdur Rahman. . . . Suffice it to say that he has evidently travelled a good deal both in Russian Central Asia, and, to a certain extent, in Russia proper, and is a well-bred, intelligent man who takes a keen interest in Russian politics, especially, of course, in that branch of it which concerns his native country, to which he professes himself to be passionately attached. It is under the influence of this fervid patriotism . . . that Abdul Baki has bewailed to me on several occasions the blindly perverse infatuation of the present Amir in trying to get rid of the British connection at the suggestion, or at all events with the approval and connivance of the Sultan. . . . My informant assures me that *Turcophilism is at present rampant in Kabul, where everything that comes, or is supposed to come from this country, is welcomed with enthusiasm by the short-sighted and retrograde ruler and all those who come under his immediate influence. . . .* [*T*]*he Amir has decided to take active steps for the education of his subjects on Turkish lines, and with this object in view he has been for some time past trying to induce Turks of the civil, military, and Ulema classes, respectively, to go and settle in Afghanistan* in order to inculcate and diffuse Turkish principles and methods in administrative, military, and educational matters in that country [emphasis mine].

13. NAI FD/Sec/F Oct. 1907, 152–59, no. 152. A confidential memorandum dated November 21, 1906, from the Personal Assistant to the Inspector-General of Police, North-West Frontier Province, forwarded an extract from a Criminal Intelligence Department report, dated November 14, 1906, that states,

he noted, "forms more or less a continuous chain," and "the rank and file are generally students." He added that "[t]he first point I would like to impress on you is that terrorism . . . is essentially a Hindu movement . . . [which] has taken root in Bengal but it started on the other side of India; the earliest centre of anarchism was formed as far back as 1897 in the Presidency of Bombay. . . ."[14]

Tegart's wife later wrote a biography of him in which she described his view of Indian anticolonial societies, such as those founded by Savarkar, as anarchist and terrorist; they had "elaborate initiation ceremonies, often with a religious twist to them, well calculated to intimidate any political backslider in the future. The recruit bound himself by solemn oath to absolute secrecy and obedience and formally dedicated his life to the cause." She added that "one of the most sinister concomitants of terrorism in any country is the prompt and unthinking adoption by its followers of lawlessness as an accepted standard . . . the Indian revolutionary leaders appeared quite conscienceless in this respect and the blood of many un-offending people . . . came to be laid at their door."[15]

One policeman believed Muslims were conspiratorial fanatics, the other that Hindu students were the original terrorists.[16] Together this meant that virtually the entire population of the subcontinent warranted surveillance as internal and external threats to British rule in India. Given Savarkar's early

---

> Jamil Effendi, Turk, of Sham returned to Peshawar from Kabul on the 13th on his way back to Sham *viâ* Bombay and is putting up with Abdul Wadud Khan, Kandahari. It has been ascertained that directly on his arrival in Kabul he had an interview with His Majesty and was granted R500 Kabuli. The Amir also directed his expenses to be defrayed from the State Treasury during his stay in Kabul. He stayed with Sardar Habibulla Khan, Naib Kotwal of Kabul, who is a connection. With the Amir's permission he visited Kohistani-i-Kabul, Chardehi and other places of interest. On his return from Logar, the Amir had again an interview with Jamil Effendi, and carried on a conversation in Turkish with the Amir. Jamil Effendi asked for a year's leave; this was granted and R500 by Sardar Nasrulla Khan and R200 by Sardar Habibulla Khan, Naib Kotwal. He was then allowed to depart. Jamil Effendi intends visiting the Turkish Consulate before leaving Bombay. He has been told by the Amir not to disclose to anybody the grant made to him. This man is also said to be in receipt of pay from the Sultan of Turkey.

14. Tegart, *Terrorism in India*, 2–5. On the same subject, see Pandey, "The Terrorist Alternative, 1885–1916," in *Indian Nationalist Movement*, 23–25. See also Chirol, *Indian Unrest*.

15. IOR/Mss Eur/C/235/1, 88–90. Tegart, *Terrorism in India*, 71. See chapter 7 ("The Growth of Terrorism") for a fairly typical colonial policeman's viewpoint about Indian "extremism," which Tegart's widow likened to Nazism.

16. IOR/Mss Eur/D/1011. "Terrorist" was the term of choice well into the 1920s. British policemen viewed all anti-British agitators as "terrorists"—including "Israeli terrorists."

anti-British actions, it is not surprising that he came under surveillance at an early age. The story of Savarkar begins therefore with the building of the British colonial surveillance system and the changes in policing and laws that allowed the gathering of information on him and his brother; his nemesis Gandhi; the two brothers (Mohammad Ali and Shaukat Ali) who led the Khilafat movement; and countless famous, semifamous, and unknown Indian students and thinkers, merchants, and travelers.

Savarkar was first placed under surveillance as a college student in Poona after he organized a bonfire of foreign cloth and made angry speeches against the British. Before that, as a young boy, he had appointed himself his village's pedagogue, instructing fellow students in political activism and national history. He published patriotic poetry and led a group of his friends to vandalize the lone mosque outside his village. He formed a secret revolutionary society and began inculcating historical consciousness in his friends by teaching them about Napoleon, Garibaldi, and Mazzini. From school in Nasik, he moved on to college in Pune, where he joined the Swadeshi movement and held the bonfires that caught the eye of British police. From there he went to England, ostensibly to study law but actually to fulminate against the British in works commemorating the 1857 Rebellion, smuggle pistols into India for assassinations, and dispatch revolutionary friends and supporters to Europe and America to learn how to make bombs. Savarkar lived virtually his entire life under surveillance; because of his suspected role in the assassination of Gandhi, he was surveilled by the Indian Police up until his death in 1966. The colonial police file on Savarkar shows that the police knew a great deal about his early life, from the members of his Bhagur and Nashik secret societies to the location of his facial scars.[17] They also translated a good deal of what Savarkar had written.

Arrested under the terms of the Fugitive Offenders Act (1881) and tried for sedition,[18] Savarkar was sent to the Andaman Islands in the Indian Ocean in 1911 to serve his two consecutive life sentences. He started appealing for his release virtually upon arrival. In 1920, he wrote to the colonial government claiming a broken body and a changed mind as proof he qualified for the amnesty King

17. Mishra, "The Bomb, the Bullet and the Gandhi Cap," 1–28. Mishra observed in her fieldwork at the intelligence department archive in United Provinces that the fortnightly intelligence reports published by the department often included descriptions of body markings such as tattoos or scars to encourage people to reveal the whereabouts of revolutionaries for whom the police did not have photographs.

18. Ilbert, "British India."

George V had announced for political prisoners.[19] He also noted that the British and his own community, by which he meant the upper-caste Hindu community, had an enemy in common: Muslim "hoardes." Despite warnings from Bombay police officers on the ground who knew that Savarkar almost certainly still harbored anti-British intentions, the central government, under pressure to maintain its liberal reputation, insisted he be released. He was released into limited house arrest in Ratnagiri in 1924 on the condition that he not engage in political activities and not stray beyond Ratnagiri district.

Nothing Savarkar did—from vandalizing a mosque to writing nationalist political poetry, from sketching out the essentials of Hindutva in prison to targeting pan-Islamic movements, from his anti-Muslim writings to his dismissal of Gandhi, not even his historical writings—can be separated from politics. How then did the colonial government that saw him as a charismatic and fanatic leader of a terrorist conspiracy convince itself he would eschew all political activity overnight? And why did it do so just when its own fears of an international Muslim conspiracy were being manifested by the Indian Khilafat movement?

In 1920, the Ali brothers, Mohammad and Shaukat, spearheaded the Khilafat movement in India, demanding that the British colonial government stop the imminent carving up of the territories of the defeated Ottoman Empire. The last Sultan of Turkey was also the Caliph of Islam, or the spiritual sovereign of the Sunni Muslim community, but his sovereignty depended on maintaining territorial control of the Muslim holy lands Mecca and Medina. If the new treaties the British were pursuing with Mustafa Kemal in 1922–23 took away the Caliph's territorial sovereignty, it would essentially destroy his spiritual sovereignty. The Ali brothers, with the support of Gandhi and the main voice of Indian anticolonialism, the INC, insisted that the Caliphate (Khilafat in the Indian context) was a religious institution, not a political one. They implored the British government to intercede not just on behalf of Muslims living under British rule, but of Muslims around the world.

The Khilafat movement and its purported appeal to Muslims worldwide triggered the British fear first expressed in 1859 in the trial of Bahadur Shah Zafar. The Bombay Police Commissioner appointed in 1864, Frank Souter, had taken seriously the task of monitoring correspondence between Indian communities and "foreigners," paying particular attention to the Muslim community and its connections outside India.[20] In one case, police surveillance

19. Ghosh, *Gentlemanly Terrorists*. As part of an overhaul and reform of the colonial prison system, George V announced an amnesty for all political prisoners.

20. The British did not see themselves as "foreigners."

brought under its ambit a Russian agent suspected of having connections to the Sultan of Turkey, all correspondence between Indian Muslims and their co-religionists in Egypt and Turkey, six Muslim rulers of Indian princely states, two newspapers, and one political organization.[21] Any suggestion of an "Islamitic conspiracy" generated a wide net of police surveillance.[22]

Nor was Turkey a new concern: in 1876, former Prime Minister William Ewart Gladstone asserted that the Turks were "upon the whole, from the black day when they first entered Europe, the one great anti-human specimen of humanity . . . and, as far as their dominion reached, civilization disappeared from view."[23] Gladstone rode back into power four years later, and the Armenian massacres in the 1890s added to the British view that the Turks were untrustworthy and even dangerous.[24] This fear is reflected in the 1911 recommendations of the Bombay Police that the British government should oust the current Turkish Consul and replace him with someone more congenial to British policies.[25] It was also present in their concern that the Young Turks were working in Afghanistan to build a "Neo-Islamic League."[26] So when the All India Muslim League and other Indian Muslim associations from Calcutta, Allahabad, Lahore, Chittagong, Madras, and Karachi joined in the appeal to the British government to protect the Khilafat, it would certainly have made the British uneasy.[27] The proverbial cherry on the top would be that Gandhi, well-known to them as a rabble rouser in South Africa, joined Muslim leaders in supporting the Khilafat movement.

We will talk more about Khilafat in the next chapter; for now I will only note that the colonial Indian Police had files on the Khilafat movement in

21. NAI/Home Department/Political/no. 3516B of 1880, C. Gonne, Chief Secretary to Government to Sir Frank Souter, Commissioner of Police, Poona, July 24, 1880. NAI/Home Department/Political.no. 2245 of 1880, Sir Frank Souter, Commissioner of Police to C. Gonne, Esquire, Chief Secretary to Govt, Political Department, Poona, August 14, 1880.

22. NAI/file 4143/M/1936/D/no. 11693 of 1880. The locution "Islamitic" [cf. "Semitic"] is itself unusual. Might it be the racialization of the "religious Islamic?"

23. Gladstone, *Bulgarian Horrors*, 9.

24. Astourian, "The Armenian Genocide."

25. IOR/L/PS/10/196. At the same time, the British government was concerned that in any instances of war, such as between Turkey and Italy, it would work with an allied power to protect pilgrimage routes for Muslims.

26. IOR/L/PS/10/196, 160.

27. IOR/L/PS/10/196, 108–19. See also IOR/L/PS/20/C19 for a historical essay prepared under the direction of the Historical Section of the Foreign Office: "The Rise of the Turks: The Pan-Turanian Movement," Confidential Handbook, February 1919. The author recognized that the Committee of Union and Progress were secular and that the pan-Islamic movement was political rather than strictly religious, but the concern about a worldwide or widespread movement is palpable.

Bombay and nationally. They knew a great deal about the movement's activities. They also knew all about Savarkar's anti-Muslim attitudes. Yet, in the same year as the Khilafat movement ended, Savarkar was placed under house arrest and allowed to write editorials, plays, and poems that reviled Muslims, Hindu-Muslim unity, Gandhi, and the leaders of the Khilafat movement, all in his native Marathi. Given the influence he had over his followers—something the police surveillance file constantly noted—his writings and speeches would surely only antagonize already inflamed passions. The colonial police made note of his "objectionable claims" but did not re-arrest him, comprehensively censor him, move him to another part of India, or exert any real control over him. They occasionally asked him to alter his prose or explain himself, but when the explanations were unsatisfactory, the police did nothing.

The colonial government may well have had its hand forced by George V's startling declaration of a Royal Clemency for all political prisoners, but Savarkar's release allowed him to—unwittingly, perhaps, but certainly effectively—serve them, acting as a useful ventriloquist and microphone for their sentiments. Within days of his release, Savarkar let fly at the Khilafat Movement, Gandhi, ideas of Hindu-Muslim unity, and Muslims in general. And since the colonial police were well aware of Indian religious politics, often enlisting Muslim detectives in the Criminal Investigation Department (CID) to watch Hindu revolutionaries,[28] there is no doubt that they knew about his sentiments. Not only did they know—they made it a point to know.

This chapter is divided into two parts. In the first, which shows how and why police surveillance expanded after the 1857 Rebellion both in India and abroad, Savarkar makes only a fleeting appearance. The second details Savarkar's surveillance. The prism for this chapter is the colonial context of Savarkar's political formation. My use of a colonial police lens to present much of Savarkar's political work is meant to show the extraordinary reach and comprehensiveness of imperial surveillance and how the police viewed Savarkar's role in nationalist politics. I will discuss his politics again when I turn to his own writings, as well as those of his acolytes, in later chapters.

Before I go further—a note on my sources. Police archives are notoriously difficult to access, and the Indian archives are no exception. I was able to access files from a self-appointed archivist about the reorganization of the Bombay police, the Khilafat movement in Bombay, surveillance files on Bombay Muslims, and, particularly noteworthy, the complete police file on Savarkar and on

28. Mishra, *The Bomb, the Bullet and the Gandhi Cap*, 14.

his associate turned informant, H. C. Koregaonkar—files that were slated to be destroyed. I augmented my research with police files from the British Library's Oriental and India Office Collection, the British National Archives at Kew Gardens, the National Archives, and the Nehru Memorial Archives in Delhi. I corroborated as many files as I could at the British Library, but often my citations are incomplete, in that I cannot give my readers the exact location where these files were acquired. That being said, there are only three archives that could have housed them: the National Archives in New Delhi before they were transferred, the Maharashtra State Archives if and when they were transferred, or the Bombay Police archives. However, since I cannot in a couple of cases give the exact location, I have, instead, given as many details from within the files as I can. Some of my materials, that is to say, come from a smuggled archive.

Surveillance

To appreciate the reach of the British secret police in India, we turn to one of its preeminent chroniclers, Sir Percival Griffiths, himself a policeman. Two years after the 1857 Rebellion was comprehensively put down, the police system of India was reorganized. In 1861, the Police Act (V) created a unified police force for India, giving control of provincial forces to Inspectors General, who were assisted by deputy and assistant inspector generals.[29] In writing his history, Griffiths relied heavily on the work of a former police commissioner, S. M. Edwardes, who wrote a history of the Bombay city police force from 1672 to 1916. Both works have the confident voice of colonial policemen celebrating police reforms, the installation of new divisions, and the establishment of a surveillance system. Both authors use the word "terrorist" to describe anticolonial activities. This is no surprise; we are not using police histories in the expectation that they will sympathize with anticolonial feeling.

In 1870 sedition was introduced into the Indian Penal Code as the offense of "exciting disaffection" against the colonial government. While John Stuart Mill's *On Liberty* (1859) stipulated that British citizens had the right to criticize their government, it was seditious for Indians in the colony to do the same. Revolutionary nationalists were arrested for and convicted of sedition; with each judicial interpretation and trial, the law's parameters widened, expanding to include the use of dangerous words as evidence of conspiracy. Sedition was used as a preemptive and ex post facto legal mechanism that allowed the

29. Rao, *The Indian Police Act*, 117.

colonial state, in anticipation of an act of "terror," to proscribe all writing or speech that might produce it. A catch-all category, sedition encompassed guns, bombs, and actual assassinations at one end to books, pamphlets, rumors, and even the harboring of anticolonial government feelings at the other.[30]

Convicting a suspect of sedition required proof, which meant that the police needed an expansive remit. It was provided by the Viceroy Lord Ripon, under whom the infamous "Gag Act," or the Vernacular Press Act (1878), that abolished the freedom of the native press was hastily passed.[31] Ripon complained, however, that there was no systematic gathering of police intelligence about suspicious people, no surveillance system, and while he did not think it "desirable to create an extensive system of secret police," he suggested it might be "expedient to pay great attention to all secret sources of information regarding foreign emissaries, intrigues, or unusual political or social phenomena."[32] Such an unusual political act occurred in the same year as the passage of the Gag Act.

After Vasudev Balwant Phadke, a clerk in the Poona military accounts department, was denied leave to visit his ailing mother, he organized a small rebellion.[33] In Griffiths's understanding, Phadke had "planned the systematic looting of government treasuries and post offices aiming to collect large funds to raise battalions of young Marhattas for a guerrilla war against the British."[34] The mention of "guerilla war" indicated that whatever Phadke was doing was something far worse than everyday crime.

In 1887, the police decided a special branch was needed to collect information that could prevent actions like those Phadke had taken. What and who ought to be placed under surveillance?

> (a) all political movements and publication of seditious literature, (b) religious sects and changes in doctrine and practice having a political significance, . . . (d) *rumours* or published opinions disturbing the public peace and popular feelings, (e) *religious excitement* such as caused by kine-killing contrary to rules, and comments by the people on laws and Government's measures (f) illicit trade in arms and ammunition, special notice being taken

30. See Bakhle, "Savarkar (1883–1966)," 54.

31. See Dacosta, *Remarks on the Vernacular*.

32. Griffiths, *To Guard My People*, 343.

33. For a biography of Phadke, see Joshi, *Adya Krantikaraka*.

34. Griffiths, *To Guard My People*, 229. For an official's view of Phadke's rebellion, see the Governor of Bombay Sir Richard Temple's account in his book *Men and Events of My Time in India*, 469–70.

> of all Arms-act cases, (g) recruiting for Indian army or native states, (h) affairs in native States and *rumors* regarding them (i) constitution, objects and proceedings of native societies whether established for political or ostensibly for other objects (j) *indication of distress* or anticipation of famine, scarcity of food or water for man or beast, with statement (in cases of famine or pressure) of number of deaths from starvation, (k) *emigration and immigration* and the causes thereof, and (i) arrival, sojourn and departure of *men of note* [emphasis mine].[35]

In other words, virtually no aspect of the life of the Indian population went unwatched. The final point, allowing the travels of "men of note" to be surveilled, gave the police leeway to monitor literally any and every part of the daily life of the population under their jurisdiction.

Though his rebellion came to nothing, Phadke became a hero for subsequent "guerrilla warriors," chief among them B. G. Tilak, who Griffiths recognized as Savarkar's hero. Griffiths, meanwhile, saw Savarkar as "the moving spirit of the London Association," the group of revolutionaries living in London.[36] Griffiths knew about Tilak and Savarkar largely because, as he remarked, "the intelligence work of the Bombay police at this time was excellent," adding that the police were aware of the correspondence between Savarkar and his brother Babarao. Griffiths opined that

> the best intelligence officers developed an uncanny flair for knowing who to believe or what clues to pursue. This work naturally devolved on a comparatively few men of all ranks, trained for the purpose and experienced in handling agents, watchers, approvers or informers, and in conducting house searches.[37]

These intelligence officers hired native watchers to keep tabs on suspicious people, paid informers who gave the police additional information, and deputized still others to conduct home searches.

"Of great importance to the intelligence officer," Griffiths continued, "was his ability to organize a reliable staff of watchers" who could produce enough intelligence to allow colonial policeman to search houses for weapons or correspondence.[38] Such searches could yield "arms dumps, literature and

35. Griffiths, *To Guard My People*, 344–45.
36. Griffiths, *To Guard My People*, 227–29.
37. Griffiths, *To Guard My People*, 256.
38. Griffiths, *To Guard My People*, 257.

organization plans of terrorist groups, wanted murderers and suspects," none of which would have been useful without "detailed knowledge of the general organization and methods of the terrorists and of the particular groups to which prominent terrorists belonged. Much of the time of intelligence officers was therefore taken up in the preparation of elaborate history sheets."

The police history sheet is akin to a master's thesis written by an excellent student. It is a detailed chronological narrative that offers evidence at each step. Efforts are made to stay objective and report the facts, with an appendix listing all sources used (newspaper reports, secret abstracts, cuttings, transcriptions of speeches). The history sheets give us a sense of the areas of concern and the pattern of reportage. The police files on Savarkar and the Khilafat movement indicate who attended meetings and public speeches, who spoke, who asked questions, how much money was solicited and raised, the size of the crowd and its mood. Police report writers did not recommend actions; they merely provided documentation, putting information from teams of watchers, informants, and researchers into a coherent narrative. Occasionally, the writer's perspective or opinion comes through in the use of adjectives, dismissals, or a bit of sarcasm. Along with the other documents in the file, the history sheet would make its way to a senior official who made policy decisions.

We will examine three such history sheets: one on Savarkar and the other two on the Khilafat movement. For now we return to Griffiths, who at the close of his chapter on terrorism wrote that "the terrorist virus . . . could not ever be completely eradicated" and admitted that in Bombay the "terrorist spirit was at times manifest."[39] The word "terrorist" was used almost epidemiologically, as if "terrorism" was a pandemic in need of a police vaccine.

In the early years of the new century, the police were grappling with the "spread of the dangerous Indian revolutionary movement." The activities of the India House in London[40], the brothers Savarkar, Bal Gangadhar Tilak in the Deccan, and "the anarchists of Bengal" all "had many ramifications in

39. Griffiths, *To Guard My People*, 277.

40. See Chatterjee, *Indian Revolutionaries in Conference*. In 1905 Krishnavarma founded the India Home Rule Society and named himself president. The society published a penny monthly called the *Indian Sociologist* that, following the Irish example and in the context of the partition of Bengal, agitated for England's complete withdrawal from India. In December 1905 he announced six lectureships of 1,000 rupees to enable authors, journalists, and others to visit England, Europe, and America. Another Indian, S. S. Rana, offered three traveling scholarships of 2,000 rupees. Krishnavarma turned his house in Highgate into a mess-cum-hostel for Indian students studying in England. Renamed India House, it became a magnet for young Indian

India, and, coupled with the malignant incitements to sedition disseminated by certain vernacular newspapers, imposed a large burden of confidential and secret work upon the various provincial and urban police forces."[41]

The police force was clearly not up to the task, and the Fraser Commission, presided over by Sir Andrew Fraser, was tasked by the Viceroy Lord Curzon with making recommendations to overhaul the country's police system.[42] But decisions about employing watchers and creating a staff of detective agents were made locally.[43] Published in 1903, the report called for a major overhaul of policing in India,[44] recommending the creation of an Imperial Criminal Investigation department, along with an "Intelligence Branch" that would work in close communication with individual-presidency CIDs since there was now a "clear necessity for a special staff of officers to obtain and transmit information about the movements of suspicious strangers."[45] Edwardes bemoaned that the "lawless influence of Tilak and his immediate followers" produced disturbances that were not easily controlled or suppressed, and the new Bombay CID was given "the task of watching the trend of political movements and of accumulating knowledge of the antecedents and actions of the chief fomenters of unrest."[46] This double-tiered imperial-regional CID would now gather information on all suspicious nationalists with the help of the Intelligence Branch.

The first head of the (imperial) Criminal Intelligence Department was Sir Harold Stuart (1904–07), followed by the Honorable Charles James Stevenson-Moore, C.V.O., K.C.I.E. (1907–10).[47] They faced a new challenge.

---

revolutionaries, many of whom were drawn to anarchists and Russian and Italian nationalists. See also Keer, *Veer Savarkar*, 28–55.

41. Edwardes, *Bombay City Police*, 121.

42. A. H. L. Fraser was the Lieutenant Governor of Bengal from 1903 to 1908.

43. Griffiths, *To Guard My People*, 346.

44. See Fraser, "Report of the Indian Police."

45. Fraser, "Report of the Indian Police." See chapter 5 and chapter 8 on individual CIDs.

46. Edwardes, *Bombay City Police*, 145–46. The CID was subdivided into four branches: Political, Foreign, Crime and Miscellaneous. For the deliberations about standardizing police salaries, duties, divisions, whether they should be trained in Scotland Yard, the difficulties that proposal posed, and what the reporting lines ought to be, see Police Letters from India, IOR/L/PJ/3/672, 1904–05. While the CID is not the main focus of this correspondence, all agreed that the Bombay City Force functioned well, and its CID was the most efficient in British India.

47. Stevenson-Moore joined the Indian Civil Service on September 19, 1887. He arrived in India a few months later in December 1887. From 1887–1904 he worked as an Assistant Magistrate and Collector for a host of stations, beginning with Midnapore to Patna and Chittagong, to Muzaffarpur and Gaya. In 1904 he was appointed Inspector-General of Police, Lower

In the previous century, colonial rule was resisted mainly by peasants and landed gentry concerned about colonial reformulations of land tenure. In the twentieth century, the most dangerous individual was the educated native, the same person colonial efforts of the previous fifty years had aimed to produce. In his 1835 Educational Minute, Lord Macaulay famously stated that the aim of imperial education institutions was to "raise up an English-educated middle class who may be interpreters between us and the millions whom we govern—a class of persons Indian in colour and blood, but English in tastes, in opinions, in morals, and in intellect." Many among the first generation of English-educated Indians were such interpreters, but in the next generation, gratitude was replaced by resentment. Second-generation educated Indians went to England, read English law, history, and philosophy, and came back radicalized. As Partha Chatterjee has pointed out, that radicalization came from a potent brew that included exposure to revolutionary European writers like Mazzini, contact with Irish nationalists, and, as we will see with Savarkar, a strong devotion to a Hindu sect associated with Ganesha or Durga. Along with the Sanskritic concept of duty (dharma) taken from the Bhagavad Gita, this combination created a set of men whose religious devotion was joined to revolutionary anticolonial politics.

These were the "extremist" characters that the fledgling CID was tasked with monitoring, both in India and abroad. Soon after taking the post of Director of Criminal Intelligence, Stevenson-Moore penned a confidential circular, published in 1908, entitled "Note on the Anti-British Movement Among Natives of India in America" that identified the US as a potential breeding ground for Indian revolutionaries.[48] All Indian students in Great Britain and America were monitored, even when they were behaving as normal young men, falling in love, losing their passports, and traveling to see friends.[49] Hindu students in London, Cambridge, and Oxford and Muslim students in London, Cambridge, and Glasgow were all tracked, the meetings they attended and speeches or comments they made noted.[50]

Provinces, and stationed in Calcutta. Four years later he was made Director of Criminal Intelligence and stationed in Simla.

48. IOR/L/PJ/12/1, 1913.

49. For instance, the police monitored the comings and goings of Shahid Hasan Suhrawardy as he became infatuated with a married Russian woman and got into trouble over his passport. Even though the file noted his utter lack of interest in politics—he was surveilled. IOR/L/PJ/12/3, 1914–18.

50. IOR/L/PJ/12/159, 1923–29

In July 1909 the Fraser committee's report on the particularities of reorganization of the Bombay Police was sent to the Commissioner of Police. It laid out the deficiencies of the current organization in detail, including the absence of "any link or continuous communication between the Criminal Investigation Department and all classes of natives" and "the failure to communicate quickly to the Police or other authorities outside the Presidency Town matters of political and criminal importance."[51] Since the CID now had to investigate crime and "political movements and intrigue which is rapidly becoming a subject of paramount importance to Government,"[52] it was recommended that "the Department should have at its head a picked European officer, holding a gazetted post in some department of the public service. He should be a highly educated man, possessing a more than ordinary acquaintance with the languages, customs and habits of all classes of natives, who by reason of his social position and intellectual calibre would be in a position both to meet natives of the highest class on equal terms and to deal equally well with the illiterate masses."[53] This highly educated man was none other than S. M. Edwardes, appointed Commissioner of Police for Bombay in 1909, the first covenanted civil service officer to hold the post.

The focus on Hindu revolutionary terrorism and student anarchists drew upon the older colonial fear of an "Islamitic Union." In 1909, in the Ottoman Empire, the Committee of Union and Progress (CUP) rebellion had deposed Sultan Abdulhamid II, and from 1909 to 1918, Mehmed V ruled but only as a titular Sultan. With the outbreak of World War I, the Ottoman Empire looked to throw its support behind the Axis powers, which concerned Indian Muslims since the Ottomans controlled the Muslim holy lands. Edwardes and his team scrutinized letters and newspapers and compiled a registry of all Turkish subjects in the city while keeping an eye on Muslims who were assumed to sympathize with the Turkish cause.[54] By now they were concerned with the goings-on in Afghanistan as well; accordingly, surveillance was extended to conversations between Indian Muslims, Turks, and Afghans.

51. NAI/Judicial Department/no. 4259/M/38, Bombay Castle, July 27, 1909, J. T. Scotson to the Commissioner of Police, Bombay.

52. NAI/Judicial Department/no. 4259/M/38, Bombay Castle, July 27, 1909, J. T. Scotson to the Commissioner of Police, Bombay.

53. NAI/Judicial Department/no. 4259/M/38, Bombay Castle, July 27, 1909, J. T. Scotson to the Commissioner of Police, Bombay.

54. Edwardes, *Bombay City Police*, 190–91.

The Savarkar Police File

The police file on Savarkar was officially opened in 1906, but surveillance of him probably began the previous year.[55] Along with the intelligence officer's history sheet, the file contains correspondence among police officers, including many that we met in Edwardes's history, most prominently Stevenson-Moore. The police file is labeled Home Department/Political/Special/file 60D and contains documents drawn from the Bombay Secret Abstracts (BSA), correspondence between the Bombay Police Commissioner's office and the Government of Bombay, correspondence between the Ratnagiri Magistrate and the Commissioner of Police, and correspondence among police officers. Various police officers annotated the documents, either recording that the material in question had arrived safely or sending it on with further instructions.[56]

Another source is Marathi historian Y. D. Phadke, who while collecting archival documentation for his five-volume history of Maharashtra, wrote a book titled *Śōdha Sāvarakarāñcā* (The search for Savarkar). Phadke was so exasperated by the *dantakathā* (fictive histories) written by Savarkar's followers that the book functions like a compilation of primary sources and includes letters between the Savarkar brothers, police files, and material from the National Archives. Phadke's focus was less on making an historical argument about Savarkar and more on identifying and correcting as many errors as possible in the sometimes absurdly exaggerated claims of many of Savarkar's biographies. Perhaps to counterbalance statements such as one about Savarkar swimming day and night to reach French shores after jumping ship in Marseilles, Phadke gives us a detailed account of every letter written by or to Savarkar, the correspondence between the government of India and the government of Bombay, and letters exchanged within the Savarkar family. While I have used the same archives, Phadke had far greater access to the personal papers of Savarkar's family and associates, so I have used his book to both corroborate and supplement my research. We now follow Savarkar from his first appearance on the police radar through 1937 when he was released without conditions.

55. Phadke, *Śōdha Sāvarakarāñcā*, 1.

56. Phadke, *Śōdha Sāvarakarāñcā*. Phadke notes that the collection of materials on Savarkar began in 1908, which Savarkar, despite his suspicion of the police, may not have known. Phadke uses the phrase "jyōtiṣī bhalēbhalē cakalē" ("the fortune teller was himself fooled"), which is uncoincidentally the title of and a line from one of Savarkar's own poems. See Karandikar, *Savarkar Charitra*, 116, and *SSV*, MPHS 7: 71. While NAI/Home Department/Political/Special/file 60D would give the reader the location of the large file on Savarkar, I have cited as far as possible the place of issue for all the documents within the file.

The history sheet notes that he had "no particular social status, but carried some influence with the student classes." His relatives were named, as was his wife and her lineage: "Saraswati, daughter of Rambhau Chiplunkar of Trimbak, late Karbhari of Jowhar State." Fifteen of his associates were named, along with the surveillance files numbers in which information could be found about them. The list includes Madame Cama, Lala Hardayal, Shyamji Krishnavarma, but also other associates from Bhagur, Nasik, and Bombay, such as Hari Anant Thatte and Daji Nagesh Apte.[57]

When Stevenson-Moore was appointed Director of Criminal Intelligence in 1907, Savarkar was already well-known to him, and most of the figures named above were under surveillance. But Savarkar merited special attention because of his affiliation with the extreme wing of Indian nationalism. As a high school student, he organized a secret revolutionary society, Mitra Mela (Society of Friends), in his hometown.[58] "It is not surprising," the history sheet author wrote, "that Vinayek became tainted at a very early age." The goals of Mitra Mela were described as "(1) the union of all castes and creeds and (2) the wiping out, at the cost of life, if necessary, *the disgrace resting on Brahmins for ceding their kingdom to others* [emphasis mine]."[59] That disgrace, according to the police sheet, was the defeat by the East India Company of the Brahmin Peshwai and the Maratha Confederacy in 1818. The police sheet is correct in identifying Savarkar's associates as Brahmin. The last names in a short book of biographies of Savarkar's associates written by one of them, Sridhara Raghunatha Vartaka, attests to this fact—Bhat, Gore, Khare, Patankar (Chandraseniya Kayastha Prabhu), Karve, Kanhere, Deshpande, Joshi, Soman, Marathe, Moghe, Apte, Vartak, Kelkar, Gadgil, Thatte, Joglekar, Datar, Athalye—but it would be more accurate to term them all Brahmin and upper caste for reasons we will see in subsequent chapters. It is far less clear that they were all motivated by the loss of the Brahmin Peshwai.[60] The society met in the attic of a friend's house in Nasik, and its primary activities were organizing public religious festivals in

57. Secret History Sheet of Vinayak Damodhar Sawarkar, B. A., 1. See also Vartaka, *Svatantryavira Savarakaranci*, for brief biographies of Savarkar's associates, from his childhood friends in Bhagur to the students who joined his secret societies. For Hari Anant Thatte and Daji Apte's biographies, see 119–214 and 77–84, respectively.

58. Godbole, *Ase Ahet Savarkar*, 19.

59. History Sheet of V. D. Sawarkar, B. A., 2. The history sheet is one of the documents in the police file on him: NAI/Home Department/Political/Special/file 60D.

60. Few original documents related to this early society exist because members destroyed them to keep them out of British hands, so much of what we know is from nonacademic Marathi

opposition to the ban on organizations and holding lectures to raise anticolonial consciousness.[61]

The late nineteenth century in Maharashtra was a time of active debates about history, the role it played in the life of a nation, and its use as a corrective to colonial denigrations of India's past.[62] Savarkar was too young to participate, but he wrote patriotic poetry extolling the figure of Mother India. The report noted that he won a prize as a schoolboy for

> a rather objectionable essay on 'Why Festivals of Historical persons should be celebrated.' This was printed and published by G.N. Joshi in 1903 and proscribed by the Bombay Government in 1910—Government Notification No. 5998, dated the 20th of October 1910.[63]

The point here is that the police were not just surveilling but proscribing the poems of a schoolboy. This may have been the first of Savarkar's works in either Marathi or English to be read, translated, and deemed objectionable and/or seditious, but it was far from the last.

All of Savarkar's political activities were noted, including his attendance at political meetings in Poona and his speaking against the impending partition of Bengal and in favor of the Swadeshi movement. The report about him was scathing, saying that his head had been turned by praise from extremist leaders in Poona and fellow students—that, though he was a force in Nasik politics,

> [he] possessed neither religious nor moral scruples and was a fluent and fiery speaker. His ambition was to be in the forefront. . . . Vinayek advocated the speedy emancipation of India from British control by the direct method of revolution. . . . The result was the transformation of that 'Mitra Mela' of Nasik into the Abhinav Bharat Society . . . [which] had for its model the secret organisations of the Russian Nihilists . . .

As we will see, connections between Indian revolutionaries and Russian anarchists, nihilists, and, after 1917, Bolshevists worried the British, who watched them carefully.

Savarkar was seen as orchestrating a nationwide campaign to infect

---

sources. For an annotated and photographic account of some early revolutionaries in Maharashtra and elsewhere, see Date, *Bharatiya Swatantryache*.

61. *SSV*, SSRSP, 1: 28–29.

62. See Deshpande, *Creative Pasts*. See also Apte "Lokahitavadi and V. K. Chiplunkar" and Tucker, "Hindu Traditionalism and Nationalist Ideologies."

63. History Sheet of V. D. Sawarkar, B. A., 2.

> . . . the whole of the Deccan with secret societies which were to be affiliated to the Nasik Branch and to that end violent speeches were delivered, and seditious and inflammatory literature published. . . . Recruitment was specially welcomed from employes [*sic*] on Railways, the Telegraph department and individuals in Departments of Government likely to give useful information and whose experience would be invaluable to the society when the day of revolution dawned. It was to be preceded by a reign of terror inaugurated by the assassination of high government officials, European and Indian.[64]

The surveillance report also took note of Savarkar as a poet. The two *povāḍās* (ballads) he had composed—Ballads about "Singhad" and "Baji Deshpande," according to the police sheet—were proscribed (see Notification No. 6583, dated November 11, 1911).[65] Why were these two *povāḍās* so unsettling for the colonial government that they needed to be proscribed?[66] After all, they were composed by a mere schoolboy. In addition, *povāḍās* were performed by peripatetic bards, making their banning akin to the surveillance of rumors, which also circulated orally. Was it the language or their circulation that made these dangerous? Was it the positive invocation of Maratha history, particularly the praise of Chhatrapati Shivaji and his warriors? As Sumit Guha has argued, the narrative of Maratha power in immediate decline in the post-Mughal period was itself a product of colonial historiography aimed at discrediting the Marathas and legitimizing British rule.[67] Savarkar might well have composed these *povāḍās* to trigger precisely the kind of public outrage the British wanted to contain.[68] We will examine one of these proscribed *povāḍās* in a later chapter.

The report listed all the speeches he gave while at college, describing them and noting where they were given (Joshi Hall in Poona, the Maharashtra Vidyalaya premises in Date's Wada, Sinnar, Manmad, Nasik, and Nandgaon) and that

64. History Sheet of V. D. Sawarkar, B. A., 2.

65. This would be confirmed by Savarkar himself some years later, when his own biography *Life of Barrister Savarkar* was published, in the writing of which he seems to have played an important role. See chapter 6.

66. I am grateful to Rupali Warke for her careful reading of this chapter, for asking these questions and helping me with answers to them.

67. Guha, "The Maratha Empire."

68. I am grateful to Rupali Warke for pointing this out to me, and also for her directing my attention to the war declared against Gwalior in 1843 by the East India Company. Gwalior was politically active well into the nineteenth century and posed a significant threat to British rule, so much so that rebels in 1857 approached Gwalior for military assistance.

they were delivered "with his usual rabidness."[69] The file is an accretive profile of a dangerous man—one whom the report concluded was "likely to become troublesome." When Savarkar held a bonfire of foreign cloth as a show of support for the Swadeshi protest, he was expelled from the college hostel. His mentor B. G. Tilak defended him in his newspaper *Kesari*, and it was perhaps the combination of one extremist publicly supporting another that might have occasioned the remark about his potential for trouble.[70] Phadke suggests that this was the moment that Savarkar ascended the first rung of the ladder to fame.[71] From the report's list of speeches in Dahanu, Umbergaon, Thana District, and Nasik, we get confirmation that Savarkar was building his base, as it were, in the small cities that dotted Bombay Presidency. After leaving college, Savarkar wrote editorials for a Bombay weekly called *Vihari*, about which the police knew as well.[72] Savarkar set sail for London on June 9, 1906.[73] He had just turned twenty-three.

In London he was a student for the bar at Grays Inn. The Indian Police alerted India House of his arrival, and when he landed in England, Scotland Yard took over his surveillance.[74] Scotland Yard's involvement was known to all the young revolutionaries; as one noted, there was always a Scotland Yard policeman near 65 Cromwell Avenue, Highgate, where Savarkar lived as a student. Some of Savarkar's letters home were intercepted, and the Bombay Police raided his brother's house looking for others.[75]

The correspondence between various colonial policemen and officials in 1908 reveals not just the extent of their surveillance but also what they were worried about.[76] Decades later, we can admit that their concerns were well-founded; in 1953, six years after independence, when narrating such stories was

69. History Sheet of V. D. Sawarkar, B. A., 5.

70. Phadke, *Śōdha Sāvarakarāñcā*, 8.

71. Phadke, *Śōdha Sāvarakarāñcā*, 8. Phadke writes, "Tātyā prasidhdīcyā prakāśajhōtāta vāvarū lāgalē tē yā prasaṅgāpāsūna" ("Tatya became famous as of this incident").

72. Phadke, *Śōdha Sāvarakarāñcā*, 4. The three men were Balkrishna Narayan Phatak, Bhaskar Vishnu Phadke, and Ramchandra Narayan Mandlik.

73. Keer, *Veer Savarkar*, 24.

74. NAI/Home Department/Political/A/no. 37/Confidential (December 1909) Letter from India Office, Whitehall, on September 10, 1909, states that the Director of Criminal Intelligence was in contact with Scotland Yard about the activities and movements of the students in India House. See also Godbole, *Ase Ahet Savarkar*, 20.

75. NAI/Home Department/no. 0863/Letter dated April 4, 1909 to the Assistant Inspector General Police, Bombay.

76. NAI/Home Department/Political/Deposit/December 1908.

less risky, Savarkar gave a lecture in Dadar in which he reveled in his past revolutionary violence and claimed that the real reason he went to England was to learn about bombmaking and bring that knowledge back to India.[77] But Savarkar did not himself engage in physical violence, whether throwing or a bomb or shooting a gun; his violence lay in his writings and in his persuasive power to compel other young men to violence. In London, his legal studies did in fact take a back seat to his anticolonial activities, which were mostly educational and literary. Within six months, he had written a biography of Giuseppe Mazzini in Marathi of which "2,000 copies . . . were printed and circulated in India."[78] The first edition sold out, and an additional 3,000 copies were printed. We also find out that the police believed there were "40 odd branches [of the Mitra Mela] scattered all over the Deccan besides the Branch at Gwalior, with a known membership of 300, but whose total number various computations place at between 500 and several thousand."[79] Savarkar was, in their opinion, capable of trouble. A lot of it.

Savarkar knew that he was under surveillance, and Phadke claims that from 1906 on, Savarkar and his associates were locked in a contest of wits with the police.[80] Even at this early date, Savarkar's anti-Muslim sentiments were known to the police since the police sheet writer noted that Haidar Raza, a member of Shyamji Krishnavarma's group, "objected to the anti-Mahomedan note which Savarkar was unable to keep out of his speeches."[81] While the standard narrative about Savarkar's anti-Muslim feelings is that he was mistreated by Muslims in prison in the cellular jail in the Andamans, we see that it was present

77. Phadke, *Śōdha Sāvarakarāñcā*, 20.

78. Phadke, *Śōdha Sāvarakarāñcā*, 9–10. Phadke writes that of the eighteen volumes of Mazzini's writings, Savarkar was able to access only the six translated into English, and these became the basis for his writings. Savarkar was not the first Indian to write a biography of Mazzini. In 1899, L. G. Ghanekar published a biography of Mazzini (*Mazzini Yanche Charitra*), N. C. Kelkar published a biography of Garibaldi in 1901, and around the same time, Shivaram Pant was writing articles about Young Italy. Phadke argues that Ghanekar and Shivram Pant's writing influenced Savarkar, who gifted Lala Hardayal an English copy of Mazzini's biography, and upon reaching England decided to translate Mazzini's autobiography and write a preface tailored to the political situation in India. Savarkar, as we will see in the last chapter, encouraged his followers to not just read his preface but memorize it.

79. History Sheet of V. D, Sawarkar, B. A., 4.

80. Phadke, *Śōdha Sāvarakarāñcā*, 3. Phadke also argued that it was only because Savarkar was less skillful in his youth at evading police traps than he was later that he was taken away to the Andaman Islands.

81. History Sheet of V. D. Sawarkar, B. A., 7.

earlier and considered worthy of mention in his police sheet. By the end of the year, he started another secret revolutionary society called the Abhinava Bharat Society, which presented weekly lectures on nationalism. His writings were viewed as helping to generate "the increase in virulence in the speeches of members."[82] In May 1907, the fiftieth anniversary of the outbreak of the 1857 Rebellion was observed in London as a day of thanksgiving for the British victory over the rebels. An outraged Savarkar countered with a speech about the Rebellion, reportedly claiming that "the English had treated the Indians with the utmost cruelty and brutality by ordering a general massacre and added that they were practically justified now in taking their revenge in any possible way—fair or foul . . . [and] went on to eulogize Nana Saheb and spoke of the Cawnpore massacre as a heroic deed."[83] Savarkar distributed this account in "O Martyrs!"[84]—a leaflet commemorating the Rebellion leaders as martyrs—catching the attention of senior policemen in both England and India.

Stevenson-Moore wrote on June 8, 1908 that "Home Department should see 'Oh Martyrs' because it apostrophizes the mutineers of 1857 and prophesies a revolution in 1917. The type of the leaflet is similar to that of the Indian Sociologist."[85] The Home Department in India noted that it was likely that Savarkar had written it in England since "[t]he phraseology is better than usual, and unlike other fulminations we are accustomed to here."[86] Just being in England had presumably improved Savarkar's English writing skills!

Even fifty years later, the colonial government did not want the Rebellion spoken of warmly, and it moved swiftly to stop the leaflet's spread. On June 15, 1908, the Home Department received a confidential letter from the Government of the United Provinces. "By the Lieutenant Governor's direction, I send you in original a copy of the pamphlet which was received from England . . . It might be possible to take some action in England to stop the printing of these pamphlets."[87] The Police Commissioner's office noted that an "Inspector Favel

82. History Sheet of V. D. Sawarkar, B. A., 10.

83. History Sheet of V. D. Sawarkar, B. A., 8. *The Indian Sociologist* was an anticolonial nationalist journal edited and published by Shyamji Krishnavarma from 1905–14 and 1921–22 in England, France, and Switzerland to promote the cause of Indian independence. For an examination of Krishnavarma's articles in the journal and Herbert Spencer's influence on his thinking, see Marwah, "Rethinking Resistance," 57–65.

84. Reprinted in *SSV*, SSRSP, 3 (History), part 2.

85. Bakhle, "Savarkar (1883–1966)," 61.

86. Bakhle, "Savarkar (1883–1966)," 62.

87. Bakhle, "Savarkar (1883–1966)," 62.

has returned from Nasik and brought with him the papers etc referred to in the attached copy of the Panchnama. 175 (written out) copies of the life of Marzani [*sic*] were seized in the search. 173 have been kept here in the custody of the Nasik police and two brought to Bombay." The papers were found in Savarkar's brother's home, after which he was arrested and charged with sedition and waging war against the King.[88]

When his brother was sentenced to banishment for life, Savarkar reportedly "made a very sensational speech on the subject, repeating an oath to take vengeance on the English and saying 'Who knows when the day will come when I shall have the lives of some Englishmen in my power and then I shall ask the English to restore my brother to me as a ransom.'"[89] This sounds more like the wishful thinking of a younger brother than anything actionable, but it fit with the British image of Savarkar as a vengeful Indian.

The government spent the next two years building a careful case against Savarkar. The District Superintendent of Police in Savarkar's hometown wrote to the District Magistrate that "VDS is a well-known rank extremist and it will be observed from one of his letters to Ganesh [Savarkar's brother], that he advocated a defiant stand being made by the extremists should Government prevent the holding of the Congress at Nagpur in December last." About Ganesh, the District Superintendent wrote that "apart from the offences he is at present charged with, the correspondence seized in his house after his arrest fairly indicates that he has been conspiring with others to subvert British rule in India." Thus, "Govt may be moved to ask the Home authorities to have the belongings of VDS, whose address is India House London thoroughly searched for incriminating documents in English and Marathi."[90] Both brothers' houses were in fact searched.[91]

Back in India, the Director of Criminal Intelligence and the Deputy Inspector-General of Police worked on building a case that would force Savarkar's extradition. The question was how to justify his arrest and whether the evidence was strong enough to do so. Would letters showing his connection to

88. Keer, *Veer Savarkar*, 65. Also, Phadke, *Śōdha Sāvarakarāñcā*, 13.

89. History Sheet of V. D. Sawarkar, B. A., 8.

90. NAI/Home Department/Political/60-A, (1909–1922), S21.

91. NAI/Home Department/Political/60-A, (1909–1922), S21. See also Phadke, *Śōdha Sāvarakarāñcā*, 11–25. Phadke presents the most detailed, day-by-day, letter-by-letter, archive-based account of the period in which police officers and administrators took pains to create a watertight case, even as Savarkar and his brothers tried to use the law to protest their arrests and searches as illegal.

his brother suffice? Or the fact that he distributed seditious leaflets?[92] The Deputy Inspector-General's office was asked to "find out whether the Advocate General has been consulted on the legal point . . . regarding the Savarkar case, and the proposal to take action against Vinayek Savarkar who is in England."[93] The response from Poona on June 14, 1909, was to ask Mr. Guider, the Deputy Inspector-General of Police, to "collect and examine the evidence against Vinayek in India."[94] Guider was given some help: on June 29, 1909, he was sent copies of statements made in 1907 about the secret society Savarkar had founded, the Mitra Mela, with the note that "if it can be established that the present Nasik Society is the same as the Mitra Mela under another name it may facilitate the connection of Vinayek with the present conspiracy."[95] While the government had clear evidence to justify arresting his brother after finding bomb-making manuals in his home, in legal terms, Savarkar was only guilty of associating with his brother, founding a secret society, and making speeches critical of colonial rule. Even with the expanded remit of sedition law, the colonial government needed more than that to put him away for good.

In England, Savarkar was tailed nonstop. The police sheet is remarkably detailed, going so far as to note that he "caught a chill and was confined to bed, suffering from pneumonia" after visiting Brighton.[96] His influence was deemed so great that his illness "had a noticeable effect on the activities of the London Party who were much concerned about him . . . the absence of the leading spirit from the scenes of active sedition were greatly felt." In this the detectives were not altogether wrong.[97] Savarkar's charisma was powerful enough to persuade his fellow students to do things they would not otherwise do or to stand down when they wanted to go full speed ahead.[98]

92. NAI/Home Department/Special/60-A, (1909–1922), 5.

93. NAI/Home Department/Special/60-A, (1909–1922), 5.

94. NAI/Home Department/Special/60-A, (1909–1922), 11.

95. NAI/Home Department/Special/60-A, (1909–1922), 19.

96. History Sheet of V. D. Sawarkar, B. A., 10.

97. Phadke, *Śōdha Sāvarakarāñcā*, 7. Pandurang Mahadev Bapat (Senapati Bapat) remembered meeting Savarkar in London:

> . . . at that point, I said I'll shoot Morley [the Secretary of State, in London.] Others opposed it. Then I went to Paris to learn how to make a bomb and came back to London. I'll throw a bomb in Parliament, I said. That was rejected. Savarkar said to me "don't do anything of the sort, just return to your country."

Writings by Senapati Bapat, *Loksatta*, Diwali Edition, 1963, in Senapati Bapat Private Papers.

98. Writings by Senapati Bapat, serial no. 1 (*Savdhan*), May 28, 1938, 21, in Senapati Bapat Private Papers. See also Phadke, *Śōdha Sāvarakarāñcā*, 65. Bapat confirmed the British belief about Savarkar's ability to influence young students:

When Savarkar wrote his history of the 1857 Rebellion, his friends in India House translated it into English and used their contacts in Germany to have it published in 1909.[99] In that same year, Gandhi published *Hind Swaraj*, an equally "seditious" work that was in some respects a response to the politics of Savarkar's young revolutionaries. It was also the year that police officials in England and India collected enough evidence to imprison Savarkar.

The search of Savarkar's brother's house had yielded ample dividends. Stevenson-Moore told his office about the documents that had been found and sent to Scotland Yard. He noted that

> an incriminating letter written by Tatya (G.D. Savarkar)[100] to his brother was intercepted along with the "Indian Sociologist" in the Sea Post Office. The Bombay Police have now made an important find in the brother's house. One item is the Manicktolla Explosives Manual. This is the first copy of the Explosives Manual found outside Calcutta and perhaps P.H. Bapat brought it . . . We should send to Bombay any information about the Savarkars which they are not likely to have and ask for copies of the statements against them when complete. Please get out what information we have about the persons named in the letters and draft to Mr. Guider to supplement letting me see.

He added, "these papers should be seen in the Home Department without delay."[101] The Home Department recommended that

---

Savarkar sowed the seeds for a number of people to become revolutionaries—inspired a number of people to become revolutionaries—showed them the way. Before Savarkar and I met I was engaged in giving lectures and writing [*cōpaḍyā lihiṇyācaṁ kāma*] but after we met within a few months I gave up that plan and decided to go to Paris to learn how to make a bomb. The main reason for me to change my plan was Savarkar's stirring speeches [*tējasvī bhāṣaṇa*] and writings had a huge impact on me. I felt Savarkar had the characteristic ability to engage in passionate discourse about revolution—much more than me, he would be able to do it much better than me—I felt I should take up something else more suited for me." Bapat remembers saying, "It should be remembered, that as soon as we saw Tatya's views on Muslims change, we felt we wanted the Savarkar of 1908 back; we didn't want the Savarkar of 1937.

99. IOR/Foreign Confidential/R/1/1/1076/1910. In his statement, Koregaonkar names himself and a W. V. Phadke as the two translators of Savarkar's book. This is confirmed by Keer, *Veer Savarkar*, 31.

100. Stevenson-Moore incorrectly identified "Tatya" as Ganesh Savarkar. Tatya was V. D. Savarkar. Ganesh Savarkar was known as Babarao.

101. CID/no. 0863/Letter dated August 4, 1909, to Assistant Inspector General Police, Bombay.

> [i]f we are going to have a conspiracy prosecution it ought to be managed by the D.C.I. [Director of Criminal Intelligence] and not by any one province, for it is clear that the conspiracy has ramifications throughout India. I think the DCI should endeavour without delay to collate all evidence of a conspiracy visiting the different provinces if necessary to accomplish his case.[102]

Collecting proof of a general conspiracy was not easy. His words were "violent," and the Benchers of Grays Inn had decided not to call him to the Bar, but that was not enough.

In July 1909 a memorandum was circulated on anti-British agitation by Indian natives in England.[103] Savarkar was in England under close watch, his older brother Ganesh had been sentenced to transportation for life in the Andamans, and his younger brother Narayan was under surveillance.[104] Savarkar's book on the 1857 Rebellion was blinking conspicuously on the colonial radar. He had spoken frequently in India House about the rebellion, even delivering an address called "The History of the Indian Mutiny and the Present Need for a Similar but Much Stronger Rising" a few months before the book was published.[105] The 1857 book, not coincidentally, spoke of Hindus and Muslims coming together in a struggle against East India Company rule.

A telegram from the Government of Bombay dated July 20, 1909, said that the "book is in Marathi and Bombay is most concerned. The Government strongly urges the issue of the notification under the Sea Customs Act, notwithstanding the publicity, and I think, therefore, that that course may be taken. We have enough information of the book to justify the prohibition of its import."[106] The matter was referred to Stevenson-Moore, who offered the following clarification: "the English version of Savarkar's book has not been printed as yet and this version is entitled either 'the History of the Revolution of 1857' or 'The History of 1857.'" He also noted on July 21, 1909,

> I see no harm in issuing the declaration under the Sea Customs Act. It may assist to catch anything on the way. I don't think any further action with

102. CID/no. 0863/Letter dated August 4, 1909, to Assistant Inspector General Police, Bombay.

103. NAI/Home Department/Political/Deposit/July 1909/no. 19.

104. NAI/Home Department/Political/Deposit/October 1909/no. 29.

105. Criminal Intelligence Office/History Sheet of Nitisen Dwarkadas/file 3103/H/1910.

106. NAI/Home Department/Political/A/August 1909/no. 23–27.

reference to the book is likely to be taken by the London Extremists for some time.[107]

He was wrong. The "London Extremists" were in fact arranging for its international distribution, which was revealed later, when Koregaonkar turned informant.[108]

The government's concern about the 1857 book can be surmised from the rapidity with which it took action. Knowing that Savarkar's brother Babarao was working to publish the book in India,[109] they alerted the Director General of the Post Office, who told officers to "be on the look-out for any copies passing through the post."[110] Toward the end of the year, the Bombay government was working out the details: "I think that the Customs might be warned to test for fake bottoms in the boxes of Indian students returning from Europe." They wondered "whether a prosecution for sedition would stand in the case of a man in whose box a copy of the book might be found on landing in Bombay. Perhaps it is worthwhile having this considered and orders issued?"[111] The police were not wrong. The books were smuggled into India disguised as the Bible, works by Shakespeare, and popular English novels, such as *The Pickwick Papers* and *Waverley*.[112] The next move for colonial officials was to amend the Sea Customs Act by adding the term "seditious" after the word "obscene" so that it read "By section 18(c) of the Sea Customs Act the bringing into British India of any obscene, seditious, book, pamphlet, paper, drawing, painting, representation, figure or article is prohibited."[113]

Telegrams referring to Savarkar were scrutinized for clues. Savarkar had dispatched a few friends from India House to Paris to learn about bomb making and had sent copies of bomb manuals to India, along with pistols to use in political assassinations. One of the pistols was used by seventeen-year-old Anant Kanhere to assassinate the Collector of Nasik Arthur Jackson.[114] When

107. NAI/Home Department/Political/A/August 1909/no. 23–27.

108. See Godbole, *Ase Ahet Savarkar*, 23.

109. Phadke, *Śōdha Sāvarakarāñcā*, 15.

110. Phadke, *Śōdha Sāvarakarāñcā*, 15.

111. NAI/Home Department/Political/60B/1910, 55, 58. See also Bakhle, "Savarkar (1883–1966)," 64.

112. Karandikar, *Savarkar Charitra*, 269. See 268–70 for a detailed description of Savarkar's plans to translate and distribute the 1857 book.

113. NAI/Home Department/Political/Deposit/May 1910/no. 1.

114. See Bhat, *Abhinava Bharat*, for a candid account of the revolutionaries and their activities and how easily young Anant Kanhere gave up all members of the group.

caught, Kanhere implicated, among others, the Savarkar family. And despite being under police watch, in July 1909, Madanlal Dhingra, a member of India House, assassinated a British military officer, Sir William Curzon Wyllie. These assassinations were a response to the arrests of fellow revolutionaries in India, particularly the way Guider had tortured Savarkar's older brother into a confession.[115] As the British mourned their lost official, they found satisfaction in the fact that the assassination of Curzon Wyllie meant that Savarkar was complicit in a murder, as "it was subsequently proved that Dhingra was a great friend of Savarkar."[116]

Letters Savarkar had received or written were entered into evidence along with publications such as bomb making manuals seized during police searches. The second and more important evidentiary strand included surveillance documents and the testimony of informants. Savarkar had tried to create his own double agent (M. P. Tirumalachari) to convey misinformation to Scotland Yard, but Tirumalachari was also under surveillance.[117] At least two fellow students in India House—H. C. Koregaonkar, and Sukhsagar Dutt—were spying for the English authorities.[118]

Koregaonkar was one of the translators of the 1857 book. When he turned informant, he told the police that India House members wanted to spread revolution all through India. While he could not provide much detail about where guns were to be acquired or how bombs were to be placed, he revealed Madanlal Dhingra's plans to assassinate an English official and his own roles as a translator and distributor of Savarkar's 1857 book.

115. Phadke, *Śōdha Sāvarakarāñcā*, 25. Phadke asserts that Guider tortured Babarao Savarkar to get him to confess that the letters in his possession signed by "Tatya" were from his brother.

116. History Sheet of V. D. Sawarkar, B. A., 9.

117. NAI/Home Department/Political/Branch A/December 1909/no. 37/Confidential.

118. Sukhsagar Dutt was the nom de plume of Sajani Ranjan Banerjea, who was engaged by the Director of Criminal Intelligence as an informant from October 1909 to June 1913. His passage, fees for admission to the Bar, and expenses for law books were paid for, and he received a monthly allowance of twenty pounds for the forty-five months of his employment. He claimed he turned informant to pay off his family debt. He reported to a Superintendent Quinn on the "seditionist movement" and was deemed useful, with "the great merit of reporting, truthfully, and not making sensational statements in order to magnify his usefulness." Sukhsagar Dutt's desire to take a science course was approved because "it gave him better opportunities of mixing with the Indians and getting information, and the science course is one that *appeals to Indians with extremist tendencies* [emphasis mine]." IOR/L/PS/8/67/1912, 31, 32. See also Padmanabhan, *V. V. S. Aiyar*, for a biographical account of the surveillance on India House.

Koregaonkar himself had been under surveillance for a while. Stevenson-Moore first became aware of him in a note about another of Savarkar's associates:

> About this time (1906) a young Chitpavan Brahmin from the Central Provinces of India (S.V. Ketkar) arrived in New York. In 1904 this young man had already been concerned in the Anarchist movement in India. He was a friend of Karve who was executed for the Jackson (Nasik) murder; and was evidently on friendly terms with B.G. Tilak, Khaparde, and W.S. Khare, the leaders in India. While in Ithaca (New York) Koregaonkar, when sent over to America, was his guest there.[119]

Stevenson-Moore concluded that Koregaonkar was

> undoubtedly an important link between American and Europe, and there is little doubt that he was expressly sent over to America by the extremist party at that time in England; headed by V.D. Savarkar. Koregaonkar visited most of the University centres and was seen at New York, Ithaca, Boston, and Philadelphia, where he met most of the agitators and many Indian students.[120]

Stevenson-Moore continued:

> Koregaonkar arrived in London in 1906. He was on very intimate terms with V.D. Savarkar (since transported for life for abetment of the murder of Mr. Jackson at Nasik) and with Madan Lala Dhingra (since executed for the murder of Sir Wm Curzon-Wyllie at the Imperial Institute, London). He was close to the murderer at the time of the latter murder and there is no doubt that he abetted the murder in every sense of the word. He helped to translate Savarkar's book "The War of Independence of 1857" a highly seditious publication embodying the grossest perversion of facts and, displaying a savage hatred of the British. Koregaonkar made a long statement to the authorities in India in January 1910, showing the part he played in the revolutionary propaganda while in England. He also gave evidence in the Nasik case against Savarkar for which he has been formally condemned to death by the remaining Indian anarchists in Europe.[121]

119. IOR/L/PJ/12/1/1913, 70.
120. IOR/L/PJ/12/1/1913, 73.
121. IOR/L/PJ/12/1/1913, 74.

In short, Koregaonkar's testimony gave the police actionable evidence against Savarkar.

The police waited a little over a month before arresting him, continuing all the while to surveil him:

> All telegrams from or dispatched to Europe at or from Bombay between 13 December 1909 and 13 January 1910 which contain or are suspected to contain references to the movements or plans of V. D. Savarkar shall be disclosed to the Deputy Commissioner of Police, Bombay.[122]

Just as the case against Savarkar was sanctioned, it was noted that "he left for Paris sixth."[123] His arrest was coming soon:

> Director of Criminal Intelligence should see after issue with as little delay as possible. I believe he intends to discuss with the Bombay authorities the possibility of framing a charge under section 121-A against V. D. Savarkar and obtaining his surrender under the Fugitive Offenders Act.[124]

His career was, according to the police report, "quickly drawing to a close," and in February 1910, "a warrant was issued for his arrest under sections 121, 121-A, 122, and 124A and 302 IPC by the Special Magistrate of Nasik, and a provincial warrant was issued by the Bow Street Magistrate under the Fugitive Offenders Act."[125] When Savarkar returned to London, on March 13, 1910, he was arrested as a fugitive. This raises a question: why use the Fugitive Offenders Act? On what grounds could he have been considered a fugitive?

The Fugitive Offenders Act presumed that the suspect in question was guilty of a crime and had fled to evade arrest. But Savarkar went to England as a student, not a fugitive. He had not been charged with a crime or evaded arrest. Yet it was imperative that he be tried in India, not England, because juries in England were liable to look leniently on revolutionaries.[126] The expanded remit of sedition law made this possible, since the only way he could be extradited to India was to produce charges of an unresolved crime in India. To this end, the only crime the colonial authorities could come up with was the charge of sedition based on speeches he had made as a college student in Pune.

122. NAI/Home Department/Political/A/ February 1910/Telegram no. 31–32.

123. NAI/Home Department/Political/1910/Notes of the Criminal Intelligence Office/Telegram from the Director of Criminal Intelligence, Nasik, dated January 13, 1910.

124. NAI/Home Department/Political/Deposit/May 1910/no. 1.

125. History Sheet of V. D. Sawarkar, B. A., 11.

126. See Bakhle, "Savarkar (1883–1966)," 65–68.

Having arrested him as a fugitive, the police had to get him to India to face trial. He was transported by sea on the SS *Morea*, a British merchant vessel that docked briefly in Marseilles. Seizing the moment, Savarkar escaped through a porthole and ran into the streets asking to see a magistrate. He was caught by a French maritime officer, who, believing he was a member of the crew, returned him to the British detectives. The next morning the ship sailed on, but French socialists declared that he had been improperly detained, and the case aroused so much controversy that England and France referred it to the Permanent Court of Arbitration at the Hague.[127]

That such a big fish had been caught was of interest all the way up the administrative ladder, and liberal Secretary of State John Morley wrote to the Viceroy, Lord Minto:

> May I confess to you that I am a little uncomfortable at the constant account of what seem to be political arrests. I distrust wholesale operations on this scale. I am, and always have been, in Ireland and elsewhere, the Policeman's friend and confederate. But I suspect that the secret procedure under the recent Act gives an opening for the manufacture of false evidence. As I have named the Fugitive Offenders Act, it would be worth your while to get one of your lawyers to study the hearing of Savarkar's appeal.[128]

Morley still wanted Savarkar arrested—he just wanted the charges to stick:

> Just as I sit down to write to you, they bring into me the opinion of the Attorney-General on the French demands in the case of Savarkar. As it might land us in the position of having to hand S. back to France, I turned to the opinion with a good deal of curiosity. Happily we need not quake; for the A.G. holds (1) that we are not bound to restore S to French territory; (2) that we ought not to promise to surrender him after the conclusion of his trial; (3) that the executive have no power under the circumstances to insist on the delay of the trial.[129]

The Morley/Minto regime was replaced by the Earl of Crewe and Charles Hardinge, who worried that the Indian colonial government was not fully cognizant of the difficulties of the case. Crewe wrote Hardinge:

127. "Hindu Case at Hague," 4.

128. IOR/Mss Eur D/573/5/folio 98/Letters to the Earl of Minto from Secretary of State Morley, June 15, 1910.

129. IOR/Mss Eur D/573/5/folio 143, 144/Letters to the Earl of Minto from Secretary of State Morley, August 23, 1910.

> We are telegraphing on the Savarkar case. The Bombay Government do not seem to have appreciated the fact that the Hague decision may, and probably will, depend to a great extent on the proof which can be produced of abetting murder. So that, if that charge were postponed until after the arbitration tribunal has decided, our strongest card would remain unplayed.[130]

Like his predecessor, Crewe was unambiguous about Savarkar:

> I hope we may catch Savarkar by extradition, if the Hague let him loose. He is *the most dangerous figure among the conspirators*, I suppose [emphasis mine].[131]

Crewe was elated at the Hague's decision to extradite him to India, saying, "We are all chucking up our hats over the decision of the sages at the Hague."[132]

Hardinge concurred, noting that it was

> really good news to hear that we had won our case at the Hague and Savarkar is not to be restored to France. He will now spend the rest of his days with his brother in the Andamans Isles. It will be a great blow to the extremists in this country and in Paris, but I shall not be surprised if we have some more political assassinations in retaliation for Savarkar's loss of liberty.[133]

Two Secretaries of State and two Viceroys agreed—Savarkar was dangerous and needed to be put away, even if his arrest led to further violent acts.

There was still worry in official circles about how precisely this result was to be achieved:

> A case should be put up against Savarkar even though its [*sic*] not very strong. If he is convicted of being a member of a conspiracy the second conviction is by no means unprovable. If he is acquitted of course the whole petition drops.[134]

This would be a disaster, and "[i]t should be clearly understood," a confidential telegram to Crewe noted, that

> there is chance of acquittal on charge of abetment of murder whereas in all probability sentence on conspiracy charge will be transportation for life

130. IOR/Mss Eur/Photo Eur 469/no. 4, Letters to Charles Hardinge from the Earl of Crewe, December 2, 1910.

131. IOR/Mss Eur/Photo Eur 469/no. 16, Crewe to Hardinge, February 10, 1911.

132. IOR/Mss Eur/Photo Eur 469/no. 18, Crewe to Hardinge, February 24, 1911.

133. IOR/Mss Eur/Photo Eur 469/no. 23, Hardinge to Crewe, March 2, 1911.

134. NAI/Home Department/Political/Notes/60B/1910, 269.

> which would be probably maximum on conviction on other charges. If such a sentence now given, effect might actually be to induce clemency at a 2nd trial. Political effect of second trial would be most unfortunate as vindictiveness of Govt would be alleged . . . [135]

Everyone involved wanted to nail Savarkar the first time and avoid the political fallout of a second trial. To do that, they pulled together multiple charges—sedition, conspiracy, treason, and abetment to murder—so that if he was acquitted of one, he could be put away on another.

Not wanting to take any chances, Guider personally met the boat that brought Savarkar to India and escorted him to jail.[136] Savarkar was tried twice by two separate courts for separate offences.[137] While the legal process was unfolding, he was moved from a prison in Nasik to one in Pune.[138] All of Savarkar's visitors were watched, and those who put false names in the record book were tracked down.[139]

The trials lasted sixty-nine days, and at the second one, he was convicted and given the maximum sentence of two life terms on the Andaman Islands. His financial assets were also confiscated. Of the thirty-eight others accused along with Savarkar of being part of a Nasik terrorist group, three were released during the trial, and eight were found not guilty. The others received sentences ranging from six months to fifteen years.[140] This differential and extraordinary treatment underscored the police perception of Savarkar as far more dangerous than most run-of-the-mill revolutionaries.

135. NAI/Home Department/Political/Note/60B/1910, 271.

136. Phadke, *Śōdha Sāvarakarāñcā*, 46.

137. Godbole, *Ase Ahet Savarkar*, 40.

138. NAI/Home Department/Special/file 60D (a)/1919.

139. The police file has a series of printed reports, all marked "P/12." These include printed surveillance reports, and the judgment on the charge of abetment of murder against Savarkar and the Criminal Intelligence Office's record of the proceedings against Savarkar under the Fugitive Offenders Act. One of the reports indicates the two names used by one of his visitors: "Name under which reported, Mr. Kashi Prasad Jagaswall, Barrister; supposed real name Kashi Prasad Jagaswall, a rich lac manufacturer of Mizapur, U.P. Is a law student at Oxford. Accompanied B.C. Pal from Paris to London on the 26th August 1908 and was present at a meeting of extremists in 'India House' shortly afterwards, at which he proposed a deputation (of which he was a member also) to approach B.C. Pal in order to dissuade him from playing into the hands of Government. Said to have been a helpmate of Savarkar and Aiyar in their propaganda . . ."

140. Phadke, *Śōdha Sāvarakarāñcā*, 47. Babarao Savarkar was sentenced to ten years of rigorous imprisonment. See Savarkar, *Khristaparicaya*.

The brothers quickly began petitioning for clemency or a change in status from ordinary criminal to political prisoner, and whether because of this or because they were perceived as dangerous, reports about their behavior and physical condition were forwarded to Bombay and Delhi. The author of the history sheet on Savarkar was a P. A. Kelly, Personal Assistant to the Deputy Inspector-General of Police, CID. The police sheet was printed while Savarkar "was undergoing his sentence in the Andamans," and it ends with reference to the Director of Criminal Intelligence's Circular No. 8 from 1911 stating that "V.D. Savarkar was without doubt the ablest of the Indian revolutionaries in Europe, and he might have proved much more dangerous if he had worked for his object with a single aim rather than being motivated solely by personal revenge."[141] While it was easier for the government to see him as a vengeful Chitpavan Brahmin motivated by personal revenge than as the successful leader of a conspiracy, the government could never decide whether he was just a vengeful Marathi Brahmin or if he had influence over those outside his region.[142]

In June 1911, Savarkar was taken to the Andaman Islands to serve out his sentences in the notorious Cellular Jail, where he continued to be monitored.[143] Savarkar's sentence included hard labor, and shortly after his incarceration, Mr. Wedgwood, a member of the House of Commons, raised the issue of his incarceration and treatment.[144] Even in jail, Savarkar's influence was still feared. The Secretary of State allowed the Viceroy to ban the importation of Guy Aldred's publication the "Herald of Revolt" into India, which demanded Savarkar's immediate release.[145] A few copies had made their way into India, and the government was keen to prevent any further copies from following suit.[146]

141. History Sheet of V. D. Sawarkar, B. A., 12.

142. Rowlatt Sedition Committee report about the Marathi conspiracy, 13.

143. IOR/L/PJ/6/1314/no. 2286. The prison superintendent reported that Savarkar had gone on work strike and was punished with "a month's confinement." Subsequently, his punishment for similar offenses had been "(i) seven days standing handcuffs, (ii) four months chain-gang (which involves chain fetters) and (iii) ten days' crossbar fetters;" but that since the 19th of June, 1914, he had "been steadily at work."

144. IOR/L/PJ/6/1314/no. 2286.

145. In a telegram sent to the Secretary of State, the Viceroy wrote, "Your Lordship's attention is invited to October issue of the 'Herald of Revolt' Savarkar number. As we consider circulation of same in India will encourage disaffection towards Government, we propose, with your approval, to prohibit it under Sea Customs Act. Please telegraph your decision urgently." IOR/L/PJ/6/3899/1912.

146. "A Government that insults the starving millions in India and England by the Royal puppet show at Delhi—that promises pardon to political offenders, only to retain its hold over

A passage from Savarkar's 1857 book had also been reprinted in the October 1912 issue of *The Herald of Revolt*, along with an account of the tribulations suffered by prisoners in the Andamans. The *Herald* also published a letter from a Walter Strickland from Munich on July 13, 1912, in which he described Savarkar's treatment as life threatening:

> Savarkar will have an iron collar riveted around his neck, with his number fastened to it. The object of this arrangement is as follows, and the English think it a very clever one: Round the clearing, about eighteen miles in length, allotted to prisoners on ticket-of-leave, are the dense forests inhabited by the fast-disappearing tribes of Andamanese. Iron is of great value to them for their spear heads, and they are allowed the privilege of killing any prisoner who escapes to the woods for the sake of the iron around his neck . . . they are not likely to show the refugee any mercy.[147]

In 1919 the superintendent of the Cellular Jail reported on his conduct:

> Punished 8 times during 1912, 1913, and 1914 for refusing to work and possession of forbidden articles. For the last five years his behavior has been very good.

As to his present attitude (in 1919):

> . . . he is always suave and polite. . . . It is impossible to say what his real political views are at the present time.[148]

In other words, the police had no real reason to believe that his political views had changed.

During his time in the Andamans, Savarkar continued to engage in political activities—drafting his *Essentials of Hindutva*, writing letters to his brother advocating interregional marriages, celebrating the crossing of the oceans by Indian soldiers during World War I, writing poems celebrating the poet laureate Rabindranath Tagore, and working out his peculiar theory of Hindu genetics. As a prisoner, every one of his letters would have been opened and read. He continued his barrage of petitions, writing the colonial government every year

---

a man who is the victim of the most infamous knavery our capitalistic governors could evolve—is one of the worst abominations of the earth. All the empty pomp and tinsel show of monarchical pauper splendour cannot lend dignity to its machinations nor glory to its career." *Herald of Revolt*, October 1912, in IOR/L/PJ/6/3899/1912.

147. *Herald of Revolt* 2, no. 10, London, October 1912, in IOR/L/PJ/6/3899/1912.

148. *Herald of Revolt* 2, no. 10, London, October 1912, in IOR/L/PJ/6/3899/1912.

from 1911 until he was released to house arrest and instructing his brother to do the same.[149] In the letters, he either recanted his past political actions, promised to comply with government regulations, or pleaded ill health. Phadke has cautioned against a too literal reading of these clemency appeals, suggesting that Savarkar was skillfully playing a political game with the authorities.

In 1918, in response to Savarkar's wife's request for clemency on the grounds that the brothers' health had been seriously jeopardized, the senior Medical Officer at Port Blair reported that Savarkar had in fact suffered from dysentery and malaria and that his weight had gone down from 111 pounds to 99 pounds but that he would soon regain it. One of Savarkar's associates, G. S. Khaparde, emphasized these clemency appeals in a question he posed to the Legislative Council in India:

> Is it not a fact that Mr. Savarkar and his brother had once in 1915 and at another time in 1916 submitted petitions to Government stating that they would, during the continuance of war, serve the Empire by enlisting in the Army if released, and would, after the passing of the Reforms Bill, try to make the Act a success and would stand by Law and Order?[150]

The Act in question was the Government of India Act of 1919, also called the Montagu-Chelmsford Act, known colloquially as the Montford Reforms. Given Savarkar's anticolonial stance and his weak constitution, he was hardly likely to enlist in the army or cooperate with any reform package that granted special privileges to Muslims. It is far more likely that he wrote whatever he thought might help get him back into India and the political arena.[151]

As Durba Ghosh has shown, prominent liberal British politicians believed it was now expedient to distinguish between crime and rebellion or revolt

149. For a detailed account of these letters, sent either by Savarkar himself or his wife or sister-in-law, in 1911, 1912, 1913, 1914, 1915, 1918, 1919, 1920, see Phadke, *Śōdha Sāvarakarāñcā*, 50–55.

150. Representation by the Honorable Mr. G. S. Khaparde, in Home Department/Special/60D (b)/1919.

151. As Phadke puts it:

> Tatya has published the application sent to the Chief Commissioner of Andaman and Nicobar Islands on March 30, 1920. It is true that in this application he has used the language of loyalty to the government; but that language should not be taken literally. Considering Tatya's repeated petitions, the political context of the time and the reaction of the British rulers, it is clear that Tatya was playing a trick to get out of prison. He was playing this game till 1937.

Phadke, *Śōdha Sāvarakarāñcā*, 50–51.

and to treat middle class "gentlemanly terrorists" like Savarkar as potential partners in the project of constitutional reform.[152] The reform package included the creation of a committee tasked with reforming the penal system and investigating the treatment of political prisoners.[153] It also included King George V's declaration of clemency for all political prisoners, even as the political prisoners were all deemed to have been properly detained by the police.[154]

Although the royal pardon was much touted by the liberal Secretary of State Edwin Montagu, the Viceroy in India was not enthusiastic. For the police who had watched Savarkar for years, it posed a real problem. For three months, from February to June 1920, the Secretary to the Government of Bombay corresponded with the Secretary to the Government of India and compared the Savarkar brothers. While Ganesh was suspicious, "the real father of the movement was his brother Vinayak," who possesses "the qualities of leadership and courage which his brother lacked," wrote the Secretary of the Government of India. He emphasized this in a subsequent letter, noting that "Vinayak is really the dangerous man, the objection to whose release lies, no doubt, not so much in the seriousness of his offense as in his temperament." The letter recommended releasing one brother to ensure the good behavior of both:

> It may be observed that if Ganesh is released and Vinayak retained in custody, the latter will become in some measure a hostage for the former who will see that his own misconduct does not jeopardize his brother's chances of release at some future date.[155]

Meanwhile, Savarkar was aware of the clemency, and his appeal invoked his lost but putatively brilliant career as a reason he should be released.

152. Ghosh, *Gentlemanly Terrorists*, 33–34.

153. Ghosh, *Gentlemanly Terrorists*, 45–50.

154. Ghosh, *Gentlemanly Terrorists*, 51–53.

155. This is one of the files that was slated to be destroyed. It contains a three-month long correspondence between Mr. H. McPherson, CSI, ICS, Secretary to the Government of India, Home Department with The Honorable Mr. J. Crerar, Secretary to the Government of Bombay, Political Department. It has several stamps on it, including "Judicial Department, 26 Feb, 1920, Bombay" which suggests that it would have been stored in the Maharashtra State Archives. Handwritten notations on the file say Home Department/Political/Special/file 60D (b)/1919. The file is twenty-two pages in length.

> ... no less a personage than one of the Hon Members for the Home Deptt had said, in 1913, to me personally ... such education so much reading ... you could have held the highest posts under our Government.[156]

He also hinted that he might be of some political use, noting that he would cooperate in warding off the "common danger from the North of Turko-Afghan fanatics" because his release might give him a rebirth and "render me [him] personally attached and politically useful in future."[157] Savarkar repeated these claims in a subsequent letter.

Despite the warnings of the Bombay government about the danger Savarkar posed, the Government of India brought him back to India in 1921. From there, Savarkar wrote yet another letter to the Governor General of India. Every line was strategic.

> The petitioner begs to assure His Excellency that he is not the man he was in the days of his conviction. Then he was a mere boy. Since then he is grown not only in age but also in experience; and he sincerely regrets that he should ever been caught up in the whirlwinds of political passions and ruined the brilliant career that was already his. Ever since the visit of the Right Honourable Mr. Montague to India he had repeatedly affirmed his faith in the Reforms and the promises made by the Government, in his previous petitions to the government. The sight of the linked Asiatic Hoards, now hanging over the frontiers and who had been an hereditary curse of India—at any rate the non-Mahomedan India—leaves him convinced that a close and even a loyal co-operation and connection with the British Empire are good and

156. Home Department/Political/Special/file 60D (b)/1919, Letter from V. D. Savarkar, convict no. 32778, to the Chief Commissioner of the Andamans, March 30, 1920, 63–71. That Savarkar was learned, erudite, and well read no one doubted—not the colonial officials around him, his followers, or Savarkar himself. He would write in *Majhi Janmathep* that he had read every book in the library of Cellular Jail and knew the works of Spencer, Mill, Darwin, Huxley, Carlyle, Emerson, Macaulay, and Gibbon as well as those of Shakespeare, Milton, Pope, Dickens, and Tolstoy and those of Aristotle, Plato, Kropotkin, and Nietszche. Many of these authors and texts were standard reading for early twentieth-century Indian students who attended institutions like Fergusson College where the reading of canonical European literature was mandatory. Gopal Ganesh Agarkar and B. G. Tilak would also have studied the same literature. See, for instance, Ganachari, *Gopal Ganesh Agarkar*, ch. 1, ch. 3, and ch. 6 for an examination of the education in and influences of utilitarian thinkers such as John Stuart Mill and Herbert Spencer on Agarkar. See Marwah, "The View from the Future: Aurobindo Ghose's Anticolonial Darwinism," for Aurobindo's reading and understanding of Spencer.

157. Home Department/Political/Special/file 60D (b)/1919, 73.

> indispensable for both of them—only he prays that it may be mutual to be lasting and fruitful.[158]

In fact, he was exactly the man he was when convicted except that he had become far more strategic. He had no regrets about participating in politics (he was no less anticolonial) and continued to be as stalwart a nationalist as he was opposed to making any special provisions for Muslims (not, for him, a contradiction). In August 1919, the twenty-six-year-old Amir Amanullah Khan had stunned the British with an unprecedented victory over their forces, declaring Afghanistan to be a free and independent state, no longer a British protectorate.[159] If not actually suggesting that he would work against the Muslims and with the British, at the very least he was suggesting that there were points of contact between his agenda and theirs. He went on, still speaking of himself in the third person:

> . . . his broken health . . . and the sufferings make him determined—apart from any such condition—to retire and lead a private life and so he is willing to undertake and observe honestly this or any other such definite and reasonable condition that the government may be pleased to dictate . . . but if the petitioner's ill luck still persists in suppressing the Voice of Mercy then as a last alternative he prays that the special grievances arising out of his sudden transfer from the Andamans would be redressed.[160]

Only cursory knowledge is required to see Savarkar's many strategic misrepresentations here. No one could have believed that he wanted to lead a private life, certainly not the police who had been watching him for decades. When writing this letter, he also believed that Gandhi was a serious danger to India.[161] He was already agitating in the Andamans against both the Mappilas and the Khilafat movement, and his biographer tells us that he urgently wanted to write and publish his tract on Hindutva.[162]

158. This letter, dated August 19, 1921, is part of the police file compiled on Savarkar, Home Department/Special/60D (d)/1921–23.

159. Ahmed, "In the Name of a Law", 655–77; Barfield, *Afghanistan*, 175–83.

160. Home Department/Special/60D (d)/1921–23. Letter dated August 1, 1921. The file includes the clemency letters sent by Savarkar's brother (from Sabarmati Jail) and Savarkar's wife, who signed the letter in Marathi and wrote it from Narayanrao Savarkar's house in Girgaum, Bombay.

161. Phadke, *Śōdha Sāvarakarāñcā*, 55.

162. Karandikar, *Savarakar Charitra*, 493.

What must also be stressed here is that he gave the colonial police an opportunity they did not take. If the government would not commute his sentence, he requested that

> He be allowed to take his family with him and sent back to the Andamans on Ticket of Leave. Even the meanest of convicts, after putting in 9 years in the Andamans and with a year of good conduct, is entitled to lead a private life under the ticket of leave system—and it would not be much if the petitioner expects that at least that much will not be denied to him, after putting in 11 years in the Andamans and in the Jails and with 7 years of jail good conduct. He would—if allowed this much at least—be simply glad to lead a retired in private life forgotten by and forgetting the world in the blessings of a domestic home life. . . .[163]

In no part of Savarkar's memoirs do we get any indication that he enjoyed a quiet domestic life. Indeed, he rarely mentions his wife or children in his memoirs. The letter concluded:

> In conclusion the petitioner humbly begs to emphasize that the continuation of this agitation or that in India may not be allowed to prejudice the interests of the petitioner. He would not have suggested this but for public statements to this effect both in the press and the platform. He could have no control over the actions of millions of people and to make him and his brother suffer longer on 'administrative grounds' would be to punish them for the actions of others which are entirely beyond his power to check.

In the petition, Savarkar emphasized his charisma in having "millions of people" publicly appealing for his release, even as he claimed he had no control over them. Neither a fundamental transformation of Savarkar's personality and character nor his indifference to political events in India could be assumed, which is exactly what the Bombay police told the central government.[164] But leaving that aside, let us consider his request for a Ticket of Leave.

The penal settlement of Port Blair considered the reeducation of prisoners of paramount importance. It was a three-tiered system in which incoming prisoners were first made to undertake hard labor in Cellular Jail, where the

163. Home Department/Special/60D (d)/1921–23. Letter dated August 19, 1921. For details on the Ticket of Leave system, see Ferrar, "The New Penal System," 48–61.

164. Phadke, *Śōdha Sāvarakarāñcā*, 58.

strictest discipline was imposed. In the second stage prisoners were transferred to the Associated Jail in which the conditions were like those in regular Indian jails. A year and a half later, pending good behavior, they were moved to the barracks spread out all over the settlement. At this point prisoners were considered "laboring convicts" and literally engaged in labor all day. After a total of ten years, prisoners could apply for a Ticket of Leave to support themselves by engaging in agriculture or shopkeeping or some other available trade. In 1921, the Government of India announced the end of banishment for life as a punishment and the closing of Port Blair.[165] At the time, 11,500 convicts lived in the penal settlement. Savarkar was in effect asking for permission to return to the Andamans with his family and live there not as a convict but a settler. Savarkar had even worked out a logical and Hindu nationalist reason for how his remaining in the Andamans would serve the larger Hindu cause. According to his biographer, Shi La Karandikar, if the Andamans penal settlement were shut down, then "three generations of Hindus, seeded and raised here, those generations would be destroyed, their blood, seed and labor would go to waste, this was now Savarkar's point of view." Karandikar also quotes Savarkar as saying "if I were not to be released as soon as I got to India, then I would prefer to live here in the Andamans, and given that I have put in ten years, I would like to do so with my family."[166] The Ticket of Leave would have been the perfect solution for Savarkar and his brothers. Leaving them in the distant Andaman Islands would have let the government claim it had given him clemency while simultaneously removing him from Indian political life. Why then would they release him into house arrest in his native state of Maharashtra when his most incendiary writings were all in Marathi and, since Savarkar wrote under assumed names and published widely in his associates' many journals, he would be very difficult to monitor?[167] Indeed, by the time

165. Ferrar, "New Penal System," 49. British marine surveyor Archibald Blair started a free settlement in 1789 in the Andaman Islands, but illness and disease beset it, and it collapsed. It was restarted after 1857 as Port Blair, a penal settlement in which the "discipline, care and reclamation of convicts" was the primary objective. See Sen, *Disciplining Punishment*, and Sen, *Savagery and Colonialism*, for a careful assessment of how the penal settlement was put in place and how the indigenous community in the Andaman Islands was perceived and depicted.

166. Karandikar, *Savarakar Charitra*, 483–84.

167. Phadke, *Śōdha Sāvarakarāñcā*, 68, 80. Phadke writes admiringly of Savarkar's cleverness in writing under an assumed name and of his ability to evade the police and maintain a political presence despite the restrictions.

watchers and translators had confirmed that those incendiary writings were penned by him, the damage had been done, as we shall see in the next chapter.

Savarkar was brought back to Calcutta in May 1921 and placed in the Alipur Jail. He was already speaking of "Khilafat" as a menace (*āphat*), and while in the Andamans, the phrase "*hī Khilāphata nāhī, āphat āhē*" ("This is not Khilafat, it is a menace") had circulated around the entire prison, so the police certainly knew of his views.[168] On January 6, 1924, Savarkar was released, subject to certain conditions. The Bombay Police had no choice but to have Savarkar sign a letter foreswearing all political activities, a letter that would not be well received by other nationalists. "As a result of representations from the convict and his relatives the Government of Bombay decided to reconsider their previous refusal to release him," the Secretary to the Government of Bombay, Home Department gloomily wrote to the Government of India on January 15, 1924.

> His Excellency Sir George Lloyd personally interviewed Savarkar in prison and came to the conclusion that granted certain conditions it would be safe to release him. I am to state that the release has been received very quietly, any tendency to make political use of Savarkar having been forestalled by the conditions which he has agreed to and even more by his full acknowledgement . . . of the justice of trial and sentence. This letter has roused some anger in extremist circles and has been described by some of the papers as a "shocking admission.[169]

We cannot tell what use the government might have made of him, forestalled as it was by Savarkar's claim that he would no longer engage in political activity. But we can suspect that they had plans to use him or would have liked to have used him. One of the ways Savarkar was useful to the British government was in his consistent attacks on Gandhi, who was the most prominent political figure advocating Hindu-Muslim unity.

Upon his release under conditions that were neither house arrest nor complete freedom, Savarkar would be monitored by the Ratnagiri police who reported to the Ratnagiri District Magistrate (RDM). The RDM conferred with the Bombay Commissioner of Police (BCP) and the Poona CID and kept the central government in Delhi apprised about Savarkar. The conditions of his

168. Karandikar, *Savarakar Charitra*, 568.
169. IOR/L/PJ/6/1871/no. 515/1924.

release made clear that he was not free to travel outside Ratnagiri or engage in political activities but did not specify exactly what political activities were proscribed. This vagueness opened the way for a decades-long debate between the police and Savarkar regarding what was and was not considered "political." The result was that Savarkar wrote and said basically whatever he wanted then argued with the police when challenged. The police could have rearrested him, moved him, watched him more carefully, etc., but instead, as we will see, they simply wrung their hands. They enabled Savarkar to continuously attack Gandhi, Khilafat and what it meant to Muslims, and everyone who did not support his agenda.

Savarkar showed his disregard for the terms of his release immediately, giving speeches exhorting young people not to be beguiled by silver and gold or promises and rewards, but to remember their duty to the nation. As he was feted across Maharashtra as the glorious revolutionary who had returned home, the *Bombay Chronicle* covered his every appearance.[170] The plague that had taken his father and uncle had returned to Ratnagiri, so he could not move there immediately, and he lived for a while in Shirgaon at a friend's home.[171] Once in Ratnagiri he began to petition about being unfairly charged, denied due process, getting differential treatment compared to others accused of similar crimes. Savarkar used petitions as political maneovreing. He had questions about where he could stay, where he could visit, how long he could remain in one city or another. He wanted to attend a birth ceremony of one relative's child, the marriage of another's, a play in one city, a gathering in another.[172] Rather than Ratnagiri, he preferred the more cosmopolitan Bombay or Poona, where he claimed he could earn a living. Most of his requests were denied, but he kept making them.[173]

Two months after his release, the police report stated:

170. Phadke, *Śōdha Sāvarakarāñcā*, 70. Savarkar was feted in Kolhapur, Meraj, Satara, Pune, Kalyan, and Devlali.

171. Salvi, *Swatantryaveer Savarkarancya Sahavasat*, 55. Vishnupant Damle was the friend with whom Savarkar lived before moving onto Ratnagiri. See also Phadke, *Śōdha Sāvarakarāñcā*, 78.

172. See Phadke, *Śōdha Sāvarakarāñcā*, 79, 103, for the various requests he made, all of which were denied.

173. Microfilm Roll N 22, Nehru Memorial Museum and Library, Correspondence with Bombay Government, 1924–37. Savarkar's petition, dated May 27, 1924 asking to go to Nasik for three months was granted from the Collector's Office, Nasik, July 11, 1924. But he was expected back in Ratnagiri by September 14. He petitioned again to be allowed to stay in Nasik because

> He has last been reported as holding meetings and expressing the usual views as to hand-spinning, so forth. His connection with preparations for the *satyagraha* reported to be in contemplation for the new year will be separately reported.[174]

And so began a pattern in which the police reported that he had engaged in political activity in expressing his views about homespun cloth (known as *khadi*, and a clear reference to Gandhi) and to *satyagraha* (nonviolent noncooperation) to be accompanied only by expressions of colonial frustration. Regularly, BSAs were added to the police file noting his overtly political claims.[175] On November 22, 1924, he was noted to have

> . . . urged union against other religions and recommended *shuddhi* [reconversion] to reclaim perverts. He emphasized the atrocities perpetrated by the Moplahs [Kerala Muslims] on Hindus.[176]

The office of the CID, Poona issued the following on November 24, 1924:

> As you know, Savarkar is precluded from dealing with political matters. This speech is clearly a political one only very thinly veiled under the pretext of social reform. Savarkar has spent the hot weather and the rains at Nasik, which Govt. kindly permitted him to do on account of plague at Ratnagiri. Since he has been there, there has been considerable raking up of old history: the prosecution of Williams, the Jackson murder, etc., and though he has done nothing in the political line, it is quite clear that his influence is at work.

This vacillation between the certainty that he was making a political speech and uncertainty about what constituted doing something "in the political line" is strange. Clearly the police recognized that his comments about the Mappillahs were incendiary, yet they let him continue. Either they were helpless or deliberately chose to do nothing.

Less than a year after his release, Savarkar was summoned to explain his anti-Muslim sentiments.

---

of the plague in Ratnagiri (August 30, 1924). He was then given permission to stay in Nasik until October 1, 1924.

174. Bombay Secret Abstract (BSA), November 15, 1924, in Home Department/Special/60D (d).

175. BSA, November 15, 1924, in Home Department/Special/60D (d).

176. BSA, November 15, 1924, in Home Department/Special/60D (d).

> Sir, I am directed to invite your attention to an article entitled "the suffering Moslems of Kohat" which appeared in the "Mahratta" of the 1st March 1925, under your name and to enquire whether the article was written by you.[177]

Savarkar's response is undated, and it is not clear if it was a draft and then rewritten before sending it, as many lines are crossed out, and some are too faded to read. It appears to have been written in a hurry—the tone is defensive, and many words are unreadable.

> The very fact that the Govt has been obliged to take a special notice of this article gave rise to doubts in my mind as to whether I had (unwittingly) [crossed out] unconsciously transgressed the terms of my understanding (by letting out) [crossed out] of not taking any part in the matter of Indian politics. So I carefully went through the article more than once and felt a sense of relief to find that so far as I can see there is hardly anything that could be construed as (objectionable) [crossed out] political matter. The only place where the word "Swaraj" happens is entirely unobjectionable as the reference is made to express not what I or anyone else thinks or ought to think of Swaraj but what exaggerated terms Mr Gandhi thought of Khilafat. The whole trend of the article is clearly unmistakenly social or religious. It would have been a great surprise myself if it had been otherwise as I so studiously confined myself to the nonpolitical aspects of Kohat that I deliberately make no reference as to the actions of the Govt or to the controversy with regard to the police activities. Perhaps the intention behind the reference was to show how Mr. Gandhi who generally is given to much unstinting condemnation of all acts of violence did not dare to condemn the Kohat Mohammedans as uncompromisingly as he did the rioters of Bombay.

In just the first paragraph, we see Khilafat, Kohat Mohammedans, and Gandhi noted as targets, but Savarkar seems to have been using the guise of a religious or social reformer to accuse Gandhi of hypocrisy when it came to condemning acts of violence conducted by Muslims.

Savarkar continued:

> The second thing that could have brought this article to the special notice of the Govt may be that the article is looked upon likely to increase the ill

177. Letter no. 724/3266, Bombay Castle, March 28, 1925, in Home Department/Special/60D (d).

> feeling between the Hindus and Mohammedans in India. But the facts quoted in my article have been reported by all most all papers and seriously criticized especially in the North. . . .

Unsurprisingly, his explanation failed to persuade the government, which responded with terse firmness:

> I am directed to state that Government consider that your explanation is far from satisfactory. It should have been obvious to you that an article of the nature which you published in the issue of 'Mahratta' of the 1st March 1926 was bound to inflame the feelings and increase the tension between Hindus and Muhammadans and was contrary to your undertaking not to engage in any manner in political activities without the consent of Government. I am therefore to request you to refrain in future from any similar writings as they would necessitate a reconsideration of the question of your release by Government.[178]

The excessive politeness of this request is simply bureaucratic legalese. Would someone they had described as a terrorist, a dangerous seditionist, a malevolent and mendacious Chitpavan Brahmin who would avenge the defeat of the Brahmin Peshwai just cease all actions they considered unacceptable? Savarkar met the government's response with exaggerated humility:

> This letter makes me revise the meaning I put on the terms of my condition which to my mind meant refraining from discussions or dealing with any question of current politics in any matter that refers to the nature or activity of the Govt directly bearing on its political aspect internal or international . . . But this order has forced me to understand the condition . . . While I am trying to define my position to myself in the light of this new introspection . . . [179]

And yet there was no evidence that he ever changed his ways on the basis of his promise of introspection.

Most immediately, it was contradicted by the report of a strange lecture he delivered on May 11, 1925, near the Ram temple in Ratnagiri.

> There were, he said, a thousand years ago a Hindu population of 60 crores in Asia but that it had now dwindled down to 22 crores which indicated that

178. Letter no. 724/7266, Bombay Castle, March 28, 1925, in Home Department/Special/60D (d).
179. Letter no. 724/3266, Bombay Castle, May 9, 1925 in Home Department/Special/60D (d).

> 38 crores of Hindus had become converts and that if this state of affairs continued there would be no Hindu left at all. He advised therefore the removal of untouchability and the taking back into the Hindu religion those who had become converts. He then related an incident that occurred in the Andamans when he was there. The Hindus and Mohammedans were given a bag of parched grain to eat after breakfast. The Mohammedans purposely went and put their hands into the bag given to the Hindus who thereupon would not eat the grain as it was polluted and starved themselves. When he explained the whole thing properly to them, they started eating the grain. Mahars [members of a so-called untouchable community], he said, should be allowed to go to temples and draw water from public wells and they should be considered one degree higher than the Mohammedans.[180]

In one fell swoop, we get Muslims as aggressive proselytizers, a fanciful history of conversion, and an effort to explain to orthodox Hindus that Muslim touch did not contaminate food. This is a speech that was clearly incendiary. He tells his followers to treat Muslims as lower than even the so-called untouchables.

The police and Savarkar had regular exchanges about his failing to stick to the terms of his release. Indeed, it was "a source of anxiety to Government, as Mr. Savarkar was then found reviving his old activities and was very near the margin of breaking the terms of the bond he had executed before his release from the jail."[181] The BCP actually stated that there was no reason to believe that he would ever refrain from political activities:

> Savarkar's undertaking not to engage in public activities is worth little. *He has never failed to introduce politics into his public speeches under the guise of religion* [emphasis mine].[182]

Yet on September 12 and 13, 1926, when Savarkar verbally attacked Muslims again, the report suggests that the police took no proactive or reactive measures.

> There is a feeling in Chiplun that he may incite communal trouble between Hindus and Mohammedans there. His movements and speeches will be watched.

180. BSA, May 30, 1925, in Home Department/Special/file 60D (d).
181. Home Department/Special/file 60D.
182. Home Department/Special/file 60D.

And watch him they did. On his travels to Bombay on a steamer, his visits to his relatives in Dadar, and his attendance at theatrical productions. He had to inform the Bombay police in advance of every person and place he intended to visit.[183]

In 1927 he published a musical play—*Saṅgīta Uḥśāpa* (Removal of a curse)—that attacked Muslims.[184] One of his associates remembers him immediately starting to write several works as soon as he arrived in Shirgaon prior to getting to Ratnagiri. In 1925 he published the English version of his historical work *Hindu-Pad-Padashahi* along with the preface, a novel, and the musical play *Saṅgīta Uḥśāpa.*[185] According to Phadke, the published play created quite a stir.[186] Savarkar wrote only three music dramas—*Saṅgīta Uḥśāpa* in 1925, *Saṅgīta San'yasta Khaḍga* (Forsaken sword) in 1931, and *Saṅgīta Uttarakriyā* (Northern action/funeral rites) in 1933. It is curious that the most famous of them—*San'yasta Khaḍga*—which was performed by Chintamanrao Kolhatkar's and Dinanathrao Mangeshkar's troupe (Balwant Sangeet Mandali), did not receive much colonial attention given its obvious challenge to nonviolence and Gandhian methods.[187] About *Saṅgīta Uḥśāpa,* however, this note was inserted into Savarkar's file:

> The plot is difficult to follow here, but it appears that one of the Brahmans becomes a servant in an Ashram, obviously meant to be a satire on

183. Letter from S. M. Bharucha, Esquire, B. A., District Magistrate, Bombay Suburban District to V. D. Savarkar, Esquire, Puja Sadan, Khar Road, Bombay, Bandra. No. Co. IV/133, Old Custom House Yard, Fort Bombay, dated October 14, 1926. See *SSV* 4: 189–94, 195–201, 208–9, for the many articles Savarkar wrote on political topics in these years, including on Lala Lajpat Rai's murder ("Lālājīnvara Lāṭhīmāra"), Gandhi's declaration of *purna swaraj* ("Sampūrṇa rājakīya svātantrya hyā śabdānnī ciḍalēlē Gāndhījī ni Iṅgraja" [Gandhi and the British annoyed at the words "complete political independence"]), Gandhi's "Himalayan Blunder," and on the Nizam of Hyderabad ("Nijāmācī taḷī ucaḷaṇārē Musalamāna" [Blind reverence of Muslims towards the Nizam]).

184. Home Department/Special/no. S. D. 288, Mahabaleshwar, April 7/8, 1927.

185. Salvi, *Swatantryaveer Savarkarancya Sahavasat,* 55.

186. See Phadke, *Śōdha Sāvarakarāñcā,* 93–101 for a blow-by-blow account of how and where the play was received, edited, published, reedited, and challenged, and the objectionable words and concepts Savarkar was forced to remove.

187. For details about *San'yasta Khaḍga,* see B. Savarkar, *Hindusamaj Sanrakshak,* 261–62. The Savarkar Smarak in Bombay published these three plays in small booklets. In the preface to *San'yasta Khaḍga,* Balarao Savarkar (Savarkar's secretary) writes that Savarkar wrote this play to show the extreme destruction wrought on India by Gandhian nonviolence, noting that the play was first performed on September 18, 1931, in Bombay.

> Mr. Gandhi's ashram at Ahmedabad. Gandhi's Tolstoyan principles are clearly brought out, and at the same time most of the residents of the ashram are represented as rogues and hypocrites. . . . The arch-villain of the piece is the Muhammadan subhedar of the place, who has married the sister of the kotwal, Ibrahim Khan. The subhedar is a regular Don Juan and is determined to carry the girl off, to add another to his list of ravished Hindu women . . . inasmuch as the two prominent Muhammadans in the play are the leading villains, it would not be advisable to approve of the play.[188]

The pattern was clear. Because he was attacking Gandhi and the possibility of Hindu-Muslim unity the government suggested merely that

> Mr. Savarkar was very ill-advised in publishing this play at a time when Hindu-Muslim feelings are hypersensitive. The book is certainly not a publication that one would expect from a party who is at large through the clemency of Govt and under the express condition that he would not engage in political activities . . . [including] attempts to inflame feelings and arouse communal tension. The Governor in Council therefore considers that Mr. Savarkar should be asked to withdraw the book from publication.

Withdraw a book that was already in circulation? This would be nearly impossible.

Savarkar, meanwhile, was not only unrepentant but again claimed the mantle of a social reformer agitating to abolish untouchability:

> Having already done all that the Government wished me to do . . . I now take leave to point out to the Government that the play cannot for the following reasons be suspended of causing or aiming to cause any serious tensions between & Moslems. For (a) it is chiefly concerned with the removal of untouchability alone. The Mohmedan characters are all secondary personages, (b) even then great care is taken in dealing with them so as never to attribute any undignified character to their community as such nor to represent only the ugly side of their society. Just as the better mentality of the present day Brahmin is represented (e.g. Purshottanshastri's character) along with the meaner (E.G. Naranbhat) so also the noble element in the Mohmedan community is eloquently brought out in some characters notably the Mulla (Act IV, 3rd Scene) who holds up the best human ideals as consistent with the teachings of true Islam and condemns forcible cinversions [*sic*] and other

188. Home Department/Special/no. S. D. 288, Mahabaleshwar, April 7/8, 1927.

> outrageous crimes of fanatism [*sic*], (c) as to the story of a Hindu girl being pursued by Moslem bad characters and forcible conversions of the Hindus—well from the days of Allauddin to Aurangzeb history bears testimony to its truth, & the play too is merely historical. And even if today is taken into consideration, the Courts of Bengal and the public everywhere are busy in dealing with such incidents to such an extent that the two communities have got used to them as occurrences of daily life and are therefore not at all likely to get shocked by witnessing a stray incident staged in a secondary drame [*sic*] like the "USHAP". (d) But above all the fact that conclusively proves that the drama is least likely to inflame any ill feeling is that several plays and novels whose main theme had been the upselling of the Moslem kingdom and fights and wars that took place between the two communities in Marathi history and which use language far bitterer [*sic*] than "USHAP" ever does are being read and staged daily for the past twenty years and more and yet they e.g. Panipatcha Mokabla, novels of Mr. Hari Narayan Apte, Shiva Sambhava and several other books,—have never caused, not are even suspected of being likely to cause any serious ill feeling between these communities. (e) In view of these facts I cannot but feel that this historical play "USHAP" would have also passed off un-noticed . . . <u>but for the fact of its being written by me.</u>

He went on, however, to say that

> if in spite of this pleading and request the Government sticks to their decision then I too will stick to my former understanding and will not reopen the sale of the book. Of course it will spell a financial ruin but then I must, grudgingly or not, but bear it . . .[189]

In turns arrogant and manipulative, this letter reveals Savarkar's skill. He claims the play is about the abolition of untouchability when his targets are Muslims; he claims a spurious equivalence between "bad" Brahmins and "bad" Muslims; and he insists that any anti-Muslim aspects were simply historical facts. He ends with a complaint of victimhood because other Marathi writers who say the same things he does are not being targeted by the police.

189. Home Department/Political/Special/file 60, Ratnagiri, June 6, 1927, from V. D. Savarkar to The Secretary to the Government of Bombay, Home Department, Bombay. Savarkar here refers to the novels of Hari Narayan Apte, but compared to the language Savarkar uses for Muslims, while Apte's *Gad Aala Pan Simha Gela* has plenty of prejudice, it contains relatively less vitriol.

Savarkar had widespread support. Conservative nationalist newspapers such as the *Indian National Herald* championed him, voicing annoyance that his play was being investigated and that he had to remove explicit prejudice against Muslims before it could be staged. The paper called the police activities "pranks of officialdom," saying that

> Red Tapism had thus full sway and "Usshapi" has been mutilated and clipped of several important passages. The Huzur Deputy ordered the drama which was a tragedy to be turned into a comedy.

The article's author saw "the whole episode of 'Usshapi,'" as an "eloquent testimony to the terror which the name of Savarkar strikes in the heart of the bureaucracy."[190] The bureaucracy may or may not have been terrified, but once again the police failed to rearrest him. Unfortunately for the police, despite several public controversies in the 1920s over publications that hurt religious sentiments, there was no law that criminalized them.[191] It was only after the enactment in 1927 of Sec. 295A that there was a law that criminalized deliberate or malicious intent to outrage religious feelings.[192]

Meanwhile, the police were tracking *Saṅgīta Uḥśāpa*'s distribution. Of the 5,000 printed, 2,290 copies were bound in books and the rest were in loose printed forms. Of the 2,290 copies the press disposed of 1,579 books to various parties including, as the police noted, to agents in Poona, Akola, Sholapur, Nagpur, Sangli, Belgaum, Amraoti, Miraj, and to booksellers in Poona, and Bombay.[193] In other words, the play traveled the length and breadth of Maharashtra.

While the constraints on Savarkar did little to restrain his political speech, his supporters were clamoring for his right to return to the political world completely unfettered. The government debated this on and off from 1928 until

190. *Indian National Herald*, December 5, 1927, in Home Department/Special/60D (d).

191. This was even more apparent in the case of the publication insulting the Prophet Muhammad, titled *Rangeela Rasool*, in Punjab (1924–27) when the Punjab High Court had to acquit the publisher because there was no law under which he could be convicted.

192. Sethi, *War Over Words*, 14. For a detailed examination of how and why the British government moved hastily to amend the Indian Penal Code after the acquittal of Mahashe Rajpal, publisher of the pamphlet "Rangila Rasul", and calls for the resignation of the acquitting judge, see Nair, "Beyond the 'Communal' 1920s," 317–40.

193. BSA of July 23, 1927, in Home Department/Special/60D (d).

his unconditional release in 1937. The BCP noted as if he had expected otherwise that

> his admiration for great men like Napoleon, Shivaji and Mazzini has not in the least abated. His other activities in the districts which are reported in the Secret Abstracts from 1924 to 1928 make me believe that he will turn out an active agitator if his restrictions were entirely removed.[194]

The Magistrate and the Ratnagiri police then noted with relief that "the decision of the Government not to cancel the conditions or restrictions placed over V.D. Savarkar will prove very helpful in the present troublous times."[195] But Savarkar was hardly quiescent.

In 1930, BCP Sir Patrick Kelly, a target of political assassination by revolutionary nationalists, wrote to the Secretary to the Government of Bombay that "his [Savarkar's] brothers may be connected with the recent shooting outrage at the Lamington Road Police Station."[196] This was one of the more spectacular attempts made by revolutionaries to kill the police commissioner. When they couldn't find him, they shot a British sergeant and his wife.[197] Some years later, the BCP admitted about Savarkar that "[w]hatever restrictions may be imposed

194. Letter from Commissioner of Police to the Secretary to the Government of Bombay, Home Department (Political), Bombay, November 26, 1928, in Home Department/Special/60D (d).

195. No. S. D. 5760, Home Department (Political), Bombay Castle, December 14, 1930, in Home Department/Special/60D (d).

196. Office of the Commissioner of Police, Bombay, no. 5885/H 3003 of 1930, Confidential letter from the Office of the Commissioner of Police to the Secretary to the Government of Bombay, Home Department (Political), Poona. October 29, 1930. Salvi writes fairly casually about assassination. Savarkar, he recalled, told revolutionaries who they should and shouldn't assassinate. Vasudev Balwant Gogate suggested to Savarkar that he assassinate the Collector of Pune, but Savarkar reputedly advised Gogate to try and assassinate the Acting Governor of Bombay, Sir Ernest Hotson. In Salvi's words,

> Tatyrarao told him not to kill the district officer/collector but shoot the white officer who was the source from whom all the injustice emanates. A collector merely follows the orders, shoot the people who wield power. Gogate agreed with this and when Hotson had come to visit the college, he found an opportunity and he tried to shoot him with a pistol. Unfortunately, he did not succeed. Hotson survived as he was cautious and wearing armor. Later the man was tried and sentenced.

Salvi, *Swatantryaveer Savarkarancya Sahavasat*, 31–32. For the case itself, and Gogate's appeal, see Bombay High Court, Emperor vs Vasudeo Gogate on January 6, 1932, Bench: J Beaumont, Kt., Broomfield.

197. Nair, "A Century of Busting Crime," *Indian Express*, Friday, February 4, 2022.

upon a man like him, he is bound to evade them." Kelly noted that neither Savarkar nor his brothers had "shown any signs of a change of heart."[198]

By July 1933, Savarkar had written a new play in Marathi called *Saṅgīta Uttarakriyā* (Northern action/funeral rites). A review in the *Oriental Translator* remarked that, though the historical facts underlying the play were not distorted, "they were presented in such a way as to bring home to the Hindus the supreme necessity of organizing and unifying their community and that in doing so, the author betrayed in places his violent anti-Muslim prejudices in language that was likely to hurt Musalman susceptibilities."[199] This note dutifully went into the file, but the police took no action.

Finally, on May 5, 1934, the District Magistrate of Ratnagiri ordered Savarkar's arrest under the Emergency Powers Act "in the interest of public peace and tranquility." His house and belongings were raided and searched by the CID.[200] Savarkar had been

> interfering with the witnesses who were being examined at Ratnagiri in connection with the Dhobi Talao shooting case in April 1934. The principal accused in the Dhobi Talao case was his follower.[201]

Informants had told CID officers that "Savarkar wields tremendous influence upon the people here and unless he is removed from the scene no one will venture to volunteer any information."[202] The District Magistrate recommended taking immediate action.

Not one to back down from a conflict, Savarkar drafted a long letter from prison. He praised himself for having "devoted himself to the Social Reform Movement and worked to secure the removal of untouchability and the curse of the caste system in particular." He claimed that he had "refrained carefully from doing anything that smelt of political favour that during the last 9 years or so there could not happen any contingency which made it necessary for the

198. UOR/no. 823/H/3003, February 15, 1934, in Home Department/Special/60 D(d).

199. No. S.D. 3076. Home Department (Political), Poona, October 22, 1934, in Home Department/Special/60D (d).

200. *Bombay Chronicle*, May 11, 1934, in Home Department/Special/60D (d).

201. Confidential, Office of the Commissioner of Police, no. 5425/H 3003 of 1934, November 5, 1934. Dhobi Talao is an area of Bombay in which the shootings took place. Home Department/Special/60D (d).

202. Confidential, Office of the Deputy Inspector General Police, CID, Bombay Presidency, no. S. B. 820 of 1934, May 14, 1934, in Home Department/Special/60D (d).

Govt to take any such drastic step as to take the petitioner into custody."[203] In the police report Savarkar was said to have written,

> [t]hat in spite of such any/almost unobjectionable record of the period that he passed after his conditional release in 1924 and the petitioner's constant and effective care to observe its conditions and restrictions he was suddenly shocked to see that he should get yesterday arrested all alone owing to some information received by the Govt to show that (as he was given to understand by the D.M's written questions) the petitioner had under the garb of Harijan Movement encouraged Terrorism!

He requested the government to believe him when he said that "he never had by word or deed anything to do with political movement as such—much less with any act of violence which school of thought he has openly disclaimed and denounced in the public statement which was issued at the time of his released and published by the Govt in the Press."[204] Disclaiming any knowledge of the perpetrators of the crime he was assumed to have masterminded, he boasted even as he pleaded.

> [T]he two . . . charged with attempt to shoot at Bombay were known to him as they used to attend the anti-caste dinners in which some eight to nine hundred persons used to participate, volunteer to teach to mahar boys, inspect mahar schools and do such work as led to the removal of untouchability and caste. Thousands of men came into contact with the petitioner in that capacity and so these two youths as well. He had no other connection whatsoever with them and knew nothing of any such criminal design on their part.

Finally, as always, he pleaded ill health.

> The Petitioner's health already broken by the previous lifelong imprisonment in the Andamans for 14 years has only very recently getting tolerably well—Any incarceration at this age after the previous strain is bound to break his health altogether and render life simply unbearable.[205]

203. May 6, 1934, Ratnagiri District Prison, to the Deputy Commissioner of Police, Special Branch, Bombay in Home Department/Special/60D (d).

204. May 6, 1934, Ratnagiri District Prison, to the Deputy Commissioner of Police, Special Branch, Bombay in Home Department/Special/60D (d).

205. May 6, 1934, Ratnagiri District Prison, to the Deputy Commissioner of Police, Special Branch, Bombay in Home Department/Special/60D (d).

Savarkar wrote another arcanely worded petition in English using only one very long sentence to do so.

> The petition of V.D. Savarkar, Ratnagiri, most humbly showeth . . . that, the petitioner hopes that the fact that he had put in 14 years in transportation and imprisonment from 1910 to 1924 and ever since then had been interned in Ratnagiri for the last 12 years or so, coupled with the fact that he had served the conditions under which he was released so scrupulously especially during the last two years period of extension as not to give any cause to the authorities even to call for any explanation from him for any of his public activities, will disarm any suspicion on the part of the government as to his future line of conduct and persuade them to give him a chance of carrying out the promise he had so often made and does renew in this petition also, to try his humble best to work out the latest Reforms and serve the cause of his Nation and Humanity by all legitimate and constitutional means available.

That Savarkar wanted to serve the cause of his nation was clear, but that he had given the police no reason to suspect him was less so, given how frequently he had violated the terms of his release. But he would have the last laugh.

In 1937, following the passage of the 1935 Government of India Act, a new constitution was drawn up and Savarkar's friend and admirer, the journalist and social reformer, Anant Hari Gadre, created a committee called the Savarkar Restrictions Removal Committee. It held public meetings, tried to win the sympathy of prominent people, gathered signatures, and pressed for Savarkar to be released without conditions.[206] Under pressure to appear more congenial to self-rule, the colonial government released him despite knowing that he was unrepentant, had played fast and loose with the restrictions placed on him, and continued to express anti-Muslim sentiments.

Celebrations attended Savarkar's release, and he was feted across Maharashtra.[207] He immediately took a swing at members of the INC calling them "national eunuchs" ("*rashtriya hijade*").[208] The police decided that Savarkar would no longer have a regular watcher but only "a look up periodically."[209]

206. BSA of August 10, 1935, in Home Department/Special/60D (d).

207. BSA of July 3, 1937, in Home Department/Special/60D (d).

208. *Bombay Chronicle*, June 27, 1937 in Home Department/Special/60D (d).

209. Letter, June 28, 1937—addressee unknown, but it is from a watcher who noted Savarkar's travel from Poona to Bombay by the Kalyan local train at 7:45 am. Home Department/Special/60D (d).

Yet, in the immediate aftermath of his release, he was still watched. The BSA reported that,

> in an informal discussion, he assured the members of the Poona Journalists' Association that the alleged improper remarks made by him at Miraj were meant for those who had applauded, during the Assembly debate, Dr. Khan Saheb's sarcastic references about the abduction of Hindu girls by Frontier Tribes. He paid tributes to the Congress and spoke in favour of Socialism.

Political speech followed political speech. Savarkar invoked 1857 as a war of independence, exhorted Hindus to unite, and proclaimed that Hindus and Muslims could never unite. In all his reported speeches in 1937 he laid out his agenda: *bhāśā śud'dhi* (purification of language[s]), no Hindu-Muslim unity, Sanskritized Hindi as the lingua franca, and the abolition of untouchability.[210] On June 26, he

> delivered a lecture on the purification of the Marathi language to an audience of about 1,500. He said he did not object to Hindi being made the "lingua franca" of India, provided no Urdu words were included.

Having been released without conditions, he demonstrated why they were necessary in the first place. But this was 1937, and the British were facing the prospect of war with Germany.

In 1937, having accepted the terms of the new Government of India Act expanding the electorate, the INC and other parties had begun their political campaigns. Having been forcefully removed from the public political sphere for the past thirteen years, Savarkar was keen to make up for lost time, campaigning

210. HB/3003, CID, the BSA of July 7, 1937 in Home Department/Special/60D (d). For Savarkar's actual writings on the subject, see *SSV*, MPHS, 3: 12–25. "Āmacī rāṣṭrabhāṣā—sanskr̥taniṣṭha Hindī, Hindusthānī navhē! Áurdū tara navhēca navhē" ("Our national language—Sanskritic Hindi, not Hindusthani! Definitely not Urdu!!") published in June 1937 in the Marathi magazine *Sahyadri*. Arguing against those he called "Ḗaikya lampaṭa" ("lusting for unity"), he claimed that seven crore Muslims wanted to impose on thirty-three crore Hindus the language Urdu not because it was a superior language, but on a whim and simply because they liked it better. Arabic, he wrote, was an impoverished language, yet Muslims wanted to fill Hindi with words from Persian and Arabic, even though Mustafa Kemal from the land of the Khalifas had abandoned Arabic in favor of Turkish. A national language, he argued, should not be a bazaar language (Urdu) or one in which the poetry composed by its poets was incomprehensible not just to crores of Hindus but Muslims as well. Savarkar concluded by advising all Hindus to declare that their national language was Sanskritic Hindi and the script was Nagari.

for a position with the INC's rival political party, the Hindu Mahasabha. Another report noted that

> he addressed a public meeting of about 15,000 people held at Bhamburda under the auspices of the Hindu Maha Sabha, Maharashtra Branch. . . . Speaking on Hindu unity he analyzed the principles of Hinduism. Concluding he said that Muhammedans, Christians, Parsis etc., had lived in India for so long, they had no permanent interest in the country. If driven away they could go to other countries where their brethren lived, but Hindus had no other Hindu country to go to, except India. Hindus had sacrificed their lives, had suffered imprisonment in the Andamans and taken active part in the last C.D. movement, while the other communities had done nothing. He urged the Hindus to unite and sink their differences as they alone would be required to fight for their country.[211]

Savarkar announced that he would not join the INC, and his rhetoric deteriorated. All pretense of supporting the reforms gone, he accused Muslims of trying to secure "special rights." The next day he gave a speech to 1,000 people in Pune, in which he was reported to have said that "Hinduism and independence were interdependent." Savarkar went on to say that "Hindus had been cruelly tortured and massacred for not embracing Islam."[212] By this time, he seemed far more concerned with Muslims than with the British.

Eight days later, undeterred by demonstrations against him in Sholapur by the orthodoxy for his views on caste, he was noted to have "expressed his views in favor of removing caste distinctions." He said that Hindu-Muslim unity was an impossibility. Later that evening, he told a meeting of 7,000 people that, "although the Muhammadans will not help the Hindus, the latter can achieve Swaraj by their own efforts."[213] Indeed, for him, they would have to do so. By November 1937, he had moved himself into the national spotlight as Gandhi's principal antagonist. The watcher assigned to him reported that Savarkar was relentlessly attacking the INC for its hubris, which he saw as inversely proportional to its meagre achievements toward independence.[214]

211. HB/3003, BSA of July 3, 1937, in Home Department/Special/60D (d).

212. HB/3003, CID, BSA of August 14, 1937, in Home Department/Special/60D (d).

213. HB/3003, CID, BSA August 21, 1937, in Home Department/Special/60D (d).

214. V. D. Savarkar's Lecture at Dadar, Bombay, filed in 3996/H. The letter is annotated to indicate that this was not a press report because his speech had not appeared in any of the daily papers. Home Department/Special/60D (d).

From the moment Savarkar left the Andaman Islands, the British had tolerated his anti-Muslim claims, at most issuing a slap on the wrist. Over and over, the police noted that his hatred exceeded mere prejudice yet did nothing. And by letting Savarkar continue, they essentially normalized his politics of hatred. Whether or not they deliberately let him run free to spew that hatred, they repeatedly allowed him to do so. Savarkar might have been a terrorist in their eyes, but in the final years of empire, when divisions between Hindus and Muslims escalated against the backdrop of something that resembled the international Islamic conspiracy that had been of such concern a century before, he was clearly a useful one.

2

A Fearful Demagogue

SAVARKAR AND THE MUSLIM QUESTION

AS I SUGGESTED in the introduction, only a kaleidoscopic view gives us the full picture of Savarkar's life and thought. This is particularly important when approaching the development of his anti-Muslim views, which have over the last century become the normative views of the current Hindu right wing. In this chapter, I will weave together not one, not two, but six different strands of Savarkar's anti-Muslim braid.[1] The first strand is the Gandhi-helmed anticolonial nationalist movement in India in the post-World War I period when the colonial government put out yet another "reform" package. The second is the Caliphate as a theory, mourned ideal, and practice in its last iteration in Ottoman and Republican Turkey. The third takes us to the debates in India about the Caliphate, referred to as Khilafat in India, and, relatedly, the discussions of the proposed *hijrat* (migration) to Afghanistan in India among Muslim intellectuals, leaders, and businessmen.[2] The fourth strand returns us to Turkey and Mustafa Kemal's abolition of the Caliphate in 1924. In the fifth we follow, in summary, the progress of the Indian Khilafat movement (the only such movement in the world). The sixth is the immediate cause for Savarkar's expostulations, namely his anger about Gandhi's support for the Khilafat

1. A note on transliterations: I have consulted the rules of the following dictionaries while transliterating Persian, Urdu, Sanskrit, and Marathi words. Steingass, *A Comprehensive Persian-English dictionary*; Platts, *A Dictionary of Urdu*; Molesworth, *A Dictionary, Marathi and English*; Apte, *Practical Sanskrit-English Dictionary*.

2. As an idea/concept pertaining to the larger, global context, I use the term Caliphate; in the South Asian context it was called the Khilafat, the movement is called the Khilafat movement and the Caliph was referred to as the Khalifa. Depending on the context, I will switch back and forth between Caliph and Khalifa, and Caliphate and Khilafat.

movement. Savarkar, from house arrest, attacked virtually every iteration of the ideas and events laid out above—the idea of the Khilafat, the movement and its leaders, Gandhi, Muslims, and all Hindus who supported Khilafat. While he did not criticize the reform package, he insisted that Muslims were taking advantage of it.

Once I trace the trajectory of each of these strands, I will move on to what Savarkar had to say about the Muslim question. I do this for two reasons. First, the strands allow us a broader look at the regional, national, and global context that framed Savarkar's views. Second, Savarkar's views about Muslims build on all of these strands, especially the way in which the Khilafat movement revealed for him the fundamental disloyalty of Muslims to India. But this was not all, for he came to see Muslims as a monolithic community that was defined as much by its proclivity for violence as by its foundational claims for a distinctive—and exclusive—political sovereignty of its own. In both cases, he felt lay extraordinary dangers for Hindus.

The Indian National Context

In July 1914, at the start of the First World War while Savarkar was still in prison, Gandhi said his final farewell to South Africa. He had lived and worked in both the British colony of Natal and in Boer South Africa in Pretoria and Johannesburg. He had led a minority movement for political representation in Natal, experienced firsthand the prejudices of a White apartheid regime, and been taken aback by the closing of Boer and British ranks against the non-White settler communities when the British annexed the Transvaal and Orange Free State, creating the Union of South Africa (1901).[3] His experiences in South Africa convinced him that any political engagement in India that did not actively include the Muslim minority population would fail. When he returned to India in January 1915, he did so with one significant advantage over other Indian anticolonial nationalists. He had found and adopted a political strategy that did not require weapons, bombs, or political assassinations: *satyagraha,* or nonviolent noncooperation.

Gandhi began his political work in India on two fronts: social reform, with specific reference to caste, and peasant protests. In May 1915, he set up a Satyagraha Ashram close to Ahmedabad, starting with the public and deliberate

3. For what remains one of the best works on Gandhi in South Africa, see Devanesan, *The Making of the Mahatma.*

flouting of caste taboos. He did not reject caste qua caste, let alone the Hindu doctrine of Karma (as we will see in the next chapter). Caste for Gandhi remained much as upper-caste Brahmins understood it: a four-tier system of occupational classification and an ordered system based on mutual respect. Within this ideal scheme, untouchability (as it was then known) had no place and was thought of as a disease afflicting an otherwise sound social system. Gandhi targeted untouchability by trying to make his community of "touchable" Hindus reject it by including in his ashram an untouchable couple with whom everyone in the ashram would have to agree to interact. The second aspect of Gandhi's political work was his early two *satyagrahas*—the first on behalf of the indigo-cultivating peasantry in Champaran (1917) and the second in Kheda (1918), where the colonial government, under increasing financial pressure because of the First World War, had imposed an unbearable tax burden on the peasantry.

Savarkar was in prison during the war and could do no more than write letters home exulting that Indian troops would finally break the caste taboo around travel by crossing the forbidden waters.[4] In India, meanwhile, revolutionaries and "terrorists" suspected of jeopardizing England's security were detained under the Defence of India Act (1915). In post–World War I India, the situation was grim. Nearly 60,000 Indians had died in combat, many while serving in a (British) Indian expeditionary force in Mesopotamia.[5] The Indian colonial government was widely condemned for not supporting the Indian expeditionary force there, essentially leaving it as cannon fodder for the Turkish army. In 1915, Edwin Montagu, then Under-Secretary of State for India (in London), excoriated the Indian government, calling it "too wooden, too iron, too inelastic, too antediluvian to be of any use for the modern purposes we have in view."[6] Two years later, now as Secretary of State for India, Montagu tried to reform the Indian government by bringing liberal or moderate Indian elites into the colonial government. This was not primarily for noble reasons. His hope was that Indian elites could be prevented from becoming restive and sympathizing with revolutionary nationalists.[7] The Montagu-Chelmsford Report of 1918 began with a grand but vague declaration that "British policy in India would henceforth have as its *overall objective* the

4. Orthodox Hindus believed that if one crossed the oceans, one lost caste.

5. Latter, "The Indian Army in Mesopotamia," 92–102. 675,000 Indians were sent to Basra, 138,000 to France, and 144,000 to Palestine and Egypt.

6. Op. cit., Tinker, "India in the First World War and After." 89–107.

7. Danzig, "Announcement of August 20th, 1917." 19–37.

gradual development of self-governing institutions *with a view to* the *progressive realization* of responsible government in India *as an integral part* of the British empire [emphasis mine]."[8] Given all the qualifiers—"gradual," "with a view," "progressive"—and the final statement—"as an integral part of the empire"—it came as no surprise to critics of the government, from B. G. Tilak to Gandhi, that the proposal stopped well short of political independence. The Report was followed by the Government of India Act of 1919, in which Montagu's halting promises of eventual self-government were channeled through the peculiar system of dyarchy.[9]

As Durba Ghosh has shown, the colonial government reluctantly gave some autonomy with one hand while seriously curtailing liberties and freedoms with the other. It had extended the 1915 wartime emergency measures to guard against new threats, hardly conveying a genuine openness to reform. As far as the British were concerned, there was much to worry about in 1917, including Russian Bolsheviks and anarchists influencing Indian revolutionary nationalists, and German agents working for the Amir of Afghanistan who supported revolutionaries plotting rebellion.[10] Even the US was suspect, as we saw in the previous chapter. The government arrested B. G. Tilak again,

8. *Indian Reforms: The Government of India Bill, 1919*.

9. See Ghosh, *Gentlemanly Terrorists*, for a full examination of the Montford Reforms (as they were called). Dyarchy awarded a minuscule measure of autonomy to the provincial governments, in which native politicians held positions, to administer some functions. A list was drawn up that laid out which functions were to be administered centrally and which provincially. A quick look at the list will immediately show that all important functions remained with the center, including defense and communications with foreigners (other Europeans). The provinces got some administrative autonomy, but even there, functions such as the control of newspapers, police, and taxes were "reserved" for the center. In other words, the so-called Reforms basically granted to the provinces functions that the government was not particularly invested in: public health, sanitation, education, public works, irrigation, and agriculture.

10. For details of the Silk Letters Conspiracy that the British knew about, paid some attention to, but did not take particularly seriously, see Kelly, "Crazy in the Extreme?" and Stolte, "Enough of the Great Napoleons!". Pan-Islamists such as Mohammad Barakatullah congregated in Afghanistan, with pan-Asianist Indian nationalists like Raja Mahendra Pratap, to think of plots to overthrow the Indian government. And the British were not wrong to monitor what Germany was doing in all of this, since it was fostering pan-Islamism to beat the British, on the assumption that, since half the world's Muslims lived under their control, if Muslims could be encouraged to rebel against them, it would weaken British power. For a riveting tale of how the Germans tried to use Ottoman pan-Islamism as a means by which to weaken the British empire, see McMeekin, *The Berlin Baghdad Express*, and Trivedi, "Turco-German Intrigue in India."

banning all seditious literature including Gandhi's *Hind Swaraj* and Savarkar's book on the Rebellion of 1857.

Sir Sidney Rowlatt, a judge, was tasked with investigating the extent to which India was liable to be attacked from within and without by terrorists and anarchists. In July 1918 his committee issued a comprehensive report identifying alleged terrorist plots in Bombay, Bengal, Burma, Madras, Punjab, the Central Provinces, and Bihar and Orissa. It also noted German interest in Indian revolutionaries, pro-Turkish intrigues in India and the *Muhammadan Current*.[11] The committee recommended that wartime rules be extended. Cases of sedition could be tried without a jury. Suspects could be interned without a trial.[12] Gandhi wrote to Srinivasa Sastry, an Indian member of the Legislative Council, to suggest that accepting the Rowlatt Act was akin to caving in to the British.

Gandhi's approach to anticolonial activism was the opposite of Savarkar's. To paraphrase Audre Lorde, Gandhi did not believe the master's tools would bring down the master's house. Following the passage of the Rowlatt Act, he called for an all-India strike (*hartāl*), but because of its lack of organization, it did not go well. There were sporadic strikes across several days instead of on just one. Meanwhile, in the Punjab, the Governor imposed martial law, disallowing large congregations and forbidding nationalists like Gandhi from traveling there. On April 13, 1919, an unarmed group of villagers came to the city of Amritsar for a fair. Unaware of the ban on meetings, they gathered in an enclosed garden called Jallianwalla Bagh.[13] Seeing this as a blatant disregard of colonial orders, General Reginald Dyer led armed troops into the area and ordered them to shoot, firing some 1,600 rounds, resulting in over 1,500 casualties. British officials claimed that the official number of deaths was 379, but many women and children also jumped into a well to escape the gunfire and died of suffocation. Thereafter, the words "Jallianwala" and "Jallianwala Bagh Massacre" entered Indian history books as a metonym for colonial brutality. A commission appointed to investigate the massacre acquitted Dyer of wrongdoing; he was completely unrepentant, claiming only that he was sorry he had run out of ammunition and that the narrow lanes had prevented him from bringing in an armored car. The event

11. Rowlatt Sedition Committee Report, 1918.

12. For a quick summary of India after the war, see Tinker, "India in the First World War and After," 89–107.

13. For the most detailed and recent description and analysis of the Jallianwala Bagh Massacre, see Wagner, *Amritsar 1919*.

galvanized Indian opinion against the Rowlett Act and ironically afforded Gandhi the opportunity to restart his *satyagraha* campaign.

In 1920 Gandhi issued two demands: right the Punjab wrong (Jallianwala) and the Khilafat wrong.[14] For Savarkar, newly repatriated to India and jailed, the world must have appeared radically changed. For one thing, violent revolutionaries were no longer held in high regard, as Gandhi had succeeded in enshrining nonviolent resistance as the primary tactic of the nationalist movement. For another, Gandhi was now so dominant a presence in the INC that he was viewed by the watchful police as not just dictatorial but able to command the support of Muslim leaders.[15] For the British, both were a cause for genuine alarm. Within a few years of his return from South Africa, Gandhi demonstrated that he could unite Hindu and Muslim communities in a common cause against the British. But what exactly did Gandhi mean by the "Khilafat wrong?" We must start with the idea of the Caliphate itself.

What Was the Caliphate in Theory and Practice?

In Classical Islamic theory, according to Naeem Qureshi, the political system "is hinged on three basic principles: *Tauḥīd, Risālat,* and *Kẖilāfat*" (Unity of God, Prophethood, and Viceregency).[16] While religion is assumed to provide the foundation for the state, Islam qua Islam has no official church nor clergy. All knowledgeable men (*'ālim* singular, *'ulamā'* plural), in keeping with Islam's theoretical egalitarianism, could be leaders. Absolute sovereignty lies only

14. The Times of India reported that "[o]ne of the leaders of the Khilafat Movement, Miyan Mohammad Chotani," had addressed a "largely attended public meeting of Mahomedans and Hindus" in which he was reported to have said that

> the Muslims and Hindus of India were not only united over the question of the Khilafat but also in all the political questions relating their motherland—India. . . . The blood of Hindus and Muslims mingled in Jallianwala Bagh and other places last year and cemented the Hindu-Moslem unity.

"The Khilafat, Another Bombay Meeting," *Times of India*, April 10, 1920.

15. Jordens, *Swami Shraddhananda*, 122. A radical Arya Samaji, Swami Shraddhanand was the leading force behind the Shuddhi and Sanghatan movements. By 1921, Shradhanand had had it with Gandhi's tactics, saying that "Mahatma Gandhi was named the first Dictator on emergency arising, with powers to name his successor." See also the Police Report, All Indian Khilafat Movement, 30. It notes that "[t]he most curious feature of the Conference [the Khilafat conference] was Gandhi's astounding assumption of dictatorship and the Muslim leaders' acquiescence thereof."

16. Qureshi calls such a state a "theodemocracy" because, as he puts it, sovereignty "is exercised by the totality of the Muslim community as the viceregent of God on earth." Qureshi, *Ottoman Turkey, Ataturk*, 48.

with God, but the community of believers may collectively select a vice regent or a representative to engage in the work of administering the daily life of the community, a *Khilāfat-i-ilāhīya*.[17] In practice this has rarely been the case. The question of religious and political authority has been subject to heated debate since the very inception of Islam as a religion, and the gap between the theory of the Caliphate and the Caliphate in practice is vast.

Indeed, at one point in time there were three different Caliphates—in Spain, North Africa, and Syria/Iraq. The Ottoman Sultan Selim I, upon the conquest of Egypt and the Levant from the Mamluks in 1517–18, assumed the title of Caliph. The Ottoman right to the Caliphate was contested by a prophetic tradition that limited it to descendants of the Prophet's clan, the Quraysh. Sultan Selim I's move was bold since he was neither a descendant of the Prophet's Quraysh clan—nor was he Arab. The Ottomans got around this by using different *ḥadīs* to claim that *only* the first four "Rightly Guided" Caliphs had to be Qurayshi. Later Muslim rulers could assume the title if they fulfilled the functions of the Caliph.[18] Sultan Selim I did so by assuming the title of protector of the two holy sites: the *Ka'ba* in Mecca and the Prophet's Mosque in Medina. He also brought key holy relics to Istanbul from Mecca. The Ottomans then all but forgot that the Sultan was a holder of this title until the late nineteenth century, when Sultan Abdulhamid II (1876–1909) recognized the value in reclaiming the Caliphate in order to prevent the further dissolution of the empire and keep at least the Arab, majority Muslim

17. Qureshi, *Ottoman Turkey, Ataturk*, 48. I am paraphrasing M. Naeem Qureshi's explanation. The ideal of the Khilafat and its reality are said to be coexistent only for the short duration of the Prophet's life as a statesman and that of his four immediate successors.

18. Two decades after the Prophet's death, the basis of the Islamic state was disputed by the followers of Ali and the Khwarij, and with the establishment of Umayyad reign (660–750) the Caliphate tumbled into the morass of dynastic succession. After the Umayyads, the Abbasids further tightened the hold between regnal and imperial power and the Caliphate. The Caliphate has been held by rulers of successive dynasties and located in Damascus, Baghdad, Eqypt and North Africa, and, finally, in Constantinopole/Istanbul. Untangling how to maintain the Universal Caliphate in the face of all of these emerging and simultaneous Muslim polities was left, as Qureshi notes, to jurists over succeeding centuries, in particular al-Ghazzali (1058–1111) and Ibn Taymiyya (1263–1328), whose works brought about an acceptable compromise such that Muslim dynasties far from the Hijāz (like the Mughals) could remain temporal sovereigns over their own territory as long as they acknowledged the Caliph as the spiritual head in the Friday *khuṭbah* (prayers.) For an examination of how the Ottomans claimed the Caliphate in an international context of the loss of Ottoman territory in the Crimea, see S. Tufan Buzpinar's extraordinarily informative and acute writings, in particular "The Question of Caliphate under the Last Ottoman Sultans" in Weismann and Zachs, *Ottoman Reform and Muslim Regeneration*, 17–37.

territories within his realm. In the late nineteenth and early twentieth centuries, as Tufan Buzpinar shows, Sultan Abdulhamid II was the last powerful Ottoman Caliph whose hold on the Caliphate was accepted, even if sometimes grudgingly, beyond the Ottoman Empire, in territories like British India in which a sizeable population of Muslims lived.[19]

Abdulhamid II was deposed in 1909 by the CUP, and his successor Mehmed V ruled as a figurehead until 1918. He was replaced by yet another Sultan-Caliph, Mehmed Vahdettin VI, who ruled from 1918 to 1922 during the period when Mustafa Kemal and the Turkish national movement effected a shutdown of the Ottoman Parliament in Istanbul and reopened that body as the Turkish Grand National Assembly in Ankara in late March of 1920. In 1922 Mustafa Kemal split the Caliphate, stripping the Sultan of his temporal powers and two years later, abolished the Caliphate altogether.

During this period of turmoil in Istanbul and Ankara (between the summer of 1919 and late 1922) the British supported both the Sherif of Mecca in his rebellion and quest to claim the Caliphate for himself and other contenders who suggested it move to Syria or Egypt. Within Turkey, they encouraged anti-Ottoman dissident groups who argued that the Ottoman claim from Abdulhamid onward was itself illegitimate, that his corruption made him undeserving of such an exalted office and title. They also averred that the Caliph should rightly be ethnically Arab.[20] In effect, they played an emergent Arab nationalism against both the Ottoman and brief Turkish Republican claim to the Caliphate.[21]

These nineteenth- and twentieth-century political machinations notwithstanding, Mona Hasan has shown in her extraordinary work on representations of loss, mourning, and nostalgia regarding the Caliphate that, virtually from the

19. Quoting Stanley Pool's work from 1922 on Turkey, Ali argues that

> not only in India, but all over Asia and Africa where the traditional Caliphate was recognized, the Ottoman Sultans were given the status of supreme head of religion. i.e. *Imamul Muslimin*. In short, from the time of Sultan Selim I up to Sultan Abdulmajid II, the last Caliph, the Ottoman Sultans had been the Caliphs of the Muslim world, and during the four centuries which had passed, not a single rival claimant had ever arisen against them.

Ali, "The Ottoman Caliphate and British Imperialism in India," 740.

20. Teitelbaum, "Sharif Husayn Ibn Ali and the Hashemite Vision," 103–22. See also Haddad, "Arab Religious Nationalism," 253–77.

21. For British, French, Dutch, Italian machinations against the Ottoman Caliphate, and their competitive games with each other as to who should assume the Caliphate after it was abolished, see Laurence, *Coping with Defeat*, in particularly ch. 2, 77–117

moment in 1258 that the Mongols sacked Baghdad and killed the last of the Abbasid Khalifas, the Caliphate was mourned, longed for by many Sunni Muslims, and represented in text after text as a golden epoch during which Muslims were safe, art and literature flourished, and piety was protected.[22] The Mongol destruction of the Abbasid Caliphate, Hasan argues, was the moment that united Muslims around the world, even as the Caliphate remained a living tradition across both Shia and Sunni communities.[23] In the late nineteenth century, Sultan Abdulhamid's resurgent Caliphate tapped into that deep affective sensibility; increasingly, it was conjoined with the concept of *ittiḥād-ul-islām*, or pan-Islamism.[24] Why then would it be destroyed a second time by Mustafa Kemal?

World War I and Mustafa Kemal's Abolition of the Caliphate

Against the wishes of many of his subjects, Mehmed V supported Germany against Britain and France in the First World War.[25] In 1915 this gave two British and French diplomats, Mark Sykes and Francois Georges Picot, the occasion to come to a secret agreement about which parts of the Ottoman Empire they would each take in the event that their alliance was victorious.[26] In October 1918, when the new Ottoman Sultan Mehmed Vahdettin VI signed the armistice of Mudros and allowed victorious armies to occupy parts of the empire, the terms of the Sykes–Picot Agreement were upheld, but they were not formalized until he signed the Treaty of Sevres in August 1920.[27] Even harsher

22. See Hasan, *Longing for the Lost Caliphate.*

23. There was a Caliph in the Muslim world even after the Mongol sack of Baghdad, and there were other ideas of God on earth besides the Sunni viewpoint. The point I take Mona Hasan as making is that, for many Sunni Muslims, the Abbasid Caliphate was viewed as representing the high point of Caliphal glory, and its end was experienced by many as the end of an eon.

24. See Qureshi, *Ottoman Turkey, Ataturk*, ch. 1, for an excellent annotated bibliography on pan-Islam in South Asia, a term Qureshi believes derives from pan-Slavism.

25. On why the Ottomans supported Germany and could not believe British promises about maintaining Ottoman sovereignty, see Pasha, "Posthumous Memoirs of Talaat Pasha," 290–91. For a timeline of events, see the marvelous graph in Philliou, *Turkey: A Past against History*, xi–xii.

26. Güçlü, "The Struggle for Mastery in Cilicia," 580–603. For an analysis of the British role in World War I as it pertained to the Ottomans, see Provence, "The Theory and Practice of Colonialism in the Post-Ottoman Middle East."

27. Güçlü, "The Struggle for Mastery in Cilicia," 580–603.

than the famous Treaty of Versailles, Sevres was designed to dismantle the geographic unity of the empire, destroy the last vestiges of Turkish or Ottoman sovereignty, and humiliate the Ottomans/Turkish. Vahdettin was viewed as an imperial toady and tool of the British acquiescing to whatever they asked him to do, and unsurprisingly, the treaty boomeranged, spurring a host of nationalist resistance movements pulled together by Mustafa Kemal, already a hero to the Turks because of his military exploits in Gallipoli against the British.[28] In effect, Turkey had two governments, the weakened Ottomans in Constantinople and the Turkish national regime under the leadership of Mustafa Kemal in Ankara.[29] Mustafa Kemal viewed both the Ottoman Sultan/Caliph and the British with suspicion since neither wanted an independent Turkey and the British were supporting the Greeks against him. In 1919 the Greeks had occupied/liberated Anatolia and had pushed further and further east. The Turkish national forces fought the Greeks and drove them west, the final point being Smyrna/Izmir, in September 1922, after which they burned the city and drove the inhabitants into the sea. These victories earned for Mustafa Kemal the title of *g̲hāzī* (victorious/holy warrior), after which the Allies and the US mediated a peace conference in Lausanne, superseding the Treaty of Sevres which never had a chance to be ratified.[30] In 1923 the Treaty of Lausanne officially ended the hostilities between Turkey and Greece, repudiated many of the provisions of the earlier Treaty of Sevres, and laid out the boundaries of modern Turkey.[31] On October 13, 1923, Ankara was declared the capital of the Republic of Turkey, officially founded on October 29, 1923, by Mustafa Kemal who was named its first president.

28. I am deeply grateful to Christine Philliou for all the time she took to explain in great detail the complicated scenario in Turkey in the early twentieth century.

29. For a US diplomat's firsthand account of the peace conference, see Grew, "Lausanne Peace Conference," 348–67. For a Greek perspective on the same conference, see Kaloudis, "Ethnic Cleansing in Asia Minor," 59–88.

30. For a concise and informative analysis and summary of the period in Turkey from the Young Turk Revolution to the founding of the tepublic, see, Philliou, *Turkey: A Past against History*, 46–49. See also Rustow, "The Army and the Founding of the Turkish Republic." For more on Mustafa Kemal being called *g̲hāzī* (victorious) see "Turkey under Kemal" in *Advocate of Peace through Justice*. For the period between 1924 and 1925 and the brief opposition Mustafa Kemal faced from the shortlived Progressive Republican Party to his high-handed tactics, see Zurcher, *Political Opposition*, 1–31.

31. Kaloudis, "Ethnic Cleansing in Asia Minor," 80.

Already in 1922, Mustafa Kemal was receiving advice about the Caliphate from a moderate Islamist, Seyyid Bey.[32] Mustafa Kemal had good reason to want it gone. In 1920 Vahdettin had his Chief Mufti issue a *fatwā*, urging true believers to kill nationalists, in effect sentencing Mustafa Kemal to death. Mustafa Kemal countered with a *fatwā* from Ankara's mufti declaring the Ottoman government the real traitor.[33] In November 1922, the Caliphate still had some slim hope of surviving because the Turkish Grand National Assembly voted to separate the Sultanate from the Caliphate effectively splitting it and stripping the Sultan of all temporal powers, and elected Abdulmajid II as the new—now utterly powerless—Caliph after deposing Vahdettin.[34] Seyyid Bey wrote a legal pamphlet on the "Khilafat and National Sovereignty," preparing the grounds, as Michelangelo Giuda argues, for its abolition. In March 1924, in the new Turkish Grand National Assembly, Seyyid Bey delivered a seven-hour speech, angrily accusing Indian Muslims supporting the maintenance of the Caliphate of disingenuity and declaring that such support would not aid the cause of pan-Islam.[35] Soon thereafter, the Turkish Grand National Assembly voted to formally abolish the Caliphate as an institution, and Abdulmajid II was expelled from Turkey along with all members of the Ottoman dynasty. This finality of the termination of an institution that had been part of Muslim life for centuries was experienced across the globe not only as a shock but as a betrayal.[36]

The Khilafat and What It Meant to Indian Muslims

Why, given that Mustafa Kemal, had abolished the Caliphate, were Indian Muslims so passionate about maintaining it? Surely it was a lost cause. World War I was over; the Ottoman Empire was in pieces; the CUP had been

32. Guida, "Seyyid Bey and the Abolition of the Caliphate," 276.

33. Teitelbaum, "'Taking Back' the Caliphate," 412–24.

34. Zekeria, "The New Turkish Caliph," 669–71. Vahdettin left for the Hijāz soon after he was deposed, and from there to Europe where he died in 1926.

35. Guida, "Seyyid Bey and the Abolition of the Caliphate," 285.

36. As Mona Hasan puts it:

> . . . the Turkish abolition of the caliphate, coming rapidly on the heels of glorious military victory against foreign occupation, left a bitter sense of betrayal among those Muslims across Afro-Urasia who had lent their material and moral support to the defense and regained strength of the Ottoman Empire.

Hasan, *Longing for the Lost Caliphate*, 151.

disbanded in late 1918, and its members repudiated any association with it, and went on to regroup under different names in the coming months.[37] But the Caliphate was not completely eliminated. Abdulmajid II was still, at least in name, a Caliph albeit in exile. At the same time, Mustafa Kemal was not especially popular among Indian Muslim leaders because of his antireligious views.

Khilafat, in its South Asian context, provided a kind of bridge between Hindu and Muslim tellings of their shared past and between groups of Muslims with vastly different agendas. It symbolized the context of Muslim fears and hopes in the 1920s and thus offers a crucial lens through which to view Savarkar and Gandhi—his foe as well as foil. Khilafat offered Gandhi a way to recruit Muslim support by throwing the weight of the INC behind a key Muslim cause. At the same time, it offered Savarkar a way to champion a cultural issue that could mobilize his local regional constituency (Maharashtra, which had few Muslims and little Muslim violence or intercommunal tensions) around fears that areas with much larger Muslim populations would emerge as a major threat if the nationalist movement followed Gandhi's leadership and his internationalist agenda.

Savarkar's use of Khilafat as a major issue reverberated across 1920s India, which witnessed increasing confrontations between Hindus and Muslims. Riots in Delhi, Nagpur, Lahore, Lucknow, Moradabad, Bhagalpar, Gulbarga, and Allahabad were sparked by the cow-protection movement and Hindi agitations but could be linked to lingering concerns about the Khilafat issue as well.[38] Calcutta, the United Provinces, the Central Provinces, and Bombay Presidency all saw violent confrontations in 1925 and 1926. In Gujarat, there was at least one case of temple desecration in 1927 and between April and September 1928 no fewer than twenty-five riots, usually over minor but familiar flash points like playing music in front of mosques or slaughtering cows. There were twenty-two major riots in 1929 alone.[39]

37. See Philliou, *A Past against History*, particularly ch. 3.

38. On this subject, see the classic work by Pandey, *Ascendancy of the Congress in Uttar Pradesh*.

39. B. R. Ambedkar did not just remark on the number of riots in the 1920s but diagnosed why Hindu-Muslim unity was a chimera:

> . . . there is among the Indians no passion for unity, no desire for fusion. There is no desire to have a common dress. There is no desire to have a common language. There is no will to give up what is local and particular for something which is common and national. A Gujarati takes pride in being a Gujarati, a Maharashtrian in being a Maharashtrian, a Punjabi in being a Punjabi, A Madrasi in being a Madrasi and a Bengali in being

Amid this violence, Muslims as a community were trying to imagine the world without one of their key premises. In the nineteenth century, the British government in India had stressed that British and Ottoman interests were aligned, depicting itself as a friend of the Khalifa.[40] When World War I destroyed this illusion, the drive to protect the Khilafat—using Britain if necessary—had brought *'ālims*, *adībs*, businessmen, physicians, and *maulana* in British India into conversations that bridged differences in terms of sect and level of orthodoxy. Gail Minault suggests that the Ottoman Caliphate was on its last legs when the movement began, and Khilafat therefore cannot be seen solely or even principally as a movement aimed at reinstating something that could not by then possibly return.[41] Yet, up until Kemal's abolition of the Caliphate, many Khilafatists believed that Britain could still be pressured to change its position on Turkey. Khilafat was also a symbolic means to support the Muslim community's future in India while catapulting the issue of pan-Islamism onto the Indian anticolonial stage. As Mushirul Hasan has noted, Muslim politicians speaking about Khilafat were adept at using Islamic symbols—mosques, shrines, festivals—to paper over sectarian or other divides within the larger community.[42] The timing, with Khilafat's dovetailing almost exactly with the INC's *satyagraha* campaign, helped it to become an all-India movement.

Muslim intellectuals already had networks connecting North Indian universities to the Hijāz, linking *shaik̲h̲s* and *pīrs* in Sindh all the way to the Mappillah revolt in South India.[43] Maulana Abu'l Kalam Azad (1888–1958), for instance—an extraordinary leader who spoke Urdu, Arabic, Hindi and Persian—traveled

---

> a Bengali. Such is the mentality of Hindus, who accuse the Muslim of want of national feeling when he says, "I'm a Muslim first and Indian afterwards."

Ambedkar, *Pakistan or Partition of India*, 184–85.

40. See Ali, "The Ottoman Caliphate and British Imperialism in India."

41. See Minault, *The Khilafat Movement*.

42. Hasan, "Communalism in the Provinces," 1399.

43. See Salahudheen, "Political Ferment in Malabar." Salahudheen argues that before the rebellion by Mappillah peasants, itself provoked by a police raid on a mosque in Tirurarangadi in August 1921 (with an official body count of 2,337 "rebels" killed and some 45,000 imprisoned), the peasants in the Malabar region had triangulated their demands against what Ranajit Guha termed the "*sarkar-sahukar-zamindar*" tripartite system of oppression. One corner of the triangle was an anticolonial struggle, the second the assertion of peasant rights against Hindu landowners and their tenancy laws, and the third the defense of the Turkish Khalifa. In 1920 Gandhi and Shaukat Ali visited Malabar as part of an all-India tour. In April 1920, many Mappillahs attended the Manjeri Conference that marked the beginning of widespread propaganda

to the Hijāz, returned to India, and traveled again to Egypt, Turkey, and Syria. He was one of many *'ulamā'* who encountered supporters of Mustafa Kemal, Arab nationalists, and Iranian revolutionaries fighting Qajar autocracy and maintained those connections for many years.[44] Linking support for the Khilafat to Gandhi's *satyagraha* also provided the opportunity for a unifying emotional appeal across the subcontinent, featuring student walkouts, new kinds of political poetry, and even the creation of semimilitarized volunteer corps. Both the Muslim and Hindu press championed the first mass movement against the British involving both communities in large numbers.[45] Such intense and unprecedented support for the Khilafat, as Faisal Devji argues, must also be seen as Indian Muslims expressing their desire for India to take a leadership role in discussing the future of Muslims worldwide.[46]

One version of this leadership role was proposed by the anticolonial revolutionary, intellectual, and social reformer, Mohammed Barakatullah Bhopali (1864–1927). A strong champion of pan-Islamism, he studied in England, where, as K. H. Ansari puts it, "his commitment to the Pan-Islamic ideal grew in direct proportion to his antagonism to the British."[47] In 1924, in his short but widely read tract *The Khilafet,* he mourned the loss of the Khilafat as "an institution hallowed with traditions of thirteen centuries, an embodiment of might and grandeur of the Orient in the eyes of European nation and a shield of defence for Islam during the last four hundred years." Given that history and reach, it made sense to consider options when that "edifice which looked as firm as a rock and promised to last as long as the world would last, was swept

---

that joined noncooperation with Khilafat. By June 1921, Salahuddin notes, there were about 200 Khilafat committees up and down Kerala that met twice weekly.

44. Pant, "Maulana Abul Kalam Azad," 1313–14.

45. Shila Sen writes, "*The Mussalman,* (editor Mujibur Rahman), *Mohammadi* and *Al-Eslam* (in Bengali and editor for both Akram Khan) propogated the cause of the non-cooperation Khilafat movement throughout 1920–23. The *Mussalman* in particular played an active role in cementing Hindu-Muslim unity." Sen, "Khilafat Non-Cooperation Movement in Bengal," 466. See also Qureshi, *Ottoman Turkey, Ataturk,* 94–95, for information about the press reaction to the British government response to Mohd Ali's delegation. Qureshi notes that the *Bombay Chronicle,* the *Amrita Bazar Patrika,* and the *Independent* were acerbic in their reactions.

46. Devji, *The Impossible Indian,* 72–74.

47. Ansari, "Pan-Islam and the Making of the Early Indian Muslim Socialists," 515. For more on Barakatullah's renown, see Siddiqui, "Coupled Internationalisms," 25–46, and Husain, "Barkatullah—A Half-Forgotten Revolutionary," 1061–72.

away by the flood of phenomena."[48] But as much as Barakatullah revered the idea of the Khilafat, he was sharply critical of how it had devolved into corruption through successive regnal periods.

The abolition of Khilafat offered a new opportunity. Since replacing one Muslim king as Khalifa with another would lead to the same problems as before, Barakatullah proposed a solution that recognized the Muslim community's vulnerability and tried to address it:

> . . . let us organize the Muslims of the world under the spiritual leadership of the Khạlīfā for three objects in view. (1) By the instinct of self-preservation, we must hang together, otherwise we may be hanged separately. (2) We should try and persuade the Jews and the Christians through the divine word of the Prophet to the policy of "live and let live" and thereby avert the calamity.[49]

The third aspect of this new organization was to organize social work centers in Muslim countries to try and alleviate poverty through love and sympathy. Barakatullah urged

> all the denominations of Islam take part in the election of the new Khạlīfā and support the institution of the Khilafat as a symbol of the unity of Islam. . . . Through him old differences and animosities can be forgotten, order can be restored in the place of the prevailing chaos, friendly relations between the Muslims and the civilized world can be established and thus many of the impending conflicts among nations can be averted.[50]

Other leaders and intellectuals took a different approach. The venerable founder of the Mohammedan Anglo-Oriental College (MAOC, later renamed Aligarh Muslim University) Syed Ahmad Khan (1817–98), for instance, never accepted Sultan Abdulhamid as the Khalifa of Indian Muslims or thought support should be withdrawn from the British over the issue.[51] He believed that the Turkish Sultan's sovereignty was limited to those under his direct rule and neither did nor should extend over India.[52] Ashraf Ali Thanawi, the eminent Sufi teacher at the Deoband madrassa, was also unconvinced about the

48. Hasan, *Longing for the Lost Caliphate*, 143.

49. Barakatullah, *The Khilafet*, 78–79.

50. Barakatullah, *The Khilafet*, 106.

51. Wasti, "Sir Syed Ahmad Khan and the Turks," 53.

52. Willis, "Debating the Caliphate," 715.

Khilafat Movement and the migration to Afghanistan. The Ali brothers who led the Khilafat movement were "Western-educated" and in his opinion were neither knowledgeable nor gifted with leadership skills; worse, they were collaborating with Gandhi, whom he saw as an unbeliever.[53] Ahmed Riza Khan (1856–1921), head of the Barelvi madrassa, objected to the Turkish Caliphate on doctrinal grounds.[54] Shibli Nomani (1857–1914), the cosmopolitan head of the Nadwat al-ʿUlamā', a reformist madrassa founded in 1894, objected as well.[55] Meanwhile, figures like Anwar Shah Kashmiri, the eminent Hadith scholar from Deoband, were not at all invested in Khilafat.[56] Kashmiri was far more concerned that in the first two decades of the twentieth century, Muslims trained in England were influencing the appointments of Sharia judges and dispensing their version of Muslim justice.[57] None of these influential Muslim leaders saw maintaining the Khilafat as crucial.

There was a range of opinions as well on the other momentous event in 1920: the proposed *hijrat* to Afghanistan. In 1920, Maulana Abdul Bari (1879–1926), an eminent scholar of the influential Firangi Mahal madrassa based in the city of Lucknow, had declared India to be *dār 'ul-ḥarb* (house of war/a place where Islam cannot be practiced without persecution).[58] The same year, he issued a *fatwā* maintaining that Indian Muslims, if they chose to do so,

53. See Zaman, *Ashraf Ali Thanawi*, 44. Ashraf Ali Thanawi held a dim view of Gandhi and often referred to him contemptuously as a *ṯāġhūt* (idol), invoking the pre-Islamic world of *jāhilīyat* in which idols were worshipped.

54. Qureshi, *Ottoman Turkey, Ataturk*, 30, and Sanyal, *Ahmed Riza Khan*, 81. Sanyal notes that Ahmad Riza's objections to the Turkish Caliphate were rooted in his understanding that the title could only be claimed by a leader who was of Quraysh descent and that Muslims could not pursue a religious goal with the help of unbelievers (Hindus).

55. Nu'mani, *Turkey, Egypt, and Syria*.

56. Sanyal, *Ahmed Riza Khan Barelwi*, 39. The Nadwat al-ʿUlamā' was founded in 1891, with the intention of bridging the divides between Sunnī and Shi'i *'ulamā'* and as an All-India platform that would inform the British of Muslim demands. On Anwarshah Kashmiri's concerns, see Blecher, *Said the Prophet of God*, 143–57. See also Zaman, *Modern Islamic Thought*, 24–26, 77, 80–95, 123, and 240–48. See also Zaman, "Evolving Conceptions of Ijtihad," 5–36, for the tension between Muhammad Rashid Rida and Muhammad Anwar Shah Kashmiri.

57. In the 1920s, for instance, many Muslim legal scholars appealed outside India for a *fatwā* to circumvent British-dominated Hanafī laws and return to Māliki law. I am grateful to my collegue, Asad Ahmad, for not just pointing this out to me but asking pointedly why Gandhi was so intent on lending his support for the Khilafat when other *'ulamā'* such as Anwarshah Kashmiri were more concerned with the immediate issues confronting them.

58. Husain, "Barakatullah—A Half-Forgotten Revolutionary," 1067.

could migrate to Afghanistan. Another *'ulamā'*, Ahmad Riza Khan from the Barelvi madrassa, declared that same year that the "fundamental shar'ia status of the country had not changed" and there was no cause for the *hijrat*; India was as always *dār 'ul-islām* (house of peace/a place where Islam can be practiced freely).[59]

The robust back and forth among the *'ulamā'* suggests that these terms and concepts were part of a larger public debate about the future of the Muslim community in India.[60] With the British gaining ever more control, could India still be considered *dār 'ul-islām* or had it descended into *dār 'ul-ḥarb*? Could Muslims live only in a Muslim-ruled country? Could they live as Muslims in India where the majority population was Hindu? Could Muslims cooperate and collaborate with a Hindu-led INC in the struggle to maintain the Khilafat? Could they work with Gandhi who spoke of Rāmrājya as the model for Indian governance?[61] Could they accept that conservative Hindus were particularly sensitive to the killing and consumption of kine? The *'ulamā'*, which had historically advised the rulers or statesmen of their time, answered these questions from their intellectual strongholds, mainly from the Deoband madrassa but also from Aligarh Muslim University and the Firangi Mahal madrassa.[62] Whether about *hijrat* or the Khilafat, or more mundane issues such as if Muslims could avail themselves of interest-bearing loans, existential questions about the future of Islam and the identities of Muslims were being posed to the *'ulamā'*, who answered them using terms like *jihād* and *dār 'ul-ḥarb*.[63]

That these *'ulamā'* were important to the daily lives of Muslims is evidenced by the fact that an unknown number of Muslims (between 30,000 and

59. See Sanyal, *Ahmad Riza Khan Barelwi*, 81–82.

60. See Willis, "Debating the Caliphate," 715. Within the Ottoman state, too, there was dissension about the Khilafat. In some Ottoman provinces Salafi scholars and activists made common cause with Arab cultural revivalists and mounted a critique of the Hamidian state, with the intention of reclaiming and strengthening the Khilafat within Arab lands and an Arab cultural traditional milieu.

61. *Rāmarājya* was a term Gandhi took from the epic, the Rāmāyaṇa, which he used as shorthand for ethical rule.

62. Aziz, "The Role of Ulema in Indo-Muslim History," 1–13.

63. See Qureshi, "Hijrat to Afghanistan" in *Pan-Islam in British Indian Politics*, 176–78. The *fatwā* in question, Qureshi notes, ignored both *hijrat* and *jihād*, being primarily economic in nature. The *fatwā* has since been misinterpreted as preaching *jihād* against the British, when its author was trying to hedge the question of usury. These *fatwās* were not always clear, as Qureshi points out, let alone consistent.

100,000) set off for Afghanistan in the summer of 1920, either selling their possessions or leaving them behind. Having initially supported the emigration, the then ruler (*Amīr*) of Afghanistan, Amanullah, changed his mind, and many who had set off found themselves destitute. Others lost their lives on the return journey.[64] What this all points to is not an inherent separatism or desire for sovereignty but rather the tumult felt by ordinary and elite Muslims across the subcontinent where they were no longer members of a ruling government (the Mughals or otherwise) and instead comprised a minority in a state that was run by a colonial empire that had colluded in the abolition of the Khilafat and might well turn the country over to a Hindu-majority government.

The Khilafat Movement (1918–24)

The *hijrat* was a disaster.[65] Not so the Khilafat movement, even if it did not achieve its goal of preventing the dismemberment of the Ottoman Empire. It was led by the Indian Muslim brothers, Mohammad Ali and Shaukat Ali, whom Seyyid Bey had spoken of as "false supporters."[66] During the war, they had been interned in Chhindwara, in the Central Provinces. Upon their release, they secured Gandhi's support and set about trying to pressure the British government to maintain the Sultan/Khalifa's territorial sovereignty. Given that the British had been guarding against the pan-Islamism implied by the

64. Zaman, *Ashraf Ali Thanawi*, 38. On the *hijrat*, see Ahmed, *Afghanistan Rising*, 9–14. Afghanistan, as Ahmed notes, was "one of the world's only fully sovereign Muslim-majority countries" and the "first independent Muslim nation-state after the fall of the Ottomans" in this period, and it made logical sense that "Afghan scholars, Ottoman lawyers, and Indian technocrats" would converge to press their case to the Amir. For a detailed look at and analysis of the *hijrat* and the conversations about it, and Gandhi's and Maulana Azad's roles, see Reetz, *Hijrat: The Flight of the Faithful*, 78–79.

65. Even before it took place, discussions about the *hijrat* made it into the police report.

> . . . Maulana Muhammad Ali and Shaukat Ali, the two political leaders of India, say that the question of Khilafat must be decided in strict accordance with the demands of the Mussulmans otherwise they would either declare Jehad or do hijrat. . . . Afghanistan is heartily prepared to welcome such immigrants.

NAI/L/PS/L/PS/Home Department/Political/1936/file H11/215, vol. 2, Detailed History of the Caliphate Movement, 27.

66. See Lelyveld, *Aligarh's First Generation*, one of the best works on Sayyid Ahmad Khan's founding of the Mohammadan Anglo Oriental College from which the leaders of the Khilafat movement graduated.

maintenance of the Khilafat since 1857, the expectation that Britain would help may seem strange.

Since suppressing the 1857 Rebellion, the British had been on the watch for further signs of Muslim disloyalty, which they assumed would come in the guise of a transnational Muslim movement. Meanwhile, British surveillance was everywhere. Well before Mustafa Kemal came out of nowhere to take hold of the Turkish nationalist movement in 1919, British intelligence services had watched the workings of the CUP. They had intercepted the communications of Ottoman ministers, knew what was happening in the Ottoman War Office, watched both the Grand Vizierate and the Turkish nationalists in Ankara.[67] Concerned about rising pan-Islamism, they were watching for Bolshevik support of it in Afghanistan as well.[68]

After the war, the CID was renamed the Intelligence Bureau (IB; not to be confused with the "Intelligence Branch" of the Fraser Report) and Colonel Cecil Kaye was appointed its head.[69] He communicated with J. W. Hose, Esq., at the India Office in London about "unrest" among the Arab population.[70] In 1919 Kaye received a letter from a source noting that

> there is a great deal of anti-British feeling amongst the Syrians and Arabians owing to the withdrawal of the British Army and the occupation of Syria by the French and also to the indirect refusal on the part of the British government to grant complete independence to these two peoples; so

67. MacFie, "British Intelligence and the Turkish National Movement," 1–3. Macfie notes that the British intelligence services had "Turkish, Greek, Armenian and Arab agents, locally recruited by MI1" in Istanbul, as well as agents operating in Syria and Iraq. The Greek Orthodox church aided their efforts, along with "other personnel posted at strategic points in Anatolia," until spring 1920.

68. For the extent of British surveillance of the CUP, the Nationalists, Mustafa Kemal, the Ottoman Sultan and all his offices, see MacFie, "British Intelligence and the Turkish National Movement." So widespread was the surveillance that literally nothing came as a surprise.

69. See IOR/Mss Eur/D/1011. Colonel Kaye was followed by David Petrie, the first Indian Police Officer to serve in that position.

70. IOR/L/PS/11/161/no. 8174. J. W. Hose had previously served as the Secretary to the Government, United Provinces. The India Office list identifies Hose as Acting Asst Secy, Judicial and Public Department, at the India Office London. The other official in this correspondence is Major John Wallinger. After consulting with Scotland Yard and the Government of India (in India), the India Office in London decided that an English/British officer of the Indian Police Force should be placed on deputation in England to head the Indian Political Office. The first English police officer posted to London to conduct intelligence work was Major Wallinger in 1910.

much so that the best friends of England in Arabia have completely turned against her . . .

Regarding Turkey, the writer continues,

. . . a very secret meeting of Turks, Egyptians and Syrians was held at Montreux . . . letters have been sent to Arabia, Syria and Egypt asking for combined action. . . . It appears that if the present circumstances so require, . . . a Holy War will be declared under the leadership of the King of the HEJAZ, which will include not only Arabians, Syrians and Egyptians, but also Russian Mahommedans and Afghans. This war is to decide once and for all the fate of Islam and the Orient. . . . My agent . . . was asked . . . to take all possible steps to warn the Indian Mahommedans and Indian Nationalists in order that they might be ready for action when the time came.[71]

Hose was not persuaded by this alarmist letter, noting that the "sympathies of Muslims in India with the Turks is only felt among a small part of the politically minded, and who so [*sic*] would have died down long ago if it had not been for the incitations of the anti-British Hindu extremists."[72] The British High Commissioner Vice Admiral Sir John Michael de Robeck based in Istanbul, however, saw a real threat of pan-Islamism, and forwarded a report to the Foreign Secretary in London, Lord Curzon, about disaffected Afghans who might collude with Russian Bolsheviks; de Robeck described Central Asia and Caucasus as "hot beds of intrigue" and warned that circumstances were

favorable for a strong Pan-Islamic movement which will gather forces and supporters in no time. All these countries are geographically connected and a movement can have all facilities for spreading quickly. . . . there is a very great probability of a strong Pan-Islamic move being established which will have the support of nearly all the Moslem countries.[73]

71. IOR L/PS/11/161/no. 8174. For a succinct yet comprehensive analysis of British surveillance of Turkey, the Ottomans, and the Nationalists, see MacFie, "British Intelligence and the Turkish National Movement."

72. IOR L/PS/11/161/no. 817. After the war, the CID was renamed the Intelligence Bureau (IB). See IOR/Mss Eur/D/1011. Colonel Kaye was Director of the CID/IB, followed by David Petrie, the first Indian Police Officer to serve in that position.

73. IOR/L/PS/11/161/no. 8391, 1919. See also IOR/L/PS/11/161/no. 8446, no. 8483. MacFie, "British Intelligence and the Turkish National Movement," 9–10, for British surveillance of Talaat Pasha, who was supposedly organizing an Islamic-Bolshevik movement to incite the Muslim world against Europe.

Given British worries about pan-Islamism, it is hardly surprising that they closely monitored the Khilafat movement in India.[74] Per the colonial census of India conducted in 1921, close to 68 million Muslims lived in British India alone.[75] The British knew that Turkey was reconstituting itself as a secular country; the Under Secretary of State for Foreign Affairs routinely copied the Under Secretary of State for India on what the CUP and, after 1919, Mustafa Kemal were doing in Ankara.[76]

Meanwhile, the Khilafat movement began in India in December 1918 with a proposal made to the political party, the All India Muslim League, by Maulana Abdul Bari, of the Firangi Mahal madrassa in Lucknow, and two physicians, Dr. Mukhtar Ahmed Ansari (1880–1936) and Dr. Hakim Ajmal Khan (1865–1927).[77] Soon thereafter, a body tasked with addressing the Khilafat issue was created in Bombay by the businessman Seth Miyan Muhammad Chotani.[78] In May 1919, after the Greek invasion of Turkey, the Central Khilafat Committee, with branches all over India, was created to publicize Turkey's plight. Khilafat Day was proclaimed on October 17, 1919; the first Khilafat Conference was held in the same year. In November 1919, an Indian Muslim delegation journeyed to England and the US to spread awareness about the movement, while another set off for Turkey.[79]

In 1920, Mohammed Ali, the spokesman of the Khilafat delegation to England, met U.K. Prime Minister David Lloyd George at 10 Downing Street.

74. IOR/L/PS/10/196, 108–119. See also IOR/L/PS/20/C19 for a historical essay prepared under the direction of the Historical Section of the Foreign Office, "The Rise of the Turks: The Pan-Turanian Movement," Confidential Handbook, February 1919. The author recognized that the CUP were secular, and the pan-Islamic movement was political rather than strictly religious, but concern about such widespread movement is palpable in these pages.

75. In the early 1900s, there were seventy-five million Muslims living under British rule. In 1911, there were close to one hundred million Muslims living under British rule (http://piketty.pse.ens.fr/files/ideologie/data/CensusIndia/CensusIndia1921/CensusIndia1921IndiaTables.pdf). Laurence, *Coping with Defeat*, 77, 87.

76. IOR L/PS/11/161/no. 8112. This voluminous file contains copies of reports about the political situation in Turkey and conditions in Armenia in 1919 sent by the British High Commission in Constantinopole.

77. On Hakim Ajmal Khan, see Metcalf, "Nationalist Muslims in British India," 1–28, and Sulṭān-I-Rome, "The Role of the North-West Frontier Province," 53. For details on the progress, meaning, and eventual failure of the Khilafat movement, see Minault, *The Khilafat Movement*, and Qureshi, *Pan-Islam in British Indian Politics*.

78. See Qureshi, *Ottoman Turkey, Ataturk*, ch. 4, for a detailed analysis of the extent to which Indian Muslims leaders appealed outside of India for help.

79. See Qureshi, *Ottoman Turkey, Ataturk*, 77.

He explained to the Prime Minister that the Islamic outlook on life was "supranational"—not national. It was vital to guard the sovereignty of the Khalifa and maintain the territorial unity of the *jazīrat 'ul-'Arab*, which Muslim cartographers had outlined as "the Hejaz, together with Transjordan, Syria, Palestine and Iraq."[80] Ali assured Lloyd George that the delegation was not political but religious and that "the institution of the caliphate united in itself temporal as well as spiritual duties and it was incumbent upon the entire Muslim nation to preserve it."[81] Getting no satisfaction from the British premier, the delegation took its cause to France, Italy, and Switzerland before returning to India in August 1920.[82]

Meanwhile, the police in India had been keeping a close watch on the All India Khilafat (AIK) movement, compiling a history sheet titled "Detailed History of the Caliphate Movement."[83] The police sheet noted everything about the AIK's progress—the location of meetings, the number of attendees, how many Muslims versus how many Hindus attended, the amount of money collected, the tone and tenor of the speeches, and the names of every Muslim leader present. The report has three narrative threads. The first is predictable: Muslims were described as fanatical, childlike hysterics, apt to explode at the slightest provocation. The second focused on Gandhi, describing him as a vile force who had made himself into a dictator. He features throughout the report as a powerful, dangerous crackpot. The third was about Hindu-Muslim unity, which was seen as the dominant theme of all the speeches and processions. By and large, a police report foregrounds the people and concerns considered most worrisome. The sheet on Khilafat makes it clear that the British saw Hindu-Muslim unity as a danger and something that required monitoring.

As interesting as the report is on its own, it becomes even more interesting when read alongside what Savarkar was saying about Khilafat and Gandhi. Savarkar also saw Gandhi as an eccentric dictator, Hindu-Muslim unity as undesirable and impossible, and Muslims as fanatics. We see a new

80. See Qureshi, *Ottoman Turkey, Ataturk*, 90–91.

81. See Qureshi, *Ottoman Turkey, Ataturk*, 91–92. As Qureshi points out, the unmoved prime minister refused to discuss Iraq or Palestine and described Turkish rule as brutish and cruel and necessitating support from the British for all who sought to challenge it. Asia Minor would be supervised by the victors of World War I; Arabian lands would go to the Arabs, and Thrace and Smyrna, with their Muslim minorities, would be returned to Greece.

82. See Qureshi, *Ottoman Turkey, Ataturk*, 112.

83. NAI/Home Department/Political/1936/file H/215, vol. 2, Detailed History of the Caliphate Movement.

convergence between Savarkar and the British against whom he fought and who, as we saw in the last chapter, set him free when they did not have to. The police file on Khilafat starts by noting that

> [t]he *religious and fanatical enthusiasm* of the Mussalmans in India took a curious turn in the beginning of July 1920 when certain Khilafat organizations suggested that Muslims should migrate from India as it became impossible to live in India under the administration of a government that was warring against their Khalifa and appeared bent upon destroying Islam. This suggestion lightly made was taken up seriously by the more *fanatically minded* and devout Mussalmans of Sind and the N.W.F.P. [emphasis mine]

The report continues:

> The Caliphate question and the future of Turkey was the subject of a strong speech by Dr. Ansari as Chairman of the Reception committee of the 11th session of the All India Muslim League held at Delhi on the 30th of December 1918. He condemned the Sherif [the ruler of Mecca who had accepted the British offer to make him Khalifa of Islam over the Sultan of Turkey] as a traitor and exhorted Mussalmans to resort to Jehad if Mesopotamia, Arabia and Palestine were not handed back to Turkey. He accused Great Britain of breaking her solemn pledges to the Mussulmans. The effect of Dr. Ansari's speech was electric. Members of the audience were heard cursing the destroyers of Islam and very strong anti-British feeling was aroused.

The report detailed all subsequent meetings of "leading Mohammedans" and the telegrams sent to leaders in different parts of India. It noted the Ali brothers' letter to the Viceroy, in which they lamented that Indian Muslims were filled with shame at having fought their co-religionists in World War I and felt that their punishment was to see their holy sites ruled by infidels. The most evocative speaker was Maulana Azad, who was said to have

> reminded the audience of the last message of their Prophet which was that the spilling of Mussalman blood by a Mussalman was "haram" . . . he asked what was to be thought of the conduct of Mussalmans during the five years of war when they contributed not only large sums of money towards the slaughter of Mussulmans in Turkey, Asia minor and Mesopotamia but actually supplied Mussulman soldiers for the purpose. The Muslims of India in general and the Mussalmans of Bombay in particular were responsible for the downfall of Islam. They had helped Government to conquer those very

lands which had been saved in the past from Christian aggression by the blood of their co-religionists and this Government which they had helped was the deadly enemy of Islam: . . . let them discard their English and other foreign clothes and wear Khadi.[84]

Khadi, of course, was an issue that connected Maulana Azad back to Gandhi. Maulana Azad had expressed his views on the Khilafat in his journal *Al-Hilāl* and in *Maslā-i-Khilāfat,* written in 1920, arguing that Muslims need not fear Hindu majority rule, asserting that, flawed as it was, the Ottoman Caliphate was the political center of Islam in the twentieth century.[85] Azad's presence along with Gandhi in the police report reminds us that the specter of Hindu-Muslim unity hovered over colonial officials. By 1921, the government had had enough of Mohammad Ali's perorations and arrested both brothers.[86]

In March 1922, when Gandhi was arrested, he was effectively removed from the leadership of the nationalist movement. About the same time, Savarkar's manifesto *Essentials of Hindutva* was smuggled out of prison and published. In November 1922, news of the election of the new Khalifa reached the Central Khilafat Committee, which reacted by saying that "whoever may be chosen as the Khalifa of Islam ought to be the strongest man in the Islamic world and the one best fitted for aggressive action in propagation of the Faith," but concern was felt especially among ecclesiastical circles at the thought that, without temporal power, the Khalifa would be as shadowy a ruler as the Pope.[87] In February 1923

> [t]he new Khalifa of the Muslims was graciously pleased to honour India by presenting a flag to one Saddiq, Bar at Law of Amritsar . . . about 2000 Mussulmans collected at the Molo station to receive the flag . . . [88]

84. NAI//Home Department/Political/1936/file 11/215, vol. 2, Detailed History of the Caliphate Movement, 46.

85. For a detailed look at Azad's explanations in *Al-Hilāl* and a careful elaboration of *Maslā-i-Khilāfat,* see Hardy, *Partners in Freedom,* 22–26, 28.

86. "[t]he meeting discussed with some heat the alleged ill treatment of the Ali Brothers in the Karachi jail. Much resentment was shown and it was decided to hold a public meeting the same evening . . . to express indignation and to protest against the action of the Karachi Jail authorities . . . it was attended by about 2000 people." Hardy, *Partners in Freedom,* 59.

87. NAI/Home Department/Political/1936/file 11/215, vol. 2, Detailed History of the Caliphate Movement, 72–73.

88. NAI//Home Department/Political/1936/file 11/215, vol. 2, Detailed History of the Caliphate Movement, 75.

But the celebrations were shortlived. Soon enough, if anyone was celebrating, it was the police, who reported that the abolition of the Khilafat had "caused a panic among the Khilafatists, the hollowness of whose claims it exposed. The Indian Khilafat leaders refused to admit the right of any one race or community to abolish the Khilafat since it was an institution belonging to the whole Islamic world, but this argument could not avert the death of the movement."[89] In this case, the police were right, and the movement, which had not accomplished its objective but had gone a fair way toward pulling the Muslim community together as a political bloc that could not be ignored, faded—except perhaps in the colonial view of the world, and that too of Savarkar, who never really got over it.

Gandhi and the Khilafat

Gandhi returned from South Africa determined to make common cause with the Muslim community. Before his arrest in 1922 he had restarted his *satyagraha* campaign with two demands: to address the violence that took place in Punjab and to restore the Khilafat. Gandhi appears in the police report for his attendance on May 9, 1919, at a "Caliphate meeting." The report quotes him as saying:

> I admit that from my childhood I had this one idea that between the Hindus and the Mussalmans there should be no difference of opinion. They are born in one country and, therefore, whatever be their religions they should be of one heart . . . I always thought that I would rather die in bringing about this unity between Hindus and Muslims . . . I have come to serve them . . .

Gandhi was also described as recognizing that "Khilafat overshadowed the 'reforms' that were to be announced," and England could offer a "Christian solution" by "restor[ing] to Turkey subject to necessary guarantees what was hers before the war." As always, Gandhi indicated that, even if the British did not accede to the demands, nonviolent noncooperation should remain the strategy.[90] With Mustafa Kemal about to abolish the Khilafat, Gandhi could

89. NAI//Home Department/Political/1936/file 11/215, vol. 2, Detailed History of the Caliphate Movement, 82.

90. NAI/Home Department/Political/1936/file 11/215, vol. 2, Detailed History of the Caliphate Movement, 20–21.

have seemed out of touch. Figures across India, including Savarkar, saw Kemal as a secular savior who was forcing Muslims out of backwardness and fanaticism and into the modern age.[91] Yet Gandhi saw the Muslim community as a group he needed to recruit to the nationalist cause rather than allow to become a rival political entity. Throughout the 1920s, Gandhi wrote about cow slaughter and the Khilafat movement, and his letters show that he saw the disturbances in northern India not as evidence of inevitable Hindu-Muslim tension but as the effect of other tensions and forces.

One of Gandhi's early steps on his return to India in 1914 was to begin a correspondence with the Ali brothers. The resulting friendship lasted the duration of the movement and has often been understood as strategic, perhaps even by Gandhi himself.[92] Writing from internment, he told them, "My interest in your release is quite selfish. We have a common goal, and I want to utilize your services to the uttermost."[93] Gandhi understood the affective hold Khilafat had on India's Muslims. He understood the fundamental security of being a part of the majority population and the deep insecurity of being a part of a minority community, which Indian Muslims very much were.

Before I return to Gandhi's support for the Khilafat, I will note that, while he supported a number of international causes (including, for example, that of the Palestinians), he was less willing to speak out against the treatment of Armenians by both the Ottomans and the CUP. In 1896, as we saw, Gladstone had raged against the Ottomans' massacres of Armenian Christians. In fact, just when Gandhi started to become good friends with the Ali brothers between July 1915 and July 1916, there were mass deportations and killings of Armenians under CUP leadership, particularly under the leadership of the twenty-seven-year-old Interim Governor of Ankara Atif Bey, who used his role to "liquidate the Armenian communities of the province," as Christine Philliou puts it.[94] Whatever the reasons, Gandhi chose not to criticize the Ottomans, or the CUP, around what we have now come to recognize as the Armenian Genocide.[95]

91. See the chapter on Ataturk's reception in India and his depiction in Urdu poetry in Qureshi, *Ottoman Turkey, Ataturk*.

92. See, for instance, Chatterji, *Gandhi and the Ali Brothers*, 38.

93. Chatterji, *Gandhi and the Ali Brothers*, 83.

94. Philliou, *Turkey: A Past against History*, 82. For the best work on the massacres of Armenians, see Kévorkian, *Armenian Genocide*.

95. See Kumaraswamy, "The Jews," 150.

Gandhi called on his community, the caste Hindu majority, to demonstrate their commitment to the broader Indian family and forgive past injuries, real or perceived. Hindus were to wholeheartedly accept Muslims' struggles as their own. Gandhi also made clear that support for Khilafat could not be transactional. In November 1919 he wrote in his weekly *Navjivan* that he had received a message "to the effect that we should help the Muslims on the Khilafat issue only on condition that they stop killing cows."[96] His answer was that

> [t]here can be no zest or point in giving help in expectation of a return. Our Muslim brethren have not sought our help on the issue of Khilafat. If, however, we want their friendship, if we regard them as our brethren, it is our duty to help them. If as a result, they stop cow-slaughter, it will be a different matter. That will not be surprising.

Underscoring the point, he continued, "it is the obvious duty of those who are eager to protect cows to give all possible help to the Muslims on the Khilafat issue."[97]

At the Khilafat Conference in Delhi in 1919, in the first of what would be many iterations of this theme, Gandhi spoke of the anguish that the loss of Khilafat caused the Muslim community and again stressed that Hindus who shared this grief should not think it made Muslims indebted to them. Over and again, Gandhi stressed that the majority community had a responsibility to take on the minority community's grievances as their own, feeling them with the anguish one might feel for a sibling's pain. He had no interest in changing minds; it was people's consciousness he was after.

> It had been said that Hindus have laid Mussulmans under a debt by sharing their feelings of sorrow and protest, but I maintain they have done no more than their duty . . . the test of unity and real fraternal feeling lies in sharing one another's sorrow and happiness alike. How can twenty-two crore Hindus have peace and happiness if eight crore of their Muslim brethren are torn in anguish? The pain of eight crores is also the pain of the other twenty-two crore inhabitants of India.[98]

In December 1920, Gandhi begged Hindu and Muslim women at a meeting in Patna not to consider themselves enemies. As reported in *The Searchlight*:

96. *Collected Works of Mahatma Gandhi*, vol. 16, 305.
97. *Collected Works of Mahatma Gandhi*, vol. 16, 305.
98. *Collected Works of Mahatma Gandhi*, vol. 16, 306. One crore is ten million.

> [H]e did not mean that the two should be one, that Hindus should take to reading and believing in the Koran, giving up the study of and belief in the Vedas and Shastras; nor that the Mussalmans should discard the Koran and begin studying and believing in the Hindu Shastras and Vedas. Every one of them should remain firm to their religion. As there could be no marriage between a brother and a sister but all the same they could love each other, so Hindus and Mussalmans also should have love and respect for each other.[99]

Despite his own faith, which he occasionally referred to as orthodox (Sanātani), he repeatedly said that his belief that the cow was sacred did not preclude him from insisting that amity between the two communities was possible. And he always insisted that amity must be cultivated through genuine alignment rather than as the result of political negotiation and compromise.

In January 1921, a year before his imprisonment, Gandhi spoke again about cow protection, *Swaraj,* noncooperation and, most importantly, the restoration of the Khilafat. The British government, he noted, invoking the Rāmāyaṇa, had "revealed itself to be a *Ravana* [the evil demon] by attacking Islam and betraying the Muslims." Gandhi claimed he had lost faith in this *Ravana* government because of "its calculated betrayal of Islam." He answered a question he assumed his audience would have—that is, why he spent so much time talking about friendship with Muslims, particularly as it related to the question of cow slaughter. "They too kill cows," he admitted, but "I shall be able to explain to them that an orthodox and devoted Hindu [in reference to himself] fought along with them with the faith that, if he fell fighting for the protection of their religion, Khuda [*k̲h̲udā*] will call upon them to protect the cow." He concluded by saying:

> You cannot save the cow by killing Muslims or Englishmen; you can save her only by offering your own dear neck. . . . As soon as the Muslims realize that for their sake the Hindus are ready to lay down their lives, they will desist from cow slaughter . . . the Koran does not insist that Muslims must eat beef. It has not prohibited beef, that is all . . . I am associating with the Muslims only with this faith and I tell all the sadhus that, if they sacrifice their all for the sake of Khilafat, they will have done a great thing for the protection of Hinduism. Today the duty of every Hindu is to save Islam from danger.[100]

99. *Collected Works of Mahatma Gandhi,* vol. 19, 67.

100. *Collected Works of Mahatma Gandhi,* vol. 19, 253,254.

Since the Khilafat was seen as an attack on Islam, Gandhi, in short, stipulated a moral and political equivalence between what he held to be two parallel "religious" principles: a ban on cow slaughter and Khilafat. The Khilafat was, functionally, the sacred cow for Muslims. Convinced that an all-India movement would fail without wholehearted Muslim support, Gandhi saw community unity as central to his political platform.

Gandhi was hardly perfect when it came to Muslims. In an oft-cited passage, he wrote of Muslims as bullies and Hindus as cowards.[101] He did not approve of conversion or regard the Qur'an as he did the Christian Sermon on the Mount. He had all the prejudices of an elite-caste Hindu man. But it was precisely because of his prejudices that his interactions with Muslims were effective—they combined brotherly accommodation with a recognition of incommensurate difference.

After 1924 Gandhi's relationships with the Ali brothers and Maulana Abdul Bari frayed.[102] Perhaps that was in part because it had become clear that Khilafat was only a pipe dream. For Gandhi and other Hindu leaders like Swami Shraddhanand, the Afghanistan *hijrat* continued to hover as a problem long after its collapse, as it indicated that the two communities could not make common cause. For Savarkar, however, both of these issues continued to gnaw at his sense of the core premises of India's nationalist future, betrayals of his dogmatic territorial fundamentalism.

Savarkar and the Muslim Question

To Savarkar, Gandhi's support for Khilafat proved he was unsuited to lead the Indian independence movement. Where Gandhi focused on communal unity at the expense of India, Savarkar focused on territorial unity. His *Essentials of Hindutva* insisted that all Indians, but Hindus in particular, needed to hold in their hearts an undivided, monogamous love for India.[103]

101. Gandhi, "Psychology of Fear," in *Gandhi and Communal Problems.*

102. See Chatterjee, *Gandhi and the Ali Brothers.* Chatterjee uses the correspondence between Gandhi and the Ali brothers to present an arc of a friendship that was often tenuous but in which both sides insisted on their complete faith in each other. Chatterjeee tracks the decline of their friendship by showing that between 1917 and 1925 Gandhi referred to the Ali brothers 651 times but he did so only 163 times between 1925 and 1931. He does not provide a singular cause for the dissolution of the friendship, suggesting that multiple events and changes in the dynamics of power, including the riots in the 1920s and the 1928 Nehru Report's failure to provide a separate Muslim electorate, brought it to its inevitable end.

103. See Bakhle, "Country First?"

Savarkar saw support for the Khilafat as a repudiation of love for India. Still, Khilafat was in some respects a gift for him, providing him with a political cause he could use to intervene in the nationalist debate, rebuild his name, and quickly make up for the time he had lost when imprisoned in the Andamans. The Khilafat movement gave him something concrete with which to confront Gandhi; at the same time, it allowed him to frame Muslims as disloyal to India. Savarkar used this to put himself forward as a better Hindu leader of the independence movement.

While under his restricted release, Savarkar picked up his pen. It was his weapon of choice, and he wielded it with great effectiveness.[104] He published his works in different outlets, some the mouthpieces of organizations such as the RSS and the Arya Samaj, others associated with influential nationalists and reformers, like B. G. Tilak's *Kesari,* the short-lived publication *Hutatma Shraddhanand,* and Marathi magazines such as *Kirloskar* and *Stree.* He mostly wrote in Marathi even though his single most influential essay *Essentials of Hindutva* was in English. Knowing that he was being watched, he wrote under several pseudonyms.[105]

Since I have spent so much time with Khilafat and what it meant to Muslim intellectuals and leaders, I begin this section with Savarkar's Marathi essay on the Khilafat, which I see as his possible rejoinder to both Gandhi and Barakatullah (although I cannot claim with certainty that Savarkar read Barakatullah's essay). He had already begun speaking of Khilafat as a catastrophe from the Andaman Islands prior to his release.[106] Fellow prisoners were not merely his audience but also potential followers through whom to propagate his views. One of his close friends, Vishwanath Kelkar, published a paper called "Swatantrya" from Nagpur, and in 1924, he published an essay with a sardonically questioning title "Kāya ajūnahi nijalāt" ["Are you still asleep?"] directed at Hindus living in a Muslim majority Sindh, about Khilafat being a menace. He published it, according to Phadke under the pseudonym "taḷamaḷaṇārā ātmā" ["A soul in turmoil"].[107] He also wrote a novel in 1926 titled *Malā kāya*

104. Between 1924–37 Savarkar wrote and published close to 300 articles, letters, responses to critics, and essays on subjects ranging from Bhasha and Lipi shuddhi to caste reform, Hindu history, Nepal, and Gandhi. For a full list see the appendix in B. Savarkar, *Hindusamaj Sanrakshak,* 1–12.

105. See Phadke, *Śōdha Sāvarakarāñcā,* for all the pseudonyms Savarkar used and the publications in which he published.

106. Karandikar, *Savarkar Charitra,* 568.

107. Phadke, *Śōdha Sāvarakarāñcā,* 68.

tyācē? (Arthāta Mōpalyāñcē Baṇḍa) (What does that have to do with me?, meaning the Mappillah Rebellion) that was published under his older brother's name.[108] Both Shankar Ramchandra Date who edited the first collection of his writings and Balarao Savarkar, his secretary, who published a series of small booklets of Savarkar's writings, claimed the novel was based on actual events, it was fiction grounded in a strong evidentiary base, in other words an accurate historic representation. Date wrote that Savarkar had changed some names but had stayed true to the actual events, and as a result, it was not even really a fictional account but a true story (a *satyakathā*).[109] It is therefore less important to state with absolute certainty when and where Savarkar's essays and poems were published; it is more important to note that his followers and fellow prisoners upon their own release guarded his writings and circulated them in the underground world of revolutionary nationalism. The *Times of India*, for instance—a paper that had colonial sanction—was hardly likely to have published an editorial by Savarkar. No indicted revolutionary could simply submit an editorial or an essay in his or her own name to a journal or a newspaper; it would have to be done using a pseudonym, and this was as true for Savarkar as it was for any other revolutionary. Therefore, the methods he used to promote his views cannot simply be sought in the colonially approved publications of his time. Savarkar's essay title gives away his point of view immediately: "Hī khilāphata mhaṇajē āhē tarī kaya?" ("What even *is* this thing called Khilafat?").[110] We are told by his secretary Bal Savarkar that a handwritten script of this essay was found in Savarkar's notes. When Savarkar wrote it, most likely at some point in the 1930s, no one was willing to publish it, and it only saw the light of day much later. In subsequent compilations of his work, this essay is not included.[111] Perhaps it was too incendiary to publish, given what he wrote about Muslims in it. But he had already written about the Khilafat in *Malā kāya tyācē?* in which he had already laid out his sense of urgency in

108. The author's name was given as Ganesh Damodar Savarkar, and it was published by Balwant Vangmaya Mandal, according to Balarao Savarkar's preface to *Malā kāya tyācē?* Savarkar's older brother did not have the same restrictions placed upon his own release, so it was deemed safer to publish the book using his name. The preface is unnumbered, but if we count the actual pages, it would be 4–5.

109. See Publisher's message in *SSV*, MPHS, 2: 5, and Balarao Savarkar's preface to *Malā kāya tyācē?*

110. B. Savarkar, *Sphut Lekh*, 38–56.

111. In the collection titled *Sphut Lekh* compiled by Himani Savarkar, for instance, which is available online from the Savarkar Smarak, this essay does not appear.

instructing Hindus that events like the Mappillah Rebellion should alert them to possible danger, and which would have been in circulation for almost a decade. In "Hī khilāphata mhaṇajē āhē tarī kaya" we find the roots of his ideology, his theory, his understanding of Khilafat, and his fear of Muslim sovereignty. Bits and pieces of this ideology would also show up in other essays, in which he would invoke Mohammad Ali or Hasan Nizami or speak of Muslims as always invested in sovereignty. The content indicates that he knew of the conversation about the possibility of the last Turkish Khalifa, Abdulmajid II, possibly retiring in India, perhaps because his daughter married one of the sons of the Nizam of Hyderabad, so there is also reason to believe that it was written closer to 1931/2.[112]

In contrast to Gandhi's efforts to reduce communal tension, Savarkar wrote to keep the memory of Khilafat, and thus communal feeling, alive. He described Muslims in the language of theft—they had stolen money; they stole Hindu women; and they were conspiring to steal Hindu sovereignty. Hindu Muslims (as he called Hindus who supported Khilafat) had invited Abdulmajid II to come to India as the Khalifa, in which endeavor, he wrote, all Muslims were engaged.[113] Paying no attention to the foundational tenet that, for the Khilafat to be maintained, the Khalifa needed to be sovereign over the holy lands, meaning that retirement to India (if it ever came to that) would not amount to much, Savarkar fulminated:

> If the Hindus of Hindustan had abolished the role of the Shankaracharya, and to restore it had Turkish Muslims collected lakhs of rupees, and if that had not worked, had they taken the Shankaracharya, rejected by Hindus, along with all of his puja samagri and his gods and goddesses and invited him to Turkey, built him a muthha, even so it would not be such a surprising thing.[114]

According to Savarkar this hypothetical situation would not be dangerous because the *Shankaracharya* was an ascetic, there was only a small Hindu community in Turkey, and a traveling ascetic could cause little trouble. But this was not the case with the Khalifa, whom ignorant Hindus were so naively inviting

112. *Genealogy of the Imperial Ottoman Family*, 37. Hadice Hayriye Ayshe Durrushehvar (daughter of Abdulmejid II) married Hidayat Ali Khan Azam Jan in December 1931.

113. Savarkar was not completely wrong, but his grasp of the facts was partial. In 1930 General Cherif Pasa had floated the idea of settling Abdulmajid II in India, suggesting that even though Ataturk had abolished the Caliphate and exiled the last Khalifa, the issue was far from over. See Qureshi, *Ottoman Turkey, Ataturk*, 71.

114. B. Savarkar, *Sphut Lekh*, 38.

into India, "spending" as Savarkar lamented "lakhon rupye" (hundreds of thousands of rupees) to nurse the asp of their demise at their chest.

"The Khalifa is not a sadhu," he wrote, "the Khilafat was a Sultani, a rajsatta—And the sole reason that Hindi Muslims want him here is to halt the work of Hindu sanghatan [organization]."[115] Again, we see that Savarkar could not appreciate Khilafat's links to Muslim feelings or yearnings and that he was unable to accept the way it might function as a means for a community to come together to protect its future in a Hindu-dominated India. Savarkar saw Khilafat only through the lens of political sovereignty and territorial disloyalty. In section after section of the essay he wrote about Muslims stealing from Hindus and the riches of India's Hindus being poured into the coffers of this surreptitious sovereignty slithering its way into Hindu India. Every Muslim, he said, from the Nizam of Hyderabad to Shaukat Ali, was complicit in a conspiracy that ignorant Hindus were unwittingly abetting.[116]

The Khalifa, therefore, was uniquely dangerous. He was not the Christian Pope who was merely the moral and spiritual protector of Christianity—"a toothless, ascetic, heirless, disarmed symbolic soldier who could not ever become a King, and had no political power whatsoever."[117] The Khalifa was a Trojan horse being smuggled into India by unscrupulous Mullas and Moulvis who were otherwise disunited. It was not even a historical argument about the revival of Mughal suzerainty over India, since that had been dispelled by the Marathas and then the British.[118] It was simply Muslim rule. And even when it came to Muslim history, he mocks the distinction between Shīʿahs and Sunnīs:

> . . . when crafty Mullas tried to convert Hindus to Islam by claiming that there was no caste among Muslims then . . . if he was a Shia then he should be asked: Oh Hazrat Andhekhan! Why then do you not acknowledge anyone other than Ali's immediate descendants as Imam, and if he was a Sunni then he should be asked Oh Bhondumiya: why does the Khalifa have to be of Quraysh descent?[119]

Where Gandhi saw anguish, Savarkar saw a surreptitious and sly Muslim takeover.

115. Savarkar, *Sphut Lekh*, 38–39.

116. Savarkar, *Sphut Lekh*, 39.

117. Savarkar, *Sphut Lekh*, 41.

118. See chapter 5 for Savarkar's understanding of how the Mughal throne had been destroyed by the Maratha army of the Peshwa.

119. Savarkar, *Sphut Lekh*, 43, 47.

He continues, "The first principle of Sunnis is that their Khalifa has to be sovereign and independent . . . and he wants sattā [governing power]—and it must be independent sattā." And who was that Khalifa? The Amir of Afghanistan.

> And the anticipation of this 'Musalmani Amir' who was going to descend to India along with the return of a glorious Muslim rule was not just in the minds of a few but in every chawl and tenement extending into the villages . . . Ali Museliar [*sic*] one of their leaders even proclaimed that "Swarajya was going to mean Muslim rajya."[120]

This conspiracy was apparently well-planned.

Even though Khilafat was essentially dead, it continued to live on for Savarkar. Once the Amir was within India's territorial boundary, all he had to do was marry someone from the Quraysh community, and voila, he would be the next Khalifa. And since all Khalifas were sovereign over their own territory, ergo Indian independence would mean a return to Muslim domination. That the Amir had declined the offer to replace the Ottoman Caliph and was far more concerned with strengthening his rule in Afghanistan was beside the point.[121] It is hard to say whether Savarkar was genuinely terrified by these forecasts or just knew they would terrify his target audience. He warned, "even if it is just the Khilafat for Muslims, for Hindus it is a disaster, nay, a catastrophe or calamity."[122]

As always, Savarkar had some grasp of the facts. Raja Mahendra Pratap and Obeidullah Sindhi had tried to get outside help to rescue India, as mentioned earlier. Some years later, Subhas Chandra Bose would do the same thing in his appeals for help from fascists like Mussolini and Hitler, even being photographed

120. Savarkar, *Sphut Lekh*, 49. In a footnote, we are told that the words spoken by a certain Ali Museliar [*sic*?], a Mappillah leader, are taken from Savarkar's novel, *Malā kāya tyācē?*

121. Ahmed, *Afghanistan Rising*, 22. The Treaty of Rawalpindi, signed in 1919 between Britain and Afghanistan, recognized Afghanistan as a sovereign state, and a subsequent treaty in 1921 gave Afghanistan more leverage, rasing the status of its new Amir, Amanullah, who briefly supported the Khilafat movement. When the Caliphate was abolished, Amanullah considered declaring Afghanistan the Caliphate's new home, but much like the lack of support for Sherif Husayn as the new Caliph, this idea was not particularly well-supported. For details of the negotiations with the British over the course of the five Anglo-Afghan Wars, see Barfield, *Afghanistan*, 179–83. For Amanullah's struggles to implement sweeping reforms against conservative resistance, plots to replace him, and internal dissent and civil war up to his departure from Afghanistan and the enthronement of Nadir Khan as king in October 1929, see Barfield, *Afghanistan*, 183–95.

122. Savarkar, *Sphut Lekh*, 54.

with some of the most heinous Nazis. In other words, the Muslim community would hardly be unique in using this strategy, but when Muslims did so, the result was sinister for Savarkar.

Savarkar had agreed to remain apolitical after his conditional release, yet his writings about the Khilafat were redolent with political implications. One article written in this period was titled "Hindūnvarīla jātīya saṅkaṭa" ("The crisis that has befallen the Hindu *jati*"). It began by locating the moment at which "Hindu" history was damaged by indifference, insularity, and ignorance. We are taken back almost a millennium, to the defeat of Raja Jaichand in 1194 by the Ghurid general, Qutb-ud-din Aibak, which helped lead to the foundation of the Delhi Sultanate.[123] For Savarkar, there was little difference between past and present. The past was endlessly relevant to the present and an endless source of what we might now call clickbait—a means to feed the monster of resentment, to invoke past harm that could justify violence in the present. For such a project, only passion was needed, not evidence. Against Gandhi's apparent inattention to history, Savarkar wanted his readers to know that the Muslims of the 1920s were just as untrustworthy as those of 1194.

Having stoked this fear, Savarkar doles out reassurance, speaking to his upper-caste audience by resorting to a well-known *śloka* from the Bhagavad Gita (4.7) in which Krishna explains to Arjuna the theory of the *Vaisnava avataras*.

Yadā yadā hi dharmasya glānirbhavati bhārata abhyut'thānamadharmasya tadātmānaṁ sr̥jāmyaham	Whenever there is a decline of dharma and an increase of dharma, then I take birth [literally: I create myself.][124]

Savarkar used this passage to preface a long lament about Hindus' lack of farsightedness and sense of unity. And when Hindus don't unite, they endanger themselves:

> Because of such self-destructive and apathetic behaviour the entire country was attacked. It is not just that by such armed attacks they took away our

123. Savarkar, *Sphut Lekh*, lekhank 1, 1. Savarkar begins by noting that Jaichand's greed and selfishness planted a seed that grew and fruited over and over, destroying the entire country. But he also notes that South India snored as North India was being ravaged.

124. I am grateful to my colleague, Robert Goldman, for his identification, explanation, and translations of all Savarkar's Sanskrit passages cited in this chapter, and to Nabanjan Maitra for helping me with transliterations.

> sovereignty, by their religious attacks they ripped out chunks of our flesh and enfeebled us while making themselves more numerous. By either harassing us or deceiving us, by cajoling or in particular, assaulting us by force, crores of Hindus were pulled away from their religion. On this occasion too, the self-destructive tendency of Hindus to not see beyond their small footprints was the cause of their downfall. The Shindes fought! The rest were quiescent. The Holkars took up arms, the rest watched the show. The Peshwas struggle on but in Satara they are so seduced by ruling they are completely dependent on the British. In the volcano of 1857 that engulfed North India, the South Indian Maratha leaders said "let's see what happens up there. If it doesn't go well, then we can enter the fray."[125]

The historical narcolepsy of Hindus, a theme Savarkar returned to in his histories, was proven and reinforced in the present by their support of the Khilafat:

> And what is the situation today? By not looking beyond our own feet, by not taking the long view, our befuddled brain that just snores away, has become thoughtless, stubborn and foggy.[126]

Savarkar then ventriloquized apathetic Hindus, whom he claimed would say things like:

> Hindu Muslim troubles are intense in Punjab, but where is this true in Maharashtra? In Malabar, Hindus were oppressed and raped, but where do Muslims here do things like that?[127]

Having set up this question, a frustrated Savarkar snapped at his fellow Hindus:

> This is all we do—just keep talking rubbish. But what we don't realize is that this is a race war that has begun. In this, our differentiation between Muslims from *this* region from Muslims from *that* region, or this region versus that region will land up being self-destructive. We have an adage: unless the nose is blocked the mouth won't open. In those areas where Muslims are more powerful than Hindus either by force of number or by rule, their oppressions against Hindus will continue. If we want it to stop, then wherever they are less powerful than Hindus either by force of number

125. Savarkar, *Sphut Lekh*, lekhank 1, 2.
126. Savarkar, *Sphut Lekh*, lekhank 1, 2.
127. Savarkar, *Sphut Lekh*, lekhank 1, 2.

or by rule, we should bring them under our thumb, harass them and let them know that even if we are weak in number they will not make any inroads. Why should we be so brainless that we don't understand something so simple?[128]

Between 1927 and 1930, Savarkar wrote twenty-three articles in Marathi commenting on current affairs, almost all of them targeting Gandhi and Muslims. Called "Garamāgarama Civaḍā" (translated as "Fresh hot snacks," or "Fresh off the press"), these pieces mixed reports from local newspapers with a hefty dose of fiction.[129] Regardless of topic or genre, Muslims were always present—when he wrote about caste reform, composed poetry, wrote history. Savarkar's Muslims fell into three stereotypical groups: ungrateful liars who demanded and received special treatment from the Indian government, violent and base Muslims so inherently (even genetically) monstrous that they routinely raped and murdered Hindu women and children, and Muslims who walked all over Hindus, who endured this treatment because over the centuries they had allowed themselves to be emasculated by Muslim men. But there is a major qualifier: for all their bluster and noise, when challenged by masculine Hindus, Muslims turned quite cowardly. The real martial warriors were the few Hindus who led by example.

Savarkar offered detailed pictures of Muslim character flaws. He created stock characters that he called G̱hāzīmiyan or Rahīmacācā (Mr. G̱hāzī or Uncle Rahīm), or occasionally, Andhekhan (Blind Khan) or Bhondumiyan (Mr. Idiot). The names have a weight to them—a density of meaning. *G̱hāzī* means a conqueror, a hero, a gallant soldier, especially one who combats infidels, a general, a leader of an expedition; it is often used to signify the triumph of political Islam over the world. Typically, Savarkar's fictional *g̱hāzī*s and *Rahīmacācā*s are neither brave nor merciful but run from the first sign of trouble. He mocked these caricatures ironically, savagely, reductively, sarcastically, using mockery's two great benefits—its ability to distance and its built-in alibi, the ever-ready "I was only joking." The caricature of Muslim names, Muslim history, the exaggeration of the threat posed by Muslims relative to

128. Savarkar, *Sphut Lekh*, lekhank 1, 3.

129. These were published separately as small books: *Garamāgarama Civaḍā* as one, *Kṣa Kiraṇē* as another, his three plays as individual books, and his caste writings as yet another. His writings were also collected in the first compilation of Savarkar's Marathi writings (*SSV*, MPHS) in 1964.

their actual population, allows him to turn Muslim ordinariness into an existential threat.

Between March and April 1925, he also wrote a series of articles that he published in the Bombay magazine *Lokamanya* under the pseudonym "Hutatma." His aim was to publish them all as a book, but that did not happen until many years later, when the Savarkar Smarak published them in a booklet titled *Sphut Lekh* in 1982.[130]

In the first of those articles, he offered a laundry list of Muslim crimes that began the moment Muslims stepped foot in India. I quote the passage in full because Savarkar fashioned himself as a pedagogue, always seeking to educate his naive community.

> Muslims came to India and engaged in all kinds of acts; lakhs [hundreds of thousands] of Brahmins were lined up and mercilessly slaughtered; innumerable women were defiled by rape. Hundreds of women and children were taken off and sold into slavery in their countries; thousands of Rajput women on account of their lustful cruelty repeatedly committed *jauhar*—like the open jaws of a spreading volcano, into the depths of the pure fire that licked its lips they had no choice but to jump, Rajputs, Marathas, Sikhs, and other lakhs of warriors who generation after generation shed their blood to protect both their religion and their country from the attacks of these violent and lustful Muslims. Because of their boorish imagination, they don't think any text other than the *Qurān* is worthy, they reduced India's unmatched treasure of books and libraries to ash, razed thousands of temples to dust, defiled thousands of idols and looted India.[131]

Violence is understood by Savarkar as historical genocide, in which millions of "us" were victims in the past, a genocide to be endlessly litigated in the present and repeatedly invoked so as never to be forgotten.[132] On Mohammad Ali, Savarkar was particularly acerbic, almost incoherent.

130. When and where these articles were published is not noted in this compilation. Balarao Savarkar, in his preface, notes that these were written either while in Ratnagiri or afterwards and published pseudonymously. See his handwritten preface in B. Savarkar, *Sphut Lekh*.

131. Savarkar, *Sphut Lekh*, lekhank 4, 11–12.

132. For how "genocide" as concept and historical narrative were assiduously cultivated by the historian Kishori Saran Lal (1920–2002) about medieval India replete with fictive population figures in the face of all factual evidence to the contrary, see Subrahmanyam, "Inventing a 'Genocide,'" 102–7.

> "Even a dissolute Muslim for no reason other than that he is a Muslim is superior even to a man the Hindus have called the Mahatma" etc, such statements and from the post of the leader of the Congress, placing a foot on the neck of the Hindu land "of the seven crores untouchables in the land give us three and a half and you keep three and a half" in order to take away such a huge limb from the Hindu body, this utterance of theft, these notes of Hindu Muslim unity are meant to put Hindus in a stupor, and out of their silence, these are the words that Mohd Ali utters.[133]

Savarkar did not report when and where Mohammad Ali uttered those words, but we know from Rakhahari Chatterji that by 1924 the relationship between Gandhi and the Ali brothers was fraying, and that Mohammad Ali was desperate to reclaim his reputation as the leader of the Khilafat cause not least because Mustafa Kemal had abolished the Caliphate. In a widely reported speech in April 1924, Mohammad Ali was noted to have claimed that not only was Islam superior to Hinduism, but that even an adulterous Muslim was better than Gandhi.[134] In response to the negative reaction to his intemperate comments, Mohammad Ali produced a convoluted apology and quasi retraction in which he professed undying love for Gandhi but at the same time noted that as a Muslim he was duty bound to consider Islam superior to any non-Muslim religion. While Gandhi subsequently went out of his way to excuse Mohammad Ali, Savarkar added his own polemical commentary.

> "I have been inspired by the good desire for Hindu-Muslim unity" so Shaukat Ali himself goes around saying here and there. "For a thousand years, Hindus have been beaten at our hands. Hindus must make accommodations to Muslims. We will continue to defile Hindus, that is our religion, we will unite as a community, but Hindus should not resist us and should give up this Sanghatan and Shuddhi agitation."[135]

Despite the fact that the Khilafat's leaders were publicly noted to have championed Hindu-Muslim unity, he saw Muslim leaders like Dr. Saifuddin Kitchlew (1888–1963), the popular INC leader from the Punjab, and even Maulana Azad as part of a conspiracy to take over India.

133. Savarkar, *Sphut Lekh*, lekhank 2, 6.
134. Chatterji, *Gandhi and the Ali Brothers*, 152–3.
135. Savarkar, *Sphut Lekh*, lekhank 2, 6.

> Dr. Kitchlew in order to show that he is opposed to idol worship removed Tilak's portrait from the Legislative Assembly and day before yesterday in Peshawar at the Muslim League's meeting challenged his beloved (?) Hindu brethren that whatever demands Muslims make, all of them have to be immediately granted by Hindus, otherwise with the help of Afghanistan or some other Muslim country we will establish Muslim rule in India, and further, that he speaks as representative of the 7 crores of Muslims and with the agreement of the Ali brothers, Maulana Abu'l Kalam Azad and other Muslim leaders. So that's that on the singing of the tune of Hindu-Muslim unity from Muslim leaders.[136]
>
> But it was not just prominent Muslims who were threats.
>
> Now let us take a look at the actions of everyday Muslims. All your life regardless of the sins you have committed or will commit, if you convert one *kafir* to Islam, *Allah* will forgive all your sins, open the doors of heaven and for all of eternity will give you everlasting happiness. Inspired by such a fanatical view each and every Muslim at the first opportunity clings to that path and attempts to convert Hindus by defiling them . . . and so in Delhi, Saharanpur, Nandurbagh, Malegaon, Kohat, Gulbarga etc, we see small and large, minor or monstrous riots.[137]

He fictionalized entire conversations and gatherings between Muslims and Gandhi on the Kohat riots:

> The main leader of Kohat appeared before Gandhi and the Ali Brothers and said "for so many years we have been defiling Hindus, stealing their wives and marrying them; the Hindus didn't complain once and we had unity. But now they want to claim their rights over the wives we abduct! They are cleansing Hindus we have defiled, and for that reason our unity is gone, they are now opposed to us, and the result is riots. No Hindu man has any

136. Savarkar, *Sphut Lekh*, lekhank 2, 6. Savarkar repeats this claim in another article, "Saṅkhyābaḷa, hēnhī baḷaca āhē" ("Strength in numbers is also strength!"), *Shraddhanand*, February 1927, available in *SSV*, MPHS, 3: 32–33. Every Muslim, from the Aga Khan Muslims in Gujarat to Hasan Nizami, Mohammad Ali, and Jinnah was bent on bolstering Muslim numbers, some going so far as to use prostitutes to convert Hindu men. "From Calcutta to Chota Nagpur and into the jungles, additionally, Christian missionaries were doing the same with such success that they were being celebrated in the US and England."

137. Savarkar, *Sphut Lekh*, lekhank 2, 7.

> right over any Hindu wife who has been touched by a Muslim and a defiled Hindu becomes a Muslim so says our *Qurān*."[138]

It is wholly impossible that Muslim leaders would proudly claim the actions Savarkar describes, but what is important here is his rhetorical strategy. Savarkar frequently took facts (e.g., riots in Kohat) or a speech in the legislative assembly (omitting dates or quotations), and mixed them with fiction (e.g., Muslims claiming their right to defile Hindus) only to assert a general historical argument. He did this so often that it became a trope that his followers mimicked. He had a powerful pulpit, and his audience may have read these depictions and accepted that Muslim leaders said and did things like this. Khilafat also gave Savarkar an opportunity to push his support for the Arya Samaj- and Hindu Mahasabha-led programs of reconversion (*Shuddhi*) and political solidarity (*Sanghatan*) promoted in particular in the UP by Hindu leaders such as Swami Shraddhanand and launched on a large scale in 1923.[139] And in an extraordinary one-sentence paragraph that follows the previous excerpt, he lays out everything: his manifesto, agenda, desires, aspirations, and his embrace of violence.

> What is legally someone else's must not be stolen, either by deceit or by force no one is to be destroyed or harassed. But a blow that is struck will be beaten back by a counter blow. We have to bring our brothers back home, prevent others from leaving, those among us who have hit on hard times, are in perilous states/like our untouchable brothers, we have to remove their tough conditions and uplift them, we have to make all of Hindu society united and strong, perhaps if the opportunity arises and the possibility is strong that such opportunities at some point eventually do arise, as the riots in Kohat, Gulbarga, Nandurbar, Yevale, Malabar etc and the repeated characteristic fanaticism of Muslims and their overflowing passions make clear . . . we need to raise a huge trained troop of young, strong, united, all rounded, capable men for the purpose of bringing back those we have lost,

138. Savarkar, *Sphut Lekh*, lekhank 3, 7. For a detailed analysis of the Kohat riots, see Nair, *Changing Homelands* (particularly 54–77).

139. For an incisive analysis of the politics of the two movements and the pervasive deployment of the language of Hindu masculinity in the United Provinces, see Gupta, *Sexuality, Obscenity, Community*, 222–43. For one of the best analyses of Swami Shraddanand's complicated political positions on untouchability reform, nonviolence and Hindu-Muslim-Sikh unity in the 1920s, a period typically glossed as "communalist," see Nair, *Changing Homelands*, 94.

> protecting those we have, keeping our society safe and fearless from the attacks of criminals, letting them know that Hindus will repay a slap with a slap and it is better not to go there, better not to provoke them otherwise they will thoroughly punish us, making sure we instill this dread in them [Muslims], and like Nagpur, to generate this in society, *to live in peace with us but dreading us,* all Hindus need to do this [emphasis mine].[140]

As with everything he wrote, some part of this narration was unexceptional. But that inoffensive first sentence set up the justification for subsequent violence and a mandate to Muslims: live in peace with us, dreading us . . . or else. This was Savarkar's secularism, his opposition to Gandhi's *sarvabhedasamabhava* (equal regard for all faiths), which might be termed a dread-secularism, in which Muslims are given two unacceptable choices: leave or live in dread. Hindus, as their history has shown, he wrote, were not inclined to violence. But a society living under the constant threat of Muslim aggression, which to him was anywhere Muslims lived in large enough numbers, has to be prepared to take drastic measures. Muslims were unusually drawn to evil and to violence against Hindus. Given this, Muslims had to be dominated. A dangerous minority had to be splintered, and it could not be allowed to come together. He cites Nagpur as a positive example.

> On the other hand, in a place like Nagpur, despite there being a Hindu troop that had the measure of Muslims and was prepared, in order to protect Hindus, to match blow for blow, Nagpur Muslims with the knowledge, trust and experience that without reason Hindus will never attack, or be unjust, live in peace and go about their business, this is a documented experience.[141]

He presents Muslims as naturally "lustful," "imperialist," "greedy," "violent," "immoral," "amoral," "deceitful," and "power hungry." Long before more virulent Hindu nationalists spouted anti-Muslim rhetoric in the 1940s and later, Savarkar's language was indoctrinating any number of his acolytes to despise Muslims.

In 1926, Swami Shraddhanand was killed by a Muslim named Abdul Rashid.[142] An admirer of Shraddhanand, even despite his support for the

140. Savarkar, *Sphut Lekh*, lekhank 3, 9.

141. Savarkar, *Sphut Lekh*, lekhank 3, 10.

142. Shraddhananada stayed away from nationalist politics before 1918, but as Jordens puts it, "Gandhi's new brand of politics immediately appealed to the Swami, as it combined total dedication, self-sacrifice, and religious motives in the *satyagraha* method. There was another aspect of Gandhi's approach that attracted him too: the Mahatma was not fighting for some

Khilafat movement,[143] Savarkar used the murder to target Gandhi's unwillingness to blame the Muslim assassin or Muslims en masse. Gandhi had respected Shraddhanand and his activities in the Punjab,[144] and Shraddhanand was at one point taken with Gandhi and his program.[145] This only exacerbated Savarkar's critique. In an essay titled "Śrad'dhānandāñci Hatyā āṇi Gāndhīñcā Niḥpakṣapātī Pakṣapāta!" ("Shraddhanand's murder and Gandhi's impartial partiality!") published in the weekly *Shraddhanand* on January 10, 1927, Savarkar quoted something Gandhi said in *Young India*:

> It is not necessary to try and establish on whose forehead we should stamp the blame for this, whether Hindu or Muslim. Because where both are guilty, the fine-grained work of figuring out the exactness of responsibility is not going to be possible.[146]

In response to this equal apportioning of guilt, Savarkar wrote,

> If at all you want to hold Hindu society responsible, hold it responsible for repeatedly birthing such a "Mahatma" as you, who cannot distinguish between justice and injustice, cruelty and compassion, oppressor and oppressed, victim and victimizer, Rama and Ravana, and holds them equally to blame and preaches "compassion" and high idealism . . . [147]

---

minor political gain, but for the freedom of the whole of India." Jordens, *Swami Shraddhananda*, 107. For a quick gloss on Swami Shraddhanand's Shuddhi movement, see Ghai, "Hindu-Muslim Relations during the 1920s." For an analysis of how gendered stereotypes of the kind Savarkar used in his writings were proliferating and being disseminated in the Shuddhi and Sanghatan movements and the literature that was circulating, see Gupta "Articulating Hindu Masculinity and Femininity."

143. Jordens, *Swami Shraddhananda*, 124.

144. See, for instance, *Collected Works of Mahatma Gandhi*, 16: 263, 275.

145. Jordens, *Swami Shraddhananda*, 114–20. Shraddhanand resigned in anger from the *satyagraha* committee but in 1920 returned to working with Gandhi until his final break with the INC in 1922, in part because the INC was not paying enough attention to the plight of the Dalit community. In 1920 he supported the Khilafat movement, but not the *hijrat*. Shraddhanand was also opposed to many of Gandhi's ideas, including sending foreign-made clothes to Turkey rather than distributing them among the poor in India.

146. *SSV*, MPHS, 4: 147. Savarkar and Gandhi met while he was in Ratnagiri, along with their wives. The meeting was reportedly cordial and they spoke about issues they had in common: abolition of untouchability and self-rule. But since their views on the way to achieve independence were so far apart, the meeting was brief. See Salvi, *Swatantryaveer Savarkarancya Sahavasat*, 4, 35, for brief descriptions of the second, and last, time Savarkar and Gandhi met.

147. *SSV*, MPHS, 4: 151.

Savarkar then explained all the ways Muslims were already committing crimes against Hindus.

> Muslims have demanded that not only in front of mosques but even within their own homes Hindus should not blow a conch shell, or ring their prayer bells, or use cymbals and for this have engaged in thuggery, harassed Hindus, bullied them or beaten them and even when Hindus have turned their head away demanded, insisted, that they should not engage in any Shuddhi activities, and done this in Malabar, Kohat, where they have burnt to the ground entire towns killing people randomly, and deciding to kill more—this is the extent of their demonic arrogance and Gandhiji, if even a tiny bit of the blame should fall on any Hindu, then the burden of Khilafat which has been heaped on the shoulders of Hindus and its poison which has freely seeped throughout the country—look no further than your own bankrupt politics and place the blame on your own forehead. This is not Hindu society's fault.[148]

Here again we see Savarkar's habit of mixing fiction and fact. There were riots in Malabar in 1921, and some were started by Muslims protesting the playing of music outside mosques, but in adding "even within their own homes Hindus should not blow a conch shell, or ring their prayer bells, or use cymbals," Savarkar moved from fact to fearmongering.

For many of his readers, Muslims were mostly a notional presence. In the 1920s, Bombay Presidency had a tiny Muslim population; Hindus were by far the majority community. But whether religious numbers were going up or down, both in the individual presidencies and across colonial India, had been a concern that grew with the colonial census from the very first one in 1872, when religion was added as a category, and data were collected on populations and cross-referenced with occupation and literacy.[149] By the end of the century, there was even speculation regarding the exact number of years it would take for Hindus to die out altogether.[150] The 1901 census had suggested a decline in the Hindu population that prompted a Bengali lieutenant colonel in the Indian Medical Services, U. N. Mukherji, to write a serialized essay in

148. *SSV*, MPHS, 4: 150.

149. I obtained this information from Bhagat, "Fact and Fiction."

150. Datta, "Dying Hindus," 1306. See also Sarkar, "Intimations of Hindutva," 657, and footnote 8, where Sarkar points out that in 1891 the Census Commissioner O'Donnell predicted it would take 700 years for Hindus to become extinct.

The Bengalee called *Hindus: A Dying Race.* This 1909 book addressed the decline (with a focus on Bengal) across a range of topics, including economics and fertility. Mukherji was so concerned about the decline that he met with Swami Shraddhanand, in 1912 to persuade him that Hindus everywhere were in danger of extinction.[151] Across colonial India the Hindu population distribution per 10,000 people in 1921 was 6,856, and ten years later it dropped to 6,824. The Muslim population distribution increased from 2,174 per 10,000 persons in 1921 to 2,216 in 1931. In Savarkar's Bombay Presidency, the 1931 census confirmed that the actual number of Hindus had gone down very slightly and the number of Muslims increased, also very slightly.[152] These are hardly numbers to make anyone nervous, Hindu or Muslim. Yet, as Pradip Kumar Datta has shown, the discourse about "dying Hindus" went on to become ubiquitous during this period.[153]

Savarkar focused on crimes against women, but he found his examples from the Muslim-majority provinces of Bengal and Punjab, and the North-West Frontier Province. By suggesting that Hindus should be worried even in their own homes—by adding this fictional punctuation to a disputed historical event (the decline of Hindus)—his readers could imagine that this too was true and that the statistically insignificant increase in the number of Muslims was a sign of steadily worse things to come.

It was on this notional demographic background that Savarkar, singling out Mohammad Ali in particular, blamed all Muslims for celebrating Shraddhanand's killing. He wrote in his piece "Mahammada Allī ni Hasana Nijāmī yāñcī lāthāḷī" ("Mohammad Ali and Hasan Nizami's kicks"), with its self-explanatory title,

> In Calcutta, Muslims as one opposed expressing any sorrow at Shraddhanand's death. In Meerut, as the news was broadcast from the mosque of the killing, Muslims held a celebration of lights. Gorakhpur Muslims distributed sweets. In Delhi from the Jama Masjid, Haji Mohammad Ali

151. For an outstanding analysis of the text, history, and circulation of U. N. Mukherji's *Hindus: A Dying Race*, see Datta, "Dying Hindus," 1305–19.

152. See Hutton, "Census of India, 1931," 392. There were 7,658 Hindus per 10,000 persons in 1921, which went down to 7,605 by 1931. In the same period the number of Muslims per 10,000 persons increased from 1,974 to 2,039. http://lsi.gov.in:8081/jspui/bitstream/123456789/460/1/39740_1931_TLS.pdf.

153. Datta, "Dying Hindus," 1305–19.

> held community prayers that ghāzī Rashid be acquitted of this crime and be released.[154]

He noted that Muslims, again uniformly, excused Shraddhanand's murder:

> In prominent Muslim newspapers Shraddhanand's murder has been ridiculed. One writes that, Shraddhanand's bodyguards (who actually risked their own lives to save his) must have killed him and then arrested Rashid without cause. The second writes, "Aji Janaab that is not the case. Shraddhanand was going to die of a disease so Hindus decided, why not, seeing his state, hasten his demise by shooting him and turning him into a martyr. This would be a good means by which to blame the Muslims." And thinking this the Hindus themselves shot Shraddhanand.[155]

But where did these events occur? By eliding details and painting a picture of a generalized threat, Savarkar not only spread conspiracy theories, he connected them to Gandhi, whom Savarkar savaged for his unwillingness to hold the entire Muslim community complicit in Shraddhanand's killing. He was especially contemptuous of his reputation as a "Mahatma."

> A Mahatma indeed! A true, true seer. And in the hands of such a seer and an enlightened personage we have handed the reins of our government and appointed him dictator, which is why a mere four years after Tilak's death both politics and religion have taken on such a glorious hue. Everywhere one looks there is talk of unity just unity, prosperity just prosperity, awakening just awakening, light upon light![156]

154. *SSV*, MPHS, 4: 153. Khwaja Hasan Nizami was a learned Sufi scholar, journalist, and author based in Delhi, who had written two books, *Da'i-i Islam* [The missionary of Islam] and *Fatimi Davat Islam* [The invitation to Islam from the children of Bibi Fatima] that Shraddhanand viewed as evidence of a conspiratorial agenda to convert Hindus to Islam. See Nair, *Changing Homelands*, 108–10, for a description and analysis of Shraddhanand's counter and challenge to Hasan Nizami's writings, and his negotiations with the INC about the need for INC Muslims to contain the threats posed to him by someone like Hasan Nizami. For a review of Nizami's career and writings, see Hermansen, "Rewriting Sufi Identity," and for Nizami's claim that Guru Nanak might himself have been a Muslim, see Sikand, "Sikh-Muslim Harmony." Savarkar would undoubtedly have known of Shraddhanand's disagreement with Nizami.

155. *SSV*, MPHS, 4: 153.

156. *SSV*, MPHS, 4: 153. Nizami supported the Khilafat movement and the cause of pan-Islamism and opposed the Shuddhi and Sanghatan activities of the Arya Samaj. For a quick look at his biography and activities, see Hermansen, "Rewriting Sufi Identity in the 20th Century."

Savarkar consistently uses a mode of argumentation we still see today. Gandhi had to be insulted, mocked, and reviled. So too did Muslims and anyone who disagreed with Savarkar. If we wonder why the Hindu right constantly resorts to sarcasm, mockery, insult, invective, and fiction against their critics, or to Muslim baiting, we can find the roots here, in this style of writing.

One interesting transposition we find in Savarkar's work is his talk of cowardice. Cowardice was typically associated with Gandhi via the equation of pacifism with cowardice, but Savarkar also applied it to Muslim leaders who were far from pacifist. He focused on Mohammad Ali, depicting him as constantly claiming he would martyr himself if one or another of his demands was unsatisfied. Here he discusses Ali's insistence that troops not be sent to China:

> "If you send troops to China, then I will lay down on the tracks on which their train will transport them and will not move until it rolls over my chest" so he thundered. Predictably, there were cheers and claps (at this statement) and Mohammad Ali this time will finally die, or so we thought because troops were going to be sent to China! Mohammad Ali is going to die, now what is to happen to the world, we are so disconcerted/frightened, both these things I read in one and the same paper![157]

Yet Mohammad Ali remained alive. Savarkar asks why:

> Maybe it happened that the troops being sent to China got into the train, and this truth loving great warrior Mohammad Ali might even have gone to lie on the tracks but instead of on the tracks, in his rush, he lay in between them, and the train rolled over him without killing him. One needs a little knowledge to know even how to die properly! Now the third opportunity has passed, let's see what happens. What will be the fourth chance for him to die? The only fear is that while jokingly alerting people "here comes the wolf, here comes the wolf" that he doesn't actually show up at all.[158]

Savarkar wrote of Mohammad Ali's possible death with a breathtaking casualness that is meant to be humorous in a sarcastic way. He portrayed Ali and

157. *SSV*, MPHS, 4: 154.

158. *SSV*, MPHS, 4: 154. Savarkar might have been referring to the 1927 nationalist uprising in China, which had a decidedly anti-British tone. The British were planning to send troops to help quell the unrest. On the anti-British movement in China, including both the May Thirtieth Movement (1925) and the nationalist uprising in China, see Clifford, *Shanghai, 1925*, and Bickers, *Britain in China*.

other Muslim leaders as cowards, implicitly assuring his readers that they need not believe the myth of Muslim bravery that portrayed them as conquerors or warriors. His use of the word *g̲hāzī* was also always intended to suggest that Muslims were anything but brave.

For Savarkar, all tales of Muslim martyrhood were fake. Islam, he wrote, held martyrs in high esteem, yet in riot after riot, only Hindus were wounded or killed. Why were Muslims constantly demanding special representation from the British, except when it came to being wounded or martyred? As ever, his prose is replete with sarcasm.

> In the Calcutta municipality there was a Muslim demand that they should have more representation than the Hindus: that was on the matter of riots! Because in the last year in all the riots, among all the dead and wounded Hindus were over-represented. All the seats were claimed by Hindus. Among the dead and wounded there was not even one place reserved for Muslims. This is a little too selfish of Hindus.[159]

He then focuses on a moment when Hindus generously shared in the killing and dying.

> But look at this good fortune, after the Calcutta riot Hindus began slowly to let go of their selfishness and this year without looking back or forth, they offered with their own hands a good taste of their forceful prasad. As an example, let's take the Bareilly riot. In the last month and a half, in the important riots, the one in Bareilly was significant. In Bareilly 6 Hindus died, and 7 Muslims. The Kanpur Hindus were not quite that generous but they were not selfish. Because among the wounded the Hindus registered 105 of their own, but only 81 Muslims, but they followed the 30% representation demanded by the Muslims of the Indian National Congress.[160]

In his article "Mumba'īcā daṅgā" ("The Bombay riots") published in February 1929, the same theme recurs.[161] Muslims, in this case the Pathans, were not courageous. He begins with the inevitable arrival of riots to Bombay, but he is not sad; he is triumphant.

> Finally! Once and for all, the riots came to Bombay, flared up and died down. We had riots in Bombay but what is this? Why are there so many

159. *SSV*, MPHS, 4: 160.
160. *SSV*, MPHS, 4: 161–62.
161. *SSV*, MPHS, 4: 213–17.

> Hindus still alive in Bombay? In fact, we can actually count how many Hindus died, but the rest are all still alive. Just as before, one cannot easily even count all those who are alive! This is a surprise.[162]

He continues:

> Mohammad Ali asked "of what are these Hindus made?" *The Muslim Outlook* reported "if it comes to that we will bring in the Pathans and plant Muslim rule on their Hindu chests." Various and sundry Mullahs and Maulvis produced *fatwās* and *fitwas*. They disagreed only about one issue and that was this: in general when in battle how many Hindus measure up to just one Muslim? How many Hindus can one Muslim kill? Some learned ones opined, one Muslim can kill 5 Hindus; others said 10, some said 50, some said 100! We have concluded taking all of these mathematicians into account that one Muslim should at least be able to kill 28 and 3/5 Hindus. That too, these are Indian Muslims. The Pathans that they are going to invite to establish Muslim rule on the chests of Hindus, that one Pathan would not be satisfied unless he killed at least 100.[163]

Savarkar here contrasts *fatwā* with *fitwa*, which in Marathi means desertion or defection. Having set up his straw man, he then knocks him down. Despite Hindu fears of Muslims, they were actually cowards, easily defeated by Hindus, even without arms! And those fearsome Pathans?

> . . . at the same time Pathans were seen on the streets at the first sign of trouble, running away, falling, dying, pursued by Hindu groups picking up whatever weapons they could find . . . same Pathans loudly almost like a fire engine, yelling, one found crying out "tauba tauba." What a surprise, it was Shaukat Ali himself yelling "my Pathans are being killed, the Hindus are hunting them! Police run, Muslims run, tauba tauba."[164]

A Pathan crying "*tauba tauba*" ("Oh God, oh God") is a clear jab at the myth of Pathan masculinity. Savarkar concludes by writing that, "Given that one brave Muslim was supposed to have been able to kill 28 and 3/5 Hindus, and there was an entire army of 1000s of such 'din din' crying warriors that fell upon Bombay and rioted, nonetheless in Bombay Hindus remained alive!"[165]

162. *SSV*, MPHS, 4: 213.
163. *SSV*, MPHS, 4: 213.
164. *SSV*, MPHS, 4: 214.
165. *SSV*, MPHS, 4: 217.

To bring his caricatured Muslims alive, Savarkar relied on exceptional stories and outrageous scandals, some based, at least in part, in truth, or at least morsels that were true. As is so often the case, women and girls, both Hindu and Muslim, bore the brunt of a great deal of communal rage. Unspeakable atrocities were committed against them, some by Muslim men. In August 1927, the *Times of India* reported a gruesome and brutal attack on a four-year-old Hindu girl.[166] But Muslim men were hardly the sole aggressors. In subsequent months the *Times of India* reported horrendous instances of infanticide by a Hindu widow, the attempted rapes of Hindu women by Hindu men, and unsolved murder cases of Hindu women.[167] But Savarkar used these crimes against Hindus instead to attack Gandhi.

> . . . of those riots how many were begun by Hindus, in many did Hindus throw the first punch, how many Hindus were violated, can Gandhiji clearly explain or tell us? In these past 4–5 years how many Hindu maidens and poor children have been raped away in Sindh, Punjab, Bengal? Alternatively, how many Muslim women or children have been raped away by Hindus?[168]

Savarkar was entirely selective in his depiction of crimes, highlighting only those involving a Muslim man and a Hindu woman, particularly if it involved rape or its threat. In 1928, he began focusing on an issue that he would narrate with ever increasing bellicosity: Muslim men making off with Hindu women, raping them not just to satisfy their own lust but as a means of conversion. His assumption was that Hindu women raped by a Muslim man lost caste and would therefore be lost to the Hindu census numbers. He insisted that Muslim women aided Muslim men in using rape as a conversion tool or caste-destroying weapon. He was not alone in this fixation.

Charu Gupta writes about the circulation of anti-Muslim leaflets in parts of North India carrying stories of Muslims posing as mendicants to abduct women and fearmongering tracts with titles such as "Hindu Auraton ki Loot" ("The Abduction of Hindu Women").[169] In this period, the Arya Samaj also

166. "Khandwa Notes: Alleged Kidnapping of a Minor Girl," *Times of India*, August 8, 1927.

167. "Bombay Criminal Sessions: Attempted Rape," *Times of India*, September 23, 1926. See also "Death Mystery of a Hindu Woman," *Times of India*, October 8, 1926.

168. *SSV*, MPHS, 4: 149.

169. Gupta, *Sexuality, Obscenity, Community*, 249, 251. Gupta's book is invaluable for its accounts of such abduction stories and their use in fearmongering. See, in particular, 240–66.

actively encouraged its members to abduct Muslim women for conversion purposes.[170] Abductions of Muslim women were augmented by verbal attacks on them, with one pamphlet claiming that Muslim prostitutes were being used to proselytize.[171]

The widespread violence against women and girls, both Hindu and Muslim, was the major impetus behind what Pradip Kumar Datta terms "[t]he first major rallying together around the abduction question."[172] Datta looks at newspapers that began publishing stories about Muslim men abducting Hindu women, particularly in East Bengal in the early 1920s. He argues that with the proliferation of such reports, the trope of lustful Muslims targeting Hindu women became a "commonsensical point of reference for Hindu communalists," eventually giving rise to organizations like the Women's Protection League, founded to protect Hindu women specifically. Datta suggests that, since communalism was compelled to self-censor, it relied on symbols, images, references, and inferences that circulated as "social common sense." This "common sense," he notes, was not solely discursive but rooted in real incidents of Muslim men abducting Hindu women, of which much was made through sustained and sensational press coverage. Indeed, Datta argues that the abducted women trope was a direct contributor to antagonism between the two communities.[173]

Some may have self-censored, but not Savarkar. The sustained and sensational coverage that Datta discusses was what he seems to have been seeking. The stories he narrated for his readers were graphic, blood-bathed, and horrific. But they also point to something much more systemic than the individual rapist: the women in the accounts Datta analyzes were beaten and raped by men, Hindu and Muslim, who were in positions of power over them, whether that be a gang, the *zamindar* (powerful landlord), the police, or one's father-in-law. Savarkar ignored any such complexities, instead narrating newspaper accounts—not from major newspapers or those from his region, but small local ones, often from communities with much larger Muslim populations

170. Gupta, *Sexuality, Obscenity, Community*, 240–42. Gupta's fine-grained critical work demonstrates how actively the Arya Samaj used the public sphere to further its agenda, calling on Hindu women to try and convert Muslim women to Hinduism to enlarge the Hindu community's numbers.

171. Gupta, *Sexuality, Obscenity, Community*. 240–42.

172. Datta, *Carving Blocs*, 150–51.

173. Datta, *Carving Blocs*, 17. For the specific and horrendous violence inflicted on these young women, see 150–51, 185.

than Maharashtra. Besides, Muslim rulers' lust for Hindu queens was a longstanding theme in nationalist literature, in which abduction, warfare, and stories of Muslim men defiling Hindu women were used to highlight Muslim cruelty and misrule in medieval India. Savarkar's rhetoric worked on his audience in part because of these literary conventions vilifying Muslim rule. Of course, these were fictional accounts, but for Savarkar, evidence could be found everywhere and worked backward and forward, with any act of violence in the present serving as evidence for an undifferentiated (and undocumented) past.[174]

Savarkar used these abduction stories to make impossible the attribution of any semblance of humanity to Muslim men. He cast the perpetrators as characterologically defective, genetically or essentially demonic, and punned on their purportedly inherent tendencies in his use of similar sounding terms like *piśāca* (fiend, a malevolent being) and *paiśāca* (abductive). Any one story was presented as indicative of the malevolence or fiendishness of the entire Muslim community, as in this depiction of a gruesome incident that occurred not in Maharashtra but in Bengal, in a village called Bhavanipur in the district of Rajshahi. Stories like the one in "Piśācca vr̥ttīcā prabhāva" ("The influence of a fiendish essence"), written in November 1927, also advanced his goals.

> In Jilha Rajshahi, in a village called Bhavanipur, the Rajvanshi community don't keep purdah. Some of their women returned from the market with some men at night. They were accosted by some Muslim faithful warriors and one young woman was made off with. She was pregnant. While engaged in their demonic cruelty the woman fell unconscious, covered in blood, and still those Muslim thugs did not cease. Unexpectedly, the priest came rushing with some police. Seeing that those valiant warriors had run away, seeing that this woman was lying in her own blood—oh my my! Her mangled foetus was on the ground breathing its last. Of those demons only one was caught and the case is ongoing.[175]

Savarkar portrayed Hindu women here in equally generic terms, portraying them as creatures of extreme delicacy. (Elsewhere they are strong, capable and

174. I am grateful to Sourav Ghosh for pointing this out to me. On Muslim stereotypes in the late nineteenth- and early twentieth-century Bengali literature, see Sreenivasan, *The Many Lives of a Rajput Queen*, and Ghosh, "Rani Durgavati: The Contested Afterlives of a Medieval Queen," ch. 2.

175. *SSV*, MPHS, 4: 164–65.

warrior-like, as I will show in the next two chapters). Note the terms he uses: they are *ablā* (vulnerable) and *sati* (chaste); their essence is *satitva* (chastity); they are innocent. He spent little to no time on the general plight of village women or women who were raped by their co-religionists, nor did he mention that it was mostly lower-caste women who were raped.[176] Instead he speaks of pure but essentially featureless Hindu women whose only narrative role is their fate as victims of the worst assault Muslim men could inflict.

Muslim women were just as evil as their male counterparts.

> The extent to which abducting orphan children and Hindu women is work that Muslim women, too, consider sacred can be seen from this incident that took place in Katni in November. Chancing upon a young thirteen-year-old Brahmin girl a saintly man named Khistu pounced on her and in response the young girl screamed. Immediately that saintly man's devout wife grabbed her hand and yanked her and stuffed something in her mouth and held a knife to her. This Muslim saint's saintly wife spirited the young girl far away, and hid her in a cousin's home. How deep this belief is in Muslim society about the duty of every Muslim to abduct Hindu girls is made evident by the fact that as soon as the police search for the girl commenced, Khistu's aunt handed her over to Khistu's mother for safekeeping. Eventually Khistu's mother was caught while trying to run away with her. Now both ghazi Khistu and his Ghazini wife are in custody.[177]

In this one passage, Savarkar uses "saintly" six times, always sarcastically. Sarcastic utterances function in particular ways—they invert meaning (saintly is actually beastly) or they make analogies in negative ways (the saint who is actually not a saint).[178] Savarkar was consistently sarcastic, particularly when

176. I obtained this information from Mehra, "A Nation Partitioned or Homes Divided?" As Mehra puts it, the Montford Reforms (1919), which increased representation of Muslims in local and district boards, were the context in which local Hindu elites used "abduction" narratives to resist this loss of power. See also Das, "The Figure of the Abducted Woman," 439–40. Das argues that these "abductions" and references to lustful Muslims and their appeal to Hindu widows became the basis for the imagining of the state and its relationship to patriarchy.

177. *SSV*, MPHS, 4: 170–72.

178. Elizabeth Camp distinguishes between four kinds of sarcastic utterances: illocutionary, lexical, propositional, and like-prefixed. In her words, "all four varieties invert something that the speaker *pretends* to mean (or presupposes someone else to have meant) relative to an evoked *normative* scale. *Propositional* sarcasm functions most like the traditional model, delivering an implicature that is the contrary of a proposition that would have been expressed by a sincere

speaking about Muslims. The equivalence I alluded to earlier is presented by Savarkar in this passage:

> If a Hindu boy had run off with a Muslim girl, a Hindu mother instead of being appreciative would brand his hand with a blazingly hot tong and raise such hell that not just his associates but the entire village all the way to Kashirameshwar would hear it, and she would declare that that Hindu boy had become Muslim and boot him out. But look at what a devout and saintly woman Khistu's mother is.[179]

When he describes the assailant with terms like *dharmaveer* or *sadhu* (sacred/saintly) it lets him insinuate that conversion by rape is a sacred duty for all Muslims. The language lets him claim that there is nothing sacred about Islam and that for Muslims violence itself is sacred. Both are ways to scorn the Muslim faith as inauthentic, and since he used these terms for men and women, they also suggest that there was no difference between Muslim men and women when it came to raping Hindu women for conversion purposes.

In an article published in December 1927 he used "compassion" in a similar fashion—sarcastically and to indicate the exact opposite of compassion, that Muslims are always cruel.

> In Bengal, in a city called Feni the wife of Harchandradas, named Shamnad, was abducted and raped by a ghazi called Lal Miyan. He was given a two-year hard labor sentence. Maybe one can consider that a one-time occurrence? But in Alipur, the testimony given to the subdivisional magistrate about what a Sandeshkhali village married woman had to endure at the hands of six or seven ghazis, needs to be immediately investigated. Shashibala's husband was extremely unwell. She is 17 years old and went to get medicines and help in her neighbourhood. In such a state, one can imagine having compassion for her. Taking pity on her a devout Muslim had compassion for her in one location. In the same manner in which he had compasssion for her, so did another one. As it transpired, such compassion being their creed, some six or seven such g̱hāzīs got together. They

utterance. *Lexical* sarcasm delivers an inverted compositional value for a single expression or phrase. *'Like'-prefixed* sarcasm commits the speaker to the emphatic epistemic denial of a declarative utterance's focal content. And *illocutionary* sarcasm expresses an attitude which is the opposite of one that a sincere utterance would have expressed." Camp, "Sarcasm, Pretense," 588–89.

179. *SSV*, MPHS, 4: 170–72.

> took her to a deserted place and each and every of one them enacted their Muslim compassion on her.[180]

Not content with this, however, Savarkar kept at his project of making Muslims into monsters.

> Has this epidemic of lust just consumed Muslim society these days, should we fear it . . . as an example, take a look at this story from the Free Press: in Badlapatiya thana in a place called Kumarbil, on the 24th of September a Muslim woman made a meal of meat for her husband. But before her husband got home, the dog ate it all. So, with the intention of killing two birds with one stone, and having no other meat available, and because she wanted to get rid of her stepson, she killed him, cooked him and without telling her husband served his own son's flesh to him. If a society has such demonic women in it what else will they birth other than these "righteous" demons?[181]

Let us assume this sorry story of cannibalism (if true) tells us about a very deeply troubled woman. Savarkar, always the self-appointed teacher, used such examples to extend one person's evil to characterize the whole group.

> Once you understand the religious duty that attends upon this fiendish tendency then you will realize that the ordinary humanity of a father-son relationship cannot exist in it. A rabid dog runs to bite people, and wherever he draws blood they too turn mad, but eventually he bites himself. Similarly maddened by religion, running here and there attempting to draw the blood of "kafirs" eventually his thirst for blood will lead him to spill blood in his own house! This is the experience of history. On the national border, claiming Hindus were kafirs, in brutal fashion he harassed, looted, and killed Hindus. Because they were few in number. But once they were gone, maddened by their blood thirst, they had to turn inward to their own home and fall upon their own bodies.[182]

This is an outlandish passage. Savarkar claims that the "experience of history" shows that Muslims are turned fiendish, rabid, animal-like, mad, and bloodthirsty by their religious duty. After depicting these crimes, Savarkar asks

180. *SSV*, MPHS, 4: 172.
181. *SSV*, MPHS, 4: 165.
182. *SSV*, MPHS, 4: 166.

(again sarcastically) if any of these criminals would be called to account for their actions. No, he answered, because, taking a swipe at the reform package and its supposed abuse by Muslims, their classification as a special minority gave them complete immunity.

Once again the facts did not apply. Accounts of Muslims being sentenced for rape could readily be found in the *Times of India* and other newspapers.[183] Notwithstanding, Savarkar insisted that any judge, magistrate, lawyer—indeed anyone at all who held Muslims accountable—would be unable to continue in a government position whether British or Indian.

> In Khulna, with regards to such upstanding men like Zubair Khan, Yusuf Sheth etc a similar case has come to pass. They made a plan to abduct a young Hindu woman named Swarnamayi. This is what thousands of Muslim men do. This is the conduct of generations of their community. Enjoying the same experience is the duty of Zubair Khan and others. But because Khulna's sessions court is charging them under regulation 36 and 144 the work of their fellow Muslims might be stopped. So now a letter should be immediately dispatched to that sessions judge, so that he too can be filled with fear and come to his senses, and hand Swarnamayi to her Muslim captors.[184]

In the burgeoning Marathi public sphere of the 1920s, middle-class Marathi readers following Savarkar would encounter repeated depictions of demonic Muslim men who hid in the shadows and streets waiting to pounce on unsuspecting Hindu women.

Savarkar's third obsession was comparing Muslim aggression with Hindu weakness. He insisted that Muslims were weakening the Hindus, not just in the present but for generations, centuries. Why were Hindus so weak? Because their strength had been leeched out, literally mutilated, by conversion.

> Setting aside the 50 Lakh Muslims who came here from abroad, of the 7 crore Muslims in India 6 crores were Hindus who were converted to Muslims. From the various subsets of the body of the Hindu race, these 6 crores were like pieces of flesh that evil times had severed and taken away. Now

183. See "Assault of a Girl: Seven Years Imprisonment for Two Muslims," *Times of India*, October 8, 1926, and "Alleged Assault on Hindu Girl: Three Muslims in Trouble," *Times of India*, July 25, 1927.

184. *SSV*, MPHS, 4: 169.

> the Hindu race is living this feeble life, dealing with the emotional pain of internal fractiousness, and drawing breaths of pain.[185]

Hindu support for Khilafat proved their weakness, since the only possible explanation for their support was their fear of Muslims.

In 1928, Savarkar wrote,

> A powerful society [Muslims] took away six and half crores of flesh from the body of Hindus. That debilitated body, only slightly aware, scattered, and disorganized, asleep with eyes closed shut, was fed the milk of the Khilafat agitation which made it even further unable to bring itself together. The promoters of Khilafat are Hindu, the teachers of Khilafat are Hindu, the workers of Khilafat in many instances are Hindu. To the Khilafat cause Hindus have contributed huge amounts of money, and in so doing have enabled this religion-mad cobra to spread his hood over us and to get stronger by striking us at will.[186]

Hindus had to stay vigilant because Muslim masculinity expressed itself in the language of rape. Indeed, guarding against this Muslim masculinity was one of Hindu men's primary tasks. Fortunately, there were some real Hindu men, some real warriors. Savarkar was referring to the RSS *swayamsevaks*, who were doing much in his opinion to undo the image of the effete and emasculated Hindu. The chief effete and emasculated Hindu nationalist was Gandhi, and Savarkar would show this by appropriating Gandhi's term—*satyagraha*—as a general term for protest. He claimed in 1927 that he too was engaged in running a Hindu *satyagraha*, by which he meant efforts that had been going on for eight months in Patuakhali, monitored by trusted RSS *swayamsevaks*. He described their tactics approvingly:

> As soon as they get to the mosque with their roar of "Harinam" the entire atmosphere of the village starts throbbing and a hundred solders come inside and escort them home to the accompaniment of musical instruments invoking the name of Hari and march along the main street beyond the Mosque. Immediately the next day once again these brave bhajan warriors engage in the same activity. Hundreds went to prison, there were protest fasts, riots by Muslim thugs, skulls were broken, more police were summoned, resolution was demanded, the governor shook in anger, the

185. Savarkar, *Sphut Lekh*, lekhank 1, 3.
186. Savarkar, *Sphut Lekh*, lekhank 2, 4–5.

Muslims shook in rage; but the Hindu harikirtan satyagraha stayed just as it was.[187]

Savarkar was a poet and took pleasure in alliteration and onomatopoeia. The phrases "gavharnara **phaṇaphaṇalē**" and "musalamāna **jaḷaphaḷalē**" ("the governor shook in distress" and "Muslims shook in rage") were designed perhaps to make his readers titter. Muslims had brought the RSS *satyagraha* on themselves, he wrote, because a procession passed a mosque only occasionally, but by turning it into an issue the Muslims had ensured a daily procession for eight months in Patuakhali. Savarkar narrates this with relish, invoking one of his caricatures, *Rahīmacācā*, again.

> This is what we call stick-to-it-ness!!! And this resolve will not just affect this case, it will remain vibrant for 1,000 years! This our 'Rahim-chacha' should understand once and for all.[188]

Then he amped up his caricature:

> Up until now, Rahimchacha in Bengal—whenever Muslim thugs would steal away a Hindu girl from her home and rape her or accost her on the streets and make off with her—would hear this news and say not a word and maybe having taken a demonic vow ("I will turn Bengal into another Punjab") could slowly see the start of it happening, and may even have laughed slyly, silently in his heart.[189]

Savarkar warns his caricatured gleeful Muslim that a Hindu will come to the rescue:

> One day last week a young Bengali named Shashimohan ended it for him. Unexpectedly, he shot him dead. Did you hear this *Rahimchacha*? Shashimohan is the emerging echo of the sound of your silent laughter, isn't that true? Listen, listen well *Rahimchacha* to what Shashimohan has to say. "I killed that demon to protect the honor and sacredness of my Hindu women."[190]

187. "Patvākhālī satyāgrahālā āṭha mahinē jhālē," in *SSV*, MPHS, 4: 155.

188. "Patvākhālī satyāgrahālā āṭha mahinē jhālē," in *SSV*, MPHS, 4: 156.

189. "Patvākhālī satyāgrahālā āṭha mahinē jhālē," in *SSV*, MPHS, 4: 156. Savarkar provides a citation for this Muslim laughing at Hindu girls being raped—the daily *Swatantra*, which reported this news by wire on March 28 without the year of publication. Such citational carelessness makes it difficult to pinpoint where this story was actually published.

190. *SSV*, MPHS, 4: 157.

Next he suggests that the Muslims should now expect such a violent response.

> Shashimohan is the first response to the lecherous and silent lusting by your fanatical thugs. Rahimchacha at least now come to your senses. Because in response to the sound of each of your silent laughs from here on a Shashimohan will roar, because every action has a counter action, and this is proof that the counteraction will always be strong.[191]

Was this Shashimohan an actual person or was he completely made up? We cannot tell, because Savarkar saw everything as an attack, either direct or indirect, against Hindus, and he was eager to blame anyone, including Hindus, for facilitating these attacks, as we see here:

> Hindus should not engage in idol worship, nor lead a procession in front of, next to, or anywhere near Muslims. Because idol worship is against Islam. That they have made this demand so clear is really a favor they have done to Hindus. When the Muslims said, "Because we are Muslims we will not fight our [Turkish] Khalifa" and when the Hindus supported them in this religious claim, right then the idea that Muslim religious sentiments are binding on Hindus, this principle became clear. We won't fight the Khalifa because it is against our religion, we won't let you play musical instruments in front of our mosques because it is against our religion. Why just in front of a mosque, we won't let you even blow your conch or use your bells near our homes because it is against our religion. The womb that would have automatically birthed such a foundational way of thinking, for Hindus to bow their heads before such thinking and agree that we will not play musical instruments in front of a mosque, such Hindus desirous of Hindu-Muslim unity inevitably leads to the next demand, which is to stop Hindus from their own worship of idols because it too is against Islam, Muslims will not pause to make that demand; it will be unavoidable; this can be deduced.[192]

Savarkar asserted that, given an inch, Muslims would take over the entire subcontinent.

> The ban against the playing of musical instruments has already been taken up by the national congress. This year they should take on a ban against idol worship, and next year against the thread ceremony, because it can be

191. *SSV*, MPHS, 4: 157.
192. *SSV*, MPHS, 4: 190–91.

> suggested that everyone knows and agrees, as does the national congress that the thread ceremony is against Islam. In such a fashion, each and every one of these questions, on the basis that they divide Hindus and Muslims we should raise, and slowly get rid of, and just make Hindus into Muslims, and we can then pat ourselves on the back for having accomplished national peace.[193]

Although I discuss Savarkar's poetry in detail in chapter 4, I end this section with a poem. He wrote this poem in Ratnagiri, close to the end of his time in house arrest. It puts in poetic form all the ideas I have detailed above. It also reveals in pithy fashion a great deal about Savarkar's scorn for Hindu diffidence and supposed self-contempt, his scorn for Muslims, and his paradoxical desire to see Hindus act more like the Muslims he detested. The poem was composed for the members of the Hindu Mahasabha and was recited immediately after the singing of a poem about Hindu unity. As we will see in the next chapter, this juxtaposition was no coincidence.

The poem's title, "Hindu Musalamāna Sanvāda," or "Hindu Muslim Conversation," tells us that it was modelled after "Hindu-Turk Samvad," a drama-poem composed in the sixteenth century by the poet/saint Eknath. As Eleanor Zelliott argues, Eknath emphasizes the unity of God and pillories the hubris and inconsistencies of thought in both Brahminic and Muslim understandings of Hinduism and Islam.[194] Savarkar comes full circle from his first writings on Muslims in "the crisis that befalls Hindus," in which he invokes a *śloka* from the Bhagavad Gita, to this poem, where he uses it again (Adhyaya 2, verse 3, in which Krishna speaks to a despondent Arjun and calls him impotent [*klaibya*] as an admonition to cowardly Hindus: "Hēṁ purēṁ pradarśana tujhyā nīca klaibyācē" ["Enough already with this display of your impotence"].)

It is a rudimentary poem that does not require a great deal of decoding. It features two Hindus, one who makes up a pusillanimous chorus which stands in for Hindu cowardice on all matters related to their cultural and political self-preservation, and the other a real Hindu who sees his duty to the community.

193. *SSV*, MPHS, 4: 191.

194. Zelliott, "A Medieval Encounter between Hindu and Muslim." For an excellent historical analysis of the poem and the actual Brahmin intellectual in Sikandar Lodi's time on whom this *bharud* might have been based, see also Phatak, *Shri Eknath*, 30–36.

FIRST HINDU: Agree to unity—I beg of you
This India is of Hindus and Muslims
MUSLIM: You call the country Hindustan
And still beg us for unity?!
FIRST HINDU: Yes, my mistake, to call the country Hindustan
We'll call it Islam-vatan if you like, truly!
MUSLIM: Let's kill Hindi
FIRST HINDU: Respectfully agreed
MUSLIM: But we must speak Urdu
FIRST HINDU: Respectfully agreed
MUSLIM: Abandon the Nagari script
FIRST HINDU: Respectfully agreed
FIRST HINDU: Whatever you ask we shall do; you are our loving brothers
Just please agree to unity—we plead of you
MUSLIM: First, get rid of this rebellious "Shuddhi"
SECOND HINDU: But you need to also get rid of your forceful conversions
MUSLIM: What are these pari/jari/tari [but/if/then] conditions?
Is this how you engage us?
FIRST HINDU: Yes, Khan. Brother, yes, forgive us
This troublesome, Hindu-unity trap
MUSLIM: We will turn all Hindus into Muslims
FIRST HINDU: Respectfully agreed
MUSLIM: But you cannot turn Muslims into Hindus
And you cannot repurify those who have been defiled
SECOND HINDU: But what about evil abductions of Hindu girls?
MUSLIM: Our accord will be in trouble if you bring up that subject
FIRST HINDU: Don't get angry, Miyaji, these are stupid people
Steal away if you like, my own daughter
MUSLIM: In Malabar Hindus converted by choice
FIRST HINDU: Yes, the occasional one . . . perhaps was tortured!
SECOND HINDU: In Kohat a lot of Hindus were killed
FIRST HINDU: Why are Hindus such cowards that allow others to beat them up!
MUSLIM: And in Calcutta lots of Muslims died
FIRST HINDU: Such an oppressive Hindu who kills others
MUSLIM: That Muslim rule which considers the *Kẖalīfā* its guru
FIRST HINDU: Is more dear to us than our own father!
MUSLIM: Our religion tells us to spread Muslim rule

FIRST HINDU: Do that to be sure, [we] Hindus just don't understand
that core concept
MUSLIM: Destroy your musical instruments.
FIRST HINDU: Respectfully agreed
MUSLIM: Stop opposing cow slaughter
Break all your idols
SECOND HINDU (to First Hindu):
Agreed. Agreed. What kind of idiotic unity is this!!
Stop this disgusting exhibition of your impotence[195]

Pushes the first Hindu away and says[196]

Listen all of you my Muslim brothers
If you want to show your brotherly affection
Let our unity be mutually beneficial
If you resist us, then let the present situation carry on
If you join us, fine! If not, then we will
fight alone, and still, in the end, win the war
Those who defeated the Sakas and Huns
Pulled apart Aurang and Afzul with their nails
Do you think those Hindus were meek?
As when without seeing a trace of cloud
lightning accompanies a storm, so too
will come many storms of Hindu bravery
They will get rid of this Kaliyug and install an era of truth[197]

The first Hindu who pleads with Muslims for unity in this poem is Gandhi, the second is an RSS member who sees the need for action and makes Savarkar proud.

Conclusion

This chapter has focused on the tension between Gandhi's view that humanity, and for that matter nationality, was shared between Hindus and Muslims and Savarkar's belief that Muslims were barely human. Every passage I quoted was

195. I am grateful to Vidyut Aklujkar for pointing out the Mahābhārata/Bhagavad Gita reference and for her invaluable help with translating Savarkar's poetry.

196. This is not part of the poem. Like in a play, Savarkar puts this line in to let the reader know who is speaking.

197. "Hindu Musalamāna sanvāda," in *SSV*, MPHS, 7: 179–81.

written by Savarkar from house arrest in Ratnagiri where he received much of his information from newspapers and magazines or secondhand from his associates and friends. Far from remaining apolitical, he threw himself into the fray, writing of Muslims solely in the language of political sovereignty, describing them as a community that from its inception understood the language of statehood and was bent on reinstating a lost global sovereignty for itself. That this language dovetailed with much of what the British colonial government believed does not, however, turn Savarkar into a willing accomplice, let alone a collaborator. Savarkar's anticolonial nationalism never wavered. But in his extreme vitriol, he aided precisely those he wished to fight.

In subsequent chapters I will show how in his influential essay the *Essentials of Hindutva*, there was room for "good Muslims" so long as they loved India and allowed themselves to be considered Hindu.[198] I have termed this attitude toward Muslims "subjunctive patriotism" or "if-then patriotism."[199] In his writing on the Rebellion of 1857 a few such "subjunctive" Muslim patriots make an appearance. However, these references disappear after the Khilafat movement. Savarkar had been able to celebrate Muslim participation when it was about trying to expel illegitimate rulers, that is, the British. Khilafat, however, which he saw as an acceptance of a "foreign" Muslim sovereignty over the territorial boundaries of the India that he describes in *Essentials of Hindutva*, was a different matter. Prior to Khilafat, Muslims who loved India could remain a tolerated religious minority. The Khilafat, however, revealed to him that they were not an authentic minority because of their global allegiances. As a result, they would always pose a political threat to Hindu sovereignty within territorial India. This fear would bring out a new and also an enduring Savarkar—the voice that is captured in excruciating detail by the extensive quotations in this chapter.

As we have seen, the Khilafat movement in India petered out when Mustafa Kemal abolished the Khilafat. But Savarkar could (or would) not let go. Territorial allegiance was the real fundamentalism of Hindutva, and the most important thing for Savarkar.[200] It was linked to the question of state sovereignty; he saw Hindus as he saw Muslims—in the language of statehood. As a result, he named and shamed any action that he construed as betraying state sovereignty.

One last point before we move to caste. The literature on Savarkar, in both Marathi and English, takes as axiomatic a "turn" toward anti-Muslim prejudice

198. For a contemporary treatment of a distinction between "good" and "bad" Muslims that has a long colonial history, see Mamdani, *Good Muslim, Bad Muslim*.

199. Bakhle, "Country First?," 178.

200. Bakhle, "Country First?," 178.

in Savarkar, one that is said to originate from his travails in the Andamans. Scholars discuss whether Savarkar developed his intense anti-Muslim hatred in prison, an idea emphasized in the Marathi literature. Dhananjay Keer, in particular—Savarkar's major biographer and propagandist of the heroic narrative about him—claims that the warden, a Mr. Barrie, placed Afghan prisoners over Hindu ones to divide and rule.[201]

The assumption in these arguments—even for Y. D. Phadke, for whom Savarkar was a hero until he turned anti-Muslim, and for Senapati Bapat, who distanced himself from Savarkar because he preferred the 1910 version to 1937 version—is that an individual Muslim was responsible for such a turn, whether the Afghan prisoner placed above him, or some other prisoner. This chapter, with its many long Savarkar-penned anti-Muslim tirades, is the rejoinder to the "individual bad Muslim" theory. Savarkar was not sporadically or episodically anti-Muslim; he was deeply and systematically anti-Muslim.

Finally, his anti-Muslim prejudices seem at some fundamental level to have been present from childhood. Phadke notes that Savarkar revealed the barest minimum of himself in his autobiographical sketches. If we accept this, we need to pay attention to what he chose to reveal. In 1928, from Ratnagiri, Savarkar began writing *Mājhyā āṭhavaṇī* (My recollections), and he wrote about the first fight he engineered with Muslim children in his village, Bhagur. The anecdote is long, but I include it all because it shows Savarkar writing with a strange and compassionless sense of humor, as if he were narrating a game of the equally offensive "Cowboys and Indians" rather than a tale of having vandalized the village's lone mosque. As a mature adult, Savarkar does not see anything to be ashamed of in his childish behavior, and there is no sense that he was engaging in retrospection for past bad behavior. Quite the contrary. Here is how he prefaced the event:

> Because between 1894 and 95, in Bombay, Pune etc, in a number of places, there were terrible riots between Hindus and Muslims. In *Kesari, Pune Vaibhav* and other such publications, we would be so eager to read the news, we would wait for them to arrive by mail for hours upon hours. When Muslims initiated riots and defeated Hindus, we would be dejected. Why do Hindus stay so silent? Suddenly, Hindus reacted and defeated Muslims and our elation would reach the skies.[202]

201. Keer was a Savarkar acolyte and seems to have gotten most of his information from the Savarkar family.

202. *SSV*, SSRSP, 1: 83.

Savarkar stresses that he had the foresight and characteristic of leadership to organize his band of child-warriors against the Muslim children.

> I gathered my boyhood friends and decided that in Bhagur we would avenge this national insult and was there any better way to do that than to attack the one and only mosque located outside the village boundaries! Done! That small group of us, not even 13 years old, not just a group but a group of warriors! One evening, like the stealth of enemies, we staked out the mosque. There was not a single person there . . . so we ransacked and vandalized it to our heart's content and following in the footsteps of Chhatrapati Shivaji's stealth guerilla raids the last thing we did was to remove ourselves from that battleground as swiftly as possible.[203]

Naturally the Hindus won since the Muslims lacked a leader like Savarkar.

> The next morning the news reached the Muslim children. Between the Marathi and Urdu schools there was a small ground, a battleground in which long before any teachers arrived we had a battle. But unfortunately for the Muslim children, a leader with the foresight to gather unto them knives, rulers, pins and other such "weapons" was not to be had, and I had done all this for the Hindu children so naturally the Hindus were victorious. The treaty drawn at the end of this by the victors was that no mention of this battle was to be leaked to the school authorities.[204]

This incident is brushed aside as the kind of prank children engage in before they know better. To be sure, the account also betrays Savarkar's desire to be viewed as a leader, a young military commander outfoxing and out-strategizing Muslims, even as a boy, and modeling what young Hindu manhood ought to be. But the account does more than just that. It does the same work that US movies and television shows and their many stories of "Cowboys and Indians" did to normalize quotidian racism against Native Americans. Savarkar recounts the desecration of a mosque as evidence of his leadership but also as just child's play (in both senses of the word—as both "easy to do" but also "childish"). A few years earlier, buried in his 1925 historical work on the Peshwai, *Hindu-Pad-Padashahi,* he had written regarding the skirmishes between the Marathas and the governor of the Mughal province of Bengal that "the Pathans, just to spite the Marathas and give a religious colouring to their cause, had attacked Kashi and committed outrages on the Hindu temples and priests,

203. *SSV*, SSRSP, 1: 83.
204. *SSV*, SSRSP, 1: 83.

swaggering loudly that the Kafirs could never face the Pathans,"[205] and that "the mosque ever reminded the Hindus of those dark days when the Moslem crescent rose insultingly on the ruins of the foremost temples of the Hindu faith."[206] Writing his memoirs did not pose for him an opportunity to wonder whether perhaps he ought not to have desecrated a mosque given that it was a community's sacred space.

Scholars have been concerned with the question of whether Savarkar was personally responsible for Gandhi's death, whether he instructed Nathuram Godse to kill him, thus playing a key role in the assassination. If we ask a prior question, however, about how the Hindu community was moved to a place where the killing of Gandhi seemed like a reasonable course of action—and relatedly, how Nathuram Godse himself was transformed from an assassin to a savior of the Hindus—I believe we can find the answer here, in Savarkar's writings. He used multiple genres (plays, polemics, poems, editorials, essays) to depict the Muslim threat so they became naturalized as dangerous—legitimate objects of fear and violence. By the time Nathuram Godse began planning to assassinate Gandhi, the Marathi community would have read pieces such as the ones quoted here for over twenty years. As a result, the issue is less about whether Savarkar turned anti-Muslim because of his experiences in the Andamans or whether he was directly involved in Gandhi's assassination than that for twenty years he had been provoking, even insulting the Hindu community for having emasculated itself, encouraging Hindus to treat Muslims as subhuman, and goading them to pick up arms and regain their masculinity. The immediate reason for Godse's assassination of Gandhi may or may not have been Savarkar's explicit plan or instruction, but it was both prefigured and justified in his writings. Thus, the importance of understanding the power of his prose and the force of his influence—the literary genealogy of a Hindu nationalist who licensed the kind of hate that led not just to the tragic murder of a man of peace but, one might fear, to his larger conception of the idea of Indian nationhood.

205. Savarkar, *Hindu-Pad-Padashahi*, 74. I accessed a PDF version of *Hindu-Pad-Padashahi* from Calcutta University Library, call no. 954.442/S26H, accession no. 17,000, and the page numbers correspond to this edition. As much as possible, I have tried to use the earliest editions of Savarkar's writings to stay as close as possible to his actual words.

206. Savarkar, *Hindu-Pad-Padashahi*, 76.

3

A Social Reformer

SAVARKAR AND CASTE

IN THE PREVIOUS CHAPTER, we read Savarkar's extraordinary assertions about Muslims. But if his views on Muslims were reactionary and often hateful, he was at the same time someone who was widely—and correctly—seen as a radical advocate for social reform. In this chapter I review his writings on caste, illustrating the contempt he had for ordinary caste prejudice and the protocols of adherence to caste distinctions. Even as I demonstrate the depths of his critiques of caste, I also argue that he was able to express this contempt in large part because of his own secure place as a Brahmin in caste society.[1] I argue further that he never developed a critique of caste that acknowledged its deep connections to structures of power, access, and wellbeing. And I go even further to suggest that his critical positions on caste allowed him license to make other kinds of prejudicial assertions, the most extreme of which were the ones directed at Muslims, as just discussed. Yet, his sustained—and on occasion radical—critique of caste prejudice has not been widely understood by non-Marathi readers outside of Maharashtra.

The March 23, 2009, issue of *Outlook* published an interview with L. K. Advani, the shrewd politician who brought the Bharatiya Janata Party (BJP) to the national forefront with his much-publicized *Rath Yatra* in 1990, and who was a leader of the movement to demolish the sixteenth-century Babri Masjid Mosque in Ayodhya. He was asked if Narendra Modi, then chief minister of Gujarat, should be held responsible for the 2002 riots following the

1. I use the word "Brahmin" to designate caste, "Brahman" only if I refer to what in Hindu theology is considered the supreme being, and "Brahmanetar" as a shorthand for the Marathi anti-Brahmin movement.

anti-Muslim pogroms there. Advani responded with a counterquestion, quoted here in full:

> Why is it that in India people are willing to tolerate individuals who are blatantly casteist but when a person or a political section is regarded as communal, they are shunned? . . . Casteism is worse in many ways.[2]

Note that he did not answer the question. While all politicians deflect, this mode of deflection is reminiscent of how Savarkar used anticaste politics, marshalling a righteous outrage as an alibi against having to answer questions about his anti-Muslim prejudice. In this chapter, I show that turning a question about Muslims into an answer about casteism has a long history and played a critical role in Savarkar's writings on caste and Muslims, which, not coincidentally, were linked. Savarkar projected himself as a radical caste reformer, but all his writings on caste were also about Muslims. These works have not traveled outside Maharashtra. His most important writings, many of which were the basis for his writings in English—including the forty-some essays he wrote and published while under house arrest in Marathi publications like *Kesari, Maharashtra Sharada, Kirloskar, Shraddhananda, Stree*—have not yet been translated. In this chapter, I discuss selections from his four major collections of essays—*Jatyuchedak Nibandha, Vijñānaniṣṭha Nibandha, Kṣa Kiraṇē, Garamāgarama Civaḍā*—along with other articles aimed directly at conservative Hindu women such as *Manusmṛtītīla Mahilā* and Savarkar's translation and commentary on the first-millennium Sanskrit text, the *Vajrasūcī*, composed by a Buddhist/Brahmin scholar.[3] Within Maharashtra, Savarkar was widely admired as a falsely imprisoned revolutionary nationalist, a rationalist, a social reformer, and a progressive (*purōgāmi*). His followers, who might today be termed Hindutvavādis, were always clear that there was a direct connection between caste and the Muslim question: caste-discrimination was the major reason for the conversion of low-caste Hindus to Islam (or Christianity) and had to be eliminated to keep the number of Hindus high. This connection, however, was neither clear nor explicit for many upper-caste Marathi Hindus who were not Savarkarite or Hindutva followers and who were the primary readership of *Kesari* and *Stree*. To these readers, Savarkar would have appeared

2. "It's Good that the Overconfidence in the Party Has Gone," *Outlook*, February 5, 2022.

3. I get this identification of Aśvaghoṣa as both a Brahmin and a Buddhist scholar writing in Sanskrit from Johannes Bronkhorst's magnificent three-volume work, but also from a talk he gave: Bronkhorst, 5th C.R. Parekh Memorial Lecture.

radical because his reformist writings savagely targeted the orthodox (Sanātani) community and used language drawn from Sanskrit epics and purāṇas to mount an internal critique. For the Sanātani orthodox upper-caste community invested in maintaining caste, as well as for many women, Savarkar's writings and claims about caste, untouchability, social reform, religion, and gender were extraordinary for their times. Meanwhile, for non-Marathi readers, the idea that Savarkar was a caste progressive might itself come as a surprise.

This chapter highlights four facets of his caste critique to suggest their complex political status and implications. It juxtaposes Savarkar's views to a small selection of B. R. Ambedkar's and Gandhi's views. By putting Ambedkar and Gandhi in the same sentence, I do not at all mean to suggest any similarity of approach, ideology, intent, subject position, or privilege. I do so only to point out how Savarkar situated himself. Ambedkar and Gandhi both saw caste systemically, albeit with fundamentally different ideological agendas and positions. Gandhi was a devout Vaishnava who thought caste was a fundamentally sound system that did not require śāstric authority to give it meaning, even as he decried the treatment of untouchables (whom he renamed Harijans, or children of God). Gandhi's solution for casteism was ethical self-reform. Ambedkar, from outside the caste fold (he hailed from what was then called an untouchable caste), saw Brahminism as the central tenet of the Hindu religion, which he rejected not least because he viewed its principles as corrupt and inextricable from Brahmin power and privilege. Ambedkar's strategy for dealing with the behemoth of caste was to turn to state power and the law, instruments of modernity that he believed would be required to begin to break the stranglehold of Brahminic Hinduism on society.

In part because Gandhi and Ambedkar both focused on caste, but also because of his own distinctive convictions, Savarkar felt he too had to address the caste question. He inserted himself somewhere between Gandhi's and Ambedkar's positions while moving in a different direction than either Gandhi's spiritual self-searching or Ambedkar's revolutionary denunciation. Instead, Savarkar treated caste as a general matter of social ignorance that caused self-destructive and divisive conduct (*ācāra*), not just among high- and low-caste groups but among untouchables as well. He suggested that people could easily discard their caste practices without leaving the Hindu fold. However, his anticaste rhetoric was also critical to his ongoing project of replacing caste (*jati*) with ethnicity (Hindu), even as he always understood that ethnicity through an upper-caste Brahminic lens.

Savarkar's critique of caste was as severe as it was sincere. This was in large part because it was primarily motivated by what he saw as an urgent and immediate need to unite Hindus against Muslims (in marked contrast with Gandhi, whose critique of caste was primarily related to the need for a unified nationalist movement against British rule). In his own life, he practiced none of the rituals considered important to living life as an upper-caste Hindu male but on occasion participated in them for the sake of his family.[4] As with his engagements with other topics, including history, Savarkar's approach to casteism was simultaneously learned and superficial. He read widely and wrote powerfully; his intellectual ability and erudition is indisputable. Yet—in part because all his writing had a larger ideological purpose—his solutions always sound superficial. He saw caste as an enduring structure of stupidity, naivete, and even innocence, which meant that even as he produced historicist readings of texts upper-caste Hindus considered sacred texts, he never examined caste as a powerful and enduring structure of oppression or as a system of power that maintained social hierarchy and caste status through Brahmin control of ritual. It is not clear that he saw caste as a system, whether a system of ideal interdependence as Gandhi quixotically did, or one of historical oppression and discrimination as Ambedkar did. Savarkar attacked not only Sanātani beliefs, but everyone else's up and down the caste ladder, including untouchables who were held to be outside the caste fold by the orthodoxy. In so levelling the playing field, his aim was to bring everyone into the Hindu fold and remove divisions between them. But that levelling disallowed any engagement with the dynamics of power or the deep structural inequalities that a Brahminic casteism had produced. At no point did Savarkar ask why caste was so powerful a marker of identity. Nor did he ever engage the anti-Brahmin debate—a discussion that was very much alive in Maharashtra at the time; such an engagement would have necessitated considering Brahminism's role in justifying and organizing the entire edifice of caste, which he never did.

Johannes Bronkhorst has defined Brahminism as a sociopolitical ideology with a "variable religious dimension" and as the "culture carried by and

4. Savarkar, *Athavani Angaracya*, 15. Savarkar's son Vishwas remembered that, per his father's wishes, he did not undergo the *upanayana* ceremony, called *muñja* in Marathi, at which the sacred thread is bestowed on a *dwija* (upper-caste) boy. But since Savarkar had undergone the ceremony as a young boy, the sacred thread (*jānavaṁ*) was always around his neck and shoulders, and he used it to hold his keys. Savarkar did, however, perform all the necessary rituals for his daughter's marriage.

embodied in Brahmins, a group of people who emphasize the purity of their descent from both father's and mother's side" and "claim descent from a priestly religion (Vedism) that stressed the centrality of sacrifice in everyday life that could *only be* conducted by them [emphasis mine]."[5] The language of Brahminism was Sanskrit, and the special axis of Brahmin power has been the knowledge, control, and use of Sanskrit along with the embodied memorization of the Vedas. The core of early Brahminism as a sociopolitical ideology is *varṇa*, the birth-based ordering of society from high to low, with the highest group being the Brahmins. The maintenance of *varṇa* through different social and cultural axes—including ritual pollution and purity, exclusive access to Sanskrit sacerdotal literature, endogamy, and even untouchability—came together over the centuries into a self-reinforcing whole that we can still, however we might define the caste system, consider Brahminism to be today.[6] Savarkar, from the comfort of his own caste identity as a Brahmin, attacked the most conservative elements of this Brahminism, the views in particular of the community that thought of itself as Sanātani (upholders of an eternal and unchanging faith).

By strategically using Sanskrit to attack Vedism, Savarkar was doing more than just challenging the scriptural basis for caste. He was also suggesting that one could reconfigure Sanskrit as a demotically Hindu language and make it non-Brahminic. In challenging taboos about purity and pollution taboos, as well as about interdining and intermarriage, he was attempting to radically alter the very content of Brahminism, updating it for the twentieth century and divesting it of outdated prejudices and protocols, all while redirecting its essence into the holistic ethnic category of "Hindu." Was this a revolutionary

5. Bronkhorst, *How the Brahmins Won*, 3–4. For a tour de force on this subject, see Bronkhorst's trilogy, beginning with *Greater Magadha*. Bronkhorst makes very clear that Brahminism was not a religion, but because of a self-ordained exclusive access to Sanskrit sacred literature and the ability to communicate directly with the supernatural through rituals, Brahmins played a very large role not only as political advisors to princes and kings but also to those below them in the social order. Because of their exclusive access to Sanskrit, they could predict the future and give political advice. Brahmins, Bronkhorst notes, also expected to live an utterly unique life—maintaining endogamous purity and a distance from things and people they considered impure. On Brahmins as political advisors, judges, legal advisors, and executive functionaries in the late eighteenth- and nineteenth-century Maratha court, see Michaels, "The Pandit as a Legal Advisor," 61–66.

6. I am deeply grateful to the anonymous reader of my manuscript who gave me the most thoughtful and compelling suggestions for how to revise this chapter.

attempt given that he was critiquing some core beliefs of Brahminism? It was certainly reformist, and radical in its rhetoric, at least in parts. At the same time, however, he was recasting issues of exclusion to apply to groups outside the Hindu fold. And as he did so, he used an elite Hindu cultural idiom to establish his own authoritative voice. This idiom arguably made his caste critique far more appealing to caste Hindus who could, without too much effort, reform their practices and remain Hindu. The radical power of Savarkar's critique lay in this expansive reconfiguration of Hindu belonging which he extended without any qualifications to the entire untouchable community; the weakness of his critique was that he assumed that he could wish untouchability away solely by attacking the insularity of the upper castes rather than the structures of oppression themselves.

His critique of caste focused on both the prejudice and ritual that attended any transposition of sacred values onto social rather than political forms. For him, Hindu became a single meta-category, removed of caste markings (including, perhaps most significantly, the marked role of Brahmanism in most contemporary understandings of caste). Unlike Gandhi, Savarkar wrote of jettisoning caste, not redefining it, and replacing it with a unified category that included all Hindus. He also refused to follow Ambedkar in abandoning the terms "Hindu" or "Hindutva"—a decision made easier because Savarkar refused to accept the connection between "Hindu" and caste prejudice—embracing the terms instead as necessary and empowering. But he never explained how replacing *jati* with the more capacious category of "Hindu" would by itself eliminate longstanding, deep structural practices of hierarchy.

Savarkar described ritual observance as silly superstition and caste as divisive. Ritual and worship had no intrinsic value for him, nor did he understand its affective hold on caste Hindu society. He rejected the idea that Vedic Hinduism was relevant to modern social forms, dismissing suggestions that Vedic sacrifice was important or should accord Brahmins special privileges or power. At the same time, everything from his use of genre and rhetoric to his deep knowledge of Sanskrit betrayed his caste status and comfort level as a Brahmin.[7] In other words, his sense that caste could be addressed simply by ridiculing and dismissing the power and importance of Brahminic ritual in everyday

7. Vasant Palshikar made much the same argument but in passing. He wrote, "The irrationality in Savarkar's argument does not seem to have been deliberately produced. Such things often happen unknowingly. But the root of such thinking is in our minds, our class, our caste status, and our self-interest. Palshikar, "Jatyuchedak nibandh," 176–78.

life was based on his inability (or unwillingness) to examine his own Brahmin subject position.

For all his iconoclasm about ritual observance, Savarkar believed in the sacred; indeed, his life's work was a project of sacralization. Yet, he defied convention by insisting that the cow, Vedic chants, and prayers were themselves not sacred. What was sacred to Savarkar was the nation. This was a distinctly modern political theology, an invocation of ancient distinctions between the sacred and the profane that conferred any residual religious values directly onto the idea of the Indian (and Hindu) territorial nation. This meant that the profane had nothing to do with an absence of belief in God or failure to practice rituals but with the denial of the centrality of the nation for worship and identity. Savarkar emptied Hindu life of most rituals, but before their lack could be felt, he substituted them with a different set of rituals in the service of the worship of another. Access to the nation was Savarkar's dogma, and insofar as caste as a system of division prevented some groups (especially "untouchables") from fully participating in the Indian nation, he attacked caste.

Lastly, Savarkar's caste critique was almost always instrumental; he cared primarily (if not solely) about creating a unified Hindu community that would be better able to oppose Muslims. All his writings on caste also reveal an underlying animus toward Muslims. Savarkar attacked the conservative Hindu caste community for its extremism (*paramāvadhī*) about *viṭāḷvēḍa* (pollution paranoia), which enabled Muslims to convert Hindus.[8] Savarkar's radicalism on the caste question was a direct result of the fear of Muslims, which was also the very thing that made his argument more persuasive for many of his readers, then and later.

If we only read Savarkar on caste, it would be easy to conclude that his politics were radical. It is similarly easy, if we read Savarkar's writings on Muslims separately from his attacks on the religious basis for caste, to miss the integral connections between them. As mentioned, many of Savarkar's writings (including his poems) about caste and untouchability were in publications such as *Kesari, Shraddhananda, Kirloskar, Pratibha, Nirbheed, Sahyadri, Jyotsna, Manohar, Stree, Maharashtra Sharada, Aryamitra, Vaishyayuvak, Bhala, Garjana, Rangarjana.*[9] The founder and editor (Shankarrao Kirloskar) of the

8. I am grateful to Christian Novetzke for helping me with this translation.

9. Karandikar, *Savarkar Charitra*, 500–501. See Kamble, *Swatantryavira Savarkaranche*, 70–74, for a list by publication and date of all of Savarkar's articles written while in Ratnagiri. Savarkar's time in the Andamans was serialized in the Marathi newspaper, *Kesari*. Later, he

magazine *Kirloskar*, who published a large number of Savarkar's articles on caste, noted in his autobiography that he removed many of Savarkar's most objectionable claims about non-Hindus. In other words, even in Savarkar's own time, editors and publishers of Marathi magazines recognized that Savarkar's words were incendiary. Kirloskar wrote,

> As good luck would have it in that precise moment we began receiving Savarkar's excellent articles one after the other. Those articles had the spirit of awakening the readers but at the same time they contained sarcastic remarks about non Hindus. I had to filter them out. I of course made sure that it did not damage the original article.[10]

The readers of these publications belonged to the same community as Savarkar: upper-caste Hindus, Brahmin and non-Brahmin, the emerging urban Maharashtrian middle class. It was to them that Savarkar advocated breaking caste taboos and denounced longstanding traditional practices such as the taboo against interdining. And his supporters described him as having endured untold suffering for advocating such reforms. One of Savarkar's supporters remembered the reaction of the orthodox community in Ratnagiri to his work, noting that

> Tatya had to endure extreme difficulties. With my own eyes, I have seen the steps taken by our Tatya in the tiny little huts of the untouchables.[11]

To state the obvious, Brahminism (*Brahmanya*) hardly disappeared because a Brahmin ventured into a Dalit hut. It bolstered a reformist Brahminism and never addressed the conditions of the lives that were lived in those tiny little huts.

It is useful here to compare B. R. Ambedkar's external critique of Brahminism with Savarkar's internal one. Ambedkar positioned himself outside the Hindu religion. He pointed a finger at *Brahmanya*, noting that, because Brahmins determined the norms of Hinduism, there was little distinction between "Brahmin" and "Hindu." Savarkar's critique, by contrast, was internal, with both speaker and audience located within the social and religious space of Brahminism. We see this in his actions in Ratnagiri, including in the poems

---

wrote in almost every issue of *Shraddhanand*, a weekly founded after Swami Shraddhanand's murder, which ceased publication four years later. After *Shraddhanand* closed, Savarkar wrote for *Kirloskar*.

10. Kirloskar, *Shanavakiya*, 268.

11. Salvi, *Savarakara Yancya Athavani*, 52.

he wrote about the *patitpavan* (purifying the impure) temple, holding intermixed Brahminic *haḷadī-kuṅkūṁ* (religious ceremonies in which upper-caste women exchange vermillion and turmeric, symbols of fertility and purity), and his desire to "uplift" (*uddhār*) rather than "emancipate" (*mukti*) or "liberate" Dalits. All of his actions speak to his desire to unite all Indians, though under a Brahmin umbrella and, if possible, under enlightened Brahmin leadership (beginning with himself).

Savarkar's writings thus had a paradoxical effect. Even as he attacked his middle-class and orthodox (Sanātani) Marathi readers for their extreme anxiety about losing caste status, he made the critique more palatable by elevating ethnicity or nationality over caste, giving a progressive sheen to this act of symbolic transference. When we contrast Savarkar's writings with those of Ambedkar and Gandhi, other features come into relief. Ambedkar and Gandhi's critiques aimed not just at raising consciousness about untouchability but eradicating it as a practice that oppresses and brutalizes an entire community. Their critiques had a moral and ethical dimension. Ambedkar's caste critique was also buttressed by the full personal experience of the pain, humiliation, and systematic deprivations of untouchability. He put his rhetoric into action, publicly burning the Manusmṛti and later—as a public statement expressing the fundamental inseparability of Brahmanism from Hinduism—converting to Buddhism. Gopal Guru has termed Ambedkar's emancipatory discourse "the rejection of the rejection."[12] At the same time, while Gandhi championed his ideal version of *varnāsharamadharma*, and was clearly aware—as was Savarkar—of the threat to the Hindu community posed by the possible secession of untouchables from the Hindu fold, he regularly engaged in practices that were meant to illustrate his ideals and change social norms. His insistence that a Dalit couple be part of his first Indian ashram experiment, for example, or his living in a sweeper's colony near the end of his life were clearly deeply unsettling to the upper-caste elite.

Ramnarayan Rawat and K. Satyanarayana have pointed out that all upper-caste anticolonial nationalists, whether Gandhi or Nehru, spoke of untouchability as a social ill in need of abolition in a variety of patronizing and condescending

12. Rawat and Satyanarayana, *Dalit Studies*, 15, 33. Gopal Guru argues that Ambedkar rejected both Gandhi's rejection of the West and the modern. He points out that Ambedkar recognized that while India as a modern nation may perhaps have attempted to organize society on the basis of egalitarian principles it had neither the ability nor the will to enforce them.

ways. None of these ways afforded Dalits a real voice.[13] Savarkar was no exception, though he was explicit in instrumentalizing what Ambedkar called the annihilation of caste in a Hindu-universalizing cause. Savarkar turned all *jatis* into one super-caste—Hindu—thereby setting the stage for the full co-optation of Dalits into a Hindutva agenda.

I start this discussion of caste with a brief history of the political milieu and the debates about caste and untouchability that took place before Savarkar's return in 1921 into which he would soon insert himself.

Non-Brahmin and Anti-untouchability Movements in Maharashtra in the 1920s

Because Savarkar lived outside of India from 1907 to 1921, he did not participate in the conversations, struggles, and debates about untouchability, casteism, and Brahminism that took place during those years in Maharashtra. But he could not have been unaware of the two separate but linked challenges to Brahminism that emerged in the region. The first confronted untouchability and the entire edifice of caste, which was viewed as a system of Brahmin domination designed to subjugate the Bahujan community.[14] The second targeted Brahmins' exclusive control over and access to ritual observances and spaces that were the cornerstone of Hindu orthopraxy. Together these movements attacked three interlinked terms: Hindu, Brahmin, and caste.

The modern movement against untouchability began in 1840, when Jyotiba Phule launched what would be a multipronged, forty-year campaign against the literal and metaphorical sacred cows of Hindu/Vedic orthodoxy.[15] In prose, poetry, and polemics (*Gulamgiri*) and the work of his Satyashodhak Samaj organization (founded in 1875), Phule equated caste with Brahminism. He argued that the central moving force in Hindu society was the struggle between Brahmins and those they oppressed. Phule rewrote ancient Indian

13. Rawat and Satyanarayana, *Dalit Studies*, 2, 16, 17.

14. B. R. Ambedkar used the term *bahujan* to refer to all those who had been discriminated against based on caste. It is an old term that literally means "majority." "Dalit" is the word used for the community which for much of the twentieth century was called "untouchable." I only use the term "untouchable" in this chapter when it would seem anachronistic not to, with the full recognition that the term conveys all of the opprobrium attached to a severely oppressed community in India's history.

15. For a detailed discussion of Jyotiba Phule, see O'Hanlon, *Caste, Conflict and Ideology*.

history as a history of usurpation and colonization of the original inhabitants of the land (the Sudras-Atisudras) by foreign Aryans who imposed an alien Vedic Brahminism on the indigenous residents.[16] Phule's supporters, including Dr. Vishram Ghole—a medical practitioner—and Krishnarao Bhalekar—who started the newspaper *Deenbandhu* (which Narayan Lokhande edited from Bombay until 1897)—proliferated his views throughout Maharashtra.[17] Following in Phule's footsteps, Maharshi Vitthal Ramji Shinde established the Depressed Classes Mission in 1906, campaigning to end untouchability and establishing schools and hostels for untouchables.[18]

With Phule's death, the Satyashodhak movement split, with one group rejecting the entire complex of Hinduism/Brahminism and the other moving back to or remaining within the Hindu fold.[19] Keshavrao Thakare, a passionate and polemical advocate for Kshatriya-hood, for instance, joined the Satyashodhak Samaj but wished to keep the category "Hindu" intact. In 1921, he began publishing a journal called *Prabodhan* (*Awakening*) that took up issues of social reform and Brahmin privilege.[20] Although passionately Hindu and an advocate of Hindu unity, Thakare did not conceive of Hindutva as inextricable from Brahminism. A polemicist par excellence, he offered the provocative view that Brahminism and Hinduism constituted two separate and distinguishable religions.[21]

The second important challenge to Brahminism came from the non-Brahmin (Brahmanetar) community. It began in October 1899, nine years after Jyotiba Phule's death, when what became known as the Vedokta controversy was set off when a Brahmin priest tried to trick the non-Brahmin ruler of

16. O'Hanlon, *Caste, Conflict and Ideology*.

17. See Bhadru, "Contribution of Satyashodhak Samaj."

18. On Vitthal Ramji Shinde, see Pawar, *Vitthal Ramji Shinde*. See also Gore, *Vitthal Ramji Shinde*, and Zelliott, "Experiments in Dalit Education." Maharshi Shinde and B. R. Ambedkar disagreed fundamentally about the path forward for the Dalit community, with the former believing in their "uplift" and the latter in the abolition of untouchability. They also disagreed about the franchise. Shinde wanted an education (fourth-grade) and employment (annual income of forty-four rupees) qualification; Ambedkar did not. See Fulzele and Meshram, "V. R. Shinde: An Analysis."

19. Sarwate, "Reimagining the Modern Hindu Self," ch. 1. Sarwate shows that for all its progressivism, the anti-Brahmin movement stayed within the confines of what was imagined as a new Hinduism rather than moving away from it altogether.

20. See Thakare, *Majhi Jeevangatha*.

21. For a brief discussion of Thakare's views, see Sarwate, "Reimagining the Modern Hindu Self," 36–37.

Kolhapur Shahu Maharaj into believing he was receiving Vedic rites when he was actually getting Puranic ones. When found out, the priest justified his actions by claiming that Shahu Maharaj was not entitled to receive Vedic rites because he was not a Kshatriya.[22] This loss of status came as quite a surprise to Shahu Maharaj, not least because he was a descendant of Chhatrapati Shivaji, who had been anointed a Kshatriya by a priest brought explicitly for that purpose from Benaras in 1674.[23] The controversy generated a fierce debate about Brahmin arrogance, privilege, and exclusive power over the religious rituals central to everyday upper-caste Hindu life. It united Phule's Satyashodhaks with members of the non-Brahmin movement and persisted long after the immediate issue was resolved when Shahu Maharaj set up alternate, non-Brahmin sources of religious authority and learning and appointed a Maratha (i.e., non-Brahmin) as *Shankaracharya* (spiritual head).

The anti-Brahmin discourse created by the Vedotka controversy was fierce, with much of it directed at a Chitpavan Brahmin source of pride: the Peshwai (the Chitpavan Brahmin ministers/rulers of the Maratha state, 1707–1818). The critique was both moralistic, targeting the Peshwai as a period of extreme debauchery and oppression,[24] and reformist, attacking the Peshwai for having reinstated orthodox Brahminism, including *varnāshramadharma* and *gopratipālana* (cow protection), and, as Sudha Desai has argued, for setting aside earlier challenges to Brahminical authority and the exclusivity of Vedic ritual.[25]

22. Sarwate, "Reimagining the Modern Hindu Self," ch. 1. Sarwate presents a concise yet detailed historiographical and intellectual history of the Vedokta controversy. On the historical roots of the controversy, see Deshpande, "Ksatriyas in the Kali Age?," 105–6. On the Vedokta controversy itself, see Phadke, *Shahu Chhatrapati ani Lokmanya* [in Marathi], and, in English, Copland, "The Maharaja of Kolhapur;" O'Hanlon, "Maratha History as Polemic;" O'Hanlon, *Caste, Conflict and Ideology*; and Wagle, "Ritual and Change in Early Nineteenth-Century Society." See also Omvedt, *Cultural Revolt in a Colonial Society*.

23. Deshpande, "Ksatriyas in the Kali Age?".

24. Sarwate, "Reimagining the Modern Hindu Self," 53–55. For the emergence of a Marathi public sphere, see Naregal, *Language, Hierarchy and Identity*. On the tussle between Brahmin reformers and Brahmin conservatives on caste, see Parimala V. Rao's excellent, incisive, and detailed "A Century of Consolidation and Resistance."

25. See Desai, *Social Life in Maharashtra*. Reviewing Desai's book, N. G. Bhavare points out that during the Peshwai, Brahmins

> were exempted from payment of ferry charges, octroi duties on transport of goods, house tax, etc. They were further permitted to pay land assessment in cash at low rates. They were exempted from *veth* or forced labour, death punishment, mutilation of limbs and other harsh punishments for any serious crime.

Much of this debate took place in a thriving non-Brahmin public sphere created by the founding of newspapers and weeklies such as *Vijayi Maratha*.[26]

In response to these challenges, the Brahmin community, never unanimous, splintered further. Savarkar's mentor and hero B. G. Tilak (a Chitpavan Brahmin) opposed all of Shahu Maharaj's actions after the event, calling them mere faddishness.[27] Orthodox interpreters of the Dharmaśāstras argued against Shahu Maharaj on the grounds that in the Kali period there were no Kshatriyas. Some Brahmin progressives argued that all Marathas should be immediately recognized as Kshatriya, and still others, including historian V. K. Rajwade, asked if by placing such importance on Vedic rituals, the Maratha community was not ceding too much authority and power to Brahmins.[28] Brahmin scholars also began to explore caste, examining, explaining, and in some cases defending its putative origins, history, and manifestations. One scholar whose work received acclaim in India and abroad was S. V. Ketkar (whom we met in the previous chapter being surveilled in the US). Ketkar received his PhD at Cornell University and wrote a two-volume dissertation on caste in India. He published the first one as *The History of Caste in India: Evidence of the Laws of Manu on the Social Conditions in India during the Third Century A.D., Interpreted and Examined; with an Appendix on the Radical Defects in Ethnology* in 1909.[29] The second, published ten years later, was called

---

Bhavare, "Review of *Social Life in Maharashtra under the Peshwas*." See also Deshpande, "Pune: An Emerging Center of Education," 60–68, which describes in detail Peshwa largesse to Brahmins and Brahmin educators in Pune, particularly in the period after the first Bajirao Peshwa made Pune his residence and built the Shanivar Vada palace fort.

26. On the politics of the struggles of the Marathas, other non-Brahmins, and Brahmins in this rapidly changing public sphere, see Sawant, "Marathas, Brahmin and Non-Brahmin Contestations," and Botre, "The Body Language of Caste," 53–55.

27. For Tilak's role in the controversy, see N. R. Phatak's Marathi biography *Lokmanya*. For an English-language overview, Dhananjay Keer's biography of Tilak deals with this episode in detail. (Keer, *Lokamanya Tilak*). For an excellent summary and analysis of Brahmin dominance and the struggles against it in the city of Pune, see Omvedt, "Non-Brahmans and Nationalists."

28. For a succinct examination of the origins of the disputes about Kshatriya status and whether there were any Kshatriyas in the Kali age or whether they were fallen Kshatriyas who could be restored in status, see Deshpande, "Ksatriyas in the Kali Age?"

29. For a critical review of Ketkar's work, see Franklin Edgerton's review in *The American Political Science Review*. Edgerton was a linguistics scholar and professor of Sanskrit and comparative philology at Yale and briefly a visiting professor at Benares Hindu University. He pointed out that Ketkar's work was marred by his nationalist desire to avoid presenting the caste

An Essay on Hinduism, Its Formation and Future. In the meantime, Ketkar wrote articles in *Kesari* on caste, getting embroiled in fierce arguments on the origins of caste and Buddhism and sounding much like Savarkar in suggesting that the Hindu community move away from religion and toward a more inclusive "Hindu" unity.[30]

Another engaged scholar was Shripad Mahadev Mate, a prominent Tilakite and Marathi intellectual from Pune, who compiled essays he had published in *Kesari* into a short work entitled *Asprushya Vichar* (Thoughts on Untouchables).[31] Mate cast himself as an anthropologist of sorts, noting in his foreword that he had lived among the "untouchable" community since 1917 and could speak personally of their tribulations. Although he wrote to disabuse caste Hindus of their notion that they were not casteist, his position was fundamentally conservative and suffused with Brahmin noblesse oblige. Patronizing and condescending in equal measure, it satisfied nobody.[32]

The Brahmin progressive wing, represented by intellectuals and scholars often affiliated with the Pradnya Pathshala, a revivalist school for Sanskrit learning located in the small town of Wai near Pune, opposed Tilakite politics. The school convened conferences of Dharmaśāstra scholars in Maharashtra in the 1920s and debated the reforms within Vedism/Hinduism. Against orthodox Brahmins who insisted that the Vedas were divine and changeless, the Pradnya Pathshala scholars argued for the Vedas' historicity and secularity[33]

---

system negatively. It was also too Brahminic in tone and content, and Edgerton faults Ketkar for not delving deeply into the Vedas and for dismissing Buddhism.

30. For an analysis of Ketkar's contributions to the "encyclopaedic age" and his arguments with other scholars including D. D. Kosambi and Narayan Pavgee on the issue of caste and its origins, see Phadke, *Vyakti ani Vichar*, 87–88.

31. Mate, *Asprushya Vichar*. For an examination of Mate's writings, see Bhagwat, "Shri Shripad Mahadeva Mate," 219.

32. Christian Novetzke has argued that much of the Varkari critique was also similarly conservative. See Novetzke, *Religion and Public Memory*. See also Chakradhar's response to menses and pollution in the *Lilacharitra* in Novetzke, *The Quotidian Revolution*, and Botre, "The Body Language of Caste," 70, 71. Ambedkar saw little to choose between orthodox and progressive reformers but noted that the latter convinced people they were genuinely reform-minded when they just wanted to purge Brahminism of certain practices.

33. See Sarwate, "Reimagining the Modern Hindu Self," 101–9. Sarwate gives us a visual map (106) of the Dharmaśāstra debate in Maharashtra that helps sort out the differences and similarities in the positions held by the Brahmin intelligentsia, whether reformist or orthodox, and how those positions dovetailed with European currents of intellectual thought and the internal deep dive into Vedic philosophy.

and pointed to instances of merit-based caste mobility in India's ancient history. They noted that caste had no genetic basis and wondered how religious Hindus could believe that a unifying God (Brahmadev) could produce caste differentiation. Finally, if true knowledge was the measure of *Brahmanya* then most Brahmins fell short.[34] These conversations are indicative of the historical moment in which an upper-caste community was being called upon to reform its practices and move into the modern world.

The long-term effect of these debates was the emergence of a powerful non-Brahmin Maratha political community. In 1921, a year before he died, Shahu Maharaj made a public statement in a Baroda newspaper.[35] Even though he had granted significant support to the non-Brahmin struggle and implemented measures to eliminate Brahmin power, he insisted that he had never been affiliated with Phule's Satyashodhak Samaj and that he had always accepted Vedic ritual authority.[36] Despite this, the non-Brahmin movement continued, led by two Satyashodhaks, Keshavrao Jedhe (1896–1949) and Dinkarrao Javalkar (1898–1932), both followers of Jyotiba Phule.[37] The two met when they jointly protested the city of Pune's decision to honor Tilak, roiling the city with savage critiques of Chitpavan Brahmin conservatism on intercaste marriage, their celebration of the Peshwai, and their antireform stances.[38] Javalkar in particular targeted Tilak, who before his death five years earlier had opposed the passage of an intercaste marriage bill proposed by Valabhbhai Patel in the

34. Sarwate, "Reimagining the Modern Hindu Self," ch. 1–3, for all the participants in this debate. See Navalgundkar, "Sva. Vinayak Damodar Savarkar," 170, for a list of the claims Savarkar made about these issues. See also Palshikar, "Jaatyuchedak nibandh," 176–78, for a list of Savarkar's activities undertaken to destroy caste in Ratnagiri. They included writing essays; singing bhajans in the Mahar community's neighborhood and bringing Mahars to sing bhajans in a mixed community; intermixing children in school; distributing *sōnēm* (leaves of the *Āpaṭa* tree) and *tiḷaguḷa* (sesame and jaggery) to a mixed community on Dussehra and Sankrant; doing mixed *haḷadī-kuṅkūṁ*; starting a band; finding jobs for members of the "untouchable community"; hosting *melas*; and supporting temple entry.

35. Sarwate, "Reimagining the Modern Hindu Self," 30.

36. See Deshpande, *Scripts of Power*, 242, 254. Shahu Maharaj abolished the post of *Kulkarni* (Brahman revenue collectors and administrators) and *watan* (hereditary land grants), and abolished Modi writing in all administrative documents in his court because of its association with Brahmin scribal authority.

37. Phadke, *Vyakti ani Vicar*, 66. Jedhe was born into a relatively wealthy family, but Javalkar was not. He was financially supported by Shahu Maharaj.

38. Phadke, *Vyakti ani Vicar*, 66.

Delhi Central Assembly in September 1918 on the grounds that it would dilute Hindu culture.[39]

In 1925 (when Savarkar was settling in Ratnagiri) Jedhe was elected to the Pune municipality, where he found numerous ways to call out Brahmin leaders for their reactionary behavior.[40] One of his first actions was to recommend erecting a commemorative statue to Jyotiba Phule to go with existing statues of Chiplunkar and Tilak.[41] Tilak's supporters refused to support this, in response to which Jedhe's colleague Javalkar wrote a forty-page polemic titled *Dēśācē Duśmana* (Enemies of the land) that extended the Phule-ite argument that Brahmins had used chicanery to trick the original inhabitants of the subcontinent.[42] Javalkar's language, described by Phadke as "*bhaḍaka, tikhaṭa*" (fiery, spicy) was insulting and provocative, indexing the deep frustration at the constant obstacles obdurate upper-caste elites placed in the way of reform.[43] He wrote:

> When the Supreme God hosted a banquet of virtues, these two Brahmins Tilak and Chiplunkar ate with such alacrity, there were no virtues left for anyone else. To uplift the West, one son of the God came forth; but for the East, to hold forth the flag of Brahminism platoon after platoon has poured forth and its generals are Tilak and Chiplunkar . . . When one says Maharashtra, what comes to mind are Tilak-Chiplunkar-Kelkar-Lavate-Kavade-Devdhar, Joshi—such great national paragons of perfection, aka monsters. Maharashtra's main mouthpiece is Kesari. This mouthpiece has 22 but even more 36 teeth, each of them habituated to orthodox chewing and are both so beautiful and swollen that if anyone other than a Brahmin raises his head they instantly clamp down on his gullet. If one dispassionately investigates

39. Jagadeesan, "Secularising the Institution of Marriage." For a discussion of the Patel Bill, see also Mandal, "Ambedkar's Illegal Marriage." For an excellent summary and analysis of reform politics in Pune, where Brahmins were culturally dominant, and the Jedhe family's participation in it, see Omvedt, "Non-Brahmans and Nationalists," 203–5.

40. Phadke, *Vyakti ani Vichar*, 70, 71.

41. Dahiwale, "Consolidation of Maratha Dominance in Maharashtra." See also Omvedt, "Non-Brahmans and Nationalists."

42. For a description of the extent to which the Jedhe-Javalkar attack on Brahmins and Brahminism roiled Pune and the Brahmin intelligentsia, see Phadke, *Vyakti ani Vicar*.

43. Phadke, *Vyakti ani Vicar*, 66. Javalkar, from Kolhapur, ran a paper called *Tarun Maratha*, in which he went after Tilakites, particularly Narayanrao Gunjal, who was an orthodox leader deeply opposed to Dalit mobilization. See also Rao, *Caste Question*, 93–94.

> the character of these patriots Tilak and Chiplunkar one would have to easily accept that they are not patriots but debased (lowly) traitors.[44]

After identifying Tilak and Chiplunkar as the true traitors to the nation, Javalkar went after the entire community of Chitpavan Brahmins, likening them to cobras, punning on the "Ko" in Konkanastha and the "Bra" in Brahmin.

> Having slithered up the mountains from the Konkan, and by now accustomed to slithering, another treacherous group of these cobras (Ko-bra) came back over the mountain. The previous snakes now have these cobras to add to their number so is it possible that there would be any limit to injustice, and irreligiosity? Some Brahmins for their own advancement have used any and all means available for their own greed. To prove this the history of the Peshwai suffices. These traffickers in women and blackeners of civilization—these are our upper caste gurus![45]

From such people, Javalkar fumed, one could expect nothing.

> For a Brahmin who sleeps with prostitutes, and a Brahmin woman who sleeps with Sudras, if the shadow of an untouchable touches them they expel him, cast him away–these Brahmamonster Peshwas and their traditions were watched and fostered by these Satanic Tilak[s] and Chiplunkar[s]. . . . As long as these endless generations of Tilaks crawl out of the sewer like earthworms, the independence of Untouchables will remain a worrying question. 'Brahmin' is such a thing that it cannot be born without slavery and cannot survive without prejudice.[46]

Javalkar's book roiled not just the Pune community; it made news up and down the state.[47] When a young Brahmin girl was attacked in Pune by a non-Brahmin, the Tilakites sued Javalkar for defamation,[48] claiming that his insults of Hindu gods and goddesses and epics had undermined societal connections between religion and morality.[49] Such was the complicated political and

44. Javalkar, *Dēśācē Duśmana*, 8, 9.
45. Javalkar, *Dēśācē Duśmana*, 13.
46. Javalkar, *Dēśācē Duśmana*, 15.
47. Omvedt, "Non-Brahmans and Nationalists."
48. Shelar, "The Role of Dinkarrao Javalkar," 599.
49. Omvedt, "Non-Brahmans and Nationalists." For an incisive and detailed analysis of Tilak's politics, see P. V. Rao, "Educating Women and Non-Brahmins" in her *Foundations of Tilak's Nationalism*.

literary milieu that Savarkar returned to when he was finally brought to Maharashtra in 1924. The movement against caste was riven with tensions about whether reform should be pursued through amelioration, structural change, or complete rejection.

While the debate in Maharashtra (and in large parts of southern India), especially that generated by Javalkar, was about both the non-Brahmin movement and untouchability, the larger national debate in northern India about caste focused on untouchability alone.[50] Gandhi called himself a Sanātani Hindu and was adamant that Hinduism could purge itself of casteism and untouchability and thus did not have to be jettisoned. On returning from South Africa in 1914, he made untouchability a central plank of his anticolonial agenda despite his perplexing defense of *varnāshramadharma* as difference without hierarchy.[51] D. R. Nagaraj describes Gandhi's stance as being in line with a range of ascetic mendicants, yogis, and sadhus in combining a national anti-untouchability social reformist agenda with spiritual self-improvement.[52] But it did not make Gandhi acceptable to Ambedkar, who emerged in the 1920s as a powerful successor to Jyotiba Phule when he called for the eradication of untouchability and turned it into a powerful political identity. Ambedkar and Gandhi clashed on most issues connected to untouchability and caste.

Ambedkar did not believe that Gandhi was ready to give up the core Brahminic components of caste, or that any Marathi Brahmin reformers, conservative or liberal, were genuinely interested in a structural dismantling of the caste system. Ambedkar was also clear about the posturing of Brahmins. In a damning statement, he noted,

> Statistics will show that the intelligentsia and the Brahmin caste are exchangeable terms. The disposition of the intelligentsia is a Brahmin disposition. Its outlook is a Brahmin outlook. Though he has learned to speak in the name of all, the Brahmin leader is in no sense a leader of the people. He is a leader of his caste at best, for he feels for them as he does for no other people. It is not intended to say that there are no Brahmins who feel for the

50. See Irschick, *Politics and Social Conflict in South India*, for an account of the rise of the non-Brahmin movement in Madras Presidency during the first decades of the twentieth century.

51. Ambedkar disagreed. He believed Gandhi was solely interested in turning the INC into a militant organization and using it to secure widespread Hindu support for the Khilafat movement. See Ambedkar, *Gandhi and Gandhism*, 48–49.

52. See Nagaraj and Shobhi, *The Flaming Feet and Other Essays*, 26–27.

untouchables. To be just, there are a few more moderate and rational Brahmins who admit the frightful nature of the institution of untouchability in the abstract and perceive the dangers to society with which it is fraught. But the great majority of the Brahmins are those who doggedly deny the horrors of the system in the teeth of such a mass of evidence as never was brought to bear on any other subject and to which the experience of every day contributes its immense amount; who, when they speak of freedom, mean the freedom to oppress their kind and to be savage, merciless and cruel, and whose inalienable rights can only have their growth in the wrongs of the untouchables.[53]

Ambedkar exposed the hypocrisy of Brahmin progressivism as not just limited but self-serving, recognizing that it served only to maintain caste endogamy.[54] In April 1927 he started a periodical in Marathi, *Bahishkrut Bharat*, and spent the next two years attacking high-caste reform leaders for their hypocrisy, asserting untouchables' right to enter temples, and warning that equal rights were not for upper castes to bestow but for the community to demand and take, whether within Hinduism or "by kicking away this worthless Hindu identity."[55] Ambedkar denounced the charity model of justice in which minimal concessions were offered by Brahmins and other upper castes as the solution for centuries of oppression.[56]

Savarkar Returns to India

When Ambedkar suggested kicking away a "worthless Hindu identity," Savarkar would have been horrified. Savarkar's central and urgent political concern was to use a broad notion of Hindu identity to establish a politically unified Hindu nation that could withstand the Muslim threat. For him the main question was not reform for reform's sake but whether one could forge

53. Ambedkar, "Evidence before the Southborough Committee on Franchise," 267–68.

54. See Botre, "The Body Language of Caste," 69–74, for a discussion of radical Dalit opposition to Brahminism.

55. Fitzgerald, "Politics and Ambedkar Buddhism in Maharashtra," 83.

56. Thirty years later, in 1956, fed up with Sanātani reformers such as Mate and Gandhi, Ambedkar and 50,000 of his followers converted to Buddhism. For a detailed examination of this debate and its participants, see Sarwate, "Reimagining the Modern Hindu Self," ch. 1. For the position of one reformer whom Ambedkar disliked, see Mate, *Asprushya Vichar*. See also Omvedt, "Non-Brahmans and Nationalists," and O'Hanlon, "Caste and Its Histories."

a path to caste equality that did not reject all Hindu cultural idioms because the question of political unity hinged on maintaining a fundamental "Hinduness" and Hindu belonging. This was neither Gandhi's reform nor Ambedkar's rejection. Where Gandhi stayed away from the Dharmaśāstric literature, turning instead to the Sermon on the Mount or the demotic Rāmāyaṇa to make his case, Savarkar dove straight into elite Sanskrit literature. Where Ambedkar conjoined "Hindu" and "Brahmin," Savarkar split them, suggesting that one became a better Hindu if one shed Brahminism's useless ritualism and illogical beliefs. Savarkar understood Brahminism primarily as occupational monopoly and to a lesser extent as intellectual chicanery. The monopoly over the tasks performed by Purohits/Pujaris could easily be broken, according to Savarkar, by a declaration of independence. The intellectual chicanery could be dispelled if everyone, including the untouchable community, became their own Brahmins and took over their own rituals.

Savarkar attempted to have it both ways: to enact radical reform without completely alienating the privileged elite.[57] By suggesting a radical reduction of Brahminism—by bringing down the necessary rituals (*saṃskāras*) from the mandated sixteen to only the essential three (naming ceremony, thread ceremony, and mourning), advocating marrying in a registrar's office, and conducting one's own rituals in Sanskritized Marathi—Savarkar believed it was possible to reconfigure and update Brahminism for the twentieth century. Despite his apparent rejection of all the trappings of Brahminism, however, he never launched a political group resembling any of the non- or anti-Brahman movements that dominated western and southern India during those years. Indeed, Vasant Palshikar has pointed out that Savarkar's actions took place in a very limited domain: "in and out of the house, and only up to a certain limit, on selected religious and cultural occasions, people should abrogate high and low casteism and untouchability."[58] And yet, he did outline a path that was meant to be an alternative to Gandhi's ideas of ethical reform and to Ambedkar's revolutionary and rejectionist agenda.

To reconfigure this Hindu identity, Savarkar went straight to the most orthodox: the adherents of Sanātan Dharma (eternal law), whom many presumed

57. See Walinjkar, *Uttar Konkan Dalitmukti*, 198–99, which suggests as much, referring to Savarkar's efforts to symbolically open one temple and make one well available to Dalitbahujans; however, he focused more on building new and separate temples and wells for them, thereby leaving most Savarna temples untouched and Savarna sensibilities appeased.

58. Palshikar, "Jaatyuchedak nibandh," 178.

to be the essential carriers of the term "Hindu." In the mid-nineteenth century, in the sacred space of the Thakurdwar temple in Bombay, Krishna Shastri Sathe, a Marathi Brahmin shastri, had expressed his understanding of Sanātan Dharma, which Richard Tucker defines as "the eternal pattern of the cosmos which encompasses everything from the heavens to human society to individual lives in an intricate harmonious whole."[59] This Sanātan Dharma was inextricable from Brahminism and Brahminic rituals because "[o]n the level of human society, the cosmic harmony was expressed as varnashramadharma (orthopraxis), in which each individual and each caste (jati) had a place, regulated by the Dharmaśāstra . . . as the learned shastris like himself interpreted it."[60] Reformers, Shastris worried, were going to produce *varṇasaṃkara* (miscegenation or dilution of caste) that would result in catastrophic chaos and anarchy. These Sanātani positions were challenged by a variety of social reformers and critics, from the peculiar (and ultimately conservative) Vishnubua Brahmachari in the positions he held and advocated to Lokahitawadi Gopal Hari Deshmukh in his *Śatapatrē* (Hundred letters) to R. G. Bhandarkar and M. G. Ranade, who wanted a reformed revitalization of Hinduism, as well as Gopal Ganesh Agarkar's rationalist examination of the origins of God.[61]

Savarkar stepped into the tracks of these reformers as a Pandit/Shastri steeped in a Brahminical tradition of learning, much like his mentor Tilak, but like Lokahitavadi and Agarkar he also used the Śruti/Smr̥ti/Purāṇa/Itihās Sanskrit literary-religious tradition against itself. No two pieces that Savarkar wrote were absent of Sanskrit quotations either from the Mahābhārata, the

59. Tucker, "Hindu Traditionalism and Nationalist Ideologies," 326.

60. Tucker, "Hindu Traditionalism and Nationalist Ideologies," 326.

61. Lokahitawadi, in particular, savaged Brahmins in his letters. See his attacks on Brahmins as ignorant, corrupt, debauched, and altogether useless in letters #11 (Brahmance Acar), #33 (Arthasunya Brahmanvidya), #61 (Bhatani lavun dilele Ved), #62 (Brahmananci Shikshan Padhdhati), #71 (Bhatanca Vidyeca Nirupyog), #86 (Sampratce Panditance Gyan), and #103 (Panditanchi Yogyata) in *Lokahitavadincin satapatrem*. See also Ghurye, "Social Change in Maharashtra," which gives an ethnographic account of some of the main issues that reformers like Agarkar addressed, along with the contradictions such reformist activity produced. Agarkar, for instance, stopped short of advocating eating meat, fish or even eggs! Lokahitawadi's criticism of Brahmins did not go unchallenged. Vishnushastri Chiplunkar responded equally furiously, denouncing Lokahitawadi's writerly (in)ability, knowledge, and character. See Chiplunkar, *Nibandhamala*, 957–86, 987–1016, 1017–46, 1047–74, 1075–95, for essays written in response to Lokahitawadi. For an examination of the deep conservatism of Vishnubua Brahmachari, see Palshikar, "Vishnubuva Brahmachari."

Bhaviṣyapurāṇa, the *Rājavyavahārakośa*, the Ṛgveda, the *Chāndogya* or *Vajrasūcī Upaniṣad*, or the Manusmṛti. Savarkar was an erudite but unsystematic thinker, and in his citing of Sanskrit verses he picked and chose idiosyncratically from the extant corpus, sometimes using full quotations, sometimes just a part of a couplet. He had already written his own definition of Hindutva in Sanskrit verse, following a similar verse formulation of his predecessor Tilak. But Tilak never referred to the purāṇas because of their later temporality, focusing instead on the Vedas and the principal Śrutis and Smṛtis (Manu, and *Yājñavalkya*). Savarkar was far more eclectic than his mentor, using not only the Manusmṛti, but also the purāṇas, perhaps because they were more accessible, since they were read and explained in Marathi by regularly appointed *Paurānikas* at different temples.[62]

While going after the Sanātanis, however, Savarkar invoked Muslims as the chief threat, one that could only be warded off by caste reform. In March 1925, the year after he moved to Ratnagiri from Shirgaon, he previewed much of the argument he would make for the next decade in a piece published in the *Mahratta* titled "Facts without Comments." [63] In it he recounted the abduction of Hindu women by Muslims and the forceful conversion of Brahmins into Muslims, which he claimed occurred from "Kashmir to Kamorin ad nauseum." Alongside these "facts," he offered the story of a "Devi Bhavani," a Hindu Chambhar (member of a Dalit community) who was forced to eat "unclean" food "at the hand of Mahomedans." Savarkar's concern here was that

> the whole society of the Chambhars is being intimidated and oppressed with a view to force them to embrace Islam. The *zamindars* have ordered washermen, barbers, and other castes not to render services to the Chambhars unless they leave the Hindu fold.

The article's title shows his construction of the narrative: this was not opinion. He presented himself as simply reciting the facts that showed Muslims acting violently to convert untouchables.

62. For an ethnographic analysis of how the Vedas are studied in Vedapathshalas and how they are taught, memorized, and recited as mantras at rituals, without knowing what the mantras mean, see Larios, *Embodying the Vedas*. The Vedas were not read but chanted; the Upaniṣads were "read" but only by those interested in Vedānta. On the purāṇas, with examples of eighteen of them, see Rocher, *The Puranas*, 31–34.

63. Savarkar, "Facts without Comments," *Mahratta*, March 5, 1925, reprinted in *SSV*, SSRSP, 6: 526–31.

While under house arrest, Savarkar was occasionally allowed to travel within Ratnagiri district. In 1925, for example, Savarkar gave a lecture titled "Spr̥śyōd'dhāra" (Uplift/emancipation/of touchables) in a small village. He was asked what had happened to the "अ" (the prefix "un-") before the word "Spr̥śyōd'dhāra," which would have made the title "uplift/emancipation of *un*touchables." He responded,

> [a]s regards our so-called untouchable brethren, over the centuries the egregious injustices that have been done to them, keeping in mind the need to atone for that sin today, it is the touchables that need to be liberated [from an inferior form of existence], and that is the reason the program is named the liberation of touchables."[64]

This is precisely what Ambedkar abhorred, the idea that touchables needed to be liberated, with untouchables being simply the medium through which the touchable community could reform their own prejudice. But for Savarkar it was the Sanātanis who needed liberating from their own principles before any real unity could even be imagined.

Speaking against the orthodox required audacity, something Savarkar had in abundance. Sa Pa Karandikar described Savarkar's passionate lectures, attended by several Brahmin conservatives.

> After his talk there was lively talk and debate. Finally, Vinayakrao Joshi said, "we agree with what you say but our traditions are not going to change overnight."[65]

Two years later, Savarkar began his literary campaign by writing essays for a range of Marathi magazines and periodicals.[66] Over the next decade, he would write some forty essays which, along with his other activities in Ratnagiri, secured for him his reputation as a *vijñānaniṣṭha purōgāmi* (scientific progressive). He

64. Salvi, *Savarakara Yancya Athavani*, 57.

65. Salvi, *Savarakara Yancya Athavani*, 60.

66. See Lele, *Marathi vrttapatranca itihasa*, 300–303. Many of these publications began with tiny circulations of 700–1,000 but rapidly grew. *Kesari* for instance, had a circulation in 1884 of 4,200. By 1897 it jumped to 6,750, and by 1927, when Savarkar was writing for it, its circulation was close to 25,000. Continental Press, Pune: 1984, 2004, 2009. Savarkar's various essays were subsequently compiled into five collections: *Hindutvācē pañcaprāṇa* (Hindutva's five essences), *Gāndhī Gōndhaḷa*, (Gandhian confusion), *Kṣa Kiraṇē* (X-Ray [of the Hindu disease]), *Vijñānaniṣṭha Nibandha* (Scientific essays), and *Jātyucchēdaka Nibandha* (Essays on caste abolition).

launched a multi-pronged attack in Marathi on a number of people and groups: the Sanātanis and those he called the half-Sanātanis ("*Samajists*"); the "aikyalampaṭa-varga," or unity—obsessed Gandhians; Western-infatuated Indians; conservative religious leaders and cow protectionists who opposed untouchables entering temples such as Chaunde Maharaj; ascetics such as Lahiri Maharaj; even non-Brahmin *Harikirtan Kathākāras* like Sant Tukdoji Maharaj (1909–1968), an ardent Gandhian and rural singer saint who championed progressive land reform.[67]

From his house arrest in Ratnagiri, he would surely have known of the storm Javalkar's *Dēśācē Duśmana* had produced in Maharashtra. But Savarkar, usually so pugnacious, ignored Javalkar's mudslinging at his heroes, his caste, and the Peshwai, even though Javalkar had attacked all that he held dear, going so far as to claim that

> Brahmins like Tilak are the poisonous offspring of cobras. They are a race of cacti—from the period of Chhatrapati Shivaji all evil deeds we can point to have been performed by Chitpavan Brahmins. Is there some message from God one wonders, that from the womb of Chitpavan mothers and sisters no great men like 'Tukaram, Shivaji, BajiPrabhu" should be born? From Janak to Ramkrishna right down to Shahu Chhatrapati if one were to compile a true list of great men you would not find a single Chitpavan on it.[68]

Instead of addressing Javalkar and the non-Brahmin debate directly, Savarkar wrote a passionate defense and glorification of the Chitpavan Brahmin Peshwai in his historical work *Hindu-Pad-Padashahi*, which depicted the Peshwas as providing India with a model for her struggle against the British.[69] The Peshwas had brought back precisely the ritualism, whether cow protection or *varnāshramadharma*, which Savarkar attacked a few years later, but they had established a Hindu state, and he did not present more than an idiosyncratic smattering of evidence for his historical claims.[70] Yet *Hindu-Pad-Padashahi*

67. See Damle, "A Note on Harikatha." On Tukdoji Maharaj's music and its appeal in rural Maharashtra, see Schultz, "Cosmaharaja."

68. Javalkar, *Dēśācē Duśmana*, 33.

69. Savarkar, *Hindu-Pad-Padashahi*.

70. Palshikar, "Jaatyuchedak nibandh," 179, 180. Palshikar raises questions about Savarkar sliding past precise historical answers on the evolution and development of Hindu society, on when and where and by whom precisely *varṇa* was determined, and on what humiliation he was speaking/writing of, among other issues. He wrote, "a fictional image of Vedic Hindu society was formed on the basis of Orientalist research at the time and its place was very important

should be seen as an indirect response to the Brahmanetar question that Phule, Jedhe, Javalkar, Thakare, and Ambedkar had identified. A few years after writing *Hindu-Pad-Padshahi*, in response to conservatives claiming that, had the Peshwai still been in existence, it would have stamped out caste reform, he suggested that reformers like him would more likely have been celebrated than trampled underfoot precisely because, from Chhatrapati Shivaji to the first Bajirao Peshwa and Nana Phadnavis, they were all caste reformers.[71]

That such an argument flew in the face of the critique of the Peshwai made by reformers from Phule to Brahmanetar reformers like Javalkar was beside the point. Ramchandra Narayan Lad, for instance, had opened his own work published in 1927 titled *Marāṭhyāñcē Dāsīputra arthāta Pāyapōsa Kimmatīcē Pēśavē* [The bastards of the Marathas, indeed the utterly worthless Peshwas] with these lines:

> The Peshwas and the Peshwai! Meaning the venomous duo that killed swarajya. The assassins of Hindu Pad-Patshahi. The Satanic power that smeared cowdung on the shining history of the righteous and noble Marathas. [72]

Every Brahmanetar stalwart separated the kingdom Chhatrapati Shivaji had established and the Chitpavan Brahmin Peshwai that had, in effect, succeeded it.

But Savarkar expressed little concern about Brahmins exercising political or intellectual leadership. In a historical sleight of hand, he told conservatives that the Peshwai was progressive and that he simultaneously supported the Brahmanetar demand for full and equal access to all Brahmin privileges. But first, he turned to the madness that prevented the community from coming together (*viṭāḷvēḍa*, meaning pollution paranoia/madness) and to untouchability. These two issues were integrally linked, since he believed that behavioral and idiotic obsessions about pollution were what created the untouchable problem in the first place.

---

from a Hindu nationalist point of view" (183). Savarkar's analysis also goes hand in hand with early twentieth-century historiography of the Muslim conquest of India. Both nationalist and Marxist scholars repeatedly claimed that caste was the main reason for the disunity of Indian princes and rulers, not having fallen to an external Muslim force.

71. "Jara kā āja Pēśavā'ī asatī" ("If the Peshwai were still present today"), in *SSV*, MPHS, 3: 420–21.

72. Lad, *Marathyance*. 1. From Mukundrao Patil to Prabodhankar Thakare, the Peshwai is not seen as a continuation of the Shivashahi but a rupture, a turning back and bringing back of Sanātani orthodoxy.

Savarkar and *Viṭāḷvēḍa*

Savarkar entered the public debate about untouchability by suggesting that he had spent ten years battling orthodoxy in the Andamans. He disparaged those Hindu prisoners who, to the detriment of their own health, had maintained the idiotic belief that even dry grain was instantly contaminated (*phuṭāṇē viṭāḷatāta*) by the mere touch of a Muslim. As his biographer noted,

> As soon as Savarkar realized that Hindu prisoners believed that the touch of Muslims contaminates dry grain, and as a result allowed themselves to go hungry, he challenged this idiotic belief, and gave them a mantra to use which also gave them a solution for dealing with Muslims in prison.[73]

The sarcasm in his saying "*phuṭāṇē viṭāḷatāta*" speaks volumes about his perception of the idiocy of Hindus who thought Muslim touch was powerful enough to contaminate even dried peas. Savarkar frequently reduced casteism not just to such idiocy but to simple bad conduct, both of which had created a closed mentality. This mentality was internally self-destructive, particularly as it related to *viṭāḷvēḍa*. Once the Hindu community was imperial and grand, reaching outward. Then *viṭāḷavēḍa* shackled it, cutting off its grandeur and preventing stalwart potentates from acting on their imperial ambitions because they feared crossing the waters or losing caste. Even worse, *viṭāḷvēḍa* allowed Muslims, in the past and the present, to make off with large chunks of the Hindu community by converting them.

One of the earliest pieces Savarkar published was titled "Mhaṇa-śivēna! Svīkārīna" ("Proclaim—I will touch! I will accept"), which instructs Hindus to just go out and touch untouchables and thereby erase untouchability.[74] His argument is based on his sense that untouchability could be quickly dismissed and that it needed to disappear. I quote it at length as it lays the framework for my argument.

> Take the question of upliftment of the untouchables: these seven crores Hindus who are by blood, religion, and nation our brothers, we don't bring them as close as we bring an Abdul Rashid, or Aurangzeb, or those, who in

73. Karandikar, *Savarkar Charitra*, 494.

74. *SSV*, MPHS, 3: 25–29. "Mhaṇa- śivēna! Svīkārīna" ("Proclaim—I will touch! I will accept!") was published in *Shraddhanda* on March 2, 1927. It was added to a collection titled *Hindutvācē Pañcaprāṇa* (The five essences of Hindutva), which brought together articles by Savarkar on Hindi as the national language with articles on the nature of religion.

> the past, killed so many East Bengali Hindus, nor do we treat them the same. The others, those religious enemies of ours, we give them a high perch to sit on, welcome them, sit cheek to jowl next to them. But if a single untouchable Hindu, even a saintly, innocent, straightforward devotee of Vithal (Varkari) if he were to take a bath and cleanse himself and come to our doorstep, we will refuse him entry, not allow even his shadow to fall upon us. These seven crores shudras are humans just as the rest of us. We pet cats and dogs, touch buffaloes and cows, but we won't touch the Shudras! As a result, those seven crores of Hindus who should be counted as among us are not counted as such. Because of this, we will have to deal with a terrible crisis that will befall us and for which we are going to held responsible. We have meted out inhumane treatment to them, and therefore they will not be useful to us (they will not help us). To the contrary, they are going to come in very handy for our enemies, to divide and conquer. . . . If we [accept that untouchables are Hindus], the wagging tongue of the Ali [brothers] proclaiming that half the untouchables belong to us, or the Maulvis from Hyderabad and Sindh extending their helping hand will automatically be chopped off and fall to the ground.[75]

The first sentence reveals that, for Savarkar, untouchability is inseparable from Muslims. Next, writing to his own Marathi community, he invokes a Varkari of Vithoba (devotee of Krishna) to set up the absurdity of caste Hindus denying entry even to their shadows. But he also notes that if caste Hindus don't let go of such notions, the seven crores will not be "useful," as Muslims will use them instead against caste Hindus. Untouchables must either be included in the Hindu fold or abandoned to Muslims' oppositional wiles. If caste Hindu society came to its senses, then, Savarkar assures them, "Ali's tongue that says, 'we'll take half the untouchables' or the Nizam who says, 'we'll take all of them' or the Sindhi maulvi's gaze—all of them would be stopped right then and there." The Nizam of Hyderabad occupied a significant space in the Marathi historical imagination as an opponent of the Marathas, so it makes sense that Savarkar brings him up here, given his use of the historical past.[76] The "Ali" in

75. *SSV*, MPHS, 3: 25.

76. See Faruqui, "At Empire's End," on how the Nizam broke away from Mughal control to establish a politically autonomous and almost sovereign state, while maintaining a symbolic connection to the Mughals. For the Nizam's overseas connections, always a source of anxiety for Savarkar given his belief in an international Muslim conspirary, see Beverley, *Hyderabad, British India, and the World*. For the Deccan region as a connected Indian ocean space, see Flatt, *The Courts of the Deccan Sultanates*.

question, was Mohammad Ali, one of the leaders of the Khilafat movement. More important, however, is the triangulation Savarkar introduces between Hindu/Muslim/Untouchable.[77] Muslims were bent on converting untouchables. The conditions of their life might give them reasons to consider conversion, which Hindus had to prevent.[78] Savarkar does not allow for the possibility that the untouchable community might not see itself as Hindu or might choose conversion as a means of getting away from caste oppression.

Would this immediate acceptance that untouchables were touchables require a change of heart or mind or consciousness? Would it cause caste Hindus hardship or expense? Hardly. As ruthless as Savarkar was in his prose about his fellow upper-caste Hindus' fear of pollution, and how they constrained their lives for fear of endangering their caste status, he did not seem to believe that this change would require real effort or struggle.

Nowhere in Savarkar's writings does he address the complexities of "touch." While we glean from his writings that words and the identity they conferred (i.e., Hindu) mattered enormously to him, he shows no real interest in the social power that inhered in the assumed magicality of incantative words such as those chanted by priests. Reframing these rules as mere bad behavior, action divorced of principle, a trivial exercise, allowed him to tell people to just give it up. He emphasized this point, invoking more examples about animals to illustrate that caste Hindus engaged in all manner of potentially contaminating behavior while stopping short of touching an untouchable

> You touch dogs, give milk to a snake, allow a cat that drinks a mouse's blood to put her mouth in your plate—But O Hindu! This man who is as human as you are, the Mahar, your own compatriot, who prays to the same God—Ram—as you. But you are so ashamed of him! Throw that shame away. Be ashamed of that shame!!! [79]

How could that shame be thrown away? Savarkar had an easy solution:

> Be bold in your conviction and head out, find your miserable Hindu brethren and caress them with affection. With that one gesture you will be able to reverse the fate of [turn back] the Hindu jati.[80]

77. I use the terms "touchable" and "untouchable" since to use Ambedkar's term "Dalitbahujan" in all cases would be anachronistic.

78. Navalgundkar, "Sva. Vinayak Damodar Savarkar," 171.

79. "Mhaṇa- śivēna! Svīkārīna," in *SSV*, MPHS, 3: 26.

80. "Mhaṇa- śivēna! Svīkārīna," in *SSV*, MPHS, 3: 26.

The Marathi words Savarkar uses are "pāṭhīvara prēmācā hātha phirava" which have a double meaning, referring both to a gentle hand passed over a back, as a loving mother might do to a child, and the sense of "turning back." Love could turn back or heal generations of hurt.[81] In advocating this touch, Savarkar was making an active start in the direction of abolishing untouchability, not unlike Gandhi's determination to do the same when he took on the task of cleaning toilets. While Gandhi went much further than Savarkar in addressing inner conflict and bodily cultivation, both of them began their programs with a call for an initial direct and simple action. Savarkar's readers and followers may not have seen the hidden instrumentality but instead the radicalness of a position that posited an immediate action.[82] The upper caste just needed to be loving, paternalistically so, in the model of the relationship of adult to child. Here as elsewhere, Savarkar's advice and lesson to his own upper-caste Brahmin community was that, if he as an educated Brahmin could rationally reject caste practices, so could they.

He also noted in his memoirs, which he began writing soon after returning to Ratnagiri, that even as a young boy he found the distinctions between the Brahmin Savarkars and the non-Brahmin Shimpis (tailors) dishonorable and humiliating. He wrote of his relationship with two brothers, Parshuram and Rajaram Shimpi.

> They came to play with us all day long.... If ever we needed help they always lent a hand ... when we were unwell they looked after us night and day. If anything befell our home they would feel it as their own. This duo of Raja and Parsha was viewed in our home with great affection. When my father was not around, I would eat with them.... Since my childhood I have abhorred this caste divide. They were Shimpi; I a Brahmin; this thought itself was dishonorable/humiliating to me. [83]

This narration makes clear the extent to which the Shimpi brothers looked after the Savarkar family. One of his favorite foods, Savarkar wrote, was millet bread and dry red chili and a garlic condiment (*zhunkā-bhākar*) prepared for him by Parshuram and Rajaram's mother, and he wrote "At that time, they must have felt so grateful that a Brahmin boy, and a Jagirdar's son on top of that, ate with them." Savarkar flouted the interdining taboo long before Gandhi, but his

81. I am grateful to Christian Novetzke for pointing this out to me.

82. I am grateful to Prachi Deshpande for pointing out that, regardless of Savarkar's instrumentality, his listeners may not have taken it that way.

83. *SSV*, SSRSP, 1: 76, 78.

narration of interdining is full of his enduring rhetoric of Brahmin noblesse oblige. The account ends with one of the two brothers virtually revering him.

Savarkar also noted that the secret society he founded as a young man, the Mitra Mela, was a test case of his early refusal of casteism. While his friends obeyed him and trusted his good intentions, his indifference to caste was so strong that some of his followers believed it diminished him.[84]

> I was never arrogant about my caste. . . . On the contrary, I was accused by my educated friends that by not taking caste, occupation, or educational status of others into account and by interacting with everyone as equal, I was diminishing my own greatness. But such greatness seemed hollow and feeble to me.[85]

Savarkar points to his own caste progressivism, his leadership qualities, and notes that he is indifferent to ritual scruples concerning interdining:

> Nhavi, Marathe, Vani, Kunbi, Brahman, Prabhu—amongst us we did not even think about who belonged to what caste. In those days even touchable Hindus would not inter-dine. Once, on the occasion of a haldi-kumkum in the auspicious month of Chaitra, when we were invited to a Brahmin's house and they served us tempered dry lentils, all of us in our usual manner sat together and ate it, and what a ruckus it created![86]

Savarkar was unsparing in his description of the prejudices of his community even as he emphasized them to show how brave he was to break taboos.[87] His sense of himself as a born leader was so strong that he noted that his father and other village luminaries slowly began to change their minds because of him.[88]

This *viṭāḷvēḍa* that he had challenged even as a boy was responsible, in his view, for the shattering of the Hindu body/community. Again, he explained how he knew how to mend and strengthen that same community.[89] He laid out the absurdity of ever-proliferating and self-destructive divisions.

84. *Majhya Athavani*, in *SSV*, SSRSP, 1: 159.

85. *Majhya Athavani*, in *SSV*, SSRSP, 1: 160.

86. *Majhya Athavani*, in *SSV*, SSRSP, 1: 160.

87. *Majhya Athavani*, in *SSV*, SSRSP, 1: 160.

88. See Salvi, *Swatantryaveer Savarkarancya Sahavasat*, particularly the numbered memories: 9, 13, 14, 15 (pages 9, 13–15, 20–21).

89. For a learned, thought-provoking, and succinct account of the difficulties of drawing a straight line from the *Puruṣasūkta* to the caste system, see Sharma, "The Puruṣasūkta."

> Among Brahmins, you have Punjabi Brahmins, Maithili Brahmins, Maharashtrian Brahmins; In one regional set of Maharashtrian Brahmins you have again: Karhade, Palshe, Devrukhe, Deshastha, Konkanastha, Gaud, Dravid, Govardhan. . . . Take sect-based caste differences: varna is just one, Brahmin; region is just one: Bengal; but one is Vaishnav, second is Brahmo, third is Shaivite, and fourth is Shakta! Varna is one: vaisya; region can be one whether Gujarat, or Maharashtra, or Karnatak, or Madras or Punjab, but one Jain vaisya, the other is a Vaishnav vaisya, the third Lingayat. Inter-dining, intermarriage, set in stone! Buddhist, Jain, Vaishnav, Sikh, Lingayat, Mahanubhav, Matangi, Radhaswami, Brahmo, which ever sect emerges takes separation as its first ambition even though it used to be an intimate limb of society. It does this by using the interdiction against intermarriage and inter-dining to cut itself off and separate.[90]

He added, "the current situation as it relates to casteism is awful . . . our national body is being dismembered into thousands by caste division, by this prohibition against intermarriage, interdining; this four varna's destroying sickness, this societal wasteful disease—do you truly think this nourishes national strength?"[91] Savarkar's question was clearly rhetorical, but it was a lead into his bitter sense that *viṭāḷvēḍa* had caused a glorious Hindu imperial state to wither away. There had been a time, before the prohibition against crossing the waters took hold, that Hindus had established colonies as far afield as Guatemala and Zanzibar; now these imperial holdings had all but disappeared.[92] Instead,

90. *Jatyuchedak Nibandha* (*JN*) #3, *SSV*, MPHS, 3: 446.

91. *JN* #3, *SSV*, MPHS, 3: 449.

92. *JN* #1, *SSV*, MPHS, 3: 436. Savarkar makes this point about the reach of the Hindus in several essays, mentioning Egypt, Mexico, and Africa. But one Sanskrit couplet, he wrote ("anuṣṭubh 'samudrayātuḥ svīkāraḥ kalau paṃcavivarjayet"), halted it all. The credit for chasing this down goes to Luther Obrock, who pointed out to me that in her work, *Kālāpāni: Zum Streit über die Zulässigkeit von Seereisen im kolonialzeitlichen Indien*, Susmita Arp records that "samudrayātuḥ svīkāraḥ" is a variant found in the *Nāradapurāṇa* for the printed text's "samudrayātrāsvīkāraḥ." But the second half of the line is not "pañca vivarjayet," which Savarkar uses. The relevant section of the *Nāradapurāṇa* reads:

> samudrayātrāsvīkāraḥ kamaṇḍaluvidhāraṇam |
> dvijānām asavarṇāsu kanyāsūpayamas tathā || 1.24.13 ||
> devarāc ca sutotpattir madhuparke paśor vadhaḥ |
> māṃsādanaṃ tathā śrāddhe vānaprasthaśramas tathā || 1.24.14 ||
> dattākṣatāyāḥ kanyāyāḥ punar dānaṃ varāya ca |

generations and generations of Hindus had forgotten how to soar bravely in the sky, their wings were paralysed, these roosters of Hindu bravery could make noise only in their small little puddle, and when did this happen? When Muslim vultures, who considered even tyranny as a virtue and European goons had all but occupied the entire sky over the world for themselves. No surprise then that at the merest advance of these Muslim vultures and European goons, this rooster of a small little puddle suffered an instant weak death.[93]

---

naiṣṭhikaṃ brahmacaryaṃ ca naramedhāśvamedhakau || 1.24.15 ||
mahāprasthānagamanaṃ gomedhaś ca tathā makhaḥ |
etān dharmān kaliyuge varjyān āhur manīṣiṇaḥ || 1.24.16 ||

This is a list of thirteen things forbidden in the Kali age:
1. taking a journey by sea
2. carrying a water pot (?)
3. the marriage of twice borns to girls not of the same *varṇa*
4. the obtaining of a son through the husband's brother
5. the killing of an animal in the Madhuparka sacrifice
6. The giving of meat in *śraddhā* rituals
7. the Vānaprasthā stage of life
8. the giving of a girl who had been given as a virgin to another husband
9. to remain permanently in the *brahmacarī* phase
10. the human sacrifice
11. the horse sacrifice
12. the way of dying by walking north (*mahāprasthāna*)
13. the cow sacrifice

The second phrase Savarkar uses, "kalau pañca vivarjayet", is commonly associated with the list of five things forbidden in the Kali age usually associated with the *Brahmavaivartapurāṇa*:

aśvamedhaṃ gavālambhaṃsannyāsaṃ palapaitṛkam |
devareṇa sutotpattiṃ kalau pañca vivarjayet ||

The horse sacrifice, the cow sacrifice, sannyāsa, the propitiating of ancestors with flesh offerings
the gaining of a son through the husband's brother, these five things one must give up in the Kali age.

It might be that Savarkar mixed the two lists from the *Brahmavaivartapurāṇa* and the *Nāradapurāṇa*. While the shorter list from the *Brahmavaivartapurāṇa* has five elements, it does not include taking sea voyages, with which he begins this quote. I am grateful to Luther Obrock for explaining all this to me. See Savarkar, "Bṛhattara Bhāratāta Pracārakārya Karū" ("For those who wish to engage in propaganda in Greater India, a splendid new field is opening up"), in *SSV*, MPHS, 3: 734.

93. *JN* #1, *SSV*, MPHS, 3: 438.

Until the tenth century, according to Savarkar, the political situation had been promising. Hindus crossed the oceans and established themselves everywhere (we get no citations or details), but when Muslims came to India, seven crores converted to Islam. Even that might have been recuperable since "even today these seven crore untouchables have the same strength of number as the Muslims," but they were "as powerless as a cut off limb because of this caste-madness."[94] It was his mission to dismantle this madness and chart a new path for Hindus.

Savarkar and Sanātan Dharma

"What kind of God can be polluted by simply being worshipped?" Savarkar asked in *Shraddhanand*.[95] He answered by noting that the "Hindu God . . . is not one who is polluted by the touch of someone impure, by his own profound touch he purifies the impure." Savarkar pointed to Ratnagiri, where at the annual Sarvajanik Ganpati (Ganesh) festival, a *purvāspr̥ushya* (previously untouchable) boy had participated in the singing of a *bhajan*, entered the temple, and worshipped with everyone including Brahmins, noting that Ganpati did not become enraged "nor has Ratnagiri been struck by lightning."[96] Anticipating that the Sanātani response would be that untouchability was authorized in the smr̥ti literature, he retorted that there was also a Sanskrit *śloka* from the *Bhaviṣyapurāṇa* that read, "na vaded yāvanīṃ bhāṣāṃ prāṇaiḥ kaṇṭhagatair api" ("one should not speak a Yavana language even if one's life was about to leave one's throat"), which in this context meant that all Sanātanis speaking a foreign language (English) were breaking their own vows.[97] He accused the Sanātanis of arrogance and of being indifferent to their

94. *JN* #1, *SSV*, MPHS, 3: 439

95. In "Jō darśanānē bāṭatō tō dēvaca kasalā!" ("What kind of God is he who can be polluted by an untouchable?"), Savarkar writes, "The presence of a devotee is not a God. The God of us Hindus is not made of cowdung and mud. His idol may be, his image may be, but he is not one who is polluted by the polluted but by his own divine touch he purifies the polluted. That is the reason he is called God." in *SSV*, MPHS, 3: 45, 46. Published in *Shraddhanand*, September 9, 1927.

96. "Jō darśanānē bāṭatō tō dēvaca kasalā!" in *SSV*, MPHS, 3: 45.

97. Jō darśanānē bāṭatō tō dēvaca kasalā!" in *SSV*, MPHS, 3: 46. I am grateful to Madhav Deshpande for his translation of the couplet above from the *Bhaviṣyapurāṇa*, Khand 3, Adhyaya 28, Verse 53. The second line, which Savarkar does not use, is "gajair āpīḍyamāno'pi na gacchej jainamaṃdiram," which means, "even if one is struck by elephants one should not visit a Jain temple."

subjugation by the English.[98] The Sanātanis were frauds because they did not literally follow the words in their *Śrutismṛtipurāṇokta* literature and were too preoccupied with ritual niceties to mind being enslaved by first Muslims and now the British. He called untouchables the "Varkaris of the Hindu dharma" extolling caste Hindus to lovingly accept them into their midst or else instead of the "*bhajan satyāgraha*" they were currently engaged in, they would become a weapon with which to destroy God ("dēvācē *bhañjana* karaṇyācā *śastrāgraha*" [emphasis mine]).[99] The poetic mode was always his resort, as was punning and alliteration, but the warning was clear: either accept untouchables into the Hindu fold or they will join forces with the Muslims.

Making clear that he not only respected the literature of the Sanātanis but knew it better than they did, he called them out for being unwilling to question its utility in the present age.[100] He attacked what he saw as blind adherence to precepts that were at best counterproductive, identifying two groups: the fanatical (*kaṭṭara*) Sanātanis and even worse, the half-Sanātanis (*ardha*-Sanātanis). Both relied on *Śrutismṛtipurāṇa*—the first to deny progress, the second to accept progress but only because they could not find untouchability in the Sanskrit literature.[101] Neither could think independently, he argued, and worse, the latter could accept that the purāṇas were historical, but not the Vedas, and as a result believed that "whatever is invented that is new and useful it is all in our Śrutis, they begin to declaim. As soon as coal-fired trains get going, they start hearing the sounds of railway engines in the Vedas. When airplanes start flying, you can be assured that will scratch out an editorial about the existence of planes in the Vedic period."[102] Savarkar had no interest in finding traces of modernity or scientific achievement in these ancient texts,

98. "Jō darśanānē bāṭatō tō dēvaca kasalā!" in *SSV*, MPHS, 3: 46. Savarkar repeated the idea that Sanātanis were ignorant of their own literature and just blind followers. In 1929 he wrote a satirical piece titled "Kāśītīla dōna sammēlanēṁ—mākaḍa mahāsammēlana ni bhākaḍa mahāsammēlana" ("Two gatherings in Kashi: of monkeys and morons"). He punned using the two words *mākaḍa* (monkey) and *bhākaḍa* (whatever comes to mind), with the latter parodied for blind adherence to their Shruti/Smriti and refusing to accept change. Savarkar repeated this theme across many of his writings, including two of three of his music dramas. *SSV*, MPHS, 4: 209–12.

99. "Jō darśanānē bāṭatō tō dēvaca kasalā!" in *SSV*, MPHS, 3: 45–48.

100. In his words, "we honor these texts with grateful respect and feeling, but as historical texts." What he objected to was treating them as "trikālābādhita, apauruṣēya, aśaṇkanīya, aparivartanīya." "Dōna śabdānta dōna sanskṛtī" ("Two civilizations in two words"), in *SSV*, MPHS, 3: 364. Europe and the US were "adyayāvata" (up-to-date); India was "puratani" (recidivist).

101. "Ājacyā sāmājika krāntīcē sutra" ("A formula for today's social revolution") in the series *Vijnanista Nibandha* (*Rationalist Essays*) in *SSV*, MPHS, 3: 368.

102. *SSV*, MPHS, 3: 368.

feeling instead that such boasts stood in the way of progress and national self-assertion for Hindus.[103]

So what was the real Sanātan Dharma? In an essay titled "What is the True Eternal Faith?"[104] Savarkar almost dared the Sanātanis to challenge him. In a passage that showcased his erudition and knowledge (and sense of humor), he wrote,

> From the Śrutismr̥tis to the Shanimahatmya every single pothi, and from the non-human authorship of the Vedas to the inedibility of the eggplant/aubergine, every principle has acquired the stamp of "Sanātani." From the sublime principles of the Upaniṣads to rules that state that one should not heat one's feet in front of a charcoal fire, sit outside in the morning sun, not eat food cooked by iron merchants, . . . that eating garlic, onions and carrots would instantly pollute a twice born (Manu 5–19); but on the occasion of the shraddha [mourning period], if one does not insistently eat meat, for the next twenty-one lifetimes he would become an animal (Manu 5–34) . . . Indeed, more than rice, during the shraddha, Brahmins must eat the meat of boars and bulls because the ancestors would be satiated for ten months . . . [105]

Meanwhile, as he pointed out, the Manusmr̥ti also contained *śloka*s that prohibited meat eating at all times.

Food prohibitions, ethical precepts, and all the contradictory *śloka*s had been lumped under the term Sanātan, and Sanātanis used the guise of divinity to claim *Ēṣa Dharmasanātana* (Sanātan Dharma). But Sanātan, Savarkar explained, meant *śāśvat* (eternal) *abādhita* (unopposed), *akhaṇḍanīya* (uninterruptable), and *aparivartanīya* (unchangeable). The only phenomena to which the term Sanātan could apply were gravity and other laws that literally applied to everyone, Aryans and non-Aryans alike. What fell under the category of religion, regardless of whether it did so as law or conduct, could not contribute to the idea of real Sanātani-ness.[106] He conceded the possibility that there could be something eternal (*Sanātana*) and unchanging even if

103. Oak, "What Does the Śāstra Have to Say," 184. In writing this, Savarkar says much the same as his mentor, B. G. Tilak, who had also scoffed at the idea that one could find railways and telegraph wires in the Vedas, if one just knew how. Here as elsewhere, Savarkar does not cite any influences or borrowings from other writers.

104. "Kharā Sanātana Dharma Kōṇatā?" in *SSV*, MPHS, 3: 307–16.

105. "Kharā Sanātana Dharma Kōṇatā?" in *SSV*, MPHS, 3: 307.

106. "Kharā Sanātana Dharma Kōṇatā?," in *SSV*, MPHS, 3: 309.

the entire planet was consumed by a comet, "[b]ecause the nature of the original energy, the origin of the world, and original laws are really eternal and timeless. The theories propagated in the Bhagavadgita and Upaniṣadas about these things may be really eternal."[107] But even here he was only really conceding the universal laws of physics, not the timeless verities of Hindu scripture.

He agreed that this was a Hindu Sanātan Dharma, but gave it a different definition: "Jō traiguṇyāviṣaya vēdāñcyā palīkaḍacyā nistraiguṇya pradēśāsahī 'viśvato vṛtvātyatiṣṭhad daśāṅgulam' tō āmhā Hindūñcā sanātana dharma hōya." ("The true Hindu Sanātan Dharma of us Hindus extends beyond the Vedas, to the space beyond the *trigunas* [*Sattva*, *Rajas*, and *Tamas*], and across the universe"). "Viśvato vṛtvātyatiṣṭhad daśāṅgulam" is the first stanza of the Ṛgvedic *Puruṣasūkta*; it means "having covered the sacrificial altar which equals the universe . . . [extending] beyond it by the breadth of ten fingers."[108] It is perhaps in this sense and this sense alone that we might think of Savarkar as a universalist, with a primary allegiance to a Vedic text or precept. In practice, however, he was far more concerned with what Sanātan Dharma was *not*, and that was *ācāra*, or conduct. Sanātan Dharma was *not* ritualism, temple protection, untouchability, and cow worship, and Savarkar's line of argument moved straight to the core of sociopolitical ideological power: the idea of *caturvarṇya*, or the Ṛgvedic normative depiction of the four-fold division of society into four castes.

Savarkar and *Varṇa*

Conduct (*ācāra*) was created by man, as was the four-fold *varṇa* system (*caturvarṇya*): it was an occupational division rather than a birth-based one. "The practice of four-varnas is by nature mutative—it has to be like that," Savarkar wrote, quoting from the Mahābhārata on the malleability and changeability of Dharma that:

na hi sarvahitaḥ kaścid ācāraḥ saṃpravartate |	There is no single Dharma that is beneficial for everyone,

107. "Sanātana Dharma Mhaṇajē jātibhēda navhē," in *SSV*, MPHS, 3: 442.

108. I am grateful to Bob Goldman for his translation of this *śloka* and its exegetical history. I am also grateful to Alok Oak for discussing these translations with me.

tenaivānyaḥ prabhavati so 'paro bādhyate punaḥ ||	every action will produce another, and another arises that wards it off

Here again we see the constant invocation of the epics or the Ṛgveda to establish his expertise and ridicule Sanātani beliefs and practices. If Sanātanis wanted to continue to believe that *caturvarṇya* had divine origins, then the current fifth *varṇa* of untouchables violated *caturvarṇya* itself.[109] Savarkar lays out the terms for a powerful internal critique by taking as axiomatic the logic of *varṇa* that prohibits intermarriage and interdining, then revealing its illogicality and its lack of a basis in the Śruti/Smṛti/Purāṇa/Itihas literature. He begins by accepting that in some putative ancient period there might have been no inter-*varṇa* marriage, but notes that

> there was never a prohibition against interdining. Rama ate fruit given to him by a Bhilla woman, Krishna ate broken rice at the homes of the sons of the female servants, Brahmin rishis ate food from Draupadi's cooking pot . . . [110]

If Hindu seers, prophets, and Gods like Ram, Krishna, and Brahmin rishis did not care about interdining taboos, surely there was no scriptural authority behind the proscription. Savarkar invokes multiple seers, kings, and prophets, and much as he did earlier in *Essentials*, where they marked out India's essential territory, he puts them to work to substantiate his argument for reform.[111]

To point out the absurdity of the divisiveness such an orthodox attitude produced, Savarkar creates lists of divisions—*varṇa*-based divisions, region-based divisions, and sect-based divisions—singling out occupation and food as producing perhaps the most egregious of all divisions. All these divisions were the enemy of unity.

> According to the varna system, there should have been a united group of minimum 9–10 crores of Shudras. But unfortunately, even that could not be achieved as different professions became different castes destroying their unity: coppersmith, bangle makers, peasants, gardener, barber, weaver, ironsmith, carpenter, dyer, tailor and so many divisions can be quoted.[112]

109. "Sanātana Dharma Mhaṇajē jātibhēda navhē," in *SSV*, 3: 445.
110. "Sanātana Dharma Mhaṇajē jātibhēda navhē," in *SSV*, 3: 445.
111. "Sanātana Dharma Mhaṇajē jātibhēda navhē," in *SSV*, 3: 445.
112. "Cāra varṇāñcyā cāra hajāra jāti!," in *JN* #3, *SSV*, MPHS, 3: 445.

Divisions were the result of the endlessly proliferating social and occupational distinctions that mapped themselves onto caste, and Savarkar renders this process as absurd.

> When some milkmen started making butter from cold milk, they became a caste separate from those who made butter from heated milk! . . . Among the meat-eating people, the group of fish-eating Brahmans became a separate caste, and the group of chicken-eating Brahmans became another caste, and the goat eaters became another one! With the same principle and order, the onion-eating daughter-in-law got herself into a separate caste, and the potato-eating mother-in-law got herself into another caste.[113]

He extended the absurdity of this passage to assert that the Sanātanis had introduced new words and new epithets right from the beginning—and, paradoxically, they marked the opposite of what the Sanātanis declared necessary. In fact, Brahmins intermingled with lower castes all the time.

> The original four varnas. Within them they intermingled according to the principles of high and low, and even found names for them! The mixing of Brahmin woman and Shudra man would make a Chandal. After that, the offspring of a Chandal man with a Brahmin woman would be called Atichandal [intense chandal]. After that the mixing of this Chandal with a Brahmin woman—after this one, yet another mixture, and then further, we get even more intense Chandal![114]

Savarkar went on to note that, even if one took as axiomatic the original four-fold division, the intermingling of blood among and between the divisions meant that not one of the four "original" castes was pure. Further, purity was neither possible nor desirable for humans. A father's genes did not automatically transfer themselves to his heirs, and if they did, they were not always positive. Light, food, water, weather, and education were all factors, he explained, in how one's progeny turned out. Once again, he used the epics to drive this point home:

> Not a single one of Shrikrishna's sons became another Shrikrishna. Vyas who could see bore a blind son, Dhritarashtra, and the noble Vyas's

113. "Cāra varṇāñcyā cāra hajāra jāti!," in *JN* #3, *SSV*, MPHS, 3: 447–48.
114. "Cāra varṇāñcyā cāra hajāra jāti!," in *JN* #3, *SSV*, MPHS, 3: 449.

> grandsons were the evil Duryodhan, and Dushshasan. The son of the first Bajirao was Raghoba and the grandson was Bajirao the second! In the entire history of the world, within five generations the descendants of an epoch-making person would invariably turn out to be weaklings, so much so that it can now seem like a plausible theory.[115]

He also queried the logic of the Ṛgvedic *Puruṣasūkta,* arguing that there was no natural difference between Brahmins and Sudras or tailors and goldsmiths. Any idea of differentiation, he explained, would inevitably lead to judgments about differential value or quality, and it was foolish to validate this by references either to God or to the Rishis.[116] There were, he said, seven aspects of casteism, each a set of self-imposed handcuffs (*svadeshi bēḍyā*), and they all needed to go because the Muslims were lying in wait.[117] They included *Vedoktabandi* (prohibition against receiving Vedic rites) and *vyavasayabandi* (occupational prohibition). On this last he had some especially sharp words for the Sanātanis—"Because Dr. Ambedkar is a Mahar if we had insisted that he be yoked to a bullock cart then our nation would have lost an outstanding leader, social reformer, and Pandit." Other irrational aspects included *sparshabandi* (touch), *sindhubandi* (crossing the seas), and *shuddhibandi* (reconversion), another superstition that especially upset him:

> Just as Hindu women upon being forcefully converted by Muslims and Christians mingle with them, if we incorporate those we have converted into society then in ten or twenty years we will be able to include in our Hindu fold close to a crore of Hindus who were previously non-Hindu.

He also disparaged the belief in *rotibandi* (interdining). In the end, the only social differences were really those of the great religions, which were beyond the control of Hindus. As he put it:

> Until such time as a Muslim remains a Muslim, a Christian a Christian, a Parsi a Parsi, a Jew a Jew, it is necessary, good, and appropriate for a Hindu to remain a Hindu. The day those groups break the bonds of their identities

115. *JN* #8, *SSV,* MPHS, 3: 473.

116. *JN* #8, *SSV,* MPHS, 3: 470.

117. "Pōthījāta jātibhēdocchēdak sāmājika krānti ghōṣaṇā! Tōḍūna ṭākā hyā sāta svadēśī bēḍyā," in *SSV,* MPHS, 3: 497.

> and accept Universal Mankind and the nationhood of man, on that day the Hindu nation will accept and live under the same flag, even if this kind of universal humanism is itself central to the Hindu faith.[118]

In short, the only thing that prevented him from discounting all forms of social difference was the fact that other religious groups insisted on them and would use any Hindu reluctance to identify as Hindus to absorb and conquer them. Until all other groups broke free of their identities, Hindus had to stick together.

Savarkar and Brahminism

Savarkar moved from challenging the epics and the Vedas to addressing not just Brahminism but the conflicts between Brahmins and non-Brahmins and what he saw as the root cause: casteism. Although his anti-Sanātani rhetoric made it seem like he critiqued Brahmins in particular, his argument was in fact far less directed at Brahmins than it appeared. He wrote that

> The Brahmaneter [non-Brahmin], while attacking the caste arrogance of the Brahmins, propagates such great values as would embarrass even a satyashodhak acharya [reformer-pandit], but when the Mahar-Mang start demanding the same status of equality, some of these charlatans get mad and chase after them with sticks . . . Marathas try to become the Brahmins of Mahars! Mahars try to become the Brahmins of the Mang! This madness of casteism is rooted in the bones and flesh of . . . Hindu society even to the extent that abrahmani chandals [non-Brahmin] also have it.[119]

Although one might read this as apportioning blame equally, in caste matters, he comes across as trying to level an unequal playing field and thus letting Brahmins off the hook. Savarkar repeatedly denied that Brahmins were especially caste prejudiced.

> If casteism was only Brahmin treachery, trick, then Shriram and Shrikrishna were not Brahmins, right? Why did they then uphold chaturvarnya [the four-fold system]? If you say, Kshatriya and other castes were just poor naive people who easily fell into the trap set by the Brahmins, then was

118. "Pōthījāta jātibhēdocchēdak sāmājika krānti ghōṣaṇā! Tōḍūna ṭākā hyā sāta svadēśī bēḍyā," in *SSV*, MPHS, 3: 500.

119. *JN* #1, *SSV*, MPHS, 3: 439–40.

> Shrikrishna naive? Or was Samudragupta naive? Was Shivaji naive . . . And what about Manu who was himself a Kshatriya?[120]

What about Kshatriyas? Could this entire system of caste have been a Brahmin-Kshatriya plot since the author of the Manusmṛti, Savarkar wrote, was a Kshatriya? He unravels this premise as well, asserting that Brahmins were always a minority and thus could not have imposed their version of caste order on all Hindu society. That power, he wrote, belonged to the Kshatriyas since force and the ability to punish (*dandashakti*) lay in their hands. Here again, Savarkar does not see or wish to acknowledge the unique role Brahmins play in the caste system.

This equal apportioning of blame for casteism is as much a fixture in his writings as were Muslims:

> If the entire prominence [blame] is attached to Brahmins for every issue, then the same argument applies to the oppression of Kshatriyas of all varnas beneath them. The same is true also of Vaisyas, who can charge Brahmins and Kshatriyas of cruel oppression, but of varnas beneath them they behave as if they are their "Brahmins." Among Sudras too, those who proclaim "the three upper varnas, using caste difference as the reason they have stripped us naked, while saying all men are equal" behave with lower caste Sudras using the same logic/fiction, they won't interdine or intermarry, Mahars and others as well won't even touch the untouchables.[121]

While Savarkar never engaged the anti-Brahmin movement directly, he defended Brahmins over and over, including in his long list of caste reformers many Brahmins, from the Brahmin student to whom the Buddha bequeathed his own position to Chaitanya Prabhu all the way to Rabindranath Tagore. In his essay "Janmajāta jātibhēda mōḍāyacā mhaṇajē kāya karāvayācēṁ?" ("If you have to break birth-based caste divisions, how do you do it?")[122] he addressed the monopoly over two professions he called *bhaṭa ni bhangi*. Again, like Gandhi, he advocated that the work of the *bhangi,* the cleaner of human waste, should be done by everyone so that the stigma attached to it would disappear. These writings made Savarkar then (and later) popular with Dalit-Bahujan leaders and other supporters of the anticaste and anti-Brahmin movements,

120. "Hyā āpattīvara Upāya Kāya," in *SSV*, MPHS, 3: 451.
121. "Vajrasuci," in *SSV*, MPHS, 3: 539–40.
122. *SSV*, MPHS, 3: 71.

not least because he was able to ventriloquize what they might have said but without the same fear of reprisal.[123]

Yet when it came to the Brahmin Bhaṭa (priest/*pujāri*), he could not see the deep structural power the position held. He wrote that the Brahmin Bhaṭa had not climbed atop the social ladder all by himself or forced his way into peoples' homes with the help of the police. His power came from so-called reformed Hindus who were trapped in their own stupidity.

> All of these "Samajists" and "Sudharaks" when it comes to marriages, naming ceremonies, mourning rituals, Gauri-Ganpati pujas, fervently seek out the Bhat, if he doesn't arrive they are bereft, can't bring themselves to swallow any food and remain hungry until he comes and conducts the ceremony, in their own idiocy lies the power of the Bhat, not in the sacred grass that he brings with him.[124]

Besides, as he reminded his readers, Brahminism even as an occupation was prevalent in all castes.

> . . . even though when we say Bhata the first image that comes before us is the Brahmin, we have to see that there are Gurava Brahmins, Jangama Brahmins, and even more than that there are Bhatas among the Mahars—all of this, even if it is non-Brahmin it is still Brahminshahi.[125]

Savarkar's solution was radical: don't invite *bhaṭa*s to conduct any religious ceremonies. Not "pujas, readings of pothis, the Gauri or Ganpati festival, marriages, mourning, auspicious days, festivals like Diwali or Dussehra, on all these numerous occasions, nothing needs to be stopped because there is no Bhat performing rituals for you."[126] While people's stupidity is what gave priests their power, he does not suggest any incentive for them to take that power back. In turning Brahminism into just a priestly occupation, Savarkar suggested that all Hindus could become their own Brahmins. This was similar to what Satyashodhak reformers advocated in rejecting Brahmin ownership and personification of rituals by publishing self-help books about rituals,

123. See, for instance, Walinjkar, *Uttar Konkan Dalitmukti*, or Kamble, *Swatantryavira Savarkaranche*.

124. *SSV*, MPHS, 3: 74. By "Samajists" he was referring to the Christianized reformist Brahmo Samaj members.

125. *SSV*, MPHS, 3: 74.

126. *SSV*, MPHS, 3: 74.

including *Swayam Purohit* (*Self-Priest*), and *Brahmnancha Hakka Nahi* (*Not a Brahmin Right Alone*), as Shrikant Botre has shown.[127] And it is entirely possible that non-Brahmins heard or read such statements very differently than did Brahmins, helping expand his base in ways beyond the direct instrumentality of his own intentions. These statements help explain how Savarkar could be seen inside Maharashtra as a caste progressive. Then and now, the more difficult question that hovered over all caste reform was which was the more unsettling practice—extending Vedic rituals to all including untouchables or inventing entirely new rituals?[128] Savarkar saw no issue with the first, since he wished to avoid conversion at all costs.

In a piece titled "The Locus of Religion/Faith Is the Heart, Not the Stomach!" he wonders why Hindu bellies were so unable to digest Muslim food.[129]

> . . . the notion that if Hindus dine with Christians or Muslims, they will be polluted is crazy! Because the locus of faith is not the stomach but the heart! Muslims and others eat food from Hindus by mistake, sometimes they even steal it but remain Muslims . . . then why is the ability for Hindus to digest Muslim food so weak?[130]

As in so many of his writings, Savarkar simultaneously attacks Hindu pusillanimity and Muslim thievery.

In the same piece, Savarkar advises all Hindus:

> I would advise each and every Hindu openly, if you have no other option, then eat your fill in a Muslim's house, drink the water, do the same in an Englishman's house, do it all over the world; and after you eat immediately place a basil leaf in your mouth, not only will your mouth be decontaminated so will your soul and after digesting every grain you will find yourself still a Hindu.[131]

Tellingly, here we see Savarkar updating Tilak for the twentieth century by suggesting Hindus take unto themselves Brahminic rituals of purification without an actual Brahmin to perform them. In suggesting the basil leaf,

127. Botre, "The Body Language of Caste," 231.

128. I am grateful to Partha Chatterjee for posing this question in his comments on this manuscript.

129. "Dharmācē sthana Hradaya āhē pōṭa navhē," in *SSV*, MPHS, 3: 41–43.

130. "Dharmācē sthana Hradaya āhē pōṭa navhē," in *SSV*, MPHS, 3: 41.

131. "Dharmācē sthana Hradaya āhē pōṭa navhē," in *SSV*, MPHS, 3: 42.

Savarkar was referring to what is called the "Panch Haud Tea Episode." Gopalrao Joshi, a somewhat eccentric and contrarian reformer whose wife Anandibai Joshi was the first Indian woman to get a medical degree from the US, hosted a lecture at the Anglican Panch Haud Mission School in October 1890 at which the guests were served tea and biscuits by the sisters of the mission. Joshi's aim, as N. C. Kelkar noted, was to set up both conservatives like B. G. Tilak and moderates like M. G. Ranade to display their hypocrisy since neither group quite knew what to do with the tea and biscuits. The conservatives believed that they would be contaminated by eating or drinking food served by Christians, and the moderates were uncomfortable openly flouting caste taboos, so the tea and biscuits were left barely touched. Six months later, Gopal Joshi published the names of the people who had attended the lecture, and news of the event reached an inflection point when the orthodoxy demanded that all attendees be declared outcastes. The whole matter was subsequently referred to the Shankaracharya (of Karveer-peeth), who came to Pune, delivered a decision in favor of the orthodox, and excommunicated Tilak for two years. Tilak argued that Hinduism was not so weak that merely eating "Christian" food turned Hindus into Christians.[132]

Savarkar did this and more. Not only did he defend Tilak, he scoffed at the idea that one should ever tiptoe around hurt Sanātani feelings (*dharmabhāvanā*).[133] A Sanātan-Dharma Parishad in Loni had reacted en masse quite sharply to Savarkar and his articles in *Kirloskar*, and he scoffed at their narrow views:

> 100s of thousands of people polluted, constant Muslim riots, women are being abducted, temples being destroyed all over the country, threats to turn Hindusthan into Pakistan, missions emptying out homes, untouchables are being destroyed by our actions, [we have] no country, no state, no clothes, no food, and to alleviate this situation, the Sanātanis, these

132. This is commonly referred to as the "Panch Haud/Cahā Grāmaṇya Episode." See Kelkar, *Lokamanya Tilak*, ch. 13. See also Phatak, *Lokmanya*, 79–80, and Ganachari, *Gopal Ganesh Agarkar*, which translates Kelkar's account into English. I am grateful to Alok Oak for pointing me to this. On this subject, Tilak's opponent, Gopal Ganesh Agarkar, weighed in long before Savarkar to defend Tilak and challenge the orthodox notion of contamination. See Agarkar, "Gramanyaprakarana" ("The Gramanya Episode") and "Iti Cahagramanyaprakaranam Samaptam" ("Here endeth the whole tea and Gramanya episode") in *Sampurna Agarkar*, 1: 402–5, 412–14.

133. "Jara kā āja pēśavā'ī asatī," in *SSV*, MPHS, 3: 416. See also his defence of Tilak in "Dharmabhōḷēp paṇācā kaḷasa" ("The height of religious naivete"), *SSV*, MPHS, 3: 273.

> "Nyaya-Mimamsa-Veda-spouters" could only suggest more prohibitions like "food must not be taken to the bridegroom's house, the bridegroom must not sulk, and riddles should not be recited while eating."[134]

It was far more important to get rid of casteism. As he put it pithily, "Hindu blood, seed, heart and soul cannot be polluted by a glass of water offered by Muslims and others, let alone an entire ocean."[135] He had made this point soon after writing *Essentials of Hindutva*. In an English article in *Mahratta*, he made clear that all Hindus were a race and had blood in common. He railed at Gandhi for suggesting otherwise, noting that the idea that Hindus could not be considered a race could only have come from him.

> From what other source can such profound shallowness flow than from the perennial fountain of "Himalayan Mistakes!" To level down to dust at a single non-violent stroke the cherished love and pride and exalted emotions of a whole race that fondly felt in its vein the blood of a Shivaji . . . only a Mahatamaic audacity can accomplish that![136]

Savarkar's argument was provocative, but it was also double-edged; he advocated the shedding of prejudice but substituted one form of prejudice for another. [137] Hinduness became an invincible genetic trait and essence—a racialized characteristic—that nothing, certainly not touching untouchables or drinking water polluted by Muslims, could change.

Savarkar and Ritualism, Temple Destruction, and Cow Worship

Savarkar begins this tripartite attack with a long and sardonic history of the saint-poet tradition of Maharashtra. For three centuries (1300–1600 CE), the region, he wrote, had been blessed by a long line of saint/poets.

134. "Āmacyā dharmabhāvanā dukhavū nakā aṁ," in *SSV*, MPHS, 3: 426–32. "Rukhavat" is the practice of taking food and drink to the bridegroom's house just before escorting him to the marriage pandal. The Sanātanis even filed petitions appealing to the Bombay government to curb his actions in Ratnagiri. See Chaturvedi, *Hindutva and Violence*, 339.

135. *SSV*, MPHS, 3: 43.

136. "Then Who Is Who, Pray?" in *SSV*, MPHS, 6: 514.

137. On the merging of heredity with Brahminism, see ch. 4 and 5; on marriage reform in Maharashtra, see Botre, "The Body Language of Caste."

> First Maharashtra got the benefit of a Mahayogi like Dnyaneshwar. If ever the support of God was manifested in any human being through penance, yoga, virtue, it would have been in this extraordinary man. He got a bull to recite the Vedas, made walls move, and his Hari-bhakti resounded all over Maharashtra. He was followed by Nivritti, Sopan, Mukta—Maharashtra was just awash in miracles and divine blessing.[138] . . . This was followed by Namdev, Janabai . . . Gora Kumbhar, Rohidas, Chokha Mahar . . . Eknath, Tukaram, from Brahmin neighborhoods to Mahar localities . . . to such an extent that Maharashtra had itself become the abode of the Gods.[139]

But to what end? Savarkar notes that as soon as the *Dnyaneshwari* was composed, Alauddin Khilji arrived with his thousands of warriors and entered like a lion among the lambs.[140] All of this devotionalism (*bhakti*) produced the opposite result, since God seemed to favor the (Muslim) oppressors. As for rituals that might be done to propitiate the gods, what use would they really be? Savarkar sarcastically listed some of these propitiations:

> . . . chanting while standing in water twice a year, fasting, meditation, conducting 108 Satyanarayana pujas, reciting Rama's name 100,000,00 times, sacrificing animals, lighting 1000 oil lamps, offering 100,000 blades of sacred grass, ritual baths, chanting prayers, feeding a cow, feeding brahmins, doing charity, giving donations, these 1000s of forms from the Śruti right down to the *Shanimahatmya* are given as ways of appeasing the Gods.[141]

The only concrete result of all of these, he noted, was to enable Muslim invasions.

Savarkar's aim was to diagnose what ailed Hindu society, and the essays I discuss in this section were compiled in a series titled *Kṣa Kiraṇē* (X-rays).[142] The first essay assailed Hindu naivete. He points out that, "while Americans

138. *SSV*, MPHS, 3: 300.

139. *SSV*, MPHS, 3: 301.

140. *SSV*, MPHS, 3: 302.

141. "Īśvarācē adhiṣṭhāna mhaṇajē kaya," in *SSV*, MPHS, 3: 299.

142. These essays were all published between 1930 and 1937 in *Kirloskar*, *Manohar*, and *Maharashtra Sharda* and collected in one volume in 1964. There are now four editions of *Kṣa Kiraṇē*, the last of which was published as a small book by Savarkar's secretary Balarao Savarkar in the series published by the Bombay Savarkar Smarak.

were engaged in exploring the possibility of space travel and crossing the oceans easily, we were engaged in useless actions such as crawling on our stomachs from Prayag to Haridwar in the belief that this would please the Gods."[143] The first issue he cast his eye on had to do with the absurd "fasts" or vows that ascetic holy men undertook, such as the one taken by a Lahiri Maharaj who wrote "Lord Ram" on over a million pieces of paper, inserted them into fragrant balls of dough, and released them into the Ganges River. The result, Lahiri Maharaj believed, would be that calamities such as earthquakes would no longer occur. Savarkar was not only incredulous at such actions but annoyed.

> Even if we respect Lahiribua's good intention . . . these eleven lakh balls of dough with Rama's name in them that have been released into the Ganga, there is not one quarter paisa's [*damaḍī*] worth of benefit to humans and all benefit acrrues solely to the fish and frogs of the Ganga.[144]

Savarkar asked exasperatedly:

> Even if Rama's address is written in Sanskrit in those letters in the balls of dough, since one doesn't really hear much about their [the fish and frogs] ability to read Sanskrit and be quite so conversant in it to be able to figure out the address, the dough balls are just going to lie in their stomachs. How are they supposed to reach God? Are [we to assume] these frog and fish stomachs [are] now the post boxes in which letters to God are to be addressed?[145]

Would not Lahiri Maharaj's time have been better spent helping those in need, he asked? Muslim readers who knew Marathi would have read Savarkar warning them to beware as well since to hold the Qur'an as unchanging and infallible was to not recognize that the Christians who had left aside such ideas about their Bible had inflicted loss upon loss on Muslims.

> You have been driven out of Spain, almost killed to extinction. You have been driven out of Austria, Hungary, Serbia, Bulgaria. In Hindusthan your

143. "Hindūñcā aḍāṇīpaṇā ni musalamānāñcā" in *Kṣa Kiraṇē, SSV*, MPHS, 3: 152–61.

144. "Hindūñcā aḍāṇīpaṇā ni musalamānāñcā" in *Kṣa Kiraṇē, SSV*, MPHS, 3: 156. Savarkar uses the word *damaḍī*, a currency denomination, as Prachi Deshpande notes, peculiar to the Pune area, to emphasize how little such efforts yielded. Deshpande, *Scripts of Power*, 90.

145. "Hindūñcā aḍāṇīpaṇā ni musalamānāñcā" in *Kṣa Kiraṇē, SSV*, MPHS, 3: 156.

> Mughal empire was taken by them. Arabia, Mesopotamia, Iraq, Syria—they are sitting on your chest and ruling you. In the same manner that our sacrifice, our fast, our mantras, curses, Vedas were unable to stop them, your Qur'an, sacrifice, namaz, taviz and tait will not be able to stop them.[146]

It is one of the few places in Savarkar's oeuvre where he offers the same advice to Hindus and Muslims.

In April 1935 Savarkar wrote an article that could be seen as perhaps his bravest attempt to dismantle Hindu prejudice. It was titled "Gāya: Ēka upayukta paśu, mātā navhē—dēvatā tara navhēca navhe!" ("The cow: a useful animal, but not our mother, and definitely not a god"). In this article, Savarkar pulls out all of the Sanskrit stops. He introduces cow worship as emerging from one of the great utterances of Advaita Vedānta from the *Chāndogya Upaniṣad*—"sarvam khalv idam brahma," meaning "all this [i.e., the universe] indeed is Brahman [the absolute and only real being]," and therefore animals too were part of this universal absolute.[147] Savarkar is very careful to assert that he has immense regard for the cow as a useful animal, indeed the wealth of the nation, given that India's economy was primarily agricultural. He praised the cow as perhaps the most useful animal of all and as a loving, caring, and gentle beast. Having said that, he swung hard, using the most sarcastic and mocking language, at cow worship. He attacked cow worshippers who "filled their cupped palms with cow urine and sprinkled it all over a temple but if a pure and wise previous-untouchable like Dr. Ambedkar were to give them Ganga water [sacred water], let alone drinking it, if it were even sprinkled on them, they believe they have been polluted."[148] Savarkar had made this point before, but he went much further now.

> If everything and everyone comes from and is a part of Brahma, then the cow and the donkey are much the same . . . so why should one protect the cow and not eat her? According to your theory of Brahman, both are either

146. "Hindūñcā aḍāṇīpaṇā ni musalamānāñcā" in *Kṣa Kiraṇē, SSV*, MPHS, 3: 161.

147. I am grateful to Bob Goldman for his translation.

148. "Gāya: Ēka upayukta paśu, mātā navhē—dēvatā tara navhēca navhē!" in *Kṣa Kiraṇē, SSV*, MPHS, 3: 164. The friendship between Savarkar and Ambedkar, which lasted until Ambedkar wrote to suggest he would not die a Hindu, was not well remarked or appreciated, even by Savarkar's older brother. Atmaram Walinjkar points out that except for a very few people, including Dhananjay Keer, hardly anyone spoke enthusiastically about their friendship. See Walinjkar, *Uttar Konkan Dalitmukti*, 199.

> true claims or false claims, both are equal activities, there is no difference between eating and protection.[149]

He drew from early debates about being and nonbeing to remind his readers that

> there is no existence that can arise from non-existence, and from sat [truth] there can be no non-existence. This is the creation of Brahma. (nāsato vidyate bhāvaḥ na bhāvo vidyate sataḥ' Hī brahmasr̥ṣṭī!")

> He pushed the point further:

> You say the texts claim that there are Gods in the cow, but the texts also say that the boar-incarnation of Vishnu had also taken the form of a pig. So why protect only the cow? Why not establish a pig-protection society and worship the pig?[150]

Here again he had a warning for such thinkers. He writes, "What these texts tell us about 5,000 years ago, if we do not subject them to an up to date rationalist examination, then our Hindu nation, our Hindu dharma will remain as backwards as it was 5000 years ago and in this age of airplanes we will not be able to keep pace."[151] He savages the new images that were circulating depicting the cow as containing within her thirty-three crore gods, challenges the notion that one of the main indices of Hindutva was the phrase "dhēnur yasya mahāmāta" ("whose mother is the cow"), dismisses the idea that cow dung and urine were medicinal, and puts forth his main argument: by preventing cow slaughter, Hindus had enabled the slaughter of the nation. Having allowed in hundreds of Muslims who butchered cows and destroyed temples, having misunderstood cow protection as a religious duty, Hindus had bolstered beef-eating from Alauddin Khilji to Aurangzeb.[152] All roads paved by Sanātanis lead to Muslim-imposed catastrophes.

One of Savarkar's associates described his writings as "an assault on the naive/innocent religious beliefs of Hindu society" and wondered "if his intellect and emotions are not in tune with each other . . . is Veer Savarkar devoid

149. "Gāya: Ēka upayukta paśu, mātā navhē—dēvatā tara navhēca navhē!" in *Kṣa Kiraṇē*, *SSV*, MPHS, 3: 164.

150. *SSV*, MPHS, 3: 164.

151. *SSV*, MPHS, 3: 165.

152. *SSV*, MPHS, 3: 168, 169.

of emotions?"[153] But Savarkar was well aware of what he was doing, and he would repeat the claim that, however innocent, ignorant, or blind it was to ascribe religion to cow worship, it was not evil. Muslims were evil; Hindus were merely victims of their own naivete (*dharmabhōḷēpaṇā*).

When the article created a storm, he wrote more explaining his position. "We should raise cows, not worship them!" one such article began. "The cow is rationally an animal. With an intellect lesser than the most dim-witted man, to worship any such animal is to insult humankind."[154] I quote at length his description of a cow's essential dimwittedness and animality and the perversity of her worshippers because the texture of Savarkar's prose is difficult to paraphrase (the Marathi original is in the appendix):

> . . . standing in her pen, eating grass and refuse, who lets loose a stream of urine without any self-consciousness, upon being tired while still chewing who sits in that very pool of urine and with her tail tosses that mess of mixed urine and dung all over herself, seizing the first opportunity to wander when her rope is loosened and sinks her face in garbage who knows where, again and again, and returns to her pen licking her lips to be re-tied—to that cow come Brahmins and chaste women wearing pure, clean, and brilliant clothes, carrying puja utensils to perform puja in the pen and to touch her tail. Their clothes are not contaminated, on the contrary, are rendered purer and more shining, and they collect her urine and dung in silver containers, drink her urine and believe their lives are even more pure! They are now pure! But when the shadow of a great man like Ambedkar falls on them they are polluted, or when inter-dining with a saint like Tukaram. An animal is treated here as a god and a godlike man an animal![155]

He wrote not to disrespect the cow but to point out that her real pleasure was fresh green grass or rummaging for food in a garbage heap.[156]

Savarkar found the elevation of low substances and the shunning of great men like Tukaram and Ambedkar illogical, irrational, and unscientific. And as Aparna Devare argues, the worst aspect of this illogicality was that it also

153. Abhyankar confronted Savarkar in 1937 and was told, "I wrote what I did to attack blind faith." Salvi, *Savarkar Yancya Athvani*, 61.

154. "Gōpālana haveṁ Gōpūjan Navhē" in *SSV*, MPHS, 3: 342. The article also illustrates what Pradeep Gokhale has referred to as the "Vedanta vs. Dhadanta debate." See Gokhale, "Ekonisavya satakatila dona vicaradvandve" in Vohra, *Adhunikata ani Parampara*, 66–72.

155. "Gōpālana haveṁ Gōpūjan Navhē," in *SSV*, MPHS, 3: 342.

156. "Gōpālana haveṁ Gōpūjan Navhē," in *SSV*, MPHS, 3: 342. See the subsection titled "Gogras."

handed Muslims an easy target.[157] Savarkar posed a hypothetical state of emergency in which a Hindu kingdom was encircled by invading non-Hindus, and food and other resources were scarce:

> In such a situation, slaughtering and eating the meat of those animals not being used in battle is itself, from a nationalist standpoint, a sacred thing to do. Such times of distress recur frequently in history. In such moments, the cow is a useful animal, she has been bred for her use to the fullest, and in times of war, cows, who are not being used for war, should be slaughtered and eaten, and to win the war, having used the cow for that reason, will be the real Hindu dharma. Cow slaughter will be the sacred bestowal.[158]

These were not just fighting words—they were designed to offend, especially for the Sanātani community. His inflammatory writings generated a strong response but they did not put him in any real danger.[159]

Savarkar continued to ask about the cost of orthodox Hindus being so keen to avoid any cow slaughter, murdered Brahmins, or destroyed temples:

> Ten temples, a handful of Brahmins, five or ten cows killed, to save themselves from this sin they let the nation die! To avert cow slaughter, they engaged in nation slaughter. If the nation was destroyed it didn't matter; what mattered was that a temple not be destroyed. When this is the constant situation in one or another form from the time of Mahmud of Ghazi down till the 2nd Bajirao, is it the fault of us utilitarians or these clutchers of ancient texts, these irrational beings, destroyers of our nation?![160]

157. Devare, *History and the Making*, 178–80.

158. "Gōpālana haveṁ Gōpūjan Navhē," in *SSV*, MPHS, 3: 343.

159. In response to Chaunde Maharaj, a staunch cow protectionist and opponent of untouchables entering temples, Savarkar invoked Sant Tukaram, and produced a little couplet that he claimed altered Sant Tukaram's original ("Jarī tō brāhmaṇa jhālā dharmabhraṣṭa. Tukā mhaṇē śrēṣṭha, tihīṁ lōkīṁ" ["Even if a Brahmin betrays his religion, Tuka says he is great in all three worlds"]) to what he thought Chaunde Maharaj might say, which was "Jari tō aspṛśya jhālā dharmaniṣṭha. Chauṇḍē mhaṇē bhraṣṭha tihīṁ lōkīṁ" ("Even if an untouchable is devoted to dharma, Chaunde says he is polluted in all three worlds"). "Dharmabhōḷēpaṇācā kaḷasa" ("The height of religious naivete"), *SSV*, MPHS, 3: 270. The actual verse in Tukaram is "Jarī tō brāhmaṇa jhālā karmabhraṣṭa, Tukā mhaṇē śrēṣṭha, tihīṁ lōkīṁ." See Lad, *Shri Tukarambawancya Abhanganci Gatha*, 401. See also Sarwate, "Reimagining the Modern Hindu Self," 154–56 and footnote 268, in which he notes that, in 1938, Denudas Dole, a disciple of Chaunde Maharaj, published in a work titled "Avarkar Sahitya" which the author translates as *Enough of It, Savarkar Literature!*

160. *SSV*, MPHS, 3: 345.

In arguing with the Sanātanis, Savarkar seems to succumb to a moment of vengeful rage.

> When Muslims threatened to raze just one Sun-temple in Multan had there been even one Hindu not blinded by scripture he would immediately have responded "bring down the Sun temple"; but mleccha [here used as an epithet] understand this! This Hindu army will not retreat but will liberate Multan from your hands and from here to Kabul whichever mosque we see we will raze it and use a donkey plough over it. And on top of Kabul's Shahi mosque we will rebuild Multan's Sun-temple. [161]

The rage here is surprising, and it is followed by an even angrier passage that refers to the Mughal emperor Aurangzeb's assault on the Kashi Visweshwar temple and the subsequent threat by the Nawab of Ayodhya to raze it to the ground.[162] Here too the correct response, according to Savarkar, should have been the following:

> Bring it down! . . . and behead a handful of Brahmins. But keep this in mind . . . the revenge for this one Kashi temple will be that at least in Maharashtra there will not remain a single mosque. We will clean out the street and we will ensure that the entire issue of music and mosques will not trouble the next generation . . . even in Shaniwarwada, there is one pir [shrine] that is safe but mleccha [again an epithet] if you violate this practice, then Hindus will raze that last one to the ground.[163]

Savarkar was not expressing religious outrage at such temple destruction; temples mattered only insofar as they were a currency of exchange between violent Muslims and violent Hindus.

Following this detour, he reverts to arguing rationally that a cow is useful, but that other animals might be considered even more useful, though they had not been turned into gods.

> . . . but because the donkey is so useful, long-suffering, honest, until today has anyone therefore not considered him an animal and turned him into a

161. *SSV*, MPHS, 3: 346. "Gāḍhavācā nāṅgara phiravaṇē" is a phrase used in Marathi that refers to an earlier practice of inflicting punishment and humiliation by razing to the ground a conquered village and then using a donkey-led plough over the land.

162. The mosque was partially brought down in 1699 by the Mughal emperor Aurangzeb. See Sarkar, *History of Aurangzeb*, 3: 282.

163. *SSV*, MPHS, 3: 346.

> god? Or composed a donkey-gita and formed a donkey-worshipping religious sect? . . . the cow is a useful animal, for this reason alone we have turned her into a god, and all of these insane things we do related to the cow, should we not acknowledge that these are all clearly wild and stupid?[164]

What was this picture of divinity, Savarkar asked, that Hindus were painting in which

> in the tail are the Nagas, in the tips of the hooves are the eight *kulaparvatas* [axial mountains]. In the middle are all the hosts [*ganas*], in the pores of the skin are the great seers. In her exhalation is the God of wind [*Marut*], and in her womb is placed the God of water [*Varuna*]. And in her urine is the Ganga.[165]

Not only was this idiotic, he noted that "if ever there was a real Gokul on this earth as described in the Bhagavat, it would be in the beef-eating land of America where they treat the cow as useful and look after her accordingly."[166]

He concluded the essay by offering an olive branch of sorts to the orthodox: ". . . by all means name her sacred once, figuratively speaking it is okay for the briefest moment, but it should not be taken literally."[167] But he added a caveat.

> . . . sometime in the past eating cow dung and drinking cow's urine were a dishonorable and insulting punishment. Like shaving off a thief's mustache, being forced to sit on a donkey, and other such insults, in the same manner, eating and drinking a cow's urine and dung must too have been part of it. Even today "eat shit, drink piss" this is a curse. Not custom.[168]

This series of essays on the cow and cow worship are extraordinary. Savarkar's trenchant, acerbic critique sits next to the need to constantly secure the nation

164. *SSV*, MPHS, 3: 348–49.

165. Savarkar uses these lines in two articles, and I put them together. See "Gāya: Ēka upayukta paśu, mātā navhē—dēvatā tara navhēca navhē!" and "Gōpālana havem̐ Gōpūjan Navhē" in *SSV*, MPHS, 3: 166, 352. The Sanskrit lines he uses are:

> pucche nāgāḥ khurāgreṣu ye cāṣṭau kulaparvataḥ |
> madhye devagaṇāḥ sarve romakūpe maharṣayaḥ||
> apāne tu maruddevo yonī ca varūṇaḥ sthitaḥ

and "mūtre gaṃgā."

166. "Gōpālana havem̐ Gōpūjan Navhe" in *SSV*, MPHS, 3: 351.

167. "Gōpālana havem̐ Gōpūjan Navhe" in *SSV*, MPHS, 3: 352.

168. "Gōpālana havem̐ Gōpūjan Navhe" in *SSV*, MPHS, 3: 353.

against Muslim attacks.[169] We now leave the classic case of the "sacred cow" to turn to a few other components of Savarkar's caste critique.

Savarkar and Intermarriage

A similar double-sidedness can be seen when we look at another area where Savarkar was progressive: the plank of anticaste reform around intermarriage. His admiration for women was genuine but always linked to his idea of the nation. Nevertheless, he yielded to none in his admiration for warrior-like women, whether Rani Laxmibai in her struggle against the East India Company in 1857 to declare her adoptive son her legal heir, the English suffragettes for demanding rights rather than requesting them, or Sister Nivedita for her commitment to the Indian nationalist cause. Other warrior women show up in the three musical plays he wrote in this period. In *Saṅgīta Uḥśāpa* (1927), the female protagonist spurns her lover when he turns to Islam and kills a Muslim and says, "Here you go, this is the sword of revenge." In *Saṅgīta San'yasta Khaḍga* (1931), the married Sulochana wears men's clothes to fight on the battlefield.[170] And in the last play, *Saṅgīta Uttarkriyā* (1933), the two wives (Suniti and Susheela) of the main character (Yashwantrao) dress as men to fight in the battle of Panipat, and Suniti promises that "just as Hindu women in Rohilkhand were sold in the markets like vegetables, we will in Poona inflict the same humiliation on you."[171] What linked these women was their service to Savarkar's Hindu nation.

Savarkar emphatically favored mixed marriages, but only between regions, not caste groups. Anticaste marriage reform movements in the late nineteenth

169. Savarkar answered all his critics, including Chaunde Maharaj, both those he termed "puranokta," and those he thought of as "sahibokta." If the first used "iti Śruti" ("It is in the Śruti"), the second used some English writer as proof. See "Gōrakṣaka ki Gāyaḷa" ("Cow protection or cow obsession?") in *SSV*, MPHS, 3: 178–88; "Hā Gābhārā kīṁ Gōṭhā?" ("Is this an inner sanctum or a cow pen?") in *SSV*, MPHS, 3: 188–97; "Uccāṅkāñcī Sātha" ("Majority support") in *SSV*, MPHS, 3: 214–19, in particular. See also "Punhā ēkadā Gāya—Hānikāraka Dharmabhāvanā" ("Once again the Cow—and destructive religious sentiments") in *SSV*, MPHS, 3: 227–38.

170. The music drama *San'yasta Khaḍga* was performed on September 18, 1931, in the Elphinstone Theater on Grant Road by the Balwant Sangeet Mandali. It was Savarkar's rejoinder to Gandhian nonviolence. Its three characters, Vikram, Vallabha, and Vallabha's wife Sulochana, ventriloquize Savarkar's political and reformist positions. For details on how it was produced, see B. Savarkar, *Hindusamaj Sanrakshak*, 261–62.

171. Savarkar, *Saṅgīta Uttarakriya*, 79.

and early twentieth centuries in Maharashtra had focused on loosening or eliminating Brahmin control over marriage by raising the age of consent, legalizing intercaste marriages, or allowing divorce. Early reformers such as Gopalbaba Walangkar, a Mahar friend and follower of Jyotiba Phule, founded the Anarya Dosh Pariharak Mandal in 1888, which aimed to demolish Brahmin priests' primacy in Hindu ritual life. In the same district where Savarkar was interned, Walangkar campaigned to replace Brahmin priests with Dalit ones.[172] In 1882 Tarabai Shinde wrote *Stree Purusha Tulana* (*Comparison between Women and Men*), challenging Brahmin patriarchy.[173] In 1888 Pandita Ramabai, a social reformer and one of the first women to receive the title of "Pandita" after an examination by the faculty at the University of Calcutta, published a feminist critique of Brahminism, *The High Caste Hindu Woman*.[174] A high-caste widow who converted to Christianity, she received much abuse from the orthodox, the Shankaracharya, and B. G. Tilak in particular, who called her *revrānda*, which, as Shrikant Botre points out, is a made-up word combining "reverend" in English with *rānda*, meaning prostitute, in Marathi.[175]

In 1916, in a talk for the Anthropology Department at Columbia University where he was studying for his PhD, Ambedkar pointed out that "the absence of intermarriage—endogamy, to be concise—is the only one that can be called the essence of Caste when rightly understood.[176] Intermarriage, by extension, was the chief way of getting rid of caste. That same year, Gandhi weighed in, defending both the caste system and taboos against intermarriage on the grounds that "[t]he Hindu social structure has endured, I believe, on the foundation of the caste system . . . we can carry out social reform with ease through the agency of the caste system and order through it our religious practical and moral affairs as we choose."[177] The prohibition against intermarriage fostered

172. Constable, "Early Dalit Literature and Culture."

173. Shinde, "Stripurushtulana," 92–106. For an English translation see O'Hanlon, *A Comparison between Women and Men*. See also Bhagwat, "Marathi Literature as a Source," and A. Rao, "Sexuality and the Family Form."

174. Kosambi, "Women, Emancipation and Equality.".

175. Botre, "The Body Language of Caste," 45. For an outstanding biographical work on Pandita Ramabai, see Chakravarti, *Rewriting History*. See also Kosambi, "Indian Response to Christianity," WS61–63, WS65–71.

176. Ambedkar, "Caste in India," 6–8. I am grateful to Weining Fang, who took on as a research project reading Ambedkar's and Gandhi's writings in search of relevant passages.

177. Gandhi. "The Hindu Caste System," 258–60.

a moral self-control, he wrote, and there were good sound reasons for maintaining endogamous marriages.

> The caste defines the limits within which one may enjoy life; that is to say, we are not free to seek any happiness outside the caste. We did not associate with members of other communities for eating or enter into marriage relationships with them. With an arrangement of this kind, there is a good chance that loose conduct will be kept down. The idea that coming together for purposes of eating promotes friendship is contradicted by experience. If it did, the great war being waged today in Europe would never have started. The bitterest quarrels are among relatives. We had needlessly exaggerated the importance of eating . . . Just as we attend to evacuation, etc., in private, we should likewise eat and perform other actions common to all animals always in private.

Marriage and dining were private activities for Gandhi, and he argued that caste imposed useful limits and restrained unlicensed pursuits of material happiness. As for intermarriage,

> . . . the same thing is true of marriage. Prohibition of marriage with anyone not belonging to one's community promotes self-control, and self-control is conducive to happiness in all circumstances. . . . That is the reason why I see nothing wrong in the practice of choosing the husband or the wife from among persons of equal birth.[178]

Troubling and retrograde as Gandhi's claims seem now, he seemed to concede the idea that interdining and intermarriage would make all Hindus come together was a fool's dream. Far better to keep the inherent system of caste and use it to reform education, regulate elections, and fight for self-rule. The problems with the caste system only showed that the humans who lived within it were imperfect:

> . . . the system is not merely an inert, lifeless institution but a living one and has been functioning according to its own law. Unfortunately, today we find it for the evils like ostentation and hypocrisy, pleasure seeking and quarrels. But this only proves that people lack character; we cannot conclude from the system itself is bad.[179]

Gandhi could accept the continuation of caste if it could be cleansed of its worst aspects, including many mandated by Dharmaśāstric texts.

178. Gandhi. "The Hindu Caste System," 258–60.
179. Gandhi. "The Hindu Caste System," 258–60.

Savarkar's advocacy of intermarriage looked precisely at śāstric injunctions and was aligned neither with Gandhi's conservative and even puritanical critique of intermarriage nor with Ambedkar's analysis of the systematic relationship between Brahminism and intermarriage. As a student in London, Savarkar wrote and sent home an essay titled "England's Women and India's Men" on the suffragette movement.[180] It is filled with admiration for the women fighting for the vote; he explained their cause, tactics, and purpose to his readers back home. He understood their impatience with the misogyny they faced and applauded their resolve to agitate on their own terms, not those laid out by men, suggesting there was much to learn from their agitation. Yet he immediately created an equivalence between men declaring women incapable of understanding politics or governance and a colonized people being told they were incapable of self-rule.

> Women have less education, they would not be able to bear arms, their brains are naturally weaker and they will not understand politics or governance, by saying so men gave them absolutely no support, and worse, some women believed all of these lies the men told and got immersed in trying to address them as if they were real. But women were not fooled, and they recognized that all these excuses were stale. Has any oppressive power ever been ready to give it up? Up until Americans seized their own government, were the British not claiming that Americans were uneducated and could not govern? That Italians did not have the brains to manage their own affairs, which was the reason Austria was in Italy, was this not maintained by the Austrians right till the end?[181]

He ventriloquized what the women demanding suffrage might have said.

> Until we get political independence, we will not get rid of our ill-education or weakness and these oppressors tell us that when we get educated and strong then they will give us political independence. Until you jump in the water, you don't learn how to swim; but they tell us they will only allow us to enter the water after we learn how to swim. Allow us?? We are jumping!! We will get our political independence.[182]

Once again, we see Savarkar's peculiar iconoclasm. He noted, for example, the inherent patriarchy in male attempts to help the suffragettes.

180. *SSV*, MPHS, 4: 53–59.
181. *SSV*, MPHS, 4: 54.
182. *SSV*, MPHS, 4: 54.

> . . . by lawful, what men mean is that women should behave in accordance with laws that men have made! Who makes laws? Oppressors do, in order to protect and safeguard their own oppressive rules. If any slave follows these laws, how will he escape his slavery? That women's subjugation remains in perpetuity, is because of being shackled by male laws.[183]

Savarkar wrote approvingly of their audacity.

> . . . when challenged in court, in response to the court's questions they retorted that they were not answerable to anyone. . . . When asked why the law was broken, they responded that it was not a law. Those men had drafted the law without women's consent/ agreement.[184]

Yet at the end we see the real point of the entire admiring article when he writes, "They were willing to take on their own fathers', brothers', even husbands' patriarchal sensibilities, imagine what they would have done *if they had been colonized by a foreign power* [emphasis mine]."[185]

Savarkar may have recognized that every issue of caste was also an issue of gender (even if the reverse was not necessarily true), and he knew that he needed women to be full members of the Hindu fold. He was tolerant of caste intermarriage, as long as Hindu women did not marry non-Hindus, as he made clear in a letter he wrote (in English) to his younger brother in 1913:

> And how do you like Bengal? By this time after the Puja holidays you are back to Calcutta and must have grown quite into a Bengali Babu-is it not? Forgotten Marathi language? Please take care you do not lose something else. For I am afraid I might hear at any time that some one of those clever Bengalis has stolen your heart away! Though I for one should like so much to have found a dear little Bengali sister in-law. I am as strongly in favour of these inter-provincial marriages among the Hindus as I am deadly opposed to the practice of marrying the European girls at this stage of our national life.[186]

This advocacy of interregional marriages was exceptional for its time when it would have been quite scandalous for a Bengali Brahmin to have married a

183. *SSV*, MPHS, 4: 53–56.
184. *SSV*, MPHS, 4: 57.
185. *SSV*, MPHS, 4: 58.
186. Letters from Andaman, Letter #2, 6.

Marathi Brahmin. But on the question of *anulōma/pratilōma* marriages, or intercaste marriages between Sudras and Brahmins, Savarkar did not engage in the kind of advocacy for such marriages as the one real route to the annihilation of caste as did Ambedkar but focused instead on demonstrating through a reading of epic literature that there are no genetic or blood-linked differences between the castes. The miscegenation that Ambedkar was recommending was, for Savarkar, already in place and had been so for centuries. Thus, while he wrote enthusiastically about interregional marriage, he did not explicitly advocate that Brahmins marry Mahars or make a case for intercaste marriages and indeed suggested that any such imposed agenda would not work, neither for upper castes nor untouchables.[187] This was all implicit in his assumption that caste should disappear in favor of everyone being Hindu and that one should be free to choose one's life partner. His most polemical attack against the prohibition against intermarriage comes when he shows that, to maintain absolute caste purity, the sons and daughters of kings would have no alternative but to marry each other. Savarkar points to the story of Lot in the Bible and an unnamed Buddhist rendition of the Rāmāyaṇa that was published in *Kesari*:

> The Buddha's clan too believed that relations between siblings led to increased genetic prosperity, and maybe to ensure the Buddha's own heirs are genetically strong, the Buddhist Ramayana describes Ram and Sita as brother and sister who fall in love and then get married.[188]

Because of this, the idea of maintaining caste purity was itself absurd.

In July 1916, congratulating his brother—the one he'd suggested might want a sweet Bengali wife—he had this to say:

> For though I long to see the day, when inter-provincial marriages amongst the Hindus would throw down the artificial and harmful barriers of castes and creeds and the Great River of life—our Hindu Life would, having freed itself of all bogs and sands, flow in an ever fresh and mighty current- uninterrupted and uninterruptible—still the first and foremost thing to be affected. In that direction is to restore to love her sole privilege and right of presiding over the wedding rights. Indeed, we can no longer be blind to the fact that we care more for the good breeding of cattle and fowls than for the *Eugenics of man*. Centuries of child marriages and marriages by proxies!

187. *SSV*, MPHS, 3: 85.
188. *JN #6, SSV*, MPHS, 3: 463.

> Centuries of love banished from its legitimate sphere of influence to attract and develop elements that tend to the betterment of body and mind and soul; and the inevitable result is a *race puny*, debilitated, all vigour and manhood sapped out of it. Thousand things have wrought this—and the marriage customs that prevail in us are one of the few important factors contributing to it. Authorities should come in to sanctify but not to silence love altogether [emphasis mine].[189]

Savarkar's use of the term "Eugenics of man" and a "race puny" startles us today, given how much eugenics is linked to Nazi terror and the brutal weaponization of science against minorities and otherwise oppressed groups. We can be quite sure that Savarkar had read the works of evolutionists and eugenicists such as Charles Darwin (1809–82), Francis Galton (1822–1911), and Herbert Spencer (1820–1903). Spencer, an English sociologist and philosopher, had suggested that society should simply evolve according to natural law, which would weed out the weakest elements of society. Darwin too, in his *Descent of Man* (1871), had applied his earlier evolutionary thinking to human beings, warning that if the lower classes continued to outbreed their social superiors, evolution would regress. Darwin's cousin, Francis Galton, another English explorer and anthropologist who coined the term "eugenics," had suggested in 1865 that humans should take control over their evolution, pitching the idea that a positive eugenics could encourage the right sorts of people to reproduce.[190] Spencer's philosophy was not without contradiction, given that he was a stringent critic of imperialism, seeing it as a sociological pathology that infected both colonizer and colonized; he was no fan of state intervention in social progress. Yet Spencer's sociological organicism in the colonial context, as Inder Marwah puts it, "enabled a notable shift by situating the motive force of social and political evolution not in *external* steering, but *internal* transformation. Progress turned on Indians' own capacities to reform social, political, and economic practices—to heal the social body—as a conjunct organism, from within."[191] In other words, Spencer's sociological organicism, with all its ambivalences and contradictions, allowed nationalists to move the focus from "benevolent empire to the Indian social body, pinning India's

189. Letters from Andaman, Letter #5, 16.

190. On Francis Galton, see Kevles, *In the Name of Eugenics*, 3–19. I am grateful to my colleague, Sandra Eder, who shared with me her lecture notes on eugenics and the Progressive era and who discussed many of these ideas with me.

191. Marwah, "Darwin in India," 8.

advancement on the social organism's endogenous evolution."[192] Such endogenous evolution was exactly what Savarkar was advocating.

Since the banishing of love from the social sphere had produced a puny race, the remedy was to return love to its rightful place. And indeed, love played a big role in *Essentials of Hindutva*. Love for the nation was, for Savarkar, proof of patriotism that could guarantee citizenship. Here, love, albeit with major qualifications (between Bengal and Maharashtra but not Hindus and Muslims as Gandhi later advocated or overtly intercaste as Ambedkar did), could eradicate caste.[193] It was not going to be easy, he conceded many years after writing these letters to his brother. In one funny example, he noted that if a Marathi Brahmin girl was married into a Bengali family, it would produce all manner of problems. Take, for instance, dining habits.

> When mother-in-law and daughter-in-law get to cooking a meal, the [Bengali] mother-in-law was likely to instruct her [Marathi] daughter-in-law to "clean these four fish for me, please." When they sit for dinner, according to the customs of Bengali Brahmins, the mother-in-law is going to scarf, scarf, scarf down that fish stew, the Marathi Brahmin daughter in law is going to barf, barf, barf at the very smell of that fish stew.[194]

Such unions could not be forced or imposed, but if they happened naturally, they should be encouraged and destigmatized.

But there were other issues linked to intermarriage between castes that concerned women, and Savarkar addressed them quite directly. In 1933 he gave a series of lectures in Ratnagiri, nine in all, to educate both men and women about the Manusmr̥ti. Given that upper-caste women were usually the carriers of tradition (*rudhi*) in their homes, Savarkar addressed them directly in a series of essays designed to explicate what he had directly read and translated.[195] If women saw the Manusmr̥ti, along with the Vedas, and the epics as "apauruṣēya, trikālābādhita ni anullaṅghya" (divinely authored, timeless, and inviolable), they were in for some surprises.[196] He illustrates this by taking as one example

192. Marwah, "Darwin in India," 8.

193. On marriage and how in the 1930s and 1940s Maharashtrian Brahmins deployed the concept of "love" within caste groups to prevent caste mixing, see Botre, "The Body Language of Caste," ch. 4 and 5.

194. "Janmajāta jātībhēda mōḍāyacē mhaṇajē kāya kārāyacē?," in *SSV*, MPHS, 3: 85–86.

195. Preface, *Pracin Arvacin Mahila*.

196. "Manusmr̥titeel Mahila," in *SSV*, MPHS, 4: 256.

names and naming. In the Manusmṛti, a *śloka* (translated correctly) declared that it is inauspicious and unadvisable to marry girls whose names express the names of constellations, trees, rivers, mountains, snakes, servants, or anything frightful.[197] This would not pose a problem, wrote Savarkar, if one read this *śloka* historically or historicized it. Read literally, as the Sanātanis claimed they did, then it would be the Sanātanis themselves who would be transgressing because in their homes "flow numerous Gangas, Godavaris, Sindhus, Krishnas, Kaveris, Narmadas," who would be ineligible to marry.[198]

In no set of writings is Savarkar quite as much the pandit/śāstri as he is in these. He quotes *śloka* after *śloka*, with translation and commentary, to demonstrate that the Manusmṛti is full of contradictory passages ("anēka parasparavirudhda ślōkāñcī khicaḍī"). His aim was to show that marriages between castes, between high-caste men and low-caste women, low-caste men and high-caste women (*anulōma/pratilōma*), and even widow remarriage was accepted in the Manusmṛti—all to hold Sanātani feet to the fire. There was no vegetarianism either, and women of all *varṇas*, he wrote, ate meat and fish as a religious duty.[199] In time that changed, but he pointed to a set of extraordinary *ślokas* that must have outraged his readers, particularly those unfamiliar with the Manusmṛti, which he translated for his readers, noting that during the period of mourning, one should serve various types of fruits and leafy vegetables, but most important was how many days the ancestors would be satiated[200]—two months if they ate fish, three months if they ate deer, five

197. *SSV*, MPHS, 4: 258. In the Manusmṛti the Sanskrit *śloka* is:

Na rkṣavṛkṣanadīnāmnīṃ nāntyaparvatanāmikām ।
na pakṣyahipreṣyanāmnīṃ na ca bhīṣaṇanāmikām ।।
avyaṃgāṃgīṃ saumyanāmnīṃ haṃsavāraṇagāminīm ।
tanulomakeśadaśanāṃ mṛdvaṅgīmudvahet striyam ।। 3.9–10

198. "Manusmṛtiteel Mahila," in *SSV*, MPHS, 4: 259.
199. "Manusmṛtiteel Mahila," in *SSV*, MPHS, 4: 277.
200. "Manusmṛtiteel Mahila," in *SSV*, MPHS, 4: 275. The Sanskrit *śloka* is:

bhakṣyaṃ bhojyaṃ ca vivadham mūlāni ca phalāni ca ।
hradyāni caiva māṃsāni pānāni surabhīṇi ca ।।
haviryaccirarātrāya yaccānantyāya kalpate ।
pitṛbhyo vidhivaddatam tatpravakṣyāmy aśeṣataḥ ।।
dvau māsau matsyamāṃsena trīnmāsānhāriṇena tu ।
aurabhreṇātha catura ḥ śākunenātha paṃca vai ।।
ṣaṇmāsāṃśchāgamāṃsena pārṣatena ca sapta vai ।
aṣṭāveṇasya māṃsena rauraveṇa navaiva tu ।।

months if they ate the meat of birds, ten if they ate the meat of wild boars, eleven with the meat of a tortoise or rabbit.[201] His point was that women who lived in the period when the Manusmṛti was composed would have not only known how to clean and cook various kinds of meat—it would have been their duty to do so.

He had already written about caste-dilution for *Kesari*, claiming that

> [i]n all the four Varnas, caste dilution has been taking place with the full authority of the Shastras. Our thousands of jatis have come about because of this caste dilution.[202]

His argument takes on the idea of purity of lineage coming from the father, suggesting that, when Brahmins married women of all castes, their children were Brahmin, for which he cites, "triṣu varṇeṣu jāto hi brāhmaṇo brāhmaṇāt bhavet" ("The one who is born of a brahmin, from among the three *varṇas* [i.e., born of a wife of any of the three higher *varṇas*] should be a brahmin"), and, "śūdraiva bhāryā śūdrasya sā ca svā ca viśaḥ smṛte। te ca svā caiva rājñaś ca tāś ca svā cāgrajanmanaḥ" ("A Sudra [woman] is alone the wife of a Sudra [man]. For the Vaishya man, she [i.e., a Sudra woman] and one of his own [*varṇa*, i.e., a Vaishya woman] are considered appropriate [wives]. Those two [the Sudra woman and the Vaisya woman] as well as one belonging to his own [*varṇa*] for the Kshatriya; those three as well as one of his own [*varṇa*] for the Brahmin").[203] It was precisely because of those kinds of *anulōma/pratilōma* marriages that Hindus have now 4,000 *jatis*. This was all for the good, he suggested, because it meant that, from high to low, the same blood ran in all castes.

> This is why from Suta and Magadha to the progeny of Brahmin women from having had relations with Sudras, who are considered Chandala, to

---

daśa māsāṃstu tṛpyanti varāhamahiṣāmiṣaiḥ ।
śaśakūrmayostu māṃsena māsānekādaśaiva tu ।।
kālaśākaṃ mahāśalkāḥ khaḍgalohāmiṣaṃ madhu ।
ānantyāyaiva kalpyante munyannāni ca sarvaśaḥ 3.227

201. "Manusmr̥titeel Mahila," in *SSV*, MPHS, 4: 276.

202. "Jātisaṅkarācyā astitvācā sākṣīdāra mhaṇajē svayamēva smr̥tica," in *SSV*, MPHS, 3: 468.

203. "Jātisaṅkarācyā astitvācā sākṣīdāra mhaṇajē svayamēva smr̥tica" in *SSV*, MPHS, 3: 469. I am grateful to Nabanjan Maitra and Luther Obrock for their incredibly prompt help with both translation and transliteration. Savarkar gets the first quote from the Mahābhārata, 13.47.17 cd. The second quote is from the Manusmṛti, 3.13.

our preciously untouchable brothers the blood of Brahmins and others is all intermixed. In all of us, everyone's blood flows—this no one can deny.[204]

Varṇasaṃkara, so feared by the Sanātanis, was a positive:

The traditions of the eternal Śruti, Smruti, Puranokta which influence the traditions of patriarchy, matriarchy, and the traditions of Anuloma and Pratiloma also prove that nobody in the four varnas or in four hundred castes is pure, and the blood of different castes is mixed with each other through the ritual marriages. . . . Hence, according to the principle of progress of hereditary qualities, we all have got the qualities of each other through this mixture.[205]

Savarkar narrates the history of the most eminent of all clans—the Pandavas from the Mahābhārata—to make his point.

Take the example of the clan of Pandavas. That clan was of the clan of the emperor Bharat, the defender of religion, the greatest of the Aryans, it was not an inferior clan! Prateep told Shantanu, "O King, who this woman is, where is she from, what caste, do not ask any of these questions, just marry her," and accordingly Shantanu married Ganga who was from an unknown caste. His son Bhishma became kshatriya through chanting rituals. Later, when Shantanu married a daughter of a fisherman and made her his queen knowing her caste and her patrilineal heritage, he still did not lose caste. Not just that, but the sons of this fisherwoman, Chitrangad and Vichitravirya became emperors of Indian Brahmins as per the shastras. Later, a son of this fisherwoman married Ambika and Ambalika, daughters of a Kshatriya king.[206]

Savarkar pushed this point even further.

The composer of the Mahābhārata himself, the sage Vyasa, was the son of Parāśar who himself was the son of a dog-eating untouchable. And Parashar's wife was a fisherwoman, who had given birth to the "Mahājñāni,

204. "Jātisaṅkarācyā astitvācā sākṣīdāra mhaṇajē svayamēva smṛtica" in *SSV*, MPHS, 3: 469.

205. "Jātisaṅkarācyā astitvācā sākṣīdāra mhaṇajē svayamēva smṛtica," in *SSV*, MPHS, 3: 470.

206. "Jātisaṅkarācyā astitvācā sākṣīdāra mhaṇajē svayamēva smṛtica," in *SSV*, MPHS, 3: 470.

Mahātapī, Mahābhāratakāra" [Great Sage, Great Ascetic, Composer of the Mahabharat] Vyasa.[207]

Savarkar exults in the discovery that Vyasa had untouchable lineage. Such *varṇa* dilution was not hellish, he suggested, but heavenly.[208] While he was interested in the problem of race and genetics, it is not equally clear that his interest led him in the direction of social engineering. All Hindus (which for him included untouchables) had the same, intermingled blood in their veins. In keeping with his sense of himself as a "progressive" thinker, Savarkar would have joined anticolonial nationalists, from Bankimchandra Chatterjee, Aurobindo Ghosh, Swami Vivekananda, B. C. Pal, B. G. Tilak, Lala Lajpat Rai, and reformist organizations like the Brahmo Samaj and the Arya Samaj, in using Darwinian evolutionism and Spencerian organicism to pull apart the fundamental assumptions in the gradualism and developmentalist agenda of the British in endlessly deferring the question of India's readiness for independence.[209] In the hands of cultural nationalists, evolutionism posed no real threat to Hinduism's cyclical conception of time and epochs. Hindu civilization could be traced back in a Darwinian geological scale to its Aryan roots, as B. G. Tilak and Narayan Pavgi would do in Marathi.[210] Darwin also allowed nationalists to argue that India was not, as the orientalists would have had it, fixed in time, but simply fallen, temporarily, until it could be, as Savarkar would have it, awakened from its narcolepsy. As he does in *Essentials of Hindutva*, Savarkar marshals all the sages, seers, kings, and prophets of the epics to do his social reform work for him.

In the early first millennium, the author of the *Buddhacharita*, a scholar named Aśvaghoṣa, composed a critical tract titled *Vajrasūcī* that had examined the concept of *Brahmanya*, suggesting that there was no Śruti/Smr̥ti authority for *varṇa* divisions.[211] The *Vajrasūcī* is sometimes considered a minor Upaniṣad,

207. "Jātisaṅkarācyā astitvācā sākṣīdāra mhaṇajē svayamēva smr̥tica" in *SSV*, MPHS, 3: 470.

208. *SSV*, MPHS, 3: 470–71.

209. Marwah, *Darwin in India*, 2, and Marwah, "Rethinking Resistance," 57.

210. See the section on *Hindu-Pad-Padashahi* in chapter 5 for Pavgi and Tilak's writing on the ancient Aryans.

211. See Omvedt, *Buddhism in India*. Omvedt notes that Bahinabai identified it as an Upaniṣad and that she may not have known that it was composed by a Buddhist rather than a Brahmin. Aśvaghoṣa's identity remains an open question. Was he a Buddhist, a Brahmin, or a Brahmin/Buddhist (in the sense that Johannes Bronkhorst describes—that, since Brahminism was not something one converted to, it could remain as a marker of sociopolitical power, even among Buddhists)? Was the *Vajrasūcī* an *Upaniṣad* or a Buddhist text? Was the author of the

attached to the Sāmaveda, sometimes a Buddhist text, and sometimes credited to Shankaracharya, an Advaitin.[212] In the seventeenth century, as Gail Omvedt points out, Sant Tukaram suggested to Bahinabai, his famous woman student, that she translate it as an important Buddhist text. Bahinabai reworded and summarized the main questions the *Vajrasūcī* raised and answered in her poetry:

> Who can without doubt be called a Brahman?
> Let us think and analyse the meaning of the word.
> Then they should be saluted and adored as supreme,
> who appointed the words of the Vedas as a gift for moksa;
> Life, the body, caste, colour, action, religion, let us look and search out the meaning,
> Baheni [*sic*] says, first see if wisdom, learning, spiritual and theoretical understanding
> are the marks of a Brahman.[213]

Omvedt notes that Bahinabai's poem

> critiques all these ways of characterising the "essence" of the Brahman—"life" (*jiv*), "body" (*deh*), "caste/birth" (*jati*), "wisdom" (*panditya*), "action" (*karma*), and "religion" (*dharma*)—arguing either that they can in no way differentiate among persons or that they simply make no sense. Since such characteristics belong to all human beings, "Brahmans" as a caste have nothing unique in them.

Buddhacarita the same as the author of the *Vajrasūcī*? This remains a matter of heated debate, but not one I am qualified to enter.

212. Sujitkumar Mukhopadhyaya, who edited the critical edition of the *Vajrasūcī* takes on this question and discusses a number of different opinions and translations, in particular the Chinese translation, which ascribes the authorship to Bodhisattva Dharmakirti. His own view is that the *Vajrasūci* was composed by the same Aśvaghoṣa who composed the *Buddhacarita* and the *Saundarananda*, despite the fact that the *Vajrasūci* reads very differently than the poetic texts of the *Buddhacarita* and the *Saundarananda*. That being said, it was not impossible that the same author could have composed texts in different styles. Both the *Buddhacarita* and the *Vajrasūci* exhibit Aśvaghoṣa's deep familiarity with the Mahābhārata, Rāmāyaṇa, and the purāṇas. I am grateful to Madhav Deshpande for pointing me in the direction of this book and for his help with the question itself. See Mukhopadhyaya, *The Vajrasūci of Aśvaghoṣa*, vii-xvii.

213. Omvedt, *Buddhism in India*, 209–10. Omvedt presents selections from Bahinabai's poems #277–94, which translate the *Vajrasucī*. The passage above is from poem #278.

Perhaps because Bahinabai's poetry might have been known to the women he was addressing, Savarkar wrote and published his own nine-page didactic translation (into Marathi) and explanation of the *Vajrasūcī* addressed specifically to the women readers of the magazine *Stree*. It is off Aśvaghoṣa's shoulder that Savarkar directs his only examination of Brahminism.

Savarkar translates, paraphrases, and comments on the *Vajrasūcī*'s central questions: Who or what is meant by Brahmana? The self? The body? Birth-based social class? The possessor of knowledge? Savarkar adds other questions, such as who is the possessor of Vedic knowledge? Of all knowledge? The *Vajrasūcī* concludes that only spiritual realization and good conduct determine *Brahmanya*.

One by one, the *Vajrasūcī* (both Aśvaghoṣa's and Savarkar's translation with commentary) dismantles arguments. Could the self be considered Brahman? Savarkar quotes Aśvaghoṣa quoting Manu: "if a Brahmin who is proficient in the Vedas and its various parts takes dakshina or any other offering from a Sudra then he will beget twelve lives as a donkey, six as a pig and seventy as a dog!" If *Brahmanya* is so easily alienable, the self cannot be Brahman. Nor is it acquired through direct genetic descent. Savarkar translates:

> Achalmuni was born of an elephant, Keshapingal of an owl, Kaushikrishi of grass, Dronacarya of an earthen pot, Taitirriya rishi of a bird, Vyasa of a fisherwoman, Kaushiki of a Sudra woman, Vishwamitra of a Chandala, Vasishtha of a prostitute; now if these ślokas are in the Smr̥tis then you must accept them. None of them had Brahmin parents, but you see them as Brahmin authorities on Brahmanya. In the same sense if you believe that one is a Brahmin only if born to Brahmin parents, that too is wrong.[214]

There was no such thing as Brahmin genetics, or pure Brahmin lineage, and we note that the names of the sages include "Vasishta, and Vishwamitra"—two of the *saptarshi* (seven rishis/seers) that Brahmin Vedic theory suggests that all Brahmins were descended from: Bharadwaj, Vasistha, Atri, Kashyapa, Jamadagni, Vishwamitra, and Gautam Maharishi. Agastya was added later, and Brahmins believe that the eight rishis/seers are the hymn-families, or clans, called *gotras* from whom Brahmins claim their patrilineal origins.[215] Priests

214. "Vajrasucī" in *SSV*, MPHS, 3: 534.

215. For two quick explanations of the "original" *gotras*, see Brough, "The Early History of the Gotras," and Rahurkar, "The Origin of the Gotra-System in the R̥gveda." The literature on this subject is vast and based on readings of the enormous Sanskrit literature. Brough and other

ask for one's *gotra* name before conducting ceremonies, and marriages within *gotras* are typically forbidden. Here Savarkar was telling traditional women that two of their *gotras* derived not from pure Brahminical origins but from untouchables.

Brahmanya does not reside in the body nor in conduct or knowledge because, now citing the Rāmāyaṇa, Savarkar writes that

> Ravana was proficient in the Vedas, but he is someone you call a Rakshasa [demon], not a Brahmin. In those days, Rakshasas also studied the Vedas, then why do you not call them Brahmins?[216]

There was nothing special about Brahmins or *Brahmanya,* and all human beings have only one caste because

> if all humans come from one Brahmadeva, and if there is no contact between them how did there come to be four different castes? If my wife gives birth to four children, aren't they all the same? Then how did one Brahmadev give birth to four different beings?[217]

Where if at all were divisions natural? Only in the animal and plant kingdom.[218]

These writings aside, Savarkar's caste-reform related activities in Ratnagiri included ceremonies that he knew would make Sanātanis uncomfortable. As A. G. Salvi recalled, Savarkar's wife held the first mixed *haḷadī-kuṅkūṁ,* a festive gathering in which married women assemble at someone's house and

---

Sanskrit Indologists extrapolate from textual evidence in the Ṛgveda or the *Brhdaranyaka Upaniṣad.* The history of *gotra* and how it was understood on the ground was somewhat different. For an anthropological look at *gotra,* see Madan, "Is the Brahmanic Gotra a Grouping?" For an examination of *gotras* as Veda Shaka families, with more than just the seven *gotras,* see Sharma, "A Study of the Gotras and Pravaras."

216. "Vajrasūcī," in *SSV,* MPHS, 3: 536.

217. "Vajrasūcī," in *SSV,* MPHS, 3: 537.

218. Savarkar began his translation of the *Vajrasūcī* with these passages from the *Bhavisyapurāṇa*:

Phalāny atha udumbaravṛkṣajāteḥ mulāgramadhyāni bhavāni vāpi ।	Fruits of the species of the fig tree, whether the roots or the tips, or the branches
varṇākṛtisparśarasais samāni tathaikato jātīr itī pracityā ।।	Whether their color, shape, form, feel,sap, all are of one *jati,* together as a single one
tasmān na go'śvavat kaścit jātībhedosti dehinām ।	Unlike a cow or horse (embodied species) there are no distinctions (in a tree)
kāryabhedanimittene saṃketa: kṛtrima: kṛta ।।	Because of their different actions we conventionally denominate them as separate *jatis*

exchange turmeric and vermillion powder. This occurred in Shirgaon, at the home of Mo. Vi. Damle, a staunch Sanātani who also admired Savarkar. Damle recounts:

> Veer Savarkar held the first intermixed haḷadī-kuṅkūṁ in our house. Neighboring upper-caste women were unwilling to offer haḷadī-kuṅkūṁ to untouchable women. Savarkar's wife, Mai, gave it to them. Following this, hesitatingly, slowly slowly, upper caste women joined her. This one event caused enormous trouble for *a couple of years*. Not merely this, but *our house was boycotted for a long time* [emphasis mine].[219]

Damle's remembrance of "enormous trouble for a couple of years" and his house being "boycotted for a long time" gives us a post hoc ethnographic description of the deep intractability of the Sanātani community for whom even an intermixed *haḷadī-kuṅkūṁ* was so transgressive. It is likely that Savarkar held the *haḷadī-kuṅkūṁ* at Damle's house to ward off additional trouble from the Sanātanis whom he had already greatly offended. Upset with his so-called immorality, Sanātanis had reported him to the Ratnagiri police and had on occasion had him evicted from the house in which he was living. In any event Damle agreed to bear the burden, not just of hosting the event but of having to deal with years of ostracization. While we should credit Savarkar for his willingness to target the orthodox community, we should perhaps also ask what an intermixed *haḷadī-kuṅkūṁ* could accomplish?[220] Even on the subject of marriage, years later, as Anupama Rao notes, when Savarkar led the Hindu Mahasabha, it joined with Ambedkar's Samata Sangha only to push for conducting Vedic marriages and thread ceremonies in Dalit communities.[221]

In 1928, at a congress on untouchability in Malvan, Savarkar gave a lecture emphasizing the seven features of caste society that needed abolition. On the

219. Salvi, *Savarakara Yancya Athavani*, 33.

220. See Palshikar, "Jatychedak nibandh," 170–71. Palshikar's critical essay on Savarkar is a rare exception. I am pointing to some of the same passages that he used and asking somewhat similar questions about the double standards in Savarkar's thought. BSA of March 3, 1928 reported that Savarkar had been "turned out at the instigation of some of the local Brahmins on the grounds of his immorality." BSA No. 36 of August 9, 1928 reported the District Magistrate of Ratnagiri as saying, "He knows how to work on the feelings of a crowd, but is now bitterly disliked by the better-class Brahmins, owing to his promiscuous immorality. Even well-to-do Chitpawans find their family honour in danger. Recently he was shouted down in a temple—which is why he now holds his meetings under a peepul tree." Both BSAs are in Home Department/Special/File 60 D (d).

221. See A. Rao, *The Caste Question*, 300–305.

boat ride back, Savarkar and others decided to eat together. Savarkar invited the ticket inspector to join them, but as one of his friends remembered, "Lala was a Muslim, and hesitated, saying he would eat separately in his own cabin, at which point Savarkar got up, took his hand and led him to our table, where we all shared in the meal, including Lala." Surprised to see Savarkar consume meat, a fellow traveler approached him and asked Savarkar how a Brahmin could eat meat. To which Savarkar was remembered as responding that

> the slaughter of animals or meat eating was not forbidden. There was no sin in it. One does not lose religion or caste by it, and you should set aside such idiotic opinions.[222]

Savarkar led by example, showing that sharing food with a Muslim did not take away his Hinduness. This passage was also meant to reveal that he was not in fact anti-Muslim and similar examples are constantly repeated in the literature on Savarkar, with his biographers frequently at pains to remind readers that Savarkar had no animus against Muslims.[223]

Savarkar's interlocutors and intended audience were Hindus whose fear of losing caste was so extreme that they did not eat eggs or go near a chewed-up sugarcane stalk, who believed that thirty-three crores of gods lived in a cow's belly. They were the ones who needed to be told that they were engaged in sacrilege.[224]

222. Salvi, *Savarakara Yancya Athavani*, 6–7.

223. See, as just one example, the preface to a relatively recent work on Savarkar published by Sudhakar Bhalerao, *Swatantryaveer Savarkar Vicarmanthan*, 5–7, in which he notes that he is not writing as a devotee or a supporter and is aware of the limitations in Savarkar's work, which do not diminish his greatness, but he nonetheless writes with open pride as a cultural Hindu. In the chapter titled "Savarakaranci aitihasika drsti," Bhalerao says that Savarkar wrote to foster Hindu-Muslim unity but only under certain conditions: the equal sovereign status of both communities. There could be no such Hindu-Muslim unity if the communities were unequal (32). That Muslims, in independent India, are a distinct minority and numerically unequal is not addressed at all. See also Salvi, *Savarakara Yancya Athavani*, 57, where Salvi remembers going to visit Savarkar with two friends sometime after independence to ask him if it was indeed true that he was anti-Muslim as he was being depicted. Savarkar's answer repeated his previous claims about even educated Muslims being religion-mad, and he seemingly urged Salvi to read books by Muslim reformers writing against fanaticism.

224. Savarkar wrote, ". . . when you treat an animal as a God, and you force not just one but 33 crore gods and goddesses, and seers into her body, draw images depicting this [travesty], sell those images, and worship her with sandalwood and flowers, then who is engaged in the real sacrilege?" See "*Gōrakṣaka ki gāyaḷa*" in *SSV*, MPHS, 3: 188.

No doubt this community needed these lessons, but Savarkar's discourse always skirted the issues that were most politically significant for the Brahmanetar, Dalit, and Muslim communities. Telling a Muslim that he or she was by birth, religion, and genes fundamentally and permanently polluted (as we saw in the last chapter) and only engaged in temple destruction and the rape and abduction of Hindu women while simultaneously reassuring Hindus that they were by blood, birth, genes, and spirit incapable of losing caste or religion through contact with Muslims was designed to reassure conservative Hindus, not provide genuine support for Muslims or Dalits, or any other oppressed community.

Savarkar and Temple Entry

If the Sanātani community was anxious about cow slaughter or leery of holding intermixed *haḷadī-kuṅkūṁs* in private homes, it was outraged at the thought of Dalits entering a temple. So intractable was the community on this issue that it prohibited Dalits from even walking on the streets on which temples were located. The Hindu temple was and is a material representation of Brahmin power, not just to organize the fundamental rituals of Hindu religious practice but to establish the ritual order of caste groups and who could be included in that caste order. Anupama Rao has called the temple "the locus of Brahminical authority" and the "most potent site of Dalits denigration by caste Hindus."[225] Accordingly, those fighting for caste equality in the 1920s—from E. V. Ramaswamy Naicker in the south to B. R. Ambedkar in western India to Gandhi on a national stage—made temple entry a major plank of their calls for reform. The INC led two major *satyagrahas* specifically on temple entry in 1924 and 1932, but as Dilip Menon has pointed out, they were aimed at and led by upper castes and intended to reform Hinduism. As Nicholas Dirks suggests, "Although social reform agendas . . . often focused on Brahmanic practices, with only a few exceptions . . . they worked to assert the primary importance of Brahman customs for the definition of the Hindu community."[226] Although Dalit-led *satyagrahas* were less about being "allowed" to enter a temple and more about equal access to public property as a fundamental right, Ambedkar soon grew frustrated by temple entry as a political objective for Dalits, as for that matter did Naicker for non-Brahmans in southern India.[227]

225. A. Rao, *The Caste Question*, 88–89.

226. Dirks, *Castes of Mind*, 256.

227. A. Rao, *The Caste Question*, 88–89; Dirks, *Castes of Mind*, 255–74.

Savarkar also took on the issue of temple entry. I present here two poems he wrote on untouchability. In 1925 he composed a song for the Akhil Hindu gathering from Shirgaon titled "Hindūñcē ēkatāgān" ("The Unity of Hindus").[228] It was sung, according to his editor, by Brahmins, Sudras, Mahars, and Mangs alike at gatherings up and down Maharashtra.[229]

You and us, we are Hindu! Brothers alike
To that Mahadev our father let us bow
Brahmin or Kshatriya whatever we are
Whatever our visage or color
Whether Mahar or Mang
To our common mother the Hindu jati we bow

We belong to the same beloved country
Our lives are composed in the same meter
We belong to the same faith
These are all part of the Ganges, each of us an equal drop

The devotee of Ramachandra or Govind
Those who worship the Gita
They sit in the ship of Hindu Dharma
And cross the eternal ocean

Everyone should forgive the faults of each other
The tradition of ill treatment should be let go
For the sake of our mother we should mingle with each other
Forgive past oppression and come together in love

We are children of this Hindujati
For our Hindu dharma, all efforts
We will defend with our life
Let us under this flag remember our common ancestor.

It is possible that a few members of the Mahar, Mang, and Sudra communities sang a poem extolling Hindu *dharma* and Hindujati, and the Gita, Ramchandra, and Govind, but that is secondary. It is less likely that lines such as "our lives are composed in the same meter" or "everyone should forgive the faults of each other" would not have come across as Brahmin condescension

228. Editor's note in *SSV*, MPHS, 7: 163.
229. *SSV*, MPHS, 7: 163.

and hypocrisy. For a community oppressed for millennia by Brahmins, the suggestion that it should "forgive past oppression and come together in love" was insulting. But the real point is the cultural work the poem does. By opposing caste with the term "Hindu," Savarkar assures those who agree with him that to be Hindu rather than Brahmin, Kayastha, Saraswat, Iyer, or Mahar was to be progressive (even if his sense of being Hindu and being Brahmin were effectively interchangeable). In other words, he was telling communities who had been denied a voice and who were doing political work on behalf of their caste that they should give up that caste identity to be called Hindu.[230] Caste was regressive, ethnic nationalism progressive.

In Ratnagiri, Savarkar wrote that part of the Konkan was considered "backward" relative to other parts of Maharashtra, and, because of his efforts, "Kshatriya, Vaisya, Kumbar, Chambhar, Teli, Brahmin, Nhavi, etc." assembled together in the main hall of the Vitthal temple and sang the poem he composed, "Tumhī āmhī sakala Hindu bandhu bandhu." Around the same time in Pune, considered the heart of progressive and forward-thinking Maharashtra, 3,000 "Mambājībuvās āṇi Rāmēśvarabhaṭṭas" (Charlatans and Brahmins) violently prevented a few members of the Mahar-Chambhar community from entering the Parvati temple. This prompted Savarkar to write a satirical piece, in which he declared that, like the Theosophists, he would call forth the spirit of the dead Mambajibua to get his "Sanātani" statement on why the Parvati *satyagraha* was such a travesty.[231] Savarkar terms this "Mambājībuvāñcē vaktavya (kaifiyata)." (Mambajibua's statement—a kaifiyat.)[232] Savarkar apologizes in this article to the Mahar-Chambhar-Mang communities, assures them they were all Hindu, encourages them to fight a hundred times for every temple in India, and implores them not to convert, not to call

> the very enemies of your parents your parents because if you change your caste, if Chambhars become Christians and Mahars become Muslims your very own ancestors will spit on you for having changed their caste—I know that the language of turning to a foreign faith is the result of Mambajibua's

230. On precisely the paradox of Dalit communities embracing their *jati* identities to demand redress for centuries if not millennia of upper caste and Brahmin oppression, see A. Rao, *The Caste Question*.

231. "Puṇyātīla tīna hajāra mambājībuvāṁ" ("Poona's three thousand Charlatans"), in *SSV*, MPHS, 3: 500–508.

232. "Puṇyātīla tīna hajāra mambājībuvāṁ" ("Poona's three thousand Charlatans"), in *SSV*, MPHS, 3: 502–3.

hypocritical tradition. For that very reason don't contaminate yourselves any further.[233]

In 1929 Savarkar composed another poem, this one called "Sutaka Yugāñcē Phiṭalēṁ" ("An Aeon of Mourning Is Over") celebrating the Shri Vitthal Ratnagiri temple opening its doors to the Dalit community.[234] In a prefatory note, the editor of his poetry collection noted that a young man named Shivu Bhangi sang it climbing up each step of the temple, with the permission of a gathered assembly, and as he climbed the last step of the temple was met with applause that resounded into the heavens. The concept of *sutak* is suffused with Brahmin doublespeak. Meaning temporary impurity and untouchability, it is observed as a period of impurity and mourning by family members of the deceased. Brahmins recover from this impurity in ten days; other castes take longer. *Sutaka fitne* or *sutaka sutane* refers to the return to normalcy in two ways—getting past the prescribed grieving period and regaining touchability. The rules about mourning and bereavement were codified in the Manusmṛti and were maintained by Brahmin priests; meanwhile, the speaker in the poem is a grateful Dalit. I have italicized each time in the poem that this fictional Dalit is self-abnegating and grateful for Brahmin beneficence. If the first poem was condescending, this one was full of Brahmin noblesse oblige.

You *allowed* us entrance to God's door
A *great favor you have bestowed*
By *touching this unclean forehead* and bestowed a boon
You have sullied your pure hands

You *cleansed our impure feet*
and *cleansed our Destiny* imprinted on our forehead
You are the Sun of Dharma, how may I describe you
I touch your shadow

you brought into the fold an *impure village*
and out you went into villages
You Hindus have brought us a-Hindus close
The aeon of *cosmic impurity* is undone
And the *contamination enshrined* through Destiny (vidhi-likhit)
is undone

233. "Puṇyātīla tīna hajāra mambājībuvāṁ" ("Poona's three thousand Charlatans"), in *SSV*, MPHS, 3: 508.

234. *SSV*, MPHS, 7: 170.

An age of quarrel has ended
The enemy's trap has been broken
We who have been slaves for centuries are now colleagues
You have bestowed a great favor

The editor of the collection containing this poem must have known that the phrase "ābhāra jāhalē bhārī" ("a great favor you have bestowed"), which suggests that upper castes had benevolently bestowed favor on the Dalits, might make some readers uneasy since he added a note saying that the core of the poem is the injustice the Dalits suffered.[235] Perhaps, but it is a measure of Savarkar's tone-deafness that he wrote so patronizing a poem.

Savarkar influenced Bhagoji Sheth Keer, a Ratnagiri philanthropist, to build a new temple in 1931, the Patitpavan temple. *Patitpavan* means purifying the impure or fallen; using it as a name for a temple speaks as much about Brahmin largesse as the poem above. The new temple was inaugurated by the Shankaracharya (head of the Karveer-peeth monastery) and social reformer Dr. Kurtakoti. Keer invited intellectuals and other Brahmins from Kashi, Bombay, and Nashik to the installation of the deity in the new temple, plunging the Ratnagiri community into its own Vedokta controversy.[236] These Brahmins opposed not just the temple but the interdining Savarkar proposed.

> Savarkar started a project of inter-dining; people of all castes came to eat. But Mahars would not sit next to Chambhars who would not sit next to Bhangis who would not sit next to Dhors. They wanted to sit with their own jati. Savarkar realized this. He said to them all "if Brahmins have to inter-dine with untouchables, they must sit next to a Chambhar. But untouchables too have to give up their insistence on sitting only next to their own jati."[237]

Again and again, Savarkar suggests that Brahmins and Dalits were equally prejudiced in their desire to dine only with their own communities. While it is true that casteism is not restricted to upper-caste communities, there is no equivalence between the positions of Brahmans and Dalits on such caste questions. Savarkar places the onus on the Dalit community to show that it is not prejudiced, instead of recognizing that *jati* distinctions proliferated from the top down. The editor of the poetry collection claimed that the temple opening was attended by nearly 5,000 people, including Brahmins, Mahars, Bhangis,

235. *SSV*, MPHS, 7: 170.

236. Salvi, *Savarkar Yancya Athvani*, 57. See also Walinjkar, *Uttar Konkan Dalitmukti Calwal*, 195–99.

237. Salvi, *Savarkar Yancya Athvani*, 58.

Marathas, and Vaisyas. Such an audience, he claimed, had not been witnessed for 3,000 years. At the *puja* for the opening of Ratnagiri's second temple to open its door to untouchables, twenty representative members from different castes sang yet another Savarkar-penned poem, "Hindū jātīcā śripatitapāvanācā dhāvā" ("A Hindu *jati*'s appeal for purification").[238]

When will you uplift us, Oh God of the Hindu jati
We are all impure—from non-Brahman to Chandala[239]
You are the one to purify us

To avoid polluting the head we did not hesitate
to cut off our feet
And because we keep purity with our feet
We cut off our feet

Veda cannot fall on our ears
Our mouth cannot dispense wisdom
If the right hand tries [endlessly] to defeat the left hand.
The entire body might as well be sold *to the enemy* [emphasis mine]

You close the door on your own
But *let thieves rule* [emphasis mine]
This is the utmost sin
You reap what you sow
These spears are piercing my heart

Liberate us or sentence us [to death]
O Lord of the Hindu Jati

My repentance has burnt away the sin

238. *SSV*, MPHS, 7: 176.

239. Pradeep Gokhale has written of two conjoined sets of debates—the Vedanta-Dhadanta and the Brahman-a-Brahman—as two ways of understanding the new set of terms and concepts used by Lokahitawadi and Mahatma Phule. Savarkar's use of "a-brahman" could well come from that conjoined concept. See "Ekonisavya satakatila dona vicara dvandve" ("Two ideological conflicts of the nineteenth century") in Vohra, *Adhunikata ani Parampara*, 66–72. In the Manusmṛti, as Eleanor Zelliott explains, the term Chandala denotes the group made up of three kinds of people: the offspring of a Sudra father and Brahmin mother, a Brahmin who begs from a Sudra to perform a sacrifice, or someone who has killed a Brahmin. Subsequent Smṛti texts identify the occupational groups of tanner, fishermen, and crematorium workers as Chandalas, or permanently polluted.

Even so, still bless us
Having destroyed the demon of difference
Let us gather unto you

The severed limbs [of the Hindu body] are being rejoined today
Breathe life into them
Push the mighty demon into the underworld
Strengthen the young, just awakened Vamana

Even if our hands don't hold fast to arms [reference to Kshatriya]
You nonetheless have your gadā [medieval weapon]
If you listen to us
We will do whatever you want, our Lord
Give us a hand, so that we may stand on our feet
As you gave us strength when you destroyed [the demon] Kansa
O Lord of the Hindu jati

Savarkar also wrote a public letter addressed to his Sanātani Hindu friends of Nasik, asking them immediately to allow untouchables into the ShriRam Mandir.

> Where Sita went into exile, where the Kauravas and Pandavas battled, where the Gita was recited, in all of those historic holy places, shrines, battlefields—these incomparable places, with their glory are inaccessible to them, and will always remain so. . . . The demand that the community previously known as untouchable enter temples is intensely religious, lawful and the movement that they have launched is the inevitable result of generations of oppression heaped on them. They have waited for sixty, seventy generations. How much longer should they have to wait? All that remains is for us to end their wait.[240]

Only Sanātanis could do this, remove the stigma from temple entry; only Brahmin leadership could accomplish temple entry and allow the *antyaj* community to fully partake of Brahmin culture. Although Savarkar maintained a progressive stance on temple entry, his putative openness on the subject was not only directed at orthodox Brahmins but of little concern to the lower castes for whom the temple—even when it was opened to them—still seemed a totally Brahminical space.

240. "Mājhyā sanātanī Nāśikakara Hindu bandhūnnā mājhēṁ anāvr̥ta patra" in *SSV*, MPHS, 3: 514.

Genetics and the Hindu Body

Savarkar also wrote about theoretical, textual, or prescriptive caste, which he called *pothijat*. The Ṛgvedic *Puruṣasūkta* was the origin myth for *pothijat*, with the implication that one substance could birth or beget four different hierarchical and distinct beings.[241] The first mistake, Savarkar wrote,

> is to believe that just because it is said in the sacred texts, caste divisions like Brahmin, Shudra, tailor, goldsmith, shopkeeper, Lingayat, milkman, gardener exist and from the beginning one caste is different from the other. . . . But to believe that one caste originated from Mahadeva's hair [Shiva], another from Brahmadeva's bellybutton and then to think that these imaginative tales are true . . . is to make a mountainous blunder. An even bigger blunder would be to ascribe a distinguishing quality to the offspring of a caste known for that quality and even if that offspring does not possess that quality, to nonetheless continue in the belief that he does possess it, make him go through the same rituals, and observe caste hierarchy. And to justify all this by saying that this is the secret of the eternal hereditary progress as discovered by our Rishis.[242]

Such accretive blunders had to be confronted directly. This excessive stupidity (*mūrkhapaṇā*) in believing such stories about caste purity leads genetically to puny Indians, a term he used in his letter to his brother from the Andaman Islands. He contrasts this sad situation to America, which produces strong men and beautiful women.

> . . . their women in beauty, comportment, personality and child-rearing ability are getting better and better. And here, with us, each generation is more puny, dwarfish, and miserable.[243]

Caste contributes to the production of these dwarfish and puny Indians. In a final expression of anger, Savarkar notes that India is already living in the long prophesied *Kaliyuga*.

241. See *Purusa-Sukta* in Doniger, *The Rig Veda*, 33, excerpted below:

> 11 When they divided the Man, into how many parts did they apportion him?
> What do they call his mouth, his two arms and thighs and feet?
> 12 His mouth became the Brahmin; his arms were made into the Warrior, his
> thighs the People, and from his feet the Servants were born.

242. *JN* #8, *SSV*, MPHS, 3: 474–75.
243. *SSV*, MPHS, 3: 476.

> . . . our farsighted seers had predicted this. So let us ask them this: this disease/trouble of kaliyuga was meant to come down on all of mankind and the entire planet, was it not? Why then is the opposite occurring in America? Their men are growing strong chested and tall with every generation. Their one cow gives the milk of our ten. In their fields, potatoes the size of coconuts, grapes without seeds, and grain to last forever. And wherever they wish, machines that will bring down rain when they want.[244]

How could Indians become more like Americans? Savarkar had the answer—"[e]very child has only one caste at birth: Hindu." Since all castes had genetic weaknesses, no one could logically claim to be superior. Secondly, and given what he saw as the unity among Christians and Muslims, all Hindus should be just and only that: Hindus. Third, Brahmins had no exclusive privilege or rights to Vedic, Vedantic, or Puranic literature or to becoming priests or *purohits*. Anyone, regardless of caste, who passed a test, could be a *purohit*. (Savarkar does not explain how those from whom sacred texts had been withheld for millennia would pass such a test.) Fourth, all Hindu sacred and pilgrimage sites were to be accessible to all regardless of caste. Fifth, marriage between two people should be based on compatibility, love, desire, and so on, not on caste. Sixth, interdining was necessary. Lastly, professions should be picked according to ability, not birth.

> . . . today everyone has the freedom to pick a profession. Brahmins sell shoes made in Pune. Chambhars can be teachers. What we need now to reform is this: no matter what the profession, the root caste's interdictions against interdining and intermarriage come along with it, and those need to be removed. What do I mean by this? Your caste is tailor, your profession goldsmith; caste Brahmin—profession merchant. This gigantic confusion that has taken over will thus be broken. Everyone's caste is Hindu, no matter what your profession.[245]

But could one so easily just pick a profession? When generation upon generation of communities had acquired expertise in a particular field, leaving expertise for all "contaminated" professions to a "contaminated" community, was it so simple to pick any profession and engage in it? As with other aspects of what made caste so intractably difficult and yet necessary to address at a systemic level, Savarkar does not take on the connections between caste and profession,

244. *SSV*, MPHS, 3: 476.
245. *SSV*, MPHS, 3: 481.

or caste and power more generally, insisting rather on seeing it as something that, like *viṭāḷvēḍa,* could be easily resolved by acts of will on the part of enlightened Brahmins following his lead.[246]

Conclusion

We are left at the end of this chapter with the question of the precise nature of Savarkar 's caste progressivism: was his agenda of caste reform of any real use to the victims of caste oppression, prejudice, and violence, or was it a way of establishing his progressive credentials in provocative but ultimately nonconsequential ways? And was his real intention to subordinate caste distinctions to a broader category of Hindu for the major reason that he thought this was the only way to take on the Muslim threat? Unlike Ambedkar or Gandhi, Savarkar seems to try to wish away the problem of caste through a unique mixture of outrageousness and rhetorical bluster. He believed that secular words mattered more than religious ones, yet he imbued secular words such as "nation" and "Hindu" with the magic of the rituals and practices he dismissed. This let him create a new secular creed that has become the basis of what we now call Hindu nationalism.

His views were progressive, to be sure, and hardly determined by any real obeisance to religious scruples and traditional belief. But there was a reason that he never constructed a full critique either of caste or of the Brahminism that supported the entire edifice. Instead, he put his faith in a project of renaming, exhorting his fellow Brahmins to give up habits without thinking either about why they might not be willing to do so or whether it would make a real difference. He never foregrounded Dalits or imagined them as agents; they were always depicted as grateful for any concessions generous Brahmins offered them. At the same time, in his acidic attacks on Sanātanis, Savarkar ventriloquized much of what the Dalit community might have wanted to say at the time if it had had his privilege and freedom of expression. Much of what he wrote about the epics, the Vedas, and about the cow and other animals would certainly have been insulting to the Sanātanis, Brahmins, and other upper-caste Hindus. For the same reason, his caste writings were heralded by many anticaste reformers, especially those from upper-caste backgrounds. It is not altogether surprising that, even today, his anticaste writings and

246. For a critique of all the views that seek to detach caste from power, whether colonial, nationalist, or sociological, see Dirks, *Castes of Mind.*

activities are touted as being ahead of their time, certainly far ahead of what Gandhi was saying.[247]

Words mattered. Indeed, they were imbued with such power that, correctly chosen, they could alter society. Even as he exhorted his community to "just reach out and touch" an untouchable, what really mattered for him was the redefinition of "Hindu" as a primary identity. When Ambedkar declared in 1935, after the failure of a five-year struggle to open the Kalaram temple in Nasik, that he would not die a Hindu, Savarkar responded that

> [u]ntil such time as a Muslim remains a Muslim, a Christian a Christian, a Parsi a Parsi, a Jew a Jew, it is necessary, good, and appropriate for a Hindu to remain a Hindu. The day those groups break the bonds of their identities and accept Universal Mankind and the nationhood of man, on that day the Hindu nation will accept and live under the same flag, even if this kind of universal humanism is itself central to the Hindu faith.[248]

While Hindu religious scruples held no sway with him, the nationalist identity he embraced was decidedly Hindu. Thus, he argued for a political identity of Hindutva to unite true Indians as the political identities attached to other religions (including both the pan-Islamism of political Islam and the political Christianity of European nationalism) had united others.

Savarkar's followers touted the progressivism of his caste politics, and with Savarkar's help and by mimicking his writings, they created a cultlike following around him that stressed his radical views. But along with his caste critique, these followers carried the vestiges of an ineradicable Brahminism along with his ever-present anti-Muslim refrain. Like him, they downplayed the structural significance of caste while naturalizing everyday prejudice against Muslims; like him they were sure that they were buttressed by nationalist progressivism even when that nationalism was so clearly marked by caste and religious assumption. The success of this nationalist turn was in no small measure assured by the building of the Savarkar myth. We will now examine how that came to be.

247. See, for instance, Kamble, *Swatantryavira Savarkaranche.*

248. "Pōthījāta jātibhēda" in *SSV*, MPHS, 3: 500.

4

A Nation's Bard

SAVARKAR THE POET

IN THE PREVIOUS TWO CHAPTERS, we saw the links between Savarkar's caste reform and his fear of Muslims and how that fear led him to work against any possible unity between Hindus and Muslims. In the next three chapters, we shift our focus to the making of the Savarkar legend. The first of these three chapters takes up Savarkar's poetry; the second, his historical writings; and the third, the biographies and memoirs he wrote and that were written about him. The three are linked, as Savarkar's poetry was Brahminic and (auto)biographical, his history writing was self-consciously poetic, and his biographies emphasized recognizable Marathi Brahmin tropes. In each genre he fashioned himself as the Indian Mazzini, yoking social progressivism to nationalism and asserting his position as the model historian/poet/biographer for a free and modern India.

Savarkar's poetry was central, in form and content, to the widespread admiration of him in Maharashtra.[1] Everything he wrote in prose, whether on social reform, caste, the emasculation of Hindu men, the glorification of Hindu warriors, and martyrdom for the nation, he previewed in his poetry. It was the mode he turned to in crisis, and in it we find his biography, his love for his village, and over and above everything else, his Hindutva nationalism.

Even while under house arrest in Ratnagiri from 1924–37 Savarkar stepped into the vacuum B. G. Tilak's death in 1920 had left in Maharashtra, and made himself the spokesman of the Hindu community beyond the immediate region. He accomplished this, I argue, by crafting his persona for posterity by, in effect, mythologizing himself. The secrecy that surrounded his poetry aided

1. I am grateful to Vidyut Aklujkar for her help with translations.

in that mythologizing because it was disseminated across Maharashtra under the colonial radar and established him as a leader in waiting.

The mythologization began with the pseudonymous publication of his biography.[2] A year earlier, a Marathi historian by the name of Tryambak Shankar Shejwalkar (1895–1963) embarked on his career in history. We will meet him very briefly in this chapter, and in greater detail again in the next two chapters, as an important foil to Savarkar. One way to comprehend Savarkar's poetry, his early instrumentalization of it, and its spread is to contrast it with Shejwalkar's writings on a genre (*povāḍā*) both men believed was important for the writing of Marathi history. This move will undoubtedly raise skeptical eyebrows and possibly be rejected out of hand, not least because Shejwalkar is considered one of the two most important, if iconoclastic, historians of Maharashtra, the first being the redoubtable V. K. Rajwade (1863–1926).[3] Some might argue that I am proposing an arranged marriage that would raise howls of protest from both families. I have no concrete evidence that the two men knew each other or actively engaged each other or even read each other. Nonetheless, I suggest that writing intellectual history requires putting certain conversations alongside each other so we may see how one strand illuminates the other.

In this and the next two chapters I present Shejwalkar as the anti-Savarkar. Their writings on the same subjects—*povāḍās*, poetry, history, biography—uncover a struggle of sorts for the disciplining of history and biography beginning in the mid-to-late 1920s and extending across their literary lifetimes. Shejwalkar, from the start of his historical career, planted a stake in the ground for rigor: careful use of evidence, linguistic proficiency, approaching the subjects of biography with a critical eye, and eschewing poetry (and melodrama) as a modality of writing.

Savarkar, on the other hand, remarked, "Mī vr̥ttīnēṁ kavi āṇi kalāvanta āhē, paṇa paristhitīnēṁ malā rājakāraṇī puruṣa banavilēṁ āhē" ("I am a poet and artist by nature, but circumstances have made me into a political being").[4] He was not an occasional poet; he thought of himself as poet first and politician second. Poetry was central to his thinking; it was also the genre in which basic

2. Savarkar, *Life of Barrister Savarkar* [*LBS*].

3. See the preface to Dixit, *Nivadaka Sejavalakara*, vii. See also the wide-ranging intellectual biographical essay on T. S. Shejwalkar by Madhav R. Kantak in his preface to *Panipat: 1761*.

4. This claim of Savarkar's is repeated in many articles that give us a biography of Savarkar. See Mankikar, "Savarakarance vangmayina vyaktimatva" in Padhye, *Savarkar Vividh Darshan*, 1.

facts and brute nationalist exhortations could be communicated on the wings of the mnemonics of poetic forms. He used poetry and his knowledge of its regional history to instill a nationalist sensibility in the youth of his native region, writing across the Marathi poetic spectrum to deliver the same message. Savarkar wrote of the nation in poetic forms ranging from *stōtras* (devotional hymns) to *povāḍās* (historical ballads), which meant that, within Maharashtra, regardless of where you encountered Marathi poetry, there was a nationalist Savarkar poem for you containing the same nationalist ideas.[5] In that sense, it was poetry that imagined the community into being even before the newspapers that, as Benedict Anderson canonically observed, played a central historical role. The community that came to know and love Savarkar's poetry was not quite a settled middle class but an emerging one, whose everyday life was sacralized and into which Savarkar's nation-deifying poetry moved easily.

A significant aspect of the cult-like following around Savarkar and his poetry was secrecy. His poems, like him, were under surveillance and often banned, which meant that the colonial police looked for printed or handwritten copies of them in their searches. As a result, his poems circulated among his followers below the police radar and were memorized and recited in defiance of the ban on political congregation. Almost all of his poetry was composed while under surveillance, either in prison or under conditional release. He wrote it on scraps that were scattered across the region, with each bit and part carefully guarded by the person to whom it was entrusted.[6] This lent the actual poetry an aura of romantic revolution that one could participate in

5. The three major content categories for a primarily Brahminic Marathi poetry are: *bhāśyakāvya* (commentarial), *kathākāvya* (storytelling), and *bhāvakāvya* (emotional/spiritual), colloquially known as *pant* (intellectual and learned), *tant* (active life), and *sant* (spiritual or devotional poetry). *Tant* also refers to the *tuṇatuṇē*, one of the instruments that was used as an accompaniment for singing *povāḍā* and *lāvaṇī*. I am grateful to Madhav Deshpande for his close reading of this chapter and for correcting some of my errors.

6. On Savarkar's sixtieth birthday in 1943, one of his associates, Va Go Maydev, himself a poet, took upon himself the task of gathering all of Savarkar's poetry and compiling it in an edition titled *Savarkaranci Kavita*. In the preface, Maydev writes,

I took on this work but did not imagine how difficult it would be at the time to locate all his poems. Some were published by some of his bhakts/followers wherever they could publish them, some poems were written down in notebooks, some poems were available in bits and pieces, and some poems had been committed to memory. I spent many days collecting all of them. Later I showed them all to Vinayakrao [Savarkar]. Only after his review and approval did I include them in the present collection.

simply by having in one's possession a handwritten poem or copy of a poem composed by a surveilled nationalist, or by memorizing it. While these poems would not have the same circulation they would once they were printed, they were important in fostering a secret community. They were not compiled and published until the late 1930s and early 1940s, when Savarkar was allowed to leave Ratnagiri, but the groundwork for them was laid by these small Marathi communities (mostly men) who held on to the scraps and recited his poems surreptitiously.

In the first part of this chapter, I survey a representative sample of his early poetry composed before he was taken to the Andaman Islands—all of it published, some translated, some well-known in his native Maharashtra, some less so—that constituted the basis for the dissemination of his ideology in prose after he was brought back; in the second part, my focus shifts to the genre of the *povāḍā* to demonstrate Savarkar's Brahminic recasting of one of the most beloved of Marathi *povāḍās*.

Poetry was Savarkar's main mode of writing though he also wrote musical plays, speeches, essays, jeremiads, and polemics. In some of those writings, there is a wildness—a kind of veering off script—that can be quite disturbing. In his poetry, however, he was much more disciplined. We also see Guiseppe Mazzini's influence, not in terms of Italian republicanism or federalism, but in Savarkar's belief that literary works played a lofty and active role in the political project. The nation, as Savarkar's poetry insisted, was the injured and subjugated mother who needed her sons to come to her rescue. Once saved by their patriotic duty and devotion, she could take her place among nations as the authentic homeland of the modern Hindus. For Savarkar, patriotic poetry was most effective among all literary genres in capturing hearts and minds and in laying down a consistent theory of history.[7]

When I refer to his poetry as having a theory of history, I do not intend a grand Hegelian teleological conception, although G. P. Deshpande has argued that Savarkar was Hegelian in his belief that spirit and nation were interchangeable.[8] Savarkar's second historical work *Hindu-Pad-Padashahi* (1925) does betray an attempt to write a history of the free Hindu spirit with the aim of

7. "In Marathi there is not a lot of patriotic poetry, but whatever there is, the first place of honor must go to Savarkar's poems." Preface to Maydev, *Savarkaranchi Kavita*, 4.

8. See Deshpande, *World of Ideas*. This is despite the fact that Hegel's use of the term "spirit" (Geist) has nothing to do with the "nation" and there is no preordained telos apart from human collective self consciousness. I am grateful to Tim Brennan for correcting me on this score.

suggesting that its success lay in the creation of a Hindu nation. But here I mean something simpler. If we consider a theory of history as a recognition of a past exegetical tradition, a knowledge of that tradition, and the subsequent use and alteration of that tradition to enter into a contemporary conversation about the world (and world history), then such a theory is present in Savarkar's poetry, in particular in his *povāḍās*.[9] Quintessentially modern, Savarkar's poetry extends back only to the eighteenth century, the brief period in which the Maratha confederation entertained imperial ambitions of succeeding the ailing Mughal empire. It is in relationship to this empire that he recasts the late seventeenth- and eighteenth-century Maratha period as an "empire" and uses it to undergird his conception of the Hindu nation.

In Maharashtra, Savarkar is particularly famous for three poems written in three different genres: a devotional prayer composed in 1903 titled "Svatantratēcē stōtra/Jayō'stu tē" ("Victory to thee"), an emotional song composed in 1909 titled "Sāgarāsa—nē majasī nē parata mātr̥bhūmīlā, sāgarā prāṇa taḷamaḷalā" ("O Ocean, my spirit is in turmoil"), and "Sinhagaḍācā povāḍā" ("Ballad of Sinhagaḍa") composed in 1905.[10]

Savarkar's *povāḍā* is well known in Maharashtra as the *povāḍā* of Chhatrapati Maharaj (1690–1708), and it recasts an older *povāḍā* about a brave warrior and general, Tanaji Malusare, who was sent by Chhatrapati Shivaji to recapture a strategically important fort from the Mughal general, Udayabhāna

9. Karandikar says as much in his official biography of Savarkar. He notes that, "as a young man, Savarkar developed his own theory of history, which can be found in the poem 'Saptarshi': in any history the first page is unobtainable, Tatya understood this even as a young man, and it later manifested itself in his poem 'Saptarshi'. The Aryas (215–22) should be read with this in mind. This fundamental principle can be located in this Arya:

Itihāsācēṁ pahilēṁ pāna na miḷaṇēṁ kadhīṁ pahāyātēṁ.	One never gets to see the first page of history
'Ārambha tujhā dusaryā pānāpāsūni' śāpa hā yātēṁ.	You begin only with the second page, this is our curse [for historians]."

Karandikar, *Savarkar Charitra*, 32.

10. "Sāgarā prāṇa taḷamaḷalā" is included in *Gani: Manatali, Galyatali*, edited by Patwardhan, Deshpande, Gangapurkar, Keskar (1990), also in *Kavita visavya satakaci* (2000) and in *Adhunika marathi kavya sampada* (2008), his "Svatantratēcē stōtra/Jayō'stu tē" in *Kavita visavya satakaci* (2000) and in *Phulora gitapuspanca* (2007), his poem titled "Mājhē mr̥tyupatra" in *Athavanitalya kavita*, bhaga 4, edited by Mahajan, Barve, Tendulkar, Patwardhan (1994). Most recently, upon Lata Mangeshkar's death on February 6, 2022, "Sāgarā prāṇa taḷamaḷalā" was sung by her siblings at an event mourning her death.

Rāṭhōḍa. Savarkar's transformation of the *povāḍā* and the genre of which it was a part (and on which it is a modern commentary) is at the heart of my discussion of his poetry. Where the original by a bard (*śāhira*) named Tulshidas (Tuḷaśīdāsa) stars Chhatrapati Shivaji's general Tanaji Malusare, Savarkar's version emphasizes the ruler. While this could seem like simple poetic license rather than structural shift, I argue that it indexes a larger transformation in which Savarkar releases his poems into the sacralized milieu of an emerging middle-class Marathi community and gave the beginning of Maratha power in the subcontinent a Brahminic gloss and a continuous history.

In 1905, the year Savarkar composed "Sinhagaḍācā povāḍā," it was recited at the Shivaji Melas (commemorative celebrations) organized by B. G. Tilak. Soon after Savarkar would leave to study abroad. While he was away, the Brahman-Brahmenetar debate raged in Maharashtra, and in Pune in particular, as we saw, Tilak and Chiplunkar were sharply attacked by the leaders of the non-Brahmin movement, Keshavrao Jedhe and Dinkarrao Javalkar.[11] Maratha leaders would demand that Shivaji festivals (*mela*s) should be only for non-Brahmins. By conflating two theoretically opposed aspects of the social order (Maratha and Brahmin) in "Sinhagaḍācā povāḍā," Savarkar was an early appropriator of Chhatrapati Shivaji in a manner that allowed him to create a seamless history that brought together both region (Maharashtra) and nation (India).[12]

In an essay about the range of poetic expressions available to a poet in the mid-twentieth century published in the first critical anthology of his poetry, Savarkar explained his use of the terms *vr̥tta, gadya,* and *padya* (metre, verse, prose) and ranks the different metres, casually demonstrating his knowledge of classical poets like Kālidāsa and Bhavabhūti and other stalwarts of the Sanskrit *kāvya* tradition.[13] For all his expostulations against the British, Milton and

11. For a quick account of Jedhe and Javalkar's political activities and trajectories in the years between 1917 and 1928, with particular attention to Javalkar's *Dēśācē duśmana,* see Shelar, "The Role of Dinkarrao Javalkar."

12. On this subject, see the previous chapter for the Brahman-Brahmanetar debate, the politics of caste in Maharashtra, and several sources that give greater explanations than I wish to here.

13. *SSV,* MPHS 7:16–24. There are a number of published compilations of Savarkar's poems; two were compiled in his lifetime and under his watchful eye. One of these was Va Go Maydev's *Sāvarakarāñcī Kavitā* (1943), which does not include all his poems. Another was an anthology with a critical commentary (albeit less critical than commentative) by Shankar Ramchandra Date (*SSV,* MPHS, 7), published in 1965, the year before Savarkar's passing, in which a short essay on *Vinayak vr̥tta* and *Vainayak vr̥tta* appears. There are small discrepancies among

Byron exerted a large influence on his poetry, as seemingly Alfred Lord Tennyson did on his prose. Influenced by Milton's *Paradise Lost* and the long speeches made by Satan in it, Savarkar coined the term *Vainayak vr̥tta* for his works in free verse and *Vinayak vr̥tta* for all else.[14] He composed close to one hundred poems in multiple subgenres: odes, dramatic poetry, heroic poetry, elegy. He wrote *povāḍās* (panegyric/elegiac ballads), *phaṭakās*, *lāvaṇīs*, *kāvyas* (epic poetry), *stutī*, (praise), *stōtra* (mantra), *bhāṣya kāvya* (exegetical poetry), *nisarga kāvya* (natural poetry), *kathā kāvya* (narrative poetry), *āratī* (chant).[15] He composed historical poems in many different metres, including the classical Sanskrit prosodic metres of *śikhariṇī*, *mandākrāntā*, *śārdūlavikrīḍita*, *anuṣṭubh*, and *āryā*.[16] He wrote in Sanskritic Marathi, *deshi* (rustic) Marathi, and in his later years, he wrote notes in Modi—the cursive shorthand running script used by eighteenth-century rulers to communicate, which he would have learned in primary school.[17] Critics find his epic poem "Kamalā," written from prison in the Andamans and with the Battle of Panipat (1761) as the tragic backdrop to the union of its two main protagonists, similar to a mahākāvya, some even

---

these compilations. For instance, in Maydev's compilation, a verse in the poem "Vr̥ṣōkti" begins, "Tēvhāṁ yē'ūnī mānavī **janusa** bā tūṁ sādhilēṁ kaya tēṁ?" But in Date's compilation it reads, "Tēvhāṁ yē'ūnī mānavī **tanusa** bā tūṁ sādhilēṁ kaya tēṁ?" Both "janusa" and "tanusa" make sense in the context of the verse. There are discrepancies as well in the placement of the anusvāra in several words ("tēvhāṁ" or "tēṁ," which nasalizes the pronounciation, rather than "tēvhā" or "tē," which does not). The Savarkar Smarak also published Savarkar's poems in *SSV*, SSRSP, 8 and 9 (2000, 2001), as did Himani Savarkar. Since I have used all of these compilations as well as Marathi scholarly writings on Savarkar's poetry, some discrepancies occasionally remain.

14. "Savarakaranci kavyasrsti" in Padhye, *Savarakar Vividh Darshan*, 36. Bha Shri Pandit writes that Savarkar stopped using the full stop at the end of each couplet, instead replacing it with a comma so that the phrases ran easily—the *śliṣṭa* (ambiguous) name he gave such compositions was *Vainayak Vrtta*. Savarkar writes in *Majhi Janmathep* that Michael Madhusudan Dutt created a metre in Bengali called *Amitraksharachanda*, inspired by English blank verse, and he wanted to create something similar to *Amitraksharachanda* in Marathi, which he tried in his epic poem, *Gomantak*, at https://www.savarkarsmarak.com/activityimages/Marathi%20-%20Mazi%20Janmathep.pdf, 169.

15. Both Sharmila Rege and Vasanta Dinanath Rao suggest that the *lāvaṇī* was the feminized form of the *povāḍā*, in that the subject matter of the *povāḍā* was masculine bravery whereas sensuous passion was the focus of the *lāvaṇī*. See Rao, "Side-Light on the Maratha Life," and Rege, "Conceptualising Popular Culture."

16. On the *āryā*, see Kanhere, "Waman Pandit."

17. I am grateful to Prachi Deshpande for pointing this out. On Modi as a medium of communication, both confidential and otherwise, see Deshpande, *Scripts of Power*, 24, 54, 55.

likening it to Kālidāsa's Meghadūta.[18] But Savarkar was not just interested in drawing a line from Kālidāsa to himself. He was also making connections between his own writings and the Marathi Paṇḍita tradition of Mōrōpanta/Mayūrapaṇḍita, the Śāhiri tradition, and the Kīrtankārs. It is as if Savarkar wanted his readers to know that no part of the 800-year-old Marathi literary tradition or the Sanskrit poetry tradition was beyond his reach. He also wanted them to see that Maharashtra's history could be the model for an independent India. It is no surprise that one of the pseudonymns he used was Mahārāṣṭrabhāṭa (Maharastra's bard).[19] *Bhāṭas* were more than everyday poets. They not only had a deep knowledge of poetry, but were also professional singers, whose job was to make the recited and sung material memorable and to spread it as far as possible.

From Savarkar's large oeuvre, I have selected not just his three best-known poems but also two of his early published *phaṭakās*: an *āryā* on a social and societal issue that won him an award; selections from a poem on child widowhood; a poem he wrote in England when his arrest was imminent, which he titled his last will and testament and translated into English; a poem written on scraps of paper before he was taken away to the Andamans, and, finally, his rewriting of the Kōṇḍāṇyācā *povāḍā* into the *povāḍā* of the recaptured fort of Sinhagaḍa ("Sinhagaḍācā povāḍā"). But we begin with Savarkar's own education in poetry.

Savarkar's Education in Poetry

For all of his bombast, Savarkar was a private individual. His poetry, however, offers a glimpse into his interiority. In his memoirs, begun while under house arrest, he noted that he began writing poetry at the age of eight. Like Gandhi, his bête noire, Savarkar combined self-aggrandizement with self-deprecation, although unlike Gandhi—who used self-deprecation to reset the dial every time an anticolonial gesture or movement failed—Savarkar's self-deprecation functions primarily as a literary flashlight to illuminate his autodidactic brilliance.

18. See Phadakule, *Kahi Ranga Kahi Resa*, 58–67. In particular see "Srngaravela 'Kamalā'" for an explicative and appreciative analysis of a small section of Savarkar's poetry and an extended analysis of his epic poem "Kamalā." Phadakule finds Savarkar's life a worthy subject of a *mahākāvya*.

19. Karandikar, *Savarkar Charitra*, 495.

Savarkar did not come from wealth, and his descriptions of family life suggest a modest household always bordering on penury. No great income fed the family, no large estate supported the household, no large landownings sheltered them from potential disasters. In the current categorical schemes of class in India, we would term him lower-middle class. But it was a privileged and learned milieu, and Sanskrit and Marathi poetry were central to his learning.[20] While Savarkar's trajectory took him from some of the smallest towns (Bhagur and Nashik) in western India to progressively larger and more cosmopolitan milieus like Pune and the colonial metropole of London, his local roots and histories remained critical to both his developing literary sensibility and his sense of history. In his writings Savarkar emphasized the sense of place that drove his work—reminding the reader that he really came from the rural milieu of Bhagur and Nasik—the *khēḍēgāva* or village world.

Savarkar grew up memorizing and listening to poems that told the region's history. The saint poets of Maharashtra, Nāmadēva, Muktēśvara, Tukārāma, Bahiṇābā'i, and Samartha Rāmadāsa, and the *paṇḍita* poets, Vāmana Paṇḍita and Mōrōpanta, were household names. Many of them, including Vāmana Paṇḍita, translated Sanskrit verses from the Bhagavad Gita into the poetic Marathi of their time, keeping the metrical integrity of the original Sanskrit. Each poet was associated with a particular metre—Vāmana Paṇḍita with *ślōka* (said to have been invented when Valmiki, the composer of the Rāmāyaṇa, saw a fowler kill a Kraunca bird), Mōrōpanta with *āryā*, Jnaneshwar with *ovi*, and Tukārāma with *abhanga*.[21] Savarkar's poetry is influenced by these poets—for instance, Mōrōpanta, whose *āryā*s he memorized as a child and whose poetry he mimicked.[22] Vāmana Paṇḍita or Mōrōpanta is described by Bhalchandra Nemade as writing "ornamental and metrically finished narrative

20. See Deshpande, *Scripts of Power*, 54, for a description of the kind of learning within a Brahmin family such as Savarkar's in which ". . . pedagogy was oral and focused on memorization of verses, prayers, . . . daily recitations at lamp lighting time."

21. For an examination of the Sanskritized style in which poets such as Moropant wrote, see Mangrulkar, Arjunwadkar, and Arjunwadkar, "Influence of Sanskrit on the Language." Moropant, among others, they write, "fell in love with the jingling sweet-sounding words in Sanskrit," and poets like him hunted down obscure Sanskrit words and appended Marathi suffixes and case terminations to them, which resulted in a "highly artificial, stilted poetry which was more Sanskrit than Marathi . . ." (98).

22. Mōrōpanta or Mayur Pandit's name was Moreshwar Ramchandra Paradkar, and he was considered the last of the Pandit poets in Maharashtra. Savarkar composed a long poem called "Godavakili" as a homage to Mōrōpanta's "Gangavakili."

verse, mostly dealing with romantic episodes from Sanskrit epics; their conscious formalism was heavily influenced by Sanskrit poetics."[23] In recounting his literary growth, Savarkar often complains that scholars known to his father who might easily have taught him some of this formalism, and the basic metres of some of the poetry he loved as a child, instead hindered his learning. His explanation for their obstructionism is simple and reappears in different guises all through his writings: they were intimidated by his obvious poetic talent and brilliance. As a result, he recounts, he was left with no alternative but to teach himself, and in so doing he composed his first major *āryā*.

We see a constant refrain: Savarkar teaches himself something difficult and then, much like Tukārāma, outdoes his intellectual superiors. We will see this again when Savarkar turns his hand to history and is contemptuous of the writing of other historians. The dislike and suspicion of established authority is a pattern, beginning with the "pōkaḷa pāṇḍitya" (hollow pedantry) of a school principal, who wrote poetry but would not explain the basics to him. Savarkar consistently presents his brilliance as a threat to authority, which means that threatening or dismissing disciplinary authority becomes a marker of his own brilliance, a practical tactic his followers also used to great effect. This school principal stands in for other Brahmins reluctant to impart knowledge to him and for the priests of Benares poring over the Vedas and disallowing Hindus from crossing the seas (and British Indologists and Western-educated Indian scholars today) and confirms for Savarkar that his autodidacticism was far superior to conventional and institutional learning.

In Bhagur and Nasik, poetry was an important source of entertainment, an agonistic pastime, and a source of learning. In perhaps one of the few places in the narrative that is not self-aggrandizing, Savarkar wrote about the games he played with other village children as they swung on trees, all the while reciting poetry and rhyming. Spontaneous poetry competitions took place, in which a set of words had to be used in the quick composition of a couplet, back and forth, with the second person having to use the last word of the second line written by the first person in the first line of his or her response.[24] What

23. Nemade, "Towards a Definition of Modernity," 72. The poets are labelled "Pandit," because "of their penchant for drawing heavily from Sanskrit aesthetics—a profusion of Sanskrit-derived metres, principles of *alankāraśāsatra,* idioms, tatsama [Sanskrit] vocabulary, and long compounds—in their compositions." Deshpande, *Scripts of Power,* 128.

24. "Vinayak had memorized exactly the song of Gajgauri as he had heard his sister-in-law (Yesuvahini) sing it. He would also quickly imitate the ovis and ukhanas composed by women. When Yesuvahini, his younger sister Mai, and neighborhood girls would come together and

marked him as unusually gifted was something he remembered about evenings on the banks of the Godavari:

> Out of Mōrōpanta's 108 different and important compositions on Ramakatha, from his most distinctive ones like Niroshta, Dam, Ovi, Mantra, etc. . . . I could recite the introductory and concluding verses, some 10–12 in the beginning and conclusion.[25]

The ability to recite from memory the first and last 12 lines of Mōrōpanta's Rāmāyaṇas suggests much about his poetic precocity, in part because of the complexities attached to reciting the poem. Mōrōpanta intended to compose 108 different versions of the entire epic of the Rāmāyaṇa; we have written records of about 87. *Nirōṣṭha* means "without pressing one's lips together," what phonologists call "bilabials." In Sanskrit, five syllables (*pa, pha, ba, bha,* and *ma*) known as the *pa varga* cannot be vocalized without pressing one's lips together.[26] The word *Rāma* cannot be uttered because it contains the syllable *ma,* and an alternative name such as *Raghunandan* needs to be used. Here are the first two verses from the "Nirōṣṭha Rāmāyaṇa."[27]

Śrīhari daśarathanandana jhālā daśakaṇṭhasaṅkṣaya karāyā	Viṣṇu became the son of Daśaratha in order to destroy the demon with ten heads
Dara śēṣa cakra hī jani ghētī jagaḍkhila saṅkaṭa harāyā	The conch, Śeṣa the serpent, and the discus also were born [as Rāma's brothers] to save the world from calamity
Aṅgaja cyāra tighīñcē sanskr̥ta sākṣara narēndra kīrtikara Nirakhī, nitānta harṣē hā ci na taisā ci nāgarikanikara	The king joyfully watched the four cultured and learned sons of his three queens who would become famous, and so did the crowds of the citizens[28]

sing ovis, Vinayak would compose his own and compete with them and try to defeat them." Karandikar, *Savarkar Charitra*, 34–35.

25. *SSV*, SSRSP, 1: 160. For a full list of Mōrōpanta's eighty-seven known Rāmāyaṇas, see Paradkar, *Aṣṭōttaraśata Rāmāyaṇēṁ*.

26. I am grateful to Vidyut Aklujkar for explaining this to me.

27. See Paradkar, *Aṣṭōttaraśata Rāmāyaṇēṁ*, 414, for the full text of the "Nirōṣṭha Rāmāyaṇa."

28. I am grateful to Madhav Deshpande for translating these verses for me.

Another of the 108 Rāmāyaṇa was the "Mantra Rāmāyaṇa," which Mōrōpanta presented in the metrical form of *āryā* as both an explanation and instructions on how this Rāmāyaṇa was composed.

Śrīkārāpāsuniyā makāraparyanta varṇa jē tērā	From Shri to Ma all thirteen syllables
tē rāghavacaritāntī granthilē hē rāmabhaktahō, hērā.	Are incorporated at the end of verses of Raghavacharita [biography of Rama].[29]

Poetry was not just the exemplary genre and the social media of its time, but, as we see in the couplet above, it was also a valuable tool for learning of the arcane. Part of the so-called folklore with which Brahmin Sanskrit-reading families such as Savarkar's would also have been familiar were the *subhāṣita*, maxims derived from the epics and Sanskrit *kavya* literature, which in pithy form and relatively simple Sanskrit communicated a lesson or admonition.[30]

Here is one such admonition:

Aśanaṁ me vasanaṁ me jāyā me bandhuvargo me	I want food, I want good clothes, wife is mine, relatives are mine
Iti me me kurvāṇam kālavṛko hanti puruṣajam	The goat in the form of a man who says "me me" [mine mine] is eaten by the wolf in the form of time [Death][31]

29. Pangarkar, *Moropanti Vence*, 55. In the "Mantra Rāmāyaṇa," as G. B. Palsule explains, "the first letter in every group of 13 stanzas in the Balakanda, read downwards form the Mantra Śrīrāma jaya rāma jaya jaya rāma," and in the "Ayodhyakanda," the same occurs except it is the second letters in each group that make up the mantra. See Palsule in Dandekar, *Sanskrit and Maharashtra: A Symposium*, 66.

30. I am grateful to my colleague Bob Goldman, whose help in tracing the kind of knowledge Brahmin Sanskrit-knowing families such as Savarkar's would have had has been invaluable. On *subhāṣitas* as wise maxims and/or practical wisdom dispensed in beautiful language, see Sternbach, *Subhasita, Gnomic and Didactic Literature*, particularly the section "Anthologies" for a historical account of the compilations of *subhāṣitas*. Savarkar's poetry was entirely Sanskritic, writes Bha Shri Pandit: "Savarkar's poetry is very cultured. His writings, reading and his experiences in life have all affected his poetry and have nurtured it. Hence it [his poetry] has a noble character." Bha Shri Pandit, "Savarakaranci kavyasrsti" in *Savarakar Vividh Darshan*, 37.

31. Bhate, *Subhāṣitaśatakam*, 1: 23, 90. See Dandekar, *Sanskrit and Maharashtra*, for a mention of a compilation titled *Suślokāmādhava* published by Vithoba Anna Daptardar in 1917.

And one attributed to Mammaṭācārya that demonstrates the alliteration poets used:

Rāmābhiṣeke jalam āharantyāḥ hastāc cyuto hemaghaṭo yuvatyāḥ	During Rama's coronation a gold pitcher slipped from the hand of the water-carrying maid.
sopānamārgeṇa karoti śabdaṃ	While falling down the staircase, it made the sound
ṭha ṭhaṃ ṭha ṭhaṃ ṭhaṃ ṭha ṭha ṭhaṃ ṭha ṭham ṭha[32]	*ṭha ṭhaṁ ṭha ṭhaṁ ṭhaṁ ṭha ṭha ṭhaṁ ṭha ṭhaṁ ṭha*

Savarkar was particularly adept at composing poetry that mimicked the alliterative and onomatopoeic elements found in this *subhāṣita*:

vidvatkavayaḥ kavayaḥ kevalakavayas tu kevalaṃ kapayaḥ	Poets who are learned are real poets. Other poets are just monkeys
kulajā yā sā jāyā kevalajāyā tu kevalaṃ māyā[33]	The wife who is born in a good family is a real wife, the other one is just an illusion

Lastly, here is a *ślōka* in Marathi attributed to Samartha Ramdas, usually recited before a meal:

Vadani kavaḷa ghētā, nāma ghyā śrīharīcē	When you take a morsel in your mouth, take Shri Hari's name
Sahaja havana hōtē nāma ghētā phukā cē	Doing that it naturally becomes an offering to the sacrificial fire
Jivana karī jivitvā, anna hē pūrṇa brahma	One should eat to keep oneself alive, food is a complete form of Brahman
Udarabharaṇa nōhē jāṇijē yadnyakarma	This is not just filling the belly, treat it as a form of sacrifice[34]

32. Bhate, *Subhāṣitaśatakam*, 1: 23, 90. From what was considered the new school of Sanskrit poetics, K. P. Jog writes, Mammata's *Kavyaprakasa* was apparently very popular in Maharashtra and was the subject of multiple commentaries. See Dandekar, *Sanskrit and Maharashtra*, 49.

33. Bhate, *Subhāṣitaśatakam*, 3: 3, 10.

34. I am immensely grateful to Madhav Deshpande for not only giving me an accurate translation but for correcting my mistake.

It is in this milieu, in which everyday life was sacralized by the frequent recitation of *subhāṣitas* or *ślokas*, that Savarkar composed his poems. The slide from worshipping a God or Goddess to worshipping a conjoined deity, the mother/nation, was seamless, and Savarkar did it in a great many of his poems. The community that took his poems and recited them would have been deeply familiar with the metres he used and the rhythms in which he instructed them to recite his poetry. It was a community of middle-class Maharashtrians, upper-caste, perhaps English-educated, but with a continuing connection and attachment to Sanskritic and Brahminic forms of life and being, even as some members were drawn to English education and jobs in the colonial bureaucracy. For this group, Savarkar's early alliterative poems were easy to memorize, lucid, readable, and understandable compared to his later penchant for coining neologisms and complex nouns.[35] Most of his poems have themes of nationalism, anticolonialism and—a distant third—social reform.

By the age of eleven, Savarkar was composing poems in a variety of meters including *ōvī* and *phaṭakā*, but he found *āryā*, Mōrōpanta's favorite metre, difficult.[36] Its metric compositions remained opaque until he figured out that it was in the consonantal valences that the metre was measured or counted. Even before he mastered *āryā*, he tells us, he submitted poems in other meters to Marathi newspapers. At the age of fifteen, he published his first poem "Svadēśīcā phaṭakā" in the Pune magazine *Jagad'hitēcchū*.[37] Before the partitioning of the province of Bengal in 1905, and before the INC launched the Swadeshi movement, one of the chief pillars of the anticolonial movement was the abolition and destruction of foreign cloth. From Nasik, Savarkar exhorts his lazy, dissolute, fat, and

35. See Gerow, *A Glossary of Indian Figures*, 102, for a discussion of the kind of alliteration Savarkar seems to have been particularly fond called *anuprāsa*. This alliteration is defined through this phrase in Bhāmahaḥ ("kiṃ tayā cintayā kānte nitānteti" ["O lovely, why are you afflicted with doubts?"]). I cannot prove this, but the kind of alliteration Savarkar used was very similar. Ashok Aklujkar has closely examined consonantal sounds Sanskrit poets used to convey, for instance, the effect of war, describing them as "highly compounded language abounding in the repetition of certain sounds considered to be relatively harsh. The consonant *ṇa* and *ḍ* commonly find his [the poet's] favor . . ." Aklujkar, "The Pandits from a pinda-Brahmanda" in Michaels, ed., *The Pandit: Traditional Scholarship in India*, 41–42, footnote 1.

36. *SSV*, SSRSP, 1: 8. See also Karandikar, *Savarkar Charitra*, 35.

37. *SSV*, MPHS, 7: 3. The *phaṭakā*, as its name suggests, is a fiery and caustic poem.

obdurate countrymen to rise up and shun imported cloth. This poem itself indexes youth in its unabashed joy through rhyming and the simplicity of its metre. As his oeuvre develops, Savarkar does not depart entirely from the obvious pleasure he takes in a certain kind of rhyming, but his words get increasingly Sanskritized, and many of his own neologisms replace the clarity so evident in this poem.

Ārya bandhū ho **uṭhā uṭhā** kāṁ **maṭhā** sārakhē **naṭā** sadā	Noble brothers wake up, why just foolishly adorn yourselves?
haṭā sōḍūni **kaṭā** karu yā mlēñcha**paṭā** nā dharūṁ kadā	leave aside your obduracy and vow not to touch foreign cloth
Kāśmīrācyā śālī tyajuni alpākālā kā bhulatā	You forego superior muslin and shawls from Kashmir
malamala tyajunī **valavala** cittīṁ **halahalake** paṭa kāṁ varitāṁ?	For inferior quality foreign cloth?

The rhyming is alliterative and simple, but catchy. The first two lines use multiple words—*uṭhā uṭhā, maṭhā naṭā haṭā kaṭā paṭā*—that rhyme and allow for easy memorization and the sheer pleasure of calling out an indolent neighbor for not taking action. Savarkar lists fabrics available in India—silk from Nagpur, shawls from Kashmir—and juxtaposes them to cheap chintz and piece-goods manufactured for the Indian market. But in what will become his trademark, he provokes and insults Hindu/Aryans to act even as he excoriates them as obdurate fools who have brought this situation on themselves. In this Savarkar and Gandhi are alike, both demanding that Indians look in the mirror for an explanation for their current plight.

Kēli anāsthā tumhīcī svataḥ maga arthātaci kalā buḍē	Yourself have you created this situation, obviously our arts/crafts will die
gēlēṁ dhanacī nēlēṁ harunī mēlāṁ tumhi tari kōṇa raḍē?	Even if we lost our wealth and you were killed who would mourn?
Arē apaṇacī pūrvī hōtōṁ sakala kalāñcī khāṇa ahā	We who used to be the apogee of all arts

bharatabhūmicyā kuśīṁ dīpa tē kalaṅka ātāṁ āmhī pahā	Now let us witness the stain on Bharat's past
Maṭhṭha lōka hō lāja kānhintari?	You stubborn folk, have you no shame?
Laṭhṭha asunī śaṭha banalō rē	In your fat laziness you have become cheats [of yourselves]
Kāmadhēnukā bharatabhūmikā asuni bhāga kāṁ tī bhikṣā	We have Kamadhenu, why then should she beg?
sahastra kōsānvarunī khāsā paikā haratō prabhudīkṣā	They who sit thousands of miles away have their own divine sanction to rob her of a lot of money
Nē'uni kaccā māla āmucā dētī sācā pakva rupēṁ	They take our raw materials and give us piecegoods
āmacyāvarī pōṭa bharī pari thōri kaśācī tarī khapē?	You fill your bellies on us and what is the greatness you peddle to us?

The reference to piece goods is obvious. The use of raw material from India, primarily cotton, which was taken to the Manchester mills and returned to India to be sold in a colonially controlled market, was the source of much anticolonial ire. But he also smirks aloud in his memoirs about the wonder of someone like him publishing in a paper from Pune, after which he exults that no one would dare say that he was not a poet.

> . . . from this point on no one can say that I am not a poet. Because in that poor little village's lifetime the only poet whose poem was published in a newspaper was me! And young and old alike were left agog by that fact—It is a good thing that the editors of *jagadahitēcchu* who published the poem did not know it was composed by a twelve-year-old boy from the village![38]

38. *SSV*, SSRP, 1: 82. Savarkar's memory was perhaps not wholly accurate. While he remembered his age as twelve, he was born in 1883, which would make his age at the time of publication (1898) fifteen.

Savarkar's next poem concerned the plague, which in August 1896 made its first appearance in Bombay[39] and ravaged not only the city but entire provinces of colonial India, taking at least twelve million recorded lives. The plague's progress across India was followed and reported in the *British Medical Journal*, along with resentment about colonial actions aimed at stopping the spread, including the displacement of countless villagers who had to camp in fields as their homes and villages were burned to the ground.[40] Ira Klein has shown that colonial India bore ninety-five percent of the global mortality rate from the start of the epidemic to World War II. He notes, "no modern Indian epidemic incited so much social disorganization and none was confronted with equally vigorous government measures."[41] Rural Maharashtra was hit particularly hard. To contain the disease, the colonial government imposed a series of measures that were at best insensitive, such as barging into the sacred inner spaces of village homes to ensure no one had contracted the disease, and at worst brutal, such as burning the homes of afflicted villagers to contain the disease, forcing the inhabitants out into the streets. The city of Poona was divided into ten wards, with the superintendent in charge of each authorized to conduct house-to-house inspections.[42] Two brothers, Damodar Hari Chapekar and Balkrishna Hari Chapekar, expressed their rage against these aggressive measures by assassinating the Poona plague commissioner and his assistant, Walter Charles Rand and Lieutenant Ayerst, on June 22, 1897.[43] The colonial government labelled the Chapekar brothers (*bandhu*) as fanatics, but within the region they were instant heroes, the subjects of praise poems and plays. The colonial government's response was to ban all celebratory writing in any genre about them.[44]

Defying this ban, Savarkar composed a *phaṭakā* about the brothers. His father admonished him, asked him to stop, but he persisted, working in secret.[45] His *phaṭakā* comprised twelve sections divided into ninety-six verses. By the last two sections, his argument against revering India's colonial masters is clear. Regardless of what one thinks of Savarkar, neither his poetic precocity

39. See Klein, "Plague, Policy and Popular Unrest."

40. Klein, "Plague, Policy and Popular Unrest," 724. Klein explains why India suffered disproportionately compared to other plague-hit countries like Indonesia and China. See also "The Plague in India."

41. Klein, "Plague, Policy and Popular Unrest," 724.

42. "The Plague in India."

43. Ganachari, "British Official View of 'Bhagwat Gita.'"

44. Solomon, "Culture, Imperialism, and Nationalist Resistance."

45. *SSV*, SSRSP, 1: 101.

nor his courage in disregarding the ire the colonial government could bring down on him and his immediate family can be gainsayed. In the *phaṭakā* we see an act of historical reconstruction that recalibrates the narrative of Rand and Ayerst's assassins; rather than considering them *māthēphiru* (crazy) or deluded, Savarkar describes them as nationalist heroes.[46]

Here are a few lines from section twelve:

Phāśī nā tī yajñavēdikā raktēṁ nhālī jī tumacyā sāṇḍuni hōvō tyāci rāṣṭraraṇiṁ sārthaka raktācēṁ amucyā.	Not by your hanging but by the spilling of your blood Our blood is made worthwhile
Kārya sōḍunī apurēṁ paḍalāṁ jhuñjata, khantī nakō! Puḍhēṁ.	That you left your work undone, do not be upset
Kāryā cālavuṁ giravuni tumacyā parākramācē amhī dhaḍē . . .	Further will we take your work.

This early obsession with blood and martyrdom maintained its hold on his poetry. In 1900 he composed a poem that was published some years later in Śivarāma Parāñjapē's weekly *Kāḷa*, titled "Vr̥ṣōkti," a conversation between a man and a bull.[47] Both are ground down, the bull by the yoke of the plough, the man by the yoke of colonialism. The bull tells the young man that his servitude is preferable to living a castrated life under colonial occupation.

Mātā āryavasundharā para tujhyā ḍōḷyāmpuḍhē bhōgitī	The mother of your ancestors, mother earth is being abused in plain sight
dāridryāsaha pāratantrya dubaḷyā mānēvarī lādatī	On your weak neck is being forced both occupation and poverty

46. See *Tilak Trial: Being the Only Authorised Verbatim Account of the Whole Proceedings*. The term *māthēphiru* is used to describe Tilak, and it is translated as "turn-headed." See also Karandikar, *Savarakar Charitra*, 45–46, for Karandikar's claims based on Savarkar's unpublished autobiography (*Sāvarakarāñcē aprakāśita ātmavr̥tta*) that, even if he was a poet by inclination, he was always willing to engage in revolutionary violence.

47. Maydev, *Savarkaranchi Kavita*, 31. The poem, according to Maydev, was inspired by the hills Savarkar saw on the way to Javhar. Karandikar is not sure when it was composed, only that it was published in the March 3, 1905, issue of *Kāḷa*. About the date of composition, he writes ". . . seeing a bull, exhausted from climbing the hills, the images in this poem must have occurred to Savarkar while en route to Javhar." Karandikar, *Savarkar Charitra*, 87.

Tēvhāṁ yē'uni mānavī janusa bā tūṁ sādhilēṁ kāya tēṁ?	What have you achieved by coming into life as a human being?
Bhūbhārāpari garvabhāra ajunī tvaccitta kāṁ vāhatēṁ?	Why is your mind still carrying a monumental arrogance?
Tūṁ ni:śastra parantu mī na ajunī ni:śr̥ṅga jhālōṁ tarī	You are disarmed, but I have not yet lost my horns
svaśr̥ṅgēṁ tuja phāḍitōṁ, bagha gaḍyā sōḍūni dētōṁ parī	I could have ripped you apart, but look, friend, I will let you go
Sōḍīṁ garva svadēśabhāra haraṇyā yatnānsi ādhīṁ karīṁ	Leave your arrogance aside, put your efforts into removing the burden on your entire nation
hō'ī īśapadīṁ sulīna puravī sadhdētulā śrīharī.	Prostrate in humility before your God, your good intentions will be rewarded. [translation mine]

Savarkar writes that he received very particular favors from the Goddess in whose praise he composed many *ovi*. Yet religion is not the subject of his poetry at all, and his real ambition was to write an epic poem, a *mahākāvya*. That he did not quite accomplish, because his poems took on urgent issues as they arose, including child widowhood, the plague, the emasculation of the Hindus, and the need for a hearty dose of modernity to enliven an Indic civilization in a state of malaise. Savarkar undoubtedly knew that the *mahākāvya* took as its subject matter mythological themes and political biographies, and he wrote himself into a tradition in which (as Lawrence McCrea argued in his essay on Bilhaṇa's *Vikramāṅkadevacarita*) the real kingmakers were poets, not historians, because poetry "does not simply publicize or preserve the memory of heroism of royal virtue—rather it creates them."[48] Savarkar fashioned himself as a mixture of Mazzini and Bilhana, the exemplary, all-powerful bard who could inflect a classical idiom with a local tradition and history to create a modern nation-state. In other words, he imagined or wished his poetry to be a commissive illocutionary act.

48. See McCrea, "Poetry beyond Good and Evil."

Savarkar was not by any means the first Marathi poet to try out a new style. In 1869, Mahadeva Moreshwar Kunte wrote "Rājā Śivāji," which, along with Jyotiba Phule's ballad on Chhatrapati Shivaji and his anticaste poems, are seen as the origins of modern Marathi poetry, not least because of their use of a Marathi idiom that moved away from a formal or classical mode.[49] Phule's *povāḍā* on Chhatrapati Shivaji depicted him as the leader of the rural peasantry, a subaltern people's leader.[50] For his part, Kunte neither mimicked the work of English poets like Milton, Spencer, Dryden, Pope, Goldsmith, Gray, and Cooper, who were widely read in India, nor merely translated their content into Marathi; he forged a new language in the heroic mode but an informal everyday idiom.[51] He was followed by Keshavsut, whose experimental poetry broke further ground due to the influence of Shakespeare, Keats, Shelley, Wordsworth, and Browning. Keshavsut also took on social issues and focused on a new epoch. Echoes of the three older and different Marathi poetry styles colloquialized as *sant/pant/tant* (spiritual/intellectual/active) remained alive, and Keshavsut and others tinkered with older Sanskritic metres. Savarkar's contemporaries included noteworthy poets/playwrights like Govindagraj/Ram Ganesh Gadkari (1885–1919), who composed *Vāgvaijayantī* and plays such as *Ēkaca Pyālā* (*Just One More Glass* [of alcohol]), Durgaprasad Asaram Tiwari (1887–1939), who composed *Marāṭhyāñcī Saṅgrāmagītēṁ* (1920) and *Jhānśīcī Saṅgrāmadēvatā* (1924), Prahlad Keshav Atre (1898–1969), the editor of the publication *Maratha*, and Kunja-vihari (Harihar Gurunath Salgarkar-Kulkarni, 1896–1978), Madhav Julian, and Balakavi.[52] What set Savarkar's poetry apart from his contemporaries was his single-minded focus on patriotism and nationalism. It was also connected to *Bhāṣāśuddhi*, the movement to purify the Marathi language.

49. See Engblom, "Vishnu Moreshwar Mahajani and Nineteenth-Century Antecedents," 143, where he notes as well that M. M. Kunte's poetry is a continuation of the pandit tradition in Western India.

50. For a translation of the *povāḍā*, see O'Hanlon, *Caste, Conflict and Ideology*. See also Jasper, "Commemorating the 'Golden Age.'"

51. On the historical debates about orthography and "pure Marathi," see Deshpande, "Shuddhalekhan."

52. I am grateful to Vidyut Aklujkar for directing me to these collections and for giving me a tutorial on Marathi poetry without which this chapter would simply not have been possible. Any errors are mine and mine alone. Vidyut participated as well at a workshop on very early drafts of three chapters of this book at UC Berkeley, hosted by the Institute for South Asian Studies, on November 27, 2018.

In his poetry, Savarkar attempted to remove all foreign borrowings and infelicities from Marathi. In this he followed in the footsteps of Vishnu Shastri Chiplunkar, the writer of the monthly periodical *Nibandhamala,* which ran from 1874 to 1882, who published an essay titled "The Current State of the Marathi Language."[53] Gopal Ganesh Agarkar, social reformer and cofounder with Tilak of the newspapers *Kesari* and *Mahratta,* also compiled many neologisms in Marathi that could replace English loanwords. In 1921 Savarkar published a short essay urging his readers to purge Marathi of borrowings from English, Urdu, and Persian.[54] Urdu and Persian had assaulted Marathi, he wrote, and he produced a list of words that needed to replace foreign words.[55] From 1925 on, he began producing neologisms, eventually publishing a small encyclopaedia of "pure words."[56] *Swabhasha, swadharma, swadesh*—our own language, our own religion, our own country—was the motto of the anticolonial struggle in Maharashtra, and Savarkar countered those who said language was separate from religion by marrying it to Indian nationalism and imbuing it with virulence and vigor. He did not make this claim this as a linguist or a student of linguistics but as a nationalist.

One important poet who helped to shape modern Marathi poetry was Kesavsut (Krishnaji Keshav Damle [1866–1905]) whose famous sonnet "Tutari" is still seen as a classic.[57] His poem "Nava Shipai" ("New Soldier") brought

53. Bhole, *Visavya Shatakatil Marathi Gadya.*

54. Bhole, *Visavya Shatakatil Marathi Gadya,* xxi. For two essays on Savarkar's project of *shuddhi,* see Lele, "Savarkar ani Bhasasudhdi," and Vakanakar, "Savarkar ani Bhasasudhdi" in Varhadpande et al., *Garudjhepa.* While in the Andamans, Savarkar also learnt Urdu.

55. Savarkar provided the list in a 1937 article for *Kirloskar* titled "Tatkāla bahiṣkārya asē kāhī parakī śabda". As with most of his essays, he began it with a quote from a Sanskrit work, in this case from Raghunath Pandit's Rājyavyavahārakośa:

vipaścita sammatasyāsya kiṃ syād ajñaviḍaṃbanaiḥ |	What harm can happen to this work, by the learned, by mockery by the ignorant?
rocate kiṃ kramelāya madhuraṃ kadalīphalam ||	Does a camel like sweet bananas?

I am grateful to Madhav Deshpande for translating these verses.

56. See Vakankar, "Savarkar ani Bhasasudhdi" in Varhadpande et al., *Garudjhepa,* 38–39, for a list of some of these pure words.

57. See Engblom, "Vishnu Moreshwar Mahajani and Nineteenth-Century Antecedents to Keshavsut," in Wagle, *Writers, Editors, and Reformers,* 143, for an analysis of some of the experiments in the modern period by poets such as Mahadev Moreshwar Kunte, who

not just a new style but a new zeitgeist, gesturing to immanence and a new sense of self.[58] Philip Engblom examines the Marathi poets who resisted English influence by sticking resolutely to Shastric and Sanskritic norms or tried to write English poetry in Marathi by using a more natural idiom than the convoluted and difficult medium of Sanskrit offered. Some of that energy is visible in "The New Soldier."[59]

Navyā manūntila navyā damācā śūra śipā'ī āhēṁ, kōṇa malā vaṭaṇīlā āṇūṁ śakatō tēṁ mī pāhēṁ!	I am a soldier of the new era with fresh breath in my lungs I would love to seek the one who can tame me/ my wild ways
Brāhmaṇa nāhīṁ, hinduhi nāhīṁ, na mī ēka panthācā, tēci patita kīṁ jē āṅkhaḍitī pradēśa sākalyācā!!	I am no Brahman. Not Hindu even. I profess no single sect Lowly are those who narrow down the space of Entirety
Jikaḍē jāvēṁ tikaḍē mājhīṁ bhānvaḍēṁ āhēta, sarvatra khuṇā mājhyā gharacyā majalā disatāhēta;	Wherever I go, I see my brethren around Everywhere I see signposts of my home
Śāntīcēṁ sāmrājya sthāpūṁ baghata kāḷa jō āhē, prēṣita tyācā navyā damācā śūra śipā'ī āhē!	The new age that strives to establish the empire of peace. I am its prophet. A soldier of the new era with fresh breath in my lungs

Keshavsut uses the word *śipā'ī* or soldier without any sense of militarism or violence; such nationalism is not part of his oeuvre. Yet he writes of a dawn of a new spirit, a new nonmaterial self that is not Brahman and, even more radically, not Hindu. This new soldier's brethren are humanity; the earth is his home. Setting aside the narrowly egotistical self, Keshavsut's *nava shipai* seeks communion and harmony with nature and people, striving to establish an "empire of peace."

---

continued the pandit tradition in Western India. Tryambak Bapuji Thombre (1890–1918), known as Balkavi, was the best exponent of the romantic modern poetry while Bhaskar Ramachandra Tambe (1874–1941) wrote poetry for an emergent middle class.

58. See Engblom, "Keshavsut and Early Modernist Strategies."

59. I am grateful to Drs. Arun and Gauri Bhagwat for their help with this translation.

No such pacifism, immanence, or harmony emerged in Savarkar's poetic voice as it matured and found its stride. He also bristled, as we have seen, at any suggestion that the term "Hindu" was not useful. His desire to write a *mahākāvya* did not diminish, but the virtues he extolled shifted from the king to the nascent nation, allegorized as a mother, sister, or widow. Narayana Rao has written that poetry is a medium that is not authentic unless it is recited, spoken, and heard, but Savarkar wrote his poems to be read in magazines by a new readership that recognized old metres even though he assigned tunes (*cāla*) and rhythms (*tāla*) to them and wrote many to be only recited. His core audience was also well aware of the Marathi grammatical categories he explained like *chanda/vṛtta* (metre) and used such as *samāsa* (compound words) and *alaṅkāra* (which means ornamentation or embellishment, such as *yamaka* [alliteration], *ślēṣa* [puns], and *upamā* [simile]). He used context-specific compounds and sounds, used style for effect, recognized that *rasa* (emotive content) and metre could not compete with each other and that the emotive aspect of his poetry could not be achieved just with the simple use of rhyme.[60] The influence of the poet/playwright Bhavabhūti—a master of alliteration[61]—might be adduced when we read his penchant for alliteration (*anuprāsa*) and onomatopoeia (*śabdānukṛti*), both common enough in Sanskrit poetry that Savarkar could casually use them both. When he used classical metres such as *śikhariṇī, mandākrāntā, śāradulavikriḍit,* the verses mostly scan correctly.

Savarkar's Poems

One of Savarkar's longer, more interesting poems, "Bālavidhavā-duḥstithikathan" (The plight of a child widow), shows his emerging position on widow remarriage. Written in 1902, when Savarkar was nineteen years old, it discusses child widowhood brought by the plague.[62] Savarkar used a natural disaster that was worsened by colonial policy to direct attention to the much older scandal of child widowhood. He excoriates widowers for continuing to live as much as he

60. I am grateful to Somadeva Vasudeva, who worked with me on this poem, helping to decode its complexity.

61. I get this phrase and the information about onomatopoeia and alliteration in Sanskrit poetry from my colleague Robert Goldman.

62. Savarkar submitted the poem to a competition held by the Bombay Hindu Union Club. He wrote it in 1902, and the full Marathi text can be found in *SSV*, MPHS, 7: 36–43.

goes after a fossilized śāstric (orthodox) law. Written in the *āryā* metre, the poem has 102 verses. Savarkar changes voices constantly, speaking as the poet, the plague, a householder, the dead wife's ghost, a young wife, and the young widow to whom the entire poem is dedicated. He creates the intimate space of a home and household in which the wife has died, the husband is bereft, and the disconsolate son is terrified his father will leave as well. The poem could be autobiographical. His mother was young when she died (of cholera, not the plague), but Savarkar lost his father and uncle to the plague. When Savarkar describes the love between husband and wife, the couple is childlike; their love play feels like that between children rather than two adults.

But his description of the plague and the effect of both the disease and the British colonial response is chilling. In his memoir he remembered reading in *Kesari* about the plague in faraway places such as Pune. As he put it:

> If the plague touched one today, he was finished tomorrow. If one person in a household contracted the plague, within seconds women, children, other family members, the entire household in the same manner as if burnt to ashes would just be destroyed. There were homes in which five or six corpses, one after the other, would fall to the ground—who would pick them up? If you picked up someone's corpse your's would be the corpse someone else would have to pick up only to have the same happen.[63]

He continues in the same vein:

> In such a situation who would pick up a corpse? Mothers were fleeing from the corpses of their infants, children from the corpses of their parents, parents from the corpses of their children because if the British were to get wind that there was a corpse in the house, in the name of sanitizing the house they would destroy it, burn all belongings, loot everything, and whoever was left alive had to flee to the forests and be "segregated." But even there, the plague! At home the plague. At the door, the plague![64]

These passages are among the few in his memoirs that are other-directed, the rare place where the self-regard that pervades his other writing is suspended. In these passages, he narrates with extraordinary emotion what must have been a petrifying situation—when his father contracted plague and had to be isolated upstairs and secluded, his wailed requests for water

63. *SSV*, SSRSP, 1: 96.
64. *SSV*, SSRSP, 1: 96.

ignored by his young son and daughter-in-law, his condition hidden from the police who would otherwise drive them out of their home, sanitize it, throw everything away, and burn it down. In Savarkar's retelling, the small towns and villages in Maharashtra become ghost towns, evacuated of all their inhabitants but those whose eerie wails of terror or pain could be heard from miles away.

After Savarkar's father got sick, his younger brother took ill. Savarkar and his young sister-in-law cared for both, in constant fear that they too would get sick. Savarkar's narrates this simply, and it is a poignant and heartrending account not because he resorts to melodramatics or sentimentality or tugs at his readers' heartstrings but because he does not. He merely describes what he saw. We get a sense of the village, the pre-electricity darkness, the eerie and mournful sounds of the chant—*bolo bhai ram*—as the funeral bier is carried to the cremation grounds. We understand the nearly overwhelming fear he and his sister-in-law felt, tending to their dying father and a deathly ill brother.

Savarkar perhaps ventriloquizes the voice of his sister-in-law in this poem. She married his brother as a young girl and might very well have found herself a child widow. He begins with the palace (*prasada*) built for the plague with the mortar of oppression and the humiliation of the earth. The first line scans perfectly, showing readers he knows the rules of Sanskritic meter.

Pāyā paravaśatā jyā duṣkāḷācyā śilānhiṁ jō racilā	The foundation of slavery is the root cause of the bad times upon us
avanati-kr̥tānta-kēli prāsādā plēga kaḷasa tyā khacilā (1)	The plague tops the edifice of our subjection
Nandanavanasama mōhaka sr̥ṣṭīcā sārabhūta hā dēśa hō dr̥ṣṭi dhan'ya pāhuni, dharuni asā plēga hr̥dayiṁ uddēśa (2)	Natural beauty akin to that of Nandanvan is in this land His eyes were filled with it and he gave himself a task
Āryavartī ālā, mumba'ilā ṭhēvilēṁ maga padālā jhālā anta sukhācā, yē ūta anantavaktra- vipadānlā (3)	He came to Āryāvarta, placed his feet on Mumbai And all happiness ended, giving rise to endless calamities

The plague starts by musing to itself (it is a masculine voice) about the unique beauties of the land—*āryāvarta*—which is a hundred times more beautiful than its reputation. The eyes of the plague are filled with this land's beguiling beauty, described with the alliterative use of *lā*: *bhulalā, khulalā, vadalā*.

Jī aikilī tyāhuni śatapaṭa adhikāci surucitā dhan'yā pāhuni bhulalā khulalā, vadalā: Mōhaka na bhū aśī an'yā (4)	The beauty of this land is a hundred times more than I had heard Having seen it he was beguiled and said I have not seen a land so beautiful as this
Kēlā niścaya aisā, kuruvāḷuni mumba'ī bhayāṇa karīṁ	He determined to himself I will caress with my terrible hand Mumbai
hō dhig na nija jiṇēṁ tēṁ, yāstava baghaṇyā puṇēṁ prayāṇa karī (6)	But my life would be worthless if I did not also visit Pune
Gōdāsnānāstava kari śrīmattryambakapurīsa gamanālā ālā Pañcavaṭīlā tēthuniyā Rāmarāya-namanālā (7)	In the Godavari he bathed so he could visit śrimattrayamabaka purī [i.e., Nashik] And then onto Panchavati to bow before Lord Rama
Bahu kāya vadōṁ? Kēlēṁ ēkyā abdānta dēśaparyaṭanā pavanāhuni javana, nacī damalā hā kīṁ vicitra vidhighaṭanā (8)	What can one say? In one year, he circumambulated the land Faster even than the wind, untiring was this strange tale of suffering

But what caused the plague? Savarkar's answer is reminiscent of Gandhi, but with a twist.

Plēga kaśācā ālā? Kr̥takarmācāci bhōga avataralā karmāyatta phalācyā åupabhōgāvīṇa kōṇa bhava taralā (9)	But what was the cause of the lague? Of our wrongdoings Who has ever escaped the fruits of karma?
Kēlīṁ bhayāṇa nagarēṁ, nagarāsama dāṭa sarva vana vasatēṁ	He destroyed cities; forests became like cities in their density of population

damalē namalē gamalē hatasattvaci mantra tantra sunavasa tēṁ (10)	none of the ritual promises made to deities if someone could be cured had any effect.
Jātā nātha strīcā tī gāåīh ūnigāya mānāvēṁ	A woman who loses her husband is more vulnerable even than the cow
suṭakā abalāñcī tyā karaṇyā ghēsī na kā yamā nāvēṁ (31)	O Yama, why don't you recite the names of these unfortunate widows to put them out of their misery
Bandhū nā, bāndhava nā, nā mātāpitara jyā abhāgītēṁ Tyā mājhīṁ duḥkhācīṁ prabhujī! Pōcati na kā nabhā gītēṁ (32)	No friend, no relatives, no parents, that unfortunate one [asks] My cries, dear God| Why do they not reach the skies
Mī alpavayī bālā, mājhā saubhāgyanidhi ahā jaḷalā vaidhavyācā durdhara bhayakara giri hā pracaṇḍa kōsaḷalā (33)	I am a young girl, my husband is dead On me has fallen this mammoth burden of widowhood
Kāya karuṁ? Zā'uṁ kuṭhē? Hō mājhē āptasōyarē sārē tārā anātha bālā, chaḷa baghatāṁ svastha basuniyā sārē (34)	What do I do? Where do I go? O my relatives Come to my aid, I am an orphan girl, harassed, and you simply sit and do nothing
Dētēṁ kā kōṇī ō abalēcyā yā madīya hāṅkēlā? Bōlā hō, bōlā hō, dhīrācā śabda åēka tari bōlā (35)	Is there anyone who can respond to this weak woman's call Please speak, please speak, just even one word of comfort

Beginning in verse twenty-nine, Savarkar explores all possible avenues to show the horrors of child widowhood. The critical voice of this poem is that of a reformer engaged in raising social consciousness about the child widow's miserable plight. In subsequent verses, Savarkar leaves no road untrod, excoriating all the sacred cows of orthodox Hinduism: the Vedas, the lawgivers, the priests. He fiercely denounces merry widowers in their dotage who remarry young girls. In that sense, this is an antihegemonic poem that uses its dialogue with a classical idiom to marshal an ideological critique of a nation that has not yet come into being.[65] For women, the plague piles insult on injury. It creates child widows who lead miserable lives; it kills mothers, sisters, and wives, putting the entire female race at risk. What does Savarkar advocate? And whom does he ask? He turns to the Shankaracharya, asking him to support widow remarriage, to found schools for widows run by older widows so a new society could benefit from generations of educated young women. The poem won an award and marked him, independent of his own self-publicity, as an up-and-coming poet.

This socially conscious poem brought him fame, but the one that positioned him regionally as an inspirational scribal poet of the nation was published in Pune in 1903. It was not didactic, but inspirational.[66] "Svatantratēcēṁ Stōtra" ("Hymn of Independence") is now readily available on the web in Marathi and in translation.[67] After independence, the composer Hridayanath Mangeshkar (son of Dinanath Mangeshkar) set it to music that was virtually unsingable except perhaps by his sister, the iconic Lata Mangeshkar, whose extraordinary vocal range meant that she, and perhaps only she, could sing it with ease. *Povāḍā* singers sing it routinely still, but without necessarily moving across three septets (*mandra, madhya, tāra*) as Lata Mangeshkar did.[68]

In "Svatantratēcēṁ Stōtra," Savarkar again shows his understanding of Marathi and Sanskrit poetic traditions. The first *dhrupad* is in Sanskrit, after which the poem switches into Marathi. Here I present not the entire poem but the section most familiar in Maharashtra.

Jayō'stu tē! Jayō'stu tē! [69] Śrīmahanmaṅgale śivāspade śubhade	Victory to thee, victory to thee, auspicious, divinely sacred, granter of purity,

65. Satya Mohanty pointed this out to me when he invited me to present part of this chapter at Cornell University.

66. Whereas the poem on child widowhood may no longer be relevant to portions of Hindu society, this *stōtra* retains its universal appeal. I am grateful to Vidyut Aklujkar for this comment.

67. See *SSV*, MPHS 7: 45–46.

68. See Savarkar, *Athavani angaracya*, 91–93, for a brief account of the association between Savarkar and the Mangeshkar family. Lata Mangeshkar's father Dinanath Mangeshkar staged Savarkar's musical, *Sangeet San'yasta Khaḍga*, with the Balwant Sangeet Mandali, and from that time on, the entire Mangeshkar family became were close associates of Savarkar.

69. Because the first *dhrupad* is in Sanskrit, *bhagavatī* is in the vocative case. The rest of the poem is in Marathi.

svatantrate bhagavatī tvām
aham yaśoyutāṁ vande

heavenly spirit of liberty, bringer
of wellbeing, I bow to thee!

Rāṣṭrācēṁ caitan'ya mūrta
tūṁ nīti sampadāñcī

You are the energy incarnate of
nations, you are their ethics of
prosperity

svatantratē bhagavatī śrīmatī
rājñī tūṁ tyāñcī

heavenly spirit of liberty, of
prosperity you are their
empress

paravaśatēcyā nabhānta tūñci
ākāśīṁ hōśī
svatantratē bhagavatī cāndaṇī
camacama-lakhalakhaśī

In the darkness of slavery,
you divine spirit of liberty
are the only brightly shining star

Gālāvaracyā kusumīṁ kinvā
kusumāñcyā gālīṁ
svatantratē bhagavatī tūñca
jī vilasatasē lālī

You are the glow on youthful
cheeks as also on fresh flowers
heavenly spirit of liberty!

tūṁ sūryācēṁ tēja udadhicēṁ
gāmbhīryahiṁ tūñci
svatantratē bhagavatī an'yathā
grahaṇa naṣṭa tēcī

you are the brilliance of the
sun and depth of ocean
destroyed by the eclipse of
your absence

Mōkṣa-mukti hīṁ tujhīñca
rūpēṁ tulāca vēdāntīṁ
svatantratē bhagavatī yōgijana
parabrahma vadatī

Salvation and liberation are
your forms
yogis and vedic-upaniṣadic
scholars call you the ultimate
Brahman

jēṁ jēṁ uttama udātta unnata
mahanmadhura tēṁ tēṁ
svatantratē bhagavatī sarva tava
sahakārī hōtēṁ

whatever is excellent, noble,
elevated and greatly enjoyable
Inheres in your service

Hē adhamaraktarañjitē
sujanapūjitē śrī svatantratē
tujasāṭhi maraṇa tēṁ janana

Bathed in the blood of oppressors,
worshipped by the good folk
death courted for your
sake is a [worthy] life;

tujavīṇa janana tēṁ maraṇa

life spent without you is akin
to death

tuja sakala-carācara-śaraṇa	In you the entire world of the static and mobile rests
Bharatabhūmilā dṛḍhāliṅganā kadhi dēśila varadē	When will you embrace our Bharatabhumi [my nation/ our nation]?
svatantratē bhagavati tvāmaham yaśōyutāṁ vandē!	heavenly spirit of liberty, bringer of wellbeing, I bow to thee!

The English translation may seem sentimental, but it remains inspirational in Marathi, and it is still sung at collective gatherings in Maharashtra. Despite its longevity, there is none of Keshavsut's expansive vision or immanence; instead, the energy of nations is apostrophized as the ultimate being, or Brahman. From his *phataka* to this *stōtra*, we see Savarkar's desire to die for the nation and his extolling a martyr's death for the nation as the most honorable and pure. He also wrote a poem for his sister-in-law letting her know she should be proud to have married into a family of nationalist martyrs.

In 1908, in a poem titled "Priyakara Hindusthāna," he coined some of the terms he later fleshed out in his extended essay *Essentials of Hindutva*, including "Puṇyabhūmi tūṁ. Pitṛbhūmi tūṁ. Tūṁ amucā abhimāna" ("Sacred land are you; ancestral land are you, in you resides our pride").[70] In England in 1909, Savarkar took a trip to Brighton Beach and was struck with homesickness so intense that he could only express it in a poem. The collection's editor informs us that Savarkar knew he was under surveillance and that his days of freedom were numbered.[71] This knowledge informs the poem, possibly the last he wrote as a free man. This poem was also set to music by Hridayanath Mangeshkar.

Nē majasī nē parata mātṛbhūmilā. Sāgarā, prāṇa taḷamaḷalā	Take me back to my motherland | Ocean, my spirit is in turmoil

70. *SSV*, MPHS, 7: 76. Savarkar directed those who might recite his poem to sing it to the same tune as the popular song "Mhātārā itukā nā" from the musical drama *Shāradā*. See https://savarkar.org/mr/pdfs/savarkaranchi-kavita-mr-v002.pdf. The song's sarcastic lyrics mock an old man who believes he is still young enough to get married. "Mhātārā itukā nā/avaghe pā'uṇaśē vayamāna/Lagnā ajuni lahāna/ avaghe pā'uṇaśē vayamāna" (Am not an old man/just seventy-five years young/still young enough to marry/just seventy-five years young). We may assume that the song's widespread popularity in Maharashtra is one of the reasons he picked it for his patriotic poem, even though the content of the two is vastly different.

71. *SSV*, MPHS, 7: 79.

bhūmātēcyā caraṇatalā tuja dhūtāṁ. Mī nitya pāhilā hōtā	I saw you every day washing my mother's feet
maja vadalāsī an'ya dēśiṁ cala jā'ū. Sr̥ṣṭicī vividhatā pāhū	You said to me let's travel the world and see its various natural beauties
ta'iṁ jananī-hr̥d virahaśaṅkitahi jhālēṁ. Pari tuvāṁ vacana tija didhalēṁ	My mother was suspicious of this separation, but you promised her
mārgajña svayēṁ mīca pr̥ṣṭhiṁ vāhīna. Tvarita yā parata āṇīna[72]	As his guide I will carry him on my back and bring him back to you quickly
Viśvasalōṁ yā tava vacanīṁ. Mī	I believed in your promise [that]
jagadanubhava-yōgē banunī. Mī	Having experienced the world
tava adhika śakta ud'dharaṇīṁ. Mī	I would be even stronger in uplifiting you
yēåīna tvarēṁ kathuna sōḍilēṁ tijalā. Sāgarā prāṇa taḷamaḷalā (1)	Having said "I will return quickly" I left her
Nabhiṁ nakṣatrēṁ bahuta ēka pari pyārā.	There are many stars in the firmament
Maja bharatabhūmicā tārā prāsāda ithē bhavya parī maja bhārī.	but the only one beloved to me is my motherland [Bharatabhūmi]
Ā'icī jhōpaḍī pyārī	There are many grand palaces here but the one beloved to me is my mother's cottage
tijavīṇa nakō rājya, maja priya sācā. Vanavāsa ticyā jari vaniñcā	I don't want a kingdom without her, even exile in her forest is preferable to me
bhulaviṇēṁ vyartha hēṁ ātā. Rē	Enough of this useless tempting
Bahu jivalaga gamatē cittā. Rē	That river which to you is most beloved
tuja saritpatē! Jī saritā. Rē tadvirahācī śapatha ghālitō tujalā. Sāgarā prāṇa taḷamaḷalā (3)	If you do not [return me] you will also suffer the pain of separation [from your beloved]

72. *SSV*, MPHS, 7: 79, for the full text of the poem.

Yā phēnamiṣēṁ hasasi nirdayā kaisā. Kāṁ vacana bhaṅgisī aisā	Hiding behind your foam how can you laugh so pitilessly? Why do you break my promise thus?
tvatsvāmitvā sāmprata jī miravītē. Bhi'uni kāṁ āṅglabhūmītēṁ?	Are you afraid of this England that right now is gloating over her mastery of you
Manmātēlā abala mhaṇuni phasavīsī. Maja vivāsanātēṁ dēśī	And you think my mother is weak and is that why you deceive her by exiling me?
Jari āṅglabhūmibhayabhītā. Rē	Even if you [the sea] are afraid of England
abalā na mājhihī mātā. Rē kathila hēṁ Agastisa ātā. Rē	my mother [India] is not weak/ powerless
jō ācamanīṁ ēka palīṁ tuja pyālā.	She can invoke Agasti who swallowed you up in a spoonful.[73]

Almost simultaneously, Savarkar began preparing for his martyrdom for the nation. In March 1910 he was arrested, and from his jail cell in Brixton he composed "Mājhēṁ Mr̥tyupatra" ("My Last Will and Testament"). Savarkar urges his sister-in-law to remember gatherings at home like sitting down to dinner under a moonlit night, singing verses to commemorate the bravery of nationalists:

Śrīrāmacandra-vanavāsa kathā rasālā
kī kēvi dēśa Iṭalī ripumukta jhālā
Tānājicā samaradhīra tasā pavāḍā
gāvā Cittōragaḍa vā Śanavāravāḍā

Kī ghētalēṁ vrata na hēṁ amhi andhatēnē
labdha prakāśa itihāsa-nisarga-mānēṁ
jēṁ divya dāhaka mhaṇūni asāvayācēṁ
bud'dhyāci vāṇa dharilēṁ kāriṁ hēṁ satīcēṁ[74]

Savarkar provided the editor of his first poetry compilation with this English prose translation

73. Savarkar is referring to the mythological sage Agastya who swallowed the entire ocean in one small sip as a favor to the Gods who needed to find the demons hiding in it.

74. *SSV*, MPHS, 7: 82–83. This exact translation in English is repeated in *LBS*.

> The Moon was delightful above and we all friends and families sat along, now musing, now lost in stirring and stimulating conversations. Now we listened to the moving story of the Princely Exile in Ayodhya or of the stirring struggle that set Italia free. Now we sang the immortal exploits of Tanaji or Chitore, or of Baji and Bhau and Nana. . . . Nor was it blindness that goaded us on to the path! No! We entered in it under the full blaze of the searching light of Logic and History and Human Nature knowing full well that those who have Life must lose it first we took up our Cross and deliberately followed him.[75]

Perhaps poets should not be allowed to translate their own works. Savarkar's fondness for such prose in English remained a constant.

Just before Savarkar was taken to the Andamans, he composed a poem from prison, writing it on a scrap of paper and handing it to a fellow inmate. It is not well-known or particularly memorable, but it gives us a sense of how instrumental he meant his poetry to be in inspiring others to take up arms and how deeply he felt the desire to martyr himself for the nation. We note Savarkar's invocation of *sthaṇḍila* or *yajñakuṇḍa* (the four-sided firepit created specifically for offering oblations in a sacrifice) long before he wrote his *Essentials of Hindutva*. He was laying the groundwork in his poetry for the prose version of his sacralized nation-deity. At this early stage in his writing, he had already disseminated in poetic form the replacement of the Goddess with the Mother-nation.[76]

Mānuni ghē sācī. Janani gē.	Accept it truly, mother mine,
Mānuni ghē sācī	accept it truly
Alpa svalpa tari sēvā apulyā	This little bit of service from your
arbhaka bālāñcī	innocent children
Ṛṇa hē bahu jhālēṁ.	Our debt to you is immense.
Tujhyā stanīcēṁ stan'ya pājuni	You have graced us with your
dhan'ya amhā kēlēṁ	milk

75. "My Will and Testament" in *SSV*, MPHS, 7: 408.

76. The full text of the poem "Pahila Hapta" can be found in *SSV*, MPHS, 7: 87. I am grateful yet again to Vidyut Aklujkar, who went through my translation of this poem to ensure that I did not, for instance, give in to my impulse to translate *sthaṇḍila* as the more colloquial "altar." The poem's metre is given as *govind*, which is not a Sanskrit *akṣaragaṇavr̥ttē* metre but a simpler one in which a particular arrangement of the consonantal valence (long and short/*hrasva dīrgha*) of the letters (*akṣara*) is not of primary importance.

R̥ṇa teṁ phēḍāyā. Haptā pahilā tapta sthaṇḍiliṁ dēha arpitō hā	In order to repay that debt, as the first installment, I offer my body to the flaming sacrificial fire
Savēñci janmuniyāṁ. Tvanmōcanahavanāta havī karū puna: punhā kāyā	Immediately by being reborn we will again and again offer our bodies in this sacrifice of liberating you
Sārathī jicā abhimānī. Kr̥ṣṇajī āṇī. Rāma sēnānī	A proud group that has as its charioteer Krishna and Rama as its leader/General
Aśī tīsa kōṭi tava sēnā Tī amhānvinā thāmbēnā Pari karūni duṣṭadaladalanā Rōnvilacī svakarīṁ. Svātantryācā himālayāvari jhēṇḍā jaratārī	Your army of thirty crores Will not rest [and] even without us Will vanquish the army of evil And erect the flag of independence on the Himalayas[77]

We now turn to the genre that was most important to him.

Povāḍās

Kathākāvya is a storytelling genre, and *povāḍā* is one of its forms.[78] It appears as early as the Dnyaneshwari (thirteenth century) as a form of eulogy.[79] However, as a genre on its own, it comes into prominence in the late seventeenth and eighteenth centuries, roughly coterminous with the rise of Chhatrapati Shivaji and the poetry of the Pandit poets Waman Pandit and Mōrōpanta.[80] *Povāḍā* composer/performers (*śāhiras, kavis*) came from the wandering group of bards known as Gondhali, which hails from and is most strongly associated

77. Maydev, *Savarkaranchi Kavita*, 81. Also available in *SSV*, MPHS, 7: 87.

78. *Bharatiya Sanskritikosha*, 5: 688. See also Dhawale and Kulkarni, *Marathi Kavita*, 6–7, for a description of the *povāḍā* style. For a quick English description of the various genres, see Deshpande, *Encyclopeadic Dictionary of Marathi Literature*.

79. Rege, "Conceptualising Popular Culture," 1041.

80. Deshpande notes that "Mōrōpanta . . . was the last and the best representative of the Pandit school of poets, even if the characteristics of this school are highly accentuated and taken to the extreme in the *Āryā Bharat*" (the Mahabharat composed by Mōrōpanta, so named because it was composed entirely in the *āryā* metre). Deshpande, *Encyclopaedic Dictionary of Marathi Literature*, vol. 1, 33.

with Gavli but also includes those from Mahar, Mang, Bhat communities, from Brahmin and non-Brahmin communities alike.[81] Although not formally attached to a court, they were patronized and paid by rulers in gifts, which occasionally were mentioned in the poetry, thus making the poems useful historical documents.[82] These bards called themselves *kavirāj* and were known as *lokakavi* or peoples' poets. *Povāḍā*s were usually masculine in tone, addressing affairs of state, great cities, forts, famous people, and great battles.[83] Often they recounted a warrior's achievements or the powers or virtues of a scholar or other notable; they were meant to render the figure, event, or place they wrote about *udātta*, or sublime.

The Marathi novelist, poet, and literary scholar Bhalchandra Nemade has suggested that it was the *śāhira*s who "made Marathi poetry a purely literary activity for the first time. They wrote, with plebian sincerity, all that was traditionally prohibited in Marathi literature."[84] As he noted, the language of the poetry is unique because it was designed to be sung with the accompaniment of musical instruments as in folk drama.

*Povāḍā*s were, first and foremost, composed to be sung or performed outdoors. Their content was intended to awaken or inspire *vīrarasa* (bravery, courage) and because of that the musicality of the genre is fairly straightforward. As Ashok Ranade has pointed out, the *talas* (rhythm structure) were also relatively simple: four-beat *tala*s (such as *Keherva*) rather than the more intricate sixteen-beat (such as *Teentaal*) or seven-beat (such as *Roopak*) *talas*. As for the musical accompaniment, the instruments (*tuntune, daph*, or *manjiri*) emphasize rhythmic pulses and are not tuned to a given pitch—they simply match the voices of the performers. The voices of the primarily male *śāhira*s are strong, and the syllables *ji ji* are periodically repeated, which give the singer a break, even if those syllables are sung at a high pitch. The *śāhira* tells a historical story to a large audience and does not take on any role other than that of narrator.[85] In form and content, the *povāḍā* was and remains a demotic and didactic genre.

81. Rege, "Conceptualising Popular Culture," 1041. For the Gondhal and Gondhalis, see Dhere, "The Gondhali."

82. Acworth and Shaligram, *Itihasaprasiddha Purushamce va Striyamce Povade*, preface.

83. See Ranade, "Performing Arts and Narrative," 27–30, for a succinct description of a *povāḍā* performance, its musicality, the role of the performer, and the content.

84. Nemade, "Towards a Definition of Modernity," 72.

85. I get all this information from Ranade, "The Povāḍā."

Composed in 1659 by a *śāhira* named Agindas (Adnyandas), the first modern *povāḍā* memorialized Chhatrapati Shivaji's killing of Afzal Khan and his daring escape and tells us that the poet received a horse and one *ser* of gold.[86] Agindas was also likely the first Marathi poet to include what we might call historical facts in his poetry.[87] Horses were central to both the Deccan economy and Shivaji Maharaj's imperial ambitions,[88] and the gift of one would point us to the poet's skill, the reception of his performance at the court, or the importance of the event being commemorated. The second notable *povāḍā* was Śāhira Tulshidas's "Tanaji Malusare," which commemorated the recapture of the Kondhana Fort in 1670.

These early recorded seventeenth-century *povāḍās* are an important archival source in Marathi because they encode elements of the social milieu in their compositions. They also serve as indices of a key historical transformation—the emergence of Chhatrapati Shivaji as an independent rural potentate, central to Maharashtra's imagination. The name "Maharashtra" is old, perhaps even ancient, and it always suggests the land where Marathi is spoken.[89] The modern state with its borders and boundaries was demarcated only in 1960. Prior to that, in both colonial and precolonial times, it was part of larger units. In the precolonial era, the area known as the Deccan was ruled by a succession of empires. In the late seventeenth century, when our *śāhira* enters the picture, rule over the region was contested by five states (Nizamshahi/Ahmednagar, Adilshahi/Bijapur, Qutubshahi/Golconda, Baridshahi/Bidar, Imadshahi/Birar) that fought each other for territorial gains while also warring against the Delhi-based ruler of the Mughal Empire (1526–1858).

In 1636, a young prince, Aurangzeb, who later became the Mughal emperor (reigning from 1658–1707), was appointed governor of the Deccan. As governor,

86. Acworth and Shaligram, *Itihasaprasiddha Purushamce va Striyamce Povade*, preface. It has been suggested that the first *povāḍā* composed by Agindas was at Jijābā'ī's insistence. See Divekar, "Survey of Material in Marathi," 98.

87. Dhawale, *Marathi Kavita*, 8–9.

88. Kulkarni, "Maratha Swarajya," 322, confirms the gift of horses and tutors and insignia upon receiving the *jagir* of Pune.

89. Phatak, *Ramdas: Vangmaya ani Karya*, 296. Phatak argues against the entire Chitpavan attribution of "Maharashtra-Dharma" by M. G. Ranade, V. K. Rajwade, Rajaram Shastri Bhagwat through to B. G. Tilak as evidence of unity and patriotism, showing instead that Samartha Ramdas used the words "Marhāṭa-Marhāṣṭa Dharma" only twice, and did not conceive of it as "Maharashtra Dharma." Phatak suggests instead that Samartha uses these words once in a letter he wrote to Chhatrapati Maharaj and once in a discourse about Kshatriya-*dharma*.

he captured the territories of the Nizamshahi ruler but had to wait to resume his campaign until after he had won the battle of succession to the Mughal throne. In 1657 he relaunched a campaign against the Adil Shahi and Qutubshahi rulers. Preoccupied with these campaigns, Aurangzeb paid scant attention to an Adil Shahi vassal named Shivaji Bhonsle, who was picking off forts lost to the rulers even as the Mughal emperor was trying to get them back.

Shivaji Bhonsle (1627–80) was the enterprising son of Shahaji Bhonsle, who had been the foremost vassal of the Nizamshahi ruler of Ahmednagar and, after his defeat, the vassal of the Adilshahi ruler of Bijapur. Between 1636 and 1642, Shivaji received the land and estate grants (*jagirs*) of Indapur, Pune, Chakan and Supe.[90] When he received the *jagir* of Pune as his father's agent while his father was alive and as full owner upon his father's death, Shivaji was gifted elephants, horses, tutors, and other forms of wealth by his father.[91] As the agent of Poona/Pune, Shivaji raided and captured neighbouring forts (Rohiḍā, Sinhagaḍa, Purandar) without official approval. Attempts to curb his ambition were unsuccessful until Aurangzeb finally turned his attention to him, dispatching Mirza Raja Jai Singh I of Amber to confront him. The two agreed on a truce, but when Shivaji went to meet the emperor in Delhi, he was imprisoned. After a daring escape, he returned to the Deccan and established his own small kingdom. This historical story is memorialized in the first *povāḍā* in 1659 by Śāhira Agindas (Adnyandas).

As historians from V. K. Rajwade to Y. N. Kelkar onward have noted, *povāḍās* contain within themselves histories of the different ways in which they were recited and are repositories of orally transmitted histories.[92] In 1891, over two hundred years after Agindas composed his *povāḍā*, S. T. Shaligram

90. Kulkarni, "Maratha Swarajya: Its Extent and Income," 321.

91. Kulkarni, "Maratha Swarajya: Its Extent and Income," 322.

92. Kelkar, *Aitihasik Powade*, 23–25. See 5–7 for his criticisms of Shaligram and Shitut. According to Kelkar, Shaligram's discovery of the desire for historical recovery was produced by his association with Vishnushastri Chiplunkar. Narayan Rao has noted that once the notion that India does not have history becomes important, colonial administrators start to create the "missing" history in a Western style and names, dates, places become particularly important. In this colonial milieu, the circulation of a poem or story becomes less important than historical claims about its origin. As a result, there was a rise in the colonial period of what were termed critical editions, in which the editors fixed the texts while ignoring the community that used them or in which they circulated. A Victorian notion of the author and his biography becomes important. Note, too, that much of the dispute about naming, fixing, biography and so on is important for Kelkar for the eighteenth century, the Peshwa period.

published the first Marathi compilation of the genre,[93] collaborating with the Municipal Commissioner of Bombay and Indian Civil Service officer, Harry Arbuthnot Acworth, to publish an English version a few years later. Acworth recomposed ten Marathi *povāḍās* into English ballads. He called the book *Ballads of the Marathas,* reflecting his understanding of the community as among the "martial races."[94] Since the compilation's publication, Marathi literary critics have refined the editors' assertions, corrected their translation mistakes, and published supplementary compilations with better and more accurate transliterations of *modi, balbodha,* and Marathi.

In the mid-nineteenth century, the writer of *Nibandhamala,* Vishnushastri Chiplunkar, began publishing *povāḍās,* hoping to alert his readers to Maharashtra's glorious past. Kedar Kulkarni sees Chiplunkar as "repurposing [them] for integrating romantic theories with Indian poetics."[95] Chiplunkar viewed *povāḍās* as both a powerful instrument to communicate history and a way to keep the Marathi language robust in the face of English encroachments.[96] Poetry, or *kāvya,* implicitly contained two other categories–*itihās* (history) and *bhāṣā* (language). *Kāvya, itihās,* and *bhāṣā* were linked categories of meaning: one without the other was meaningless. The *pōvāḍa* was the glorious amalgam of all three, and important because it discussed the masculine world. Chiplunkar, for instance, distinguished between the political *povāḍā* and the *lāvaṇī,* which told of feminine seductions, to justify his attention to *povāḍās.*[97]

The *povāḍā* I focus on here is the story of the 1670 recapture of a fort (*gaḍ*) named Koṇḍāṇā located in the Sahyadri mountain range in the modern state of Maharashtra.[98] Although the recapture was successful, it exacted a high price, as Chhatrapati Shivaji's friend and chief general Tanaji Malusare died in

93. Acworth and Shaligram, *Itihasaprasiddha Purushamce va Striyamce Povade.*

94. Acworth, *Ballads of the Marathas,* preface. On the success of this translation, see Engblom, who finds Acworth's efforts "remarkable not only because they were the first of their kind or because they dealt with the folk as opposed to the literary tradition of Marathi poetry, but also because they are so successful as translations, so readable." Engblom, "Marathi Poetry in English Translation," 115–16.

95. Kulkarni, *World Literature and the Question of Genre,* 55.

96. Kelkar, *Aitihasik Powade,* preface.

97. Rege, "Conceptualising Popular Culture."

98. Deshpande, *Creative Pasts,* 56–61. Deshpande also analyzes this *povāḍā* as an exemplary case of how political loyalty to a chief was depicted, as well as Chhatrapati Maharaj as an ideal ruler. My analysis, while indebted to Deshpande's, has a different focus.

the battle. As the story is told and retold, Tanaji received a summons on the morning of his son's marriage and set off to get his orders from Shivaji, whose mother Jijābā'ī had ordered him to get the fort back. With a small army and the help of trained mountain lizards called *ghorpads*, Tanaji scaled the fort in the dead of night, battled Udayabhāna Rāṭhōḍa, and recaptured the fort but was martyred in the process. Legend, historical fiction, and popular poetry over the ensuing three centuries have memorialized the words Shivaji Maharaj supposedly spoke on receiving the news: "*gaḍ ālā paṇa sinha gēlā*" ("the fort has returned to us, but our lion has departed"). Chhatrapati Shivaji renamed the fort Sinhagaḍa (Lion Fort) and built a shrine to commemorate Tanaji's bravery.[99] Four years later, in 1674, Shivaji crowned himself ruler in the orthodox Hindu tradition, bringing Brahmin priests from the holy city of Varanasi to coronate him and anoint him Chhatrapati Shivaji.

This story has been narrated in ballad form from the seventeenth century to the present day. A poet named Tulshidas, believed to have lived in the marketplace of Poona, composed the first *povāḍā* on the Koṇḍāṇā recapture.[100] Over its many revisions and performances, the core narrative remains remarkably consistent; it is still performed in rural Maharashtra and at the site of the original fort.

Following these three seventeenth-century *povāḍās* are the eighteenth-century *povāḍās* that have been recorded and written down, numbering approximately 150 to 300 works, many composed in praise or criticism of the Peshwa period. These *povāḍās* were patronized beyond the immediate

99. The year before Savarkar composed this *povāḍā*, the novelist Hari Narayan Apte (1864–1969) published a work of historical fiction titled *Gaḍ ālā Paṇa Sinha Gēlā* (1903). The novel includes a couple of *povāḍās* performed by Gondhalis, but the novel's plot is completely different from the two *povāḍās* analyzed in this chapter. Apte's protagonist Udaybhanu (a low-caste Rajput prince who converts to Islam) is consumed with desire for a married Rajput princess (Kamalkumari), so with the emperor Aurangzeb's consent, Udaybhanu abducts the couple, imprisons them in the Kondana fort, and Tanaji is despatched by Shivaji Maharaj to rescue her. The rescue fails—the princess commits suicide, and Tanaji Malusare is killed. The novel ends with an invocation of Śāhira Tulshidas's *povāḍā*:

Śūra mardācā pōvāḍā. Śūra mardānaṁ aikāvā.	A *povāḍā* about brave men should be heard by brave men
Shivajicē rājyānta. Aisā umarāva hōṇēṁ nāhīṁ	*In all of Shivaji's reign, there was no match for such a warrior*

100. Acworth and Shaligram, *Itihasaprasiddha Purushamce*, 19. See 20–50 for the first printed full text of the *povāḍā*.

milieu of their composition, and a great many include the starting points of various battles and names of families and factions, deaths, land grants, and so forth, which were part of daily life in the eighteenth century. The *povāḍās* depict the political milieu during their composition, with caste as the lived social organizer of community. The *povāḍās* are all named, and the name of the *śāhira* appears in the poem toward the end. The world of these poems was polyvocal and polyglot, with some written in part rustic Marathi, part rustic Hindi.

Śāhira Tulshidas's *Povāḍā*

Finally, we arrive at the *povāḍā* for which the previous excursus was a prerequisite. The version I am using is the one first recorded in print. Composed and performed in the *gadya padhdhati, śravya kāvya* style, which is to say in the tradition of poetic prose oral narration, rather than being sung, it immediately takes up the importance of garrisoned forts and one of several territorial boundaries.[101]

The *povāḍā* opens:

Rājagaḍa rājācā! Pratāpagaḍa Jījābā'īcā!	Rajagaḍ is Raja's! Pratapagaḍ is Jijābā'ī's
Sinhagaḍa Panhāḷā! Pahā tō Mōṅgalāñcā!!	Sinhagaḍa and Panhala! Aah, that is Mughal!
Sarjā Shivaji Śivabhajana! Kābīja kēlē taḷakōṅkaṇa!!	All praise to Shivaji conquered the Lower Konkan,
Gaḍa Māhulī ghētilī! Kalyāṇa Bhivaṇḍī kābīja kēlī	the fort of Mahuli, Kalyana Bhiwandi,
Khabara tyā Vijāpurālā gēlī	news reached Bijapur [Adil Shahi rulers]
Ṭhāṇē rājācē basalē	the sovereignty of the Raja was established
Shivaji Maharaj	Shivaji Maharaj

101. I am indebted to Vidyut Aklujkar for her help in understanding the intricacies of Marathi metre, particularly *povāḍās*. *Śravya* means "pleasing to the ear."

Rājagaḍa kilyāvara basalē	reigned at Rajagaḍ fort
Jijābā'ī mātā	Jijābā'ī his mother
Āhē Pratāpa gaḍāvarī	resided in Pratapagaḍ
Sōmavāracyā divaśī	On Monday!
Hātī hastanācī phanī	Ivory comb in hand
Ugavatē bājūlā najara kēlī	her gaze fell to the east
Najara Sinhagaḍāvara gēlī	her attention went to Sinhagaḍa

Straight off the bat, we get a basic geography lesson: Sinhagaḍa was to the east of Pratapagaḍ. We get the day (Monday) and Jijābā'ī's royal stature is shown by her use of an ivory comb. After this mention of the day of the week and the chronological order of the conquest of Konkan in 1657 and the capture of the rich towns of Kalyan and Bhiwandi and the fort of Mahuli, time is suspended, replaced with a densely textured geography.

Now let us look at the second section:

Bārā māvaḷa Puṇyākhālī	twelve districts below Pune[102]
Bārā māvaḷa Junrā khālī	twelve districts below Junnar
Puṇyācyā tōṇḍālā Jējurīcyā bārīlā	at the mouth of Pune and next to Jejuri
Killā Sinhagaḍa pāhilā	[she] saw the fort of Sinhagaḍa
Navē kōmbaḍīcē aṇḍē	freshly laid chicken eggs!
Aisā killā jhaḷakalā	such did the fort gleam
Aisā Pantōjī tō kākā	such was Pantoji uncle
Tyānē hujaṟyā bōlāvilā	who called the servants [to]
Jāvē Rājagaḍa kilyālā	go to Rajagaḍ fort
Sāṅgā Shivaji Maharajālā	summon Shivaji Maharaj [to]
Jēvāvē Rājagaḍa killyālā	dine at Rajgaḍ [but]
Añcavāvē Pratāpagaḍālā	rinse your mouth at Pratapagaḍ!

The belt of land running along the Western Ghats is known as Maval, and the valleys into which it is divided are known as *barah maval* or twelve mavals. Our balladeer's basic geography lesson is accurate, although the fort's actual

102. By below Pune, it is possible that the *povāḍā* refers to the geography of the Mavals. See Soitkar, "Emergence of Nomenclature: Sinnar." Soitkar suggests that there were twelve mavals from Junnar to Chakan and twelve from Pune to Shirval, and names the twelve "below Pune" as Andarmaval, Nanemaval, Pavanmaval, Ghotanmaval, Paudkhore, Mosekhore, Muthemaval, Gunjanmaval, Velvandmaval, Bhorkore, Shivtarkhore, and Hirdasmaval.

location is narrated poetically, not cartographically. He moves quickly to the prized fort at the mouth of Pune and close to Jejuri, described in the first of the capacious food metaphors he uses repeatedly. The fort gleams like newly laid eggs. The forts in which Shivaji Maharaj and his mother reside index luxury: we see Shivaji Maharaj's mother's comb, and he dresses in brocade and silk. Maureen Miller examined the semiotics of power that can be read in fabric, food, and clothing worn and used by the clergy in medieval Europe.[103] Likewise, here too the poet is alert to small details. Consider the description of Shivaji preparing to meet his mother:

Shivaji Maharaj pāñca pōśākha naṭalā	Shivaji Maharaj dressed himself to the hilt
Pāī tumāni suravārī caḍhavilyā	pulled on a tumani survar over his legs
Aṅgī kinakhāpa ghātilē	silk and brocade over his body
Śirī jirīṭōpa ghātalā	brocade cap on his head
Hātī vāghanakhē ghālūna	vaghanakhe [tiger claws] on his hands
Kr̥ṣṇā ghōḍīlā jina kēlā	called for his horse, Krishna
Ḍhāla pāṭhīvarī ṭākitā jhālā	slung his shield on his back
sōnasaḷī paṭṭā hātāta ghētalā	picked up his gold sword
Kr̥ṣṇā ghōḍīlā cābūka kēlā	spurred Krishna his horse
ālā Maḍhyācyā ghāṭālā	came to Mudh-ghat
ghāṭa Maḍhyācā utaralā	got down at Mudh-ghat
ālā Biravāḍī gāvālā	came to the village of Birwadi
gāva Biravāḍī sōḍīlā	left the village of Birwadi
ālā Kōlāmpurālā	came to Kolanpur [Polatpur]
Kōlāmpūra sōḍilē	left Kolanpur
ghāṭa pārācā vēṅghalā	scanned the edge of the ghat
ālē Pratāpagaḍa kilyālā	came to Pratapagad fort
salāma jijābā'īlā kēlā	bowed to Jijābā'ī

The landscape that Shivaji Maharaj traverses is tiny, local, ridged with hills and mountains. The events described take place in the nonurban world, in the *desh* that in Chhatrapati Shivaji's time would have been the southeastern part

103. See Miller, *Clothing the Clergy*. Miller shows how clothing made of silk and brocades and often adorned with gold and jewels were a signal marker of power and prestige and were used to mark hierarchy among the clergy.

of his kingdom.[104] The *povāḍā* stretches time by its slow, detailed rendering of Shivaji Maharaj's elaborate dress and his travel. The audience is meant perhaps to imagine the journey as if to join him on it, to arrive at the edge of a village, go through it, go to the edge of the hills, survey the landscape. The poem contains Turkish, Arabic, Persian, and Hindi words, in contrast to Savarkar's subsequent insistence on pure Marathi and only pure Marathi.

Shivaji Maharaj meets his mother and plays a game of dice, clearly a reference to the Mahābhārata, in which the game occasions all manner of difficult moral, ethical, and political situations for its protagonists. When Shivaji Maharaj loses to Jijābā'ī, the *śāhira* gives us his peremptory concession.

Aika jijābā'ī	listen Jijābā'ī
Sattāvīsa kilyāñcā mī rājā	over twenty-seven forts do I rule
Māga māga jijābā'ī	ask, ask, Jijābā'ī [i.e., "ask for whatever you wish"]

Note he does not call her *aaisaheb or matasaheb,* both respectful titles or words for mother that are commonly used in the depictions of their relationship today. Instead, he speaks to her imperiously, reminds her of his power and possessions, and sets the stage for what comes next.

Jijābā'ī asks for Sinhagaḍa. Here is Shivaji Maharaj's response:

Rājā tharatharā kāmpalā	Raja trembled with fear
Hā killā Udayabhāna Mōṅgalācā	That fort is Udayabhāna Moghul's
Bā'ī Udayabhāna Mōṅgalācā	Bai! Udayabhāna Moghul's
Jē umarāva gēlē Sinhagaḍālā	the warriors that went to Sinhagaḍa
Tyāñcyā pāṭhī ga pāhilyā	we saw their backs [saw them go]
Nāhī puḍhē pāhilē	we did not see their faces [did not see them return]
Killā āhē vāghācā jabaḍā	the fort is a tiger's mouth

The ruler trembles in fear. The fort she wants has been impossible to take back from the fearsome Udayabhāna Rāṭhōḍa, the Mughal vassal. Everyone who has tried has died in the attempt. Chhatrapati Shivaji is not the warrior here; Tanaji has not yet been introduced. When Tanaji is summoned to the

104. Kulkarni, "Maratha Swarajya: Its Extent and Income."

fort, his uncle tells him the same story about the soldiers who went to Sinhagaḍa. Bound by fealty, Tanaji gathers his 12,000 troops, an event described in detail, showing the archival and geographical imperative. The troops come from nearby villages—these are the peasant warriors Dirk Kolff wrote about, forced into war when the land lies fallow.[105]

Lakhōṭā subhēdārānē hātāta ghētalā	Subhedar (Tanaji) takes the farman [royal order] in his hands
Jyānē ēkā lakhōṭyācē bārā lakhōṭē kēlē	of the one he makes twelve
Dhāḍalē kāgada khōṟyālā	dispatched it through the Maval valley
Mōṭhyā mōṭhyā saradārālā	the big lords
Pandharā gāvācē pāruñcē	leaders of fifteen villages
Tyānē āpaṇājavaḷa bōlāvilē	he summons them
Umarṭhyācē Śirakē	the Shirkes of Umartha
Tyānē āpaṇājavaḷa bōlāvilē	he summons them
Dasapaṭecē Mōkāśī	Mokashis of Daspat
Tyānē āpaṇājavaḷa bōlāvilē	he summons them
Nāndavicē Sāvanta	Savants of Nandvi
Tyānē āpaṇājavaḷa bōlāvilē	he summons them
Vaḍagharacē Nā'īka	Naiks of Vadghar
Tyānē āpaṇājavaḷa bōlāvilē	he summons them
Silamācē Ṭhākūra	Thakurs of Silma
Tyānē āpaṇājavaḷa bōlāvilē	he summons them
Bārā hajāra phaujēlā jyācā lakhōṭā pōcalā	to 12,000 soldiers the farman is delivered

In the recitative repetition "*āpaṇājavaḷa bōlāvilē*" ("he summons them"), the *śāhira* slowly and deliberately builds tension. Irritated with Chhatrapati Shivaji for having interrupted his son's wedding, Tanaji does not leap to do his bidding. Then, eighty-year-old Jijābā'ī feeds all 12,000 troops, a meal the *śāhira* details:

Bārā hajāra phauja ghē'una ālā daravājyācē tōṇḍī	With 12,000 troops he came to the door
jyānē saimpāka pāhilā	they saw the preparation of food
bārā hajāra pāṭa māṇḍalā	12,000 plates were laid

105. See Kolff, *Naukar, Rajput, and Sepoy.*

bārā hajāra pañcapātrī	12,000 times five dishes
bārā hajāra māṇḍalā ṭhāva	12,000 sat to eat
saimpāka vāḍhūna tvarīta jhālī	quickly they were all served by
ainśī varṣācī umara	[Jijābā'ī who was] eighty years old
jyācā māpṭyācā āhāra	the measure of each one's portion
tyācā adhōlīcā jhālā	was immensely expanded
jyācyā mōharē pāñca pōḷyā	he who would have had fifteen rotis
tyācyā pandharā pōḷyā jhālyā	was served fifteen
khāvavatīla tyānē khāvyā	they ate what they could
uratīla tyānnī	what remained
gaḍākhālī ṭākāvyā	was tossed over the side of the fort walls
bārā hajāra phauja tr̥pta jhālī	12,000 ate to satiation

The poet's use of food is not unusual in Indic poetry. Vidyut Aklujkar has pointed out the profusion of food imagery in Marathi *sant* poetry, beginning with Jnanadeva (1275–96), who used extended food metaphors to express yogic bliss. Aklujkar argues that in later poetry, food was used to convey an expressly anticasteist sensibility—there was food enough for everyone; no one went hungry; no one was turned away.[106] In the *povāḍā*, food changes the peasantry's mind and allows them to become warriors. Luxury, hospitality, and obligation are present in this description of food so plentiful it can even be thrown away. This stands in marked contrast to the adage common in the region that wasting a single grain of rice is an insult to Lakshmi, the goddess of plenitude. Our poet could not have been unaware of the taboo against wasting food, but he uses food to show Jijābā'ī's egalitarianism (she personally serves the troops) and Tanaji's fairness (he agrees to Jijābā'ī's demand only after the 12,000 soldiers are sated). The narrative does more than underscore the centrality of food security in a peasant environment. We also see the preoccupations of the rural, landless, caste constituency. Sovereign authority, as we know from the stanzas about Shivaji Maharaj and Jijābā'ī's game, could be capricious, the fate of the world resting on a roll of the dice. Here, the narration presents a holistic picture of sovereign authority as paternalistic and Godlike in its ability to feed the subjects.

106. See Aklujkar, "Sharing the Divine Feast." See also Keune, *Shared Devotion, Shared Food.*

The *povāḍā* functions anthropologically, giving us paradigmatic relationships and pointedly asserting that food and feeding are the sovereign's obligations.[107] Food, in the form of the gleaming white eggs we saw earlier, is the measure of beauty; food is the measure of security and the obligation of the sovereign/state. Food instructs us in martial hierarchy and serves as the metaphor for battle. The link between "mother" and "food," as James Laine has pointed out, is certainly mythological but perhaps even more powerful.[108] The poem makes us understand that, insofar as Shivaji Maharaj and his deified mother Jijābā'ī are viewed as the state, food is the domain of state management.

Having ensured that his army is fed, Tanaji embarks on a mission he knows he may not survive. His army is armed only with sickles and hooks. Rather than show Shivaji Maharaj as a ruler with a disciplined army ready for whatever campaign he might undertake, the *povāḍā* is explicit that the expedition was doomed and that brave Tanaji Malusare accepted it anyway. But the sovereign must be held accountable for his demands, and before he leaves Tanaji finalizes his contract with Shivaji.

Āmhī jātō Sinhagaḍālā	I will go to Sinhagaḍa
āmacā Rāyabā sāmbhāḷā	Look after my son, Rayaba
jara ālō Sinhagaḍ'āhūna	If I return from Sinhagaḍa
lagīna karīna Rāyabācē	I will arrange for my son's marriage
jara gēlō tikaḍē mēlō	If I die there
lagīna karā Rāyabācē	You will arrange for my son's marriage
Maja bāpācī saradārī	My lands
dyāvī Rāyabā bēṭyālā	Let it be given to my son
Divaṭī Budalīcī jahāgīra	The jagir of Divti-Budli
dyāvī Rāyabā bēṭyālā	Let it be given to my son
Ḍōñjagāva dyāvā pānasupārīlā	The village of Donj to collect revenue
dyāvī Rāyabā bēṭyālā	Let it be given to my son
Mālasara yācā daṇḍa	Revenue from Malasara
dyāvā ināma khāyālā	Let it be given to my son

107. On the use of food, plenitude, and excess as metaphors in Indic poetry, see Aklujkar, "Battle as Banquet."

108. Laine, *Shivaji: Hindu King*, 28–30.

The repetition of "let it be given to my son" becomes an almost legal/contractual obligation that must be met. Furthermore, both rank and three different kinds of land tenure agreements are recorded here. Tanaji's son would become a *sardar* because he would receive a *jagir* for revenue use, a village (*paan supari*), and an *inam* tract of land, referring to land that is free of tax obligations.

An element of the narrative that prevails through the hundred years of this *povāḍā*'s performance is the detailed description of the fort's dimensions and its ruler:

Tīna kōsācā āhē bā ghērā	It has a three-kilometer circumference
Dīḍa kōsacī āhē bā rundī	It has a two-and-a-half-kilometer width
āhē aṭharāśē paṭhāṇa Sinhagaḍālā	1,800 Pathans live in the fort
āhē Udayabhāna Mōṅgala	And Udayabhāna Moghul
dīḍa gā'ī dīḍa śēḷī savā mana tāndūḷa vēḷēlā	Who consumes one and a half cows, one and a half lambs, and one and a quarter mun [maund] rice daily[109]
aṭharājaṇī bibyā	Eighteen wives!
āhēta tyācyā palaṅgālā	In his bed!
ghētō tēlyācī pahāra	He takes the oil press
Managaṭāvara ghālatā	Loops the link on his wrist
sarī karūna ghālatō	Presses out the oil.
bībīcyā gaḷyāta	On his wives' necks
cānda vaḍī rupayā	Silver rupees
dōhōna bōṭānnī tōḍītō	He breaks them between two fingers

Leaving aside the palpable delight in depicting Udayabhāna Rāṭhōḍa as licentious and gluttonous, with eighteen women in his harem and a vast appetite that consumes a cow, a lamb, and vast quantities of rice, here too we see the centrality of food. The plenitude of appetites and the ability to satisfy them points us to

109. By "mun" our poet probably meant "maund," which is approximately thirty-seven kilos, or eighty-one pounds.

powerful sovereignty.[110] Udayabhāna's general Siddi Hillal has only nine wives and a marginally less gluttonous appetite—only one lamb, half a cow, and vast quantities of rice. Military hierarchy is here presented through appetite. James Laine is correct to point out the egregiousness of the depiction of a crazed Udayabhāna Rāṭhōḍa reacting to the killing of his children by slaughtering a pregnant cow on the altar, but the blood sacrifice can be also read as the demand of a child for a child. Hands and fingers, bellies, and entrails fly around this poem; blood spills in great amounts.[111] Five militant goddesses offer Tanaji help at key moments, and in fifteen minutes, he kills 300 Pathans at one door and 400 at another, which adds up to 900, according to the poem. Our bard's arithmetic is clearly not perfect, but he needs to harmonize his initial tally of 1,800 Pathans in the fort with his claim that Tanaji raised an army of 12,000. He does so by reducing it to 50 who can climb the fort, setting up Tanaji's defeat.

It all ends tragically. Tanaji cannot withstand the sheer power of Udayabhāna Rāṭhōḍa. However, the *povāḍā*'s final stanzas have nothing to do with bravery, religion, the fort, manliness, independence, or Muslimness. Instead, they document that Shivaji Maharaj kept the terms of his contract with Tanaji.

Shivaji rājānē mulagā pōṭāsaṅgē dharilā bārā divasācē sutaka dharilē	Chhatrapati Shivaji Held the boy close to him He grieved the full twelve days for Tanaji.
Tērāvyā divaśī Rāyabācē māṇḍāvā ghātalā	On the thirteenth, he saw to it that Rayaba was wed.

110. Aklujkar, "Battle as Banquet," shows that this kind of imagery was fairly common in the Indic poetic tradition.

111. These descriptions will not surprise scholars familiar with the Indic poetic tradition. Here is a small portion of a translation from the battle at Kurukshetra from the Mahābhārata:

> Then with his torrents of sharp arrows the wearer of the diadem [Arjuna] set a dreadful river flowing on the battlefield: its water was blood from the wounds of weapons on men's bodies, its foam human fat; broad in current, it flowed very swiftly, terrible to see and to hear. Corpses of elephants and horses formed its banks, the entrails, marrow, and flesh of men its mud. Ghosts and great throngs of demons lined its banks. Its waterweed was hair attached to human skulls, its billows severed pieces of armor, as it bore along thousands of bodies in heaps. Fragments of the bones of men, horses, and elephants formed the gravel of that fearful, destructive, hellish river; crows, jackals, vultures and storks, and throngs of carrion beasts and hyenas were approaching its banks from every direction.

Van Buitenen, trans., Mahābhārata 6.55. 121–25.

Pahilī navarī radda kēlī va dusarī navarī nēmasta kēli	The first bride was set aside. A different one was chosen.
Lagna thāṭāta jhālē	The wedding was resplendent
Bāpācī saradārī	The father's lands
dilī Rāyabā bēṭyālā	were given to the son
Divaṭyā Budalīcī jahāgīra	the jagir of Divti-budli
dilī Rāyabā bēṭyālā	were given to the son
Ḍōñjha tē gāva	the village of Donj
dilē pāna supārīlā	was given for pan supari
Mālusaryācā daṇḍa	the control of malusare
dilā ināma khāyalā	was given as inam

Nowhere in the poem do we find out why the first bride was discarded. Maybe her alliance with the family had already brought disaster to it in the form of Tanaji's death and she was viewed as *apaśakuna* or inauspicious. Perhaps Chhatrapati Shivaji improved on the earlier marriage contract to keep the contract he made with his martyred warrior. The *povāḍā* ends with the declamation that a poem about a brave man should be heard by brave men.

Śāhira Savarkar's *Povāḍā*

Shi La Karandikar, Savarkar's biographer, tells us that Savarkar made a practice of visiting historical sites in Maharashtra, one of which was the Koṇḍāṇā Fort (now called the Sinhagaḍa Fort). In 1904 Savarkar visited it with some college friends, and on the way back he rewrote this most iconic of Maharashtra's *povāḍās*. By 1905 this *povāḍā* and the one he wrote on Bajiprabhu Deshpande had been proscribed by the colonial government, though (perhaps because) they were on everyone's lips in his hometowns of Nasik and Bhagur.[112] In Savarkar's version, Chhatrapati Shivaji, not Tanaji Malusare, occupies center stage. Savarkar also erases the previous poet's representation of his history, replacing elements central to seventeenth- and eighteenth-century society with aspects related to twentieth century middle-class Maharashtrian sensibility. Savarkar's *povāḍā* appeals to middle-class Maharashtrians not least because it is suffused with Sanskritic *veer-rasa* (heroic flavor).[113] As he did some years

112. Karandikar, *Savarkar Charitra*, 92.

113. For a basic explanation of *rasa*, see Dace, "The Concept of 'Rasa' in Sanskrit Dramatic Theory," 249–54.

later to great effect in *Essentials of Hindutva,* Savarkar infused the poem with his brand of secular history, not ancient but old, a history not of Vedic civilization but of Hindu statehood. Both Savarkar and Śāhira Tulshidas glorify Tanaji, but Savarkar's greatest admiration is for the way Chhatrapati Shivaji builds a state that is a model for Savarkar's idea of the Hindu nation.

The curiosity of Savarkar's rewriting and reformulation of this *povāḍā* is that there is barely any history in it, and it does not need to be sung. One of his critics saw this lacuna but accepted it by noting that Savarkar's *povāḍā* was meant to be read. Older *povāḍās*, he argued, lacked literary beauty and relied on an interactive audience and musical instruments. Savarkar's genius was such that his "*povāḍā* does not need this paraphernalia. A mere reading of it by one's own is quite impactful."[114] Why would Savarkar compose a *povāḍā* that was not dependent on music or singing? Kedar Kulkarni has suggested that the poetry of the *śāhiras* ought not to be considered "*sahitya*" but "*vangmaya*," by which he means poetry composed not for private, objectified, and detached reading but for oral and performative settings, serving as "an information economy, carrying news from the peripheries to the hinterland."[115] The bards who performed *povāḍā* moved between locales, urban and nonurban, and if they recited his *povāḍā*, it ensured that his composition would reach a large audience that would not have had access to a *stōtra*.

Let me now take a brief detour to make good on my promise to look at Shejwalkar's use of the *povāḍā*. Shejwalkar saw the *povāḍā* not as an instrument, but a resource, an archival source. He traveled to Panipat in the 1930s to the exact locale where the famous and historical battle between the Afghans and the Peshwa army took place in 1761. When the Marathas lost the battle, it put paid

114. "Instead of addressing Maratha history Savarkar's *povāḍās* are an incitement against the oppressive British government of his own time. So that the echoes of past bravery, and action remain alive in his own time, Savarkar deliberately used the medium of the *povāḍā* . . . he privileged it over all others, keeping in mind the needs of his own time. Older *povāḍās* are not filled with literary beauty, but there is plenty of it in the new ones. Older *povāḍās* need the dapha and the sambal, the accompaniment of singers singing "ji ji" and an audience. New *povāḍās* don't need such things. If one just reads them by oneself, their effect can be felt. Savarkar's *povāḍās* are a good example of this [new genre.])" Pandit, "Savarkaranci kavyasrsti" in *Savarakar Vividh Darshan,* 16.

115. Kulkarni, *World Literature and the Question of Genre,* 50. See also ch. 1, "Romanticism in India and Gifts for the Coloniser," for an illuminating and excellent discussion of the differences between *vangmaya* and *sahitya*. The former was temporally and spatially bound and not vulnerable to objectification and circulation via print and new technologies, while the latter, Kulkarni suggests, offered a "detached representation of the world" (48).

to their imperial ambitions, and the story became the subject of a 131-couplet historical poem called a *phaṭakā* composed by one of Savarkar's contemporaries, Ram Ganesh Gadkari (1885–1919), who used the penname Govindagraj. It was first published in Savarkar's handwritten paper, the *Āryān Weekly*, which he started while at Fergusson College.[116] The tone was tragic, befitting the catastrophic defeat of the Marathas. I present here the first few couplets:

Kaurava-Pāṇḍava-saṅgara- tāṇḍava dvāpara-kālīṁ hōya atī tasē Marāṭhē Gilacē sācē kalīnta laḍhalē Pānapatī[117]	The Kaurav–Pandava battle like Shiva's Tandava dance was fought during the Dvapar Yuga In the same vein the Marathas and the Afghans fought in the Kaliyuga on the battlefield of Panipat
Kāya kathācī yud'dha-kadhā? Maga vr̥thā Bhā'ucā śrama jhālā; dhīra sōḍuni paḷati Marāṭhē, purṇa parābhava tyāṁ ālā.	What can I tell you about this battle? Bhau's efforts were in vain Marathas lost their courage and ran, and Bhau was completely defeated
Hā Hindū, hā Yavana, Pāraśī hā, Yahudī hā bhēda asā.	He is Hindu, he is Muslim, He is Parsi, he is Jewish— why these distinctions
Nakō nakō hō! Ēkī rāhō! Sāṅguṁ āpaṇāṁ kitī kasā?	Forget about them, let there be unity, how much can one say this?

116. Pandit, "Savarakaranci kavyasrsti" in Padhye, *Savarakar Vividh Darshan*, 16. Pandit also notes that both Savarkar and Gadkari were influenced by Shivrampant Paranjpe, with Gadkari composing poems about the Shivakaleen period and Savarkar about Panipat. Both poems were left incomplete, according to Pandit (29).

117. The full text of the Panpatcha *phaṭakā* can be found in Gadkari, *Vagvaijayanti*, 216–26. I am grateful to Madhav Deshpande for correcting my translations and pointing out that *gilacā* was used to refer to Afghans not just in old Marathi documents but also in many modern plays and novels about Panipat. In Kulkarni, *Marathi Vyutpatti Kosa*, the word *gilacā* is glossed as a particular class of Pathans and seems to have been the Marathi adaptation of the Afghan Khilji and other Pathan *jatis*.

Kathī raḍakathā nijadēśācī vācuni aisā hā phaṭakā	When you read this heartbreaking story about our country let this phataka
laṭakā jā'uni kalaha paraspara lāgō ēkīcā caṭakā!	Inspire you to let go this false quarrel, and let the spark of unity be lit

Govindagraj used this *phaṭakā* to advance the cause of national unity between India's disparate communities—Hindu, Muslim, Parsi, Jew—suggesting that the Battle of Panipat could serve a didactic purpose about what the absence of unity could bring. Shejwalkar also saw Panipat as tragic, and hearing that both Muslim and Hindu poets from the region had composed poems about the Maratha general Sadashivrao Bhau, he went in person to transcribe what he called "Bhā'ūcā Hindusthānī Povāḍā."[118] What interested him was the *povāḍā* composer's use of the genre as a material record of how the battle was experienced in Panipat and its surroundings. He did not dismiss or rewrite the *povāḍā* but was mindful that there were flights of fancy in it, with some depictions entirely imagined and some events incorrectly narrated. I will return in more detail to Shejwalkar in the chapters on history and (auto)biography where a comparison shows, interestingly, that Savarkar was by no means without a model for a different way of thinking about these texts. What is crucial here is that Shejwalkar recognized the distance between poetry and history, even as the two were deeply connected.

Savarkar's approach was different. If Shejwalkar was going to the archive, Savarkar was creating a new archive altogether. As a *śāhira,* he wrote in a distinctively classicizing way, eschewing the polyglot authenticity of the genre, and transforming the *povāḍā* into something that would be more familiar to an upper-caste (Brahmin and non-Brahmin) community. Savarkar was not the only one Brahminizing the late seventeenth century. As B. G. Gokhale demonstrates in his work on Pune's rise to prominence in the eighteenth century, the city was important in the middle of the seventeenth century, but truly became the *punyanagari* (sacred city) of the Peshwas only after Balaji Viswanath (1713–1720) acquired the city as a *jagir* and his son and successor (1720–1740) made it the capital in 1730. After that, the Chitpavan Brahmins who flocked there in large numbers as *sardar*s and Peshwa loyalists and their

118. Shejwalkar, *Panipat: 1761,* 205. For an English translation of the essay, see Shejwalkar, "Ballad on Bhau and the Panipat."

subsequent investment in the culture of Brahminism via *dakshina* funds made Pune the de facto capital of the Maratha empire (the actual capital was in Satara).[119] Six generations of Peshwas and their investment in Brahminic ritual, festival, and worship displaced the *bhakti* practices based in Pandharpur and installed Brahminism as the official culture of the Chitpavan Peshwas.[120] In literary terms, as Gokhale notes, the Peshwas actively patronized Brahminism, initating a revival of a Chitpavan Sanskritized neoconservative Vedism that was focused more on Brahmin worship, rituals, festivals and less on the *santkāvya* drawn from the epics.

In the twentieth century, this eighteenth-century Brahminization of the seventeenth century was part of Savarkar's worldview. The Peshwai itself, representing Chitpavan Brahmin rule, as we have seen, engendered both nostalgia and critique.[121] But in Savarkar's writings, the Peshwai and the important defeat at Panipat were not histories of errors and defeat but an arrow pointing the way to a national resurgence and the only loss (albeit an important one) among three battles that showed Peshwa warriors' bravery in routing Muslim armies. Starting with Chhatrapati Shivaji, Savarkar weaponized Maharashtra's very particular history of resistance to the Mughals and the Peshwai's battles with the Afghans along with the region's longstanding Varkari tradition, which turned Maharashtra's landscape into an extraordinarily charismatic model for the nation at large. Many Marathi writers were smitten by Chhatrapati Shivaji and what he represented, but Savarkar went further than most. While earlier writers confined him to Maharashtra, Savarkar enabled Chhatrapati Shivaji's posthumous ride so to speak, following in B. G. Tilak's footsteps, out of Maharashtra and throughout India, from the Hindi heartland to the *sunderbans*

119. Deshpande, "Pune: An Emerging Center of Education." Deshpande points out that *dakshina* was distributed to Brahmins who came to Pune to study based on their tested levels of Sanskrit knowledge.

120. See Gokhale, "The Religious Complex in Eighteenth-Century Poona." Funds were set aside for the annual pilgrimage even during the Peshwa period, but the elite Brahmins of the Varkari *panth* were a different denomination than the Chitpavans who made up the Peshwai. For a recent and erudite examination of Sanskrit education during the Peshwai and Pune as a center of Sanskritic education in general, see Deshpande, "Pune: An Emerging Center of Education."

121. For a succinct and caustic criticism of Peshwa rule, see Mate, "Downfall of the Marathas." Shejwalkar, who is examined in greater detail in the next two chapters, faulted the Peshwai for not living up to Chhatrapati Maharaj's promise by essentially becoming Mughal vassals.

of Bengal.[122] And as we will see, Savarkar's twentieth-century *povāḍā* reworks not only the seventeenth century but papers over all the military disappointments of the intervening centuries.

By juxtaposing the "original" seventeenth-century *povāḍā* to the twentieth-century version, I bring together two sets of archival documents: the first shows the social, political, and cultural world of the rustic poet, and the second shows a nationalist bard with an acute sense of poetry's didactic role in disseminating a core historical narrative. Chhatrapati Shivaji, who was viewed in his own time by his own poets as a rural guerilla leader and described in the rustic language of a nonurban peasantry, was now elevated into the only exemplary Hindu, leader of the Indian nation.

Here is the *povāḍā*:

Dhan'ya Shivaji tō raṇagājī dhan'yaci Tanaji	Hail to Shivaji, that master warrior, hail to Tanaji
prēmēṁ ājī Sinhagaḍācā povāḍāgājī	Today lovingly we sing the Sinhagaḍa *povāḍā*

The language is Sanskritized, although not as much as the previous *stōtra* ("Jayō'stu tē") we read; Savarkar uses a Marathi *povāḍā* meter (Chandrakant), and he corrects the Marathi of the previous *povāḍā—sinhaga**ḍā**cha povāḍā,* not *sinhag**ad**cha povāḍā*. Formally, we get five couplets and a chorus; the old structure has been bent to the dictates of neoclassicism.

Dēśāmājī kahara gujaralā pāratantrya-jaharē	All through the land has spread the poison of servitude
halāhalahi hyā paradāsyāhuni gaḷā gāṭhitā barēṁ.	Even the poison [swallowed by Lord Shiva] had it been poured down our throat it would have been more tolerable

Instead of the *desh* of Maharashtra, this poem immediately takes up all India, as "all through the land" disorder spreads with the poison of foreign occupation. Clearly Savarkar is referring to British rule, but he does it by invoking Mughal rule.

122. B. G. Tilak had tried to popularize the Shivaji festival in Calcutta, and Hindi and Bengali writers were writing about Marathas and Rajputs as Hindu fighters against Muslims and Afghans from the 1880s onward.

Gōmātāñcī māna āṇi tī śikhā brāhmaṇāñcī	The tonsure of Brahmins and the neck of the sacred cow
paradāsyācī surī bandhunō cirī ēkadācī	has equally been cut by the knife of subjugation

Where the poison was originally everywhere, it now rests specifically in the body and beliefs of Brahmins, who are made to stand in for the nation. In the poems of Samartha Ramdas, the difficulties encountered by Brahmins under the Muslims are already manifest.[123] Savarkar extends that difficulty into the present.

Dēśa Hinducā hāya tayācā mālaka mlēñcha ṭharē	The country belongs to the Hindus but, alas, its master is a foreigner
pari paramēśā phāra divasa hēṁ rucēla kēviṁ barēṁ	How can God tolerate this for so long?

The word *mleccha* (foreigner), not found in the seventeenth-century *povāḍā*, is used here to mark the foreignness of the Muslims so that a contemporary situation can be imposed on the seventeenth century. Savarkar also adds something new by claiming the land belongs to the Hindus.

Cāla: Maga ārya dēśa tāraṇā. Adhamamāraṇā. Karāyā raṇā	Chorus: Provide protection to the land of Aryans [country]/ kill the evil ones/wage war for it
Paradāsyarātri nāśālā.	To destroy the night of subjugation
Śivanērī śrīmāna ālā.	At Shivneri our Shriman came The Sun of Independence dawned
Svātantryasūrya udayālā	Shivneri is where Shriman [Shivaji], the sun, was born, solely to destroy the night of foreign occupation.
Tyā sūryācā kiraṇa raṇāṅgaṇi taḷapē Tanaji	That Sun's ray was Tanaji who shone on the battlefield
prēmē ājī Sinhagaḍācā pōvādā gājī	Lovingly we sing the Sinhagaḍa *povāḍā*.

123. See for instance the poems "Asmānī Sulatānī", "Paracakranirupaṇa", and "Dhīra dharā dhīra dhara" in Karandikar, *Samartha Ramdas*, 147–50.

Note that Tanaji has been demoted, as it were, from his earlier place in the seventeenth-century version. He is now a ray to Shivaji's sun.

Ṭhāyī ṭhāyī vīra māvaḷā sarasāvuni bhālā.	Brandishing their spears brave Mavals leap to action
Rāmadāsamata chhatrapatīñcā anuyāyī jhālā.	And follow the Chhatrapati who was legitimized by Samartha Ramdas

The population of rural Maharashtra is no longer rough and tumble but brought into the poetic fold by allegiance to the theological guru and saint-poet Samarth Ramdas, who also imbues the king with authority.

Svātantrya-śrītōraṇa Tōraṇagaḍa avaghaḍa paḍalā.	Difficult as it was to vanquish Toranagaḍ, Shivaji took it, and it became a symbolic garland of his independence
Bhagavā jhēṇḍā tyā bhālyāsaha sarasara vari caḍhalā	The saffron flag along with the sword climbed higher and higher

This is the only time the poem mentions that the struggle to regain the forts was difficult.

Pratāpagaḍicī śānta karāyā svatantratā dēvī.	To please the Goddess of independence he conquered Pratapgarh
Puḍhatī phāḍuni Aphajhulyālā bhaga tō maga ṭhēvī.	Ripping apart Afzal Khan's chest and belly, leaving in it a hole
Dēśārtha mr̥tyuhī varilā.	In the service of independence, he married death
Śāhistā caracara cirilā.	Shaista [Shahista Khan] was slit into pieces
Ganimānni vacaka bahu dharilā	Our enemies held their fear close to them
Jhuratī ripu pari ajuni nāndatō Sinhagaḍāmājī.	In Sinhagaḍa fort even today our enemies long to go but cannot out of fear of Shivaji
Prēmē ājī Sinhagaḍācā povāḍā gāji	Lovingly we sing the Sinhagaḍa *povāḍā*

The signal difference between the two *povāḍās* is the emphasis on the shedding of blood for the nation. Savarkar combines the first two *povāḍās* into one to include both Shivaji's defeat of Afzalkhan and Tanaji's recapture of the fort. In the seventeenth-century *povāḍā*, there is valor and bravery; in Savarkar's version, blood is already copyrighted by the nation.

3	3
Jarā ḍhilā'ī pāhunī vadalī jijā Shivajilā	Seeing some weakening of resolve spoke Jijābā'ī to Shivaji
gaḍa sara kēlyāviṇa varaṇē nā anna śapatha tujalā	Till Sinhagaḍa is conquered I swear you will not eat

Savarkar eliminates Jijābā'ī the capricious mother. In the earlier version when her son's resolve weakens, she resorts to emotional blackmail, telling him, "I will not eat until you do my bidding." In Savarkar's version she becomes a stern mother withholding food from her son. "*You* will not eat," she tells him, until he has recovered his resolve. She is straightforwardly powerful and directive, not impulsive, certainly no mythological goddess playing dice. Savarkar also ventriloquizes through her the language of abused motherhood, invoking the insult where strange men use dirty feet to perpetrate a doubled violence on the mother—the mother as cow, the earth as mother, both defiled by strange men.

Parakē bālā bhūmātēlā tē lāthā dētā.	When cunning foreigners kick our mother [earth]
Anna na gamatē gōmāsācā ghāsaci tō ghētāṁ.	The food is not food, it feels like I am eating beef
Gulāmagirīcī bēḍī pāyī taśīca dharatā nā?	And you! Shackled by slavery you do nothing
Gulāmagirīcyā narakāmājī tasēca picatā na?	In the hell of slavery you simply stay imprisoned
Cāla: Nirjīva anna kāṁ rucē. Ūdara śatrūcē. Phōḍa tēthicē.	How can you enjoy lifeless food? Swoop on the enemy—rip him apart
Ātaḍyānnī bhūka śamavāvī.	Feast on his entrails
Raktāni bhūka śamavāvī.	Sate yourself on his blood
Mānsāni bhūka śamavāvī.	Appease your hunger with his flesh
Ghyā gaḍa kaḍakaḍa cāvuni adharā dhāvā yē kājīṁ.	Take the fort, bite your lip, rush to this work
Prēmē ājī Sinhagaḍācā povāḍā gājī.	We lovingly sing the Sinhagaḍa *povāḍā*

4	4
Dhan'ya mātā Jijā tilācī Śivabā suta sājē.	Hail to a mother like Jija whose son Shivaba perfectly suits her
Svatantra jhālyāvīṇa sutālā annahi dē nā jē. Svātantryācyā sukhanīmājī janma	To him she would not give a grain until he had secured independence
svatantrāñcē. Gulāmagiri cyā ukīraḍyāvari gulāma nipajācē.	From the womb/quarry of independence is born independence. From slavery's filth are born slaves
Śvānahi bharitē pōṭa bāpuḍē caghaḷuniyā tukaḍē.	Even a poor dog will fill his belly with scraps
Śēṇāmājī bāndhuni vāḍē nāndati śēṇakiḍē.	In cowdung a dung beetle will live and thrive
Cāla:Sansāra asā jarī karī. Manujatā tarī. Kaśāsī dharī.	If this is the life you want to live, why would you hold onto your humanity?
Hō tuccha kiḍāci na kā tō. Jō gulāma asunī hasatō.	Become a lowly insect who laughs even when enslaved
Paradāsyīṁ svasthaci basatō.	Sits quiet in the same state
Dhika dhika vadalā śrī śiva ghē'uni gaḍa rākhū bājī.	Shivaji said "No, I will reclaim the fort!"
Prēmē ājī sinhagaḍācā povāḍā gājī.	We lovingly sing the Sinhagaḍa *povāḍā*

In Savarkar's *povāḍā*, the words "deshārtha marana" (dying for the nation) appear again and again. His version has an excess not found in other *povāḍās* which, despite their depiction of blood and gore, are composed to be performed by the *śāhira* in whatever variation they see fit. Savarkar's poetry is clearly meant for more than just performative pleasure, and even if it is not sung, it makes for powerful reading.[124]

His recasting of the recapture of Sinhagaḍa is nowhere more apparent than in his depiction of the wedding. Look at how simply Tulshidas describes Tanaji's son's wedding. Three lines give the reader all she needs.

Svayanvara bāḷācē māṇḍalē	a *swayamvar* [marriage] was set up for the son

124. I am again grateful to Vidyut Aklujkar for pointing out how Savarkar's *povāḍā* has an excess not to be found in others *povāḍās*.

Kāḍhalyā pañcamīcyā haḷadī	on the fifth day of the month turmeric was brought out
Kāḍhalē ṣaṣṭhīcē lagina	the wedding was set on the sixth day

Here is Savarkar's version:

Prabhāta jhālī vādyē jhaḍalī muhūrta lagnācā	Dawn emerged, the instruments sounded, the auspicious time for the wedding arrived
bōhalyāvarī ubhā rāhilā suta Tanajicā	On the sacred mound stood the heir of Tanaji
ghaṭikā-pātrē mōjunī dvijagaṇa śēvaṭalyā ghaṭīlā	The twice born completed the preparations for the ritual; told people to pay attention
daṅgala mōḍunī maṅgala vhāyā sāvadhāna vadalā	Stop the noise, get ready for the occasion, and "shubha mangala savdhana" was intoned by all

There is no hasty *swayamwar*; he describes all the rituals of a Marathi Brahmin wedding, including the chant "shubha mangala sāvadhana." Savarkar uses "twice born" (*dvija*), that is, upper-caste, in the same manner one might use "lad," naturalizing Brahmin identity as the order of society.[125]

When Tanaji is pulled away from the festivities, there is none of the irritation or hesitation expressed in the seventeenth-century version. Here's how Savarkar tells it:

Vadalā dvija parī kuṇi bhēṭāyā Tānājisa ālā	A dvija [presiding priest] noted someone has come to meet Tanaji
ālā tō tō talavārīnī maṇḍapa khaṇakhaṇalā	As he came those assembled made the sacred space ring with the sound of swords
cāla: Tō hara hara ēkacī jhālā! Camakalā bhālā! Vadati rē calā	The community came together in one voice (hara hara

125. Bronkhorst, *How the Brahmins Won*, 140–51. As Bronkhorst explains, the rite of initiation at the heart of classical Brahminism is the *upanayana*, which amounts to a "second birth" (hence the term *dwija* or "twice born"). Since only those boys who have undergone this ritual are entitled to hear, learn, and recite the Vedas, it is a rite of exclusion, keeping those who have not undergone it outside the Vedic fold.

	Mahadeva)! The spears shone bright! Let us move
Śivarāja dūta pātalē	Shivaji's messengers came:
hē lagna rāhū dyā bhalē	Leave this wedding behind
dēśārtha janana āpulē	We live only for the nation
dharmārtha janana āpulē	We live only for our [religious-national] duty
lahāna mōṭhā nighē Marāṭhā puḍhatī Tanaji	Young and old Marathas followed their leader, Tanaji
prēmē ājī sinhagaḍācā povāḍā gājī	We lovingly sing the Sinhagaḍa *povāḍā*

The marriage is set aside in the face of the task at hand, suggesting that the only life worth leading is one dedicated to *desh* and *dharma*. Swords entering the hallowed space of a wedding is a caste violation that Savarkar depicts as musical and glorious, something that unites the community and makes them leave joyously. Indeed, in an essay Savarkar wrote titled "Jara kā āja Pēśavā'ī asatī" ("If the Peshwai were still present"), he seamlessly blends "Shivshahi" with the "Peshwai" as if it were a continuation, rather than a rupture, something other historians and reformers in Maharashtra would go on to show.[126]

The two *povāḍās* could be compared stanza by stanza and line by line to show how Savarkar rewrites it in a neoclassical Brahminized frame. What we see in Tulshidas's attention to material detail is the archival imperative; in Savarkar, the imperative is to mythologize. For Savarkar, Tanaji is the sword released by Shivaji, who is the real hero, and Sinhagaḍa stands in for Mother India, wounded and hurt.

Śivarāyācyā tīrā jā bā Tanaji vīrā	Shivaji's arrow, go forth brave Tanaji
vīrāmmājī hō raṇagājī ari mārunī dhīrā	Having killed the enemy be lauded as a great warrior among all
Sinhagaḍāvari tujhī āryabhū phōḍī hambarḍē	At Sinhagaḍa your motherland mewls piteously
gulāmagirīcē khūna pāḍaṇyā jā jā jā tikaḍē	Go in order to spill slavery's blood

126. *SSV*, MPHS 3: 409–22. T. S. Shejwalkar's critique of the Peshwai is discussed in chapter 5.

Savarkar invocation of *gulamgiri* (slavery) might remind his readers of Mahatma Jyotiba Phule's work some forty years earlier, but this slavery is not what Phule invoked in his blazing critique of Brahmins. It is closer to what Samartha Ramdas invoked in "Kṣātradharma" with couplets such as these:

Dēvamātra Ucchēdilā । jityā Parīsa mr̥tyu bhalā	If God himself has been uprooted, then victory is no better than death
Āpulā svadharma buḍavilā । Aisēṁ samajāvēṁ	And our Dharma is now sunk, this [you] should understand
Marāṭhā titukā mēḷavāvā. Āpulā mar'hāṣṭadharma vāḍhavāvā	Unite all Marathas and spread Maharashtra-dharma everywhere
Yēviṣayī na karitāṁ takavā । Pūrvaja hānsatī	If you do not do this, the ancestors will scorn [us]
Dēvadrōhī titukē kuttē. Māruni ghālāvē paratē	God's traitors [Mughals, possibly] are dogs, kill them and send them packing
Dēvadāsa pāvatī phattē. Yadarthī sanśaya nāhī[127]	God's followers will be victorious, in this there can be no doubt

In like fashion, Savarkar's conclusion invokes the ancestors of the Marathas and reminds his readers to pay attention to the message:

Arē māritī pūrvaja tumacē svargātunī hākā	Your ancestors are calling out your name from heavens,
ahō Marāṭhē dē'ūnī nīṭa sarva aikā	O Marathas, listen to them very carefully.

127. See "Kṣātradharma" in Karandikar, *Samartha Ramdas*, 157, particularly couplets 12, 13, and 17. There is a longstanding controversy as to whether Samartha Ramdas used the words "Maharashtra-Dharma" or "Marhasta-Dharma." The first would suggest that he was advocating or advising the ruler (Shivaji Maharaj or his successor) in the language of modern nationalism, the second that he was referring merely to the land in which the language "Marhatti," later termed "Marathi," was spoken. I am using it here in the sense that Savarkar would have.

Conclusion

When Savarkar wrote these poems, there were other efforts in other regions of India to recover and reclaim folk and/or regional traditions. Literature was used to demonstrate civilizational pedigree, while new forms of history were written to assert a national charter. Eschewing the seduction of the ancient, Savarkar created a unique, if strange, combination—he used mythology to construct a territorial fundamentalism while celebrating a local leader precisely to create a national Hindu leader as the natural progenitor of a modern Hindu nation.

To be sure, nationalists like B. C. Pal and Lala Lajpat Rai in Punjab and Bengal also revered Shivaji Maharaj. But while Shivaji Maharaj understood the caste politics of his time, as seen in his crowning himself Chhatrapati with the help of Brahmins from Varanasi, Savarkar deterritorialized Shivaji, releasing him, as it were, to claim the entire Hindu nation. The empirical details in Tulshidas's *povāḍā* are absent from Savarkar's—the landscape, names of villages and landlords, the attention to numbers and dimensions, the sovereign's contractual obligations, the food, and, most importantly, all traces of peasant life and language—are erased completely. Other *śāhiras* who performed or rewrote the same *povāḍā* maintained the narrative's empiricism. Only in Savarkar's rendition is Chhatrapati Shivaji transformed from a Maratha leader to a Hindu one, from local lord to national ruler. If Chhatrapati Shivaji needed Gagabhatta to give the stamp of Brahminical approval to his coronation, Savarkar brings it full circle by producing a continuous, seamless history of the Śivāshahi and the Peshwai.[128]

Savarkar "re-castes" a military tradition on the one hand and takes a rustic historical tradition and turns it into chaste poetry on the other. He overlays Tulshidas's rusticity with Sanskritized Marathi and transmutes Maratha (non-Brahmin) history into Indian history. In Savarkar's language Maharashtra becomes a model for a nation with no Hindu leader. Shivaji Maharaj may be entered into a pantheon of Gods, as James Laine suggests, but Savarkar brings him into world history as a national leader akin to Napoleon, Mazzini, Garibaldi, Washington, and Kruger. If Gandhi found the concept of Rāmrājya in the Rāmāyaṇa and used it as a form of ethical justice that focused on the needs of the peasantry without eschewing caste, Savarkar went to a seventeenth-century

128. On Gagabhatta and Shivaji's coronation, see Bahuguna, "The Ideological Political Role of Brahmans," and Deshpande, "Kṣatriyas in the Kali Age?"

Marathi *pōvāḍa*, removed all peasant traces, and marshalled the language of neoclassicism to generate a patriotic nationalist community. As Prachi Deshpande points out, V. K. Rajwade claimed that the concept of "Maharashtra Dharma"—that is, the spirit of the Maratha Empire founded by Chhatrapati Maharaj and carried on by the Peshwai (although this latter claim was challenged by Shejwalkar)—was far superior to that of the "Hindustani Dharma" of the Rajputs. In Savarkar's hands, "Maharashtra Dharma" allowed the nation to be female (*matrubhumi*), its leader to be masculine, and its basic attibutes to be genealogical and sacred (*pitrabhu* and *punyabhu*). In the next chapter, we will see how Savarkar took the discipline of history, infused it with the poetic impulses we have seen here, and used it to do similar work.

5

A Nationalist Historian

SAVARKAR AND THE PAST

THE PREVIOUS CHAPTER foregrounded the role poetry played in the making of the Savarkar legend. In this penultimate chapter, we move into the second facet of legend-building by looking at Savarkar's understanding of historiography and his instrumentalist use of history. In his historical writings, Savarkar modeled for his supporters the weaponization of an overtly political, polemical, and instrumental hijacking of history as memory work, with a particularly idiosyncratic use of "fact." And as we will see in chapter six, he gave the many followers who have written biographies about him the authority to write histories that are equally distant from fundamental protocols and norms around evidence, facts, and careful source use.

Savarkar was widely recognized in Maharashtra as a poet, less so as a historian. One would not find his name in the list of great historians of his time who wrote about Maharashtra or India such as Jadunath Sarkar, G. S. Sardesai, or T. S. Shejwalkar. How then did his work on the 1857 Rebellion (1909), *Essentials of Hindutva* (1923), *Hindu-Pad-Padashahi* (1925) and his last historical work, *Six Glorious Epochs* (1966), gain traction outside his immediate milieu? What was it about these works that brought such recognition? Was it simply that they were written or quickly translated into English and could therefore travel out of Maharashtra's immediate milieu?[1] Was it the search for relics of lost or imagined commonality? The recognition these works garnered is even more striking because, as I have noted, Savarkar was not the originator of the

1. I wrote this chapter before Vinayak Chaturvedi's recent book *Savarkar and the Politics of Violence* was published. Chaturvedi's incisive argument addresses Savarkar's English works that traveled outside Maharashtra.

discourse he came to represent. He was far from the first to write nationalist histories or argue for a different kind of history or historical consciousness. Nor was he unique in his admiration for Chhatrapati Shivaji as a farsighted Hindu ruler.[2] It cannot be because of his excellence as a historian; despite his citing of British historians of the rebellion and his claim that his work on 1857 was "scientific," Savarkar followed no bona fide scientific method. He stayed close to Vishnushastri Chiplunkar's historical sensibility in which, as Prachi Deshpande writes, the emphasis was more on "the expressive and emotive power of history than with its place within the disciplines of knowledge or its practical details of method."[3] Yet Savarkar's works are read as histories, and he is widely regarded as a reliable historian; many laypeople, whether or not they adhere to RSS ideology, think of his historical writings as accurate representations of the past. Indeed, his writings have shaped the historical consciousness not only of the late twentieth-century Marathi Brahmin middle class but many others as well due to the translation of his historical works into many Indian languages. According to his secretary Balarao Savarkar, his 1857 book was translated into Hindi, Gujarati, Malayalam, Tamil, Bengali, and English; *Hindu-Pad-Padashahi* into Hindi, English, Telugu, and Kanadi; and *Saha Soneri Pane* (*Six Glorious Epochs*) into English and Hindi.[4]

Here again I seek to comprehend the hold Savarkar's writings have on the imagination of his followers by contrasting them with those of Maratha historian T. S. Shejwalkar. As mentioned earlier, Shejwalkar and V. K. Rajwade are considered the two most important twentieth-century historians of Maharashtra.[5] Shejwalkar never mentions Savarkar by name in his writings but apparently suggested that, upon his release, Savarkar should have been made president of the INC.[6] He was no fan of Vishnushastri Chiplunkar's notion that historians should be nationalist cheerleaders. He criticized Chiplunkar's negative impact on history, particularly his view that any critical writing was

2. See Deshpande, *Creative Pasts*, for an excellent analytical description of the development of historiography in Maharashtra.

3. Deshpande, *Creative Pasts*, 83.

4. Savarkar's collected works were broken up into a series of small books, and in the front matter of each his secretary lists the languages into which each work has been translated. See, for instance, the front matter to *JN* (*Jatyuchedak Nibandha*), published along with Savarkar's other writings in 1982. Two-thousand copies were printed of each of these small books.

5. See Dixit, *Nivadak Shejwalkar*, vii.

6. According to Shi La Karandikar, Shejwalkar wrote on two occasions in his publication *Pragati* that Savarkar be made president of the INC.

self-loathing and the manner in which he reduced complex figures like Tilak, Rajwade, and Agarkar to caricatures:

> Vishnushastri Chiplunkar by merely being argumentative and mocking routed all [potential] rebelliousness. Not merely that, he inserted a new kind of poison into Brahmin society. The effect of this poison was that any criticism of India's history on any subject whatsoever was now to be considered the proof of self-loathing or the absence of self-respect. It is from this that the *Sadashivapethi* culture was born.[7] From this poison, even subtle thinkers like Tilak and Rajwade could not escape. Lokmanya got bound up in the wrap of being a social reformer and became just a nationalist defender of civilization, and Rajwade despite his criticism of the Peshwai became just a crippled analyst.

Shejwalkar and Savarkar both wrote historical works in the mid-1920s: Shejwalkar a groundbreaking preface to G. S. Sardesai's monograph on Nanasaheb Peshwa, Savarkar (from Shirgaon) his romantic and glorifying history of the Peshwai *Hindu-Pad-Padashahi*. The two accounts of the Peshwai could not have been further apart. Shejwalkar did not think there was a single statesman worthy of the name in the Peshwai, whereas Savarkar's account recalls a children's mythological epic, with evil Muslims and manic Portuguese all falling against the glorious Maratha sword. Where Savarkar extolled the Peshwai as the establishment of an independent Hindu rule, Shejwalkar saw it as a failure to implement Shivaji Maharaj's farsighted vision and a return to corrupt vassalage under the Mughals. Near the end of his life, Savarkar wrote *Six Glorious Epochs*, and Shejwalkar wrote his influential history *Panipat: 1761*. We know that Shejwalkar knew of Savarkar when he was brought back to mainland India and placed in Ratnagiri. We can also see his criticisms of historians who played fast and loose with Marathi sources as suggesting he would have disapproved of Savarkar's mode of writing history, even if he admired (as did many in Maharashtra and beyond) Savarkar's nationalism and patriotism. Shejwalkar often argued with fellow historians whom he saw as less than rigorous, but he never engaged with Savarkar's works. Savarkar, meanwhile, engaged with some historians, but usually only to try to dismiss them. Given this apparent mutual disregard, why place the most eminent of Maratha historians next to the most polemical and incendiary of nonhistorians?

7. By Sadashivapethi culture, Shejwalkar meant the culture of a particular group of Pune's intelligentsia.

Shejwalkar and Savarkar are connected through the eminent G. S. Sardesai, who was known as Riyasatkar Sardesai for his historical works on Maharashtra. Even though Sardesai was Shejwalkar's mentor, Shejwalkar found much to fault in his histories, arguing that they were full of historical inaccuracies and uncritical worship of the Peshwai. But Sardesai was one of the very few historians on whom Savarkar bestowed some approval (Jadunath Sarkar also gets some praise).[8] Savarkar apparently urged Sardesai to write not just in Marathi, since, according to Sardesai, Maharashtra's history could be completely extrapolated to the Indian nation. This was in stark contrast to Rajwade, who wrote entirely in Marathi and supposedly chastised Jadunath Sarkar for writing in English.[9]

In a first-person mini-memoir that Savarkar included at the end of *Six Glorious Epochs,* he noted that he had sent Sardesai many oral messages from prison. Sardesai then visited Savarkar in Ratnagiri to tell him that he was a world-historical figure. Indeed, Savarkar reports Sardesai as saying that "[w]e are all the writers of history; but you are the makers of history! When you make history, we note it down, and I came here with a sincere desire to see you as the maker of history."[10] Sardesai also, we are told, was so influenced by Savarkar that fifteen years after this visit he wrote a three-volume English-language history of the Marathas.[11] It was precisely the Sardesai-Savarkar mode of history writing that Shejwalkar would write against.

Between 1922 and 1924, when Savarkar wrote *Essentials of Hindutva,* Shejwalkar was engaged in research at the Bhārata Itihāsa Sanśōdhana Maṇḍaḷa (Association of Researchers of Indian History [BISM]) founded in 1910 in Pune by V. K. Rajwade to train historians and provide resources for them.[12] Researchers associated with the BISM scoured Maharashtra for documents and family papers, which were compiled and published in BISM's journals. They were autodidacts, amateur historians who were passionately interested in their region's history (and worked in its language—Marathi), and, like them, Shejwalkar did not have formal disciplinary training in history. In 1925,

8. Savarkar, *Six Glorious Epochs,* 301.

9. See Chakrabarty, *The Calling of History,* 59, for the conversation between Rajwade and Sarkar.

10. Chakrabarty, *The Calling of History,* 408.

11. Chakrabarty, *The Calling of History,* 408.

12. The founding members of the BISM were Rajwade, D. B. Parasnis (1870–1926), V. V. Khare (1858–1924), and K. N. Sane (1851–1927).

as he began his career as a historian, Sardesai asked him to write the preface to his monograph on Nanasaheb Peshwa. That was the same year that the RSS was founded (the RSS disseminated Savarkar's *Essentials of Hindutva*).

When Shejwalkar wrote the preface he was unknown, and one might imagine he would introduce Sardesai and say a few nice words about the work. Instead, Shejwalkar posed historiographic questions about how biographies ought to be written, pointed out the importance of using comparative history (*taratamya*) to avoid hyperbolically praising one's subject. He also made a powerful case for a different kind of history than his eminent predecessors had written. He opposed the practice, which might be seen as having come down from R. G. Bhandarkar to Rajwade, in which, as Prachi Deshpande argues, Sanskrit was used to confirm the historicity of an ancient text as a means of writing universal history.[13] This bold move not only launched Shejwalkar's academic career; it laid out most if not all the historical questions he went on to address.

Meanwhile, Savarkar began his project of constructing his version of nationalist history, eschewing all foreign borrowings, rejecting histories written by foreigners, and authorizing literally anyone else who wished to write history to do so. He used Sanskrit demotically and idiosyncratically, hitting out against that same Indological exegetical tradition but for opposite purposes. The past was not to be obsessed over, he wrote, and only those parts of the past that were currently useful needed to be brought into the present. Taking the Rāmāyaṇa as an example, he wrote,

> Ancient history sometimes can't be found, this agitates us sometimes. But if we don't have an understanding of how to distinguish, then in one sense is it not better that entire parts of it are forgotten? . . . If we were to historically designate which country was Ravana's Lanka, is it not the case that the people of that country would resent us [Aryans] and on the grindstone of an old enmity a new one might be pounded? No one thinks about this. Because the tale of Rāmāyaṇa is not forgotten, we foolishly indulge wild monkeys.[14]

History was ultimately far more about the future than about the past. And while the worship of monkeys was the unfortunate result of a literal reading of

13. See Deshpande, *Creative Pasts*, ch. 3, in which she describes and analyses the beginning of Maratha historiography and the coming together of Indology and antiquarian history writing, from R. G. Bhandarkar to V. K. Rajwade. Shejwalkar moved away from them both, though some of their questions were relevant to his inquiries.

14. *SSV*, SSRSP, 1: 2.

the Rāmāyaṇa, Savarkar used it to show that Hindus always had a military policy. Both Savarkar and Shejwalkar found in Shivaji Maharaj's vision and endeavors fertile ground for a didactic slippage between region, nation, and India. Savarkar and Shejwalkar located themselves within the region to write about the nation, but while Shejwalkar remained in the region, Savarkar went beyond it.

Savarkar and Shejwalkar were not just proud Maharashtrians and nationalist Indians but also, as mentioned, Brahmins. However, they understood the terms differently. Shejwalkar was not an anti-Brahmin crusader, nor a social reformer in the Phule/Ambedkar tradition. His scholarly claim was that a Vedic system of merit-based identifications of *varṇa* had been corrupted or had devolved over the centuries into a noxious birth-based system.[15] Was he tilting the sails of interpretation to catch the wind of the times? Perhaps. In taking this historical position, Shejwalkar tipped his hat to Brahmin reformers from the Wai Pradnya Pathshala school who, as Rahul Sarwate has shown, produced a fourteen-point program in 1920 that laid out all the ways in which the Vedas, as historical documents rather than divine revelation, had changed over time.[16] After studying the śāstric literature, the school's founder, Narayan Shastri Marathe (1877–1956), concluded that, like the Platonic conception of the myth of the metals, *varṇa* was not birth-based but could be differentially bestowed depending on individual capability.[17] Shejwalkar took much the same view, placing the blame for *varṇa*'s devolution squarely on the shoulders of secular rulers and orthodox Brahmins. Taking the Yadava period (the twelfth to fourteenth centuries) as an example, Shejwalkar bemoaned the fact that, facing Muslim aggression, instead of producing new thinkers and theologians, Yadava kings built temples and patronized insular and ritual-observance-obsessed Brahmins who worked to cement their social positions rather than recognize the universal merits of equality and fraternity.[18] In his words,

15. See Kantak, *Panipat: 1761* (Marathi), 57.

16. Sarwate, "Reimagining the Modern Hindu Self."

17. See Sarwate, "Reimagining the Modern Hindu Self," for information on the Pradnya Pathshala and the Brahmin reformist agenda in the 1920s.

18. Shewalker wrote,

> The Brahmins of the time possessed the ability to respond to each new crisis. Likewise, they understood the need to expand and build upon the contemporaneous store of knowledge. This is proven by their settlements in the East.

But, he continued, instead of building on their knowledge,

> With the spread of these evil times there was a heavy narcolepsy that was creeping in. Brahmins who searched for new weaponry, new arts, and incorporated outside knowledge died out, and in their stead came forward housebound "earthly gods" (*bhu-devas*) more interested in gluttonous honied and buttery feasts while following an array of ritual observances.

This kind of critique was central to Shejwalkar's approach. Little escaped his critical-historical gaze, and he was unmoved by suggestions that his comprehensive critique of the Peshwa could be used to buttress the anti-Brahmin political position.[19]

For Shejwalkar, the historian's job was to judge the past, to identify when and where historical actors failed to act or lacked the farsightedness to make counterintuitive and difficult decisions. A historian was obligated to identify the mistakes statesmen made and en passant to note the repercussions for contemporary India.[20] He was concerned with the role history had played in

---

> it is almost as if to both entice and facilitate a Mahmud (of Ghazni) to easily conduct his loot all in one place that they filled temples with gold and precious gems, something they continued to do.
>
> On the copperplates of the time, we get a good sense of what concerned the Brahmins and what they advised. Having secured for himself a kingdom, what should a ruler be doing? He should build temples and support Brahmins. But about what was absolutely necessary to reforming the country to keep pace with the times, of that knowledge they cared not a whit.
>
> Did they write even one work on politics or the science of warfare? They had no time to turn away from their ritual observances to such impure worldly matters.
>
> Their profound "Chaturvargacintamani" is still considered the crowning text of all these ritually observant Brahmins; because it is a comprehensive compilation of useless rituals from the ages. If a pious observant man were to follow all it prescribed, a single lifetime would not be adequate.

Shejwalkar, "Kranticya mulatatvanca Maharastretihasatila anukrama" in Dixit, *Nivadak Shejwalkar*, 121, 122, 123, 124.

19. See Shejwalkar's preface to G. S. Sardesai's book on Nanasaheb Peshwa, in *Nivadaka Sejavalakara*, 45. Shejwalkar writes about a researcher who suggested that he be careful when writing critically about the Peshwai because the non-Brahmin movement might appropriate his criticisms. For Shejwalkar, keeping people in the dark about historical events was exactly what history ought not do. As an aside, it is not clear that the anti-Brahmin polemicists needed his help. The Peshwai had already become a target for anti-Brahmins debating with Brahmins, as Rahul Sarwate has shown, detailing the polemics of what he has called an "ugly battle between Brahmins and non-Brahmins." See Sarwate, "Reimagining the Modern Hindu Self," 56–59.

20. See Shejwalkar, *Panipat: 1761* (Marathi edition), 189.

shaping the India of his time, but given the far-reaching sweep of his critiques, he cannot be easily categorized under one political designation. For Savarkar, in contrast, history's task was straightforward: it was to help build an effective and ultimately militant Hindu community.

If Shejwalkar dismissed people who wrote history without rigorous research, Savarkar did the opposite. Like V. S. Chiplunkar, he saw little separation between history, poetry and literature; in fact, he held that history needed poetry and literature. Savarkar's rhetorical style upped the ante on *chiplunkari walan*, the unfettered and unmediated style of combative argumentation against opponents.[21] The work of the two men—one empirical, archival, analytical, prosaic, and rhetorically dispassionate, the other poetic, polemical, passionate, emotional, loosely moored to historical fact, weaponized as propaganda, incendiary and declamatory—ran on parallel tracks. Like Savarkar, Shejwalkar wrote in both English and Marathi, but his most important works were in Marathi. Savarkar's works, however, captured a larger imagination, attracting readers beyond the region. One reason was the difference in rhetorical style, although Shejwalkar's pen was by no means dry. But another was Savarkar's use of poetry. Just as we find in his poetry a theory of history, in his historical works we find poetic devices that, while likely seeming maudlin to an English reader, reached a much larger audience than Shejwalkar's more academic writing.

Tryambak Shankar Shejwalkar: Hindu Nationalism without Hindutva

Tryambak Shankar Shejwalkar was born in 1895 and grew up alongside the anticolonial struggle in India. Like many of his generation, he admired B. G. Tilak and was influenced by the histories of the Marathas, in particular Sardesai's, and N. C. Kelkar's biography of Garibaldi.[22] After graduating from college, he worked a variety of research-related jobs, beginning with a clerical job at the Bombay Military Accounts department. When he joined Rajwade's BISM, he worked with Sardesai, and, as we have seen, it was Shejwalkar's preface to Sardesai's biographical work on Nanasaheb Peshwa that brought Shejwalkar to the attention of serious historians.

21. *Chiplunkari walan*, according to Prachi Deshpande, is "unrestrained in its passion for putting forward its point of view and denouncing its opponents." Deshpande, *Creative Pasts*, 103.

22. Dixit, *Nivadaka Sejavalakara*, viii.

When Shejwalkar wrote the preface, Indian history—as opposed to the history of the British *in* India—was just being established at Indian universities as an academic subject, and Marathi was not considered a major language of research. Sanskrit, rather than the so-called vernacular languages, was the subject of secondary and university education.[23] In Bombay, Bombay University was founded the year of the 1857 Rebellion, and it recognized Elphinstone College three years later. In Pune, Deccan College was founded in 1860, followed by Fergusson College in 1885. Undergraduate history was taught in English and focused either on Indology (on Manu's Dharmaśāstra, for instance) or Europe and the British Empire in India. History, as Prachi Deshpande notes, was less about practice and more about knowing and gathering factual knowledge.[24] Historical research, as it was conducted at Deccan College, was oriented toward Indology.[25] Traditional Sanskrit sāstris, with some contention and debate, moved toward a professionalization of their work, some making the transition from traditional Pandit to college/university professor, aiding in work such as compiling Marathi dictionaries and compendia.[26] Meanwhile, other Pandits composed (in Sanskrit) works on the Vedic tradition, the Epics and the purāṇas, the Dharmaśāstras and the Arthaśāstra, Ayurveda, astronomy and mathematics, poetics, and music.[27] Beyond the Pune/Mumbai nexus, Bhaushastri Lele (of Wai) published Marathi translations of Vedic and Dharmaśāstric texts, Narayan Shastri Marathe (also from Wai) compiled the *Mimansakosa* in seven volumes as well

23. Dandekar, *Sanskrit and Maharashtra*, 11.

24. Deshpande, *Creative Pasts*, 86–87.

25. Deshpande, *Creative Pasts*, 88–89. See also Dandekar, *Sanskrit and Maharashtra*, 28. The second major institution, Fergusson College, was founded by alumni of the Deccan College in 1885. See Deshpande, "Pandit and Professor" in *The Pandit*, 132.

26. Deshpande, "Pandit and Professor" in *The Pandit*, 124.

27. See Dandekar, *Sanskrit and Maharashtra*, for a list of works composed in Sanskrit, translations and commentaries on Sanskrit works in Marathi, and creative works in Sanskrit. The Asiatick Society's aim of reviving ancient Indian learning produced debates such as the one examined by Christopher Z. Minkowski, in which the Siddhantic model of the cosmos that rejected the Puranic view of the same was seen by the British Political Agent as a way of smuggling in the Copernican revolution without disturbing the entire group of jyotisa sastris. See Minkowski, "The Pandit as Public Intellectual," in *The Pandit*. The debate itself was inaugurated by the publication of a Marathi text—*Siddhantasiromaniprakasa*—by one Subbaji Ramacandra Sastri, which produced a fast and furious response by Baba Joshi Rode, called the *Avirodhaprakasa*.

as Sanskrit dictionaries of technical terms. Intellectual energy was directed almost entirely toward the ancient period.[28]

The Bhandarkar Oriental Research Institute of Poona was founded in 1917. Its erudite and formidable founder R. G. Bhandarkar (1837–1925) published stupendous works of scholarship on almost all aspects of Sanskritic learning.[29] In 1925 the institute began work on a critical edition of the Mahābhārata under the guidance of V. S. Sukthankar. This was no small project. The preparation and publication process took several decades, eventually reaching 22 volumes and 13,000 pages.[30] The scholars associated with the critical edition were interested primarily in the accurate dating and fixing of the location of the Bharata war, debating whether it was fought in 1400 BC, 1931 BC, 3102 BC, or 3016 BC.[31] Scholars working on an edition of the Rāmāyaṇa-samālocana had similar kinds of questions.

The emphasis on Sanskrit scholarship meant that modern and/or medieval Indian history took a backseat to the work of Indologists. The field of Indian history qua history in Maharashtra was ploughed by writers of historical fiction and drama long before it was considered a university discipline. Ramchandra Bhikaji Gunjikar's 1871 novel *Mocangad* told the story of Chhatrapati Shivaji's capture of a fort, V. N. Bapat's *Sambhaji* (1884) inserted a romance into the historical novel, and Hari Narayan Apte's *Gad Ala pan Simha Gela* (1903) told a prose version of the recapture of the Kondana fort that was very different from the famous *povāḍā*.[32] Theater companies also staged historical plays, and the two forms borrowed subject matter from each other.[33] The point here is that not only was disciplinary history a relative latecomer; it entered a field in which historical imagination was fired by romanticism and fueled by poetic and dramatic performances about heroes, sacrifice, martyrdom, and

28. Dandekar, *Sanskrit and Maharashtra*, 12–15.

29. Deshpande, *Creative Pasts*, 98–100. For concise intellectual histories of Pandits turned professors, such as the father/son duo of Krishnashastri and Vishnushastri Chiplunkar, and R. G. Bhandarkar as the first professor of Sanskrit who did not hail from a Pandit background and learned Sanskrit not through traditional practices but a modern institution like Deccan College, see "Pandit and Professor" in Deshpande, *The Pandit*.

30. Dandekar, *Sanskrit and Maharashtra*, 25.

31. Dandekar, *Sanskrit and Maharashtra*, 27.

32. See Raeside, "Early Prose Fiction in Marathi," for plot summaries of Gunjikar's and Bapat's novels and a brief (if negative) critical examination of them.

33. See Deshpande, *Creative Pasts*, 152–54, for a succinct description of these plays and novels.

regnal potentates.[34] The historical sensibility about Maharashtra's historical past was not yet being forged by disciplinary historians.

There was a reason for this. Postgraduate courses in (modern and medieval) history at Bombay University were offered only in a select few colleges affiliated with the university in 1913, with just the one professor who taught it. The first postgraduate department of history was founded in 1919 in Calcutta.[35] Indian history was offered as a subject in England with the founding of the School of Oriental Studies in 1917, but the school understood Indian history to mean the history of the British in India, not the history of Indians.[36] British scholars like S. M. Edwardes (whom we met in the first chapter) revised Vincent Smith's *Early History of India*; others published the first *Cambridge History of India* without the input of any Indian scholars.[37] At the heart of empire, in England, Indian history remained on the margins until after World War II. In Maharashtra, however, the debates about Indian history, chiefly between Jadunath Sarkar and G. S. Sardesai on the one hand and BISM researchers on the other were intense. Sarkar/Sardesai argued forcefully for a "scientific" history wedded to "fact," no matter how unpalatable, and saw the BISM researchers as merely regional preservationists.[38] The search for and access to documents on the basis of which a scientific or a preservationist history could be written pitted these early historians against each other, creating alliances (Rajwade/Jadunath Sarkar/Sardesai) as well as antagonisms (Sarkar/Rajwade on whether one should write in English or Marathi; Rajwade/Sardesai and Shejwalkar on the glorification of the Peshwai).

Indian researchers could not simply enter and use the records of the India Office or any other colonial records office. They required special permission and the patronage of an administrative scholar official, and even when they had those, they worked under a watchful colonial eye.[39] Records kept in

34. See Kulkarni, *World Literature and the Question of Genre*, for an outstanding literary and postcolonial analysis of the assumption that "literature" was only that which was written or read and the need to include poetry, drama, and other oral performances to understand the changing dimensions of the period. For Chiplunkar, romanticism, and Marathi as a poetic language, see 55–73.

35. Deshpande, *Creative Pasts*, 89; Chakrabarty, *Calling of History*, 38.

36. Chakrabarty, *Calling of History*, 52–53.

37. Chakrabarty, *Calling of History*, 61.

38. Chakrabarty, *Calling of History*, 74–75.

39. See Chakrabarty, *Calling of History*, 90, for a discussion of how Jadunath Sarkar had high-ranking patrons such as Henry Beveridge and William Irvine, "colonial administrative scholars,"

London were out of reach for most Indian researchers. This is why the BISM and scholars like Shejwalkar in the second generation of researchers after Rajwade made it their life's work not just to hunt down archival documents but base their writings almost obsessively on them. They staked out their approach in opposition both to scholars who had colonial patronage and poets who were writing hopelessly romantic histories.[40]

Shejwalkar was in his own way as abrasive and cantankerous as Savarkar, but unlike Savarkar, he insisted that history be written comparatively and based on archival materials. Shejwalkar's master's thesis on the influence of Muslims on Hindu civilization did not pass muster because of his dispute with his examiners. He remained unmarried, and Raja Dixit suggests that the absence of a secure domestic life and academic recognition by his master's committee haunted him throughout his life.[41] He edited a weekly called *Pragati* (*Progress*) from 1929–32 and was appointed Reader of Maratha History at Deccan College, Pune, from 1939–55. There he trained many historians, among them V. T. Gune, whose work on the judicial system of the Marathas remains without peer. Shejwalkar passed away in 1963, seemingly frustrated that he had not completed the work dearest to his heart, namely, a full history of Chhatrapati Shivaji.

Before going further, let me get the inevitable question about politics out of the way. Like all the characters in this story, Shejwalkar was a nationalist. He certainly shared some of Savarkar's Hindu imperial territorial sensibilities, along with the desire to see a majority government in India. He thought past Muslim rule had been, at least on occasion, oppressive and in need of replacement by Hindu rule. But—significantly—Shejwalkar's understanding of "Hindi samrajya" was closer to Gandhi's idealized idea of national sovereignty than to Savarkar's assumption that a minority community would need to be kept compliant, preferably by force.

Was Shejwalkar a Hindutvavadi as the term is understood today? Raja Dixit anticipated this question when he compiled and edited Shejwalkar's writings, answering that Shejwalkar "was not a spokesman for a bigoted, intolerant and aggressive Hindutva."[42] Despite his advocacy for the maintenance of Hindu

---

who not only managed the first *Cambridge History of India* project but also decided which Indian scholars to include. See 44–51 for colonial restrictions on access to official records offices.

40. See Deshpande, *Creative Pasts*, 85–89, 92–97, for a discussion of Rajwade and his career. See 98–99 for a brief analysis of Shejwalkar.

41. Deshpande, *Creative Pasts*, ix.

42. Deshpande, *Creative Pasts*, xi.

civilization, Dixit notes that his writing was historical and philosophical. Furthermore, as Dixit suggests, if one were to consider Shejwalkar a Hindutvavadi according to a current understanding, then one would be at a loss to understand how he "had the nerve to consider Golwalkar guruji 'unintelligent' or criticize the RSS and the Hindu Mahasabha." Dixit concludes that, "if one considers all of his works in context then he would be considered a 'progressive Hindu humanist.'"

In other words, Shejwalkar's writings were certainly consistent with Hindu nationalism, but not within the political Hindutva fold. He was far from anti-Muslim in Savarkar's sense and had a more nuanced historical and political understanding of India's past and future. While Savarkar was a flame thrower, Shejwalkar stayed close to the archive. His major historical work was the history of the battle of Panipat in 1761, but he was not a prolific creator of single-authored works. Nonetheless, as Dixit notes, "the value of his work is so immense that Shejwalkar is counted among the great historians."

Shejwalkar took on the most eminent historians of his time. He corrected the errors of Sardesai, Rajwade, and Sir Jadunath Sarkar, among others. Most importantly, he argued against Sardesai's *Marathi Riyasat*, pointing out that it was punctuated with factual errors that had been repeated endlessly by scholars and laymen alike, thus perpetuating the problem.[43] Rajwade's Chitpavan Brahmin pride led him to misrepresent the Peshwai as recognizing and continuing Shivaji Maharaj's farsighted agenda in trying to establish a Hindu "*Pad-Padashahi*" (Hindu empire). Jadunath Sarkar in particular came in for sustained critique for his ignorance and arrogance. Not only did he not know the physical landscape of the battle of which he wrote, he ignored the corrective critiques he had received from numerous Marathi scholars.

Like Rajwade before him, Shejwalkar scoured the region for primary sources, including *bakhars*, *povāḍās* and *kaifiyats*. History for Shejwalkar was a combination of Rankeian facticity combined with the recognition that the sources had veto power over what could and could not be written.[44] While multiple Marathi historians (including, of course, Savarkar) wrote about 1857, accepting that the 1757 Battle of Plassey marked the start of the East India Company's rule over Bengal, Shejwalkar viewed the years between 1757 and 1761 as far more important. It was the Battle of Panipat in 1761, where the Marathas were soundly defeated by the armies of Ahmad Shah Abdali, that he

43. Shejwalkar, *Panipat: 1761* (Marathi edition), 16–17.

44. See Koselleck, *Futures Past*, in particular the chapter on Neuzeit.

saw as determining India's future. Had the Maratha army prevailed, it might have been possible to stem the imperialist expansion of the East India Company.

After challenging Sardesai's views about the Peshwai in his preface, he became significantly more critical of Peshwa rule, arguing that it had squandered all the gains made by Shivaji Maharaj and become, yet again, a Mughal vassal. By the time he researched Panipat, he was ready to take on Jadunath Sarkar, the great Bengali historian of Mughal India. Panipat occupied a particular role in the Marathi imagination as both the exemplary tragedy involving the martyrdom and bravery of the Marathas and the beginning of the end of what could have been a glorious *Hindu-Pad-Padashahi*. Jadunath Sarkar was fundamentally incorrect, Shejwalkar argued, because he did not understand the importance of this episode. Shejwalkar corrected this, first in English in 1946 and on the bicentennial of the battle in Marathi in 1961, arguing that Panipat was not a regional story but rather was fundamental to the larger history of the British takeover of India.

Shejwalkar listed Jadunath Sarkar's errors:

> He has overlooked important relevant material. His interpretation of the material used is incorrect, not to say inadequate. He betrays insufficient knowledge of the Marathi language and inexpertness in using the material in that language. An unsympathetic critic must, at least, be fully and correctly acquainted with the subject he writes upon, and these conditions are unfortunately not fulfilled by Sir Jadunath's very brilliant presentation in masterly English.

He had, he remarked, sent his corrections to Sarkar and was astonished that the second edition of his work remained uncorrected.[45] Such unwillingness to correct his errors endangered all scholarship on Maratha history because

> [i]n the world of Indian scholarship at present, the vogue of copying, imitating and adapting is current. This results in circulating the error in a wider area which later on comes to be called a universally accepted fact. Many

45. Shejwalkar knew that he had gotten under Sarkar's skin: "Of course, the grace to admit his mistake was not a part of him. But that he was dealt a major blow is evidenced by the boatload of curses he heaped upon me in his private papers!" Shejwalkar, *Panipat: 1761* (Marathi edition), 15. Sarkar apparently received Shejwalkar's corrections but wrote to Sardesai saying that after his Herculean efforts over many years, Shejwalkar had only managed to offer four small corrections. Chakrabarty, *Calling of History*, 254–55.

> scholars throughout the length and breadth of India are now-a-days trying to utilize the Marathi material and weaving it into the thread of their histories. An aggressive occupation of the historical field is going on before our eyes. But the danger underlying these efforts is scarcely understood by the scholarly knights errant engaged in these adventures. It is high time someone should put a stop to their activities, for while it is easy to disseminate an error, it is not so easy to recall it back or to stop its ravages. As a humble effort in the cause of weeding out errors, I place this book before the public.[46]

Suffice to say, Shejwalkar resented Sarkar's assumption that he could waltz in from Bengal and write the history of Maharashtra with such scant attention to and real understanding of the sources or their languages.

When Shejwalkar published his English monograph on Panipat, he noted, in his characteristically curmudgeonly style, that

> [a]s the subject is an old one, generally known to most students of history, I have thought of curtailing the narrative within minimum limits, leaving the bare anatomical structure behind. To fix the attention of readers on facts, I have avoided over-burdening this fragment of history with detail. I have *eschewed all description with hyperboles surcharged with chauvinistic sentiments and thus left an open field to poets, dramatists and novelists* [emphasis mine].[47]

Shejwalkar made clear that whatever poets, dramatists, and novelists might be writing about these canonic moments in Maharashtra's history, it was not history.

Although Shejwalkar believed Panipat to be the single most important battle fought for a polyglot India, he also wrote that the battle could have been averted had the Peshwa engaged in strategic diplomacy. The Marathas' bravery was more suicidal than smart, and it rang the death knell of the unity of the subcontinent[48] because it paved the way for the East India Company takeover of India and put an end to Shivaji Maharaj's visionary hope that once the Marathas revealed Mughal weakness, other Hindu potentates would unite to fight for Hindu sovereignty. The nation whose sovereign boundaries Shejwalkar

46. Shejwalkar, *Panipat: 1761* (English edition), 7.

47. Shejwalkar, *Panipat: 1761* (English edition), 7.

48. Shejwalkar, *Panipat: 1761* (Marathi edition), 35. I am paraphrasing Madhav Kantak's Marathi summary of Shejwalkar's position in his preface to the second edition.

mapped was Hindu, to be sure, but with a polyglot community in which Afghans were major players along with Indian Muslims and Hindus. At the same time, he did not believe that a government that set aside the desires of the majority population could ever succeed. While that might sound much like Savarkar, Shejwalkar's fundamental assumption was different. Savarkar saw a tragedy in Hindu loss of control over what he saw as a Hindu country; for Shejwalkar, the tragedy was that the loss at Panipat meant the loss of a potential nation that, ruled by Hindus, could also serve Muslims and other minority groups. As such, Shejwalkar thought that it was important not just to document history but also to evaluate it. Savarkar, however, saw history as the foundation of and propelling force for the political future all of his writing, whatever the genre, was intended to serve.

Savarkar's *The Indian War of Independence* and *Hindu-Pad-Padashahi*

Savarkar's first work of prose history was *The Indian War of Independence*, but it was not his first foray into writing about historical figures. He composed a prose poem in 1904 on the death of the Boer general Paul Kruger, whom Savarkar admired for his opposition to the British.[49] A few couplets from the poem illustrate how he believed history ought to be written:

Hāṁ dēvī hāṁ. Adhika raḍasī ārta kaṇṭhē aśī kāṁ?	Goddess listen! Why the excess of such heartrending tears?
Sāṅgē jhālēṁ aśubha asalēṁ kāya tēṁ sōḍa śōkā	What so inauspicious has transpired? Set aside your grief
Hā dhik mr̥tyō, sakala kaḷalēṁ ghē'ūnī nīca gēlā	Death be ashamed! We know that you have taken away
svātantryācyā vimalatilakā tyā ahā Krūgarālā	Independence's pure crown jewel [auspicious dot on the forehead] President Kruger

Here Savarkar addresses Kruger:

Sanrakṣāyā samariṁ gaḷalēṁ ūṣṇasēṁ rakta jyātēṁ.	The protection of your nation for which you spilled warm blood

49. See *SSV*, MPHS, 7: 47–51, for the full text of this poem.

Bōlē taisī karaṇī karūnī thakka kēlēṁ jagātēṁ.	The stunning of the world when you acted as per your word
Hā hā jhālēṁ paravaśa tujhēṁ rāṣṭra gā Krūgarā tēṁ.	But your nation has been subjugated dear Kruger
Anta: kālīṁ smaraṇa karitā vāṭalēṁ kāya tūtēṁ.	In your last moments who knows how you must have felt!

The poem shows us how Savarkar thought history ought to be written—a pithy narrative of a world leader that connected his cause to justice and the sacred. Savarkar wrote many poems with complex Sanskritic and Marathi metres, but he wrote this one simply, with short couplets. Why write history as poetry at all? Because it makes history memorizable and available even to the unlettered. Anyone could hear a poem and memorize it, which is what Savarakar wanted. Even his prose histories tended to have short chapters that did their jobs quickly.

Savarkar plants an early stake in the historical ground with an introduction to Mazzini's biography and the 1857 book, both written in Marathi. The 1857 book is based on English sources since Savarkar could use the resources of the British Library, despite being under surveillance. It is "truthful" in that it is both based on historical documents and, while invoking traditional historical genres such as *itihaskatha* (story of history), a recognizeable account of real historical events; yet, it is also attentive to the idea that history was the source of peoples' identity and the repository of their memories. Savarkar's history was "nationalist" in the manner Sarkar would decry and narratively overblown in the style Shejwalkar would scorn, but before the tussle that would take place between the two lives of history that Dipesh Chakrabarty has termed the "cloistered" and "public,"[50] Savarkar used language attentive to both "heroes" and their characters. It suggests why the amateur or uncloistered historian would gain such traction in Maharashtra. Positivism, empiricism, preservationism, and prose descriptions would find their place in the discipline of Indian history in colleges and universities and in the work of the BISM. Savarkar had a different audience in mind, and although he did not participate in any academic debates, he drew from the work of academic historians when it suited him, while positioning himself as the single authoritative voice of India's history.

50. Chakrabarty, *Calling of History*, 42, 165.

Savarkar described the Rebellion of 1857 as a fresh start as a new nation was born, midwifed by patriotic Hindus and Muslims. The 1857 Rebellion was analogous to the French Revolution in the way it reset time; historians—its scribes—played almost a religious role. In the first paragraph of the first chapter, Savarkar underscores this in his description of "the holy works of the historian."[51] In this first book, he models the active role historians needs to play. Their job was not simply to narrate past events. Historians, in other words, were not "mere" historians. They were the narrators as well as the makers of history. History was not a passive intellectual process. Instead, the duty of history and historians was to rouse people to action, preferably violent action. This early recasting of the task of the historian laid the groundwork for later works in which he simply ignored academic historians.

To be sure, Hindus had suffered 500 years of repression, but these sins could be forgotten because patriotic Muslims had joined hands with Hindus as co-protonationalists (of a not yet realized Hindu nation), and together the communities could defeat the British. It is no surprise that the British banned both this book and Gandhi's *Hind Swaraj*. Both said a firm "no" to the West, although Gandhi eschewed violence, while Savarkar came out swinging. Neither Gandhi nor Savarkar was much interested in the scholarly discipline of history, let alone what practitioners from within that discipline were producing. Gandhi in fact never engaged politics in the language of history, which provided him with little more than the occasional anecdote which he performed symbolically, such as putting a pinch of salt in his tea while reminding the Viceroy about the Boston Tea Party to protest the salt tax imposed by the British. History as a linear narrative of facts and details mattered little to Gandhi, but he was fairly certain that playing an anticolonial card game with the British meant ceding control of the table, the pack, the dealer, and the rules.

Yet, compared with other Indian nationalist figures, Gandhi alone can be considered a world-historical figure. By contrast, Savarkar, who was immersed in history, was obsessed with becoming a world-historical figure. Not that he was any more interested in linear narratives or with historical knowledge for its own sake—like Gandhi he invariably translated history into memory work—but he recognized that the judgments and legacies of history were

51. Savarkar, *Indian War of Independence*, 3. All page numbers cited here are from the original 1909 English translation of the book. The complete Marathi text can be found in *SSV*, MPHS, 8: 25–425.

critical for the emergence of the kind of Hindu nation he wished to imagine into being.

Among the many aspects of the book that would have alarmed the British was Savarkar's frequent comparisons of the French Revolution and the 1857 Rebellion, which he described as the epochal turning point of Indian history. The first edition attributed the book to "An Indian Nationalist," and we cannot tell for sure how many copies circulated underground.[52] But it came to the attention of fellow nationalists like Jawaharlal Nehru.

Savarkar begins his introduction by explaining that he too is writing a scientific history of the events of 1857. But he meant something very different by this than what either Jadunath Sarkar or Shejwalkar did. Insofar as he used evidence, it was instrumentally. He refutes the British demotion of the war of independence to the status of a mere mutiny of a small section of the British army and argues for a political subjectivity that anticipated many of the rhetorical techniques that Ranajit Guha later used for his seminal *Elementary Aspects of Peasant Insurgency*. Guha asked if it was possible to believe, as scores of secular historians across a swath of ideological persuasions had, that the peasantry could have acted in any manner that was *not* political, given that, as a class-group, it had experienced firsthand the tripartite oppression of *sarkar*, *sahukar*, and *zamindar* (the East India Company, moneylenders, and landlords). Guha pointed to unmistakable signs of an emergent peasant political consciousness, citing the manner in which their protest destroyed and challenged very specific markers of their oppressions by landlords. He admitted that this political consciousness was not mature and lacked a leader but insisted that it was an act of supreme arrogance on the part of secular historians dismissive of the constitutive role played by the peasants' religiosity to suggest either that peasant adherence to "superstition" or a

52. *SSV*, MPHS, 8: 6–7. The editor Shankar Ramchandra Date writes that the book was originally intended to be published in Marathi, but while they could publish in Devanagari typeface in Germany, they were unable to do so in Marathi (despite the script being the same). Date also notes that because a few handwritten pages of the manuscript fell into police hands, they were alerted to it, and as a result its publication had to be done elsewhere. French publishers would not publish it; eventually a publisher from Holland agreed. It was then smuggled into India by Sikandar Hayat Khan in his suitcase, safeguarded by Madame Cama in France, and Date notes that "*śēkaḍōśē*" (hundreds upon hundreds) of copies circulated in Europe, England, and even the US. Perhaps that is how UC Berkeley and Columbia University's libraries have an original edition, published in 1909, where the author's name is given as "By an Indian Nationalist." Legal copies were only published after independence.

simple response to the most brute economic necessities were the only causes of their rebellion.

I am not here suggesting a direct affinity between Guha's and Savarkar's works. But Savarkar's fundamental argument about the causes of the 1857 Rebellion was rooted in the same assumption that the "mutiny" was a historical expression of a national self-consciousness. He took on British historians who explained the rebellion as deriving either from fanatic religiosity that caused gullible, incredulous, and/or fanatical Hindus and Muslims to go mad upon hearing that the Royal Enfield rifle cartridges were greased with pork and beef fat or from the fact that these primitive beings were incapable of higher-order sensibilities like loyalty or patriotism.

It was impossible to believe, Savarkar wrote, that the rebels of 1857 were moved to rebellion by something as insignificant as a culturally insensitive greased cartridge casing. "Is it possible?" he asked,

> Can any sane man maintain that all-embracing Revolution could have taken place without a principle to move it? Could that vast tidal wave from Peshawar to Calcutta have risen in blood without a fixed intention of throwing something by means of its force?[53]

If casings were the cause, he argued, as soon as the casings were withdrawn and reissued without the offending grease, any rebellion should have stopped. It did not; in fact, it spread.

In his first work of history, Savarkar was still careful to refer to foreign writers of India's history, although he was usually deeply critical of the authors whose books he had consulted, including Charles Forjett and his *Real Danger in India*, Alexander Duff, Sir John Kaye (three volumes), and Sir John Kaye and George Bruce Malleson (all six volumes), Henry Mead, Philip Meadows Taylor, and George Trevelyan. Savarkar used these works not because they were primary sources but to argue that they were all written with an imperial ideological bias and could not therefore be trusted. It allowed him to make his powerful argument that "the nation ought to be the master and not the slave of its own history."[54] And he apologized in his introduction for his overreliance on British sources, noting that he hoped that someday a more comprehensive history of 1857 would be written by an Indian author with better access to

53. Savarkar, *Indian War of Independence*, 5.

54. Savarkar, *Indian War of Independence*, vii. See also Bakhle, "Savarkar, Sedition and Surveillance," 57.

Indian sources. For now, he included reports of military action, correspondence between East India Company officials, and responses to military actions. He drills down and attends to minutiae; he writes of armed struggles between British troops and leaders such as Kunwar Singh of Arah, Begum Hazrat Mahal, Tantia Tope, Rani Laxmibai, and Maulvi Ahmadullah Shah. In what is ultimately a tale of failure, he praises four who were killed and—high praise—he compares Maulvi Ahmadullah Shah to Mazzini.[55]

From an early age, Savarkar was drawn to romantic, even melodramatic, prose, and the work is replete with striking and intense phrases; it is also hopelessly overwritten, with bombast the primary mode of expression.[56] Waves of revolution sweep across parts of India, English yokes are thrown off, and glorious beginnings are undone by the Sikhs, the Nepalese leader, and South India's marked indifference, which Savarkar ascribed to a lack of national historical consciousness. His prose shows that even in this first book, he was clear that he had to write in a poetic if overwrought vein, with intense, striking, affective, and sentimental turns of phrase, all calculated to move his readers to action.

In the prevailing English historiography, 1857 was depicted as an example of native ingratitude—a marker of an essential characteristic of colonized Indians—and the rebellion's successful suppression as proof of divine support for the Empire. Savarkar was prescient in challenging that historiography. Savarkar targeted not just eminent English historians but also the popular English understanding of the event. English historians, Savarkar argued, were too blinded by their own imperial and nationalist prejudices to understand that an Indian nationalist ideology was the motivating factor behind the 1857 Rebellion. He took English historians to task for not recognizing this ideology even when 1857 provided all the evidence needed. Savarkar's fundamental contribution was to author a "semantic transvaluation of British nationalism via an early rewriting of both British and Indian history, reconceptualizing the 'Sepoy Mutiny' of 1857 as a unified Indian national and nationalist (ideological) rebellion."[57]

55. Savarkar writes, "As Mazzini had clung to Rome, all alone, . . . so this Moulvie too . . . continued the fight with the strength that despair gives." Savarkar, *Indian War of Independence*, 35.

56. Such prose was not Savarkar's alone. Jadunath Sarkar was very taken with "[h]istory shaped by a powerful literary sensibility" from Tennyson to Shakespeare to Oliver Goldsmith. Chakrabarty, *Calling of History*, 170–81. Savarkar's prose is replete with such literary allusions, also unnamed.

57. Bakhle, "Savarkar, Sedition and Surveillance," 58.

This let him set up what would be a persistent refrain: the Rebellion of 1857 was only defeated because of "traitors" to the cause who remained untouched by the spirit of nationalism.[58] Savarkar's gendered understanding of these "traitors" was that they were "idle, effeminate, selfish, and treacherous men."[59] Ideas of effeminacy and masculinity run like a stream through the book, and every now and then we dip into it to find that, while the British displayed camaraderie and a sense of duty that prevailed over internal factionalism, they were nonetheless cowardly for having killed female prisoners. Savarkar describes Rani Laxmibai's attentiveness to her daily *puja* and her ritual display of widowhood, noting that she always wore "a Chanderi saree of faultless white."[60] Women were fully capable of nationalist leadership, which could not be said of all of India's men.

Hindu-Muslim relations were not at the center of this narrative, and even as he claimed that "for more than five centuries the Hindu civilization had been fighting a defensive war against the foreign encroachment on its birthrights,"[61] he could still envision an India with two integral communities. In the introduction, Savarkar shows his occasional ability to historicize; "The feeling of hatred against the Mahomedans was just and necessary in the times of Shivaji—but, such a feeling would be unjust and foolish if nursed now, simply because it was the dominant feeling of the Hindus then."[62] In other words, 1857 let him forgive Muslims for past aggressions. He could even indict the British for conspiring to "trample the Hindu religion and the Muslim faith" or, as he also put it, for being contemptuous of "the Hindu and Muslim faiths—the two principal religions of India."[63] He devoted an entire chapter to Maulvi Ahmadullah Shah of Fyzabad, a fallen Muslim warrior, praising him highly, as we see in an extraordinary but by no means unique passage:

> As soon as the news of his death reached England, the relieved Englishmen felt that "The most formidable enemy of the British in Northern India was

58. Savarkar, *Indian War of Independence*, 118. Savarkar terms the Jats and Sikhs "loyal traitors" for opting to protect Amritsar (118); Gurkhas made up "traitor regiments" (119); and traitors show up throughout (129, 130, 159, 251, 258, 265). Ilahi Buksh Mirza was also a traitor who facilitated the arrest of Bahadur Shah (280); the Nepalese (324–25); South Indians and Hyderabad, (376); and cowardly Jayaji Rao Scindia (395).

59. Savarkar, *Indian War of Independence*, 443.

60. Savarkar, *Indian War of Independence*, 373.

61. Savarkar, *Indian War of Independence*, 234.

62. Savarkar, *Indian War of Independence*, vii–viii.

63. Savarkar, *Indian War of Independence*, 46, 47, 50, 73, 76.

no more!" In person, the Moulvie was tall, lean, and muscular with large deep-set eyes, beetle brows, high acquiline nose, and lantern jaws. It is impossible to find a character who has illuminated the history of this nation with more noble patriotism than this hero. The life of this brave Mahomedan shows that a deep faith in the doctrines of Islam is in no way inconsistent with, or antagonistic to, deep and all-powerful love of the Indian soil! That a Mahomedan dominated by an uncommonly spiritual impulse, can, at the same time, nay by the very fact of his being so dominated, be also a patriot of the highest excellence, offering his very life-blood on the altar of Mother India, so that she might [lift] her head as an independent and free country; and that the true believer in Islam will feel it a pride to belong to, and a privilege to die for, his mother country.[64]

In this description, Savarkar conjoined Islam and patriotism, suggesting that an authentically devout Muslim would not hesitate to martyr himself for his mother country. He does not make such statements after the Khilafat movement shatters his expectations that Muslims should deify Mother India.

The hermeneutic innovation of the 1857 book was to broadcast the importance of history for the anticolonial and nationalist hopes of its readers.[65] Savarkar conceptualized his audience as the Indian nation, as a people who needed to hear him say that Indians were not and had never been an infantile (they were in fact infantilized by the British) population in need of being shepherded into the modern world by their British overlords. He blew up the scale of the argument by asserting that 1857 was not a small mutiny but the struggle of the Indian nation that, despite its failure, demonstrated that a unified India could still succeed in her struggle against foreign rule. Savarkar almost bypassed the British altogether to appeal directly to the national community he knew was there—somewhere—under colonial rule. Small wonder that an informant sent the manuscript to Scotland Yard, and the book was banned before it was even published. One measure of the book is how much it upset the British; another is that in 1929 Jawaharlal Nehru expressed a qualified respect for it. Writing on censorship, in particular the ban on Mazzini's essays, Nehru noted:

A more flagrant instance of misuse of power it would be difficult to find. Savarkar's history of the *War of Independence* is another famous example. It

64. Savarkar, *Indian War of Independence*, 370.

65. I am grateful to Dorothea von Mucke for this insight.

> is a brilliant book though it suffers from prolixity and want of balance occasionally. I had occasion to read it in Europe and I have often felt that a new edition, more concise and with many of the oratorical flights left out, would be an ideal corrective to the British propaganda about the events of 1857. But I am afraid we shall have to wait for this till Swaraj comes.[66]

Leaving out the "oratorical flights," however, would be anathema to Savarkar, who doubtless saw them as central to both his historical and literary strategy.

Soon after the book's publication, as we know, Savarkar was arrested and sentenced to two life terms at Cellular Jail in the Andaman Islands. From his prison cell in India just before being taken away, he composed a short poem, written on a scrap of paper, which he gave to his fellow inmates to copy, distribute, and circulate upon their release. It was titled "Pahila Hapta" ("The First Installment").[67] Eleven years later, when Savarkar returned to mainland India, it was this poem and those detailed in an earlier chapter that laid the groundwork for his 1923 book *Essentials of Hindutva*.

Essentials of Hindutva

Nothing in *Essentials of Hindutva* was new for Savarkar. He had been thinking and fulminating about Khilafat while still in prison in the Andamans, and in his three years in prison between Alipur, Ratnagiri, and Yerawada, he had publicized his views to fellow prisoners. As he went on to write *Essentials of Hindutva* upon his return, he composed what was in effect a distillation of views he had already expressed piecemeal in earlier poetry.[68]

Essentials of Hindutva was composed in English and written and published under the radar of the colonial police. A short work of just eighty-eight pages divided into thirty-one sections, the structure of its argument is apparent from its organization. The first seven sections deal with the issue of naming: who is a Hindu, when do names get their fixity, what is the history of names, why is a name important, can a name of a people be considered the name of a nation?

66. Nehru, "The Proscription and Censorship of Books," 394–95.

67. See *SSV*, MPHS, 7: 87, for the full text of the poem and the section on "Savarkar's Poems" in chapter 3 of this book for a translation.

68. *Essentials of Hindutva* was written in English, and none of the Marathi or Sanskrit words were diacritically marked. In quoting passages, I have left the text unmarked. I have used *Essentials of Hindutva* as published in the collection of English translations of his writings, Savarkar, *Selected Works of Veer Savarkar*, vol. 4.

Sections eight to thirteen are a detour about why Buddhism as nationalism let the country down. Section fourteen takes us to the Vedas, and the next three sections concentrate again on the issue of naming. Section eighteen apologizes to Buddhism for giving offense, and section twenty-one deals with foreign invaders. Sections twenty-two to thirty-one, except for one (twenty-two) devoted to a historical narrative, return to the issue of naming. The section that would seem most germane to his endeavor, given that it carries the title of the book, "Essentials of Hindutva," is only a paragraph long.

Claiming at one point that it is "not necessary here for our arguments to be very precise," Savarkar offers no dates or names since most of what he wrote would have been drawn from his memory. Writing from prison, many of the events he describes are either unsourced and/or counterfactual. Nonetheless, the book is studded with phrases like "knowing for certain," "indisputably clear," "treading on a solid ground of recorded fact." The closest thing to sources for describing the ancient era are Vedic *śloka*s that he describes as "half symbolic and half actual description." Even though Savarkar admitted that a significant portion of the information he used was mythological, he also claimed that it was a "solid ground" of facts. He often cited "our ancient records" or "our records," but does not say what those records were or when or by whom they were written.

This book imagines a different audience than his work on the 1857 Rebellion, which despite its undisciplined rhetoric and flights of fancy, clearly aspired to be a contribution to the scholarly understanding of Indian history. *Essentials of Hindutva* starts with four questions: What's in a name? What is Hindu? What is *Arya*? And who is a Hindu? He answers by invoking *Romeo and Juliet*. He does so for two reasons: first, because of the obvious association of Romeo and Juliet with both naming and love; second, because it allows Savarkar to open with his first declaratory statement, "Hindus we are and love to remain so." The love plot with its fraught romance demands emotional investment from readers and pulls them into the text.[69] It also allows him to move into the first of many quasi-theoretical claims.

The first claim is that "as the association of the word with the thing it signifies grows stronger and lasts long, so does the channel which connects the two states of consciousness tend to allow an easy flow of thoughts from one to the

69. See Berlant, *The Anatomy of National Fantasy*, for an examination of the erotic pull of the national fantasy.

other, till at last it seems almost impossible to separate them."[70] Savarkar does not elaborate on the logic of bestowing consciousness on "word" and "thing," but we need to dwell on it because he begins with a reflection on words, the power they have to move us, the magic certain words hold. *Essentials of Hindutva* functions as an instruction manual for future Savarkarite historians that provides the essential poetic language, the distilled assertions and definitions, the appropriate sources and examples of how to use them—in other words, all that Savarkar believed essential to writing prose history. At the same time, by letting his readers know how much words mean, their power to perform affective work, Savarkar scripts the conditions for the reader's interpretation of the text. These words are the means through which he will bestow on them a binding identity. This metaliterary device is placed at the beginning, thus alerting readers that all the subsequent words carry a great weight. All his theoretical gestures are aimed at guiding his audience to the word "Hindu" and to what the word has over time become "naturally" associated with, namely, a self-conscious political community.

Savarkar makes his points about names via a set of polemical questions: "What is in a name? Ah! Call Ayodhya, Honolulu, or nickname her immortal Prince, a Pooh Bah, or ask the Americans to change Washington into a Chengizkhan. . . ." Or, in the climax to his examples, he writes, "persuade a Mohammedan to call himself a Jew," and you would soon find out, he suggests, exactly what is in a name.[71] He seems to be laying the ground for a quick version of what Koselleck has termed *Begriffsgeschichte*: a history of the word/concept of "Hindu." Yet the text does not offer a systematic history; instead, he uses the name to assert his ultimate syllogism: the connection between name (Hindu) and place (Hindusthan).

Savarkar's next philosophical sally is as follows: "To this category of names which have been to mankind a subtle source of life and inspiration belongs the word Hindutva, the essential nature and significance of which we have to investigate." Savarkar wants readers to understand that he is engaged in a grand historical project—part etymology, part genealogy, part political polemic. His main claim is that "Hindutva is not a word but a history." Gyanendra Pandey argues that the category/term "Hindu" is quite restrictive, manifesting in the nationalist imagination as male and upper-caste and perhaps excludes South

70. Savarkar, *Essentials*, 459.

71. Savarkar, *Essentials*, 459.

India.[72] If this is so, Savarkar's goal was to create a far more expansive understanding of the word, to insist that if millennia of usage had not muddied the waters, we would understand that "Hindutva embraces all the departments of thought and activity of the whole Being of our Hindu race."[73] The racialization of Hindu identity, Hindus' quotidian behaviors, their cultural habitus, even their political opinions, all fall under the term "Hindutva" whether they like it or not and whether they identify themselves as Hindu or not.[74] He grounds this grand gesture of historical appropriation by suggesting that to understand the term "Hindutva," we need to examine the history of the word "Hindu" and the manner in which it has come to be understood. Savarkar then embarks on this quest with a quick run through the millennia, ticking off the numerous instances when the word "Hindu" was used.[75]

A central technique of this appropriative historical move was his format. If the 1857 book did not follow a conventional historical format, *Essentials of Hindutva* is even less conventional. It has no clear narrative chronology.[76] Instead, Savarkar piles assertion upon assertion, using a set of rhetorical and argumentative devices. He quotes from Sanskrit, Gurmukhi, and old Hindi texts but also from Marathi letters. He uses a commonsensical declamatory tactic in which he emphasizes the obvious rather than the complex. But his most important technique is his canny use of the poetics of the list.[77] These lists, of which there are many, all have an incantatory, liturgical, and recitative quality. They feature rhyme and alliteration, which as we have seen in his poetry, plays, and essays, was one of his preferred devices.

In *Essentials*, four such lists stand out. In the first, he uses caste names and a repeated chorus to call the community into being.

72. Pandey, "Which of Us Are Hindus?," 251, 253.

73. Savarkar, *Essentials*, 460.

74. See Sarwate, "Reimagining the Modern Hindu Self," 40, for a description of the Hindu Missionary Society, founded in 1917, and its activities. The discourse about Hindutva was reimagined by Savarkar, not imagined. Bal Thakare's father Prabodhankar Thakare was also a strong advocate for a reimagined Hindutva.

75. Savarkar, *Essentials*, 461.

76. I am grateful to Dilip Gaonkar for pointing this out.

77. I am particularly indebted to my friend and former colleague at Columbia University Dorothea von Mucke, who discussed with me the argument I was mulling. I have benefitted enormously from the precision of her theoretical formulations, which have been the basis for my reading of *Essentials*.

> Some of us were *Aryans* and some *Anaryans*; but *Ayars* and *Nayars*—*we were all Hindus and own a common blood.* Some of us are Brahmins and some Namshudras or Panchams; but Brahmins or Chandals—*we are all Hindus and own a common blood.* Some of us are Dakshanatyas and some Gouds; but Gouds or Sararwats—*we are all Hindus and own a common blood.* Some of us were *Vanars* and some *Kinners*: but *Vanars* or *Nars*—*we are all Hindus and own a common blood.* Some of us are monists some pantheists; some theists and some atheists. But monotheists or atheists—*we are all Hindus and own a common blood.* [emphasis mine][78]

Along with the alliteration, Savarkar provides a chorus, as if this were to be sung or recited. In each successive sentence, he uses alliterative names to build the community (see my italics). Some of us were A (*Aryans*) and some B (*Anaryans*), but A2 (*Ayars*) and C (*Nayars*) we are all Hindu. Some of us are D (Brahmins) and E (Namashudras) or F (Panchams) but D (Brahmins) or G (Chandals), but we are all Hindus.[79] The logic is inclusive and accretive, escalating to the idea of a super-religion or super-category that transcends sectarian and confessional divides (monists, pantheists, atheists, deists, theists) and ties everyone by blood. At the same time, the act of bringing everyone who can be brought into the Hindu fold makes the boundary line between Hindus and non-Hindus clear.

In another passage he uses a different set of names to summon the community.

> The first cradle songs that every Hindu girl listens to are songs of *Sita*, the good. Some of us worship *Rama* as an incarnation, some admire him as a hero and a warrior, all love him as the most illustrious representative monarch of our race. *Maruti* and *Bheemsen* are the never-failing source of strength and physical perfection to the Hindu youth; *Savitri* and *Damayanti*, the never-failing ideals of constancy and chastity of the Hindu maid. The love that *Radha* made to the Divine cowherd in Gokul finds its echo wherever a Hindu lover kisses his beloved. The giant struggle of the Kurus, the set duels of *Arjun* and *Karna*, of *Bhima* and *Dusshasan* . . . *Abhimanyu* could not have been dearer to Arjun than he is to us [emphasis mine].[80]

78. Savarkar, *Essentials*, 518.
79. I thank Dorothea von Mucke for pointing this out to me.
80. Savarkar, *Essentials*, 521.

Savarkar does not associate Krishna here with the Bhagavad Gita, as he does elsewhere in his poetry, but with love and desire.[81] In the first part of this very long passage, Savarkar names key characters from epic Sanskrit literature that reside in the blurred boundary between the mythological and the sacred. This part of the passage appears to end with one quick sentence—"[T]he story of Ramayan and Mahabharat alone would bring us together"—but he does not stop there, immediately adding,

> The fall of *Prithviraj* is bewailed in Bengal: the martyred sons of *Govindsingh* in Maharashtra. An Arya Samajist historian in the extreme North feels that *Harihara* and *Bukka* of the extreme south fought for him, and a Sanātanist historian in the extreme south feels that Guru *Tegbahadur* died for him. . . . The names of *Mokavassya* and *Pisali*, a *Jaichand* and *Kalapaharh* make us all feel as sinners do. The names of *Ashok*, *Bhaskaracharya*, *Panini*, and *Kapil* leave us all electrified [emphasis mine].[82]

The link between name and geography is worth noting here, with Savarkar laying out the four quadrants as he moves from epic mythology (Rama, Sita, Maruti, Radha) to historical figures (Prithviraj, Harihara, Bukka). Between the two halves of this passage, we have twenty-five mythological heroes, lovers (Radha/Krishna), warriors, sages, grammarians (Panini), rulers, kings, and religious leaders (Guru Tegbahadur). Savarkar uses these names (some well-known, some less so) to create a linked footprint across the geography of much of India to build a united community. In drawing from old literary traditions—the listing of the ships in the Iliad, the genealogical repetitiveness of names in the Hebrew Bible, the lists in Arabian Nights and the Samhitas, the thousand names of Vishnu—Savarkar brings the historical past into the present.

However, just as he did not invent the technique of listing, he did not by any means invent the term "Hindutva," which B. G. Tilak had used before him to denote the community. Nor is his fascination with connecting the earliest "Hindus" and "Aryas" original.[83] All of this, the groundwork for *Essentials* and its obsession with names and territory, was created by others. The debate and scholarly arguments about whether the "Aryans" were indigenous to the South Asian subcontinent or had migrated from elsewhere had occupied linguists,

81. I thank Alok Oak for this insight.

82. Savarkar, *Essentials*, 521.

83. See Oak, *Political Ideas of B. G. Tilak*, 133–40, for a detailed examination of Tilak's *Arctic Home*.

philologists, archaeologists, and Orientalists since the early seventeenth-century "discovery" of Sanskrit as a language as old or older than Hebrew. In the eighteenth and nineteenth centuries, as Edwin Bryant argues, this "discovery" spurred an intellectual move away from seeing Genesis as the origin point for the historical evolution of the human species and toward Sanskrit as the language of an ancient civilization and the mother of all languages.[84] Accordingly, since Sanskrit was the language of the ancient Aryans, the question as to whether they were indigenous to South Asia became greatly important, especially against the backdrop of an anticolonial nationalism.

While most of the participants in this debate and those about Sanskrit and Aryans more generally were European philologists and Orientalists, Indians took up these questions as well. In 1912 Narayan Pavgi, an apparently indefatigable retired Magistrate, published a work titled *The Vedic Fathers of Geology*, followed by two more works in 1915 and 1918—*The Aryavartic Home*, which began with a chapter on "Our Planet and the Geological Epoch of Aryavarta," and "Self-Government in India: Vedic and Post-Vedic," which took on the Arctic theory and European hypotheses about Central Asian migration—all of which were distinct from another staggering twenty-one volumes on India's ancient history.[85]

In *The Arctic Home in the Vedas*, B. G. Tilak suggested that the ancient Aryans did not originate in South Asia but in the Arctic zone. Savarkar was not especially interested in the nitty gritty details of the Indological, archaeological or etymological argument about who the ancient Aryans were or where they came from, what language they spoke. He stayed away from scholarly disputes, producing instead a modern interpretation of an older modality that animated key historical figures and moved them seamlessly through time and space.

For Savarkar, mythology is the archive, history the instrument, and the nation the telos. To that end, the lists function as performative, mnemonic devices, not unlike the memorizable prose poetry of his Kruger poem. Even more important, Savarkar does not simply place a religious label on the map on India. Instead, he underscores that people inhabited a sacred geography and that the nation comes into being as the material phantasm of a collective

84. See Bryant, *Quest for the Origins of Vedic Culture*, ch. 1, for an excellent historical examination of the Aryan debate—how the debate began, the routes it took, and what the stakes were regarding whether the Aryans were or were not indigenous to South Asia.

85. See Deshpande, *The Arctic Home in the Vedas*, 39–42, for a discussion of Pavgi.

memory. He turns the figures he names into peripatetic propagandists who continually remind community members of the ties that bind them.

These reminders and these figures are Savarkar's memory workers. In distinguishing between history and memory, Pierre Nora wrote, "Memory is life, always embodied in living societies . . . subject to the dialectics of remembering and forgetting. . . . History, on the other hand, is the reconstruction, always problematic and incomplete, of what is no longer."[86] He added, "memory is always a phenomenon of the present, a bond tying us to the eternal present . . . Memory, being a phenomenon of emotion and magic, accommodates only those facts that suit it."[87] Savarkar understood this phenomenon particularly well.

In another passage, Savarkar speaks of Sanskrit as the language that feeds all other Indian languages. But he is not interested in etymology; he brings forth Sanskrit's supposed progeny to populate the land in yet another alliterative phrase—"Gujarathi and Gurmukhi, Sindhi and Hindi, Tamil and Telugu, Maharashtra and Malayalam, Bengali and Singhali"—and asserts that they "constitute the vital nerve-thread that runs through us all, vivifying and toning our feelings and aspirations into a harmonious whole."[88] If one reads past the alliteration and musicality, one might note that Gurmukhi is a script, not a language, and that Tamil has always been distinct from Sanskrit (with a classic literature of its own). But Savarkar, here as elsewhere, is less concerned with accuracy than with an inclusive roll call of Indianness—an e pluribus unum Hindutva.[89]

This section of *Essentials* is reminiscent of the hymn composed by the Indian Nobel laureate Rabindranath Tagore sung at the 1911 session of the INC in Calcutta and later adopted as India's national anthem. A few passages later, Savarkar explicitly cites Tagore, including him in a list of poets whom all India would claim as their own (in contrast to Shakespeare, despite his opening reference to the Bard).

> *Adipuran* was not written by a *Sanatani* yet the Adipuran is the common inheritance of the Santanis and jains. The *Vasavpuran* is the bible of the Lingayat; but it belongs to Lingayats and non-Lingayat Hindus alike, as one of the foremost and historical Kanarese work extant. *Vachittarnatak* [*sic*] of Guru Gobind Singh is as truly the property of a Hindu in Bengal as the

86. Nora, *Realms of Memory*, 3

87. Nora, *Realms of Memory*, 3.

88. Savarkar, *Essentials*, 522

89. I am grateful to Martha Schulman for pointing this out to me.

> *Chaitanyacharitramrit* is of a Sikh. Kalidas and Bhavabhuti, Charak and Sushrut, Aryabhatt and Varahamihir, Bhas and Asvaghosh, Jaidev and Jagannath wrote for us all, appeal to us all, are the cherished possession of us all. Let the work of Kamb the Tamil poet and say, a copy of Hafiz be kept before a Hindu in Bengal and if he be asked 'what belongs to you of these? He would instinctively say "Kamb is mine!" Let a copy of the work of Ravindranath and that of Shakespeare be kept before a Hindu in Maharashtra, he would claim "Ravinder! Ravinder is mine."[90]

Here, Savarkar uses languages, texts, and authors to create a nexus between unity and diversity. Texts and authors from one part of the country were part of the collective memory of the entire community, and the figure at the end of the passage—a "Hindu in Maharashtra"—functions as a stand-in for Savarkar, making him not only the creator of this literary unity, but someone on whom it acts.

From texts, Savarkar moves to a poetic evocation of geography meant to call attention to the land itself, using cartographic tropes to assert the fundamental unity of Hindustan:

> . . . it was in this land that the Founders of our faith and the Seers to whom "Ved" the Knowledge was revealed, from Vedic seers to Dayanand, from Jin to Mahabir, from Budh to Nagsen, from Nanak to Gobind, from *Banda to Basav*, from *Chakradhar to Chaitanya*, from *Ramdas to Rammohun*, our *Gurus and Godmen* were born and bred [emphasis mine].

Again we see his penchant for alliteration. He continues:

> . . . the very dust of its paths echoes the footfalls of our prophets and Gurus. Sacred are its rivers, hallowed its groves, for it was either on their moonlit ghats or under their eventide long shadows, that the deepest problems of life, of man, soul and God, of Brahma and Maya were debated and discussed by a Buddh or a Shankar.[91]

Having named a community, he moves to the territory it has always inhabited, using words like "sacred" and "hallowed" to imbue that territory with heightened value.

It is in these passages that we see Savarkar's belief that poetry is a more effective register than history to re-enchant a territory in which he has already

90. Savarkar, *Essentials*, 523.
91. Savarkar, *Essentials*, 534.

located his eternal if peripatetic community. While Tilak and Pavgi were having scholarly disputes with German Orientalists and Indologists, Savarkar was using poetic language about territory and the past common to how millions of Indians thought of space, time, location, and event: "Ah! Every hill and dell distinct with memories of a Kapil or a Vyas, Shankar or Ramdas."[92] In one sentence, he moves across millennia, bridging a mythological seer (Vyas) and a seventeenth-century mendicant (Guru Ramdas). As the passage continues, Savarkar uses familiar Indic tropes from the epics, in which the indexical adverbs are used to demarcate what the heroes of epics had done—*here* is Kurukshetra, where the battle between the Kauravas and Pandavas took place; *there* is where the Buddha attained Nirvana. Savarkar uses similar deictic and performative gestures, knowing his readers would recognize and find them familiar.

> *Here* Bhagirath rules, *there* Kurukshetra lies. *Here* Ramchander made his first half of an exile, *there* Janaki saw the golden deer. . . . Here is Bodhivraksha, *here* the deer park. *Here* Mahavir entered *nirvana* [emphasis mine].

The indexical adverbs *here* and *there* can be felicitous only when the objects pointed to are both intimate and proximate, both spatially close (here) and temporally immediate (now). But Savarkar also uses this rhetorical technique because it employs cultural idioms and forms that are central to how Indians understand their own charismatic landscape, not in the secular language of cardinal geography but in terms of sacred pilgrimages and sites. The passage comes to a thundering close when Savarkar brings it all together through yet another familiar trope: "Every stone *here* has a story of martyrdom to tell. Every inch of thy soil, Oh mother! *has been a sacrificial* ground [emphasis mine]."[93] Not only has there always been a mythic community in a magical land, but every part of this land that is still so near and present has been sacralized by sacrifice. Martyrdom is a very powerful mobilizer of a community, and since Savarkar's interest is rhetorical rather than informational, he can make these claims with impunity.

The next passage—we are now in the last section of the book, called "Unique Natural Blessing to Hindusthan"—makes the apotheosis of territory even more apparent. Savarkar writes, "She is the richly endowed daughter of

92. I am grateful to the anonymous reader of my manuscript for pointing this out to me.
93. Savarkar, *Essentials*, 534.

God—this our Motherland."[94] Savarkar, as we saw in the chapter on caste, dismissed the ritual observance (*vratavaikalya*) that was a part of Marathi Brahmin life. He considered himself a rationalist, but here is his exuberant praise and sense of sacral awe for territory.

> Her rivers are deep and perennial. Her land is yielding to the plough and her fields loaded with golden harvests . . . rich in her fauna, rich in her flora, she knows she owes it all to the immediate source of light and heat—The Sun.[95]

In the same passage, Savarkar creates a sharp contrast between Mother Ganges and Father Thames, obvious references to India and England, while taking aim at the generally popular notion that warm climates generate lassitude.

> She [Mother India] covets not the icy lands; blessed be they and their frozen latitudes. If heat is at times enervating here, cold is at times benumbing there. If cold induces manual labor, heat removes much of its very necessity. She takes more delight in quenched thirst than in the parched throat. . . . Father Thames is free to work at feverish speed, wrapped in his icy sheets. She loves to visit her ghats and watch her boats gliding down the Ganges on her moonlit waters. With the plough, the peacocks, the lotus, the elephant, and the Gita, she is willing to forego, if that must be, whatever advantage the colder latitudes enjoy . . . her gardens are green and shady, her granaries well stocked, her waters crystal, her flowers scented, her fruits juicy, and her herbs healing. Her brush is dipped in the colours of Dawn and her flute resonant with the music of Gokul . . . [96]

She covets, takes, loves, foregoes, and paints while watching herself. If colonialism makes one lose self-regard, then the work of history for Savarkar moves the community out of loss. Pride turns into a national narcissism—India likes to watch herself carefully and without haste, unlike the paradoxically frigid yet feverish Thames.

It may be easy to dismiss this text and his prose as overly sentimental, a kind of faux-Tennysonian poetry transposed into Indo-Anglian prose, but we must recognize its power when it was written and released into the underground

94. Savarkar, *Essentials*, 549. See also Ramaswamy, *The Goddess and the Nation*, for an outstanding examination and analysis of how artists mapped India's geography onto the image of a female Mother India across several media.

95. Savarkar, *Essentials*, 549.

96. Savarkar, *Essentials*, 549.

public sphere of colonial India. Gandhi had been arrested; the country's mood was somber. The nonviolent noncooperation movement had not accomplished any real gains. Many felt a sense of defeat; these passages, written by a jailed revolutionary, countered that sense. In *Essentials*, Savarkar reaches out to a community that had just seen Gandhi taken off to prison and reminds them that there was an older, richer, deeper geography that it had access to for a very long time, even millennia. Inhabitants of the subcontinent—primarily Hindus, to be sure—had their own understanding of belonging, and a mode of comprehending space, time, location, event, and territory that a colonial, cardinal cartography could never replace. Modern anthropologists would recognize that the seemingly simple question "Where are you from?" would set in motion a chain of answers, beginning with the name of a village, and go on to include the abode of the family deity and in some cases even refer to a land grant that might be dated to a mythological epic.[97] For all his rationalism, Savarkar is prescient in recognizing that this was the language of belonging, and rather than scorn it as he did rituals, he used it to bring into the present cultural idioms and forms that he knew millions upon millions of Hindus could recognize. Pierre Nora writes that "the atomization of memory . . . imposes a duty to remember on each individual." He calls this a "law of remembrance," which has enormous persuasive power. He continues, "for the individual, the discovery of roots, of 'belonging' to some group, becomes the source of identity, its true and hidden meaning." And he notes that "[b]elonging, in turn, becomes a total commitment." Nora writes using the Jewish community as an example of this kind of total commitment. "In the Jewish tradition, whose history *is* its memory, to be Jewish is to remember being Jewish."[98] Likewise, by using indexicals that point to enchanting locations and events, Savarkar recognized that nationalism needed not just history but geography and the commitment alluded to earlier. Unlike Shejwalkar's prosaic insistence on a thorough knowledge of the physical landscape, Savarkar's geography was as enchanting and mythological as his history. He used it to name a modern nation into being by using an older poetic literary trope and technique. That is no small feat. And we must credit him also with political and populist savvy.

97. See Daniel, *Fluid Signs*, for the most sensitive and perceptive ethnographic examination of precisely this sense of belonging in multiple registers, all of which begin with a question of the location of one's *ur* (village/place/home) in Tamil Nadu. See also Cohn "The Pasts of an Indian Village," 88–99.

98. Nora, *Realms of Memory*, 11.

Writing from prison during a moment when nationalist leaders were demoralized and dispirited, he produced a text that invoked prophets and seers from the four corners of India as if they were timeless, present, *and* the ancestors of the present moment, available to invest the nation with a hopeful future. This was not the history writing that Nora describes as "the reconstruction, always problematic and incomplete, of what is no longer" or an "intellectual, nonreligious activity, [that] calls for analysis and critical discourse." History, Nora writes, entails "a criticism destructive of spontaneous memory," which "divests the lived past of its legitimacy" and one in which "all historians denounce the supposedly fraudulent mythologies of their predecessors." Savarkar was very clear that the history he was writing was closer to what Nora describes as memory, which is "an absolute, while History is always relative."[99] Such memory work "imposes a duty to remember on each individual."[100] Memory was always suspect in "the eyes of history, whose true mission is to demolish it [history]." These distinctions, between memory and history, which Savarkar never elaborated upon as such, were nonetheless clear for him.

The first historical event he discusses is a mythic one: the first sacrificial fire lit on the banks of the Indus, which, for Savarkar, occurred long before the ancient Egyptians and Babylonians. History begins with sacrifice and the ancient Aryans, and with history begins the naming process. He proposes that even if the ancient Aryans came from elsewhere and encountered the Indus Valley civilization, they would not have coined utterly new names for everything but would have used, perhaps with minor changes, the words the locals used. This speculation lets him claim that the Aryans turned the word "Hindu" into "Sindhu" because of a peculiarity of their language that turned *ha* into *sha*. Savarkar was not interested in the term "Aryan" and dismissed the efforts of Hindus who were.[101] In 1923 that term would have alienated large numbers of South Indians who were not keen to be incorporated into this fold, given the racism and prejudice the term carried. South Indians voiced their nationalism in the language of "Dravidianism," a term that was often seen in deliberate opposition to the Aryans of the North (seen as the historical oppressors of the South). Using the term "Hindu" let Savarkar bypass this divide.[102]

99. Nora, *Realms of Memory*, 3–4.

100. Nora, *Realms of Memory*, 11.

101. Savarkar, *Essentials*, 508, where he derides the attempt to have the word "Aryan" reclaimed as a census category.

102. I am grateful to Satadru Sen for this insight.

From the fire of ritual sacrifice, Savarkar turns to water, using rivers as civilizational landmarks. He employs Sanskrit quotations liberally throughout the work, but especially in this first part, suggesting that the language is an essential scaffolding for his edifice. In the second Sanskrit quote he names the rivers—Ganga, Yamuna, Saraswati, Satadru, Godavari—drawing from an earlier Marathi Varkari tradition but without dwelling on a specific regional aspect.[103] From riverine civilization, he moves quickly through Puranic mythology. The immense distance between the early Ṛgvedic period (twelfth century BCE) and the Puranic period (second century AD) does not bother him. What mattered was any textual record of the word "Hindu" or "Sindhu," because their presence let him assert that the nation originated in a named community. Moving from small group to nation was for Savarkar an inexorable and inevitable step, the tracing of which was one of the essay's central tasks.

Claire Wrigley points out that, in *Essentials*, Savarkar frequently uses words with the "re" prefix. As she notes, attached "to transitive verbs, the prefix 're' denotes that the action of the verb is being performed again, or it shows that the action of the verb *reverses* a previous action or process. Savarkar's Hindu nation is also a 're'-action from the very beginning." Thus, for example, when the Aryan tribes arrived in the Indus valley, "they soon *re*claimed the vast, waste and but very thinly populated lands." When Savarkar discusses language, as Wrigley notes, he claims that a national language had to undergo a *re*vival, and "that merely by the act of arrival, or of speaking, these inhabitants of the Indus River valleys were gesturing to their own history as a people."[104] A revival suggests a previous presence, which Savarkar addresses more directly in his last work.

An important shift in perspective occurs when Savarkar addresses Muslims in section twenty-one, entitled "Foreign Invaders." His claim begins with Mahmud of Ghazni's invasion.

> From year to year, decade to decade, century to century, the contest continues. Arabia ceased to be what Arabia was; Iran, annihilated, Egypt, Syria, Afghanistan, Baluchistan, Tartary—from Granada to Gazani [*sic*]—nations and civilizations fell in heaps before the sword of Islam of Peace.[105]

The Indo-Islamic millennium is presented as another series of collisions, although this time it is not Islam as a world historical force against extant

103. See Feldhaus, *Connected Places*, 160–82.
104. Wrigley, "Subaltern Studies and Beyond" [Presentation].
105. Savarkar, *Essentials*, 487.

nations, but one nation—India—against a multitude of Muslim ethnic groups he identifies as "Arabs, Persians, Pathans, Baluchis, Tartars, Turks, Moghuls."[106]

His anger and fear are both expressed fully here:

> Religion is a mighty motive force. So is Rapine. But where Religion is goaded on by Rapine and Rapine serves as a hand-maid to Religion, the propelling force that is generated by these two together is only equaled by profundity of human misery and devastation they leave behind them in their march.[107]

Rapine reappears in *Six Glorious Epochs,* where Savarkar describes it as an essential tactic. Meanwhile, in *Essentials,* he interrupts the Indo-Islamic millennium that he has collapsed into decades and centuries of ceaseless conflict to say "India single handedly kept the fight morally and militarily. The moral victory was won when Akbar came to the throne and Darshikoh [*sic*] was born."[108] No more information is given to the reader about Akbar or Dara Shikoh. This is surprising. Given that Savarkar places the Mughals in a history that starts with Arabs and includes Tartars and Turks, one might assume that there were no distinctions to be made among Mughal emperors.

In the section following "Foreign Invaders," we get a little historical analysis. Section twenty-two—"Hindutva at Work"—spends sixteen and a half pages ploughing through the Indo-Islamic millennia until arriving at the Aurangzeb-Shivaji conflict. For the longue duree prior to Chhatrapati Shivaji, Savarkar is vague, seeming to anticipate scholarly inquiries and ward them off. The section is also flatter than others, with no elevated prose or poetic lists. It serves only to highlight Shivaji Maharaj's greatness, defined against the perfidy of the Mughal emperor Aurangzeb (1658–1707), a far cry from the "moral" Akbar. From this point on, most quotations are in Hindi and Marathi. The first work Savarkar quotes is *Prithviraj Raso* by Chand Bardai. Since Chand Bardai uses the words "Hindi" and "Hind" so often, "as far back as the eleventh century," there can be no doubt that "Hindu" was already used as a self-identificatory definition. Here we note that *Prithviraj Raso* was written no earlier than the sixteenth century.[109]

Savarkar then moves to Samartha Ramdas, quoting numerous lines from a poem that dreams of a world in which the Aurangzeb is defeated by

106. Savarkar, *Essentials,* 487.
107. Savarkar, *Essentials,* 488.
108. Savarkar, *Essentials,* 488.
109. I am grateful to Sheldon Pollock for pointing this out to me.

Chhatrapati Shivaji. The Hindu poet Bhushan, who challenges Aurangzeb and praises Shivaji Maharaj, is cited only as "vide Bhushan Granthawali."[110] Savarkar then mentions three texts: *Chatraprakash,* described as the text that described the events of Chattrasal's reign and was composed by Lalkavi, then *Pathaprakash,* then *Suryaprakash,* without author or publication dates but quoting from memory. In this section, a "youthful Shivaji" wrote a letter in 1646, identified as part of Rajwade's collection. Toward the end of this section, Savarkar uses letters again, but we are given no information about where to locate them: Dhondo Govind to Bajirao, Bajirao to Brahmendra Swami, Jaysingh (where we get a specific date—October 26, 1721), Nanasaheb's letters, and the last letter from Govindrao Kale to Nana Phadnavis in 1793.

The text makes clear that Savarkar's memory is prodigious, as he was remembering all this from his prison cell, even as his real interest, even when books might have been available to him, was using a handful of decontextualized facts instrumentally. In *Essentials,* he shrewdly identified a middle-class audience that he could captivate by using an older poetic modality in English and impress with his seeming grasp of an array of historical sources in multiple languages. Paradoxically, Savarkar taps into a populist anti-intellectualism while showcasing his vast knowledge. Liberal sprinklings of Sanskrit phrases and couplets gave the text authority—it did not matter if they were accurate, out of context, or correctly transliterated. His aim was to awe readers. After all, how could someone writing from prison, producing from memory twenty Sanskrit quotations, verses from the *Prithviraj Raso,* and selections from the *Bhaviṣyapurāṇa,* who could remember the letters about Maratha history that Rajwade possessed and Taraknath Vachaspati's writing in Bengal, be anything but extraordinary?

Essentials of Hindutva's power lay in precisely the elements that upset both intellectuals and academic historians. Wherever Savarkar bumps up against a scholarly inquiry or the possibility that some readers might demand greater historical detail, he announces that these details are not germane, while also noting his complete command of the material. In one instance, Savarkar quotes a line in Sanskrit—"Shivashiva na Hindurna Yavanah"—and adds that the verse is too well-known to require citation.[111]

110. Savarkar, *Essentials,* 494.

111. I am grateful to Madhav Deshpande for helping me find the verse, and translating it for me. The verse from which Savarkar quotes can be found in a collection of memorable verses, titled *Samayocitapadyamālikā,* 36.

Savarkar effectively combines historical snippets and seemingly authoritative knowledge with the directness and simplicity of tabloid reporting. It concludes by distilling Savarkar's main argument into a Sanskrit couplet in which "allegiance" is conceptualized as a pledge to territorial fundamentalism: "Asindhu sindhu paryanta yasya bharat Bhumika / Pitrabhu punyabhushchaiva sa vai hinduriti smritaha" ("India's geographical contours extend from the Sindhu River in the North [in present-day Pakistan] to the seas below in the South / All people who claimed India as both *pitrabhumi* [the land of their ancestors] and *punyabhumi* [holy land] were its natural inhabitants"). The verse is effective for two reasons. Coming at the essay's close, it cements the notion that nationalism needs geography even more than it needs history. It is easy to read and understand, and simple for anyone with a rudimentary facility in any of the Indian languages with a Sanskritic vocabulary, which includes Hindi, Marathi, Gujarati, Malayalam, Kannada, and Bengali, and thus a vast number of Indians could memorize it. Indeed, Savarkar would recommend that every Hindu memorize it, teach it to their children, and have them recite it as a prayer (*sandhyā*) every evening.[112] Second, it does not overtly keep non-Hindu communities from claiming that its pilgrimage sites lay within India's ancient geography. Indian Muslims and Christians could claim that India housed their places of worship and was the land of their fathers. Muslims, Christians, and Jews could be citizens, but their citizenship was of second order, because their primary holy land was not in India and their prophets had not been born in it, preached in it, roamed around it, or rendered it sacred.

Having turned India into the ancient home of the mythic Hindus, Savarkar emphasized that respect for Hindu culture was as central a tenet for belonging as birth and religion. At the end of *Essentials,* he almost turns the tables on the work he's done up to that point. On one hand Hindus were the authentic

न संध्यां संधत्ते नियमितनमाजं न कुरुते	He neither performs the Sandhyā, nor does he regularly perform Namaz.
न वा मौंजीबंधं कलयति न वा सुंनतविधिम्।	He does not follow the right of Upanayana [*mauñjībandh*] nor does he undergo circumcision.
न रोजां जानीते व्रतम् अपि हरेः न एव कुरुते	He does not perform the Roja fasts nor the fasts for Vishnu.
न काशि मक्का वा **हर हर न हिंदुः न यवनः**	He goes neither to Kashi nor to Mecca. O Lord, he is neither a Hindu nor a Muslim [*yavana*].

112. "Hindutvace Panchprana" in *SSV*, MPHS, 3: 11.

inhabitants of Hindustan because their original holy sites and ancestral lands were within its boundaries.[113] On the other he used a modern notion of choice to suggest something that is simultaneously absurd yet simple: if you choose to love India, whether you are Hindu, or Muslim, or Christian, you can be a part of the fold.

> Are you a monist—a monotheist—a pantheist—an atheist—an agnostic? Here is ample room, oh soul! Whatever thou art, to love and grow to thy fullest height and satisfaction in this temple of Temples . . . Ye who by race, by blood, by culture, by nationality possess *almost all the essentials of Hindutva* . . . ye have only to render whole-hearted love to our common mother and recognize her not only as Pitrabhu but even as a Punyabhu and ye would be most welcome to the Hindu-fold. This is a choice which our country-men and our old kith and kin, the Bohras, Khojas, Mamons, and other Mohamedan and Christian communities are free to make a choice again which must be a choice of love [emphasis mine].[114]

Nationalism now becomes a matter of choosing to love; this move lets future generations of militant Hindu nationalists use the modern concept of political choice as an alibi for prejudice. It sets in place a subjunctive nationalism in an "if-then" frame: if non-Hindu Indians really loved India, they would show it by relinquishing all other allegiances.

Savarkar writes in a seductive vein, occasionally trading his hammer for a honey dipper to imply an inclusive nationalism is open to members of all communities, if not equally. Christians could be considered second-order Hindus because they had respect for Hindu culture, as could Bohras and Khojas because they accept the ten avatars of Vishnu and add the Prophet Muhammad as the eleventh, but most other Muslims *choose* to remain aloof as outsiders. In other words, even though all of the communities he refers to in the above passage might have been born in India and lived in it for centuries, only the Muslim community truly leaves itself out of the fold due to choices it is assumed to have made.

113. See *SSV*, MPHS, 3: 2–5. Savarkar made this point more clearly in two essays he wrote some years after *Essentials*. In an essay titled "Hindutvācē pañcaprāṇa," he argued against those who might suggest that the term/word "Hindu" was used by Muslims to identify the inhabitants of those who lived on the other side of the Indus. This is one of the few times Savarkar returns to the Vedas, but as a historical text, to argue that the word "Saptasiṁdhavaha" was used to denote both a people and a nation.

114. Savarkar, *Essentials*, 535–36.

In *Essentials*, Savarkar extends his previous poem about homesickness, "Sāgarā prāṇa taḷamaḷalā" (discussed in chapter 4), into a full-fledged love letter in which he lays out a powerfully transcendent and nonsexual love. It is not a love of women, men, or children, of parents or siblings; the only true love is love of country/nation. Nationalism is the expression of this love, which must be doubly monogamous: one country and one love. The emphasis on monogamous love explains why Muslims and Christians could not be natural inhabitants of India, and could be brought under the umbrella of Hindutva only if they abandoned their divided love.[115] India had to be the transcendent love object.

Why did this love letter to the community seem necessary to Savarkar in 1922/3? Had someone denied his beloved the love of which he wrote so eloquently? Given Savarkar's conception of singular love, it seems clear that he is referring to Gandhi and the Khilafat movement. The Khilafat movement's demand for dual allegiance was exactly what Savarkar saw as an unchaste, nonmonogamous love. Therefore, he classified love for India—her land, her people, her sages, her rivers, her mountains, her literature—as a necessary condition for being welcomed into the Hindu fold. Whenever Savarkar wrote in the poetic or sentimental vein, he wrote of this love, whether for a river, the Indian Ocean, the hills, the epics, the mythological heroes, or Mother India. And he ended with the idea that such a love—of country and culture—was available to non-Hindu communities if they chose it. Savarkar whitewashed his anti-Muslim utterances by defending a few non-Hindus. "Foreigners," like Sister Nivedita, for example, could be received into the fold not because they were Christian (as opposed to Muslim) but because of their undivided love for India.[116] Similarly, what brought Akbar inside the fold was his choice to love India.

Therefore, not only did he reiterate that he has stayed true to his love; by implication, he also suggests that Hindus should beware Gandhi's embrace of Khilafat. *Essentials* was a political argument made in a poetic register. It was an argument with and against an unnamed Gandhi at a moment when he seemed finished with politics. It was a cry from behind prison walls, intended to remind the outside world that, even if Gandhi was off the political scene, Savarkar was there. He was still a leader, a champion of the Hindus, and a politician capable of pulling together a nationalist community. But the Hinduness he offered was different from Gandhi's, as was the nationalism he embodied.

115. Savarkar, *Essentials*, 535.
116. Savarkar, *Essentials*, 546–47.

If Gandhi officiated at the marriage of religion and politics and Khilafat leaders were using religious symbols to forge a community, Savarkar argues in *Essentials* that what bound the Hindu community was not religion but name and place. He assailed

> the unfortunate misunderstanding that owes its origin to the confusing similarity between the two terms Hindutva and Hinduism . . . We have protested against the wrong use of the word Hinduism to denote the Sanatan Dharm alone . . . This twofold mistake that identifies Hindutva with Hindudharam and both with Sanatani sects is justly resented by our non-Sanatani sects or religious systems.[117]

But he was far too canny to suggest complete atheism or dismiss religion altogether. Instead, in its most fundamental contribution, *Essentials* inaugurated a new set of terms. In place of religion qua religion, Savarkar secularized a pantheon of Hindu religious leaders. In so doing he did not generate a sterilely secular nationalism. Indeed, he did the opposite, enchanting a secular nationalism by placing a mythic community into a magical land.

By framing love for the mythic land of India as an active choice of allegiance, Savarkar also challenged the texture of Gandhi's support of the Khilafat movement. As V. S. Naipaul pointed out, Gandhi was utterly uninterested in physical landscapes or markings.[118] One searches Gandhi's works in vain for any description of the countryside, whether South African or Indian. Nationalism for Gandhi was always about people, whether Hindus or Muslims. He would later assert that even the British were welcome to stay in India after independence if they stopped being British, by which he meant a number of things, including adopting vegetarianism and abjuring violence.

In *Essentials*, Savarkar argues that nationalism has nothing to do with actual people, let alone their religion, and everything to do with a mythic community in a sacred land. If the first essence of Hindutva is territory, invoked not through the modern instrument of the map but through making an ancient visual landscape present, then every name and place is a footprint of a mythic and powerful history. It is no accident that Savarkar includes at least sixty proper names—caste names; names of people, places, and lands that were known by different names; names of texts and authors—connecting a sacred and secular geography through pilgrimage, reminding a Hindu community of

117. Savarkar, *Essentials*, 541.

118. See Naipaul, *India*, 102–6.

its birth, its genealogy, and its heritage. Such a piling of name after name, place after place, text after text, generated not just aural alliteration but a visual architecture. It was through this pile upon pile of name and place that an ever-present ancient edifice—the nation—was (re)built, secularized, and enchanted.

In his book on the 1857 Rebellion, Savarkar argued that India was a nation, as demonstrated by the unified Hindu and Muslim struggle against the British. He had a romantic if provisional notion of two natural communities that lived side by side, coming together in a common nationalist struggle. By the time he wrote *Essentials*, however, this marriage of two communities had been sundered because one of India's two communities was deep in a bigamous relationship. *Essentials of Hindutva* has the passion and possessiveness of a jealous and patriarchal husband who reminds his wife that she may not look at anyone else, let alone form an attachment. It was the first indelible salvo in a long series revealing the spurned lover's rage and anger at the one who seemed to want to get away.

Hindu-Pad-Padashahi

Immediately after getting out of prison, Savarkar wrote *Hindu-Pad-Padashahi*, another historical work with *Essentials*-style prose. The book was published in an edition of 1,500 copies in November 1925 by B. G. Paul & Co. in Madras—the same publisher of Savarkar's pseudonymously written biography. The publisher's announcement informs us that Savarkar had ". . . laid under contribution all contemporary records—historical, literary and epistolary,—and there is not a single fact cited here for which he is not prepared to quote chapter and verse as authority." Savarkar, for all his disdain for historians, wanted to remind readers that he was a scholar. Not that he could have consulted documents; he was restricted to Ratnagiri, and even if he could have traveled, he would not have been granted access to records he might have consulted. The Peshwa Daftar records at the Alienation Office in Poona, even if placed under G. S. Sardesai's editorship, would not have been accessible to him.[119] He relied on his memory of whatever materials he had seen before or materials friends helped him gather. But the lack of archival materials might not have mattered because *Hindu-Pad-Padashahi* was meant on the surface to show that a Hindu state led by the Brahmin Peshwas could serve as a better model than Gandhi's

119. Chakrabarty, *Calling of History*, 154.

weak, nonviolent vision and, under the surface, as a counter to the powerful Brahmanetar arguments against Brahmins that we saw in chapter three.

Hindu-Pad-Padashahi could be considered Savarkar's attempt at writing a mildly Hegelian history, insofar as it was a teleological history of the Hindu spirit's yearning for freedom that culminated in the Peshwa state. But that would be farfetched, since Savarkar never elaborated on any fundamental Hegelian concepts. The real interest in this book seems to have been to write the affective history of the Peshwai. Savarkar notes in his foreword, in complete contradistinction to Shejwalkar, that

> the duty of a Historian is primarily to depict as far as possible the feelings, motives, emotions and actions of the actors themselves whose deed he aims to relate. This he cannot do faithfully and well, unless he, for the time being, rids himself not only of all prejudices and prepossessions but even of the fears of the consequences the story of the past might be calculated to have on the interests of the present.[120]

This sounds very much like the kind of history Jadunath Sarkar would have recommended, with its emphasis on truth-telling, even the eschewing of "prejudices and prepossessions." But a dispassionate or disinterested history was far from Savarkar's goal. Almost as if to anticipate the charge of prejudice, he forewarns any possible Muslim readers that

> before you make out a case for unity, you must make out a case for survival as a national or a social human unit. It was this fierce test that the Hindus were called upon to pass in their deadly struggle with the Muhammadan power.

His Muslim readers also had to understand that there could only be real unity between equals, which is why

> The day that witnessed the forces of the "Haribhaktas," of Hindudom, enter Delhi in triumph and the Moslem throne and crown and standard lay hammered and rolling in dust . . . in 1761 A.D. was the day which made an honourable unity between the Hindus and the Moslems more or less feasible.[121]

Essentially Savarkar was implying that there could not be any Hindu-Muslim unity of the sort that Gandhi was asking for, the unity that required Hindus to stand with Muslims in their quest to maintain the Khilafat. Unity could only

120. Savarkar, *Hindu-Pad-Padashahi*, x.
121. Savarkar, *Hindu-Pad-Padashahi*, xiii and xiv.

come once all semblance of Muslim rule and privilege was destroyed. Given that Muslims were in a minority in India, we might read this as Savarkar denying the possibility of Hindu-Muslim unity altogether or suggesting that only defeated Muslims could be compatible with victorious Hindus.

The book deals primarily with Chhatrapati Shivaji and his Peshwa successors and reads exuberantly, full of glorious Hindu heroes and malevolent Muslim villains. A couple of passages will show my point:

> Aurangzeb (Alamgir I) fancied that he could blow out the lamp of Hindu life that flickering burnt in the temple just with a breath of his imperial wrath. He swore by Allah and blew: but, to his utter dismay, discovered that the faintly flickering lamp scorching his heart burst suddenly into a wildfire: the hills of Sahyadri caught it and setting aflame a million hearts and towers and turrets, and hills and valleys, by land and sea, it grew into a great sacrificial conflagration. Alamgir I despised the Marathas as "mountain rats." Since then the Hindu rats developed such terribly sharp and powerful claws that many a lion of Islam lay torn and bleeding at their feet in the capital of Alamgir II. Emperor Alamgir I did not condescend to recognize Shivaji even as a mere Raja: but his descendant, Alamgir II, could call himself Emperor only because the descendant of Shivaji did not mind it much to allow him the luxury of the name.[122]

After reading his glorification of Shivaji Maharaj and all that he set out to establish, we now see Savarkar's exhausting and frenetic Puranic imagination of the relentless Manichean struggle for deliverance of "the Hindu people and the Hindu land" from alien bondage, Muhammadan foes and mobs, Muslim fanaticism, Muslim sway, Muslim yoke, Muslim plots, enemies of the Hindu faith, and Muslim tyranny.[123] Muslim potentates are "silly," "stupid," sometimes "wild with terror" sometimes "emasculated." They write "ridiculous" letters to the Marathas. They are "consummate hypocrite[s]."[124] Each successive Peshwa beginning with Bajirao and Nanasaheb embodies Shivaji Maharaj's spirit to further expand *Hindu-Pad-Padashahi*. Maratha diplomats are sage; Maratha armies rout Muslims in moral military campaigns described as brilliant.[125] When the Peshwa army reached Attock, Savarkar writes,

122. Savarkar, *Hindu-Pad-Padashahi*, 82–83.

123. Savarkar, *Hindu-Pad-Padashahi*, 10, 15, 24, 35, 51, 62, 69.

124. Savarkar, *Hindu-Pad-Padashahi*, 61, 62, 72, 96.

125. Savarkar, *Hindu-Pad-Padashahi*, 65, 74.

> The Hindus reached Attock. For the first time since the dismal day when Prithviraj fell, a triumphant Hindu flag waved proudly on the sacred river of the Vedas. The Hindu horse of victory drank the waters of the Indus, gazing fearlessly at himself as reflected in its crystal tides.[126]

Self-regard is here adduced as an essential marker of shedding the oppressive yoke.

In *Essentials of Hindutva*, Mother India too, as we may recall, likes to watch herself carefully and without haste. Here the "Hindu horse of victory" does the same, fearlessly. For all their differences, the two books, one slight, one close to 300 pages, have in common their mood. Both are feel-good books that reassure the Hindu community that their past contains victories, particularly against Muslims. *Hindu-Pad-Padashahi*, written when both Javalkar and Shejwalkar were criticizing the Peshwai, reassured the Marathi (Chitpavan Brahmin) community that they had much reason to be proud. The Marathas, Savarkar wrote,

> knew they had dealt a deathblow to the Moslem Empire in India. They knew that they had grown into an Asiatic power and that Poona had begun to be the centre, not merely of Indian, but of Asiatic politics. The Mogul Empire lay smashed at their feet: now they decided to sweep off all that still impeded them in taking the last and crowning step of openly assuming the imperial crown.[127]

Savarkar shows again his extraordinary eye for detail, names, events, battles, skirmishes, and wars, as he did in the book on 1857. And as in *Essentials*, he piles names upon names—Malharrao Holkar, Samsher Bahadur, Vithal Shivdeo, Manaji Dhaigude, Antaji Mankeshwar, Mane, Nimbalker, Bhau, Vishwasrao, Balaji, Damaji Gaikwad, Santoji Wagh—sometimes all on one page. It feels almost as if he were writing of past Maratha generals as his current contemporaries and intimates. True to his stated intention, the work attempts to put itself into the minds of its characters—all of them.[128] The book's final crescendo is the Maratha occupation of Delhi, in which, according to Savarkar,

> The Moslem crescent set, the banner of *Hindu-pad-padashahi* rose at last over the capital of the Indian Empire in spite of all that Pathans and the

126. Savarkar, *Hindu-Pad-Padashahi*, 89.
127. Savarkar, *Hindu-Pad-Padashahi*, 93.
128. Savarkar, *Hindu-Pad-Padashahi*, 102.

> Rohillas, the Moguls or the Turks, the Shaiks [*sic*] or the Sayads [*sic*], could do against it. Abdally [*sic*], with all the powerful allied forces of the Moslems, was but on the other bank of the Jumna and yet could do nothing to prevent it.[129]

Both Shejwalkar and Savarkar wrote of Panipat. For Shejwalkar it was a mistake, for Savarkar, a glorious martyrdom in which the Marathas would not concede to Abdali:

> Not a Maratha would vote for that: they would rather brave fearful odds, distressed and starved out though they were, and facing the foe fight in such a wise [*sic*] that even if they be not able to gain success for themselves they would yet render the success of their foe utterly futile to him. Amongst men of this temper stood Bhau like a pyramid of strength and unconquerable courage dauntlessly determined not to give in, not to do anything derogatory to the national honour of his people, but if the worst came to the worst to win—if not a success—yet at least such a defeat as would be a greater source of constant inspiration and pride and national glory generations of his people yet unborn than many a success could ever be.[130]

This is where Savarkar turns Panipat into a victory, not a pyrrhic one, or one which could have been avoided (as Shejwalkar argued), or where Maratha actions could be critiqued. It was not the Maratha Waterloo. It was a defeat that was better than success. Of Vishwasrao's death during the battle, Savarkar writes,

> The dying youth opened his princely eyes and in heroic accents replied: "Dear uncle, why tarry with me now? The battle may go against us while its commander is away." Even death's agony could not make that gallant young prince of Maharashtra forget his duty, his foremost thought was still of the battle, and his anxiety to win it even if after his death.[131]

Again, we see the use of melodramatic language, almost as if Savarkar were hoping that the romance and heroism would make up for the loss while influencing readers to take up Vishwasrao's mantle.

129. Savarkar, *Hindu-Pad-Padashahi*, 104.
130. Savarkar, *Hindu-Pad-Padashahi*, 117.
131. Savarkar, *Hindu-Pad-Padashahi*, 122.

Ahmad Shah Abdali is described as

> [t]rue to the traditions of a Pathan Conqueror, he even got angry and celebrated this assumption of the imperial dignity by ordering a ghastly general massacre of the citizens of Delhi for a few hours. In those few hours, not less than 18 thousand persons were put to the sword in cold blood.[132] Thence he started to vindicate his title as the defender of the Moslem Faith by devastating the sacred places and the holy cities of the Hindus.[133]

Bhau refuses to retreat and instead

> galloped forth into the very jaws of death. Mukund Shinde, seeing him desperate, ventured to hold his horse a while by the rein and humbly pressed, "Commander, thine had been a superhuman valour our men have done all that heroes humanly could do, but now it is wise to retire!" "What! Retire?" exclaimed Bhau. "General, seest thou not that Vishwas is dead and the flower of our army fallen on the field? General after general I called out by name and at *my* bidding fell fighting against the foes. How can I now leave the field and survive to show my face to Nanasaheb and my nation? Smite, smite, smite the foes unto death: this is my last command."[134]

Panipat can be turned into a victory because it ended the efforts of Muslims to work across frontiers:

> This was the last of the series of attempts the Indian Muhammadans made to save their Empire from the attacks of the Hindus by joining hands with their fierce co-religionist across the frontiers. *They* won the battle of Panipat, and in winning it they lost the last chance of either crushing the great Hindu power of the Maratha Confederacy or rescuing their Moslem Empire from the deathgrip with which they clutched at its throat.[135]

Panipat also features true Hindu heroes. Under Nanasaheb Peshwa,

> the Hindus reached the highest pinnacle of glory they ever attained for the last seven hundred years or so—ever since the fall of Prithviraj. He was

132. See Sarkar, *Fall of the Mughal Empire*, 2: 210–12. Savarkar is not far off the mark here. Sarkar estimates 28,000 dead on the battlefield, a further 10,000 deaths of noncombatants and in subsequent massacres, and 22,000 captured and enslaved. 50,000 horses were also lost.

133. Savarkar, *Hindu-Pad-Padashahi*, 85.

134. Savarkar, *Hindu-Pad-Padashahi*, 124.

135. Savarkar, *Hindu-Pad-Padashahi*, 128.

undoubtedly one of the greatest personalities—if not the greatest—of his time in the world.[136]

Where Shejwalkar saw a poor strategist, Savarkar saw one of the greatest leaders of his time.

We leave *Hindu-Pad-Padashahi* by pointing out that it contains many elements that we will see some forty years later in Savarkar's last work *Six Glorious Epochs,* where his initial, grudging romance with Hindu-Muslim unity and his disappointment at the sundered compact came full circle. The book is full of rage at how partition has undone India's fragile unity.

1857, Essentials of Hindutva, Hindu-Pad-Padashahi, and *Six Glorious Epochs*

Savarkar's four main prose works are intimately connected. In all of them, he frustrates the readerly expectation of an argument and conclusion. Conclusions are hidden in plain sight in his fiction or in his poetic writing. *Essentials of Hindutva* was written to persuade Hindus who thought of themselves not as Hindus but as Bengalis, Malayalis, Lingayats, Jains, or Marwadis that there were territorial, mythological, historical, and poetic reasons to think of themselves as Hindus. It is where Savarkar attempted to create an alert, aware Hindu national consciousness. Claire Wrigley has pointed out the pervasive use of the passive voice in *Essentials*: "The whole life of the nation '*was being* brought into a harmony,' Hindus '*were welded* into a nation,' and 'the term Hindu *has come to mean* much more than its geographical significance'" [emphasis Wrigley's]. The passive voice means that no specific agent engaged in the labor of welding; none was needed; Hindu consciousness is always already present.[137] In *Six Glorious Epochs,* however, that Hindu consciousness needed constant resuscitation.

When Savarkar wrote the book on 1857 (published in 1909) and *Essentials* (published in 1923), India's territorial boundaries were twenty years away from being settled, and any number of futures were possible, even as the British government continuously postponed independence with each act of reform

136. Savarkar, *Hindu-Pad-Padashahi,* 133.

137. Wrigley, "Subaltern Studies and Beyond" (presentation), quoting from Savarkar, *Essentials,* 42.

or imprisonment of Indian nationalists. In 1963, when *Six Glorious Epochs* was published, India and Pakistan had been independent and mutually hostile nations for sixteen years.

Savarkar ended his life and literary career writing about glorious warriors who represented a "golden" or successful page in India's history. This history, Savarkar insisted, had been stolen from Hindus by historians who had promoted a history of defeat and ignored crucial glorious Hindu moments. *Six Glorious Epochs* is full of raw emotion, unmediated by discipline, expressed in prose even more sentimental, melodramatic, and poetic than earlier works. Savarkar was not well when he wrote it. A lifetime of effort had come to a bitter end, though there were still a few bright spots. India always had, Savarkar argued, a defense strategy or a Hindu military policy that could be seen in the six epochs he was highlighting in his effort to correct the humiliating and incorrect histories written by traitorous Indian and foreign historians.[138] It is also worth noting that when the book was published in 1963, it was just after India had suffered a humiliating defeat on the China border in November 1962.

Six Glorious Epochs was written in Marathi, and Savarkar wanted to translate it into English, but his health was too poor. It was translated by S. T. Godbole instead, but Savarkar went through it word by word and approved the translation (from which I quote.) Nearly forty years after the publisher of *Hindu-Pad-Padashahi* directed readers' attention to Savarkar's prodigious archival work, Godbole did much the same. He tells us he added some references because Savarkar was too old to "stand the rigour of pin-pointing his references, voluminous as they were."[139] But we know that Savarkar never actually pin-pointed his references. Were the references added by Godbole all Savarkar's? We don't quite know, but Godbole made the book at least semischolarly. And since Savarkar approved the translation, we can assume that the prose in the body of the text was his, even if the scholarly scaffolding was not. This suggests that up to the end of his life Savarkar wanted in some respects to be viewed as an important—and genuine—historian, even as he scoffed at most of them. Godbole added footnotes, he said, to show readers that "the facts mentioned in this volume are fully backed by evidence."[140]

Given the title, we must ask what he meant by the term "epoch." He explained, albeit confusingly:

138. Savarkar, *Six Glorious Epochs*, 254–59. The chapter is titled "Hindu War Policy."
139. See Godbole, "A Word in Confidence," in Savarkar, *Six Glorious Epochs*.
140. Godbole, "A Word in Confidence," in Savarkar, *Six Glorious Epochs*.

> I mean the one from the history of that warlike generation and the brave leaders and successful warriors who inspire and lead it on to a war of liberation in order to free their nation from the shackles of foreign domination, whenever it has the misfortune to fall a prey to such powerful fatal aggression and to grovel abjectly under it, and who ultimately drive away the enemy making it an absolutely free and sovereign nation.[141]

An epoch, in short, had to feature a war of some kind.

The first four epochs are Chanakya-Chandragupta (Yavana-destroyer); Pushyamitra; Vikramaditya (Shaka-Kushan Menace); and Yashodharma (the Conqueror of the Huns), which are dispensed within a single chapter. Epoch five, which covers the Marathas, requires eighteen chapters because it traverses almost a millennium of war—a period of epic and endless battles between Hindus and Muslims. The last epoch, in which India is liberated from British rule, is a mere twenty pages. As in *Essentials*, Savarkar writes in short titled and numbered paragraphs that made it easy to reference himself and his work. The book is easy to dip into, packed with historical sound bites, and entertaining, if not always informative. Chapters are short, much of the writing is aphoristic and pithy, and the prose is always mixed in with poetry.

Let us take Attock, of great importance in Maharashtra as an example of the geographical extent to which the Marathas placed their flag. The twenty-second chapter is titled "Not Only Attock: Even Beyond it!" and begins with a numbered paragraph (1081) that is a poem by Prabhakar:

> Saradāra padaracē kasē kuṇi sinha
> jasē kuṇi śārdula gēṇḍē
> arē jyāniṁ Aṭakēnta pāva
> ghaṭakēnta rōvilē jhēṇḍē

> The sardars under him, some
> were lions, some were rhinos
> Within a ghatak [twenty-four
> minutes]they had planted
> their flags in Attock.[142]

The prose starts in the next paragraph, number 1084, which extolls the Marathas retaking of the fort in Attock in 1757 as the reclaiming of a major Indian boundary because it made the holy waters of the Indus available again to Hindus and horses. Why horses? For one thing, some 50,000 horses were lost in the Battle of Panipat (1761), and perhaps Savarkar recalled his own prose from *Hindu-Pad-Padashahi* where he had written, "The Hindu horse of victory

141. Savarkar, *Six Glorious Epochs*, 3.
142. Savarkar, *Six Glorious Epochs*, 449.

drank the waters of the Indus, gazing fearlessly at himself as reflected in its crystal tides."[143] This paragraph starts exultantly:

> On that glorious day at last was the ban of a 100 years enforced by the religious law of the Hindus themselves broken by the Hindu arms. Why, the Maratha warriors pursued the Muslims even beyond Attock upto Kandahar.

Then comes paragraph 1085, just one line: "It is already explained in paragraphs 522 to 535 how this town was named 'Attock' and why." We turn to 522 to find Savarkar writing that the ban on crossing Attock came about because of how the priestly community dealt with Muslim incursions into their territory:

> It should be told here that the ban on the crossing of the Attock, i.e., the injunction appearing in the later *smṛtis,* declaring it a sin to cross the Indus and to go over into the Muslim lands, *must* have been promulgated by our traditionalist priesthood with the sole intention of saving Hinduism.[144]

In paragraphs 523 and 524, he uses the same strategy to explain the ban on crossing the Indus.

> But it becomes clear from the historical facts mentioned above that it is only when the Hindu states beyond the Indus were liquidated, thousands of Hindus began to be violently converted to Islam by the devilish Muslims, who subjected the followers of other religions to harrowing persecution. The ban on crossing the Attock *must,* therefore, have been enforced owing to the helplessness caused by the lack of any armed support for the Hindus in those regions.

The "must" in this paragraph and the many others in *Six Glorious Epochs,* as Claire Wrigley notes, is a key strategy of his historiography and his dilemma that can "neither address fully nor silence completely the idea that there might be other interpretations of the events in question, and the awareness of this problem only emerges in moments of equivocation, which are followed by ever more strident justifications of Savarkar's own vision."[145] In paragraphs 526 and 528, Savarkar takes credit for bringing a verse in the *Bhaviṣyapurāṇa* to light for the first time, claiming that they were added after Mohammad Ghuri's

143. Savarkar, *Hindu-Pad-Padashahi,* 89.
144. Wrigley, "Subaltern Studies and Beyond" (presentation).
145. Wrigley, "Subaltern Studies and Beyond" (presentation).

invasion. The newly discovered verse lays out those new boundaries.[146] This may well be the case, since Savarkar's claim that *smṛti* writers were active, according to him, still appending new guidelines after Muslim invasions was accurate in the case of the *Bhaviṣyayapurāṇa.* Of the eighteen *Mahāpurāṇas,* the one purāṇa that was kept "up-to-date" by continuous additions of new rulers of India from the Muslims to British (called *Guruṇḍa*) was the *Bhaviṣyapurāṇa,* and Savarkar cited it in many of his writings.[147] But was there no injunction earlier? When was an addition added to the *Bhaviṣyayapurāṇa?* Perhaps Savarkar's fondness for the *Bhaviṣyayapurāṇa* had to do with the deliberate removal of all historical markers to additions, to maintain the conceit that it, like the other purāṇas transcended history. Now, consider paragraph 1,087, which has a heading almost as long as the paragraph itself: "**AND THIS ITSELF IS THE FIFTH GLORIOUS EPOCH OF HINDU VICTORIES OVER THE AGGRESSORS.**" The paragraph is just one sentence:

> The page in the history of the Hindu nation which records this unique event of the conquest of Attock and the final victory of the Hindus in the epic millennial Hindu-Muslim war and the establishment of the de facto sovereignty of the Hindus over the so-called Muslim empire is really the Golden Page in Hindu history and that day is truly the Red Letter Day in the life of Hindu nation![148]

Savarkar appears here to be shouting at us.

The first four and the sixth epoch together make up 147 pages of a 455-page book. The fifth epoch is where Savarkar unloaded a great deal of anger in his trademark poetic prose. Savarkar starts his discussion of the fifth epoch, all 800 years of it, by explaining the problems with previous histories—all of them:

> The histories written not only by foreign historians or those who are avowedly inimical to us, but even by our own people, ignore the glorious episodes of exceptional valour and monumental successes of the Hindus and in their stead, catalogue only the calamities that befell them and present them as the only true history of the Hindus, because they were never fearlessly written from the *pure and simple Hindu standpoint.* . . . Generally

146. Savarkar, *Six Glorious Epochs,* 206, 207.

147. I am grateful to Madhav Deshpande for his explanation about the *Bhaviṣyayapurāṇa* and why it is that Savarkar might have referred to it so often.

148. Savarkar, *Six Glorious Epochs,* 451.

> speaking in all histories, especially in the history text books used in schools . . . a pupil, catches an impression which is very often carried even in his later life, that the history of the Hindus is nothing but a doleful tale of foreign subjugation and national defeats. Our enemies have publicized these false impressions as established facts all over the world for the last two or three centuries [emphasis mine].[149]

History, in other words, could only be the history of war and victory, neither the Orientalist history that dwells solely on defeat and failure, nor histories borne of Indian self-loathing and critique.

We see clearly here how Savarkar's view of history was not just bombastic but required the taking of sides; as such, Indian history could only be penned by Hindu propogandists. Versions of this sentiment appear throughout the book. We are told that a "true historian, whose avowed duty is to tell the truth, the whole truth and nothing but the truth, should effectively and proportionately describe the intervals between any two Muslim invasions and the heroic resistance, successful or otherwise, offered by the Hindus."[150] Among those who have failed this charge is B. R. Ambedkar, whom Savarkar describes as "a man . . . burning with hatred against Hinduism," who wrote that the history of Hindus "has been a life of a continuous defeat. It is a mode of survival of which every Hindu will feel ashamed."[151] By now, Savarkar's admiration of Ambedkar, which we saw in the chapter on caste, had ended.

Epoch number five begins with Hindus' abundant enemies. Traitors lurk in corners ready to visit atrocities upon Hindus, Hindu women, and Hindu children, and *Six Glorious Epochs* finds them everywhere, starting with Buddhists,

> who were elated to see the Muslim foreigners march against the Hindu kingdom. These Buddhists, who bore malice towards the Hindus, perhaps thought that these new Muslim aggressors might embrace their Buddhist cult . . . [152]

"Buddhist high treason" and the "Fanatic Buddhist Ahimsa" combined with ahimsa-fanatics like the Jain king Kumarapala, who confiscated the property

149. Savarkar, *Six Glorious Epochs*, 131.
150. Savarkar, *Six Glorious Epochs*, 145.
151. Savarkar, *Six Glorious Epochs*, 131.
152. Savarkar, "The Buddhist Traitors" in *Six Glorious Epochs*, 133–34.

of a merchant who killed a louse in his hair and built a temple to this "martyred" louse and named it "Yukvihar." Among the first Hindu victims, we are told, were millions of people so fed up with Buddhist fanaticism that they "shook off its tyrannical yoke, and sought refuge in the Vedic religion, which had now taken an all-embracing noble form . . ."[153] Savarkar abandons his critique of śāstris sitting around writing useless treatises and turns instead to the Vedas and the Vedic pandits now as protectors of Hinduism. To give the work the patina of scholarship, his translator gives us a citation to a fourteenth-century Sanskrit work titled "Kumarapala-charita" composed by Jayasimha and corroborated by Vincent Smith's *Early History of India*. A hunt through the bibliography gives us R. C. Majumdar's 1950 work *An Advanced History of India*.

Many of the claims he made about Muslims in previous works are repeated even more virulently. And despite his earlier admiration for Ambedkar, Savarkar now goes after the Buddhists for having worsened untouchability without naming Ambedkar specifically: "Even historians seem to be labouring under the delusion that the Buddhists did not recognize the principle of untouchability and that no one was considered untouchable in the Buddhist regime." The Buddhists imposed ahimsa with such violence and imposed such harsh punishments on meat eaters and hunters with the result that "the practice of untouchability instead of being wiped out became still more firmly rooted, widespread and most distressing."[154]

Halfway through the fifth epoch, we get another glimpse of the idiosyncratic historical etymology that so fascinated Savarkar. He muses that that the word *musal* was a Puranic pun on the word *mousal* that described Arab traders.[155] From this starting point, off he goes! Yadavas had established a colony in Arabia; Tamil was originally called "Aravi;" aboriginal Arabs (it is not clear what he means by this) were Shaivites, and their priests were called "druid" (*draviḍa*). This chain of associations lets him suggest that imperializing Hindus had gotten as far as modern-day Ireland and England.[156] The Chinese

153. Savarkar, "The Martyr Louse" in *Six Glorious Epochs*, 138, 139.

154. Savarkar, *Six Glorious Epochs*, 140

155. As Prachi Deshpande has shown, etymology was central to a historical understanding of origins, "turn[ing] words and their sounds and meanings into archives, enabling the imagination of particular linguistic as well as social pasts." *Scripts of Power*, 160. We also saw this in the caste chapter, from Jyotiba Phule to Rajaram Shastri Bhagwat to V. K. Rajwade.

156. Savarkar, *Six Glorious Epochs*, 259–61.

referred to the Hindus as "Shintsu," which confirmed for him that the word "Hindu" was derived from "Sindhu," which the Chinese could not pronounce.[157] These etymological flights of fancy continued his primary aim of reminding readers that the Hindus had once been a great empire.

These aspects reveal *Six Glorious Epochs'* fundamental lack of discipline. In the eighteen chapters of the fifth epoch, we leap across time, rushing forward to the Battle of Panipat only to scramble back to the ninth century. Because Savarkar followers understood him as a genius, neither they nor he thought he needed an editor. We read about Savarkar's unhappiness with Ambedkar once, and then again, several hundred pages later, when Savarkar praises South India for not having known any invasion by land or sea for about 1,500 years:

> And such a country like India, more than half of whose territory enjoyed such a glorious past, is derided by some half-crazy jealous historians, foreign as well as Indian, or by some Hindu-haters like Dr. Ambedkar or by some quite ignorant writers, so as to say, "Indian history from the beginning is a history of a slavish people, sunk deep into foreign bondage and constantly trampled under foreign heels."[158]

Savarkar does not mention any "half-crazy" or "jealous" historians (jealous of what, we don't know) other than B. R. Ambedkar.

But we should not write *Six Glorious Epochs* off as merely a late-in-life folly. It is a direct extension of Savarkar's previous work. In *Essentials of Hindutva,* Savarkar instructed his readers that the category "Hindu" is far more capacious than the internal divides of caste and region or subcaste and subregion might suggest. Without quite saying so, but by invoking consciousness and self-consciousness, he was suggesting that there was a shared Hindu consciousness. And by marching mythological characters up and down the fundamental territoriality of the "Hindu Nation," Savarkar turned "Hindu" into an internally imperializing category that included communities—Sikhs, Jains, and Buddhists—who did not consider themselves Hindus.

At the start of *Six Glorious Epochs,* Savarkar emphasizes what he laid out in *Essentials,* namely, the territorial fundamentalism that allows him to claim everything and everyone within it as Indian. But if *Essentials* was the recipe for Hindu consciousness, *Six Glorious Epochs* was its weaponized manifestation,

157. Savarkar, *Six Glorious Epochs,* 261.
158. Savarkar, *Six Glorious Epochs,* 281, 282.

which, along with Hindu consciousness, could lead to a national rejuvenation. The adage goes that a man with a hammer sees nails everywhere. "Rejuvenation" was Savarkar's hammer, and *Six Glorious Epochs* is based on the assumption that only an ever-present and self-conscious Hindu nation could be rejuvenated.[159] But we are left with a question. If India was always present, then why did she need so much rebirthing, revival, resurrection, rejuvenation, revival? One might imagine that Savarkar's "nation" had a narcoleptic sleep disorder.

What or who would jolt the nation out of its sleep? Rulers like Chandragupta Maurya, Pushyamitra Sunga, Vikramaditya, and Yashodharma who make up the four heroes of the first four epochs. However, the most perfect ruler and most glorious of all epochs was Shivaji Maharaj and the rise of the *Hindu-pad-padashahi*. Shejwalkar wrote essay after essay challenging this Chitpavan-pride-suffused inaccurate history and pointing out that the Peshwai had destroyed the promise of a *Hindu-pad-padashahi*. But Savarkar ignores Shejwalkar and praises G. S. Sardesai.

Herein lies *Six Glorious Epochs*' passion. It offers us historical agents, whether Hindu, Buddhist, or Sikh, who bravely defeat "superstitious," "crazy," and "stupid" Muslims, but these heroes occupy a slumbering nation that constantly needs a caffeine jolt or trumpet blast to awaken it. That is one problem. The other is caste. Even in a book that was trying to give good news, Savarkar can't avoid showing how Hindus kept turning on each other over minor issues, how fragile their unity was. Savarkar's rage becomes ever more intense as he deals with his sleepy Hindu nation and an internally fractious Hindu community. But there is a solution, and it is found in the links between *Six Glorious Epochs*, *Essentials of Hindutva*, *Hindu-Pad-Padashahi*, and the book about 1857. Self-conscious Hindus and the nation can reverse the processes of time and their torpor by abandoning caste and embracing violent resistance, not Gandhian nonviolent noncooperation.

Six Glorious Epochs is also a defensive tract about the Hindu Mahasabha, which had held itself aloof from Gandhi and the INC-led Quit India movement in 1942. Savarkar led the Hindu Mahasabha for five years, and he saw it as India's only decent political party because of its opposition to partition. For Savarkar, the Indian National Army (despite failing spectacularly and tragically) and Subhas Bose's alarming desire to ally with Mussolini, Hitler, and General Tojo were better strategies than Gandhi's nonviolent noncooperation.

159. Savarkar, *Six Glorious Epochs*, 132, 204.

Essentials is the bridge between his first "scientific" history of 1857 and his reprisal of persistent "newness" in *Six Glorious Epochs*. Rounding off the anti-academic position he adopted in *Essentials* and building on the numerous biographies of him that had been published, he was addressing the grand mass of "Hindu people." *Six Glorious Epochs* has a frenetic quality, as if Savarkar knew it was the last time he would get to explain that Hindus had been cheated of their due by Muslim court chronicles and Indian and British scholarship. Over and over, he shows how Hindus had been cheated—first by evil Muslims, then in narrative history by Muslims, the British, and treacherous Indians, and to top it all they cheated themselves by infighting and their obsession with *viṭāḷvēḍa*. Small wonder Savarkar appears both angry and tired in *Six Glorious Epochs*, leaving him no recourse but to write outside the conventions of ordinary history.

Savarkar largely departs from the kind of history Shejwalkar had spent the last thirty years molding, although he took care to show that he had command of all the evidence and understood what historians wrote. Right from the beginning, he dismisses formal history as inadequate to the task of memorialization. He literally takes the opposite position from Shejwalkar on the uses and abuses of history. History should be written as if it were a *povāḍā*, a genre meant for glorification. This is fully revealed near the end of the fifth epoch. The *povāḍā* was not just a source; it was an inspiration and a model for prose. "There is a border-land," Savarkar tells us, "between pure history and pure unalloyed poetry." "Human nature" he claimed, "demands that everything that is unique, everything that is stupendous and splendid and exciting, must be expressed in a highly emotional and ornate style." In this style, "history itself becomes poetry."[160] Savarkar goes on: history can be prose, but it should be "poetic prose, often bedecked with dazzling ornaments of simile, metaphor, and other figures of speech, as is the prince of princes adorned with the real ones."[161] Savarkar then writes that it was fitting that the "very first quatrain by the very first poet should be born of a highly exciting sentiment which could never be conveyed in simple words?" His reference was to Valmiki's Rāmāyaṇa and the *ślōka* (verse); prose history was adequate to describe failure, as in his work on 1857, but incapable of describing epochal glory.

Although the book carries on many of the themes of Savarkar's earlier work, he expresses a new and different view of the emperor Akbar, increases his

160. Savarkar, *Six Glorious Epochs*, 403–4.

161. Savarkar, *Six Glorious Epochs*, 404.

exultation about Hindu war policy, and takes time to ruminate about his own life. To reframe his picture of Akbar, he begins with the famous siege of Chittor.

> It was the same heartless Akbar who caused such a great havoc amongst the Hindus, but whom the spineless Hindu historians of today call the most liberal of monarchs; the one, they say, who yearned to bring about amity between, and unity of, the Hindus and Muslims; the one, in their opinion, who treated the Hindus far more honourably than any Muslim ruler before or after him; who was according to them, a veritable Raja Ramchandra amongst the Muslims!

This was nonsense, according to Savarkar, because

> as if not content [with] this bloodcurdling sacrifice of men, women and children of Chitod, Akbar entered the blood-stained city of Chitod, put to sword every one of the bewailing Hindu citizens that remained there . . . Only after quenching his fiendish fanaticism a little with such an inhuman destruction of the Hindu capital of Chitod did this Muslim emperor Akbar return to India calling himself "Gazi" for this virtuous and pious act of his.[162]

No longer a "good" Muslim, Akbar could no longer be differentiated from Aurangzeb as he had been in *Essentials*.

Savarkar writes that contrary to what ignorant historians had written, Akbar "was as fanatical and as fiercely inimical to Hinduism and the Hindu nation as was either Allauddin or Aurangzeb."[163] The European writers who wrote well of Akbar, Savarkar calls sly, the Hindu ones slavish. "This eulogy," Savarkar declared, "is utterly false." Hindus, he said, had to choose between showing "respect, gratitude and affection for Rana Pratap or for his dire enemy, Akbar. . . . How can we worship God and the devil at the same time?"[164] Savarkar admits that Akbar wielded great power, founded a vast empire, and patronized arts and culture, but he ends by reminding us that "with all that greatness, he was, from our Hindu point of view, foreign, belonging to another religion and mean minded and as such he should be decried by us, Hindus!" Nativism overrode all other criteria for judging historical actors.

162. Savarkar, *Six Glorious Epochs*, 382, 383.
163. Savarkar, *Six Glorious Epochs*, 400.
164. Savarkar, *Six Glorious Epochs*, 400.

The chapter on Hindu war policy does exactly what he had earlier suggested Hindus not do: read ancient sacred literature literally. Mythological beings like *daityas*, *danavs*, and *rakshasas* become "the cruellest, most atrocious and cunning cannibals of the time." In fighting them, his Hindu ancestors produced a war policy that turned them "more atrocious, more deceptive and cunning, and far crueller" than their enemies,[165] a cruelty Savarkar celebrates. He invokes the Rāmāyaṇa, saying that when "Ram was shown at various places the heaps of bones of Rishis whose blood those cannibals had drunk and whose flesh they had eaten,"[166] he approved, which showed that "at that time those gods and godlike emperors, too, considered it the holiest religious duty to show [s]uper savage cruelty to beat down the cruelty of the Rakshasas, to be arch devils against the devils!"[167] Those looking for a fuller explanation are directed to previous paragraphs in which Savarkar narrates the story of Shurpanakha, who along with a fellow Rakshasin, Tratika, was killed by Ram and Laxman. Why, we might ask? The answer is that "[w]hen Shoorpanakha, another she-demon, rushed to eat away Seeta like cucumber, Laxman deprived her of nose and ears and sent her back—not honourably with generous gifts of ornaments to show off his chivalry to women."[168]

In another example of valor and chivalry, we get this:

> When Narakasur carried away thousands of Aryan women to his Asur kingdom [Assyria of today], Shree Krishna marched upon the demon and killed him in the war. But he did not stop with the military and political defeat he inflicted on Narakasur! He rescued all the thousands of imprisoned Aryan females, undergoing all sorts of humiliation there, and brought them back to his own kingdom; and thus took a social revenge. Shree Krishna's army did not forsake their kinswomen, simply because they were forcibly polluted and violated—a dastardly thought which he never entertained for a minute.[169]

Setting aside the question of how Savarkar could get into the mindset of a mythical character, we see that his main point was that revenge should be taken a thousandfold for any slight to the Hindu nation:

165. Savarkar, *Six Glorious Epochs*, 254.
166. Savarkar, *Six Glorious Epochs*, 256.
167. Savarkar, *Six Glorious Epochs*, 255.
168. Savarkar, *Six Glorious Epochs*, 182.
169. Savarkar, *Six Glorious Epochs*, 182.

> . . . whenever the Hindus gained an upper hand, they *could have* retaliated by massacring Muslim population and making the region Muslim-less! Devoid of Muslims![170]

They could have, and they should have:

> Ahimsa, kindness, chivalry even towards the enemy women, protection of an abjectly capitulating enemy Kṣamā Vīrasya Bhūṣaṇām (forgiveness, a glorious emblem for the brave!) and religious tolerance were all virtues no doubt—very noble virtues! But it is blind and slovenly—even impotent—adoption of all these very virtues, irrespective of any consideration given to the propriety of time, place or persons that so horribly vanquished them in the millennial Hindu Muslim war on the religious front.[171]

Savarkar elaborates on this point in a chapter that reveals its argument in the title—"Perverted Conception of Virtues." He identifies what he called a "suicidal morbidity" that had "completely possessed the Hindu mind for a long time" and "paralyzed their own offensive and counter offensive might."[172] Hindus had misunderstood the essence, he wrote, of the maxim that one should feed the poor and hungry; even worse, they had been made to understand, almost from birth, religious tolerance as a virtue. These were ideas they needed to rid themselves of so that they could retaliate at a level of a thousand to one. When Mahmud of Ghazni raided Somanath, for instance, the Hindu king should have "wiped out of existence all the masjids without exception, as soon as he conquered the land. . . ."[173] We contrast this with Gandhi's famous injunction that an eye for an eye makes the whole world blind. Better blind than unavenged, Savarkar would argue.

So strongly did Savarkar feel about this that even Chhatrapati Shivaji comes in for some rare questioning. He too had fallen prey to this "perverted virtue": "Even now we proudly refer to the noble acts of Chhatrapati Shivaji and Chimaji Appa, when they honorably sent back the daughter-in-law of the Muslim Governor of Kalyan and the wife of the Portuguese governor of Bassein respectively." Instead of praising them, why did the chroniclers not remember, Savarkar asks, the rapes and molestations of thousands of Hindu women in earlier periods? He continues melodramatically, "Did not the plaintive screams

170. Savarkar, *Six Glorious Epochs*, 185.
171. Savarkar, *Six Glorious Epochs*, 187.
172. Savarkar, *Six Glorious Epochs*, 167.
173. Savarkar, *Six Glorious Epochs*, 171.

and pitiful lamentations of the millions of molested Hindu women, which reverberated throughout the length and breadth of the country, reach the ears of Chhatrapati Shivaji and Chimaji Appa?"[174] Note that in just one paragraph the number of molested women rises from a thousand to millions. This is another of Savarkar's preferred rhetorical tactics—he takes an actual event, misrepresents it, then casts it as part of a continuous history of molestation to ask the present to avenge the past. When history is converted thus to memory, the entirety of the past becomes simultaneous with the present and must be acted upon as such. In this case, it would be

> [t]he souls of those millions of aggrieved women might have perhaps said, "Do Not forget, O, your Majesty, Chhatrapati Shivaji, and O! your Excellency, Chimaji Appa the unutterable atrocities and oppression and outrage committed on us by the Sultans and Muslim noblemen and thousands of others, big and small, let those Sultans and their peers take a fright that in the event of a Hindu victory our molestation and detestable lot shall be avenged on the Muslim women. Once they are haunted with this dreadful apprehension, that the Muslim women, too, stand in the same predicament in case the Hindus win, the future Muslim conquerors will never dare to think of such molestation of Hindu women.[175]

Next, Savarkar defends the Peshwas in a passage that suggests he might have been writing a rejoinder to Shejwalkar:

> Those, who ignorantly, or maliciously blame the Peshwas for the evil treatment given to the untouchables when they entered the town, should also criticize, equally vehemently and for the same offence Asoka, Shree Harsha and Buddhist kings . . . and in the Buddhist period especially instead of being weakened it was most scrupulously and mercilessly observed.

And, in a clear reference to Ambedkar, he writes that "[t]he Buddhists once again I should like to repeat, aggravated and not mitigated 'Untouchability.'"[176]

Savarkar concludes this section by recommending his own book.

> Looking at it, as impersonally as it is possible to do so, this one of all the extant books on the history of this period appears even to me as the most

174. Savarkar, *Six Glorious Epochs*, 179.
175. Savarkar, *Six Glorious Epochs*, 179.
176. Savarkar, *Six Glorious Epochs*, 140, 141.

> stimulating, most searching and teeming with the national spirit imbued with Hindutwa . . . My book [*Hindu-Pad-Padashahi*] is really the golden temple of the survey and appraisal of that great war . . . [177]

Savarkar also takes a final shot at Rajwade, who got much right, but also much wrong. He had failed to understand the importance of Maratha history in India's national history, and "[h]is incidental and desultory discourses on the subject appear, by the very nature of their topics, incomplete and inconsistent." Savarkar is at pains to point out that he had bested the great historians, from Jadunath Sarkar to Sardesai to Rajwade, noting that his book was not only based on solid evidence but "interesting to read."[178] Savarkar gets close to historians only to recoil from the actual work they do. He mentions them but does not engage with their arguments or evidence. Savarkar only refers to individual historians when they agree with him. Those he disagrees with, apart from B. R. Ambedkar, are left unnamed.

The impression that *Six Glorious Epochs* leaves is that it was not written to persuade but rather to provide ammunition for the persuaded to use and to counter every argument including those that criticize Savarkar. When, for example, secular historians described Akbar's liberal policies, a quick look at the index would direct a reader to a paragraph that would counter that argument. If someone suggests that Savarkar was not a historian, his translator has put in all kinds of references, and in the body of the text, there is Savarkar conspicuously meeting Sardesai, already renowned in Maharashtra as a great historian.

And so Savarkar set a pattern to insulate himself from any criticism. This strategy continues today, as we will see in the final chapter.

Conclusion

Shejwalkar was clear; writing history was not for everyone or anyone, and it required a lifelong dedication to research. He warned that

> the vogue of copying, imitating and adapting is current. This results in circulating the error in a wider area which later on comes to be called a universally accepted fact. Many scholars throughout the length and breadth of India are now-a-days trying to utilize the Marathi material and weaving it

177. Savarkar, *Six Glorious Epochs*, 412.
178. Savarkar, *Six Glorious Epochs*, 412.

> into the thread of their histories. An aggressive occupation of the historical field is going on before our eyes.[179]

His attention to discipline, by which he meant the protocols of using archival evidence and careful historical exposition, was intended to "fix the attention of readers on facts."[180]

Whether Shejwalkar read Savarkar or not, he was surely aware both of him and of the tendency to hijack the historical record for polemical arguments, whether he might agree with them or not. He was clear that real history should not be written by poets. Of course, that is exactly what Savarkar contested in his intentional admixture of the poetic, the historical, and the fictional. Arguments and conclusions were displaced by him because political memory was what he was most interested in, not history qua history. Through his strategic use of unstructured, unperiodized, untemporalized time, and an equally strategic use of anachronism, Savarkar produced a presentist conception of the Hindu nation and put it back in time. His belief that he could shape history meant that the historical act—a battle, a decision—had no intrinsic capacity to enter the record but was left for Savarkar, the recorder, for whom the sole purpose of the past was to produce a future.[181] For these two Maharashtrian Brahmins, history existed in entirely different keys. And despite the importance of Shejwalkar's work for the establishment of historiographical standards in the writing of history, it was Savarkar who not only was much more widely read but accumulated followers for whom the poet became the personal embodiment both of history and of a glorious future. And that is what we examine in the last chapter.

179. Shejwalkar, *Panipat: 1761* (English edition), 7.

180. Shejwalkar, *Panipat: 1761* (English edition), 7.

181. I am grateful to Sudipta Kaviraj for his comments on this chapter and his discussion with me about Koselleck and Machiavelli, in particular the conception of untemporalized time as marking the difference between the writing of modern and premodern history.

6

A Legend in His Own Time

SAVARKAR AND HIS HAGIOGRAPHY

IN THIS FINAL CHAPTER, I tackle an unwieldy biographical literature, written primarily by Savarkar's followers, that is in some fundamental respects derivative of his own memoirs, much more in the manner of embellishment than of correction or revision, let alone critique. This literature floats below the radar of the scholarly literature on Savarkar in English. In thinking through how Savarkar has been mythologized, I came to understand that this literature makes up an important corpus, not least because it includes some 250 books, mostly in Marathi. Of the many English works on Savarkar, none have attempted to analyze or even characterize this large Marathi biographical literature, even if some use it to cross-check dates or events or to corroborate other accounts. Yet this literature is far more than a set of primary sources with which to only verify dates and events; rather, it serves to bring attention to and emphasize Savarkar's contribution to modern Indian history. There is a palpable sense of resentment throughout these works about the way that the canonic nationalist figures—Gandhi and Nehru—have displaced Savarkar's rightful place in India's history. The neglect of this corpus has meant that the space Savarkar occupies in the everyday Marathi imagination and the passion with which he is defended and mythologized has rarely been considered seriously. It is this gap that I will begin to fill in this chapter, as I round off my examination of the three-part mythologization of Savarkar, through his poetry, his histories, and this biographical literature.

These biographies are themselves proof of his continued mythologization because most of these books are written as homage-biographies or praise books. They are all available in the Swatantryaveer Savarkar Rashtriya Smarak (Savarkar National Memorial) in Bombay, although the librarian who comes to the Smarak every evening for a few hours does not organize them in any order.[1] Many are unavailable in academic libraries, but there are also books in this collection that are more commonly available.

Some of the authors hold faculty positions at universities, usually in academic disciplines far afield from English or history, such as Sheshrao More, an engineer and the author of two books on Savarkar. Still others have doctoral degrees and are eminent university faculty, such as Sha Na Navalgundkar, former Pro-vice-chancellor at Pune University. Some are written by organic intellectuals, others by those who for different reasons felt compelled to write another biography because they saw or met Savarkar once or held him in high regard. A few were written while Savarkar was alive, and some of the authors consulted him. Savarkar's son (Vishwas) and secretary (Shantaram Shivram, aka Balarao) wrote biographies of him.[2] Most were written as long obituaries when he died or ten years later to memorialize him. Some deal with his writings on social justice, others with his political thought, still others with his literary works. As for the books themselves, they range in length and type enormously; some are short ten-page tracts, others four-hundred-page volumes, and many somewhere in between. In addition to the numerous biographies, there are Marathi plays, children's books, *povāḍās*, poems, and graphic novels.

Savarkar's own memoirs are the foundation on which this corpus is built. While the collection of his writings fills ten large volumes, most of what he penned consists of poems, plays, histories, articles, and speeches. Very little of his writing is straightforwardly autobiographical, and much of that is repetitive. The narrative of Savarkar's English biography only goes up to the point of his trial for sedition and treason in 1910. He began serializing his biography under the title *Mājhyā āṭhavaṇī* (My recollections) between 1928 and 1930, with some parts published in a Bombay-based magazine called *Hutatma Shraddhanand*. Divided into two parts—about Bhagur and Nasik—the focus is on his early years, and there are few details about his time in London (for obvious reasons: he wrote under police surveillance; he had promised to desist from political activities; and he would not have wanted to give them any more evidence than they already had of his revolutionary activities). Because he had been released on the condition that he not engage in any political work or

1. To belong to the Smarak, you have to be vetted for your fealty to Savarkarite ideology. The Smarak has a president, a board of trustees, and members. When I did my research there, I only had to say that I was writing a book on Savarkar and was interested in learning more about him.

2. Savarkar, Vishwas, *Athavani angaracya*; Savarkar, Balarao, *Hindusamaj Sanrakshak*; Savarkar, Bal, *Yogi yoddha vidasa*.

writing, the police came to his house in Ratnagiri and looked through the house specifically in search of his *ātmavṛtta* (autobiography) and told him expressly that he was not to write it anymore.[3] What we have as his memoirs qua memoirs is therefore quite limited. But precisely because of these limits they have an exalted status.

Because of continued police surveillance and his identification as dangerous by both the colonial and national state, and the conditions of his house arrest, he was never as accessible as most of his contemporaries, including Gandhi, who was allowed to write his autobiography in prison. And despite the proliferation of biographical and related forms of writing about Savarkar, we learn very little that is new about his actual life. What we get instead are multiple exemplifications of what I am calling *darśana-dakṣiṇā* literature. *Darśana* means a visit to a sacred shrine of a deity, as well as just being in the presence of a spiritual figure, and *dakṣiṇā* is a form of homage, a form of prestation given to one's spiritual leader. The *darśana-dakṣiṇā* literature provides a distinct and yet extremely influential portrait of him that has contributed to Savarkar's ongoing mythologization and sacralization.[4]

After 1948, when he was acquitted of aiding in Gandhi's assassination for lack of actionable evidence, Savarkar lived in virtual seclusion, constantly battling ill health, with only a tiny circle of friends and associates around him. Access to him was therefore much coveted by his followers. The *darśana-dakṣiṇā* literature augments this narrative of unreachability while simultaneously offering his followers vignettes of his everyday life and how he spent his time. In this mode, the witnessing function (*pratyakṣa*) expressed in the phrases "I was there" or "I saw him once" or "I asked him once" or "I was fortunate to spend many days in his company" lends an authority much like that of having had a moment of *darśana*. The witnessing validates the biographer as true devotee who then revalidates the subject's otherworldliness. This literature also humanizes Savarkar the idol, showing him smiling or laughing at a question. It offers affectionate memories of his eccentricities and foibles as *dakṣiṇā*, while insisting that every small detail about Savarkar is valuable, including factoids like Savarkar's fondness for snuff, the way he wore his dhoti, or that he never betrayed any anger no matter the question posed to him.[5] Each detail presents another facet of the secular deity Savarkar has become.

3. Salvi, *Swatantryaveer Savarkarancya Sahavasat*, 37.

4. A perfect example of such guru-*dakṣiṇā* is Bapat, *Smrutipushpe*.

5. Gokhale, *Savarkaransi Sukhasanvada*, 3.

From this collection, I select a few memories that offer a slightly more fleshed-out image of Savarkar than we otherwise have, even as they also provide a window through which to look at the men and women who held (and still hold) him dear. Who were they, and why would a single act of kindness or attention generate such reverence? Many of the men who recount their memories of Savarkar tell of being arrested and imprisoned for their activities. For them, their one- or three-year sentences were utterly insignificant when compared to the two-life-term sentence that was handed to Savarkar. Many hail from small villages and remember that only Savarkar bothered to pay their homes a visit and talk to them about nationalism. Gandhi returned from South Africa and reoriented the gaze of the cosmopolitan nationalist elite toward the villages; Savarkar's gaze, it is clear from these reminiscences, had never left the people who lived in villages and small towns. They were his base, and they did not waver in their loyalty to him because Savarkar's politics themselves emerged from rural Maharashtra.[6] Along with the kinds of histories Savarkar wrote and authorized, it is these biographies and the *darśana-dakṣiṇā* literature that worked to keep Savarkar's legend alive even in the years when he was in complete isolation.

What sets them apart from works written about other nationalists, from Gandhi to Subhas Chandra Bose, is their defensiveness, and many of them are written in the form of an apologia. Endlessly repetitive, this corpus performs an anticipatory rehabilitative function, keeping the embers of his memory steadfastly warm, ready—I suggest here—to conjure him as a new nationalist hero as soon as his time came, as surely it would. Indeed, very little rehabilitation was needed given that these works built and reinforced a heroic Savarkar and his interpretation of Indian history as Hindu history constituting a persistent, if at times almost subterranean, infrastructure of political thought and historical consciousness in Maharashtra.[7] There was always the sense in Maharashtra that, when the time was right, Savarkar would return to national prominence as the progenitor of a Hindu nationalist understanding.

The books on Savarkar are written as biographies, though as a distinct kind of life history that had as much to do with Indic traditions around *darśana* and *dakṣiṇā* as with Thomas Carlyle's sense of the need to worship a hero. Modern biographies seek to humanize great figures as in the mode of biographers such as Robert Caro or Walter Isaacson, who acknowledge the genius of exceptional people while aiming both to keep the biographer out of *their* narratives and

6. I am grateful to Christian Novetzke for making this point so clearly.

7. I am grateful to Thomas Hansen for suggesting this analysis.

refusing to accept the subject's account of their own history. This was not the model for biography or autobiography in twentieth-century India. There were occasional exceptions, such as Pandita Ramabai's collection of autobiographical fragments compiled in a memoir titled *A Testimony of Our Inexhaustible Treasure* (published in 1907), which revealed the difficulty of her life and her journey to subsequent conversion to Christianity.[8] But by and large the biographies that commanded respect and admiration were English biographies, such as Lytton Strachey's biography of Queen Victoria, James Boswell's biography of Samuel Johnson, or John Morley's biography of William Ewart Gladstone. Marathi biographies that might have taken some part of their compositional mode from these English biographies focused on the exceptionality of the subject's life and work or the service rendered by them to the cause of social reform.[9] It would seem unthinkable in a period of anticolonial nationalism to pick a figure to write about only to produce a negative assessment of his or her contributions to society. Biographies did political work in the years of anticolonial nationalism, serving to publicize the work of heroes and to engage in what historians such as Pierre Nora have more recently called "memory work."[10]

Biographies and autobiographies also stayed connected—in form and prose style—to an earlier literary and poetic tradition, both in Sanskrit and Marathi. Alokeranjan Dasgupta notes that elements of what might be called the biographical and autobiographical can be found in the vast Sanskrit courtly epic literary corpus from Banabhatta's *Harsacarita* (seventh-century CE) to Kalhana's *Rajatarangini* (1148–50 CE).[11] In Marathi, one of the earliest works is the *Lilacharitra* (1278 CE), which can be considered in equal measure an ethnography, a hagiography, and a biography of the founder of the Mahanubhav sect, Chakradhar Swami, written by his disciple, Mhaimbhat.[12] From

8. See Kosambi, *Pandita Ramabai*. Ramabai also published a long essay on the plight of Hindu women titled "The High Caste Hindu Woman" (1887) that expands on her earlier work in 1882, titled *Stree-Dharma-Niti*.

9. See Satchidanandan, "Reflections: Thinking of Autobiography." Wives of prominent reformers such as Anandibai Karve or Ramabai Ranade, or women such as Hansa Wadkar or Durga Khote who pursued unconventional careers in professions like acting or theater that were not considered reputable, published their life stories.

10. Nora, *Realms of Memory*, 2–4, 10–11.

11. Dasgupta, "Biography: A Māyā?"

12. On whether the *Lilacharitra* can be read as a biography or an ethnography of its time, and for a history of its composition, see Kolte's preface to *Mhaimbhat Sankalit Lilacharita*. See also Novetzke, *Quotidian Revolution*, ch. 7, for why Novetzke calls the *Lilacharitra* a biography.

the *Lilacharitra* in the thirteenth century, there has been in Maharashtra a continuous literary output focused primarily on saintly poets that contains elements of the biographical and hagiographical. In the eighteenth century, as the story goes, a devotee of Tukaram by the name of Mahipati received Sant Tukaram's order in a dream to write the biographies of saints. This he proceeded to do in several Marathi works: the *Santalilamrit* in 1757, *Bhaktavijaya* in 1762, *Kathasaramrita* in 1765, *Bhaktalilamrit* in 1774, and last, the unfinished *Santavijaya*.[13] In the nineteenth century, biographical poems continued to be composed (in Sanskrit and Marathi) about Chhatrapati Shivaji and other kings of the Bhonsle dynasty but also about memorable queens (Ahilyabai Holkar of Indore).[14] And saints remained the subjects of biographical poems in Sanskrit as well, including the *Gurucharita*, the *Sri-Gurusamhita*, and the *Dattalilamritabdhisara*.[15]

Alokeranjan Dasgupta distinguishes between the overly florid and panegyrical Sanskrit works that contain little genuinely biographical information and the saintly and confessional biographies, which are much more accessible to everyday people, not least because these saint-composed poems are heartrendingly lyrical. Dasgupta addresses this multilingual corpus, from the poems of Kabir to the *abhangas* of Tukaram, and points out that several biographies are, as he puts it, democratically motivated, that is, representative of the voice of the everyday Marathi man. In these works, "peoples' cravings take a palpable shape not in the form of escape but of a kind of collective projection."[16]

Savarkar's own interest in writing a biography of himself emerges from this hybrid Marathi and Sanskrit, English and anticolonial, and regional and national milieu of the late nineteenth and early twentieth century. Long before Savarkar was memorialized, both his mentor (Tilak) and his nemesis (Gandhi) had been turned into subjects of rousing biographies. In 1913, two years after Savarkar had been removed to the Andamans, the first Marathi biography of Gandhi, eulogizing his actions in South Africa for the Indian

13. See Abbott and Godbole, *Stories of Indian Saints*, xxvii.

14. Dandekar, *Sanskrit and Maharashtra*, 68–69.

15. See Chitrav, *Bharatvarsiya Pracina*, 28. Chitrav compiled a a bibliography of biographies of characters from Vedic, epic, and Puranic literature. Both Tilak and Savarkar were the subjects of biographical poems. M. S. Aney composed *SriTilakayasornava*, which contained eighty-five cantos and more than 11,000 stanzas on Tilak's career, while S. B. Varnekar wrote *Vinayakavaijayanti* in 1958 and an epic opus of sixty-eight cantos on Chhatrapati Maharaj. Dandekar, *Sanskrit and Maharashtra*, 68, 69.

16. Dasgupta, "Biography: A Māyā?," 161.

minority community, was written by Tukaram Thakur.[17] It was soon followed by others, in 1914 and 1918, and by the time Savarkar was brought back, there were more. Given the colonial context, almost all (auto)biographies were imagined as the autobiography of the nation, exemplified in the life of the hero.[18]

The same period also produced an unprecedented publication of encyclopedias, dictionaries, and collections in Marathi. S. V. Ketkar labored for twelve long years to produce twenty-three volumes of his *Maharashtriya Dnyanakosha*, setting in motion what B. S. Bhole has called a veritable *kōśayuga* (age of encyclopaediae).[19] Ketkar's objective was to release knowledge about Maharashtra from the stranglehold of the pandits (*paṇḍitavarga*) and make it readily available to the general public.[20] The result of all this activity was that even as scholars from Rajwade to Shejwalkar tried to plant the discipline of history and biography firmly in the soil of evidence-based narratives, the fields had already been ploughed by a different and much more hagiographical impulse. With this mindset in place, anyone who was so inclined could write a history or biography of a famous figure—and they often did. As a result, the works I address in this chapter, including Savarkar's (auto)biography, followed certain generalized features of mythologization and hagiography.

In the previous chapter, we read Savarkar's conviction that only genuinely historical people should be written about, Chhatrapati Shivaji and Generals Kruger and Washington, for instance. Savarkar put himself in the same category, as did a historian of regional repute like G. S. Sardesai, who claimed he merely wrote history, but Savarkar made it.[21] Savarkar appreciated Sardesai's declaration, but he had not waited for it, having long deemed himself a born leader, and an important historical figure for India. A pseudonymous biography of Savarkar was published in 1926; did Savarkar write it himself? Perhaps. Or perhaps he wrote it with an associate, V.V.S. Aiyar. Savarkar might have chosen to remain anonymous to allay colonial suspicion about his activities or to generate precisely the conversation that occurred, with people asking if Savarkar wrote it, dictated it to an associate, or asked an associate to write it,

17. Bhole, *Visavya satakatila*, xvi–xvii.

18. Boehmer, "The Hero's Story."

19. Bhole, *Visavya Shatakatil*, xix.

20. Savarkar's biographer A. G. Salvi wrote of his experience of hearing two intellectual giants, Ketkar and Savarkar, at their meeting in Ratnagiri. "Ketkar was a real Pandit. Just like him Savarkar's reading on Indian civilization was also deep. . . . I am grateful that I had the good fortune to listen to these encyclopaedic conversations." Salvi, *Savarkar Yancya Athvani*, 20–21.

21. Savarkar, *Six Glorious Epochs*, 408.

or if someone associated with him wrote it independently and secretly.[22] Whatever the case, at a minimum it tells us that rather than leave his legacy to others, Savarkar managed the interface between his writings about himself and others' writings about him.

Both his own writing and the Marathi writings that followed him employed biography for the purposes of hagiography, in contrast to the modern genre of biography. Savarkar and his followers wrote in a Puranic (post-Vedic epic mythological) form but in a secular vein, intermingling features of hagiography and secularity. In the hagiographic mode, the subject is presented as a much-maligned figure whose life was tragic, who underwent a sequence of ever-increasing hardship, and who emerges wounded and almost transcendent. Signs of his or her exceptionality emerge early, as early as from birth, sometimes gleaned from the astrological chart, the horoscope (*janmakuṇḍalī*), reminiscent of the signs Brahmins saw when the Buddha was born suggesting that this was no ordinary man. He was, instead, an emulatable man. Despite all these spiritual trappings, Savarkar also presented himself as decidedly secular, a worldly rationalist. What this meant was that hagiographic biographers revered his rationalism and nationalism, along with his so-called progressivism, anticasteism, and simple lifestyle. Once Savarkar had essentially turned the figure of the nation into a female goddess, then her worship fulfilled both a secular and a sacred function and readers could derive spiritual sustenance from nationalist and patriotic activities. As for the rage and anger at Muslims we saw in previous chapters, that was simply set aside, either because it was seen as unexceptional or, for that matter, embarrassing (though there is no evidence of this).

In his magisterial work on European literary criticism, Eric Auerbach distinguished between two equally ancient and epic narrative styles: the Homeric and the Biblical, which he further distinguished in terms of the difference between the legendary and the historical.[23] Homeric heroes were (merely) legendary, whereas Biblical characters were historical. Auerbach pointed to the great figures of the Hebrew Bible, from Adam to the Prophets, who were chosen by God with the singular aim of "embodying his essence and will." It was a strange will, in that the main characters had little real control or choice over the tragedies that inevitably landed on them, as Abraham's terrible sacrifice demonstrates. For Auerbach, this drawn-out tragedy of a chosen life that has to undergo foundational challenges is why the figures in the Hebrew Bible

22. Chaturvedi, "A Revolutionary's Biography."
23. Auerbach, *Mimesis*, 14–18.

are historical, in stark contrast to the Homeric heroes. While the great Greek poets describe Achilles and Odysseus magnificently, neither in character or personality do we see any maturity or growth, and Auerbach writes that their "life-histories are clearly set forth once and for all."

Auerbach explains how to tell the legendary from the historical:

> Legend arranges its material in a simple and straightforward way; it detaches it from its contemporary historical context, so that the latter will not confuse it; it knows only clearly outlined men who act from few and simple motives and the continuity of whose feelings and actions remains uninterrupted. In the legends of martyrs, for example, a stiff-necked and fanatical persecutor stands over against an equally stiff-necked and fanatical victim.[24]

By contrast,

> Abraham, Jacob, or even Moses produce a more concrete, direct, and historical impression than the figures of the Homeric world . . . because the confused, contradictory multiplicity of events, the psychological and factual cross-purposes, which true history reveals, have not disappeared in the representation but still remain clearly perceptible.[25]

In the Marathi corpus, the historical and legendary coexist in the combination of the biographical and the *darśana-dakṣiṇā* literature.

The combination is most evident in the prefaces that detail the reason(s) the author decided to write about Savarkar despite knowing how many biographies already existed. These prefatory remarks offer a glimpse of Savarkar's charisma, and along with the vignettes, they humanize Savarkar's otherwise iconic and idolized persona. The biographies, with their repetition of Savarkar's trials, present us with a legendary hero; they also provide a glimpse of a human hero, replete with personal eccentricities, foibles, and idiosyncratic tics. Together, they reveal not just how but why Savarkar is (and should be) revered.

Without commenting on the truth of the story being told, my question here concerns how the reader is supposed to benefit from these books? Is the goal learning, admiration, or emulation? How does the author give himself authority and credibility? Moving from the author to the text, a different set of questions emerge. Historians, as Yori Lotman wrote, "are condemned to deal with texts." The relentlessly textual nature of our work requires us to engage whatever

24. Auerbach, *Mimesis*, 19.

25. Auerbach, *Mimesis*, 20.

relevant narratives we can find for the purposes of a larger understanding, narrative, and argument about the past outside the confines of any particular text. This is especially true of biographies, where crosschecking of dates and facts is a given, a disciplinary norm. In considering biographers, historians would normally inquire about why they assign so much importance to the figure. How do they compress or expand the concept of time and space? Which events recur? What is the argumentative standpoint of the text? Can it be separated from the author? None of these questions apply in the case of these Savarkar biographies. They all sing the same tune, in the same key and meter. Their tone is decidedly apologetic, with most authors seeking to ward off criticism, correct a misperception, or simply assert that Savarkar was uniquely victimized.

The corpus is also involuted, in that all the authors reference Savarkar's writings and poems and the few biographies written while he was alive, and many of the authors reference each other. Since this corpus has no internal organization, I have divided it into three sections: the first is Savarkar's writings, the second is biographies of him, and the third is *darśana-dakṣiṇā* literature. After the first category, I pick a few representative ones from the subsequent two to highlight and discuss.

In the first section, I look at Savarkar's (auto)biography and memoirs, which are distinct from his historical works, novels, plays, poetry, or speeches. In the second section, I look at biographies written by Savarkar's friends and associates. As I have argued elsewhere, Savarkar was the chief prophet of a spiritual nationalism, and to the extent that he was its modern high priest and the author of a secular Bible (*Essentials of Hindutva*, *Life of Barrister Savarkar*, and his memoirs), the authors of these biographies are like Savarkar's evangelists, spreading his gospel to as many people as possible. The release dates of these biographies are not incidental. The first appeared in 1924, the year Savarkar was placed under house arrest and two years before his English (auto)biography was published. The second was published in 1937, the year Savarkar was released unconditionally. In 1943 the first major official biographical work on Savarkar was published to mark Savarkar's sixtieth birthday. Shi La Karandikar, an associate of Savarkar's, consulted him in writing *Savarkar Charitra (kathan)* focused mainly on Savarkar's life between 1906–10, his London years. But given that under Savarkar's leadership, the Hindu Mahasabha had stayed away from the largest anticolonial protest, the Quit India movement, it is the start of a type of writing about Savarkar that takes the form of *apologia*: at once a defense and a defiant advocacy. By 1948 Savarkar was effectively back in house arrest and closely watched, this time by the new Indian state. Other biographies and homage poems were also written in this period, and at a fairly steady pace. I discuss a few, but since they mostly repeat the narrative of these early biographies, I include them in the bibliography but do not look at them individually.

In the third section, I discuss selected *darśana-dakṣiṇā* literature, that is, biographies written by people awed at having met or spent time with Savarkar. My selections represent primarily lower-middle-class but upper-caste Marathi men who attended college with Savarkar or were his neighbors in Ratnagiri. In this literature, the meeting or encounter with Savarkar is of primary narrative importance, and his biography is secondary, as it would be when repeating a mythological tale whose details are already known. The literature keeps reiterating the wonder of having met Savarkar, however briefly, and this fleeting intimacy functions as an anticipatory rebuttal of so-called objective works of secular and scholarly history.

I discuss a few books from this corpus. The first is edited by S. V. Modak, who published *Sāvarakara Yāñcyā Āṭhavaṇī* in 1962, four years before Savarkar's death. The second is by S. P. Gokhale, *Svātantryavīra Sāvarakarāñcyā Sahavāsāta*; the third, *Sāvarakarāñcyā Āṭhavaṇi*, is by A. G. Salvi, a retired high school teacher from Ratnagiri. The vignettes and commemorative writings found here reveal a great deal about Savarkar's appeal, his sway, his hold on the Marathi imagination, and, most important, the distance between this work and secular and scholarly writings on Savarkar. The authors describe their acts of writing as homage to a fallen hero and comrade. Intimacy and immediacy are seen as far more important than objectivity, and each book in each corpus bolsters, substantiates, and provides evidence for the other, in a sort of ongoing rhizomatic reaction.

The last names of the authors of the biographies and remembrances that make up the *darśana-dakṣiṇā* literature are telling: Moghe, Budhkar, Khare, Satvalekar, Sathe, Takle, Thatte, Kanitkar, Vartak, Soman, Limaye, Damle, Ketkar, Datar, Devdhar, Patwardhan, Paranjpe, Borkar, Patil, Bhave, Rege, Watwe, Joshi, Karandikar, Abhyankar, Athalye, Apte, Karmarkar, Karandikar, Kale, Kirloskar, Kulkarni, Kelkar, Gogte, Gharpure, Chapekar, Joglekar, Tambekar, Bhat, Upasani, Ranade, Potdar, Pendse, Bhopatkar, Bhagwat, Desai, Bhide, Sahasrabuddhe, Bhope, Gokhale, Aafle, Malshe, Shidore, Varhadpande, Athavale, Utpat, Vartak. This is a virtual who's who of Marathi Brahmin and upper-caste last names, a list of Savarkar's Brahmin or upper-caste apostles.

Some of these writers live or lived in Pune and Bombay, of course, but many lived in the place Savarkar proudly claimed as his home—the *khēḍēgāva*, or village world, that was the staging ground of his pedagogy. Savarkar held sway too over Pune and Bombay, but these works show that the nerve centers of his influence were Nasik, Nagpur, Dahanu, Akola, Indore, Buldhana, Shirgaon, Karhad, Panvel, Solapur, Ratnagiri, Ahmednagar, Kolhapur, Makhjan, and Baroda and Gwalior. In hailing from the *khēḍēgāva*, moving beyond it, yet never forgetting it, Savarkar was a model. Like Gandhi, Savarkar recognized that historical consciousness needed seeding among the nonurban, nonelite, non-English-educated people. Unlike Gandhi, he did not turn to the rural peasantry, but to the inhabitants of small-town Maharashtra, preaching education as the way to achieve historical consciousness, an education filled with role models of world historical figures like Mazzini and Garibaldi, poems on General Kruger, and didactic lectures on Mustafa Kemal.

There is also, of course, more scholarly literature on Savarkar, about which I will make only a few observations, not least because I see the corpus above, with its ease of access and colloquial Marathi, as more important in fostering the Savarkar myth. With few exceptions, the scholarly writing on Savarkar is less critical than explicatory; it reads more like a Festschrift than a biography.[26] While some authors claim to present a critical appreciation of Savarkar, the word "critical" typically means adding details or nailing an event down more precisely, to the day or even the hour. An early example of such "criticality" is S. L. Karandikar excavating the exact date of one of Savarkar's poems:

> In the Bombay magazine, *Vivadhajñānavisatāra*, in 1904, issue #34, on pp 85–94 the three poems are sequentially published. But even if they were published in 1904, it can be determined that they were composed in 1902. This is because the notice of the award money was publicized in the March 2, 1903 edition of the *Kesari*.[27]

26. See Kasbe, *Hindurashtravad*, 131, for an important exception to this rule. However, his critique is qualified; while he mentions Savarkar's anti-Muslim views when discussing his historical writings, he does not analyze them. Kasbe writes of Savarkar as a patriot and revolutionary (20, 27) but dismisses his historical writings, with the exception of the book about 1857, as unimportant since he sees them as fantasies that do not follow the general principles of historical writing (36, 126–33). In his criticism of Sheshrao More's work and that of other Savarkarite scholars, Kasbe does suggest that they need to point out Savarkar's faults and not merely worship him. Vasant Palshikar's critique of Savarkar goes much further in examining the material impact of his anticaste agitation, as I have shown in the chapter on caste. G. P. Deshpande is also critical of Savarkar, but Deshpande writes about Savarkar in English, and I am highlighting here works written in Marathi.

27. Karandikar, *Savarkar Charitra*, 89.

The scholarly literature is full of this level of detail; what it lacks is any real analysis. Like their more popular and in some ways more self-aware cousins, the scholarly works begin with admiration and conclude with praise.[28]

The scholarly works also seem to use archival material to confirm in a scholarly vein what the other biographies do in a popular one. P. L. Gawade, for instance, took Savarkar as the subject of his dissertation, and his work is exemplary of a strand of Marathi scholarship that is detailed, exhaustive, and comprehensive. No work of Savarkar's is left unread, and a smattering of secondary sources are consulted as well.[29] What is missing is any theoretical or critical analysis or perspective on the writing of biography or the approach to sources. Even for someone as scholarly as Gawade, Savarkar functions as an oracle or truthteller, with the word *chikitsak* (critical) in his book's title—*Savarkar: Ek Chikitsak Abhyas* (Savarkar: a critical study)—meaning explicatory or detailed. Gawade's writing is also tautological. He quotes Savarkar's work, explains it, then quotes Savarkar's work again as proof. For instance, following a one-line description of other work done on Hindus, Savarkar's claims about his own discourse on Hindutva are cited and accepted as accurate. Gawade then explains:

> . . . in creating this discourse [of Hindutva] Savarkar gave Hindutva a classical orientation, and on the foundations of this question Savarkar had given a lot of thought. This kind of fundamental thinking right down to the foundational principle is one of Savarkar's core traits. [30]

28. Three representative works are Gawade, *Savarkar*; More, *Savarkarancha Buddhivad* (Savarkar's thought); and Navalgundkar, *Swatantryaveer Savarkar*.

29. Gawade, *Savarkar*. Other examples are Joshi, *Krantikalloḷa*. Joshi refers to Karandikar and notes in his preface that he also met and spent time with Savarkar and got information from him about various political events. As with Gawade's book, Joshi's book is densely archival. See also Joglekar, *Dnyanayukta Krantiyoddha*. Joglekar is perhaps the best-known advocate of the Savarkarite point of view; he ardently defends Savarkar's reputation against accusations made in *Frontline* and elsewhere, and he begins his book with quotations about other nationalists, particularly those commonly perceived to be Savarkar's bête noires: Gandhi and Nehru. Joglekar quotes from a book called *The Myth of the Mahatma* by Michael Edwardes, in which Gandhi remarks that "32 years of struggle had come to an inglorious end," by which he meant the bloody partitioning of the subcontinent; and from a December 10, 1992, *Times of India* review of the book *The Indian Challenge* by Dr. Gisela Bonn, in which the author recounts an interview with Nehru in which Nehru claimed that Bonn had "before him a failed statesman." The quotes serve as the backdrop for Joglekar's argument for why, if Savarkar had been listened to, India would have done better.

30. See Gawade, *Savarkar*, 25, for an example of tautological reasoning.

Gawade understands Savarkar's conception of Hindutva not in political or social terms, or even in terms of law or policy. He asks a different question. Was Savarkar's conception *sankuchit* (limited) or *vyapak* (spread out/unlimited)? Does the emphasis in Savarkar's famous couplet on *punyabhu* make his discourse religious? His explanations or answers mirror Savarkar's declamations.[31] Gawade uses Hindutva much as some in the US use the term "American"—attached as it currently is to "values" and reverence for them, as for example expressed in standing for and singing the national anthem. Gawade is more concerned with the question of who is part of the Hindu community, asking for example whether, "a convert [can] still be considered culturally Hindu."[32] His answer mirrors Savarkar's.

Y. D. Phadke, perhaps the most prolific of Marathi historians, provides another example of what critical does *not* mean. His essay "Sāvarakarāñcī Vicārasr̥ṣṭī," written three months after Savarkar's death (perhaps as an obituary) takes as a given Savarkar's view of himself as a world-historical figure. Phadke repeatedly shows Savarkar's hubris without evaluating how that hubris might have affected his political trajectory or the people around him, let alone questioning whether it was merited. He describes Savarkar with the kind of adjectives we find in nonscholarly adulatory works: "*Asāmān'ya* śaurya, *asādhāraṇa* dhairya va sāhasa, *amōgha* vaktr̥tva, *ōjasvī* lēkhana" [unparalleled bravery, extraordinary patience and fortitude, electrifying eloquence, passionate writing] and notes that because of "his leap into the ocean which *resounded around the world . . . his hair-raising experience of torture* in jail, because of all these, Savarkar's life story in his own lifetime began to seem like a delightful and unique novel" [emphasis mine].[33]

31. Gawade, *Savarkar*, 245.

32. Gawade, *Savarkar*, 246. Another biographer writes that "Savarkar recognized that Sikhs and Aryasamajis don't register themselves as Hindus," and that is why a larger national theory that included them was needed. Navalgundkar, *Swatantryaveer Savarkar*, 25–31, 92. Navalgundkar sees Muslim aloofness in their supposed resistance to science and Western learning during colonial times and insists that Islam, by being anti-Western, has always been political. He notes that there is no confusion between the word "British" as connoting a nation and "Christianity" a religion but says that Hindu being a religious designation has caused great confusion. Here, too, Navalgundkar merely repeats what Savarkar has already noted in *Essentials of Hindutva*. Deshpande, *Savarkar te Bha Ja Pa*, also uses the term "critical" to mean detailed. He offers a precis of Hindutva (94–109), raising the question of Muslims and whether they can assimilate into India, and agrees with Savarkar that "Muslims are a nation."

33. Phadke, *Vyakti ani Vichar*, 151.

These descriptions could as well be from *Life of Barrister Savarkar*.

It is true, as I noted earlier, that for part of the time when he was in the Andaman Islands, Savarkar did hard labor, which is more than Gandhi, Nehru, Jinnah, or many other nationalists experienced. But we also know from the history sheet and prison records, which Phadke consulted, that Savarkar's experience was little different from other prisoners, unlikely to have been a "hair-raising experience of torture." Why the hyperbole? Because it is the established mode in which one writes of Savarkar in this corpus. The closest Phadke gets to an analysis is in this description of Savarkar's self-confidence with a vague question toward the end.

> Savarkar looked at himself from a very early age as a leader . . . his leadership was not built according to him because of anyone's protection or patronage. His views were his own and his success was also his own—they were not inspired or influenced by anyone. . . . Savarkar did not believe any leader matched up to him, not just that but that there could be second or third tier leaders whose views he could have consulted or talked to, or set his own views aside, because this is how politics was waged—such a notion does not seem to have been the case with Savarkar. The national party needed one leader, *everyone should simply listen to him, who knows if this is what he thought*? [emphasis mine][34]

We know that this is exactly what Savarkar thought. Phadke also narrates a rumor about Savarkar: supposedly, when a questioner asked Savarkar if he had read Marx, Savarkar suggested that a better, albeit anachronistic, question would be whether Marx had read Savarkar.[35] My point here is that even the scholarly literature on Savarkar competes to see who can describe his courage, fearlessness, or personality in more superlative terms.

In previous chapters, I have presented Shejwalkar for contrast, as he took very different approaches to both poetry and history. Here I'd like to briefly comment on his perspective on biography. Shejwalkar had a pithy sociological sense of the role history needed to play. It was not to cheerlead, but rather, "Itihāsācā vāstavika upayōga śahāṇapaṇa śikaṇē hā āhē ("The real use of history lies in teaching us to be wise"). He added, however, that this could only be done by "keeping past mistakes at the forefront, to attempt to get rid of

34. Phadke, *Vyakti ani Vichar*, 153.
35. Phadke, *Vyakti ani Vichar*, 165.

those faults so we don't repeat mistakes, if this is not our endeavor, then the efforts of historian/researchers will be in vain."[36] In theory, Shejwalkar and Savarkar agreed on this. But Shejwalkar went on to say:

> One thing a biographer has to pay attention to and that is exquisite knowledge of comparison/comparativeness—someone born in the village knows each and every pebble of it, but he has no wider sense of the world and might think of his village headman as in the same league as Nana Phadnis; many researchers make the same mistake.[37]

Likewise, he noted, "at a superficial level one might compare Nanasaheb Peshwa to William Pitt, but someone who has a sense of world history might wonder if they can be put in the same category."[38] Shejwalkar raised questions of scale, context, and the nature of historical judgment. The Peshwa was an important figure, but he had a good deal less power than William Pitt. A historical figure worthy of biography, in other words, could not simply be someone who was important within a region of India. We cannot know what Shejwalkar might have made of Savarkar's declaration of himself as an extraordinarily important national figure. Was he comparable to Shivaji Maharaj, or William Pitt, or even Gandhi? We do know that, had he considered this question, he would have asked critical questions that would invoke an entirely different perspective than that of Savarkar.

Shejwalkar anticipated the criticism he might receive for suggesting that a historian's role was to evaluate, indeed even judge, past actors for their actions or to pose counterfactuals when writing a biography. As he said:

> All historical analysis notes that at such and such a time, this and such action was appropriate, and the analysis focuses on whether or not such action was taken. In my opinion the study of only such a history has any chance of being useful. Simply recounting historical events is not real history, it is a tale.[39]

Glorious tales, however, were exactly what Savarkar and his biographers expected. Let us turn now to them.

36. Shejwalkar, "Nānāsāhēba Pēśavē: Prastāvanā," in *Nivadaka Sejavalakara*, 46.
37. Shejwalkar, "Nānāsāhēba Pēśavē: Prastāvanā," in *Nivadaka Sejavalakara*, 47.
38. Shejwalkar, "Nānāsāhēba Pēśavē: Prastāvanā," in *Nivadaka Sejavalakara*, 47.
39. Shejwalkar, "Nānāsāhēba Pēśavē: Prastāvanā," in *Nivadaka Sejavalakara*, 50, 78.

Savarkar's First Memorialization

The first English biography of Savarkar was published in 1926. Titled *Life of Barrister Savarkar* (hereafter *LBS*), its author was someone calling himself "Chitra Gupta," whom Vinayak Chaturvedi argues was a pseudonymous Savarkar.[40] This is possible for multiple reasons, most importantly the tremendous overlap between this biography and Savarkar's Marathi memoirs, which read like translations of each other. It also seems unlikely, given Savarkar's views on history and biography, that he would leave his legacy to chance. Finally, Savarkar's prose in English uses certain recognizable phrases and word choices. He translated a few of his Marathi letters and poems into English, and the translations in this English biography and in later publications are identical. Yet, neither Savarkar's biographers, nor Savarkar himself ever acknowledge that he was the author and indeed are irate at suggestions that he was, some suggesting that V.V.S. Aiyer or C. Rajagopalachari wrote it.[41] As a result, I cannot confirm Vinayak Chaturvedi's claim, but he is likely correct that the book was either written in close consultation with Savarkar or dictated by him to a friend or colleague. And so, rather than using Savarkar's name as the author, I will use "Chitragupta" in the pages to follow.

LBS is short—115 pages—and the publisher (in Chennai) notes that 2,000 copies were printed in 1926. The work's main objective seems to be to insist that Savarkar was a Homeric heroic figure: not just an extraordinary revolutionary, but the most brilliant and gifted of men, a devoted son, brother, and brother-in-law, and the patriot who was singularly responsible for bringing India's colonial plight to international attention. Chitragupta describes Savarkar as suffering only occasional self-doubts, which he resolves with his excellent mind. Savarkar is allowed no complexity of character. He was prodigiously learned, and we learn of his fondness for Pope's *Iliad* and the stories of Agamemnon and Achilles.[42] Perhaps that is why Savarkar's depiction is also heroic.

Let us recall from the chapter on caste that, in 1925, in *Dēśācē Duśmana*, Chitpavans took a ferocious verbal beating at the pen of Dinkarrao Javalkar, who suggested that it was almost as if God had willed there to be no Chitpavans among

40. See Chaturvedi, "A Revolutionary's Biography," 126–27.

41. Sane, "Lekhak Savarkar ani Savarkarance Lekhak." On the other hand, in the preface of the PDF version of *LBS* available on the BJP's elibrary site (https://library.bjp.org/jspui), Dr. Ravindra Vaman Ramdas claims that *LBS* was written by Savarkar.

42. Chitragupta, *LBS*, 2.

history's great men. Perhaps this explains why the biography begins with an account of brave Chitpavans, followed by Chitragupta's claim that he "was marked by all those who came into contact with him as an exceptionally gifted child."[43] Savarkar is described as having "remarkable poetical faculties" and that "well-known papers in Poona began to accept his contributions, both prose and poetical, when he was twelve, hardly realizing that the writer of them was but a boy of such tender years."[44] But it was not just poetry that set him apart. He waited for the newspapers in his village of Bhagur, read them avidly, and rushed to explain them not only to his schoolmates but his schoolteachers and elders. Why would they need an explanation from a twelve-year-old? Because, Chitragupta tells us, "He had even so early as that impressed men round him as one who spoke words of wisdom far above his age and whom men instinctively liked to listen to."[45]

Whether written or dictated by Savarkar, not a page can be turned without praise. As a secret (auto)biography it escapes restrictions such as modesty. He was "a voracious reader" whose eloquence "exercised a wonderful effect on the masses: while when he dealt with some philosophical or literary subjects, the learned and the wise were ever struck by the polished diction, the charming fluency and the soundness and cogency of the argument he had in hand."[46] Such was his brilliance that even as a college student "subjects delivered by Savarkar would long be remembered by those who had once heard them as best examples of Marathi eloquence and revolutionary literature."[47] He was not just knowledgeable about politics, he was also a shining example of Marathi literature. But there is more. Such was his "oratorical power that mass meetings of thousands of people sat spell-bound to listen to him."[48] Thousands? Facts matter less here than the narrative impact of these sentences on his audience. Such was his literary prowess that the introduction to the book he translated (Mazzini's biography) studying in London "grew so popular as to secure a record sale in Marathi literature. . . . Students were made by their teachers, and sons by their fathers, to commit whole passages to their memories

43. Chitragupta, *LBS*, 2.

44. Chitragupta, *LBS*, 3. This is exactly the phrasing Savarkar used in his memoirs when narrating how his first poem was published in Jagadhitechu. See ch. 4.

45. Chitragupta, *LBS*, 8.

46. Chitragupta, *LBS*, 10,18, 19.

47. Chitragupta, *LBS*, 20.

48. Chitragupta, *LBS*, 22.

from the masterly introduction which Mr. Savarkar wrote for the book." This sentence, about committing whole passages to their memories from Savarkar's introduction, is repeated word-for-word in numerous subsequent biographies.[49] What we see here is Savarkar being built into a figure whose words were to be memorized—not analyzed, discussed, or challenged. When the book was banned, his readers, "hid the copies at imminent risk and preserved them as a precious relic to be handed down to their posterity."[50] His words were to be preserved without alteration and treated as if they were sacred.

We already know that he knew the works of the Brahmin poets of Maharashtra: Mōrōpanta and Waman Pandit, and the poetry of the Varkari tradition. Savarkar's father catches him writing a ballad to the Chaphekar brothers who had assassinated a colonial official. Here is the description of his father's remonstrances:

> Damodar Pant with a father's solicitude pressed, "Child, thou art still too young. These serious cogitations would tax thy tender brain with unwholesome strain. Go take to some lighter and gayer moods and songs. When thou comest to manhood thou will be more able to fashion ways and means to render thy mission fruitful."[51]

Savarkar ignored this advice, writing the ballad and reciting it to a friend, who "simply refused to believe that it could have been composed by him" because it was so extraordinary. Despite their publication being banned, the ballads "lived and thrived from lip to lip and almost religiously remembered and cherished, can still be heard recited in towns and hamlets amidst admiring circles of the Mahrata [*sic*] people."[52] Savarkar insists elsewhere too that his words needed memorizing, whether the couplet in *Essentials of Hindutva,* his preface to the Mazzini biography he translated, or his ballads. It is not simply that Savarkar converts history to memory as we saw in the previous chapter: memorizability was a major part of his agenda.

A wave of "fanaticism," writes Chitragupta, swept through India, and "soon the malady infected Maharashtra and woeful tales of Moslem outrages of the usual inhuman type inflamed the Hindu element all over the land."[53] The

49. Karandikar, *Savarkar Charitra,* 127.
50. Chitragupta, *LBS,* 43.
51. Chitragupta, *LBS,* 12.
52. Chitragupta, *LBS,* 27.
53. Chitragupta, *LBS,* 4.

young Savarkar (according to Chitragupta) "could not rest without wreaking some vengeance or other on the Moslems for the outrages they had inflicted on his coreligionists," so the village mosque was desecrated. We have already read how Savarkar narrated this in Marathi, so here I will simply note that Savarkar wrote regarding the skirmish between the young Hindu boys and their Muslim schoolmates, "our young Vinayak had wisely equipped his army."[54] He used the same adjective "wise" in recounting this episode in Marathi.

Then, the young Savarkar took a vow:

> . . . he solemnly stood up and took the vow of dedicating his life and if need be his death to the mission of liberating India from the fetters that held Her in bondage. He would carry forth the torch of his fiery resolve and set the youth of India aflame! He would organize a secret society, arm and equip his countrymen and fight out the grand struggle and if need be to die sword in hand in Her cause.[55]

Death appears twice in three sentences and many more times elsewhere, including his poetry. Florid passages such as these dot the book, as when he narrates an internal conversation he had with himself about hiding in Paris:

> Wouldst thou continue to enjoy these morning walks and this fresh air and the sight of these beautiful water lilies and gay swans; while thy followers and friends and brothers are rotting in cells deprived of light and food, fettered and forced to bear untold hardships—canst thou enjoy this all? The contrast was too grim! The sensitive youth shrank within himself at its sight and felt himself a sinner . . . [56]

Vinay Dharwadkar argued that in the interwar period, Indian poets took as their models the works of Wordsworth, Keats, Shelley, Byron, Sir Walter Scott, Lord Alfred Tennyson, and Henry Wadsworth Longfellow.[57] Savarkar seems to have found in Victorian prose the appropriate tone to strike in his English writings. He continued the conversation with himself, now focusing on death and dying:

54. Chitragupta, *LBS*, 5.
55. Chitragupta, *LBS*,10.
56. Chitragupta, *LBS*, 80.
57. Dharwardkar, "Some Contexts of Modern Indian Poetry."

> I must risk even as my followers have done and show that I cannot merely sacrifice but even suffer. If I get arrested well that would be the real test of my mettle. . . . Youngsters who took lessons at my feet have braved the gallows and kept their pledge of fighting even unto death; should their trusted teacher and guide and friend and philosopher keep running away from shore to shore. . . . If I survive in spite of risking and come out unscathed from the ordeal then I might hold myself justly entitled to spare me as a general without the least danger of demoralizing either myself or my followers. Well if I don't survive I shall have kept my word, my pledge of striving to free India even unto death and leave a glorious example of martyrdom which in these days of mendacity and cringing political slavery is the one thing wanted to fire the blood of my people and to rouse and enthuse them to great deeds.[58]

The emphasis on death and dying remains popular even today in the biographical literature on him.

I close this section with a quote about a conversation that he claims to have taken place. He writes that he had to endure the intemperate venting of a guard, who insulted his entire family. "Prepare thyself," he told himself, "Now to face the worst that befalls a victim," and he kept "devising what he must do if they actually tortured him. He must bear it all." Savarkar was said to have responded with this important speech:

> Look here: you talk of tortures. . . . I am now dead to myself while living. Desperate recklessness is now my only friends. But your case is quite otherwise. You have yet to live and enjoy the pleasures of a sweet home. Therefore think twice before you subject me to any such foul treatment of tortures. For I know I cannot defend myself against you all. But one thing I will do. I will not die until I have killed at least one of you.[59]

He narrates his abiding desire to be tortured and killed for Mother India.

Savarkar seems to be modeling the high rhetorical pitch necessary for writing a biography of a world-historical figure. Certainly, as Vinayak Chaturvedi argued, Savarkar wished the world to know that he was an exemplary revolutionary. But *LBS* is less a biography of Savarkar than a Savarkarite depiction of a great man, written to be emulated and instructed by, not written to criticize

58. Chitragupta, *LBS*, 81–82.
59. Chitragupta, *LBS*, 105.

or for that matter contextualize his life. That would be seen as a mark of disrespect. Savarkar conveyed this message in his historical writings; it was conveyed in *LBS* and his memoirs. And the corpus they generated shares their traits: evidence is optional; you can leave out the parts that don't look good (here Savarkar's views about Muslims); the figure's leadership is self-evident (but still praiseworthy); poetry is mixed with prose; and underpinning it all is the idea of Savarkar's infallibility. Generations of Savarkar *bhakts* (devotees), as we will see, have written versions of this narrative.

Savarkar's *Mājhyā Āṭhavaṇī* and Gandhi's *My Experiments with Truth*

In 1925, the year after Savarkar was released into house arrest in Ratnagiri, Gandhi was in prison and had already written most of his autobiography. Asked to write something for a weekly magazine called *Navjivan*, he wrote a weekly short piece that always imparted a moral lesson, usually dealing with something intensely personal. Influenced by the hagiographical tradition, Gandhi's autobiography is unsurprisingly titled *My Experiments with Truth*. Truth was not a given for Gandhi—it had to be experimented with and experienced firsthand. In Gandhi's autobiography his forward motion is always predicated on the mistake as the motor of history. Concomitantly, Gandhi's writings invite us into his own agonistic world of struggle and therefore the nation's agonistic struggle to be born.

Gandhi's posture was that of a salvation seeker, who emphasized self-mastery whether that concerned diet, sex, the body, or violence. In the Introduction, Gandhi wrote, "my experiments in the political field are well known—for me they don't have much value—but I would like to narrate my experiments with the spiritual world." In this text, he remade himself into first and foremost a spiritual leader, a guru. But he did so within the Vedic paradigm—*Varnashramadharma*—the four stages of life as adhered to by upper castes. The text can be broken into four parts: the first period of his student life in London (Brahmacharya), the second as a successful householder and lawyer in South Africa (Grihyaprastha), the third as a man who began his detachment from the world of family and business when he returned to India (Vanaprastha) in the service of a new form of religious politics and salvation for India and Indians. The fourth and last (Sanyas) was Gandhi retiring from politics, which he did periodically across his entire life.

Gandhi's autobiography focuses on events that fundamentally elucidate the human self as ever-failing but always rising, Lazarus-like, from the ashes of that failure. Gandhi writes of his defeats and setbacks as the basis for his own experience of grasping for truth. He began as a mediocre student but converted his failure into success. He depicts himself as a bumbling and unremarkable lawyer in South Africa before he learns how to be successful through the inspiration that comes from working on behalf of his community. He writes about his failure as a husband, another failure that imparted the lesson that he needed to subordinate both his desires and his personal obligations to the needs of the nation to realize his own potential. In each case, as he recounts and recognizes his shortcomings, he finds a new path by channeling and advocating for the needs and wishes of others. He develops his own sense of self-restraint as the means to discover the power of passive resistance and nonviolent noncooperation. And even as he translates his personal experiments into nationalist parables, he fashions himself as an indispensable figure for Indian politics as well as for emulation by others around the world.

A formative text for Gandhi was Max Muller's *India: What Can It Teach Us?* Gandhi's Christian contacts in Pretoria gave him material intended to convert him to Christianity. It turned him into an evangelical Hindu instead. His major source of inspiration was Tolstoy, who had written *The Kingdom of God Is within You, or, Christianity Not as Mystical Teaching but a New Concept of Life* in 1893. Tolstoy was a critic of lived Christianity, and Gandhi took from Tolstoy his reasons for why he could not convert despite his fondness for Jesus. And he lived his life as transparently open to the point of excess. The entire world was informed if Gandhi had dysentery or when carnal desire arose in and surprised him even as it embarrassed just about everyone else. Gandhi represented his own body as the body of the nation, and the raw material on which the emergent history of the nation (of India) would be written. Hence, everything Gandhi underwent was what the emergent nation underwent, whether that was a physical ailment or a spiritual crisis.

At roughly the same time that Gandhi began writing his *My Experiments with Truth*, Savarkar began serializing his own autobiography under the title *Mājhyā āṭhavaṇī* (My recollections). It appeared in *Hutatma Shraddhanand*, the Bombay weekly that Savarkar's younger brother, Narayanrao Savarkar, began publishing and editing in 1926 after Swami Shraddhanand was killed. Given how large a space Gandhi occupied in Savarkar's imagination, it is not farfetched to ask if Savarkar deliberately wrote his autobiography to compete with Gandhi's prison diaries/sermons. Between Gandhi's autobiography and

Savarkar's the central distinction is between a text that talks about human failing and one that admits none. For Savarkar, there was no question of conversion to any religion, given that he saw conversion as a political instrument wielded by Muslims. Savarkar also would have seen such slavish praise of Christianity as a slight to Hinduism, not so much because of any interest on his part in following Hindu dogma but rather because he wanted exclusive focus on Hindu identity with the nation.

For Gandhi, personal intimacy always stood at odds with being the leader of a collectivity, and in that struggle personal intimacy was lost. While we know a little of Savarkar's personal life, we know that Gandhi sought self-consciously to either display it as a lesson for others or suppress it. But therein the similarities come to an interesting bifurcation. While both men idealized women, in Gandhi's case, women were models of nonviolence, purity, and self-sacrifice. Gandhi contrasted this with all things masculine, even his own past, in particular his carnal desire for his own wife. Men represented lust and selfishness, and Gandhi's *satyagraha* was an inversion of masculinity both in his construction of his self-image and in his delineation of nonviolence as more effective than violence. Savarkar celebrated masculinity, particularly that of the RSS *swayamsevak*.

Savarkar was released on the condition that he not engage in any political work or writing, and the police came to his house in Ratnagiri and looked through it in search of his *atmavrtta* (autobiography)—and he was expressly told not to write it anymore. Instead, it became the basis for the multiple little biographies that were published by people like A. G. Salvi or others addressed in this chapter. These biographies are relentlessly disciplined in putting forth as consistent and constant the legend of Savarkar juxtaposed against the messy contradictions of Gandhi. The messiness had already been asserted by Savarkar in his excoriation of Gandhi in a series of fifteen articles published and compiled in 1927/1928 as "Gandhi *gondhal*" ("Gandhian chaos").[60] In his own writing as well as the writing about him by his followers, Savarkar would claim to being the disciplined, unwavering, consistent nationalist.

Salvi remembered that the writing of the autobiography was being carefully watched and monitored, the houses of the Savarkar brothers were searched, and the reason for all this was that if they could find a handwritten copy it would give them enough evidence to rearrest him. (We know that the police were indeed watching). What is telling about Salvi's account is its description

60. *SSV*, MPHS, 3: 88–151

of how literally every page of Savarkar's writings was secreted away and kept secure as if it contained the sayings of a beleaguered prophet.

> When he finished his daily writings, four copies were made. One went to the illustrator, one to me, and the third to Savant Guruji . . . I took a copy of his biography to my village and hid it in a bin of rice.[61]

The scarcity and secrecy made every little bit of Savarkar's autobiography all the more precious.

After 1937 Savarkar's autobiography was published openly, and Salvi recalled how happy he was when the first 1,000 copies sold out immediately and that he had helped: "We got the immense satisfaction of having been personally involved in guarding this great man's autobiography."[62] Sketches of Savarkar's life were published in Marathi, Hindi, and Gujarati.[63] They were published again in 1949, after independence, under the title *Savarkar Atmacharitra* (*Savarkar's Autobiography*.) The first volume of his collected works has a *purvapeethika*, or prologue, by Savarkar that opens with the exhortation to forget. All memories should not be memorialized; he says, some should be forgotten, as an excess of memory produced one demon after another. As he put it:

> . . . speaking from a Puranic tradition, from the body of history, each drop of blood produces a new demon. From this oppressive remembering, to protect people that blood drop of memory/demon as soon as it falls is gone forever, thanks to the Goddess of forgetting! In truth, remembering and forgetting are both God's gift.[64]

But which drops of memory needed retaining and which did not?

Savarkar believed that a determined forgetting is far better than a simple piling up of memories. Memories needed to be evaluated, and their relative value (*taratamya*) should be the determinant of whether they should be turned into historical texts (*grantha*.) Family histories were not important; only societal or national histories needed to be published. Savarkar's life, as he

61. Salvi, *Svatantryavira Savarkarancya*, 38.

62. Salvi, *Svatantryavira Savarkarancya*, 38.

63. Chitragupta, *LBS*, publisher's preface. Since Savarkar had some role to play in writing the book, it stands to reason that he would know where his work was published.

64. *SSV*, SSRSP, 1: 1–2.

noted, was intertwined with the social life of the nation and needed therefore to be narrated.[65]

> . . . in the life of the nation, my own individual life has been an important and influential mediator. My having been a guru/teacher to so many young men whose lives I have transformed, and to such an extent have my views, efforts and company, in person or not, influenced them, and because of the opportunity to play a major role in national agitations over and again, the manner in which my life was formed and grew, all of this narrated from my own mouth, this will be very useful as a means by which to tell the national history of those times. My memories are not useful just to tell my story alone but will be reflections of two or three generations.[66]

Noting that he was writing these memoirs under challenging circumstances, Savarkar pledged to recount his memories just as he remembered them, without added ornamentation. But because his life and that of the nation were intertwined, he begins with a history of the British Raj after the 1857 Rebellion. For Savarkar, Indian history starts with the disarming of Hindus, the British use of divide-and-rule tactics among Hindu groups, and the propagandistic spread of English education. Bengalis come in for angry words for not having resisted the British, but they are excused because they were, in his view, ground down by 500 years of Muslim rule.[67] His potted history races through the years, with approving nods to B. C. Pal, Surendranath Banerjee, and Dadabhai Naoroji, along with a stern rebuke to the Brahmo Samaj for being seduced by the British. There is the predictable criticism of the "mendicancy" years of the INC and strong applause for Dayananda Saraswati for having convinced the Hindus of the Punjab not to fear Muslims and Christians and for setting against the mimeticism of the Brahmo Samaj the authenticity of the Arya Samaj.[68]

But when he moves to recounting his own life, a more authentic Savarkar appears than the one who wrote *LBS*, who simply recollects past events in his life. He writes with some humor: "As I write my recollections I'm afraid I must confess I have no memory of my birth."[69] He writes of his village, Bhagur,

65. *SSV*, SSRSP, 1: 3.
66. *SSV*, SSRSP, 1: 3.
67. *SSV*, SSRSP, 1: 7.
68. *SSV*, SSRSP, 1: 11
69. *SSV*, SSRSP, 1: 59

with enormous affection. Here and there in his memoirs, flashes of authenticity emerge, as if Savarkar forgot for a moment that he was writing for posterity. It happens when writing about his village, Bhagur, and in keeping with his favorite mode of writing, he wrote a seventy-one-couplet poem about it, a few couplets of which follow.

Hōtī ēka nadī nāmēṁ Dārakā tāpahārakā.	There was a cooling river named Daraka
Pratipaccandralēkhēva tanvaṅgī dhavalōdakā.	Slim, slender, white water like the crescent moon
Asē jāṇuni jīṁ gāvēṁ tānhēlīṁ bahu tyāñjalā.	Knowing the villages that were thirsting
Nadī cimukalīśī hī jā'ī pājita sajjalā.	This small little river would nourish everyone
Śētīcē gīta 'yē bailā asē ūñca dr̥ḍhasvarī.	The songs of the fields, the calling to the buffalo in high tones
Pahāṭēsa ūṭhē phullāṁ gandhāñcyāsaha ambarī.	The dawn rose into the sky with the fragrance of flowers
Mōṭāntūni paḍē dhōdhō pāṇī pāṇathaḷāmadhī.	When from the well flowed copious water into the fields
Snigdha gambhīra nādānē mōra nācati tyā tadhīṁ.	Peacocks danced entranced in them at the time[70]

His connection to the village remained a constant throughout his life.

Savarkar writes of his family with affection and gentleness. He narrates his parents' brief marriage as happy and speaks warmly of his mother who died when he was nine years old and whose face he could no longer remember.

> There was no false pride in her about being wealthy. But after she died, when our family had financial troubles, my father would always say "when she came into our house she brought Lakshmi [prosperity] with her, as soon as she departed, so did Lakshmi. She was the Lakshmi of the home." My father doted on her.[71]

70. *SSV*, SSRSP, 1: 62.
71. *SSV*, SSRSP, 1: 66.

But these happy memories, he reminds us, were not his own but instead based on what he was told of his parents' life. His reported first memory is of his own intellectualism, at the age of seven. In *LBS* Chitragupta wrote of his copious reading and his intellectual precociousness. In his memoirs, Savarkar adds to that claim: "My father's rule was that after dinner my older brother would read Ramvijay, Harivijay, PandavPratap, ShivLeelamrit, Jaimini Ashvamedha and such ovi-based [poetic meter] texts; and then he would discuss them with my mother."[72] The entire Savarkar family, we can deduce, was schooled in these classical texts.

His mother died when she was barely twenty-three years old.

> The four of us, young still, wealth at home, a husband who loved her infinitely, a happy household—none of this could she experience. She contracted cholera. That day I remember well . . . in the midst of our meal, she felt giddy, and in that old house she went to sleep next to the [home] temple. She never got up. The meal stayed uneaten. At 2 pm she was cremated. Everyone came home afterwards. But Aai did not.[73]

By wealth at home, Savarkar does not mean untold riches but a general happiness. As a young man, he shifted his attachment to his mother to his young sister-in-law (*vahinī*), the only other woman about whom he wrote with authentic affection. He includes in his memoirs a brief account by her about him. Yesuvahini describes an intense child, only twelve years old, but already focused on his schoolwork and anything else he did. She notes that he read voraciously, confirming Savarkar's account. He tells us he was a precocious reader, a poet, and an intellectual, almost savant-like, able to read Sanskrit easily, as well as Homer's Iliad and Odyssey (in English translation), the Mahābhārata, an Aranyaka here and there, and with regularity Vishnushastri Chiplunkar's *Nibandhamala* and Tilak's *Kesari*.[74] These writings confirm in Marathi what had already been written about him in English in *LBS*.

72. *SSV*, SSRSP, 1: 68. Eknath (1533–1599) and the compositions of "Rukmini Swayamvar" and "Bhavartha Ramayana" ("The Life of Rama") are considered classic examples of *Akhyan-kavya* (long narrative poems typically based on epics), and the last of such *Akhyan-kavyas*—Harivijay (1702), Ramvijay (1703), and Pandavpratap (1712)—were composed by Shridhar Pandit (1658–1729). See Deshpande and Rajadhyaksh, *History of Marathi Literature*, 31–35, for a history of *akhyankavya* and *kavita*.

73. *SSV*, SSRSP, 1: 69, 70.

74. *SSV*, SSRSP, 1: 78, 79.

> . . . Homer too was a great favorite with his father and Vinayak loved to listen to the spirited verses of Pope's Iliad and the translated stories of Agamemnon and Achelles [*sic*] at his father's feet. . . . [75]

At the age of thirteen he commences his education in English and leaves Bhagur for Nasik.

> The day I was to leave Nashik, my young companions, and loving neighbors felt very bad about how far I was going. Even in my young days, young and old, men and women, had great love and devotion for me.[76]

That Savarkar was exceptional in his village and that many people turned out to see him leave for the big city (Nashik) we can understand. That they grieved because of his departure was less likely. Nonetheless, the trope of his exceptional standing and brilliance is reiterated so often that it becomes standard in the secondary corpus. In his memoirs an older and mature Savarkar recreates a Puranic figure of himself as a young man, one much like the brilliant Brahmins of old who stun adults with their mnemonic and compositional abilities despite their lack of formal training. Nowhere does Savarkar concede any real intellectual or political influences on him other than Mōrōpanta in poetry and Shivaji Maharaj in politics.[77] Instead, with no apparent self-consciousness, he praises himself repeatedly and lists people on whom *his* influence was manifest.

> In my opinion, my speeches that kept having such a productive influence on so many people was because relative to my age, I had a storehouse of relevant information and knowledge . . . this is all due to my extraordinary reading, perception, and attentiveness from early on in my childhood.[78]

There is a matter of factness to such narrations, as if Savarkar had the distance to write objectively about himself.

I end this section with one last translation. In the secondary corpus and the *darśana- dakṣiṇā* literature, virtually no mention is made about the happiness or lack thereof of Savarkar's marriage. Nor does Savarkar tell us much. Gandhi would write of his wife, Ba, that she was his "better half" who truly made him

75. Chitragupta, *LBS*, 3.

76. *SSV*, SSRSP, 1: 91.

77. Chitragupta, *LBS*, 3, provides a sense of influence, as he mentions that these were the poets his father made him recite.

78. *SSV*, SSRSP, 1: 95, 102, 116, 117, 134.

whole. Savarkar, on the other hand, wrote of his marriage sparingly and without emotion. In 1901, when his marriage to the eldest daughter of Bhaurao Chiplunkar was arranged, it posed a problem for Savarkar. He wanted to further his education, and he and his associates debated whether a revolutionary should get married.

Would marriage drag a revolutionary down?[79] Would a woman who married a young man dedicated to the cause of Indian independence be basically opting for widowhood? Savarkar's answer was both peculiar and progressive. Peculiar because it involved a sense of genetics, and progressive because he took the opportunity to endorse widow remarriage. In conversations with fellow revolutionaries, he wrote,

> I used to show that revolutionaries who were willing for the sake of independence and to protect people to take a vow and had the courage to fulfil it were the uber mensch, the supermen, of society. The procreation from such outstanding seed for the betterment of society was of prime importance.[80]

Raosaheb Kasbe suggests that Savarkar was familiar with the works of Bentham, Mill, Hegel, Spencer, but the influence of Darwin and Nietzsche on his thinking was profound.[81] Here we again encounter Savarkar's genetic theory. He believed, as we have seen, that Hindus had unique blood, genes, spirit; now we learn that revolutionaries could pass down a revolutionary zeal to their offspring. Unfortunately, according to Savarkar, this was not happening. Without any warning, revolutionaries could be felled by an oppressive colonizer, and "[t]he lineage and offspring therefore of revolutionaries was dying out and those who were extremely ungrateful, vulgar, traitorous, selfish, who turned away from social service, only those were living on, flourishing and their offspring, mind you, were increasing in society."[82]

For this reason, Savarkar concluded, it was acceptable for a revolutionary to marry, not only to procreate, but to counter other misguided procreation. And should the revolutionary die, here was Savarkar's genuinely progressive position on widow remarriage:

79. *SSV*, SSRSP, 1: 153.
80. *SSV*, SSRSP, 1: 153.
81. Kasbe, *Hindurashtravad*, 166.
82. *SSV*, SSRSP, 1: 153.

> Their wives and children should recognize that their husband/father has become a martyr and be proud of it. But if they cannot, then such a widow should happily find some other good man, remarry and restart her married life. To give her such permission, a revolutionary would be grateful. Or he should be. If it is not a sin for a man to immediately remarry for whatever reason upon the death of his wife, for the same reason it is not a sin for a woman to remarry.[83]

Nonetheless, Savarkar was hesitant about marriage and was practically cornered into it. He justified getting married as respecting the wishes of his uncle and others in his family, rather than his own. Love, which he would write about as vital in the determination of marriage in his letter to his brother, was in this case irrelevant.

> Because the girl his uncle had decided on was Shri Bhaurao Chiplunkar's daughter and between Bhaurao Chiplunkar and his uncle there was a deep and long affective friendship, and he could not break his word. With such a family to have a close, and now even closer relationship of marriage, was a rare opportunity, such that anyone's circumstance or the question of liking the girl was to be set aside.[84]

Savarkar agreed to the marriage on the condition that the Chiplunkar family paid for his higher education. The narration allows readers to believe that he agreed to the marriage because of his affection for his future father-in-law, whom he described in these glowing terms:

> He was tall, fair as can be and very handsome. His face, his smart bearing, his piercing eyes, his imposing way of walking! When you saw him it brought to mind a Chitpavan Sardar of the Peshwai.[85]

Whether Savarkar was equally impressed by any feature of his wife we cannot tell, because this is the sole description of her:

> . . . even before the question of getting married had been raised, that girl had been sent to our house for eight days by her father. She too wanted very much to be married into the family.[86]

83. *SSV*, SSRSP, 1: 154.

84. *SSV*, SSRSP: 155. See Karandikar, *Savarkar Charitra*, 69–70, where he repeats this story virtually verbatim.

85. *SSV*, SSRSP, 1: 154.

86. *SSV*, SSRSP: 156.

Savarkar does not mention his wife again. The rest of the memoir describes people he was genuinely fond of, explains why India needed armed revolutionaries, and concludes quite abruptly with the founding and activities of the secret society he founded, the Mitra Mela. Savarkar had separately published his memories of his time in the Andamans, titled "The Echo from the Andamans," which would have followed this memoir chronologically. Luckily, he didn't need to write anymore; he had done enough. His many followers would now take up the charge.

Hagiobiography

In 1924, the year Savarkar moved to Ratnagiri, Sadashiv Rajaram Ranade wrote the first homage biography. Titled *Swatantryaveer Vinayakrao Savarkar yanche Sankshipt Charitra* (*Concise Biography of Nationalist Hero Vinayakrao* [honorific] *Savarkar*), it cost eight annas. Savarkar declined, according to Ranade, to talk about himself, yet he clearly already had iconic status as a former revolutionary.[87] He didn't need to talk about himself; what he wanted repeated had been published in *LBS* and his Marathi writings.

In this first biography, the differences between an earlier generation of Marathi nationalists such as Tilak and Savarkar's subsequent generation are clearly stated in the official preface. Tilak's devoted biographer, N. C. Kelkar, wrote the preface reluctantly. He spoke as an elder statesman, noting that not only did he not know Savarkar well but that he disagreed fundamentally with him, yet could not refuse the honor of writing the preface because Savarkar's fearlessness in speaking his mind and challenging colonialism had impressed him.

Ranade's own preface gives us an indication of what made Savarkar so impressive. Ranade was a student in the government school when Savarkar was incarcerated in Ratnagiri prison, prior to his house arrest.

> All I desired was to see once the man who escaped from a boat in Marseilles and at a very young age who by his extraordinary courage brought the world's attention to him.

This line could be taken verbatim from the English biography. Savarkar as a profile in courage may seem odd to readers of Indian nationalist history, which

87. See Ranade, *Swatantryaveer Vinayakrao*, in particular the author's preface, in which he notes that he asked Savarkar many times to tell him some *mahatvachya goshti* (events of importance), but Savarkar always declined.

typically excoriated him as a collaborator for having recanted his nationalist political views to secure his own release.[88] But in Ratnagiri district, in the small town of Makhjan, Savarkar was the uniquely courageous hometown boy who had suffered enormously and remained a nationalist patriot. Ranade not only admired him; he revered him. And in writing his praise-filled biography, more a praise paean, he consulted many of Savarkar's associates, including his father-in-law, Bhausaheb Chiplunkar.

A picture will soon emerge of a group of upper-caste Marathi men, often small-town lawyers, teachers, or clerical workers in one or another administrative unit in Nagpur, Solapur, Ratnagiri, Chiplun, or some other small city, far removed from Pune or Mumbai, let alone Delhi or Calcutta, for whom Savarkar was a larger-than-life figure. His intellectual brilliance left them stunned and his fiery speeches enthralled them. Ranade met Savarkar in Makhjan and had the privilege of hearing first-hand the story of his escape in Marseilles. Ranade's Makhjan is not the Maharashtra that those from colonial Bombay or Peshwai Pune, let alone the colonial capitals of Calcutta and Delhi, knew or visited. But Savarkar knew it. It was from locations like Makhjan that he imagined building an army and teaching young men about Garibaldi's and Mazzini's miltant nationalism.

Ranade draws a portrait of an unceasing, relentless, missionizing zeal that tracks with Savarkar's description of his childhood. Ranade's prose is that of a devotee; indeed, it is essentially a *povāḍā* rendered in prose. Savarkar is, simply put, flawless, pure, and purifying. From childhood on, he is presented as a purifying indoctrinator of nationalism and patriotism, whether in his distaste for frivolity or his nonstop nationalist proselytizing. The biography is Brahminic in tone and content. The contest between Hindu and Muslim boys is narrated through Savarkar's understanding of Muslims being obsessed with converting Hindus by any means necessary. Apparently unaware of Savarkar's views about *viṭāḷvēḍa*, Muslim boys threaten to force fish dumplings down Savarkar's throat, believing that it would make him lose caste. Ranade establishes Savarkar as a heterodox Brahmin almost immediately, telling us about his friends, the sons of Gopal Bhiku and Ranba Shimpi, whom we met in the caste chapter.[89]

The second Marathi biography, entitled *Swatantryaveer Barrister Vinayakrao Savarkar Yanche Charitra* (*Freedom Fighter Barrister Vinayakrao Savarkar's*

88. See as just one example, Nandy, "A Disowned Father of the Nation."

89. Ranade, *Swatantryaveer Vinayakrao*, 12, 13.

Biography) was written by Ra Ga Bhope in 1938 to celebrate the end of Savarkar's house arrest in Ratnagiri.[90] The late 1930s were turbulent times in India. Following the Government of India Act of 1935 and its (very limited) extension of the Indian electorate, there was an election, which the INC swept. Having formed a government, they realized how little power they had when, with no consultation, the Viceroy Lord Linlithgow plunged the country into war against Germany. By 1939 the Congress had resigned all governmental positions and once again, the colonial government cracked down.

In 1937, when Savarkar took up the leadership of the Hindu Mahasabha, he began with a tour of Maharashtra. It was a resurgent moment for him in two ways: personally, with his resurgence after decades of incarceration that had taken him out of the political limelight, and politically, with the vigorous resurgence of his caustic rhetoric against his old enemy, Gandhi. Bhope's book had many sponsors, including the Hindu Mahasabha and the Arya Samaj, and it took a mere twenty days to be printed in Ahmednagar.[91] Bhope did not simply retranslate or use the first English biography; he traveled through Nashik and Bhagur and consulted other Marathi biographies of Savarkar. Still, the narrative is unsurprising, repeating much of what Ranade wrote, bulking it up with examples from other biographies. No two pages of Bhope's book go by without a Sanskrit quotation, and the book, made up of short sections, each highlighted in boldface, is formatted for easy reading, even ending, as Savarkar himself had done, with a patriotic poem.

One prominent strain in this collection of books is a powerful sense of indignation, that Savarkar, hawk to Gandhi's dove, has been so ignominiously ignored. The authors angrily point out that Savarkar endured worse prison torments than Gandhi or Nehru and dealt with family tragedy (the death of his parents, uncle, two children, and his sister-in-law) with no sympathy from the national media. As if making up for this, the books go on at length about Savarkar's contributions, claiming a series of firsts for him—first bonfire of foreign cloth, first to think of militarizing Hindus, first among the nationalists in his learning and erudition.

By 1940, when Mo Shi Gokhale writes *Veer Savarkar*, we are fully into the world of legend. Like Ranade, Gokhale remembers meeting Savarkar in 1925 as a schoolboy in the small village of Parshram. Savarkar had been invited to

90. In 1935, before Savarkar was released from house arrest, Dr. Ga Ba Palsule composed a Sanskrit play about his life titled *Dhanyoham Dhanyoham* and published it in Pune.

91. Bhope, *Swatantryaveer Barrister*, 1, 2.

give a lecture on Parshuram (a mythological figure) and spoke about how Parshuram had rendered this earth free without compromising his own bravery. From that one meeting in 1925 came this short book—shorter than a full-length biography, longer than a pamphlet. Gokhale fictionalizes entire sections, including a segment about the Andamans and the cruelty of the prison officials. He betrays no self-consciousness about this fictionalizing; in fact, he tells his readers about it. Why would he feel free to fictionalize Savarkar's Andamans experience? Perhaps because Savarkar himself fictionalized many conversations he had in the Andamans and saw no major distinction between the genres of poetry, history, and fiction.

Because his biographers so insistently narrate Savarkar as a young revolutionary, they write quite casually of the political assassinations that were the weapon of choice for revolutionaries. Even after independence, the biographies show no concern, regret, or even reflection about the taking of a life—whether Curzon Wyllie's or anyone else's. The possibility that what Savarkar and other revolutionary-minded nationalists thought of as legitimate political action could be seen as murder does not seem to occur to the authors. Their conviction that political assassinations are not murder allows the authors to insist that Savarkar's sentence for aiding and abetting political assassination was inhumane and unfair.

In 1943 the first official biographical work on Savarkar was written and published by an associate of Savarkar's who was not just closer to him than previous biographers but who had also written a biography of B. G. Tilak. Shi La Karandikar, a member of the Bombay Legislative Assembly, focused mainly on Savarkar's revolutionary years: 1906 to 1910. The book's title is *Savarkar Charitra (kathan)*. The use of *kathan* is no accident since four years of Savarkar's life are narrated as if they were a *katha* (mini-epic) across more than 500 pages. The publisher is listed as Sou. Seetabai Karandikar (possibly the author's wife, though it is unknown), and Savarkar's poem *Gomāntak* is included to provide clues to Savarkar's interiority, how he must have felt, and what he thought.

No detail was too small to be included. Karandikar consulted extensively with Savarkar; the book is filled with the author's recollections of conversations he had with him and his entire family. Karandikar repeatedly points to Savarkar's unpublished autobiography as well as conversations with people close to Savarkar with limited, and often self-referential citations and references. The book is divided into sixteen chapters, covering his childhood, his middle- and high-school years, his college years, his association with Shyamji Krishnavarma, his time in London, his association with Madanlal Dhingra, the inhumane sentence of two lifetimes, and his time in Cellular Jail. Some chapter titles later became titles of books, and one—"trikhaṇḍāta gājalēlī uḍī" or the "leap that resounded across the heavens, earth, and the netherworld"—was repeated word-for-word in later books. The homage corpus, in other words, borrowed not just the narrative Savarkar laid out as its fundamental template but also style and rhetoric.

Karandikar begins with a detailed examination of the origins of Savarkar's last name—the *gotra* (patriarchal lineage) from which his Chitpavan Brahmin family takes its lineage. He references Rajwade as an authority but also the epic travails of the mythological hero of the Rāmāyaṇa. Ram's exile lasted thirteen years, and between the ten years in the Andamans and three in prison in India, so did Savarkar's. Karandikar immediately establishes Savarkar as a character from an epic saga. He next examines the Savarkar family's involvement with the Peshwai and describes Savarkar's birth along with his astrological chart and what it predicted about his brilliance.[92] Karandikar apologizes to his readers for not having much information about Savarkar's earliest years but tells them that,

> in this work, the couplets taken from Savarkar's *Gomantak* are in a sense autobiographical. Keeping the information in those couplets in mind, Savarkar's extraordinary life can be dramatically depicted, I am absolutely sure.[93]

Savarkar's mischievousness is likened to that of Krishna, and his relationship with his mother is also narrated in epic style—he was the Balkrishna (young Krishna) to her Yashoda (mother). Savarkar's role in the narrative is visible in the lengthy detour into Gandhi's mendacity, the lies he inserted into public and political life, and the need for a different political strategy for independence.[94] As in Auerbach's understanding of the legendary style, there is no interiority to Savarkar's life, only the obsessive filling in of details of a formulaic version of a Puranic godlike figure and his saintly and happy family. All affect is monotonously heroic, tragic, or dramatic, confirming what had already been formulated for a lay-Marathi reading public. Karandikar refers to Ranade and to *LBS*. Ranade refers to Savarkar. Subsequent biographers refer to *LBS*, Ranade, and Karandikar.

92. Karandikar, *Savarkar Charitra*, 19, 20.
93. Karandikar, *Savarkar Charitra*, 19.
94. Karandikar, *Savarkar Charitra*, 28–30.

Although Karandikar called this biography a *kathan*, it was actually more like a *gātha*, or an extended historical epic, even though it only went up to the year 1910. But he sets the stage by focusing on the first of the many travails that Savarkar would endure, the illness and death of his mother (to cholera), which is described in these terms:

> Anna [Savarkar's father] was absorbed in enjoying the pure happiness of his good fate, but he experienced what is written in the verse "God has not written everyone's fate completely." In 1894, around the month of May/June the cholera epidemic started and slowly it made its way to Bhagur. At month's end, there were some religious ritual observances that needed conducting. The day of that religious observance dawned. From the morning she was unwell. But in the characteristic manner of devout Hindu women, she paid no attention to her illness, and let no one know she was unwell till the afternoon. She needed to go out (to the bathroom) once, but she took a purifying bath and resumed her cooking.

Savarkar's mother died, Karandikar notes, with her four-year-old son in her arms. From here we move to the familiar story of Savarkar's childhood friends, but Karandikar moves across the caste spectrum—not only was Savarkar a progressive Brahmin who opposed untouchability, he also had *kṣatriya tēj* (warrior spirit).[95] The loss of his mother, which had brought a pall to the house, was lifted by the entrance of his sister-in-law, Yesuvahini, who was Savarkar's age and shared many of his interests including poetry. We see repeated references to his intellectual precocity, and yet again we read about the Upaniṣads and Alexander Pope's translation of the Iliad, much the same as what is written in *LBS*. Savarkar annotated books he'd read with copious notes, all of which, Karandikar notes, were lost in the police raids that started in 1908. His schoolteachers noticed his genius, sometimes doubting it could come from one so young. Virtually everything he wrote was published, but the annotated books, poetry collections, letters, and drawings were destroyed because of constant police searches.[96]

The story of the desecration of the village mosque is told exactly as Savarkar tells it in his memoirs. Karandikar was hesitant to include it, noting that just about every other biographer had done so, and he said he did not intend to trace Savarkar's views on Muslims to this one small event. Because, however,

95. Karandikar, *Savarkar Charitra*, 28–30.

96. Karandikar, *Savarkar Charitra*, 35, 42, 43.

of the many stories of Muslim atrocities that had been published in the newspapers, he thinks it necessary to draw from Ranade's 1924 biography the story about Muslim boys in the village vowing to convert Savarkar by polluting him, crowing that "these Muslim boys had to quietly concede defeat, because they could not fulfil their vow to contaminate Tatya by forcing either dry or wet or any other kind of fish down his throat."[97]

The curiosity of this first official biography is that as soon as the author encounters sources such as the *London Times* or the Sedition Committee Report, the tone changes and becomes less dramatic. It reverts to romantic melodrama in the chapter on Savarkar's escape attempt and his journey to the Andamans, detailing what he ate on the boat, a seemingly fictitious conversation between Savarkar and the new Irish warder Mr. Barrie, who was keen to meet the author of the book on 1857 and the daring escape at Marseilles, along with descriptions of the jail and Savarkar's resignation that henceforth he would have to bathe in salt water.[98] The main source for all of this narrations is Savarkar's *An Echo from Andamans* published in both English and Marathi. Karandikar adds dramatic flair but again produces what is at root Savarkar's account of Savarkar's trials. In part because of this repetitive accumulation of narratives and books, the corpus appears to have great richness and depth. All the authors[99] take Savarkar's greatness as their starting point, and as is the nature of confirmation bias, signs of greatness emerge constantly.

Much of this literature is intended to educate middle- and high-schoolers. Savarkar's pedagogic activities are taken as the model, and the corpus works to ensure that his agenda—*Bhasha Shuddhi* (language purification) and patriotism—is inculcated early. The control Savarkar exercised, wittingly or not, on how his legacy was disseminated is unlike that of any other nationalist. By the close of Karandikar's biography, we learn that Savarkar was an exceedingly private man who did not seek the company of others or let anyone come meet him. This reclusiveness adds to his allure, and the fact that subsequent authors got close to Savarkar lends their work more authority. Indeed, Va Go Maydev, the poet who collected and compiled Savarkar's poetry, thanks Karandikar in his acknowledgements for sharing some poems, then says, ". . . but more than anyone else I am indebted to Vinayakrao himself, who set aside his own

97. Karandikar, *Savarkar Charitra*, 43.

98. Karandikar, *Savarkar Charitra*, 410.

99. See Karandikar, *Savarkar Charitra*, 29, for example, where Karandikar points to *LBS* as providing a detailed and thrilling account of the Great Leap.

greatness and freely talked to me about these poems, found bits and pieces of them, taxed his own memory about them, stayed up late on occasion all to make his poetry be correctly published."[100]

In 1947, a few years after Karandikar's work was published, Sha Na Barwe wrote and published from Pune a short book entitled *Svātantryavīra*. Like other authors, his preface contains a disclaimer, here framed as a rhetorical question: ". . . many people have written about Savarkar, what am I going to contribute?" He answers by saying that it was important to write and adds that people will surely be eager to read another rendition of Savarkar's life.[101] Barwe connects to Savarkar as a poet, and his goal is for readers to memorize Savarkar's life events as simple poetry.[102] Here we see the success and continuation of Savarkar's didactic project, as Barwe depicts a life that reaches its crescendo in Hindu *samaj*, Hindu unity, Hindu language, Hindu race, and Hindu *rajya*. Was he even human, this *daivat* (Godlike man) Barwe worships?

Now and then a marginally different biography appears, such as *Bĕrisṭara Vināyaka Dāmōdara Sāvarakara: Śalākā Paricaya* (*Barrister Vinayak Damodar Savarkar: A Pointed Introduction*) by Sa Cha Athavale. Published in 1947, the book starts somewhat unusually. Athavale describes a small village where he sees a funeral pyre that is constantly attended by a man and an assistant. They circumambulate it and attend it, keeping the deceased's ashes together in a supreme act of duty and respect, as if to assist the deceased in his passage to the other side. The sensitivity and the profundity of this act struck the author. It was the funeral pyre of a young man, barely eighteen years old, who had been ill for eight days before succumbing to his illness. The man tending the fire insisted that he (the dead youth) would return, in a next life, to take his place in society and that tending the fire was a way of showing respect. This man, whom the author re-encountered some years later, was apparently Savarkar, whose act of care struck the author deeply. But after this reminiscence, the biography holds no surprises.

Books are published at a regular pace—a children's book in 1951, then back to books for adults in 1963, 1966, 1973, 1982, 1983.[103] In 1966, for instance, Pra Ga Sahasrabuddhe wrote a biography that begins with Savarkar's escape from

100. Preface to Maydev, *Savarkaranchi Kavita*, 3.

101. Barwe, *Swatantryaveer*, 6.

102. Barwe, *Swatantryaveer*, 36, 37.

103. Shikhare, *Swatantryaveer Savarkar*. In his preface, Shikhare explains why he wrote another biography, and why he aimed it at chidren:

Marseilles—and includes the same fictive conversation Savarkar narrated in *LBS* with the policeman who apprehended him. He describes how after Savarkar's brother's marriage, Yesuvahini came to live with them, comparing her arrival to that of a beautiful frangipani offered to the sacrificial fire. He pushes the metaphor further by noting that the Savarkar household was a sacrificial fire pit for the securing of independence, with Yesuvahini as the steady stream of pure cow's milk ghee offered to it.[104]

In 1983 a Savarkar Festschrift was published to commemorate what would have been his one-hundredth birthday.[105] None of the writers refer to the giant and critical corpus of writing in English not just about Savarkar but about Tilak, the plague, the period of revolutionary nationalism, or for that matter any of the now voluminous works of history about the time and the place. Savarkar himself gives us the reason why, as we have seen in the previous chapter. As early as 1910, he concluded that the general misunderstanding of Marathi history was due to the prevalence of histories written by Muslims and the British. He ignored these histories and wrote his in English to challenge them, as it were, on their own turf. Thereafter, he literally paid no attention to the scholarly literature in English, because only a native viewpoint, one rooted in Marathi sources, would do. In like fashion, this Festschrift follows suit, reiterating Savarkar's greatness and ignoring any literature that might either challenge or complicate the canonic legend of Savarkar.[106]

> The youth of Maharashtra cannot wallow in the mud of inaction, laziness, and vagabondery. Only if they are schooled in service, principles and sacrifice will our Maharashtra, indeed our India be truly independent.

In 1963, Vi Sa Valimbe wrote *Swatantryavira Savarkar*. His preface begins with one of Savarkar's poems, the gist of which was that since he had not wasted his days, the end of his days comes to him without any sorrow. "This poem came to my mind when Savarkar passed away," writes Valimbe, and, wanting to make the unremitting patriotism of such a great man clear, he decided to write a book based on Savarkar's writings and speeches. In 1973, Aravinda Natake wrote *Yugapravartaka Sāvarakara*, which was sold for just two rupees. The publisher noted that this inexpensive biography of Savarkar could be sold door-to-door and thus do double work—it would sell well because it was so cheap, thus informing more people about Savarkar, and the publisher would also gain financially. Natake noted in his preface that he had met Karandikar, chatted with him, got *LBS* from him, read Dhananjay Keer's English biography, then used Karandikar's biography to write his own.

104. Sahasrabuddhe, *Swatantryaveer Savarkar*, 12.

105. Varhadpande et al., *Garudjhepa*.

106. Varhadpande et al., *Garudjhepa*, 168.

Memories of Savarkar: The *Darśana-Dakṣiṇā* Literature

A few years before Savarkar died, though when he was already ill, Rajaram Laxman Renavikar took it upon himself to collect the bits of wisdom, snatches of conversation, and stray comments that people who had met Savarkar in Maharashtra remembered. He compiled these memories into a short book titled *Sāvarakara Yāñcyā Āṭhavaṇī* (*Memories of Savarkar*), published in Pune in 1962.[107] In the preface, the editor Shi Vi Modak explains why, given all the existing works, this enterprise was necessary. He points out that Savarkar lived a vast, varied, and intellectually rich life, and the memories of him collected by Renavikar could add to the record and correct some of the misunderstandings about Savarkar. More importantly, the memories would demonstrate Savarkar's impact on people: "through meeting Tatyarao, and hearing him speak on a number of subjects, the impact on people's minds and brains emerges as the memory of his darśana."[108] Modak then apologizes for all the memories that could *not* be put in this short book.

The portrait of Savarkar that emerges here is less varied or complex than one would have hoped. Numerous writers remark on his kindness and his generosity to strangers in distress, but most talk about his strict insistence that his fellow students study hard and know Indian history well. Or they remark on his calm demeanor and the fire that blazed within him, on his steadfastness, his abjuring of caste, his poverty, his persistent but polite challenge to the orthodox in the essentially conservative city of Ratnagiri. The authors refer to Savarkar as *tātyā* or *tātyārāva*, a respectful term for an older male relation: he was the teacher, the guru, the older brother, the smartest in the room, the one who stoically bore travail.

One of the memories collected in this book is from Shankar Narayan Moghe, who remembered Savarkar from their college days. In 1903, he tells us, Savarkar liked to keep his associates close to him, caring for them to such an extent that when Moghe had a mild fever for a few days, Savarkar went out of his way to ensure that he had food. "Even after I got well, Tatya for many days took me to the college's Shivaji Club as someone's guest so that I could eat well."[109] Savarkar was strict about punctuality and his associates' education, and Moghe describes a stern schoolmaster:

107. Preface to Modak, *Savarkar Yanchya Athvani.*
108. Preface to Modak, *Savarkar Yanchya Athvani.*
109. Modak, *Savarkar Yanchya Athvani*, 10.

> Tatya was very strict about meetings starting on time. He was also insistent that everyone present at the meeting had to participate. He would quiz us about our schoolwork, the marks we got in our exams, our rank in class, and while doing this he would also check whether we were exercising.

For all his strictness, he never shamed his associates in public, always correcting them in private.

Moghe recalls being thrown out of his house by his father for joining the revolutionary ranks. He describes bursting into tears telling Savarkar and being immediately invited to live with Savarkar in Nasik. Moghe was astonished that "without even waiting for my acceptance, he bought me a ticket and took me to Nasik." In Nasik, Moghe writes, a group of men gathered around to chat with Savarkar, and in one of the rare instances in which Savarkar's wife is mentioned, Moghe wrote,

> Thinking he was alone, Tatya's wife would bring him a bowl of milk. But Tatya was a master! He called all of us children, and in each one's palm he placed 2 spoonfuls of milk and then he would drink the rest. His wife would often get angry about this.[110]

Such acts of kindness had a profound impact on a young revolutionary aspirant thrown out of his house by his father. Moghe also remembers Savarkar making it a point to go to every small village in Nasik district in 1906 to instruct students for hours upon hours about history.

K. G. Khare, a lawyer from Pune, was arrested for revolutionary activities as a young man, along with thirty-eight other men. He was one of the eleven to be released and remembers, "My release letter started to be read . . . at the time Savarkar who was sitting behind me, told me that I'd been released this time, but cautioned me against being caught again.[111] Dho Kru Sathe couldn't quite remember the year, but it was around 1906, as he had just matriculated. He was traveling from Bombay to Pune and musing aloud about his future when he met Savarkar on the train and was advised to attend Deccan or Fergusson College and was given the names of young men already there who could help him. But what stood out was this:

> The main source of surprise for me was that Savarkar showed up the next day at my home. There were two other young men with him. He introduced

110. Modak, *Savarkar Yanchya Athvani*, 15.
111. Modak, *Savarkar Yanchya Athvani*, 22.

> them to me. He wanted to organize the youth of the country, and this was part of the effort.[112]

Ja Na Thatte from Indore was in the Byculla prison in Bombay serving a three-year sentence related to the assassination of Nasik's collector. He heard that Savarkar had received a fifty-year sentence in the Andamans. Believing that no one ever returned alive from the Andamans, Thatte persuaded the night warden to let him meet Savarkar, who was held in Byculla prior to being transported. Thatte recounts his surprise when he scaled the wall of his own cell and looked down into Savarkar's: "I saw that Savarkar was waiting for me. On his body were the clothes of convicts, and his legs and arms were in chains."[113] Savarkar came near the wall to talk with him and in their ten-minute conversation reassured him that he was in the company of other martyrs and taught him a precis of an English poem.[114]

There are other prison reminiscences. In 1911 Ra Va Soman was a clerk in the prison in Thane from which prisoners were dispatched to the Andamans. His job allowed him to see prisoners even under strict watch, including Savarkar.

> In those days, Savarkar's attire (yellow cap—this is how we recognized a prisoner who was to be sent to the Andamans) a short kurta, shorts down to the knee, the fabric of such clothing was extremely rough. Both legs were chained. In exactly these clothes, two days before he went to the Andamans, his wife was allowed a brief visit.

Soman could not hear their conversation, but he was clearly moved by what he saw.[115] Other stories are similarly full of pathos. Ma Vi Limaye remembers that, upon Savarkar's release into house arrest in Ratnagiri, people's fear of the colonial government made it difficult for him to rent a house.[116]

Three years after Savarkar's death, Shri Pu Gokhale published a book of memories.[117] It is the most personal of the books I examine here, as it offers intimate details about Savarkar's life. Gokhale recalls the first time he saw Savarkar.

112. Modak, *Savarkar Yanchya Athvani*, 25.
113. Modak, *Savarkar Yanchya Athvani*, 27.
114. Modak, *Savarkar Yanchya Athvani*, 27.
115. Modak, *Savarkar Yanchya Athvani*, 31.
116. Modak, *Savarkar Yanchya Athvani*, 32.
117. Gokhale, *Svatantryaveer Savarkar*.

> It was about 1 or 1:30 in the afternoon. The bungalow in which Savarkar was staying, from the entrance itself we could see a fair gentleman in the middle of the room at the far end, half stooped, and rapt in smoothing the folds of his new and clean dhoti between the thumbs and forefingers of both hands over and over again. His hands were moving up and down on his dhoti, and so were the sinews [muscles] on his hand. His filled out frame, his gold edged spectacles, and his bald yet still appealing head—all of this filled our eyes . . . we tried to get a closer look but someone came towards him and he lifted his head . . . [118]

This encounter brought Gokhale a moment of near euphoria: "That we would see him like this, in a completely informal way was not even in our dreams, our happiness could not be contained, it soared to the sky."

When Savarkar was released from house arrest, Gokhale was determined to spend some time with him:

> On the morning of 31 December 1937 at Karnavati I insistently presented myself to him, and from that day until the day he died, for what seems like more than two aeons, I was blessed to be with him on several occasions. I consider myself immensely fortunate. Meeting Savarkar was an impossible feat to accomplish. But my good luck was such that I was never turned back from his house. I was able even to travel with him on many occasions.[119]

Gokhale thus establishes the main element in the *darśana-dakṣiṇā* account: meeting Savarkar and spending time with him.

Gokhale's vision of the book was that it would be like works such as *Conversations with Stalin* or *Conversations with Nehru*, except in Marathi. He notes that he is not a representative of a political party or a journalist and that his conversation with Savarkar was like that between a teacher and student, born out of "an unrestrained and shrewd student's questions."[120] I will point out a few of the personal details Gokhale offered his readers. Gokhale writes of Savarkar as someone always open to argument, never given to angry outbursts. Describing Savarkar as a man who lived simply, he gives his readers a picture of a day in Savarkar's life:

118. Gokhale, *Svatantryaveer Savarkar*, 6.
119. Gokhale, *Svatantryaveer Savarkar*, 4.
120. Preface to Gokhale, *Svatantryaveer Savarkar*, 5.

> Tatya was not used to waking up early, nor did he like it very much . . . he worked primarily at night. . . . He had two boiled eggs with his tea. He peeled the eggs with his own hands, and after removing the shell he ate them seasoned with salt and chilli powder. Sometimes he had Glucose biscuits with his tea. He needed at least a cup and a half of tea.[121]

While Gokhale did not deviate much from the template, for Savarkar's devotees, these homely details brought their idol into sharper focus.

Gokhale described Savarkar's morning rituals and preferences.

> The barber would come at about 10 am. He liked having himself shaved everyday. . . . He did not like people dropping by without giving prior notice.[122]

The details become more intimate:

> Before his bath, he would rub coconut oil all over his body. While he was still healthy, he liked taking a bath in cold water. . . . Tatya needed a lot of water for his bath . . . his style and trick of wearing his dhoti was very funny. . . . To avoid getting caught in one of the loose folds of the dhoti he would walk in a peculiar manner by twisting his right leg, for an onlooker it was strangely endearing. . . . Then he would enter his own room. He would sit in a chair next to the table in the lotus position. More than anything else, he loved Ratnagiri Alphonso mangoes and ice cream. He also liked fish.[123]

Gokhale also emphasized Savarkar's reclusiveness.

> He never stepped out of Savarkar Sadan . . . the funniest tale of all was that he could speak to an entranced audience of 100s of thousands but he was personally reserved and easily startled. When he went for a walk in the evening for exercise, if someone saw him, he quickly hid himself.[124]

There could be many reasons for Savarkar not wanting to be seen; he was, after all, in disrepute after 1948 given his association with Gandhi's assassin.

In 1972 Shri Ra Vartak wrote *Sāvarakarāncī Prabhāvaḷa* (*Savarkar's Influence*). Compared to the rest of the books in this section, it was unusually long,

121. Gokhale, *Svatantryaveer Savarkar*, 2
122. Gokhale, *Svatantryaveer Savarkar*, 2.
123. Gokhale, *Svatantryaveer Savarkar*, 3.
124. Gokhale, *Svatantryaveer Savarkar*, 4.

close to 160 pages. Hidden among other works, this firsthand account reveals the reach of Savarkar's influence, focusing on Savarkar's friends and associates and other Marathi revolutionaries. Some took over the running of Abhinava Bharat in Nasik, others were fellow students in Fergusson College. Unintentionally, Vartak provides an ethnography of the heartland of Marathi Brahmin revolutionary activity, showing us why Savarkar was not allowed to live in Nasik upon his return from the Andamans and pointing us to the demographics of Marathi revolutionaries. It is full of names of unknown, unrecognized Marathi revolutionaries—Patankar, Karve, Deshpande, Joshi, Soman, Khare, Marathe, Apte, Bhat, Gore, Nagpurkar, Moghe—almost all upper-caste, not all of them wealthy, many of whom were executed by the British. As mentioned, the *darśana-dakṣiṇā* literature is filled with rage about Savarkar's mistreatment and misrecognition in the nationalist mainstream, and these men received even less recognition. While undervalued, Savarkar is still known, and he therefore stands in for a lost generation of revolutionary nationalists, all of whom, they insist, were sidelined by Gandhi.

One such lost nationalist was Govind Pandurang Bapat, who published his own autobiography in 1972.[125] Bapat recounts his memories simply, without rhetorical flourish, but gives the reader a clear sense of the atmosphere in Maharashtra when he was a young revolutionary. Bapat knew much more than Savarkar about bomb making and guns, and his book offers an informative auto-ethnography of the revolutionary nationalist period in Maharashtra. The most important element of the book, however, is the surprise and incredulity of revolutionaries who came out of prison to realize that what they had believed—that only armed struggle would free India from the British—had all but disappeared. Anticolonial nationalism was now voiced in the language of Gandhian nonviolence. Which was all very well in the end, but what of their sacrifice? Their hardship? The tide seemed to have turned with astonishing speed, rendering their efforts valueless, dismissed and reviled by the Mahatma who was on his way to copyrighting Indian anticolonial nationalism. The shock of such a betrayal must have been profound, and Bapat recounts that Tilak told him to work from the outside and stay out of anticolonial struggles altogether. Any thanks men like Bapat got came from Savarkar, not Gandhi.

Bapat did not follow Tilak's advice to cease and desist, detonating a bomb here and there—but the damage was done.[126] He gives us a sense of the

125. Bapat, *Atmakatha*.
126. Bapat, *Atmakatha*, 20–25.

Marathi men from Goa to Ratnagiri who joined the revolutionary movement only to be arrested or forced to leave the country. Only Savarkar and Tilak commemorated them—the main voices of nationalist history forgot them. Despite that, Bapat is exceedingly generous—India did not get her freedom because of armed struggle, he concedes, but because of nationalists like Gandhi. And because of them, he notes, revolutionaries like him now have at least some mention in history's memory. But he also notes how difficult the colonial police made it for him to get a job after he was released, how he went nearly blind in both eyes and had to rely on someone to read and write for him.[127] Still, if he were not to get his due, at least Savarkar would.

A few years after Bapat's book, A. G. Salvi, a primary school teacher in the police headquarters school in Ratnagiri and a municipal officer, wrote a book made up of numbered vignettes about Savarkar. Salvi was known as *guruji* (spiritual teacher) or *shikshak* (educator) rather than by the English word "master" that was typically used for teachers. He recalled the movement for the purification of the Marathi language—*bhasha shuddhi*—that Savarkar was passionate about. A number of the words that were to be boycotted came from either Persian or Arabic—such as *āsmāna* (sky), *jamīna* (earth), *jabābadārī* (responsibility), *kāyama* (fixed), *jarūra* (sure)—but they also came from English—such as circular, searchlight, typewriter, paragraph—and Savarkar had suggested replacements for each of them—such as *paripatra, śōdha-jyōta, ṭaṅkalēkhak, chēdak.* As a result, Savarkar introduced into Marathi a host of Sanskritic neologisms, many of which are now commonplace in India, such as *ākāśavāṇi* (sound from the skies) for radio transmission.[128] Salvi gives readers a textured description of a Ratnagiri that was simultaneously fascinated with Savarkar, intimidated by him, and terrified of colonial reprisals. In the third vignette, Salvi tells us,

> When Savarkar walked back from the city people would regard him with respect. They'd gesture to one another and ask "Is this the same Savarkar?

127. Bapat, *Atmakatha*, 20

128. Salvi, *Swatantryaveer Savarkarancya Sahavasat*, 3. Other neologisms, such as *dūradhvanī* for telephone, or *vidhijña* in lieu of *vakīla*, have not caught on. It is worth noting that, if one removed all Arabic and Persian from Marathi, it would be impossible to speak or pronounce it. Salvi remembered with awe Savarkar's point that "'r' is written three different ways, it should be written just in this one fashion. Even when he thought of big issues like politics, or social reform, he would also think of such minute details. Such was his omnipotent intelligence, which one finds in very few perople. He would tell it to us and tell us to tell it to others" (20).

> The one who was in the Andamans? . . . The one who in the flower of his youth underwent so many trials for the country?" Educated, uneducated people, would with respect but also awe watch him . . . wherever he sat, people would gather to listen to his views on the purification of language, self-rule, and reconversion, and abolition of untouchability. Tatya would personally meet everyone, speak to them without airs, like he was speaking to a close friend. Such was his manner. If he met someone once, he would remember them and ask after them—he had immense ability to remember.[129]

The admiration for Savarkar's prodigious memory was complemented by a stunned appreciation of Savarkar's rationality and emotionlessness, such as the description of May 1937, when Savarkar's infant child died.

> The infant was barely 3–4 months old when it died, it was the afternoon. Savarkar's wife, Sou. Mai was grief stricken sitting next to the corpse. . . . As soon we heard, Madhavrao Patkar, Dr, Shinde, Savant [teacher]—in the raging heat of the afternoon we went to their house. What do we see but Tatya calmly engrossed in his work. We were stunned. He asked us why we'd come in such blazing heat? He seemed a little angry. Yes, the child has died, this is true, we did our best. We were unsuccessful. Go home, go eat, go rest and come at 4 pm in the evening.

Salvi notes, as an addendum to this description "Savarkar had encountered death firsthand, welcomed it even, so in such a situation he was unlikely to be downcast."[130]

Though Salvi was an educator, he compared himself self-deprecatingly to Savarkar:

> . . . our intellect was not so far reaching as to pay attention to the future. In *Shraddhanand, Kesari, Balvant, Satyashodhak,* and even some Hindi weeklies, his articles would appear. Even though we sat next to him and could hear his speeches, I still regret not writing them down.

For Salvi, Savarkar was a godlike figure, and he was grateful that Savarkar disseminated his wisdom throughout Maharashtra.[131] Salvi described Savarkar's

129. Salvi, *Swatantryaveer Savarkarancya Sahavasat,* 3.
130. Salvi, *Swatantryaveer Savarkarancya Sahavasat,* 6.
131. Salvi, *Swatantryaveer Savarkarancya Sahavasat,* 24, 25.

speeches as like "a bullet shot from a cannon which penetrated the audiences' deepest interiority."[132] In a section entitled "Arē, mājhī vyākhyānē kuṇītarī lihūna ṭhēvā" ("Hello! Someone please write down my speeches"), he remembers Savarkar instructing him to record everything he said—all his speeches, long and short—because they would come in handy in the future.[133] Salvi confesses modestly that

> we knew of the Manusmr̥ti as Yagnavalkya smr̥ti, but what was inside its pages who knew? Tatyarao, when he explained the Manusmr̥ti focused on a comparison between then and now, between what was appropriate in the past and what is incorrect about the maintenance of such views in the present, and in this manner his lessons were always relevant."[134]

I end this *darśana-dakṣiṇā* section with a few final examples. Na Sa Bapat, who belonged to Savarkar's secret society as a young student in Ratnagiri, reflected on his memories of Savarkar. Bapat's text begins with the temple established by Savarkar, Patitpavan Mandir, built by Bhagoji Sheth Keer, and its activities and his memories of Savarkar's lectures, classes, and encouragement of young people.[135] The text bristles with anger that Savarkar is so misunderstood and ignored by the *karaṇṭya,* or good-for-nothing people, who doubt his nationalism, revolutionary consistency, and zeal; misunderstand the manner in which he conducted politics while in Ratnagiri; and fail to understand that everything he said and did was political and nationalist.[136] Bapat chiefly celebrates Savarkar's militarization policy; without Savarkar, Bapat insists, there would not have been an Indian army, navy, or air force. This is not quite true, since many other nationalists pushed for a strong military. Bapat continually challenges Gandhi's nonviolence and hold over mainstream nationalists, comparing him unfavorably to Savarkar the ur-revolutionary, the man who read about revolutionaries, thought constantly of revolution, knew and admired revolutionaries, and was admired by them. To rebut the claim that Savarkar was an armchair revolutionary, Bapat claims

132. Preface to Salvi, *Swatantryaveer Savarkarancya Sahavasat.*

133. Salvi, *Swatantryaveer Savarkarancya Sahavasat,* 24.

134. Salvi, *Swatantryaveer Savarkarancya Sahavasat,* 24

135. Bapat, *Smrutipushpe,* 1–11. The term *patitpavan* in Patitpavan Mandir refers to the purification of the impure.

136. Bapat, *Smrutipushpe,* 26.

that Savarkar had stains of pitric acid used in bombmaking on his hands when he went to the British Library.[137]

Bapat's indignation about matters omitted in Indian history books suffuses the narration. The blacklisting of Savarkar was an outrage not just to a noble man but to the entire region. Savarkar even wore a Gandhi *topi* on occasion, Bapat says, so one should not ostracize a man who was so much a part of the nationalist mainstream. Savarkar met Gandhi; Bose took advice from him; Ambedkar met him; every major nationalist respected him—yet here in modern India he is shunned.[138] Bapat also mentions that Savarkar was friends with Comrade Meherali, debunking by implication the false charges of Savarkar's anti-Muslimness. He concludes that "only those who have actually engaged in secret revolutionary work can understand the betrayals and troubles."[139]

In the same year, from Nagpur, Gangadhar Jadhav published *Jay Jay Mrutyunjay Savarkar* (Hail to immortal Savarkar). I close this section with a translation of a few verses of one of the poems, "Hindusthānācaṁ bhāgya ghaḍavā hō" ("Let Hindustan's good fortune become real").[140]

Sōḍā jātīpātīcā bhēda	set aside the divides of caste
Prānta bhēda pantha bhēda	the divides of region, sect
Pārṭībājicē matabhēda	the divides of party disputes
Ēkā jhaṭīnē vhā abhēda	in one move come together, undivided
Vīra Vināyakācē guṇa	Veer Vinayak's virtues
Mani hradayī mī ṭhasavuna	having installed them in my heart and mind
Gātō sabhēta mī garvānaṁ	I sing with pride in this assembly
Dēśabhakti mūrtimān	epitome of service to the nation
Dharmāci mūrti jāṇa	understand your duty
Tēja divya dēśabhakticē, raṇa-śambhūcē	with the brilliance of national service,
Aṅgī tumhi banavā	become warriors
Hindusthānācaṁ bhāgya ghaḍavā hō	and secure the good fate of Hindustan

137. Bapat, *Smrutipushpe*, 19.
138. Bapat, *Smrutipushpe*, 24.
139. Bapat, *Smrutipushpe*, 26.
140. Jadhav, *Jay Jay Mrutyunjay Savarkar*, 5.

These writers and poets, these unnoticed and hidden scribes of Savarkar's and India's history, composed and continue composing the works that circulate through the Savarkar Smarak, with its imposing presence in Shivaji Park in Mumbai. Bapat, Salvi, Dugal, Vartak, Barwe, Shidore, Athavale, seventy-odd old revolutionaries who sent in their memories for a collective history, and at least eighty other writers. They pay no attention to historians like me. They write with the confidence that comes with the immediacy of their own experience. Their books are not taught, cited, or referred to, but they are read. And all of them are influenced by Savarkar's touch, glance, advice, or some other talismanic exchange. Those chance encounters were enough for each of them to pick up their pen, join the demotic gathering of scribes, and engage in the quintessentially Savarkarite project of inculcating a national consciousness in the nonurban communities of village and small-town Maharashtra.

Conclusion

In 1948 Savarkar turned sixty. Known as the *shashthi*, the sixtieth birthday of a Savarna Hindu male is a watershed moment, a time to look back at one's achievements and perhaps think about moving on to the next stage. It is a moment of making peace with what one has accomplished. Savarkar's sixtieth birthday coincided with a particularly intense moment in Indian history, coming just after Gandhi's assassination by one of Savarkar's associates. Savarkar's *shashthi* was marked therefore by a dual failure: the failure to be martyred for the nation, a desire he expressed over decades across many literary forms; and the failure of becoming known as the assassin of the father of the nation rather than the founder of the nation himself. This last brought complete ostracization and drove Savarkar into virtual isolation for the rest of his life.

Gandhi was the subject of biographies of journalists of world repute—from William Shirer and Louis Fischer to Joseph Lelyveld and Ramchandra Guha more recently—as well as countless historians and scholars. Savarkar was memorialized almost exclusively *within* India, in Indian languages, and until recently, with very little notice beyond a small Marathi reading public. But there is a homage to Savarkar architecturally enshrined in the part of Bombay known as Shivaji Park, where Savarkar lived after independence. A large and imposing building fronts a street named for him. Once Cadell Road, it is now Swatantrya Veer Savarkar Marg, V. S. Marg for short. On this road sits the Swatantryaveer Savarkar Smarak (Savarkar Memorial Building), which opened to the public in 1989. The Savarkar Smarak is privately funded. Although registered with the

Maharashtra Government as an agency, it does not receive any state or central funding or have a university affiliation. The large campus called the Nehru Memorial Museum and Library (NMML) in New Delhi, by contrast, contains four complexes including a planetarium and is one of the major research centers in India. In Bombay, the Mani Bhavan Gandhi Sanghrahalaya houses a reference library with all of Gandhi's papers and memorabilia, all of his writings, a collection of photographs, and about 50,000 books and periodicals. Mani Bhavan is associated with the University of Bombay, which offers doctoral degrees in Gandhian Thought and Rural Development. The two memorials compete in the same city for recognition, reproducing the old tensions between Gandhi and Savarkar, with Savarkar no longer the overlooked underdog.

While Gandhi's and Nehru's respective museums and research sites have their place in India's intellectual and pilgrimage milieus, the monumental self-presentation of Savarkar Smarak appears a little forlorn. Yet it is far from empty. Its activities reveal the role Savarkar plays in the Marathi imagination and testify to his steady and persistent mythologizing, by himself and by the many followers who have taken his lead and, often, his words.

Conclusion

SAVARKAR DIED in isolation on February 26, 1966. A few weeks earlier, despite his daughter's urging, he had refused food, water, and medication, leaving this world of his own accord and choosing.[1] Coming two years after Nehru's death, his own caused no major ripples in an India that had no place for a person who had been so tainted by his association with the assassination of the father of the nation, Gandhi.

Not everyone, however, failed to notice Savarkar's passing. The year after his death, Govindswami Aphale, a noted singer of *kirtan* (a form of devotional singing that combines a spiritual message with a social one) composed and published a *gāthā* (mini-epic poem) called *Sāvarakara-Gāthā*, the cost of which was a mere fifty paise ($0.0066), for all practical intents and purposes to be given away freely.[2] Aphale in his preface wrote that he was not writing a biography of Savarkar but was setting to verse a few select events in his life that would thrill the hearts of his listeners.[3] This type of accolade reflects some of what I have been tracing in this book. "Some tunes" he wrote,

> are from the Gita-Rāmāyaṇa, and on some occasions, there is a similarity with the Rāmāyaṇa. For that reason, I initially thought of calling these poems Gīta-Sāvarakarāyaṇa.

1. Savarkar, *Athavani Angaracya*, 21–26.

2. Aphale, *Sāvarakara Gāthā*.

3. His exact words were "Hr̥dayālā caṭakā lāvaṇārē kāhī prasaṅga nivaḍūna mī tyāvara hī kāvyaracanā kēlī āhē ।" ("I have composed this poem on a few select events from Sāvarakara's life that will thrill the heart"). Aphale, *Sāvarakara Gāthā*.

As he put it,

> Swatantryaveer Sāvarakara's character is the Bhagavadgītā of freedom upliftment. It is a series of climaxes of many emotions such as strength, sacrifice, sorrow, ridicule, appreciation, honor, courage, contempt, despair.

This Marathi *kirtankar* saw both of Hindu India's two major epics, the Rāmāyaṇa and the Mahābhārata, as the appropriate comparisons for his account of Savarkar's heroic life.

Within a year of his death, in fact, Savarkar was in the process of being deified. I quote just three couplets from Aphale's memorable gāthā by way of illustration:

Sāṅgatō kathā manācī (jivācī) vyathā Vināyaka Sāvarakara gāthā	I tell the story of the travails of Vinayak Sāvarakara
Bhāgyavāna tō Bhagūra gāva hō Nāśika śējārī tithē janmalē prabhu Sāvarakara Hindū kaivārī	Blessed be that Bhagur village that neighbors Nashik For there was born Lord Sāvarakara the protector of the Hindus
Nāśika Pañcavaṭīcā parisara Rāma Jānakīcā parākramācyā paramparēcā Hindu asmitēcā	Nashik and Pancavati belong to Rama and Janaki The extent of the power and tradition of Hindu identity
janmatāca jō jagatā sāṅgē pahilyā huṅkārī asē janmalē prabhū Sāvarakara Hindū kaivārī[4]	upon his very birth this his first shout so was born Prabhu Sāvarakara the protector of the Hindus.

In Maharashtra, only two figures (leaving aside Gandhi) are enshrined like this: Savarkar and B. R. Ambedkar. Both are national as well as regional icons. Both have been deified by their followers, and both are enshrined, coincidentally, on the same Veer Savarkar Marg in the neighborhood known as Shivaji Park. Founded in 1989, on the anniversary of his birth, it is called the Swatantryaveer Savarkar Rashtriya Smarak (Savarkar Memorial Building). A large and

4. Sections 2 and 3 in Aphale, *Sāvarakara Gāthā*, 2–3.

high stage-like platform looks out over passing drivers, who if they turned their heads to look would see an imposing statue of Savarkar seated on a chair as if he was rising from it, with his arm raised as if to make a point to them as they go by. Behind the statue there is an artistic mural, in the shape of a large halo painted by a well-known Marathi artist, depicting Mother India being protected by her numerous nationalist sons. The building that houses the library, the gymnasium, and the conference center, as well as the offices of the secretary of the society, is behind the mural and statue. The Smarak remains true to Savarkar's mottos: physical fitness for all Hindus, men and women, self-arming through the learning of the use of weaponry, and pride in being Hindu.

I went to this Smarak many times over a period of ten years. Initially I did not think there was much to find there; what could one find in a national commemorative building other than commemorative materials? The small room that is the library had a few Godrej steel cupboards, all of them containing books. I got to know the librarian, chatting with him as I did about the weather—how hot and muggy Bombay was—while gaining his sympathy for the fact that my father, whose apartment was just a few blocks to the north, had contracted ALS. Over the months as I kept returning, he began to let me remove books from the library and take them home to photocopy. I mentioned en passant that it was possible that my personal views did not always dovetail with Savarkar's (I was a bit vague on the subject), to which his response was a simple "it doesn't matter—you're reading Savarkar." There was never a crowd at the Smarak; people came and went but not in large numbers.

Outside of Maharashtra, Savarkar had seemed to fade into obscurity after Gandhi's assassination, even as his writings remained a steady influence on the anti-Nehru/Gandhi right wing. However, Savarkar was resurrected locally and nationally in the 1990s just as the Smarak was founded, and his vision has roared back into such prominence that one wonders if he really was ever that obscure a figure. Narendra Modi, Prime Minister of India since 2014 and leader of the BJP, claims that Savarkar is his muse, his greatest influence, his guiding star. As Hindu fundamentalism began to assert its political power in India, especially regarding the agitation around the idea that a mosque had been built over a temple in Ayodhya that culminated with a march and attack on the mosque in 1992, Savarkar began to eclipse Gandhi and Nehru as the most influential nationalist thinker for modern India, the touchstone for rising nationalist pride in Hinduism and the growing rejection both of secularism and the place of Muslims as a respected minority. The current BJP-led Indian government is ever-alert to any attacks against perceived "Hinduphobia," intolerant of Muslims, and bellicose toward Pakistan. It is now altering school curricula and watching to ensure that nothing critical of Hindus, Hinduism, or Hindutva can be expressed by journalists and scholars. How did this happen? How did the Gandhi-Nehru vision of secularism—*sarvadharmasamabhava* or equal respect for all faiths—disappear and Savarkar's dread-secularism (live with "us" but always in fear) and ultranationalism take its place so quickly? These are questions that are critical as well to Maharashtra, which prided itself on its social and political progressivism (*purōgāmitva*).

The rapidity with which Savarkarite ideology was resurrected and reclaimed the political landscape of modern India begs the question of whether it had been seeded earlier, quietly fertilized, and nurtured so that at the appropriate moment it could burst on the scene fully-grown, mature, and worked through. What was that seeding? I went repeatedly to the Smarak to try and find out. In the Smarak's library, none of the books and articles I was familiar with in English, by authors like Aparna Devare, Parimala Rao, Charu Gupta, Thomas Hansen, Christophe Jaffrelot, or Ashis Nandy, among others, were to be found. Instead, the cupboards consisted of Marathi books, many of which have figured prominently in the chapters of this book.

These books proved indispensable in analyzing how Savarkar was and continues to be understood in his native state of Maharashtra and what he exemplifies. In many of the Marathi works I read, poverty is narrated as if it is the basis for Brahmin pride. Historically, Marathi Brahmins are not like the Bengali Brahmin *zamindar*s who owned land and large *haveli*s; in Maharashtra the models are Ram Shastri Prabhune, an upright and honest man who found Raghoba Peshwa guilty of murdering his nephew (whose wife changed the *dha* in *dharā* to *mā* in the royal order thereby turning the word "hold" [*dharā*] into "kill" [*mārā*]);[5] Sudama the poor Brahmin; Shravan the young man who looked after his blind parents; the ostracized Brahmin son of a *sanyasi* who wrote the *Dnyaneshwari* and could make a bull recite the Vedas. To this list, thanks to the Marathi corpus about him, we might now add Savarkar, as a heterodox Brahmin who underwent untold suffering for his patriotism, suffered numerous personal tragedies, and was beleaguered by British colonial administrators and INC politicians alike, misunderstood, and neglected till the bitter end.

The Marathi corpus also makes clear that many of the very traits that render him anathema to secular Indians also turn him into a hero for others. This is

5. This is now an adage in colloquial Marathi. Someone who changes *dha* to *mā* is considered treacherous.

because there is a constitutive contradiction at the heart of Savarkar: if it were at all possible to simply ignore or set aside as one part of his ouevre his ideology, his politics, and his writings about Muslims, then there would be little about him that we might find difficult to accept or objectionable (unless, of course, we were orthodox and devout Sanātani Hindus, in which case, he would be utterly repellent). But there is virtually no work of Savarkar's that is not either overtly or covertly linked to Muslims. In that sense, regardless of subject or genre, Savarkar wrote primarily about Muslims. But it is precisely that delinked kaleidoscopic gaze that allows Savarkar to be read piecemeal, to focus on his humorous and indeed biting attacks on the orthodoxy, or be astonished at his erudition or awed at his early embrace of technology, rather than solely focusing on his anti-Muslim vitriol. My attempt has been to show the linkages and suggest that we get a very different picture if we keep turning the kaleidoscope rather than allowing it to stay within one frame.

In reading Savarkar I came to realize that his chief mode of expression was either poetry or poetic polemic. The invoking of the image of nation through poetry was common to many regional formations, in languages such as Bengali, Hindi, and Tamil, for instance. Invoking the nation through poetry, making loyalty to territory emotionally powerful as Savarkar did was not what made him unique; what sets him apart from other nationalists is that he combined in the same person the revolutionary, poet, novelist, playwright, historian, caste reformer, and political leader of the nation.[6] His historical writings have traveled outside the region, and have the largest circulation of any of his writings, not least because he offered a history of the Hindu state in a language not of failure but success. Unwilling to cede any ground to anyone, not history to historians or caste reform to reformers, Savarkar's hubris was as extraordinary as his versatility and range. His use of different genres and facility with different personas also gives us some insight into why he was such an effective communicator. While he certainly gave vent to intemperate polemics, the numerous genres that he tried his hand at also won him consent, a major element in constructing an anticolonial, antihegemonic point of view.[7] The transformation of that sensibility into the present is one of the most effective transformations/deformations of a minoritarian outlook into a majoritarian/authoritarian one.

Within Maharashtra, Savarkar has remained an important and inspirational poet, and specific poems and verses of his have become iconic. He transcended

6. I am grateful to Partha Chatterjee for pointing this out.

7. I am grateful to Keya Ganguly, who pointed this out to me.

the region, however, not through his poetry but through his political writings. Many of those were translated, but not his other writings on caste, on poetry, or on the Manusmṛti. All of this literature—Savarkar's own writings, his poetry, as well as the literature on him in Marathi—is difficult to classify as familiar genres for scholarly analysis. For starters, most of the material I found in the Smarak is not available in academic libraries. Much of it can be found in community-based libraries or libraries set up by memorial centers. Many of the necessary questions about the reach of the literature remain difficult to answer: how many copies were published, who bought them, how were they distributed, who read them? There are certainly no reviews of such works, although the reading public that is devoted to learning about Savarkar knows all these books quite well. We might dismiss the works with the claim that vanity publishing that yields at most 200 to 2,000 copies distributed by and within the cognoscenti is not worth paying attention to, but without these little tracts, the seeding of Hindutva and the dissemination of Savarkar as the exemplary Hindu would not have succeeded.[8]

Many of these Marathi books also offer this list of "firsts" about Savarkar:

First student to take a vow (*pratigya*) at such a young age
First student whose degree (B. A.) was retrospectively taken away for his activities
First student ever to hold a bonfire of foreign cloth
First nationalist writer of the 1857 Rebellion
First nationalist to make a national flag
First Indian nationalist to have a book banned before it was published
First Indian nationalist to receive two life terms in prison
First Indian prisoner to receive no pen or paper but managed to carve poetry on his prison wall

8. In 1990 a small book titled *Mi Pahilele Savarkar: Jyani Savarkarana pahile aahe asa namvant Savarkar-bhaktancya Athavani* (The Savarkar that I saw: Recollections of Savarkar-devotees who had seen Savarkar) was published that brought together recollections of Savarkar from more than one hundred men from across Maharashtra. These men hailed from Pune, Ratnagiri, Nashik, Sangli, Belgaon, Satara, Karhad, Nanded, Nagpur, Yavatmal, Solapur, Wardha. It is a different group than the ones referred to in the previous chapter, but the last names are still Brahmin or otherwise upper-caste last names: Dixit, Natu, Joshi, Kolhatkar, Satvalekar, Ranade, Pathak, Phadke, Limaye, Ghate, Kulkarni, etc. Bhat, *Mi Pahilele Savarkar*, Anukramanika [Table of contents], 7–11.

First Indian nationalist to actively propose militarization of Hindus and the state
First nationalist revolutionary who ended his life by *ātmārpaṇa*—refusing medicine, then food, then water.

In Marathi, in other words, there was a different Savarkar to be had than just the one who had written *Essentials of Hindutva* or blessed Nathuram Godse. But what remained constant, whether in English or in Marathi, were two things: first, his virulent attacks on Muslims, and second, his connection to and preoccupation with the figure of Gandhi. On a spectrum of political ideas, aspirations, principles as they related to peaceful coexistence and non-violence, we would find Gandhi on one end and Savarkar on the other. And yet Savarkar and Gandhi were in some kind of strange if discordant synchrony with each other, interlocutors and antagonists all their lives, symbols of a kind of assertive Indian nationalism that attained modern power while drawing heavily from the wealth of upper-caste Indian tradition and precept. This emerges clearly when we look at their personal trajectories, their investments in a "Hindu" style of governance, their heroes both in India and abroad, their convictions that, for India to be freed of colonial rule, it had to turn inward, that Indians had to reconnect with their own culture(s) and language(s)—so dismissed by two hundred years of colonial contempt—and return to the villages and small towns rather than focusing on urban centers that were, according to them, in thrall to a colonized lifestyle.

Neither Gandhi nor Savarkar had any interest in the scholarly discipline of history, let alone what practitioners from within that discipline were producing. Gandhi became a world-historical figure, heralded by countless acolytes from outside India even as he was seen as an inspiration for all Indian nationalists. To a limited extent and solely within India, this was true of Savarkar as well if we look at the list of nationalists who made it a point to visit Savarkar while in Ratnagiri, from B. R. Ambedkar to Bhagat Singh and Rajguru, Bhai Parmanand, Yusuf Meherali, Sikandar Hayat Khan, and Senapati Bapat.[9] After his release when he moved to Bombay, he was visited as well by figures such as M. N. Roy (founder of the Indian Communist Party) and Tarkateertha Laxmanshastri Joshi.[10] Savarkar, who wanted to be a world-historical figure and proclaimed himself one, was obsessed with history. He had a rather

9. Savarkar, *Parisparsha Swatantryaveeranca*, 13–30.
10. Savarkar, *Parisparsha Swatantryaveeranca*, 59, 62–63.

straightforward and instrumental understanding of history as the vital tool for generating a national community. He believed it was necessary to germinate a historical consciousness to develop a real commitment to the nation. No time should be wasted on knowledge for knowledge's sake or the study of any discipline—be it history, geography, poetry, art, literature—unless it was in the service of developing a national consciousness. This one-themed history would be as monotonous and repetitive as an endlessly dripping faucet, but it was one of the seeds of Hindutva, and extraordinarily effective in fixing in place a particular understanding of Indian history.

The stakes for Savarkar to rewrite Indian history from the point of view of the oppressed may seem like a counter-Hegelian project. However, civilization qua civilization interested Savarkar not in the least. He certainly wished to see Indian history as a vital part of the pantheon of other national histories, but he had no genuine interest in India's civilizational glory, as did so many other historians, whether they found it in the antiquity of Gupta- and Pallava-period architectural splendor or in Chola-period lost-wax bronze making, and certainly not in the spectacularly glorious Mughal architecture, whether the Taj Mahal or the Agra Fort. He knew and appreciated the Sanskrit literary tradition, but India's architecture, art, and sculpture held only a passing interest for him, given his blinkered focus on nationhood. His sole interest was in ensuring that only Hindus proud of their history should write it, engaging in critique under the necessary condition that it specifically serve the greater cause of the Hindu nation.

Gandhi had even less interest in India's material history, though he drew inspiration from its epics and traditions and used the civilizational plaudits of Western Orientalists to assert equality, if not superiority, over the West. Both he and Savarkar owed much to their hero B. G. Tilak, and like him they turned their activist gaze back into India's past to search for tools for her future liberation. Gandhi returned to the Rāmāyaṇa, in whose protagonist's ideal rule he would find an ethical polity in an organic idiom, with himself as the messenger or harbinger of potential good news: the coming of Rāmrājya. By contrast, the historical move generated by Savarkar produced no idealized ethical governance, but an aggressive, and subjunctively tolerant ethnic Hindu as the true subject of Indian national history.[11] The nation is beholden to past kings and rulers of the Indian subcontinent such as Chandragupta Maurya and his wily minister, Chanakya, from the third-century BCE, all the way through Chhatrapati Shivaji of the late seventeenth-century. But while the historical as a

11. Bakhle, "Country First?," 178.

modality for Savarkar was always national, he could also be as baldly historicist as the most Rankeian of scholars, noting in a vastly different reading of the Rāmāyaṇa from Gandhi's, and even his own in *SGE*, that the idiocy of a literal reading of it produced a monkey-worshipping citizenry.

Like Gandhi, Savarkar would also assume that in his fragmented autobiographical person lay the correct body of India: politically Hindu, opportunistically secular, generally agnostic, and sentimentally religious all at once. But while Gandhi is either now ignored—or even disdained for his perceived sympathies with caste hierarchy—Savarkar's philosophy seems to have a little bit of something for everyone. Except, that is, for Muslims. In other words, there is a preferred kaleidoscopic setting for everyone as long as one does not look too closely at the dark parts. If you ignore his polemical scorn for Muslims, he comes across as a progressive, satirical, polemical, and outrageous critic of casteism and a proud Hindu imperialist. Put his anti-Muslim views back into the picture, and they overwhelm and undermine his progressivism. Yet again, if you ignored what he wrote about Muslims, radicals would find much to agree with in his critique of liberal policies; conservatives would find much to agree with in his circling of the Hindu wagons and valorization of Sanskrit; anticaste reformers would find solace in his arguments against caste Hindus and Benares Brahmins poring over the Vedas; moderns could sympathize with his claims for national history; and modern antimoderns could sympathize with his rejection of the West. Furthermore, it allowed for a comfortable accommodation of otherwise irreconcilable contradictions. Read piecemeal, as a poet, or as a critic of caste, Savarkar comes across in such a way that Gandhi, his main enemy, seems the reactionary, the conservative, even the Hindu fundamentalist, given that his point of departure was to return India to a Rāmrājya rather than create a strong and even militant modern nation.

So far I have not said anything in this book about Hindu fundamentalists, which is what Savarkar and his followers are considered to be. But what would a nonmonotheistic fundamentalism look like? For Dayananda Saraswati, the founder and leader of the Arya Samaj, which comes closest to espousing a monotheistic fundamentalism, the Vedas could play the scriptural role that the Qur'an and Bible played in Islam and Christianity, and he dismissed all texts that postdated the Mahābhārata.[12] But the Arya Samaj's reach was

12. See Gold, "Organized Hinduisms." I am grateful to Britt Leake, who took a graduate seminar with me and wrote a research paper in which he read through all five volumes of the Fundamentalism Project. I have learned a great deal from his analysis.

limited to North India and to the Hindi heartland and Gujarat at best. Savarkar admired the leaders of the Arya Samaj for their proselytizing work but paid no real attention to all the self-proclaimed Hindu sages and saints who appeared on India's cultural and political stages in the late nineteenth and early twentieth centuries. Savarkar realized that sectarian divides between Shaivites and Vaishnavites, between one *sampradaya* and another, not to mention the otherworldly messages that were proclaimed, were as antinationalist as the caste divides he so decried. Instead he focused on "Hindu" as a single unifying political identity, a transcendent category bypassing all these divides.

Savarkar did this not by referring to a book but by the simple gesture of tying every Hindu—whether one identified as Hindu or not—to a sacred cartography. One should note, however, that national sovereignty had been defined in the language of territoriality in Europe by the seventeenth century and universalized by European colonialism thereafter. This particular lesson of world history had been absorbed quite fully by Savarkar, but to it he added an Indic component. He also translated into the language of Hindutva the idea of ethnic solidarity in keeping with his vision of a Hindu state. Neither pluralist secularism (pace Gandhi's *sarvadharmasamabhava*) nor an unmarked universalism has been able to shake off Savarkar's territorial fundamentalism, so much so that the slogan "not an inch of our territory can be conceded to the enemy" (chiefly Pakistan, but also China) is now the commonsense view voiced by all Indian political parties, from the left to the right. Thus, Savarkar's territorial fundamentalism is now the accepted sacred cartography of Indian political discourse. Savarkar's territorial/cartographic fundamentalism involved no temple, no theology, no priesthood, no rituals of worship, no single text. But there was a dogma, a vocabulary, and a set of cultural practices used for veneration: music (the national anthem), poetry (*jayo stute*), dance. Even today, Savarkar's life invokes dance dramas and poems as the affective vocabulary of his remembrance.

The cultural critic Ashis Nandy reads Savarkar as completely Westernized in his concepts. His secularism in particular, mixed and mixed up though it was, prompted Nandy to view Savarkar as the literal embodiment of the disease of secular modern rationality.[13] A Western sickness, as Nandy diagnoses it, had taken over the body politic of colonial India, and Savarkar's imagination itself had been colonized by years of incarceration and hard labor, wherein he

13. Nandy, "A Disowned Father of the Nation in India," 91–112.

had become a mixture of "collaboration and xenophobia."[14] Nandy calls this secularism "the pathological by-product of the modern idea of a secular nation state rather than that of Hinduism."[15] The more I read Savarkar in Marathi, the more this didn't seem altogether correct. Savarkar occupies a unique place between tradition and modernity. It would never be time for Savarkar to write Indian history in a Western mode. There would be no need for footnotes or to accept the work of scholarly historians or to worry much about facts when self-assured autodidacticism could do the job just as well. History itself would be removed from its own disciplinary constraints to serve as Savarkar's nationalist handmaiden.

The separation Nandy suggested between religion and nation was also not quite right. Savarkar was not truly or fully an atheist, as much as he projected himself as a rational, modern thinker. Neither, however, did he fully abjure the fundamentality of the ideas of sacred and profane, transposing them onto a modern political ideology that simultaneously drew its power from religious traditions and affective modes of representation, while recommitting them all to a modernist project of national unity and strength.

This modernist project has culminated in perhaps the strangest of all results: the enshrining of Savarkar as a secular God and of Gandhi as a national saint. These images are themselves locked in battle, and when Savarkar's and Gandhi's respective biographies/autobiographies are read against each other, the differences present two distinct visions of and for India. Gandhi was the subject of biographies of journalists, historians, and scholars of world repute. Savarkar was memorialized almost exclusively *within* India and mainly in Marathi (and to a lesser degree Hindi). While Gandhi lived his life transparently—if always with a kind of pedagogical intent—Savarkar's life was closed off from public scrutiny and fashioned through narratives that seemed designed—whether written by him or others—to create and sustain a legend that drew anecdotes from his life only when they served a single, higher, purpose.

All of Gandhi's biographies, from the first one written by William Shirer to the canonical ones by Mahadev Desai and Louis Fischer to more recent ones by writers like Joseph Lelyveld, open a window into Gandhi's internal struggles over a range of subjects: sexuality, self-discipline, social reform. If biographies are accretive or accumulative, then every single biography gives us yet

14. Nandy, "A Disowned Father of the Nation in India," 100.
15. Nandy, "A Disowned Father of the Nation in India," 103.

another facet of the historical Gandhi. Savarkar's life is narrated in fundamentally different ways. A Homeric hero turned secular God, the corpus on Savarkar creates a consistent legend to be deified and enshrined. What is most remarkable is that the legend was based on his own narrative, one that projected all his struggles onto the outside world, while building the story from the beginning that here was an extraordinary human being whose only failure was to be insufficiently recognized as a great man during his lifetime. As generations of biographers, beginning in his own lifetime and continuing until today, have used the genre of hagiography to narrate his life, they have followed his own modes of self-fashioning, rendering a shared myth more than a real life.

Savarkar was exonerated of any implication in Gandhi's actual assassination. But Savarkar and Gandhi, the God and the saint, remain in a seesawing rivalry, neither one able to ascend unless the other is descending. Gandhi's India can accommodate Nehru, Ambedkar the constitution maker, (not the annihilator of caste) but not Savarkar, even as Savarkar's India has no room not just for Gandhi but for most nationalist heroes, and after Ambedkar's conversion it has no room for him, but plenty for Subhas Bose and Bhagat Singh. Between Savarkar and Gandhi one has to choose. Even today, as Gandhi has been rendered a reactionary figure because of his seemingly accommodationist caste politics, Savarkar is read by many as genuinely modern, a man who escaped the prejudices of Indian tradition, at least so long as you keep your hand over the anti-Muslim parts (unless of course you share those views too and see him as an intrepid truth-teller.)

In this book I have kept in mind Theodor Adorno's aphorism that one must be steeped in a tradition to hate it properly. By hate, Adorno meant critique, which I take to mean both appreciation and analysis. I have steeped myself in the traditions that surround Savarkar so I could present a new view, scholarly and dispassionate, but also embedded in the traditions and milieu that spawned his life and his legends. I have tried to present Savarkar as a man of intense nationalist passion who was seen as extraordinarily dangerous (and hence important and influential) by the colonial authorities, yet who was used (perhaps unwittingly) at the same time by them to further their own agenda. I have detailed his radical progressivism about caste and gender while also unveiling his legendary fear and rage at Muslims. I have depicted a man who took himself, much like his chief enemy Gandhi, as representative of Hindus, while casting them as minorities in their own land—a position he was steadfastly devoted to undoing. I have shown his immense learning but also his superficial exposition and single-minded obsessions, blinded by his anger at

Muslims and Hindus like Gandhi who wanted to create a nation that was comfortable with constituencies within it that had multiple (and thus treasonous) loyalties. I have spent so much time writing about and translating his poetry in order that we can see his brilliance, a master of multiple genres who truly loved his native language Marathi. I have shown the picture of a man who was obsessed by history and yet used it in ways that were only meant to mobilize the past for the purposes of devotion to a future in which the Hindu nation would rise triumphant against all odds and against all enemies. I have written of a man who was simultaneously full of hatred and love.

In India today, the BJP-led government has all but ruled that the cow is a sacred animal and may not be slaughtered. It has mandated that schools can only teach a Hindu history that does not focus on Hindu defeat but teaches the glories of Hindu potentates. For those who might assume that Savarkar authored both of these worldviews, it is salutary to remember that he would have certainly opposed the ban on cow slaughter on the grounds that the cow is sacred. And yet he would have been the chief advocate for the view that only a glorious Hindu history ought to be taught.

In 2003 the BJP-led National Democratic Alliance amended the Citizenship Act of 1955 (CAA), which also gave them a mandate to create a National Register of Citizens (NRC). The 2003 CAA offered refuge to persecuted minorities from India's neighboring countries. In December 2019 the BJP, led by Modi, amended the CAA once again. This time, the amendment specifically named religious minorities in Muslim countries who would be eligible for citizenship. On the face of it the new law simply makes it easier for non-Muslim refugees from three Muslim-majority countries surrounding India to become citizens of India. Hindus and other non-Muslims who did not have the paperwork the NRC declared necessary could get citizenship through the CAA. At the same time, millions of Indian Muslims who did not have the same paperwork could now be made stateless. The BJP claimed that the NRC and the CAA were unrelated and not directed against Muslims. Yet in the one state, Assam, where the NRC has been implemented, nearly two million people, mostly Muslims, have now been categorized as "suspected foreigners."[16] The controversy over the CAA and NRC erupted a few months after the revocation of Article 370, by which the state of Jammu and Kashmir was downgraded to a union territory. The central government in Delhi assumed the power to

16. "'Muslims Are Foreigners': Inside India's Campaign to Decide Who Is a Citizen," *New York Times*.

administer the territory and suspend civil liberties, arresting political leaders and imposing one of the longest internet blackouts ever recorded in a democracy.

I believe that Savarkar would have supported the 2019 CAA and the NRC in augmenting the numbers of Hindu citizens, and also, for that matter, making Jammu and Kashmir into a union territory. But temples mattered not at all to him, nor did the epics as sacred texts. He had no time for Hindu ritual observances nor would he have supported spending money on building more temples. His views of the Indian nation have triumphed, and yet his legacy—and certainly his legends—sit at an uncomfortable angle to the gloss of Hindu religiosity that so often accompanies the policies of the Hindu right.

At this moment in history, Savarkar may indeed have triumphed over his rivals, fully displacing the positions held by Gandhi, Nehru, and other leaders of the INC. Yet he remains an enigmatic and contradictory figure, a man who even at a time of his political apotheosis escapes the easy legends that undergird the populist fundamentalisms of contemporary politics. He remains inscrutable still, both in what one might admire about him and what one may revile. But I trust that he is a little less inscrutable now, after you have encountered the slow turning of the kaleidoscope through the pages of this book.

APPENDIX

Introduction

1. ज्या भूमीत एखाद्या धर्माचा संस्थापक ऋषी, अवतार वा प्रेषित (पैगंबर) प्रकटला, त्या धर्मास उपदेशिता झाला, त्याच्या निवासाने त्या भूमीस धर्मक्षेत्राचे पुण्यत्व, आलें, ती त्या धर्माची पुण्यभू. जशी ज्यूंची व ख्रिश्चनांची पॅलेस्टाइन मुसलमानांची अरेबिया . . . नुसत्या पवित्रभूमि या अर्थी नव्हे. (Note 16)

Chapter 1

1. “ही खिलाफत नाही, आफत आहे” (Page 68)
2. आमची राष्ट्रभाषा- संस्कृतनिष्ठ हिंदी
   हिंदुस्थानी नव्हे! उर्दू तर नव्हेच नव्हे. (Note 210)
3. ऐक्यलंपट (Note 210)

Chapter 2

1. “ही खिलाफत म्हणजे आहे तरी काय?” (Note 110)
2. हिंदुस्थानातील हिंदूनी शंकराचार्य पीठ बंद केले असता ते पुनः स्थापण्यासाठी तुर्कस्थानच्या मुसलमानांनी जर लाखो रुपयांची वर्गणी जमवून चळवळ करून युद्ध पुकारले असते आणि त्यानेही काही भागत नाही असे पाहून हिंदुनी पीठावरून काढून टाकलेल्या शंकराचार्यास आपल्या पूजेच्या बाणासह आणि देव देवतांच्या मूर्तिसह तुर्कस्थानात येऊन मठ बांधून रहावे म्हणून आमंत्रण दिले असते तरी देखील इतके आश्चर्यकारक झाले नसते. (Note 114)
3. पण खलिफा म्हणजे साधू नव्हे, खिलाफत म्हणजे सुलतानी आहे, राजसत्ता आहे- हिंदी मुसलमानांचा अंतस्थ हेतु हिंदुस्थानातच असा इस्लामी केंद्र स्थापण्याचा कि त्यायोगे हिंदु संघटनाचे गळ्यात आणखी एक भयंकर धोंड अडकवली जावी हा आहे. (Note 115)
4. ख्रिश्चनांचा पोप हा केवळ त्यांचा धर्माधिरक्षक होय. त्यास राजशक्ती नसते. इतकेच नव्हे तर तो राजा होऊच शकत नाही. तो संन्यस्तच असावा लागतो. त्याने लग्न करता कामा नये, त्याचा औरंस पुत्र त्याचा वारस नसणार त्याने शस्त्र धरणे अनुचित असणार. जो धर्मदंडाचा तेवढा अधिकारी राजदंडाचा नव्हे, त्याची सत्ता केवळ नैतिक केवळ धार्मिक. (Note 117)

5. . . . एखाद्या भोळ्या हिंदूस एखादा मौलवी जेव्हा जातीभेदाचे व्यंग दाखवून म्हणतो की आमच्यात जातीभेद मुळीच नाही . . . तेव्हा तो शिया असल्यास त्यास विचारावे की हजरत अंधेखान! तर मग अल्लीच्या वंशाबाहेरच्या मनुष्यास आपण इमाम का बरे मानीत नाही व सुनी असल्यास विचारावें कि भोंदूमिया कोरेश जातीचाच खलिफा का बरे असावा? . . . खलिफास सत्ता हवी व ती स्वतंत्र सत्ता हवी. (Note 119)
6. मुस्लिमांची ती जरी असली खिलाफत तरी हिंदूंवर कोसळणारी ती आहे निंव्वळ आफत. केवळ आपत्ती. (Note 122)
7. असल्या आत्मघातकी ढसराईखोरपणानें मुसलमानी संकटांनीं सर्व देश आक्रांत झाला, सैनिक हल्यानें त्यानीं आमचे पासून राज्यच हिरावले असें नाहीं, तर धार्मिक आक्रमणांनीं आमच्या अंगांतील मांसाचे लचके तोडून आम्हांला रोड केलें व आपली संख्या वाढविली. छलानें व बलानें, फुसलावणीनें व विशेषत: अत्याचारानें कोट्यवधि हिंदूना आपल्या धर्मातून ओढून नेले. . . . याहि वेळीं हिंदुजातीची पाया पुरते पहाण्याची आत्मघातकी कृतीच त्यांचे नाशास कारणींभूत झाली. शिंदे लढले। बाकी स्वस्थ। होळकरांनें हात उचलला इतर तमाशा पहाणारे. पेशवे धडपड करतात तर सातारकरांना राज सत्तेच्या मोहानें गुरफटवून इंग्रजांच्या कच्छपीं लावलेलें. . . . ५७ च्या उत्तर हिंदुस्थानच्या ज्वालामुखीच्या स्फोटाच्या वेळी दक्षिण हिंदुस्थानांतील मराठे सिंह 'पाहूं या तिकडे काय होतें ते. नाही तर मागाहून आपण आहोंतच!! (Note 125)
8. आणि आज काय आहे? पायापुरतें बघून भावी संकटाचें दूरदृष्टीनें आकलन न करतां स्वस्थ घोरत पडण्याच्या आक्काबाईंने घेरलेली आमची बुध्दि विचारहीन, मठ्ठ व धुंद झालेली. हिंदुमुसलमानांचा प्रश्न पंजाबमध्यें तीव्र पण महाराष्ट्रांत तसा कोठे आहे? मलबारांत हिंदूंवर अत्याचार व बलात्कार झांले, येथले मुसलमान असे कोठे करतात? (Notes 126–27)
9. असले आम्हीच बुध्दीचे तारे तोडणार; पण एवढे लक्षांत येत नाही कीं, हा जाती जातींमधील संघर्ष सुरू झालेला आहे. यामध्यें येथील मुसलमान वा तेथील मुसलमान अथवा इकडचा प्रांत वा तिकडचा प्रांत असा भेद आत्मघातकी झाल्याशिवाय राहणार नाही. नाक दाबल्या शिवाय तोंड उघडत नाहीं अशी आपल्यांत एक म्हण आहे. जेथे संख्याबलानें वा सत्ताबलानें मुसलमान हिंदूपेक्षा प्रबल आहेत तेथे तेथे हिंदूवर त्यांच्याकडून उघड उघड जुलूम व अत्याचार होत आहे. हें बंद करावयाचें असेल, तर जेथे जेथें ते संख्येनें व सत्तेनें आपणांपेक्षा कमी आहेत तेथें तेथें त्यांच्यावर आपला दाब पाडल्याशिवाय, त्यांना 'दे माय' केल्याशिवांय जेथे आपण कमी आहोंत तेथें आपला "धरणी ठाय" लागणार नाही. ही साधीहि गोष्ट आपल्या लक्षांत येऊं नयें इतकें कां आपण बुध्दिहीन व्हावें? (Note 128)
10. मुसलमान लोक हिंदुस्थानांत येऊन त्यांनी येथे अनन्वित कृत्ये केलीं; लाखो ब्राम्हणांना दावणीला उभे करून अत्यंत निर्दयपणानें त्यांच्या हत्या केल्या; अगणित स्त्रियांवर बलात्कार करून त्यांना भ्रष्टविल्या. शेंकडों बायकांमुलांना पकडून आपल्या देशांत गुलाम म्हणून नेऊन विकले; राजपुतांच्या हजारों स्त्रियांना यांच्या पाशवी क्रूरपणाकरितां अनेकवार जोहार करीत आ पसरलेल्या ज्वालामुखीच्या जबड्याप्रमाणें ज्वालांच्या जिभल्या चाटीत असलेल्या प्रदीप्त अग्नीच्या खाईत उड्या घ्याव्या लागल्या, रजपूत, मराठे, शीख आदिमधील लाखों वीरांना या भयंकर व हिंस्त्र अशा मुसलमानी राक्षसी हल्ल्यांपासून देशाचें जीवीत सुरक्षित ठेवण्यासाठी व धर्माचे रक्षण करण्यासाठी पिढ्यानपिढ्या यांच्याशी झुंजत राहून आपल्या रक्ताचे पाट वाहवावे लागले, यांच्या धर्माच्या रानटी कल्पना असल्यामुळें कुराणाशिवाय इतर ग्रंथ अस्तित्वांत असावयाला योग्यच नाहींत या कल्पनेनें

हिंदुस्थानच्या अमोल अशा अनेक ग्रंथभांडारांना यांनी अग्नीच्या भक्ष्यस्थानीं लोटून नष्ट व भस्मसात केलें, हजारों मंदिरें धुळीला मिळविलीं, सहस्त्रावधि देवमूर्तींचा भंग केला व हिंदुस्थानांतून अतोनात संपत्ति लुटून नेली. (Note 131)

11. एखादा दुराचारी मुसलमान देखील केवळ तो मुसलमान आहे म्हणून हिंदुमधल्या महात्मपदाचा मान दिला गेलेल्या गांधींच्याहून सुध्दां श्रेष्ठच आहे" इत्यादि अतःस्थ विचार चित्राची कल्पना देणारी वाक्यें आणि कॅाग्रेसच्या [*sic*] अध्यक्षपदावरून हिंदूंच्या मानभूमीवर पाय आदळींत "सातकोटी अस्पृश्यातले साडेतीन कोटी अस्पृश्य आम्हांला द्या व साडेतीन कोटी अस्पृश्य तुम्हांला ठेवा" असा हिंदू जातीच्या शरीरांतील अवयवाचा तुकडा तोडून घ्यावयासाठी, उच्चारली गेलेली अपहांरोक्ति ही हिंदुमुसलमानांच्या एकीचे स्वर हिंदूंना गुंग करण्यासाठी पुंगींतून काढणारें महमदअल्ली यांच्या तोंडातून बाहेर पडतात. (Note 133)

12. "हिंदूमुसलमानांच्या एकीच्यां सदिच्छेनें प्रेरित झालों आहों" असे स्वमुखाने सांगत फिरणारे शौकतअल्ली "आज हजार वर्षे हिंदूंनी आमचे हातचा मार खाल्ला आहे. हिंदूनीं मुसलमानांशी मिळतें घेतलेंच पाहिजे. आम्हीं हिंदूंना भ्रष्ट करीत आलो ते आम्हीं करणारच, तो आमचा धर्मच आहे, आम्ही मुसलमाल संघटना करणारच, हिंदूंनी मात्र आम्हांला प्रतिकार करण्याचें सोडून हिंदु संघटन व शुध्दि चळवळ ही बंद केलींच पाहिजेत." असला मानभावी उपदेश करीत फिरतात. (Note 135)

13. डॉक्टर किचलू आपण मुर्तिपूजेचे विरोधक आहोंत असें दाखवीत लोकमान्याचे तसबिरीला सभास्थानांतून काढून टाकितात आणि परवा पेशावरच्या मुसलमानांच्या सभेतून सर्व प्रिय (?) हिंदूबंधूंना आव्हान देत सांगतात का, मुसलमान जे जे हक्क मागत आहेत, ते ते त्यांना हिंदूंनी निमुटपणें द्यावे, नाही तर अफगाणिस्थान वा इतर कोणत्या तरी मुसलमानी सत्तेचे साह्य घेऊन आम्हीं हिंदुस्थानावर मुसलमानी राज्य स्थापन करू आणि ते म्हणतात कीं, हें मी ७ कोटी मुसलमानांचा प्रतिनिधी या नात्यानें व अल्ली बंधू, अबुल कलाम आझाद इत्यादि मुसलमान पुढाऱ्यांच्या समतीनें सांगत आहें. हे झाले हिंदुमुसलमानांच्या एकीचे पोवाडे गाणाऱ्या पुढाऱ्यांविषयी. (Note 136)

14. आता मुसलमान जातींतील सर्वसामान्य लोकांची कृति पहा. जन्मामध्यें वाटेल ती पापें हातून घडली असलीं किंवा घडणार असलीं तरी एक काफर (मुसलमानेतरांना व विशेषतः हिंदूना ते काफर म्हणतात) मुसलमान केला कीं अल्ला सर्व पापाची क्षमा करून व स्वर्गाचीं द्वारें खुलीं करून अनंत कालपर्यंत आपल्याला स्वर्गसुख देईल असल्या धर्मवेडाच्या भावनेनें प्रेरित होऊन प्रत्येक मुसलमान संधि साधतांच वाटेल त्या मार्गांचे अवलंबन करीत हिंदूला भ्रष्ट करण्याचा प्रयत्न करतो . . . दिल्ली, सहारणपूर,नंदुरबार, मालेगांव, कोहट,गुलबर्गा इत्यादिसारखे लहानमोठे व कमी अधिक भयंकर दंगे होतात. (Note 137)

15. कोहटचे प्रमुख नेते गांधीजी व शौकतअल्ली यांच्या पुढे येऊन असें म्हणतात कीं, "इतके दिवस आम्ही हिंदूना भ्रष्ट करीत होतों व त्यांच्या बायकांना धरून नेऊन त्यांच्याशीं निका लावीत होतो; पण हिंदु कांही एक तक्रार करीत नव्हतें व आमची एकी होती. परंतु आताशा आम्ही पळवून आणलेल्या त्यांच्या बायकांवर ते आपला हक्क सांगून परत घेऊं पहातात. भ्रष्टविलेल्या हिंदूंना शुध्द करतात व त्यामुळे आमची एकी तुटली, बेकी झाली व त्याचा दंग्यात परिणाम झाला. कोणत्याहि हिंदूच्या बायकोला मुसलमानानें स्पर्श करतांच तीवर पहिल्या पतीचा हक्क रहात नाही व भ्रष्टविलेला हिंदू मुसलमान होतो असें आमच्या कुराणांत सांगितलेले आहे. (Note 138)

16. जे न्यायानें दुसऱ्याचे आहे त्याचा अपहार करावयाचा नाही, छळानें वा बळानें इतरांना बुडवायचें अथवा छळावयाचें नाही, परंतु आघात करणाराचा आघात प्रत्याघातानें दूर सारावयाचा आहें. आपले गेलेले बंधू परत घरी आणावयाचें आहेत, जाणारे थांबवावयाचे आहेत, दूरवस्थेंत असलेल्या आपल्यांतील आपल्या अस्पृश्य बंधूंची दूरवस्था दूर करून त्यांना वर घ्यावयाचें आहे, सर्व हिंदू समाजाला सुसंघटित व समर्थ बनवावयाचे आहे, कदाचित वेळ प्रसंग पडल्यास आणि असले प्रसंग केव्हांना केव्हांतरी ओढवण्याचा पुष्कळ संभव आहे, हे कोहट, गुलबर्गा, नंदुरबार, येवलें, मलबार, इत्यादि दंगयावरून व मुसलमानांच्या स्वभावसिध्द धर्मवेडाच्या वारंवार उद्रेक पावणाऱ्या भावनांवरून स्पष्ट आहे व यावरून असले प्रसंग येणे हेच अपरिहार्य. न आलें तर तो अपवाद समजावयाचा; अशी स्थिती असल्यानें—व्यूहबध्द करण्यासाठीं कवाईत, इत्यादि आजच्या काळीं शक्य त्या संरक्षणकला शिकवून संघटित, समर्थ, सर्वव्यापि, दक्ष व समाजसंरक्षणोद्युक्त असें हिंदू जातीतील तरुण वर्गाचें एक महान दल उभारावयाचे आहे आणि हें सर्व आपले गेलेलें परत मिळविण्यासाठी, आहे ते राखण्यासाठी, आपला समाज दुसऱ्या आक्रमणकारी आततायींच्या आक्रमणापासून सुरक्षित व निर्भय करण्यासाठीं, थपडीस थपड मिळेल तेव्हां हिंदूच्या वाटेस जाणें नको, त्यांच्याशी खाजवाखाजवी नको नाहीं तर ते आपलें पुरे पुरे पारिपत्य करतील असा स्वानुभव व दरारा दुसऱ्याच्या मानांत बसवून नागपूर प्रमाणें, वचकून राहून शांततेने राहण्याची प्रवृत्ति इतर समाजांत उत्पन्न करण्यासाठी, हे सर्व हिंदूंना करावयाचे आहे. (Note 140)
17. पण उलट नागपूरसारख्या ठिकाणीं मुसलमानांची रग जिरविणारे हिंदू स्वरंक्षणक्षम, आघातावर प्रत्याघात करून आघातहस्त छिन्न करावयाला समर्थ व प्रबलतर असून सुध्दां निष्कारण आक्रमण आपल्यावर हिंदूलोक केव्हांहि करणार नाहींत व आपल्यावर अन्याय होणार नाही हें स्वानुभवानें, त्याच्या स्वभावाच्या माहितीनें जाणून नागपूरचे मुसलमान विश्वस्त असल्यामुळे निर्भयतेने व स्वस्थ मताने आपापले व्यवहार करीत आहेत, हा वर्तमान कालांतील प्रत्यक्ष अनुभव आहे. (Note 141)
18. श्रद्धानंदांची हत्या आणि गांधींचा नि:पक्षपाती पक्षपात! (Page 127)
19. जर थोडासा दोष त्या समाजावर पडत असेल तर तो इतकाच की अन्यायास आणि न्यायास, क्रौर्यास आणि कारुण्यास, छळकास आणि छळितास, पीडकास आणि पीडितास, रामास आणि रावणास, समान दोषी ठरविणें आणि सारख्याच दयेस आणि ऊत्तेजनास पात्र समजणें, म्हणजेच नि:पक्षपातीपणा होय अशी भ्रामक समजूत करून घेणाऱ्या तुमच्यासारख्या 'महात्म्यास" तो हिंदुसमाज वारंवार जन्म देतो! (Note 147)
20. मुसलमानांनी मशिदीसमोर तर काय, पण घराघरातून टाळ, घंटा, शंख, वाजवू नयेत म्हणून मारामाऱ्या कराव्या, आपण हिंदु लोकांस छळाने वा बळाने बाटविण्याचा संघटित प्रयत्न सदासर्वदा चालविला असता हिंदूंनी मन वळवून देखील शुद्धीकरण करू नये म्हणून हट्ट धरावा, मलबार, कोहाट सारख्या ठिकाणी हिंदूंचीं नगरेंच्या नगरें जाळपोळ आणि कत्तली करून उद्‌ध्वस्त करून टाकावीं आणि हिंदूंच्या श्रद्धानंद, लालाजी, पंडितजी सारख्या महनीय पुढाऱ्यांच्या हत्या कराव्या आणि हत्या करण्याचे कट करावे—इतकी त्यांची राक्षसी अरेरावी जी माजली आहे तिचा दोष गांधीजी हिंदूंमध्ये आंशिकत: जर कोणावर पडतच असेल, तर खिलाफतीची आफत हिंदूंच्या खांद्यावर बळे बळे लादणाऱ्या आणि ते विषाचें वेडें पीक या देशात मुक्त हस्ताने पेरीत सुटणाऱ्या तुमच्या स्वत:च्या राजकारण दिङमूढ, परंतु अत्यंत अहंमन्य मस्तकावरच होय! तो दोष हिंदु समाजावर पडत नाही. (Note 148)

21. कलकत्त्याच्या नगरसंस्थेत (म्युनिसिपालिटीत) श्रद्धानंदांच्या मृत्यूविषयी खेद व्यक्त करणाऱ्या ठरावास मुसलमानांनी एकजात अडथळा केला. मिरतच्या मशिदीतून मुसलमानांनी ती हत्येची बातमी ऐकताच दीपोत्सव केला. गोरखपूरला मुसलमानांनी मिठाई वाटली. दिल्लीच्या जुम्मामशिदीत हाजी महंमद अल्लींनी गाझी रशीदला या खटल्यातून निर्दोष होऊन सुटता यावें म्हणून सार्वजनिक प्रार्थना केल्या. पेशावरपासून तो महाराष्ट्रातील लहानसहान जिल्ह्यांच्या गावापर्यंत मुसलमानांतून रशीदचा खटला लढविण्यासाठी निधि जमविण्यात आला. कोठेही महत्वाच्या अशा मुसलमानांच्या सभा श्रद्धानंदांच्या हत्येविषयी खेद प्रदर्शित करण्यास झाल्या नाहीत. अनेक ठिकाणी हरताळाचे दिवशी मुसलमानांनी आपली दुकानें बंद ठेवण्याचें नाकारिलें. (Note 154)
22. मुसलमानांच्या कित्येक प्रमुख पत्रांतून श्रद्धानंदांच्या हत्येविषयी टर उडविणारे उद्गार काढण्यात आले. एकाने लिहिलें की, बहुधा श्रद्धानंदजींच्या सेवकाने (ज्याने त्यांचा प्राण वाचविण्याचे कार्यी स्वत:ही घायाळ करून घेतलें त्याने) बहुधा त्यांची हत्या केली असावी आणि मग रशीदला निष्कारण पकडलें असावें. दुसऱ्याने लिहिलें, अजी जनाब ऐसा नहीं! 'एवीतेवी श्रद्धानंद रोगाने मरणारच आहेत असें पाहून त्या रोगाच्या अत्यवस्थ स्थितीत हिंदूंनी विचार केला की, यांना गोळी घालून मारून हुतात्माच कां न करा! मुसलमानांवर आग पाखडण्यास ही उत्तम संधि आहे!' आणि हिंदूंनी असा विचार करून श्रद्धानंदास स्वत:च गोळी घालून मारिलें! (Note 155)
23. महात्माच तो! खरा खरा अंतर्ज्ञानी ! ! ! अशा अंतर्ज्ञानी आणि दिव्यदृष्टि पुढाऱ्याचे हाती राष्ट्राचीं सूत्रें सोपवून त्यास 'सर्वाधिकार' (डिक्टेटर) नेमलें म्हणूनच तर लोकमान्यांचे मृत्युनंतर एका चार वर्षांत हिंदुस्थानात राजकारण आणि धर्मकारण इतकें रंगारूपास आलें! जिकडे पहावें तिकडे ऐकीच ऐकी, ऊन्नतिच, ऊन्नति, जागृतिच जागृति, तेजच तेज! (Note 156)
24. चीनला जर सैन्य धाडाल तर ज्या आगगाडीने तें जाईल तिच्या रूळावर मी पडेन आणि माझ्या छातीवरून ती आगगाडी जाईतो उठणार नाही म्हणून तें गर्जले. रीतीप्रमाणे टाळ्या पडल्या आणि महंमद अल्ली आता मात्र वाचत नाहीत अशी आम्हांस धास्ती पडली. कारण चीनला सैन्य हें जाणारच! महंमद अल्ली मरणार, आता जगाचें कसे होईल म्हणून उद्विग्न असता एकाच पत्रात दोन्ही बातम्या वाचल्या! (Note 157)
25. क्वचित् असें झालें असेल की, चीनचें सैन्य आगगाडीत बसून निघतांना हा सत्यप्रतिज्ञ महावीर महंमद अल्ली आगगाडीच्या रूळावर पडण्यास गेला असेल. पण रुळावर न पडता घाईघाईत रुळांचे मधोमध पडल्याने रुळावरून गाडी निघून गेली तरी त्याचा प्राण काही गेला नाही. मरावें कसें याची देखील माहिती असावी लागते! आता हा तिसरा योग तर गेला. आता पाहू. मरणाचा चौथा डोहळा महमदअल्लीस कोणच्या प्रकारचा होता तो? भीति ऐवढीच की, लांडगा आला लांडगा आला! असे गमतीने म्हणता म्हणता लांडगा खरोखरीच ऐखादे वेळी आला नाही म्हणजें झालें? (Note 158)
26. कलकत्ता नगरसंस्थेतही हिंदूंहून अधिक प्रतिनिधित्व मुसलमानांस प्रतिशेकडा मिळत आहे. तथापि एका गोष्टीत मात्र हिंदूंनी विशिष्ट प्रतिनिधित्व देण्याची आजवर फारच टाळाटाळ चालविली होती; ती गोष्ट म्हणजे दंग्यांची. कारण जितके दंगे गेल्या वर्षापर्यंत झाले त्या सर्वात मेलेल्या आणि घायाळांच्या संख्येत हिंदुच आपली भर करून घेत। त्या सर्व जागांवर हिंदुच हिंदु नेमिले जात. मेलेल्यात किंवा घायाळांत शेकडा एक जागा देखील मुसलमानांस राखून ठेवण्यात येत नसे. हा हिंदूंचा आपलपोटेपणा अक्षम्य होता. (Note 159)

27. पण सुदैवाची गोष्ट की, कलकत्त्याच्या दंग्यापासून हिंदूंनी हा आपलपोटेपणा सोडण्यास हळूहळू आरंभ करून या वर्षी तर मुसलमान बांधवांस बहुतेक दंग्यांत लोखंडी चण्यांचा बराचसा प्रसाद स्वहस्ते वाटण्यास मागे पुढे पाहिलें नाही. उदाहरणार्थ, बरेलीचा दंगा घेऊ. गेल्या महिन्या दीड महिन्यात जे महत्त्वाचे दंगे झाले, त्यांत बरेलीचा दंगा मोडतो. . . . बरेलीस हिंदु ६ मेले आणि मुसलमान ७. कानपूरच्या हिंदूंनीही तितका ऊदारपणा दाखविला नसला तरी आपलपोटेपणा काही केला नाही. कारण घायाळात हिंदूंनी १०५ लोक आपले भरती केले तर ८१ मुसलमानांचे भरती करून, राष्ट्रीय सभेने मुसलमानांस जें शेकडा तीस विशिष्ट प्रतिनिधित्व अर्पण केलें आहे, तो करार पाळला. (Note 160)

28. झाला! एकदाचा मुंबईचा दंगा ऊद्भवला, चेकाळला, शमला। मुंबईचा दंगा झाला पण हें काय? मुंबईस किती तरी हिंदु अजून जिवंत! किंबहुना किती मेले तेच सहज मोजता येत आहेत—बाकी सगळेच जिवंत! अगदी पूर्वीसारखे सहज मोजमापीच्या मापात न मावतील इतके चिकार जिवंत! आश्चर्य आहे बुवा! (Note 162)

29. महंमद अल्ली म्हणाले, 'हिंदु कोणच्या झाडाचा पाला!' मुस्लिम औटलुक म्हणालें 'जर वेळच पडली तर पठाणांना आत बोलावून हिंदूंच्या छातीवर मुसलमानी पाच्छाई ऊभारू!' इतर मुल्ला आणि मौलवींच्या फतव्यांची आणि फितव्यांची तर गणतीच नव्हती. त्यांचा मतभेद असा एकाच गोष्टीवर होई आणि तो म्हणजे या की, एकंदरीत एक मुसलमान लढाईत किती हिंदूंच्या बरोबर असतो—किती हिंदूंस मारू शकतो—त्या खंजिराखंजिरानिशीच्या खडाजंगीत!! काही तज्ज्ञ म्हणाले, एक मुसलमान ५ हिंदूंस मारू शकतो; काही म्हणाले १०; काही म्हणाले ५०; काही म्हणाले १००! या आणि इतर गणितज्ञांची सरासरी काढून आम्ही सिध्दान्त केला की, एक मुसलमान निदान २८ ३/५ [28 3/5] हिंदूंस तरी भारी असलाच पाहजे! तोही हिंदुस्थानी मुसलमान! ज्या पठाणास आत बोलावून हिंदूंच्या छातीवर मुस्लिम बादशाही स्थापिली जाणार आहे, त्या एका पठाणास तर चटणीस देखील शंभर हिंदु पुरणार नाहीत. (Note 163)

30. तोंच रस्तोरस्ती पठाण पहिल्या धडाक्यासच दिसू लागले;पण ते जीव घेऊन पळताना,पडताना, मरताना, आणि हिंदूंच्या टोळ्या त्यांच्यामागे हातात सापडेल तें हत्यार घेऊन लागलेल्या! . . . तोंच मोठमोठ्याने एखाद्या बंबासारखा गळा काढून कोणी 'तोबा तोबा,' म्हणून रडताना ऐकू येऊ लागलें. पहातो तों ते शौकतअल्ली ओरडत होते, 'माझे पठाण मारले जात आहेत, हिंदु लोक त्यांची पारध करीत आहेत. सरकार धावा, पोलीस धावा, मुसलमानांनो धावा! तोबा, तोबा!' (Note 164)

31. अशा रीतीने एक मुसलमान २८ ३/५ [28 3/5] हिंदूंना मारणारा वीर असूनही आणि अशा वीरांच्या हजारोंच्या सेना 'दीन दीन' म्हणून तुटून पडल्या असताही दंगा होऊनही गेला, तरी मुंबईत हिंदु जिवंतच आहेत. (Note 165)

32. . . . त्या दंग्यातून किती दंगे हिंदूंनी आरंभिले होते, किती ठिकाणी पहिला वार हिंदूंनी केला होता, किती हिंदु भ्रष्ट केले गेले आणि किती मुसलमान भ्रष्ट केले गेले, हे गांधीजी स्पष्टपणें सांगू शकतील काय? ह्या उभ्या चार पांच वर्षात किती हिंदु कुमारिका आणि अर्भक मुलें सिंध, पंजाब, बंगाल इत्यादि प्रांतांत बलात्काराने पळविण्यात आलीं? आणि उलटपक्षी किती मुसलमानी स्त्रिया वा मुलें हिंदूंनी बलात्काराने पळविली? (Note 168)

33. राजशाही जिल्ह्यात भवानीपूर गावी पुजारी राजवंशी राहतात. त्यांच्यात पडदा नसतो. त्यांच्या काही स्त्रिया पुरुषांबरोबर बाजारातून परत येत असता रात्र पडली. तोंच मुसलमानांच्या धर्मवीरांनी त्यांस अडवून एक तरुण स्त्री पळविली. ती गर्भवती होती. हे राक्षसी क्रौर्य चालता चालता ती स्त्री बेशुद्ध

झाली—रक्तबंबाळ झाली—तरी ते मुसलमानी गुंड परावृत्त होईनात. इत्क्यात पुजारी पोलिसांसह धावपळ करीत तिथे आले. तों हे पराक्रमी पळून गेलेले दिसले, ती स्त्री रक्तात लोळत पडलेली दिसली—आणि हाय हाय. तो तिचा गर्भ तडफडत बाहेर पतन पावून चेंदामेंदा झालेला दिसला. त्या अधमांपैकी एकास पकडलें असून दावा चालला आहे. (Note 175)

34. हिंदु कन्यकांस आणि अनाथ मुलांस बलात्काराने बाटविणें हें कृत्य मुसलमानी स्त्रियाही किती पवित्र आणि आदरणीय मानतात याचें आणखी एक उदाहरण कटनी येथे नोव्हेंबरमध्येच घडलें आहे. एका तेरा वर्षाच्या ब्राह्मण कन्यकेवर मार्गात एकाकी पाहून खिस्तू नांवाच्या मुसलमानी साधु पुरुषाने झडप घातली, त्यासरशी ती पोरगी ओरडली. तत्काळ त्या साधूच्या धर्मशील पत्नीने तिचे हात धरून ओढले आणि तिच्या तोंडात बोळा कोंबून सुरा उपसला। या मुसलमानी साधूच्या साध्वीने मग त्या मुलीला दूर आपल्या चुलत्याच्या घरी पोचवून लपविलें. हिंदु कन्यकेस मुसलमानाने धरताच तें कृत्य पचविण्यासाठी झटणें हे प्रत्येक मुसलमानाचें कर्तव्य आहे ही भावना मुसलमानी समाजात किती खोल रुजली आहे तें त्यावरूनही व्यक्त होईल की पोलिस शोध चालू होताच त्या खिस्तूच्या चाचीने त्याच्या आईच्या हाती ती पोर लपवून ठेवण्यास दिली. ती खिस्तूची आई त्या मुलीस पळवीत असता धरली गेली! आता गाझी खिस्तू आणि गाझिणी ती त्याची बायको हवालातमध्ये बंद आहेत! (Note 177)

35. एखाद्या हिंदु मुलाने एखाद्या मुसलमान पोरीस पळवून आणिली असती, तर हिंदु आई त्याची धन्यता मानण्याचे स्थली त्याच्या हाताला उलथणें तापवून डाग देती आणि त्याचे संबंधीच नव्हत तर उभे हिंदु गाव काशीरामेश्वरपर्यंत ऐकू जाईल अशी बोंब मारून उठतें आणि तो हिंदु मुलगाच मुसलमान झाला असें म्हणून त्यास हसकून देते. पण खिस्तूचि आई पहा किती साध्वी आणि धर्मशील बाई ती! (Note 179)

36. बंगाल्यांत फेनी येथे हरचंद्रदासच्या शामनाद नामक स्त्रीला बलात्काराने लालमिया नांवाच्या गाझीने पळविली होती. त्याला दोन वर्षे सक्तश्रमाची शिक्षा झाली. तेंही एकवेळ क्षम्य म्हणता येईल; पण अलीपूरच्या सबडिव्हिजन मॅजिस्ट्रेटच्यासमोर सहासात गाझींवर एका सन्देशखाली गांवच्या शशिबाला नामक विवाहित हिंदु स्त्रीने जो कहर गुजरविला आहे त्याचा वचपा गाझी गुंड आणि मंडळ यांनी अगदी त्वरित काढलाच पाहिजे. शशिबालेचा नवरा अतिशय आजारी. ती सतरा वर्षाची घाबऱ्या घाबऱ्या औषध आणि साह्य मागण्यास शेजारीपाजारी फिरु लागली. अशा अवस्थेत तिची दया येणें साहजिकच होतें. तशि तिची दया येऊन एका धर्मभीरू मुसलमानाने तिला औषधासाठी दुसऱ्याकडे नेलें. त्याला दया आली तशी आणखी ऐकाला दया आली. होता होता दया हेंच ज्यांचें ब्रीद आहे असे सहासात गाझी एकत्र जमलें. त्यांनी त्या शशिबालेला एकान्त स्थळी ओढली आणि प्रत्येकाने तिच्यावर त्याची मुसलमानी दया करण्यास आरंभ केला! (Note 180)

37. या पैशाचिक प्लेगाची मुसलमान समाजात सध्या साथच आलेली आहे की काय अशी भीति वाटावी, इतक्या भीषण अनुक्रमाने प्रत्यही राक्षसी वृत्तीचे अत्याचारी स्त्रीपुरुष शेकड्यांनी उत्पन्न होत आहेत. स्त्रियादेखील! उदाहरणार्थ ही खालची फ्री प्रेसची बातमी पहा: २४ सप्टेंबरला बदलापटिया नांवाच्या ठाण्यातील कुमारबिल नांवाच्या ठिकाणी एका मुसलमान बाईनी आपल्या नवऱ्यासाठी मांसाचें भोजन करून ठेविलें. पण नवरा परत येण्याचे आधी तें कुत्र्याने खाऊन टाकिलें. तेव्हा एका खड्याने दोन्ही पक्षी मारावे अशा हेतूने तिने, दुसरें कशाचें मांस नाही आणि तिचा सावत्र मुलगाही नाहीसा करण्याचें अजून ऊरलेलें आहे असें पाहून त्या लहान मुलाला मारून कापून त्याचें मांस शिजविलें आणि ते आपल्या नवऱ्यास न सांगता मुलाचें मांस बापास जेऊ

घातलें! . . . अशा पैशाचिक स्त्रिया जेथे आहेत त्या घरात त्यांचे पोटी वर वर्णिलेल्या नीचातील नीच "धर्मवीरांची" वीणच उत्पन्न व्हावयाची! (Note 181)

38. एकदा पिशाच्चवृत्तीसच धर्मकर्तव्य समजण्यात आलें म्हणजे मग बापास बाप आणि मुलास मूल म्हणण्याइतकी माणुसकी मनुष्यात उरत नाही. कुत्रें पिसाळलें म्हणजे प्रथम दुसऱ्यास चावावयास धावतें, व रक्त जों जों तोंडी लागतें तों तों तें अधिकच पिसाळतें आणि शेवटी दुसऱ्यास चावता चावता स्वत:सही चावू लागतें. तसाच धर्मोन्मत्त पिसाट, 'काफर' म्हणून दुसऱ्याचे रक्त पिण्यास चटावता चटावता शेवटी रक्ततृष्णा अनिवार होऊन स्वत:च्या घरातही रक्तपात करीत सुटतो. हा इतिहासाचा अनुभव आहे. सरसीमेवर हिंदूंस काफर म्हणून भयंकर रीतीने छळून मारून लुटून हुसकून दिलें. कारण ते अत्यल्प होतें. पण ते गेल्यावर त्यांच्या रक्ताने पिसाळलेला धर्मोन्माद स्वत:च्या घराकडे वळताच आपल्या अंगासच फाडफाडून टाकू लागला. (Note 182)

39. जुबेरखां, युसुफशेट इत्यादि खुलना येथील इस्लामी सज्जनांवरही असाच एक प्रसंग ओढवला आहे. स्वर्णमयी नांवाच्या हिंदु कन्येला पळवून नेण्याचा त्यांनी यत्न केला. असे हजारो मुसलमान हिंदु कन्यकांस पळवीत असतात. ही त्यांची पिढीजात वहिवाट आहे. या वहिवाटीचा ऊपभोग जुबेरखां आदींनी घेणें त्यांचे कर्तव्य होतें. पण खुलनाच्या सेशन्स कोर्टात त्यांचेवर ३६ आणि १४४ इत्यादि कलमांखाली खटला चालू असून ही इस्लामी अनुयायांची धार्मिक वहिवाट बंद पाडण्याचा प्रयत्न होत आहे. तरी त्या सेशन्स जज्जासही तत्काळ एक चिठी धाडण्यात यावी. म्हणजे तोही थरकाप भरून शुद्धीवर येईल आणि स्वर्णमयीला मुसलमानांचे हातीच सोपवून तिचा ऊद्धार करील. (Note 184)

40. परक्या देशांतून आलेल्या मुसलमानांची सुमारे ५० लाख संख्या वजा करता ७ कोटींपैकी ६॥ कोटी मुसलमान हे हिंदूंचे केलेले मुसलमान आहेत. हिंदू जातीच्या अंगप्रत्यंगांचे हे ६॥ कोटी मासाचे गोळे त्या दुष्ट संकटानें तोडून नेलेले आहेत. आतां हिंदुजाति ही दुर्बल जीवन धारण करीत, आपसांतील द्वेष भावनांच्या ठणक्यानें सर्वांग दु:खी झालेली अशी श्वासोश्वास करीत उभी आहे. (Note 185)

41. . . . ज्या प्रबलतर समाजाने हिंदु जातीच्या शरीराचे लचके तोडीत साडे सहा कोटी मांसाचे गोळे तोडून नेले, त्याच समाजाला तो किंचिन्मात्र जागृत, विस्कळित, विखुरलेला व डोळे मिटून पडलेला असतांहि खिलाफतीच्या चळवळीचें दूध पाजून, त्याला संघटना-सामर्थ्ययुक्त केले. खिलाफतीचा पुरस्कर्ता हिंदू, खिलाफतीचे उपदेशक हिंदू, खिलाफतीचे कार्यवाह हि कित्येक ठिकाणीं हिंदूच होते. खिलाफतीला पुष्कळसा पैसा दिला हिंदूनी आणि या धर्मवेडाच्या सापाला डवचवून आपणांवर फणा फेकीत विषदंश करून घ्यावयास समर्थ करून ठेवलें आहे. (Note 186)

42. मशिदीपर्यंत पोंचेतों हरिनामाचे गजराने त्या गावचें वातावरण दुमदुमवून देते आणि अंती सशस्त्र शिपाई येऊन त्यास धरीपर्यंत स्वयंसैनिक वाद्यें वाजवीत आणि हरिनामाचा घोष करीत मशिदीपुढील राजमार्गाने पुढे घुसतात. लगेच दुसरे दिवशी पुन: दुसरे भजनवीर हाच क्रम पुढे चालवितात. शेकडो तुरुंगांत गेले, अन्नत्याग झाले, मुसलमानी गुंडांचे दंगे झाले, डोकीं फुटलीं, जादा पोलिस बसले, त्यांच्या करासाठी लिलाव पुकाराले, गव्हर्नर फणफणले, मुसलमान जळफळले; पण हिंदूंचे हरिकीर्तन आणि सत्याग्रह जशाचा तसा चालू आहे! (Note 187)

43. "गव्हर्नर **फणफणले,** मुसलमान **जळफळले**" (Page 142)

44. याला म्हणतात चिकाटी ! ! ! अशी चिकाटी थोडी फार तर तो 'या धकाधकीच्या मामल्यांत हजारो वर्षे 'जीता रहनेवाला है!' हें आमच्या 'रहिम चाचांनी' पक्कें समजून असावें. (Note 188)

45. रहिमचाचा आजपर्यंत बंगालमध्ये मुसलमान गुंड जेव्हा जेव्हा हिंदु कुमारिकांस घरातून बलात्काराने धरून किंवा मार्गाने चोरून पळवून नेत म्हणून बातम्या ऐकत तेव्हा चकार शब्दही काढीत नसत आणि कदाचित् त्यांच्या 'मी बंगाल दुसरा पंजाब करीन' ह्या आसुरी प्रतिज्ञेप्रमाणे हळुहळू बंगालमध्ये दृश्य दिसू लागलें याने मनात फिदी फिदी हसतही असतील. (Note 189)

46. ". . . गेल्या आठवड्यात एके दिवशी शशिमोहन नांवाच्या एका बंगाली नवयुवकाने त्याचा शेवट करून टाकिला. त्यास अचानक ठार मारून टाकिलें. . . . ऐकलेत ना, रहिमचाचा? शशिमोहन हा त्या तुमच्या खिदिखिदि हसणाऱ्या ध्वनीचा केवळ पडसाद उठलेला आहे; नाही का? . . . ऐका, नीट ऐका, रहिमचाचा, शशिमोहन काय म्हणतो, तें नीट ऐका! 'मी माझ्या हिंदु भगिनीच्या सन्मान आणि सतीत्व रक्षणासाठी त्या अधमास कापून काढिलें.'" (Note 190)

47. हिंदु स्त्रियांकडे पाहून खिदिखिदि हसणाऱ्या तुमच्या धर्मवेड्या गुंडगिरीचा हा शशिमोहन पहिला हिंदु प्रतिध्वनि आहे. रहिमचाचा, अजून तरी शुद्धीवर या. कारण तुमच्या हसण्याच्या प्रत्येक ध्वनीमागोमाग यापुढे शशिमोहनी प्रतिध्वनि गर्जत उठतील असा संभव, क्रियेनंतर प्रतिक्रियेचा संभव जितका बळकट असतो, तितक्याच बळकटपणे दिसत आहे! (Note 191)

48. हिंदूंनी मूर्तिपूजा आणि मूर्तीच्या मिरवणुकी मुसलमानांच्या समोर, शेजारी किंवा जवळ करू नयेत. कारण मूर्तिपूजा मुसलमानी धर्माच्याविरुध्द आहे! ही मुसलमानांची मागणी त्यांनी अनेकदा स्पष्टपणे सांगून टाकिली हे त्यांचे हिंदूंवर खरोखर उपकार आहेत. . . . कारण आम्ही मुसलमान म्हणूनच आमच्या धर्माचा खलिफा जो तुर्क त्याच्याशी लढणार नाही म्हणून जेव्हा मुसलमान म्हणाले आणि जेव्हा हिंदूंनीही त्यांच्या त्या कोटिक्रमास त्याच धार्मिक कारणाकरिता दुजोरा दिला, तेव्हाच मुसलमानांच्या धार्मिक समजुती हिंदूंनाही बंधनकारक आहेत हे तत्व सिध्द झालें. खलिफाशी लढत नाही कारण तें मुसलमानी धर्माच्या विरुध्द आहे आमच्या मशिदीसमोर वाद्ये वाजवू देणार नाही, कारण तें मुसलमानी धर्माविरुध्द आहे. मशिदीसमोर तर काय, पण घराशेजारी शंख घंटाही वाजवू देणार नाही कारण तें मुसलमानी धर्माच्या विरुध्द आहे. अशी विचारपरंपरा ज्या मूलतत्वाच्या ऊपजाऊ कुसव्यातून आपोआप प्रसवली, त्या विचारपरंपरेला मान तुकवून मशिदीसमोर वाद्यें बंद करितो असें हिंदु मुसलमानांच्या एकीचे हिंदु भोक्ते म्हणू लागताच त्या पुढची पायरी चढून मूर्तिपूजा बंद करा, कारण तीही मुसलमानी धर्माच्या विरुध्द आहे म्हणून मुसलमान मागणी करण्यास चुकणार नाहीत असें अपरिहार्य अनुमान आम्ही काढलें होतें. (Note 192)

49. वाद्यबंदीची मागणी राष्ट्रीय सभेने विचारात घेतलीच आहे. आता या वर्षी मुर्तिपूजा बंदीची मागणी तिने विचारात घेऊन मान्य करावी की, पुढील वर्षी मुंजबंदीची मागणी , मुंज ही मुसलमान धर्मा विरुध्द आहे याच सर्वमान्य आणि राष्ट्रीय सभा-संमत तत्वांचे आधारावर पुढे करता येईल. असें एक एक करून आपण हिंदुमुसलमानांत दुही माजविण्याचे सर्व प्रश्न हळूहळू सोडवून हिंदूंना मुसलमानच करून टाकू आणि राष्ट्रीय हित साधल्याचें महत्तम पुण्य शीघ्रच गाठी बांधू शकू. (Note. 193)

50. हिंदु मुसलमान संवाद : (Pages 145–46, Note 195)

प हिंदु:	एकीस मान्य व्हा पाय धरितसे तुमचे।
	हें हिंदुस्थानचि हिंदु मुसलमानांचें ॥ ध्रु ॥
मुसलमान	देशासी हिंदुस्थान अजुनिहि म्हणसी:
	आणि एकी करण्या पाय आमुचे धरिसी ॥

प हिंदु	हां! चुकलो!! हिंदुस्थान नाम देशाचें।
	इसलामवतन वा म्हणू रुचे तरि साचे ॥
मुसलमान	हिंदीस ठार मारावें
प हिंदु	मान्य जी
मुसलमान	उर्दूसि मात्र बोलावें
प हिंदु	मान्य जी
मुसलमान	नागरी लिपिस सोडावें
प हिंदु	मान्य जी
प हिंदु	करु सांगा तें तें बंधु तुम्ही प्रेमाचे।
	एकीस मान्य व्हा पाय धरितसो तुमचे ॥ १॥
मुसलमान	शुद्धीचें परंतु बंड अधीं मोडावें ।
दु हिंदु	परि बाटविण्याचें मात्र तुम्ही सोडावें ॥
मुसलमान	'परि', आणि 'जरी तरी' अशा अटी कोणाशी।
	घालशी गाठ ही असे मुसलमानांशी ॥
प हिंदु	हां! खान! भाई हां। क्षमा करा साहेब।
	हे भांडखोरिचे हिंदुसंघटण पेव ॥
मुसलमान	करूं मुसलमान हिंदूंचे।
प हिंदु	मान्य जी
मुसलमान	करु नका हिंदु मुसलमानांचें।
प हिंदु	मान्य जी
मुसलमान	करु नका शुद्ध भ्रष्टांचे।
प हिंदु	मान्य जी
प हिंदु	कमविणें न मुळी गमविणें ब्रीद हिंदूंचें।
	एकीस मान्य व्हा पाय धरितसो तुमचे ॥ २ ॥
दु हिंदु	परि पळवुनी नेती हिंदु मुली जे दुष्ट।
मुसलमान	बिघडेल एकि जरि काढशील ती गोष्ट।
प हिंदु	नचि कोप करा मिय्याजी मूर्ख हे लोक।
	पळवाच पाहिजे तरी माझिही लेक ॥
मुसलमाम	मलबारी स्वेच्छेनेच हिंदु बहु बाटे ।
प हिंदु	हां एक कुठेसा जरा पीडिला वाटे ॥
दु हिंदु	कोहाटामाजी हिंदु ठार बहु झाला।
प हिंदु	हा भ्याड हिंदु कां मारु देत दुसऱ्याला ॥
मुसलमान	आणि कलकत्त्यासी मुसलमान बहु मेला।
प हिंदु	हा अत्याचारी हिंदु मारी दुसऱ्याला ॥
मुसलमान	खलिफासि मानि गुरु मुसलमान जें राज्य ।
प हिंदु	तो आम्हांसी बापाहुनि म्हणुनची पूज्य ॥
मुसलमान	'मुस्लिम राज्य करूं जगीं' सांगतो धर्म ।
प हिंदु	ते तुम्हींच करा हो हिंदु जाणि ना मर्म ॥

मुसलमानः वाद्यांसी तुमच्या फोडा । (प हिंदुः- मान्य जी)
गोवधा न हरकत पाडा ।
तुम्ही मूर्ति तितुक्या फोडा ।
दु हिंदु—प हिंदूस मान्यजी! मान्यजी । काय खुळ्या एकीचे.
हें पुरें प्रदर्शन तुझ्या नीच क्लैब्याचें ॥
(पहिल्या हिंदूला ढकलून घालवून पुढे म्हणतो)
हें पहा बंधु तुम्ही मुसलमान ते सारे ।
परि बंधुसम जरि व्हाल प्रेम करणारे ॥
अन्योन्य हितार्थी तरी घडू द्या एकी ।
अडवुनि धरा जरि हीच चालु द्या नेकी ॥
जरि याल तरि संगेचि, नातरी आम्हीं ।
एकटे लढुनिहि जिंकु युद्ध परिणामी ॥
जिंकिले शकाहूणांसि जिंकिलें ज्यांनी ।
औरंग आणि अफजुल्ल विद्ध नखरांनीं ॥
ते हिंदु तुच्छ तूं कारे । समजसी
दिसता न खंड मेघाचा । ये जसी
वादळी झोड वीजांची । रे तशी
सहसाचि वादळें उठुनि हिंदु शौर्याची ।
बुडवितील कलियुगा सृष्टि घडित सत्याची ॥

51. कारण सन १८९४ ते ९५ चे संधीस मुंबई, पुणें वगैरे ठिकाणी हिंदु-मुसलमानी दंग्याची मोठी भयंकर लाट ऊसळली. केसरी, पुणेंवैभव वगैरे पत्रांतून त्याचें वृत्त वाचण्यासाठी इतकें ऊत्सुक व्हावें की, त्या पत्रांच्या डाकेची वाट पहात तासतास टपालठाण्यापाशी तिष्ठत ऊभें राहावे. मुसलमानांनी दंगे आरंभून हिंदूंचा पाडाव केला की आम्ही अगदी संतप्त व्हावें. हिंदु चूप का राहतात? इतक्यात हिंदूंनी प्रतिकार करून मुसलमानांस चेचल्याचें वृत्त आलें कीं आमच्या मंडळींचा हर्ष गगनात मावू नये. (Note 202)
52. आमच्या बालसंवगड्यांस जमवून मी ठरविलें की, या राष्ट्रीय अपमानाचा बचपा भगूरला भरून काढावयाचा आणि तो काढण्याचा ऊत्तम मार्ग म्हणजे वेशीबाहेर असलेल्या त्या एकुलत्या एका ओसाड मशिदीवर चाल करून जाण्यावाचून दुसरा कोणता असणार! झालें. ती आमची बारा तेरा वर्षांच्या आतील मुलांची टोळी, नव्हें वीरांची टोळी! एका संध्याकाळी गनिमी पदध्तीने लपत लपत त्या मशिदीवर छापा घाळण्यास गेली. मशिदीत कोणी नव्हतेंच . . . आम्ही मशिदीची मनसोक्त मोडतोड करून आणि शिवछत्रपतींच्या हल्ल्यांचीं धुळाक्षरें आपण वळवीत आहोत ही पूर्ण जाणीव ठेवून त्या शिवसंप्रदायातील शेवटचें कृत्य जें रणातून चटकन् पाय काढणें तें अगदी शक्य तितक्या आरंभीस ऊरकून घेतलें. (Note 203)
53. दुसऱ्या दिवशी ही बातमी मुसलमानी मुलांसही कळली. त्या गावातील आमच्या मराठी शाळेच्या पडवीतच भरणाऱ्या ऊर्दू शाळेसमोरील लहानशा अंगणाइतक्या विस्तीर्ण रणक्षेत्रात शाळाशिक्षक येण्याच्या आधीच तुंबळ लढाई झाली. पण मुसलमान मुलांच्या दुर्दैवाने चाकू, रूळ, टाचणी इत्यादि रणसाहित्याचा आधीच पुरवठा करून ठेवणारा सेनापति त्यांस कोणी न लाभल्याने आणि हिंदुमुलांपाशी हे साहित्य मी प्रथमपासुनच सज्ज ठेवल्याने अर्थातच हिंदुंचा जय झाला. शेवटी संधि होऊन त्यात मुख्य अट अर्थातच ही ठरली की ही बातमी ऊभयपक्षी कोणीही शिक्षकांस कळवू नये! (Note 204)

Chapter 3

1. ब्रह्मदेवाने जेव्हा सद्‌गुणांचे सहस्त्रभोजन घातले, टिळक-चिपळूणकर नावाची दोन भटे इतकी तुडुंब जेवली की, दुसऱ्यांच्या वाट्याला जायला सद्‌गुण शिल्लकच राहिला नाही. पश्चिमेचा उध्दार करण्याकरिता आकाशातल्या बापाचा एकच पूत धावत आला, पण पूर्वेचा ब्रह्मांड पांडित्याचा झेंडा फडकविण्याकरिता ब्रह्मदेवाच्या मुखातून एक पलटणच्या पलटण येथे आली आहे. या पलटणीचे कर्ममार्तंड कै टिळक आणि चिपळूणकर हे होत! महाराष्ट्र म्हंटले की टिळक-चिपळुणकर-केळकर-लवाटे-कवडे-देवधर हाटेलवाले, जोशी खानावळवाले अशी बडीबडी देशाची भक्ताळ धेंडे दिसू लागतात. महाराष्ट्राचे मुख्य केसरीपत्र. या मुखाला बत्तीसच काय पण छत्तीस दात आहेतच. प्रत्येक दात चावण्याच्या सनातन सवयीने इतका सुंदर आणि सुजरा बनला आहे की, ब्राह्मणाशिवाय कोणी दुसरा डोके काढू लागला की त्याच्या नरडीला हा दात लागलाच. टिळक-चिपळूणकरांच्या चरित्राचे नि:पक्षपातीपणाने निरीक्षण करणाऱ्यास टिळक-चिपळूणकर देशभक्त नसुन अत्यंत नीचकोटीतले देशाचे दुश्मन होते, हे सहजच पटणारे आहे. (Note 44)
2. कोकणातून वक्रगतीने डोंगर चढून आल्यामुळे सवयीने पुन्हा वक्रगतीनेच चाळणाऱ्या को ब्रा ची (कोकणस्थ ब्राह्मणांची) आणखी एक निमकहराम टोळी घाटमाथ्यावर पाठी पडशी टाकून आली. अगोदरच्या ब्रह्मका सर्पांना हा 'को ब्रा' जोडीला मिळाल्यावर मग अन्यायाला, अधर्माला सीमा तरी कशी राहणार? . . . काही ब्राह्मण लोक बढतीसाठी कुठल्याही दाराने, कसलेही साधन हाती धरून स्वार्थ साधीत असतात. एवढे विधान ठोकायला पेशवाईचा इतिहास पुरेसा आहे. बाईल-बढतीची देवघेव करून मानवी सभ्यतेला काळीमा फासणारे ब्राह्मण हे आमचे वर्णगुरू! (Note 45)
3. वेश्येच्या माडीवर उतरलेल्या भटावर, शूद्राच्या काखेतून पावन होऊन आलेल्या भटणीवर अस्पृश्याची सावली पडली म्हणून त्या अस्पृश्याला गुलटेकडी च्या मैदानात छाटून टाकणारे हे ब्रह्मराक्षस पेशवे आणि त्यांची परंपराच चालवू पाहणारे हे सैतान टिळक-चिपळुणकर जोपर्यंत जगांत पेशवाईचे पक्षपाती टिळकानुटिळक गटारानें वळवळणाऱ्या गांडुळासारखे चळवळत आहेत, तोपर्यंत अस्पृश्यांच्या स्वातंत्र्याचा प्रश्न खडतर होऊन राहणारच! . . . 'ब्राह्मण्य' ही अशी चीज आहे कीं ती भेदाशिवाय जगत नाहीं आणि गुलामगिरीशिवाय जन्मत नाहीं. (Note 46)
4. अस्पृश्य मानलेल्या बांधवांच्या बाबतीत शतकानुशतकें स्पृश्यांनी जो घोर अन्याय केलेला आहे त्या पापाचें प्रायश्चित घेऊनच आता स्पृश्यांचा उद्धार होणार आहे, म्हणून हा स्पृश्यांच्याच उद्धाराचा कार्यक्रम असल्याने स्पृश्योद्धार हाच शब्द यथायोग्य असून मुद्दामच योजला आहे. (Note 64)
5. टिळकांसारखा चित्पावन भट म्हणजे कोबऱ्याची विषारी अवलाद. चित्पावनाची जात म्हणजे फड्या निवडुंगाची जात . . . शिवकालापासून महाराष्ट्राच्या इतिहासात जेवढी म्हणून 'दुषकृत्ये' घडली आहेत, ती बहुतेक चित्पावन भटांकडूनच. चित्पावन माय-भगिणींच्या उदरी 'तुकाराम, शिवाजी, बाजीप्रभू' असल्या तोडीचे नरेंद्र जन्मूच नयेत, यात काही इश्र्वरी संकेत आहे देव जाणे. जनक रामकृष्णापासून शाहू छत्रपतींपर्यंत जर मातृभूमीच्या सच्च्या पुत्राची यादी काढली तर त्यात एकही चित्पावन सापडावयाचा नाही. (Note 68)
6. "मुसलमानांच्या स्पर्शामुळें फुटाणे विटाळतात या वेडगळ समजुतीच्या आहारीं जाऊन, हिंदु-बंदिवान स्वत:ची उपासमार करून घेत आहेत हें कळल्याबरोबर, सावरकरांनीं अंदमानांतल्या

हिंदु-बंदिवानांना एक कानमंत्र सांगितला होता: व हिंदु बंदिवानांनी त्या मंत्राचा प्रभाव दाखविल्याबरोबर पठाण नि मुसलमान बंदिवानांची खोड मोडली होती." (Note 73)

7. अस्पृश्योद्धाराचाच प्रश्न घ्या; हे सात कोटी आपले हिंदु, रक्ताचे, धर्माचे, राष्ट्राचे बंधु, ह्यांस आपण तो अब्दुल रशीद, तो औरंगजेब, ते पूर्व बंगालात हिंदूच्या कत्तली करणारे इतर विधर्मीय धर्मोन्मत्त यांना जितकें जवळ करितो, त्यांना जसें आणि जेथपर्यंत घरात येऊ देतो, तेथपर्यंत आणि तसें देखील वागवीत नाही. ते धर्मशत्रू घरात आले असते तर त्यांस तुम्ही गादीवर बसवून 'या खानसाहेब' म्हणून मांडीशी मांडी लाविली असतीत. पण जरी या अस्पृश्य हिंदूंतील अगदी संत, सालस, सरळ, विठोबाचा वारकरी स्नान करून घराशी आला तरी त्याला आम्ही आत घेणार नाही, त्याची सावली देखील घेणार नाही! हीं सात कोटी आम्हां मनुष्यांसारखीं मनुष्यें, आम्ही कुत्र्यामांजरांसारख्या गदळ प्राण्यास, म्हशी गाईसारख्या पशूस शिवू, पण त्यांस शिवत नाही! त्यायोगे हा सात कोटी हिंदुसमाज आपल्या पक्षास असून नसून सारखास झालेला आहे; इतकेंच नव्हे, तर त्याहून भयंकर संकट आपणांवर कोसळण्यास कारणीभूत होणार आहे. कारण त्यांच्यावर जो अमानुष बहिष्कार आम्ही टाकला, त्यामुळे ते आपल्यास ऊपयोगी पडत नाहीत. उलट शत्रूंस आपल्या घरात भेद पाडण्याला सुलभ साधन होतात. . . . मग अर्धे अस्पृस्य आम्ही घेतो म्हणून म्हणणारी अल्लींची जीभ, आणि सगळे अस्पृश्य आमचेच आहेत म्हणून अधिकार सांगणारी निजामी आणि सिंधी मौलवींची धृष्टता ठिकच्या ठिकाणी लुळी पडेल. (Note 75)

8. कुत्र्यास शिवतोस, सापास दूध पाजतोस, ऊंदिराचें रक्त प्रत्यही पिणाऱ्या मांजरास ताटात तोंड घालू देतोस—तर मग हे हिंदु! या माणसासारख्या माणसास, या तुझ्या रामाची पूजा करणाऱ्या तुझ्या देशबंधूस—या तुझ्या महारास शिवण्याची तेवढी तुला इतकी कसली लाज वाटते! सोड ती लाज! त्या लाजेचीच वाटू दे लाज . . . (Note 79)

9. इतका निश्चय करून तू बाहेर पड आणि त्या हीन दीन हिंदु बंधूंच्या पाठीवर प्रेमाचा हात फिरव की, त्या एका हात फिरवण्याने तू या हिंदुजातीचे भाग्यचें भाग्य परिणामकारकपणे फिरवू शकशील. (Note 80)

10. ही दोन्ही मुले आमच्याशी दिवसभर खेळावयास येत. जेव्हा अण्णा नाशिकास जात तेव्हा रात्री सोबतीस येत. वेळ प्रसंगी हरघडी अडलेले काम करीत . . . आम्ही आजारी पडलो म्हणजे आमची शुश्रूषाही रात्रंदिवस करीत. आमच्या घरावर संकट आले म्हणजे त्यांस रडू येई. . . . "राजापरशा" च्या ह्या जोडीवर आमच्या कुटुंबाचीही घरातील मुलांप्रमाणे ममता असे. वडील घरी नसले म्हणजे मी त्यांचेबरोबर घरी एका पंक्तीस जेवावे. लहानपणापासूनच मला जातिभेदाचा तिटकारा वाटे. हे शिंपी मी ब्राह्मण ही कलपनाच मला उपमर्दाची भासे. (Note 83)

11. माझ्यावर त्यांच्या घरातील माणसांचाही फार लोभ असे. त्यांच्या भावजया आणि आई ह्यांनी माझ्यासाठी ताजी भाकरी आणि लाल लाल लसणाच्या तिखटाची चटणी, मोठ्या प्रेमाने आणि विशेष काळजीने करावी आणि ती मी खावी. तेव्हा ब्राह्मणाचा आणि जहागिरदाराचा मुलगा आपल्या घरी जेवला याचे त्यांना केवढे उपकार वाटावे. (Notes 83–84)

12. जातीपातीचा अहंकार माझ्या ठायी मुळीच नसे . . . ऊलट माझ्यावर हाच आक्षेप आल्यास माझ्या शिक्षित सहकार्यांकडून येई की मी जात किंवा धंदा किंवा शिक्षणाची योग्यता न पाहता सर्वांशी फार बरोबरीने वागतो नि त्यामुळे माझ्या मोठेपणास कमीपणा येतो. असा मोठेपणा मला पोकळ आणि दुर्बळ वाटे. (Note 85)

13. न्हावी, मराठे, वाणी, कुणबी, ब्राह्मण, प्रभु, आमच्यात कोणाची जात कोणची हा विचारच नसे. त्याकाळी हिंदु स्पृश्यदेखील एकत्र बसून फराळ करीत नसत. एकदा चैत्रातील हळदीकुंकवाचे निमित्ताने

आम्ही ब्राह्मणाच्या घरी गेलो असता त्यांनी दिलेली फोडणीची डाळ आमच्या नेहमीच्या पद्धतीप्रमाणे एकाच ठिकाणी सरमिसळ बसून खाल्ल्यामुळे केवढा गवगवा झाला होता! (Note 86)

14. प्रांतविशिष्ठ जातिभेद:- एका ब्राह्मणात पंजाबी ब्राह्मण, मैथिली ब्राह्मण, महाराष्ट्रीय ब्राह्मण, एका महाराष्ट्रीयात पुन: कऱ्हाडे, पळशे, देवरुखे, देशस्थ, कोकणस्थ, गौड, द्राविड, गोवर्धन . . . पंथविशिष्ठ जातिभेद:-वर्ण एकच ब्राह्मण; प्रांत एकच. ऊदाहरणार्थ बंगाल; पण एक वैष्णव, दुसरा ब्राम्हो, तिसरा शैव तर चौथा शाक्त! वर्ण एकच वैश्य; प्रांत एकच, गुजरात वा महाराष्ट्र वा कर्नाटक वा मद्रास वा पंजाब, पण एक जैन वैश्य तर दुसरा वैष्णव वैश्य तर तिसरा लिंगायत. रोटीबंदी, बेटीबंदी, चिरेबंद! बौद्ध, जैन, वैशणव, शीख, लिंगायत, महानुभव, मातंगी, राधास्वामी, ब्राम्हो जो जो पंथ निघे त्याची पहिली महत्वाकांक्षा ही की, त्यांचा पंथ ज्या समाजाचा एक सलग अवयव होता त्यापासून रोटीबेटीबंदीच्या दोहाती तरवारीनीं साफ कापून निराळा फेकला जावा. (Note 90)

15. जातिभेदाच्या प्रस्तुतच्या स्वरूपाची ही अशी भेसूर रूपरेखा आहे . . . आपल्या राष्ट्रदेहाचे हे रोटीबंद, बेटीबंद, तटबंद असे सहस्त्रश: तुकडे पाडणारा हा जातिभेद; ही चातुर्वर्ण्याची मारक विकृति—हा सामाजिक क्षयरोग—अशाचा अशाच भरभराटू देणें हे आपल्या राष्ट्रीय शक्तीस पोषक आहे असें आपणांस अजूनही खरोखरच वाटते का? (Note 91)

16. आकाशात उडण्याची साहसी सवय पिढ्यानपिढ्या नष्ट झाल्याने ज्यांचे पंख पंगू झाले आहेत असे हे हिंदू पराक्रमाचे कोंबडे हे आपल्याच जातीच्या अंगणास जग मानून त्यातच डौलाडौलाने आरवत बसले आणि ते केव्हा? तर आततायी पराक्रमासही पुण्य मानणाऱ्या मुसलमानी गिधाडांनी आणि युरोपिअन गुंडानी सर्व जगाचे आकाश नुसते झाकून टाकले तेव्हा अशा स्थितीत त्यांच्या झेपेसरशी ते अंगणातले कोंबडे ठिकाणच्या ठिकाणी फडफडून गतप्राण झाले यात काय आश्चर्य! (Note 93)

17. ". . . जें जें काही नवें वा उपयुक्त निघेल तें तें त्या आमच्या श्रुतीत आहेच म्हणून सांगू लागतील. . . . इकडे आगगाडी निघाली की, यांना वेदात आगगाडीची भसभस ऐकू येऊ लागलीच म्हणूण समजावें. इकडे विमानें निघालीं की वेदकालीन विमानें म्हणून त्यांनी अग्रलेख खरडला म्हणून समजावें. (Note 102)

18. श्रुती स्मृतीपासून तो शनिमाहात्म्यापर्यंतच्या साऱ्या पोथ्या वेदांच्या अपौरुषेयत्वपासून तो वांग्याच्या अभक्षत्वापर्यंतचे सारे सिद्धांत सनातन धर्म या एकाच पदवीस पोचलेले आहेत. उपनिषदातील परब्रह्मस्वरूपाचे अत्युदार विचार हे हि सनातन धर्मच आणि विस्तवापुढे पाय धरून शेकू नये, कोवळ्या उन्हात बसू नये, लोखंडाचा विक्रय करणाऱ्यांचे अन्न कदापि खाऊ नये . . . लसूण कांदा आणि गाजर खाल्ल्याने तर द्विज तत्काल पतित होतो; परंतु श्राद्धानिमित्त केलेले मास जो कोणी हट्टाने खात नाही तो अभागी एकवीस जन्म पशुयोनी पावतो (मनू ५-३४) . . . श्राद्धामध्ये भातापेक्षा ब्राह्मणास व वरहाचें व महिषाचें मास जेवू घालणे उत्तम कारण पितर त्या मांसाच्या भोजनाने दहा महिने तृप्त राहतात. (Note 105)

19. या चातुर्वर्ण्यात बेटीबंदी होती असे गृहीत धरले तरी रोटीबंदी नव्हतीच नव्हती. राम भिल्लिणीची बोरें खात, कृष्ण दासीपुत्राच्या घरी कण्यांचा भात खात, ब्राह्मण ऋषि द्रौपदीच्या स्थालीतील भाजी खात, आणि सूत्रकार 'शुद्रा: पाककर्तार: स्यु:' म्हणून आज्ञा देत. पण भागाचे विभाग, विभागाचे शकले, शकलांचे राईराई एवढे तुकडे रोटीबंद, लोटीबंद, बेटीबंद, संबंधशून्य, सहानुभूतिशून्य तुकडे तुकडे करून टाकले या जातीभेदाने. (Note 110)

20. वर्णांप्रमाणे हिंदु राष्ट्राचा कमीत कमी नऊ दहा कोटींचा शूद्र गट तरी एक असावयास पाहिजे होता. पण दुर्दैवास तें न साहून त्याच गटाचे व्यवसायविशिष्ट, कर्मनिष्ठ, जातिभेदाने तुकडे तुकडे पाडून

टाकले. या एका शूद्र वर्णाच्या प्रांताप्रमाणे निरनिराळ्या जाति झाल्याच होत्या. पंथाप्रमाणे त्यातही पुन: विभाग झाले. तांबट, कासार, कुणबी, माळी, न्हावी, धोबी, विणकर, लोहार, सुतार, रंणून सांगावें! हगारी, शिंपी कोण कोण म्हणून सांगावें! (Note 112)

21. काही गवळी कच्च्या दूधापासून लोणी काढू लागताच त्यांची स्वतंत्र जात होऊन, तापलेल्या दुधाच्या लोण्यास काढणाऱ्या सनातन गवळ्यांशी त्यांचा बेटीव्यवहार बंद. . . . मांसाहारातही मासे खाणाऱ्या ब्राह्मणांची एक जात तर कोंबडी खाणाऱ्यांची दुसरी, बोकड खाणाऱ्यांची तिसरी! त्याच क्रमाने आणि तत्वाने कांदे खाणाऱ्या सुनेची एक, बटाटे खाणाऱ्या सासूची दुसरी . . . (Note 113)

22. संकरविशिष्ट जातीभेद: मूळ चार वर्ण: त्यांचे अनुलोम-प्रतिलोम पद्धतीचे पहिल्या प्रतीचे संकर त्यांनी कसेबसे मोजून त्यांस नांवेंही शोधून काढली. ब्राह्मण स्त्री—शूद्रपुरुष यांच्या संकराने चंडाल झाला. पुन: चंडालपुरुष आणि ब्राह्मण स्त्री यांपासून अतिचंडाल झाला. पुन: अतिचंडाल पुरुष आणि ब्राह्मण स्त्री यांचा संकर—त्यांचा त्यांचा पुन: संकर, त्यांचा पुन: संकर; अति अति अति अति चंडाल ! पण पुन: संकर आहेच! हे अनंत भेद, नुसते ब्राह्मण प्रतिलोमाचे. तितकेच अनंत क्षत्रिय प्रतिलोमाचे, तितकेच वैश्य प्रतिलोमाचे, तितकेच शूद्र प्रतिलोमाचे . . . (Note 114)

23. श्रीकृष्णाचा एकही पुत्र श्रीकृष्ण निघाला नाही. डोळस व्यासांचा मुलगा अंधळा धृतराष्ट्र आणि सच्छील व्यासांचे नातू दुर्योधन, दुःशासन . . . पहिल्या बाजीरावाचा पुत्र राघोबा आणि नातू दुसरा बाजीराव! किंबहुना उभ्या पृथ्वीचे इतिहासात कोणी शककर्ता म्हंटला की त्याच्या चार, पांच पिढ्यांचे आतच कोणीतरी दुबळा राज्यविनाशक पुत्र निपजावयाचाच, असा प्रकार जवळजवळ एखाद्या सिध्दान्तासारखा आढळून येतो. (Note 115)

24. जोवर मुसलमान मुसलमानच राहू इच्छितात, ख्रिस्ती ख्रिस्ती, पारशी पारशी, ज्यू ज्यू, तोवर हिंदूनेही हिंदूच राहणे भाग आहे, उचित आहे, इष्ट आहे. ज्या दिवशी ते विधर्मीय गट आपली आकुंचित कुंपणे तोडून एकाच मानवधर्मात वा मानवराष्ट्रात समरस होण्यास समानतेने सिध्द होतील, त्या दिवशी हिंदुराष्ट्रही त्याच मानव धर्माच्या ध्वजाखाली मनुष्यमात्रांशी समरस होईल, किंबहुना असा 'मानव' धर्म हीच हिंदुधर्माची परमसीमा नि परिपूर्णता मानलेली आहे. (Note 118)

25. ब्राहमणाच्या जात्यहंकाराचा केव्हा अगदी ठीक ठीक समाचार घेताना जो ब्राहमणेतर सत्यशोधकपंथ समतेच्या एखाद्या आचार्यासही लाजवील अशा उदात्त तत्वांचा पुरस्कार करतो, त्यातील काही लोक तेंच समतेचें अधिष्ठान महार-मांग मागू लागताच अगदी मंबाजीबुवासारखे पिसाळून त्यांच्यावर लाठी घेऊन धावतात, या जातवेडामुळे! ब्राह्मण मराठ्यांचे ब्राह्मण बनू पाहतात. मराठे महारांचे ब्राह्मण बनू पाहतात, महार मांगांचे ब्राह्मण बनू पाहतात! हे जातवेड एका ब्राह्मणाच्या अंगी मुरलेलें नसून अब्राह्मण चांडालापर्यंत उभ्या हिंदूसमाजाच्याच हाडीमासी रुजलें आहे! (Note 119)

26. केवळ ब्राह्मणांचीच ही क्लृप्ति असती तर श्रीराम आणि श्रीकृष्ण हे तर ब्राह्मण नव्हतेना? मग त्यांनी तेंच चातुर्वर्ण्य कां उचलून धरले? जर म्हणाल की, क्षत्रियादिक वर्ग बिचारे भोळसर म्हणून सहज ब्राह्मणी काव्यात फसले तर———श्रीकृष्ण का भोळा होता? का समुद्रगुप्त भोळा होता? का शिवाजी भोळा होता? . . . आणि स्वत: मनू कोण? क्षत्रिय! (Note 120)

27. . . . त्यात ब्राम्हण ज्ञातीसच जरी मुख्यत्वे करून साऱ्या कोटिक्रमात संबोधिलें आहे तरी तीं ब्राह्मणांना यथायोग्यपणे दिलेलीं प्रत्यूत्तरें क्षत्रियांखालील वर्णांना पायाखाली तुडवू पाहणाऱ्या क्षत्रियांनाही तंतोतंत लागू पडतात. वैश्यांतही वरच्या ब्राम्हण क्षत्रियांस 'पीडक' वर्णाहंकारी म्हणून दूषित स्वतः शुद्रास्पृश्यादिक खालच्या जातींना मात्र आपल्या 'उच्च' वाणीपणाचें पाणी दाखवण्यास नि खालच्यांचे आपणही 'ब्राम्हण' बनण्यास न सोडणारे लक्षावधि वैश्य आहेतच;

शुद्रांतही त्रैवर्णिकांनी ज्ञातिभेदाचें ढोंग काढून आम्हास नागवलें, मनुष्य मात्र समान!' म्हणून घोषिणारे शुद्रच त्यांच्या 'खालच्या शुद्र पोटजातीससुद्धा त्याच जातीभेदाच्या त्याच ढोंगाखाली हीन लेखिण्यास सोडीत नाहीत, बेटी रोटी व्यवहार करीत नाहीत, महरादिक पूर्वास्पृश्यांस तर शिवतही नाहीत. (Note 121)

28. भटाच्या नावाने सांज सकाळ बोटें मोडणारे अनेक 'समाजिस्ट' नी 'सुधारक' लग्न-मुंज, श्राद्धपक्ष, गौरी-गणपतीचा दिवस उजाडला की भटजींकडे जे हेलपाटे घालतात तो येत नाही म्हणून त्यावर जे चडफडतात, दोन वाजेपर्यंत उपाशी राहतात पण भटाने पूजा सांगितल्यावाचून अन्नाचा घास जो त्यास गिळवत नाही, त्या त्यांच्या भाबडेपणातच भटशाहीचे बळ आहे, भटाच्या दर्भात नव्हे. (Note 124)
29. कारण भट म्हणताच प्रथम ब्राम्हण जरी चटकन डोळ्यापुढे येतो तरी गुरव गुरु, जंगम, फार काय महार भट आहेतच! ही सारी अब्राह्मण असली तरी भटशाहीच आहे. (Note 125)
30. पूजा, पाठ, गौरी, गणपति, सोयर—सुतक, संक्रांत, द्वादशी, दसरा, दिवाळी प्रभृति शेकडो प्रसंगी भटावाचून काहीएक अडणार नाही. स्वत: पोथी वाचावी किंवा शुध्द मराठीत ते शब्द नि भाव व्यक्तवून ज्याची त्याने पूजा करावी. (Note 126)
31. वास्तविक पाहता कोण्याही हिंदुने मुसलमानाचें किंवा ख्रिस्त्याचें अन्न खाल्लें किंवा पाणी घेतलें म्हणजे तो बाटतो ही कल्पनाच खुळी आहे. कारण धर्माचें स्थान पोट नसून हृदय हें आहे! . . . मुसलमानादिक लोक हिंदूंचें अन्न चुकूनच नव्हे तर लुबाडून घेऊन देखील खातात आणि पुन्हा मुसलमानचे मुसलमान राहतात . . . मग मुसलमानाच्या अन्नानें हिंदूंचा धर्मच नष्ट व्हावा इतकी हिंदुसमाजाची पचनशक्ति क्षीण कां असावी? (Note 130)
32. आम्ही तर प्रत्येक हिंदूला उघडपणे सांगतो की, जर निरुपाय होईल तर चापून मुसलमानांचे घरी खा, पाणी प्या, इंग्रजांचें घरी खा, पाणी प्या; सर्व जगाच्या घरी खा, पाणी प्या; आणि जेवण झाल्यावर लगेच एक तुळशीचें पान तोंडात टाका की, तुमची मुक्खशुद्धिच नव्हे तर आत्मशुद्धिही होऊन आणि अन्न पार पचवून टाकून तुम्ही पुन्हा हिंदूचे हिंदुच राहाल. (Note 131)
33. लाखो लोक बाटताहेत, आततायी मुसलमानांचे दंगे, कन्यापहरणे मंदिरोध्वंसाप्रभृति अत्याचार साऱ्या देशभर चालू आहेत, हिंदुस्थानचे पाकस्थान बनविण्याचें घाटत आहे, मिशनें, घरें पोखरून राहिली आहेत, अस्पृश्य आमच्या छळाने नि त्यांच्या पिसाळण्याने कोटि कोटि फुटून जात आहेत, न राष्ट्र न राज्य, न अन्न, ना वस्त्र! अशा जर्जर झालेल्या हिंदुराष्ट्रास तारण्यासाठी या न्यायमीमांसावैदिकतर्कवेदत्वचास्पतींना हा एवढा उपाय काय तो सुचला, पुरेसा वाटला! 'रुखवत करू नये, जावयाने रुसू नये, जेवणाच्या वेळी उखाणे म्हणू नये!!' (Note 134)
34. खाण्यापिण्याने हिंदुधर्मीय बाटणार तरी कसा? कारण हिंदु धर्माचें वसतिस्थान तुमच्या पोटात नसून रक्तात आहे, बीजात आहे, हृदयात आहे, आत्म्यांत आहे आणि तें हिंदु रक्त, हृदय, बीज, आणि आत्मा मुसलमानादिकांच्या पाण्याच्या एका पेल्यांत तर काय पण उभ्या समुद्रातही बुडून जाणें अशक्य आहे. (Note 135)
35. प्रथमदर्शनीच ज्ञानेश्वरांसारख्या महायोग्याचें दर्शन घडते. जर कधी तपस्येने, योगाने, पुण्याईने, कोणा मनुष्यात भगवंताचे अधिष्ठान सुव्यक्त झालें असेल तर तें ह्या अलौकिक पुरुषात होतेंच होते. रेड्याकडून त्यांनी वेद म्हणवले; भिंतींना चालविलें; हरिनामाच्या गजराने महाराष्ट्र दणाणून सोडलें; ते ज्ञानेश्वर, ते निवृत्ती, ते सोपान, ती मुक्ता आपल्या अलौकिक दैवी संपत्तीची महाराष्ट्रभर नुसती लूट करवीत होते . . . त्यांच्या मागोमाग नामदेव, जनाबाई, गोरा कुंभार, दामाजीपंत, सावता माळी, रोहिदास चांभार, चोखा महार . . . त्यांच्या मागोमाग ते एकनाथ, ते तुकाराम ब्राह्मणवाड्यापासून

महारवाड्यापर्यंत महाराष्ट्रात घरोघर साधुसंत . . . महाराष्ट्रात हेंच त्याकाळी देवाचें राहते घर झालेलें होतें वैकुंठ नव्हते. (Note 139)

36. पंचाग्निसाधन, पाण्यात उभे राहून द्वादशवार्षिक नामजप, योगसाधन, उपासतापास, एकशेआठ सत्यनारायण, एक कोटी रामनाम जप, संतत धारेची अनुष्ठाने, रेडे व बोकड मारणारे नवस, हजार वाती लावणे, लक्ष दुर्वा वाहणे, स्नानसंध्या, जपजाप्य, नामसप्ताह, पुरश्चरणे-पारायणे, गोग्रास, ब्राह्मणभोजन, यज्ञयाग, दक्षिणादाने प्रभृति जे शतावधि उपाय श्रुतिपासून शनिमाहात्म्यापर्यंत देवास संतोषविण्यास वर्णिलेले आहेत त्यास आचरणे हा होय. (Note 141)

37. जगत्कल्याण साधण्याच्या लहरीबुवांच्या सदिच्छेस सन्मानूनही असें विचारावेसें वाटते की, ज्याअर्थी जगतात माणसेंही असतात, आणि लोकांवरील संकटें टळण्यासाठी मी हें करणार म्हणून त्यांच्या प्रतिज्ञेंत उल्लेख आहे, त्याअर्थी या व्रताने माणसांचेंही काहीतरी कल्याण ते साधू इच्छीत असलेच पाहिजेत. जर तसेंच असेल तर त्या कार्यी हीं लाख रामनाम म्हणून पत्ता लिहिलेलीं पत्रें पिठाच्या एक लक्ष गोळ्यांतून गंगेत टाकल्याने माणसांचा एक दमडीचाही प्रत्यक्ष लाभ नसून, जर प्रत्यक्ष असा जगतापैकी कोणाचा लाभ होत असेल, तर तो माशांचा नि बेडकांचा होय. . . . रामाचा पत्ता जरी त्या चिठ्ठ्यांवर संस्कृतमध्ये लिहिलेला असला तरी माशांस वा बेडकांस संस्कृत येत असल्याचें वा तो पत्ता वाचण्याइतका साक्षरतेचा प्रसार झाला असल्याचें फारसें ऐकिवात नसल्यामुळे, त्या पिठाच्या गोळ्या त्या बेडकांच्या नि माशांच्याच पोटात पडणार; देवाकडे कशा जाणार? देवाकडचीं पत्रें टाकण्याच्या बेडकांचीं नि माशांचीं पोटें ह्या पोस्टाच्या पेट्या आहेत कीं काय? (Notes 144–45)

38. तुम्हाला स्पेनमधून हुसकलें, सरसहा कत्तलवून नामशेषविलें. ऑस्ट्रिया, हंगेरी, सर्व्हिया, बल्गेरिया ठिकठिकाणी ठेचून ठेचून तुमचा फन्ना उडविला. हिंदुस्थानात तुमची मोगल बादशाही छिनली. अरब, मेसोपोटेमिया, इराक, सीरियातून तुमच्या छातीवर ते राज्य करताहेत. जसा आमचा यज्ञ, वेद, जप, तप, शाप, शिव्या, त्यांचे काहीएक वाकडे करू शकले नाहीत तसेच तुमचें कुराण, कुरबानी, निमाज, ताईत, तावीज त्यांचे काहीएक वाकडें करू शकत नाहीत. (Note 146)

39. म्हणून आव्हानपूर्वक विचारीत, भरसभेत पंचगव्य पितात, गोमूत ओंजळ ओंजळ भरून देवळांत शिंपडतात, पण डॉ. आंबेडकरांसारख्या एखाद्या शुद्ध नि त्यांच्याहूनही सुप्रज्ञ पूर्वास्पृश्याच्या हातचें स्वच्छ गंगोदकही, पिण्याचें राहोच पण त्यांच्या अंगावर शिंपडले जाताच, विटाळ झाला म्हणून स्नान करू लागतात. (Note 148)

40. किंबहुना गोरक्षण न करता गोभक्षण का करू नये? ब्रह्मवादाने दोन्हीही लटकीं किंवा दोन्हींही खरीं आहेत, स्वीकार्य आहेत, भक्षण आणि रक्षण हा भेदच ब्रह्मसृष्टीत नाही. (Note 149)

41. गायीत देव आहेत म्हणून पोथ्या सांगतात तर वराहावतारी देव डुक्कर झाले होते असेंही पोथ्या सांगतात! मग गोरक्षणच का करावे? डुक्कर-रक्षण संघ स्थापून डुक्कर-पूजा का प्रचलवू नये? (Note 150)

42. पाचहजार वर्षांपूर्वीच्या पोथ्यांत सांगितलेली प्रत्येक गोष्ट आता आम्ही जर अद्ययावत विज्ञानाच्या कसोटीवर पारखून न घेतली, प्रत्यक्षनिष्ठ ज्ञानाच्या ती विरुद्ध जाताच किंवा आजच्या परिस्थितीत आपल्या हिंदु राष्ट्राच्या हितास हानीप्रद ठरताच आम्ही तत्काळ टाकून न दिली, तर आपले हिंदु राष्ट्र नि हिंदु धर्म हि पाचहजार वर्षांइतकाच मागासलेला राहून ह्या विज्ञानाच्या वैमानिक युगातील टकराटकरीत आपण टिकाव धरू शकणार नाही. (Note 151)

43. अति मानुष ती देवता, देव. अपमानुष तो पशु, कीट. गाय ही धादांत एक पशु. मनुष्यातील अगदी निर्बुद्ध माणसाइतकी बुद्धि देखील ज्यात नाही अशा कोणच्याही पशूला देवता मानणें म्हणजे माणुसकीचाच अपमान करणें आहे. (Note 154)

44. गोठ्यात ऊभ्या ऊभ्या गवत कडबा खात असलेल्या, एकीकडे खाताखाताच ऊभ्या ऊभ्या दुसरीकडे मलमूत्रोत्सर्ग नि:संकोचपणे करणाऱ्या, थकवा येताच रवंथ करीत त्याच मलमूत्रोत्सर्गात स्वेच्छया बैठक मारून बसणाऱ्या, शेपटीच्या फटकाऱ्याने स्वत:च्या शेणमूत्राचा तो चिखल अंगभर ऊडवून घेणाऱ्या, दावें सुटून थोडा फेरफटका करण्याची संधि मिळताच अनेक समयी कोठेतरी जाऊन घाणीत तोंड घालणाऱ्या नि तसेच ओठ चाटीत गोठ्यात आणून बांधल्या जाणाऱ्या त्या गाईस शुद्ध नि निर्मळ वसनें नेसलेल्या सोज्ज्वल ब्राह्मणाने वा महिलेने हाती पूजापात्र घेऊन गोठ्यात पूजावयास जावें नि तिच्या शेपटीस स्पर्शून आपलें सोवळें न विटाळता ऊलट अधिक सोज्ज्वळले आणि तिचें तें शेण नि तें मूत्र चांदीच्या पेल्यात घोळून पिताना आपलें जीवन अधिक निर्मळलें असे मानावें! ते सोवळें की जें आंबेडकर महाशयांसारख्या महनीय स्वधर्म बंधूच्या श्रेष्ठ मनुष्याची सावली पडताच विटाळावे, तें ब्राह्मक्षात्र जीवन की जें तुकारामासारख्या संताच्या नुसत्या पंक्तीस बसून सत्तवस्थ दहीभात खाल्ला असताही भ्रष्टावें ॥पशु तो देव, देवासारखा माणूस तो पशु! (Note 155)

45. अशा स्थितीत त्या शत्रूच्या वेढ्यात गवसलेल्या हिंदु सैन्यास अन्नाचा पुरवठा करण्यासाठी ते पशु लढाईस गुंतलेले नाहीत ते मारून खाणेंच राष्ट्रीय दृष्ट्या अत्यंत पवित्र गोष्ट होय. अशा अणिबाणीच्या वेळा इतिहासात प्रत्येक राष्ट्रास आलेल्या आहेत. अशा वेळी गाय हा ऊपयुक्त पशु आहे, मनुष्यास अधिकात अधिक ऊपयोग करून घेण्यासाठीच गोपालन कर्तव्य असतें, आज त्या वेढ्यात सापडलेल्या हिंदुंच्या राजधानीच्या ह्या दुर्गाच्या संरक्षणासाठी तेथील बाठ्या नि युद्धार्थ अनावश्यक अशा गाईही मारून त्यांचें मांस खाणें हाच त्यास हिंदुराष्ट्रास ऊपयुक्त करून घेण्याचा खरा मार्ग आहे असें आढळताच हिंदू सैन्याने त्या गाई मारून खाणें नि त्या बळावर हिंदुराष्ठाच्या शत्रूशी झुंजत राहणें हाच हिंदूंचा खरा धर्म ठरणार! गोपालन नव्हे, तर गोहत्या हीच पुण्यप्रद होणार! (Note 158)

46. दहा देवळें, मूठभर ब्राह्मण, दहापांच गाई मारण्याचें पाप टाळावें यास्तव राष्ट्र मरू दिलें! गोहत्येचें पाप टाळावें म्हणून राष्ट्रहत्या घडू दिली! राष्ट्राहून राष्ट्रातील एक पशु श्रेष्ठ मानला! राष्ट्रस्वातंत्र्य पडलें तरी चिंता नाही, एक देऊळ पडण्याची चिंता! . . . मग जिथे असे प्रसंग महंमद गजनवीच्या काळापासून तों दुसऱ्या बाजीरावाच्या काळापर्यंत ह्या वा त्या रूपाने वारंवार घडलेले आढळतात, तिथे या पोथीनिष्ठ, विवेकशून्य, राष्ट्रघातक 'धर्मभोळे' पणाचा आम्हांस अत्यंत तिटकारा यावा ह्यात कोणाचा दोष बरें! आम्हां उपयुक्ततावाद्याचा का त्या राष्ट्रबुडाऊ धर्मभोळेपणाला अजूनही चिकटून राहू पाहणाऱ्या आमच्या भाबड्या पोथीवाद्यांचा! (Note 160)

47. मुलतानचे एक सूर्यमंदिर पाडण्याचा धाक मुसलमानांनी घालताच पोथीने अंधळलेला हिंदू नसता तर त्याने तत्काळ उलट प्रत्युत्तरले असतें कि 'पाड तें सूर्यमंदिर; पण म्लेंछा समजून ऐस कि, हि हिन्दुसेना आता परती न जाता ते मुलतान तुझ्या हातून सोडवून काबूलपर्यंत जितकी म्हणून मशीद दिसेल तिच्या तिच्यावर गाढवाचा नांगर फिरवून देण्यास सोडणार नाही! आणि त्या काबूलच्या शाही मशिदीच्या शिळांच्याच पायावर मुलतानचे सूर्यमंदिर पुन्हा उभारलें जाईल! (Note 161)

48. 'पाड ते देऊळ! . . . नि काप हीं आमचीं मूठभर ब्राह्मणांचीं शिरें! पण ध्यानात धर . . . ते या एका काशीच्या देवळाचा सूड घेण्यासाठी महाराष्ट्रात तरी मशीद म्हणून उरू देणार नाहीत. रस्ते साफ करून मशिदी नि वाद्ये हा प्रश्नच आमच्या पुढच्या पिढ्यांना त्रास देण्यास मागे ठेवणार नाहीत . . . शनवार वाड्यात देखील एक पीर सुरक्षित ठेवला; पण जर तुम्ही म्लेंछ ती वहिवाट पुन्हा तोडाल तर हिंदूही तिला ठोकरून देतील.' (Note 163)

49. पण गाढव इतकें ऊपयुक्त नि इतकें प्रामाणिक, इतकें सोसाळु असते, म्हणून त्यास पशु न मानता आजवर कोणी त्याची देवता बनविली; किंवा एखादी गाढव-गीता रचून गाढवपूजनचा संप्रदाय

काढला आहे काय? . . . मग गाय हा ऊपयुक्त पशु आहे, यासतवच त्याची देवता कल्पून आपण हे सारे वेडेचार जे गाईच्या प्रकरणी करतो तेही निव्वळ बाष्कळपणाच, मूर्खपणाच म्हणावयास नको काय? (Note 164)

50. खरोखर आजवर कुठे भागवतातील गोकुळ पृथ्वीवर नांदत असेल तर ते गोमांसभक्षक असताही गायीस एक उपयुक्त पशु मानूनच काय ती तिची जोपासना करणाऱ्या अमेरिकेत होय. (Note 166)

51. गाईस एक वेळ गोमाता म्हणा, लाक्षणिक अर्थी तें क्षणभर चालेल; पण तें अक्षरश: खरें मानणें नव्हे. आम्हांस असें वाटतें की, गाईचें शेण खाणें नि मूत्र पिणें ही पूर्वी केव्हातरी एक उपमर्दकारक निंदाव्यंजक शिक्षा दिली जात असावी. पाप्याची मिशी काढणें, गाढवावर बसविणें इत्यादि धिंडवड्यांप्रमाणे त्याला दंड म्हणून गाईचें शेणमूत खाणें भाग पाडलें जात असावें. . . . अजूनही व्यवहारात "शेण खाणे, मूत्र पिणें" ही शिवी अहे। संस्कार नव्हे! (Notes 167–68)

52. स्त्रियांना शिक्षण कमी आहे, त्यांना शिपाईगिरी करता येणार नाही, त्यांना राजकीय हक्क संभाळण्याचें बद्धिसामर्थ्यही निसर्गत:च कमी आहे वगैरे मुद्द्यावर पुरुषवर्गांपैकी कोणीही त्यांची दाद घेत नाही, इतकेच नव्हे तर ह्या पुरुषवर्गाच्या कोट्या खऱ्याच आहेत असें समजून कित्येक स्त्रीपक्षीय पुढारी स्त्रियाही या अडचणी कशा दूर कराव्या ह्या विचारात गढून गेल्या! परंतु लवकरच त्यांच्या ध्यानात असें आलें की जुलमी लोकांचीं ही शिळीं विधानें सर्वथैव खोटीं आहेत। स्वत:च्या हातातील सत्ता सोडून देण्यास जुलमी मनुष्य तयार होणार आहे? व ती आपली सत्ताप्रियता छपवून ठेवण्यासाठी स्त्रिया ती सत्ता चालविण्यास योग्य नाहीत ही सबब आजच पुढे आली आहे की काय? अमेरिका राजसत्ता हिसकून घेईतोपर्यंत ती अशिक्षित व राजधुरा धरण्यास असमर्थ आहे म्हणून जुलमी राजे म्हणत नव्हते काय? इटालीला स्वातंत्र्य सांभाळण्याची अक्कल नाही म्हणून आम्ही तेथे राज्य करतो, हें ऑस्ट्रिया शेवटपर्यंत म्हणत नव्हता काय? (Note 181)

53. राजकीय स्वातंत्र्य मिळाल्याशिवाय आपली दुर्बलता व अशिक्षितता जाणार नाही व हे जुलमी लोक तर म्हणतात की ती दुर्बलता व अशिक्षितता नाहीशी झाल्याशिवाय आम्ही तुम्हाला राजकीय स्वातंत्र्य देणार नाही! पाण्यात उतरल्याशिवाय आम्हांस पोहता येणार नाही व हे जुलमी सत्ताधीश म्हणतात की, पोहता आल्याशिवाय तुम्हांला पाण्यात उतरू देणार नाही!" उतरू देणार नाही? आम्ही ऊतरणार! आम्ही स्वातंत्र्य मिळवणार!" (Note 182)

54. . . . कायदेशीर पद्धतीने म्हणजे पुरुषांनी केलेल्या कायद्यांना अनुसरून! . . . कायदे कोणी केलेले असतात? जुलमी लोकांनी आपल्या संरक्षणासाठी व आपले जुलूम अव्याहत राहण्यासाठीच ते कायदे केलेले असतात. असल्या कायद्यांच्या शिरस्त्याने जोपर्यंत एखादा गुलाम चालतो तोपर्यंत त्याची *गुलामगिरी* कशी सुटणार? गुलामाची गुलामगिरी कायम राहावी म्हणूनच त्याच्यावर कायद्याची ही बेडी चढवलेली असते. (Note 183)

55. पुढे कोर्टात चौकशी चालली तेव्हा कोर्टाच्या प्रश्नांस स्त्रियांकडून उत्तरें दिलीं जात की तुम्हांला आम्ही उत्तरें देत नाही. कारण तुम्हांला स्त्रियांचें मत न घेता न्यायासनावर बसविलेलें आहे. कायदा कां मोडला या प्रश्नांस उत्तर की तो कायदाच नव्हता. त्यांस पुरुषांनी स्त्रियांची संमति घेतल्याशिवाय कायदा बनविला आहे. . . . (Note 184)

56. ह्या स्वत:च्या बापाच्या,भावाच्या किंवा पतीच्याही अन्यायी परवशतेला न जुमानणाऱ्या इंग्लंडच्या स्त्रिया स्वदेशावर जर परक्यांचें राज्य असतें तर काय करत्या व काय न करत्या. (Note 185)

57. बुद्धाचें कुलही सख्ख्या बहीणभावंडांच्या संबंधापासूनच आपली ऊत्पत्ती झाली असें मानी, आणि क्वचित बुद्धाच्या या ऊत्पत्तीचें अप्रत्यक्ष समर्थन करण्यासाठीच की काय बुद्धाच्या रामायणात राम

आणि सीता हीं सख्खी बहीण भावंडें असून त्यांचा प्रीतिसंबंध पुढे विवाहसंबंधात परिणत झाला असें वर्णन दिलें आहे! (Note 188)

58. सैपाकाला ती सासू बसली की हिला सांगणार, 'येवढे चार मासे सोलून दे पाहूं.' जेवताना ती बंगाली ब्राह्मणांच्या रीतीप्रमाणे माशांची आमटी भुरक भुरक भुरकणार. ही मराठी ब्राम्हणांची मुलगी त्या मासोळी जेवणाच्या वासासरशी ओक ओक ओकणार. (Note 194)

59. मनुस्मृतीतील एक श्लोक (Note 197)

 नर्क्षवृक्षनदीनाम्नीं नान्त्यपर्वतनामिकाम्
 न पक्ष्यहिप्रेष्यनाम्नीं न च भीषणनामिकाम्
 अव्यन्गान्गीं सौम्यनाम्नीं हंसवारणगामिनीम्
 तनुलोमकेशदशनां म्रुदव्दृङ्गिम्रुद्वहेत्स्त्रियम्

60. म्हणूनच सूतमगधादिकांपासून तो शूद्रपुरुषसंबंधाने ब्राह्मण स्त्रीस झालेल्या आणि चंडाळ म्हणून मानलेल्या आमच्या पूर्वास्पृश्य बांधवापर्यंत वर्णांचे रक्तबीज संकीर्ण झालेलें आहे. आम्हा सर्व जातींच्या नसानसातून परस्परांचें रक्त प्रवाहित आहे ही गोष्ट काही कोणासच नाकारता येणें शक्य नाही. (Note 204)

61. श्रुति स्मृति पुराणोक्त अशी अगदी निर्भेळ सनातनी मुद्राच ज्या प्रथांवर मारलेली आहे त्या पितृसावर्ण्य, मातृसावर्ण्य, अनुलोम आणि प्रतिलोम ह्याचा प्रथांवरून देखील हे निर्विवाद सिध्द होऊ शकते की चारी वर्णांत काय किंवा संकरोत्पन्न चारशे जातींत काय अगदी नि:संकीर्ण आनुवंश असा कुठेच राहिलेला नसून अगदी शास्त्रोक्त विवाहांचे आणि संगमाचे द्वारेच रक्तबीजांचा परस्परसंकर पिढ्यानपिढ्या होत आला आहे. आणि म्हणूनच आनुवंशिक गुणविकासाच्या नियमान्वयेच आमच्यांत परस्परांचे गुणावगुणही संकीर्ण झालेले आहेत. (Note 205)

62. एक पांडवांचे कुळच पहा

उदाहरण हवे असेल तर पांडवाचेच कूळ घ्या. तें कूळ म्हणजे धर्मसंरक्षक आर्योत्तंस प्रत्यक्ष सम्राट भरताचे-कोणी एखादे हीन, अमंगळ कूळ नव्हे! आणि तो काळ म्हणजे 'चातुर्वर्ण्य मया सृष्टं' म्हणून घोषणा करून चातुर्वर्ण्याची हमी घेतलेल्या पूर्णावतारी श्रीकृष्णाचा! . . . प्रतीपाने शंतनूस सांगितलें 'राजा, ही स्त्री कोण, कुठली, काय जात, असे काही एक न विचारता तिच्याशी लग्न कर' त्यारून अज्ञात जातीच्या गंगेशी शंतनूने लग्न केले. त्याचा मुलगा भीष्म, अभिषेकार्ह क्षत्रिय झाला. पुढे शंतनूने, तीची जातगोत माहीत असूनही उघडपणे एका कोळ्याच्या मुलीशी, सत्यवतीशी विवाह करून तिला पट्टाभिषिक्त राणी केली तरी शंतनूची जात गेली नाही. इतकेच नव्हे, तर त्या कोळ्याच्या मुलीचे मुलगे चित्रांगद आणि विचित्रवीर्य दोघेही भारतीय ब्राह्मणांचे शास्त्रोक्त सम्राट झाले. पुढे त्या कोळ्याच्या मुलीच्या मुलाने अंबिका नि अंबालिका या क्षत्रिय राज्यकन्यांशी लग्ने लावली. (Note 206)

63. परंतु व्यास कोण? ब्राह्मणश्रेष्ठ पराशरपुत्र; आणि ते ब्राह्मणश्रेष्ठ पराशर कोण? 'श्वपाकाच्च पराशर: ॥' एका अस्पृश्य श्वपाकाचा पुत्र. त्या अस्पृश्याचा हा पुत्र पराशर ब्राह्मणश्रेष्ठ ठरला. त्या ब्राह्मणश्रेष्ठ पराशरास कोळीण-कुमारीपासून जो पुत्र झाला तोच महाज्ञानी, महातपी, महाभारतकर व्यास होय! (Note 207)

64. अचलमुनीचा जन्म हत्तीच्या पोटी, केशपिंगलाचा घुबडाच्या पोटी, कौशिक गवताच्या पोटी, द्रोणाचार्य मडक्याच्या पोटी, तैतिरी रिषीचा पक्ष्याच्या पोटी, व्यास कोळिणीच्या पोटी, कौशिकीचा

शूद्रिणीच्या पोटी, विश्वामित्र चांडाळणीच्या पोटी, वसिष्ठ वेश्येच्या पोटी जन्मले; हे श्लोक स्मृतीतील म्हणून तुम्हास मान्य असलेच पाहिजेत. या सर्वांची आईबापें ब्राम्हण नसताही त्यांना तुम्ही ब्राह्मण्याचे अधिकारी ब्राम्हण म्हणून मानता त्या अर्थी आता मातापित्यांच्या द्वारेच काय ते ब्राह्मण्य लाभते ब्राम्हण आई बापाच्या पोटी येतो तोच ब्राम्हण होऊ शकतो हेंही म्हणणें खोटें ठरतें. (Note 214)

65. तुम्हीच म्हणता सर्व माणसे एका ब्रह्मदेवापासून उत्पन झालीं आहेत. मग त्यांच्यात एकमेकांशी रक्तबीजाचा संबंध नसलेल्या या चार भिन्न जाती कशा निर्मिल्या गेल्या, माझ्यापासून माझ्या पत्नीला चार मुलें झालीं ती एकाच जातीची नव्हेत काय? मग एकाच ब्रह्मदेवाचीं हीं मुलें जातीचीच भिन्न असतील तरी कशीं? (Note 217)

66. Savarkar Poem "हिंदूंचे एकतागान्": (Note 229)

तुम्ही आम्ही सकल हिंदु. बंधुबंधु
तो महादेवजी पिता आपुला चला तया वंदू
  ब्राह्मण वा क्षत्रिय चांग. जरि झाला
  कसलेंहि रूप वा रंग. जरि ल्याला
  तो महार अथवा मांग. सकलांला
ही एकचि आई हिंदुजाती आम्हांस तिला वंदू
  एकची देश हा अपुल्या. प्रेमाचा
  एकची छंद जीवाच्या. कवनाचा
  एकची धर्म हा आम्हां. सकलांचा
ही हिंदुजातीची गंगा आम्ही तिचे सकल बिंदू (2)
  रघुवीर रामचंद्राचा. जो भक्त
  गोविंदपदांबुजिं जो जो. अनुरक्त
  गीतेसि गाऊनी पूजी. भगवंत
तो हिन्दुधर्मनौकेत बसुनिया तरतो भवसिंधू
  ऊभयांनि दोष ऊभयांचे. खोडावे
  द्वेषासि दुष्ट रूढीसी. सोडावें
  सख्यासि आईच्यासाठी. जोडावें
अम्हि अपराधांसी विसरूनि प्रेमा पुन्हा पुन्हा सांधू (4)
  लेकुरें हिंदुजातीचीं ।हीं आम्ही
  आमुच्या हिंदुधर्मासी. त्या कामीं
  प्राणही देऊनी रक्षू ।परिणामीं
या झेंड्याखाली पुर्वजांचिया एकाची नांदूं

67. स्वतः तुमच्या आईबापांच्याच कट्टर शत्रूंना आई बाप म्हणू नका! जातच बदलून चांभाराचे किरिस्ताव आणि महाराचे मुसलमान व्हावयाचे- तुमचेच बापजादे तुमच्या तोंडावर त्यांची जात बदलल्याविषयी थुंकतील. परधर्म स्वीकाराची ही अभद्र भाषा मंबाजीबुवाच्या परंपरेचा दांभिक पडसाद आहे, हे आम्ही जाणून आहो. म्हणूनच तर तुम्ही तरी त्यांच्या संसर्गाने आपली निष्पाप जिव्हा पुन्हा वितळू नये! (Note 233)

68. Savarkar Poem: "सुतक युगांचे फिटलें" (Notes 234–35)

तुम्हिं देवाच्या येऊं दिलेती दारीं
आभार जाहले भारी
तुम्हिं वरदानीं शिवुनि पतित हा माथा
मळविलें पावना हाता
या ठेवुं पदांवरति पवित्रां ताता
दिधलाति पतित हा माथा
तुम्हि धर्माचे सूर्य कथू किति नवला
सावली तमाची शिवलां
जे गाव-बहिष्कार्य आंत त्यां आणी
बाहेर गांव जावोनी
तुम्हि हिंदू या जवळ हिंदुसी आजी
केलेत अहिंदूहुनि जी
हें सुतक युगांचे सुटलें
विधिलिखित विटाळहि फिटले
जन्मांचें भांडण मिटलें
शत्रूचें जाळें तुटलें
अम्हि शतकांचे दास: आज सहकारी
आभार जाहले भारी !

69. Savarkar poem sung at the opening of the second temple of Ratnagiri. (हिंदु जातीचा श्रीपतितपावनाचा धावा) (Notes 238–39)

उद्धरिसी गा हिंदुजातिसी केव्हा
हे हिंदुजातिच्या देवा ॥ ध्रु ॥
आब्राह्मण चंडाल पतितची आम्ही
तुम्हि पतितपावन स्वामी
निजशीर्ष विटाळेल म्हणुनि कापाया
चुकलो न आपुल्या पाया ॥
आणि पायांनी राखु शुध्दता साची
छाटिलें पावलांनाची ॥
ऐकू न पडो आपुलिया कानातें
मुख कथि न म्हणुनि ज्ञानातें ॥
निज सव्यकरें वामकरा जिंकाया
विकियली शत्रुला काया ॥
करु, बंधूंसी बंद करु दारा, जे
चोर ते घराचे राजे
हें पाप भयंकर झालें । रे
पेरिलें फळाला आलें । रे

हृदिं असह सलति ते भाले। रे
उद्धार अता! मृत्युदंड की दे वा
हे हिंदुजातिच्या देवा!
अनुताप परी जाळितसे या पापा
दे तरी आजि ऊःशापा
निर्दाळुनि त्या आजि भेद दैत्याशी
ये हिंदुजाति तुजपाशी
ते अवयव विच्छिन्न सांधिलें आजी
तू फुंकि जीव त्यामाजी
देऊनि बळा वामनासि या काळी
तो घाल बळी पाताळी
जरि शस्त्र खुळा कर न आमुचा कवळी
परि तुझी गदा तुजजवळी
जरि करिशि म्हणू जें आता । रे
म्हणशील करू तें नाथा । रे
ऊठु आम्हि परी दे हाता । रे
दिघलासि जसा कंस मारिला तेव्हा
हे हिंदुजातिच्या देवा !

70. जिथे सीता वनवासी निवसे, जिथे कौरव पांडव लढले, गीता उपदेशिली तीं तीं ऐतिहासिक देवस्थानें तीर्थें क्षेत्रें हि अप्रतिमच ज्यांचे वैशिष्ठ्य त्यांच्या कोणत्याही प्रतिलिपीस (Copyस) येणे शक्य नाही. तशीच सदोचित राहणार . . . पूर्वास्पृश्यांची मंदिरप्रवेशा ची मागणी अत्यंत धर्म्य, न्याय्य, आणि ते ज्या सत्याग्रहाच्या निकारावर आले आहेत, तो सत्याग्रह आपल्या पिढ्यानपिढ्याच्या दुराग्रहाचाच केवळ अपरिहार्य पडसाद आहे! सात सत्तर पिढ्या त्यांनी वाट पहिली. आणखी वाट ती त्यांनी किती पाहावयाची? आता आपणच ती वाट त्यांना मोकळी करून देणे एवढेंच बाकी उरलें आहे. (Note 240)
71. आजच्या आमच्या हिंदूसमाजात ज्यांच्यामध्ये केवळ पोथीत तसे लिहिले आहे ह्या व्यतिरिक्त दुसऱ्या कोणत्याही सहज लक्षणाने विभिन्नत्व दिसून येत नाही अशा ब्राह्मण, शूद्र, शिंपी, सोनार, वाणी, लिंगायत, गवळी, माळी आदि सहस्त्रशः उपजतच भिन्न असणाऱ्या जाती मानणे ही मूळ चुकी. त्यात त्या प्रत्येक जातीविषयी महादेवाच्या जटेपासून अमुक जात निघाली, ब्रह्मदेवाच्या बेंबीपासून तमुक निघाली अशा काल्पनिक भाकड उपपत्या अक्षरशः खऱ्या मानून त्या उपपत्त्यांप्रमाणे त्या त्या जातीच्या अंगी एकेक विशिष्ट गुण उपजतच असतात, असे ठाम ठरवून टाकणे ही घोड चुकी ! ! आणि तो गुण त्या जातीच्या संतानात प्रकट झाला नसला तरी तो असलेच असे समजून, त्या गुणानुरूप मानपान, सोयीगैरसोयी, उच्चता-नीचता त्या जातीतील त्या संतानात उपजत भोगावयास लावणे ही पहाड चुकी ! ! ! आणि म्हणे हेच ते आमच्या ऋषींनी शोधून काढलेल्या आनुवंशिक गुण-विकासाचे सनातन रहस्य! ! ! (Note 242)
72. त्यांच्या स्त्रिया सुंदरतेत, सुजनक्षमतेत, सुभगतेत आणि अपत्यसंगोपनातही अधिकाधिक क्षमतर होत आहेत. आणि आमच्या इकडे प्रत्येक पिढी ही पूर्वीहून खुरटी, पूर्वीहून किरटी, पूर्वीहून करंटी निपजत आहे! (Note 243)

73. आमच्या त्रिकालदर्शी ऋषींनी हें आधीच सांगून ठेवलें आहे. तर त्यास आम्ही असें विचारतो की, ह्या कलियुगाची ही ब्याद सर्व मनुष्य जातिवर आणि सर्व पृथ्वीवरच कोसळणार म्हणून सांगितलें आहे ना? मग अमेरिकेत त्याच्या अगदी उलट स्थिति कां होत आहे? त्यांच्या माणसाची छाती, ऊंची, प्रतिभा, प्रतिपिढी वाढत आहे. त्यांची एक गाय आमच्या दहा, दहा, गाईंइतकें दूध देत आहे. शेती, नारळा ऐवढे बटाटे, बियांवाचून द्राक्षें आणि खंडाखंडास पुरून ऊरेल इतकें धान्य निपजवीत आहे. आणि माणूस इच्छील तेथे इंद्र बनून पाऊस पाडण्याची कला आटोक्यात आणीत आहे. (Note 244)

74. आज सर्वांस व्यवसायस्वातंत्र्य आहेच. ब्राह्मण पुणेरी जोडे विकतात. चांभार ऊत्तम शिक्षक होतात. आता सुधारावयाचें तें इतकेंच की, प्रत्यक्ष व्यवसाय दुसरा असताही मूळच्या व्यवसायाची जी एक मानीव रोटीबेटीबंद जात त्याच्या मागे हात धुऊन लागते तिची ब्याद मात्र टाळावयाची.. म्हणजे जात शिंपी—धंदा सोनार; जात ब्राह्मण—धंदा दुकानदारी; हा जो आज ब्रह्मघोटाळा झाला आहे तो मोडेल. सर्वांची जात हिंदु, धंदा जो कोणता असेल तो. (Note 245)

Chapter 4

1. मोरोपंतांचे एकशे आठ रामायणांपेकी महत्वाच्या रामायणाचे प्रकार मी तोंडपाठ म्हणून दाखवावे—निरोष्ठ, दाम, ओवी, मंत्र, लघु इत्यादि मोरोपंती अदभुत कारागिरीच्या रामायणाच्या प्रत्येक दहा बारा पहिल्या नि शेवटच्या आर्या मला पाठ येत (Note 25)

2. निरोष्ठ रामायण (Note 27)

   श्रीहरि दशरथनंदन झाला दशकंठसंक्षय कराया ।
   दर शेष चक्र ही जनि घेती जगदखिल संकट हराया ॥ १॥
   अंगज च्यार तिघींचे संस्कृत साक्षर नरेंद्र कीर्तिकर ।
   निरखी, नितांत हर्षे हा चि न तैसा चि नागरिकनिकर

3. मंत्ररामायण (Note 29)

   श्रीकारापासुनिया मकारपर्यंत वर्ण जे तेरा
   ते राघवचरितांती ग्रंथिले हे रामभक्तहो, हेरा ॥

4. सुभाषितं (Note 31)

   अशनं मे वसनं मे जाया मे बन्धुवर्गो मे।
   इति मे मे कुर्वाणं कालवृको हन्ति पुरुषाजम् ॥

5. सुभाषितं (Note 32)

   रामाभिषेके जलमाहरन्त्या:
   हस्ताच्चयुतो हेमघटो युवत्या: ॥
   सोपानमार्गेण करोति शब्दं
   ठ ठं ठ ठं ठं ठ ठ ठं ठ ठं ठ:

6. सुभाषितं (Note 33)

विद्वत्कवय: कवय: केवलकवयस्तु केवलं कपय: ।
कुलजा या सा जाया केवलजाया तु केवलं माया ॥

7. *Śloka* (Note 34)

वदनि कवळ घेता, नाम घ्या श्रीहरीचे
सहज हवन होते नाम घेता फुका चे
जिवन करी जिवित्वा, अन्न हे पूर्ण ब्रह्म
उदरभरण नोहे जाणिजे यज्ञकर्म

8. Lines from Svadeshicha Phatka (स्वदेशीचा फटका) (Note 37)

आर्यबंधू हो **उठा उठा** का **मठासारखे नटा** सदा
हटा सोडुनी **कटा** करू या म्लेंच्छ**पटा** ना धरूं कदा
काश्मीराच्या शाली त्यजुनी अलपाकाला कां भुलतां
मलमल त्यजुनी **वलवल** चित्ती **हलहलके** पट का वरितां?
केलि अनास्था तुम्हीची स्वतः मग अर्थातचि कला बुडे
गेलें धनची नेलें हरुनी मेलां तुम्हि तरि कोण रडे?
अरे अपणची पूर्वी होतों सकल कलांची खाण अहा
भरतभूमिच्या कुशीं दीप ते कलंक आतां अम्ही पहा
मठ्ठ लोक हो लाज कांहिंतरि?
लठ्ठ असुनि शठ बनलो रे
कामधेनुका भरतभूमिका असुनि भाग कां ती भिक्षा?
सहस्त्र कोसावरुनी खासा पैका हरतो प्रभुदीक्षा
नेउनि कच्चा माल आमुचा देती साचा पक्क रुपें
आमच्यावरी पोट भरी परि थोरि कशाची तरी खपे?

9. आता यापुढे मी कवि नाही असे म्हणण्याची कोणाची माय व्यायली आहे असे माझे मला देखील वाटे. कारण त्या बिचाऱ्या खेडेगावच्या उभ्या आयुष्यात, ज्याची कविता वर्तमानपत्रात छापली गेली, असा कवि मीच, म्हणून लहान थोरांत त्या गावभर गाजावाजाच झाला तसाच. (Note 38)
10. बरे झाले की, जी कविता जगदहितेच्छुकारांनी प्रसिद्ध केली, ती ऐका खेड्यातील बारा वर्षांच्या मुलाची होती हे त्यांना कळले नाही. (Note 38)
11. Lines from Chaphekar ani Ranade yanjvareel Phataka (चाफेकर आणि रानडे यांजवरील फटका) (Note 46)

फाशी ना ती यज्ञवेदिका रक्ते न्हाली जी तुमच्या!! ।
सांडुनी होवो त्याचि राष्ट्ररणिं सार्थक रक्ताचें अमुच्या ॥७
कार्य सोडूनी अपुरें पडलां झुंजत, खंती नको! पुढें ।
कार्या चालवु गिरवुनि तुमच्या पराक्रमाचे अम्ही धडे ॥८

12. Lines from Vrushokti (वृषोक्ति) (Note 47)

माता आर्यवसुंधरा पर तुझ्या डोळ्यांपुढे भोगिती।
दारिद्र्यासह पारतंत्र्य दुबळ्या मानेवरी लादती॥
तेव्हां येउनि मानवी जनुस बा तू साधिलें काय तें?
भूभारापरि गर्वभार अजुनी त्वचित्त कां वाहतें? ॥१०
तूं निःशस्त्र परंतु मी न अजुनी निःशृंग झालों तरी
स्वशृंगें तुज फाडितों, बघ गड्या सोडूनि देतों परी
सोडीं गर्व स्वदेशभार हरण्या यत्नांसि आधीं करीं
होई ईशपदी सुलीन पुरवी सध्देतुला श्रीहरी ॥ ११

13. Keshavsut's Nava Shipai (नवा शिपाई) (Note 59)

नव्या मनूंतिल नव्या दमाचा शूर शिपाई आहें,
कोण मला वठणीला आणूं शकतो तें मी पाहें!
ब्राह्मण नाहीं, हिंदुहि नाहीं, न मी एक पंथाचा,
तेचि पतित कीं जे आंखडिती प्रदेश साकल्याचा!!
जिकडे जावें तिकडे माझीं भांवडें आहेत,
सर्वत्र खुणा माझ्या घरच्या मजला दिसताहेत;
शान्तीचें साम्राज्य स्थापूं बघत काळ जो आहे,
प्रेषित त्याचा नव्या दमाचा शूर शिपाई आहे !

14. Lines from Balvidhva Dusthitikathan (बालविधवा दुःस्थितीकथन) (Note 62)

पाया परवशता ज्या दुष्काळाच्या शिलांहिं जो रचिला
अवनति-कृतांत-केलि प्रासादा प्लेग कळस त्या खचिला (1)
नन्दनवनसम मोहक सृष्टीचा सारभूत हा देश
हो दृष्टि धन्य पाहुनि, धरुनि असा प्लेग हृदयिं उद्देश (2)
आर्यावर्ती आला, मुंबईला ठेविलें मग पदाला
झाला अंत सुखाचा, ये ऊत अनंतवक्त्र- विपदांला (3)
जी ऐकिली त्याहुनि शतपट अधिकाचि सुरुचिता धन्या
पाहुनि भुलला खुलला, वदलाः मोहक न भू अशी अन्या (4)
केला निश्चय ऐसा, कुरुवाळुनि मुंबई भयाण करीं
हो धिग् न निज जिणें तें, यास्तव बघण्या पुणें प्रयाण करी (6)
गोदास्नानास्तव करि श्रीमत्र्यंबकपुरीस गमनाला
आला पंचवटीला तेथुनिया रामराय-नमनाला (7)
बहु काय वदों? केलें एक्या शब्दांत देशपर्यटना
पवनाहुनि जवन, नची दमला हा कीं विचित्र विधिघटना (8)
प्लेग कशाचा आला? कृतकर्माचाचि भोग अवतरला

कर्मायत्त फलाच्या अुपभोगावीण कोण भव तरला? (9)
केलीं भयाण नगरें, नगरासम दाट सर्व वन वसतें
दमले नमले गमले हृतसत्त्वचि मंत्र तंत्र सुनवस तें (10)
जाता नाथ स्त्रीचा ती गाअीहूनि गाय मानावें
सुटका अबलांची त्या करण्या घेसी न का यमा नांवें (31)
बंधू ना, बांधव ना, ना मातापितर ज्या अभागीते
त्या माझीं दुःखाचीं प्रभुजी! पोचति न का नभा गीतें? (32)
मी अल्पवयी बाला, माझा सौभाग्यनिधि अहा जळला
वैधव्याचा दुर्धर भयकर गिरि हा प्रचंड कोसळला (33)
काय करू? जाउ कुठे? हो माझे आप्तसोयरे सारे
तारा अनाथ बाला, छळ बघता स्वस्थ बसुनिया सारे (34)
देतें का कोणी ओ अबलेच्या या मदीय हांकेला?
बोला हो, बोला हो, धीराचा शब्द अेक तरि बोला (35)

15. जो आज प्लेगला लागला तो उद्या नाहीसा झाला, घरात एक माणूस प्लेगने लागला कि देखोदेखी बायका-मुले, माणसे, घरचे घर एखाद्या आगीत भस्म व्हावे त्या प्रमाणे पटापट मृत्युमुखी पडून नष्ट व्हावे. एकेका घरात पाच पाच, सहा सहा प्रेते एकामागून एक पडलेली कोणाचे प्रेत कोण उचलणार! . . . जे दुसऱ्याचे प्रेत आज उचलीत तेच उद्या त्या संसर्गासारशी प्लेगने लागून पर्वा त्यांची प्रेते त्याच मार्गाने तिसऱ्यास न्यावी लागत. (Note 63)
16. तिथे कोण कोणाचे प्रेत उचलणार, मुले आई-बापाचे प्रेत टाकून पळत, आई-बाप मुलाचे प्रेत सोडून पळत कारण घरात प्रेत आहे असे कळताच सरकारी अधिकारांच्या आडदांड सोजिरांशी गाठ पडे. घर शुद्ध करण्यासाठी म्हणून उध्वस्त करणार, सामानाची जाळपोळ, लुटालूट होणार आणि उरलेले कुटुंबाचे कुटुंब वनवासात नेऊन "सिग्रेगेशन" च्या अटकात पडणार. पण तिथे हि प्लेग—घरी प्लेग दारी प्लेग! (Note 64)
17. Svatantrateche Stotra (स्वतंत्रतेचे स्तोत्र) (Note 69)

जयोऽस्तु ते! जयोऽस्तु ते!
श्रीमहन्मंगले! शिवास्पदे शुभदे
स्वतंत्रते भगवति ! त्वामहं यशोयुतां वंदे ll ध्रु. ll
राष्ट्राचें चैतन्य मूर्त तूं नीति संपदांची
स्वतंत्रते भगवती! श्रीमती राज्ञी तूं त्यांची
परवशतेच्या नभांत तूंची आकाशीं होशी
स्वतंत्रते भगवती! चांदणी चमचम-लखलखशी ll

गालावरच्या कुसुमी किंवा कुसुमांच्या गाली
स्वतंत्रते भगवती! तूंच जी विलसतसे लाली
तूं सूर्याचें तेज उदधिचें गांभीर्यहिं तूंची
स्वतंत्रते भगवती! अन्यथा ग्रहण नष्ट तेंची ll

मोक्ष-मुक्ति हीं तुझींच रूपें तुलाच वेदांतीं
स्वतंत्रते भगवती! योगिजन परब्रह्म वदती
जें जें उत्तम उदात्त उन्नत महन्मधुर तें तें
स्वतंत्रते भगवती! सर्व तव सहचारी होतें ll
हे अधम-रक्त-रंजिते l सुजन-पूजिते l श्रीस्वतंत्रते
तुजसाठि मरण तें जनन
तुजवीण जनन तें मरण
तुज सकल-चराचर-शरण
भरतभूमिला दृढालिंगना कधि देशील वरदे
स्वतंत्रते भगवति ! त्वामहं यशोयुतां वंदे ll

18. पुण्यभूमि तूं। पितृभूमि तूं। तूं अमुचा अभिमान (Note 70)
19. Lines from Sagaras (सागरास) (Note 73)

ने मजसी ने परत मातृभूमीला। सागरा, प्राण तळमळला
भूमातेच्या चरणतला तुज धूतां। मी नित्य पाहिला होता
मज वदलासी अन्य देशिं चल जाऊ। सृष्टिची विविधता पाहू
तइं जननी-हृद् विरहशंकितहि झालें। परि तुवां वचन तिज दिधलें
मार्गज्ञ स्वयें मीच पृष्ठिं वाहीन। त्वरित या परत आणीन

विश्वसलों या तव वचनीं । मी
जगदनुभव-योगे बनुनी । मी
तव अधिक शक्त उद्धरणीं । मी
येअीन त्वरें कथुन सोडिलें तिजला । सागरा प्राण तळमळला (1)

नभिं नक्षत्रें बहुत एक परि प्यारा । मज भरतभूमिचा तारा
प्रासाद इथे भव्य परी मज भारी । आइची झोपडी प्यारी
तिजवीण नको राज्य, मज प्रिय साचा । वनवास तिच्या जरि वनिंचा
भुलविणें व्यर्थ हें आता । रे
बहु जिवलग गमते चित्ता । रे
तुज सरित्पते ! जी सरिता । रे
तद्विरहाची शपथ घालितो तुजला । सागरा प्राण तळमळला (3)
या फेन-मिषें हससि निर्दया कैसा । कां वचन भंगिसी ऐसा
त्वत्स्वामित्वा सांप्रत जी मिरवीते । भिउनि कां आंग्लभूमीतें ?
मन्मातेला अबल म्हणुनि फसवीसी । मज विवासनातें देशी
तरि आंग्लभूमि-भयभीता । रे
अबला न माझिही माता । रे
कथिल हें अगस्तिस आता । रे
जो आचमनीं एक पलीं तुज प्याला ।

20. Lines from Majhe Mrutyupatra (माझे मृत्युपत्र) (Note 74)

श्रीरामचंद्र-वनवास-कथा रसाला
की केवि देश इटली रिपुमुक्त झाला
तानाजिचा समरधीर तसा पवाडा
गावा चित्तोरगड वा शनवारवाडा ॥ ५॥

की घेतलें व्रत न हें अम्हि अंधतेने
लब्धप्रकाश इतिहास-निसर्ग-मानें
जें दिव्य, दाहक म्हणूनि असावयाचें
बुद्ध्याचि वाण धरिलें करिं हें सतीचें

21. Pahila Hapta (पहिला हप्ता) (Note 76)

मानुनि घे साची । जननि गे मानुनि घे साची
अल्प स्वल्प तरि सेवा अपुल्या अर्भक बालांची ॥
ऋण हें बहू झालें । तुझ्या स्तनींचें स्तन्य पाजुनी धन्य अम्हां केलें
ऋण तें फेडाया । हप्ता पहिला तप्त स्थंडिलिं देह अर्पितों हा
सर्वेचि जन्मुनियां । त्वनमोचनहवनात हवी करू पुनः पुन्हा काया

सारथी जिचा अभिमानी । कृष्णजी आणी । राम सेनानी

अशि तीस कोटि तव सेना
ती अम्हांविना थांबेना परि करुनि दुष्टदलदलना
रोंविलची स्वकरीं । स्वातंत्र्याचा हिमालयावरि झेंडा जरतारी

22. Lines from Govindagraj, Panpatacha Phataka (पानपतचा फटका) (Note 117)

कौरव-पांडव-संगर-तांडव द्वापर-कालीं होय अती
तसे मराठे गिलचे साचे कलींत लढले पानपती ॥धृ०॥

काय कथाची युद्ध-कधा ? मग वृथा भाउचा श्रम झाला;
धीर सोडुनि पळति मराठे, पुर्ण पराभव त्यां आला.
हा हिंदू, हा यवन, पारशी हा, यहुदी हा भेद असा.
नको नको हो ! एकी राहो ! सांगुं आपणां किती कसा ?

कथी रडकथा निजदेशाची वाचुनि ऐसा हा फटका
लटका जाउनि कलह परस्पर लागो एकीचा चटका!

23. Śāhira Tulsidasanca Povāḍā (शाहीर तुलशीदासांचा पोवाडा) (Pages 271–80)

राजगड राजाचा! प्रतापगड जीजाबाईचा!
सिंहगड पन्हाळा! पहा तो मोंगलांचा!!
सर्जा शिवाजी शिवभजन!
काबीज केले तळकोंकण!!
गड माहुली घेतिली!
कल्याण भिवंडी काबिज केली
खबर त्या विजापुराला गेली
ठाणे राजाचे बसलें
शिवाजी महाराज
राजगड किल्यावर बसले
जिजाबाई माता
आहे प्रतापगडावरी
सोमवारच्या दिवशी
हाती हस्तनाची फणी
उगवते बाजूला नजर केली
नजर सिंहगडावर गेली
बारा मावळ पुण्याखाली

बारा मावळ जुनराखाली
पुण्याच्या तोंडाला जेजुरीच्या बारीला
किल्ला सिंहगड पाहिला
नवे कोंबडीचे अंडे
ऐसा किल्ला झळकला
ऐसा पंतोजी तो काका
त्याने हुजऱ्या बोलाविला
जावे राजगड किल्याला
सांगा शिवाजी महाराजाला
जेवावे राजगड किल्ल्याला
अंचवावे प्रतापगडाला
शिवाजी महाराज पांच पोशाख नटला
पाई तुमानी सुरवारी चढविल्या
अंगी किनखाप घातिले
शिरी जिरीटोप घातला
हाती वाघनखे घालून
कृष्णा घोडीला जिन केला
ढाल पाठीवरी टाकिता झाला

सोनसळी पट्टा हातात घेतला
कृष्णा घोडीला चाबूक केला
आला मढ्याच्या घाटाला
घाट मढ्याचा उतरला
आला बिरवाडी गावाला
गाव बिरवाडी सोडीला
आला पोलातपुराला
पोलातपूर सोडिले
घाट पाराचा वेंघला
आले प्रतापगड किल्याला
सलाम जिजाबाईला केला
    ऐक जिजाबाई
        सत्तावीस किल्यांचा मी राजा
माग माग जिजाबाई

राजा थरथरा कांपला
हा किल्ला उदेभान मोंगलाचा
बाई उदेभान मोंगलाचा
जे उमराव गेले सिंहगडाला
त्यांच्या पाठी ग पाहिल्या
नाही पुढे पाहिले
किल्ला आहे वाघाचा जबडा
लखोटा सुभेदाराने हातात घेतला
ज्याने एका लखोट्याचे बारा लखोटे केले
धाडले कागद खोऱ्याला
मोठ्या मोठ्या सरदाराला
पंधरा गावाचे पारुंचे
त्याने आपणाजवळ बोलाविले
उमठ्यांचे शिरके
त्याने आपणाजवळ बोलाविले
दस पटेचे मोकाशी
त्याने आपणाजवळ बोलाविले
नांदविचे सावंत
त्याने आपणाजवळ बोलाविले
वडघरचे नाईक
त्याने आपणाजवळ बोलाविले
सिलमाचे ठाकूर
त्याने आपणाजवळ बोलाविले

बारा हजार फौजेला ज्याचा लखोटा पोचला
बारा हजार फौज घेउन आला दरवाज्याचे तोंडी
ज्याने सैंपाक पाहिला
बारा हजार पाट मांडला
बारा हजार पंचपात्री
बारा हजार मांडला ठाव
सैंपाक वाढून त्वरीत झाली
ऐंशी वर्षाची उमर
ज्याचा माप्ट्याचा आहार
त्याचा अधोलीचा झाला
ज्याच्या मोहरे पांच पोळ्या
त्याच्या पंधरा पोळ्या झाल्या
खाववतील त्याने खाव्या
उरतील त्यांनी
गडाखाली टाकाव्या
बारा हजार फौज तृप्त झाली
आम्ही जातो सिंहगडाला
आमचा रायाबा सांभाळा
जर आलो सिंहगडाहून
लगीन करीन रायाबाचे
जर गेलो तिकडे मेलो
लगीन करा रायाबाचे
मज बापाची सरदारी
द्यावी रायाबा बेट्याला
दिवटी बुदलीची जहागीर
द्यावी रायाबा बेट्याला
डोंजगाव द्यावा पानसुपारीला
मालसर याचा दंड
द्यावा इनाम खायाला

तीन कोसाचा आहे बा घेरा
दीड कोसची आहे बा रुंदी
आहे अठराशे पठाण सिंहगडाला
आहे उदयभान मोंगल
दीड गाई दीड शेळी सवा मन तांदूळ वेळेला
अठराजणी बिब्या
आहेत त्याच्या पलंगाला
घेतो तेल्याची पहार

मनगटावर घालता
सरी करून घालतो
बीबीच्या गळ्यात
चांद वडी रुपया
दोहोन बोटांनी तोडीतो
शिवाजी राजाने
मुलगा पोटासंगे धरिला
बारा दिवसाचे सुतक धरिले
शिवाजीमहाराजानी सुभेदाराचे

(तेराव्या दिवशी रायबाचे मांडावा घातला. पहिली नवरी रद्द केली व दुसरी नवरी नेमस्त केलि. लग्न थाटात झाले)
बापाची सरदारी
दिली रायाबा बेट्याला
दिवळ्या बुदलीची जहागीर
दिली रायाबा बेट्याला
डोंझ ते गाव
दिले पान सुपारीला
मालुसर्याचा दंड
दिला इनाम खायला

. . . स्वयंवर बाळाचे मांडले
काढल्या पंचमीच्या हळदी
काढले षष्ठीचे लग्न

24. Śāhira Savarkarancha Povāḍā: Sinhagaḍācha Povāḍā (सिंहगडाचा पोवाडा) (Pages 285–92)

-१-

धन्य शिवाजी तो रणगाजी धन्यचि तानाजी l
प्रेमें आजी सिंहगडाचा पोवाडा गाजी ll ध्रु.
देशामाजी कहर गुजरला पारतंत्र्य-जहरें l
हलाहलहि ह्या परदास्याहुनि गळा गाठिता बरें ll १
गोमातांची मान आणि ती शिखा ब्राह्मणांची l
परदास्याची सुरी बंधुनो चिरी एकदाची ll २
देश हिंदुचा हाय तयाचा मालक म्लेंछ ठरे l
परि परमेशा फार दिवस हें रुचेल केविं बरें ll ३
चालः- मग आर्य देशतारणा । अधममारणा । कराया रणा l
परदास्यरात्रि नाशाला ।
शिवनेरीं श्रीमान् आला ।

स्वातंत्र्यसूर्य उदयाला ।
त्या सूर्याचा किरण रणांगणिं तळपे तानाजी l
प्रेमें आजी सिंहगडाचा पोवाडा गाजी ll ४ ll

-२-

ठायी ठायी वीर मावळा सरसावुनि भाला ।
रामदासमत छत्रपतींचा अनुयायी झाला ll १ ll
स्वातंत्र्य-श्रीतोरण तोरणगड अवघड पडला ।
भगवा झेंडा त्या भाल्यासह सरसर वरि चढला ll २ ll
प्रतापगडिची शांत कराया स्वतंत्रता देवी ।
पुढती फाडुनि अफझुल्याला भग तो मग ठेवी ll ३ ll
चाल:- ते धन्य मराठे गडी l घेति रणिं उडी l करुनि तातडी l
देशार्थ मृत्युही वरिला ।
शाहिस्ता चरचर चिरिला ।
गनिमांनि वचक बहु धरिला l
झुरती रिपु परि अजुनि नांदतो सिंहगडामाजी ।
प्रेमें आजी सिंहगडाचा पोवाडा गाजी ll ४ ll

-३-

जरा ढिलाई पाहुनि वदली जिजा शिवाजीला l
गड सर केल्याविण वरणें ना अन्न शपथ तुजला ll १ ll
परके बाला भूमातेला ते लाथा देतां ।
अन्न न गमतें गोमांसाचा घासचि तो घेतां ll २
गुलामगिरिची बेडी पायी तशीच धरिता ना ? ।
गुलामगिरिच्या नरकामाजी तसेच पचता ना? ll ३
चाल : निर्जीव अन्न कां रुचे। उदर शत्रूचे । फोड तेथिचें ।
आतड्यानि भूक शमवावी ।
रक्तानि भूक शमवावी ।
मांसानि भूक शमवावी ।
घ्या गड कडकड चावुनि अधरा धावा ये काजीं ।
प्रेमें आजी सिंहगडाचा पोवाडा गाजी ll ४

-४-

धन्य माता जिजा तिलाची शिवबा सुत साजे ।
स्वतंत्र झाल्यावीण सुताला अन्नहि दे ना जे ।
स्वातंत्र्याच्या सुखनीमाजी जन्म स्वतंत्रांचे ।
गुलामगिरिच्या उकिरड्यावरि गुलाम निपजाचे ।l २
श्वानहि भरितें पोट बापुडें चघळुनिया तुकडे ।
शेणामाजी बांधुनि वाडे नांदति शेणकिडे ll ३
चाल:- संसार असा जरि करी। मनुजता तरी । कशासी धरी ।
हो तुच्छ किडाचि न कां तो ।

जो गुलाम असुनी हसतो ।
परदास्यी स्वस्थचि बसतो ।
धिक् धिक् वदला श्री शिव घेउनि गड राखू बाजी ।
प्रेमें आजी सिंहगडाचा पोवाडा गाजी ll ४

-५-

प्रभात झाली वाद्यें झडलीं मुहूर्त लग्नाचा l
बोहल्यावरी उभा राहिला सुत तानाजीचा ll १
घटिका-पात्नें मोजुनि द्विजगण शेवटल्या घटिला l
दंगल मोडुनि मंगल व्हाया सावधान वदला ।l २
वदला द्विज परि कुणि भेटाया तानाजिस आला l
आला तों तो तालवारींनीं मंडप खणखणला ll ३
चाल:- तो हर हर एकचि झाला l चमकला भाला l वदति रे चला l
शिवराज दूत पातले l
हें लग्न राहूं द्या भलें l
देशार्थ जनन आपुलें l
धर्मार्थ जनन आपुलें l
लहान मोठा निघे मऱ्हाठा पुढती तानाजी l
प्रेमें आजी सिंहगडाचा पोवाडा गाजी ll ४

- ७ -

शिवरायाच्या तीरा जा बा तानाजी वीरा l
वीरांमाजी हो रणगाजी अरि मारुनी धीरा ll १
सिंहगडावरि तुझी आर्यभू फोडी हंबरडे l
गुलामगिरीचे खून पाडण्या जा जा जा तिकडे ।l २

-८-

अरे मारिती पूर्वज तुमचे स्वर्गातुनि हाका l
अहो मराठे कान देउनी नीट सर्व ऐका ll ३

Chapter 5

1. प्राचीन इतिहास सापडत नाही, म्हणून आपणास केव्हा केव्हा फार तळमळ लागते. इतिहास कसा वाचावा याचा विवेक जोवर कळला नाही तोवर, एका अर्थी आपणास त्यातील काही भागांचे साफ विस्मरण पडले आहे हेही बरेच नाही का? कारण, आज रावणाची लंका कोणती हे जर ऐतिहासिक निश्चिततेने सांगता आले, तर त्या देशातील आम्हा आर्यांविषयी थोडाफार तरी द्वेष उत्पन्न होऊन नव्या भांडणास जुन्या भांडणाच्या सहाणेवर घासून धार लावली जाणारच नाही, असे कोण सांगू शकेल? ही अगदी कल्पनाच नाही. त्याच रामायण कथेच्या स्मृतीमुळे आम्ही आर्य अजूनपर्यंत माकडांचे लाड करतो. (Note 14)

2. Paul Kruger yancha Mrutyu (पॉल क्रूगर यांचा मृत्यु) (Note 49)

हां देवी हां! अधिक रडसी आर्त कंठे अशी कां?
सांगे झालें अशुभ असलें काय ते सोड शोका
हा धिक् मृत्यो, सकल कळलें घेऊनि नीच गेला
स्वातंत्र्याच्या विमलतिलक त्या अहा क्रूगराला

संरक्षाया समरिं गळलें उष्णसें रक्त त्यातें
बोले तैसी करणी करुनी थक्क केलें जगातें
हा हा झालें परवश तुझें राष्ट्र ग क्रुगरा तें
अंत:कालीं स्मरण करिता वाटलें काय तूतें

3. Lines from Prabhakar (Note 142)

सरदार पदरचे कसे कुणि सिंह जसे कुणि शार्दूल गेंडे
अरे ज्यांनीं घटकेंत पाव घटकेंत रोविले झेंडे

Chapter 6

1. पौराणिक परंपरेने बोलायचे तर, रक्तबीज राक्षसाप्रमाणे कालाच्या शरीरातून जो जो क्षणाचा रक्तबिंदु गळतो, त्यातून आठवणीचा एक नवानवा राक्षस उत्पन्न होते. पौराणिक परिभाषेत बोलायचे तर, स्मृतीच्या याच अत्याचारापासून ह्यां लोकांचे परित्राण करण्यासाठी तो क्षणाचा रक्तबिंदु पडतापडताच गिळून नाहीसा करणाऱ्या देवी विस्मृतीचा अवतार झाला म्हणून बरें! खरोखर स्मृतीप्रमाणे विस्मृति हीही देवाची देणगीच आहे. (Note 64)
2. इतकेच नव्हे, तर पुढेपुढे त्या राष्ट्रीय जीवनाचा, ते माझे व्यक्तिजीवन,एक प्रमुख आणि परिणामकारक घटक होत आले आहे. माझ्या गुरुस्थानी असलेल्या वयस्क पिढीतील अनेक राष्ट्रीय पुढाऱ्यांचा माझ्याशी संबंध आलेला असल्याने, माझ्या समकालीन पिढीतील लक्षावधि तरुणांच्या आयुष्याची दिशा पालटून जावी, इतका त्यांच्यावर माझ्या मतांचा, प्रयत्नांचा आणि सहवासाचा अप्रत्यक्ष व प्रत्यक्षपणे परिणाम झालेला असल्याने आणि माझ्या आयुष्यातील अनेक मोठमोठ्या राष्ट्रीय उलाढालीत प्रमुख भाग घेण्याचा प्रसंग मजवर वारंवार येत गेल्याने, माझ्या चरित्राचा बनाव आणि घडाव कसकसा होत गेला याचा माझ्या तोंडचा वृत्तांत हा त्या काळाच्या राष्ट्रीय इतिहासाच्या रचनेस उपयुक्त झाल्यावाचून राहणार नाही. माझ्या आठवणी केवळ माझ्या एकट्यानेच चरित्र सांगणार नसून उभ्या दोन तीन पिढ्यांचे जीवन त्यात प्रतिबिंबित होणारे आहे. (Note 66)
3. “माझ्या आठवणी” लिहिताना प्रथमच हे सांगणे अवश्य आहे की, मला माझा जन्म झाल्याची मुळीच आठवण नाही.” (Note 69)
4. Hoti Ek Nadi (होती एक नदी) (Note 70)

होती एक नदी नामें दारका तापहारका
प्रतिपच्चंद्रलेखेव तन्वंगी धवलोदका

असे जाणुनि जीं गावें तान्हेलीं बहु त्यांजला
नदी चिमुकलीशी ही जाई पाजीत सज्जला

हिरविचार चौभोती शेती दूरवरी फुले
सिंधूत बेत कि तैसें गांव तीत मधे खुलें

शेतीचे गीत "ये बैला" असे उंच दृढस्वरी
पहाटेस उठे फुल्ला गंधांच्यासह अंबरी

मोटांतुनि पडे धोधो पाणी पाणथळामधी
स्निग्ध गंभीर नादाने मोर नाचति त्या तधीं

5. श्रीमंतीचा गर्व असा तिला शिवला नाही. ती वारल्यानंतर जेव्हा आमच्या कुटुंबाच्या संपन्नतेला ओहोटी लागली, तेव्हा माझे वडील नेहमी म्हणत "आमच्या घरी ती आली ती लक्ष्मी घेऊन आली, ती जाताच लक्ष्मी निघून गेली. तीच माझ्या घरची लक्ष्मी होती" माझे वडील माझ्या आईवर फार लोलुप असत. (Note 71)
6. माझ्या वडिलांचा परिपाठ असे की रात्री जेवणे झाल्यावर आमच्या वडील बंधूकडून रामविजय, हरिविजय, पांडवप्रताप, शिवलीलामृत, जैमिनी अश्वमेध असे ओवीबद्ध ग्रंथ वाचवाचे; आणि आईशी त्यांच्याविषयी चर्चा करावी. (Note 72)
7. आम्ही चार लहान मुले, घरी श्रीमंती, तिच्यावर निरतिशय प्रेम करणारा पति, संसाराच्या सुखाचा भर, तो दुर्दैवास पाहवला नाही, तिला महामारी झाली. तो दिवस मला स्पष्ट आठवतो. . . . भर पंक्तीत तिला ऐकदम भोवळ येऊन ती परतली; आणि त्या जुन्या घराच्या देवघरापाशी निजली, ती पुन्हा काही उठली नाही. जेवण तसेच राहिले . . . दुपारी दोन वाजता प्रेत दहन होऊन इतर सर्व मंडळी स्मशानातून परतली; आई काही परत आली नाही. (Note 73)
8. मी ज्या दिवशी नाशिकला शिकावयास जाणार त्या दिवशी माझ्या लहान सवंगड्यास आणि शेजाऱ्यापाजाऱ्या प्रेमळ गावकऱ्यांस मी दूर जाणार म्हणून फार वाईट वाटले. मजवर त्या बालवयातही लहानमोठे अनेक स्त्री-पुरुष निस्सीम प्रेम आणि भक्ती करीत. (Note 76)
9. मला वाटते माझ्या वक्तृत्वाचा अमोघ परिणाम जो अनेकांवर होत आला तो बहुधा त्या त्या प्रसंगाच्या वयाच्या आणि विषयाच्या मानाने व मजजवळ ह्या तदुपकारक ज्ञानाचा भरपूर साठा असे त्यामुळेच होय . . . याचे कारण लहानपणापासूनचे माझे विविध आणि अश्रांत वाचन, मनन, आणि निरीक्षण. (Note 78)
10. मी असे दाखवी की, स्वदेशास्तव, लोकहितास्तव प्राणत्याग करण्याची प्रामाणिक प्रतिज्ञा करणारा आणि ती पुरी करण्याची धमक असणारा क्रांतिकारक बहुधा समाजातील ऊच्च मनोवृत्तीचा कर्मवीरच असणार. अशा ऊच्च बीजांचीच संतति वृद्धिंगत होणे समाजोन्नतीस परम आवश्यक. (Note 80)
11. देशभक्तांचे संतान ऊत्पन्न करणारे वंश लुप्त होतात आणि जो जितका अधिक कृतघ्न, स्वार्थी, लोकहितपराङ्मुख, भ्याड, देशद्रोही, पिशून असेल तोच जगतो, नांदतो नि त्याची संतति मात्र तितक्याच अधिक पटीने समाजात वाढली जाते. (Note 82)

12. त्याच्या पत्नीपुत्रांनी आपला नाथ असा महान हुतात्मा झाला, या विचारासरशी आपल्या त्या अनाथपणासच वास्तविक स्पृहणीय असे सनाथत्व मानले पाहिजे. पण तेही होत नसेल तर अशा अनाथ स्त्रियांनी सुखेनैव तशाच कोणा थोर पुरुषाशी पुनर्विवाह करून आपला संसार पुन्हा थाटावा, अशी अनुज्ञा मन:पुर्वक देण्यापुरता तो क्रांतिवीर बहुधा उदार असेलच. निदान असला तरी पाहिजे. पुरुषाने पत्नी वारताच जर नि ज्या कारणासाठी पुनर्विवाह करणे पाप नाही तर पती वारताच स्त्रियांनीही हवे तर पुनर्विवाह करणे त्या त्या कारणासाठीच पाप नव्हे. (Note 83)
13. कारण मामांनी ज्यांची कन्या मला वधू म्हणून निश्चित केली होती त्या श्रीयुत भाऊराव चिपळूणकरांचा आणि मामांचा आबाल्य अत्यंत स्नेह असल्यामुळे श्रीयुत भाऊराव चिपळूणकरांसारख्या प्रभावशाली पुरुषाचा शब्द मामांस मोडवेना. अशा घराण्याशी आपला स्नेहसंबंधच नव्हे तर इतका निकटचा संबंधही जुळण्याचा हा योग अगदी अलभ्ये-यापाई इतर कोणाचीही अडचण वा 'मुलींविषयींची' आवडनिवड दूर सारावी लागली तरी चिंता नाही असे मामांस वाटे. (Note 84)
14. ते देहाने उंच, दुहेरी बांध्याचे, गोरेपान आणि फार देखणे पुरुष असत. त्यांची मुद्रा, त्यांची ती डौलदार राहणी, ते चाणाक्ष नयन, चालण्याची ती प्रभावशाली ढब. त्यांना पाहाताच पेशवाईतील कोणी अस्सल चित्पावन सरदारच आपण पाहात आहोत की काय, असे वाटून मनुष्य क्षणभर त्यांच्याकडे पाहातच राही. (Note 85)
15. लग्नाचा प्रश्न निघण्यापूर्वीच त्या मुलीला भाऊराव चिपळूणकरांनी ऐकदा आमच्या घरीच आठ दिवस राहण्यास धाडली होती. तिचाही फार मानस की इथेच आपल्यास द्यावी. (Note 86)
16. "अरे, माझी व्याख्याने कुणीतरी लिहून ठेवा." (Note 133)
17. Lines from Gangadhar Jadhav's poem. (Note 140)

> हिंदुस्थानचे भाग्य घडवा हो
> सोडा जातीपातीचा भेद
> प्रांत भेद पंथ भेद
> पार्टीबाजीचे मतभेद
> एका जातीचे व्हा अभेद
> वीर विनायकाचे गुण
> मानी हृदयी मी ठासवून
> गातो सभेत मी गर्वानं
> देशभक्ती मूर्तिमान
> धर्माची मूर्ती जाण
> तेज दिव्य देशभक्तीचे, रणशंभूचे,
> अंगी तुम्ही बाणवा
> हिंदुस्थानाचं भाग्य घडवा हो

Conclusion

1. हृदयाला चटका लावणारे काही प्रसंग निवडून मी त्यावर ही काव्यरचना केली आहे. (Note 4)
2. Savarkar Gatha by Aphle (सावरकर गाथा) (Page 413)

सांगतो कथा मनाची (जीवाची) व्यथा विनायक सावरकर गाथा
भाग्यवान तो भगूर गाव हो नाशिक शेजारी
तिथे जन्मले प्रभू सावरकर हिंदू कैवारी

नाशिक पंचवटीचा परिसर राम जानकीचा
पराक्रमाच्या परंपरेचा हिंदू अस्मितेचा

जन्मताच जो जगात सांगे पहिल्या हुंकारी
असे जन्मले प्रभू सावरकर हिंदू कैवारी

BIBLIOGRAPHY

Archival Sources

National Archives of India (NAI)
India Office Records (IOR)
Maharashtra State Archives

Libraries Visited

Svatantryaveer Savarkar Rashtriya Smarak Library, Mumbai
Pune Marathi Granthalay
Pune Nagar Vachan Mandir
Shri Va Phatak Granthasangrahalay, Lokmanya Seva Sangha, Mumbai
Mumbai Marathi Granthasangrahalay

Newspaper and Magazine Articles

"Alleged Assault on Hindu Girl: Three Muslims in Trouble," *Times of India*, July 25, 1927.
"Assault of a Girl: Seven Years Imprisonment for Two Muslims," *Times of India*, October 8, 1926.
"Bombay Criminal Sessions: Attempted Rape," *Times of India*, September 23, 1926.
"Death Mystery of a Hindu Woman," *Times of India*, October 8, 1926.
"Hindu Case at Hague: Question between France and England over Extradition of Student," *New York Times*, February 25, 1911, 3.
"It's Good that the Overconfidence in the Party Has Gone," *Outlook*, February 5, 2022.
"Khandwa Notes: Alleged Kidnapping of a Minor Girl," *Times of India*, August 8, 1927.
"'Muslims Are Foreigners': Inside India's Campaign to Decide Who Is a Citizen," *New York Times*, April 4, 2020.
"The Khilafat, Another Bombay Meeting," *Times of India*, April 10, 1920.
"'Vikram Sampath Is Claiming My Ideas, Words as His Own': Historian Janaki Bakhle on Savarkar Author," *The Wire*, February 22, 2022.

Private Papers

Senapati Bapat Private Papers, Nehru Memorial Museum and Library Mss Collections

Unpublished Dissertations

Bell, Lucinda Downes. "The 1858 Trial of the Mughal Emperor Bahadur Shah II Zafar for Crimes against the State." PhD diss., University of Melbourne, Faculty of Law, 2004.

Botre, Shrikant. "The Body Language of Caste: Marathi Sexual Modernity (1920–1950)." PhD diss., University of Warwick, 2017.

Ghosh, Sourav. "Rani Durgavati: The Contested Afterlives of a Medieval Queen." PhD diss., Jadavpur University, 2014.

Khan, Noor-Aiman Iftikhar. "The Enemy of My Enemy: Indian Influences on Egyptian Nationalism, 1907–1930." PhD diss., University of Chicago, 2006.

Oak, Alok. "Political Ideas of B. G. Tilak: Colonialism, Self and Hindu Nationalism." PhD diss., University of Leiden, 2022.

Pincince, John. "On the Verge of *Hindutva*: V.D. Savarkar, revolutionary, convict, ideologue, c. 1905–1924." PhD diss., University of Hawaii at Manoa, 2007.

Mishra, Shaivya. "The Bomb, the Bullet and the Gandhi Cap: Violent Nationalism and Political Surveillance in Colonial India, 1906–1945." PhD diss., University of California, Berkeley, forthcoming.

Sarwate, Rahul. "Reimagining the Modern Hindu Self: Caste, Untouchability and Hindu Theology in Colonial South Asia, 1899–1948." PhD diss., Columbia University, 2020.

Reports

Fraser, Sir Andrew H. L., et. al. "Report of the Indian Police Commission 1902–1903." Simla: Government Central Press, 1903.

Rowlatt Sedition Committee Report (published edition). Calcutta: 1918. https://archive.org/details/in.ernet.dli.2015.47485/page/n11/mode/2up

Tilak Trial: Being the Only Authorised Verbatim Account of the Whole Proceedings with Introduction and Character Sketch of Bal Gangadhar Tilak Together with Press Opinion, London: 1908.

Indian Reforms: The Government of India Bill, 1919. With Full Text of the Bill, the Memorandum, Mr. Montagu's Speech and Sir Sankaran Nair's Minute. Chennai, Tamil Nādu, India; Madras, G.A. Natesan, 1919.

Genealogy of the Imperial Ottoman Family. Jamil ADRA, Hanedan-Maison D'Osman, Paris, Istanbul, Beirut: 2004.

Presentations

Bronkhorst, Johannes. 5th C. R. Parekh Memorial Lecture, Institute of Indian Thought, Centre for the Study of Developing Societies, Delhi, August 7, 2019.

Wrigley, Claire. "Subaltern Studies and Beyond." At UC Berkeley, Department of History, November 2017. [Paper on Savarkar—presented at my graduate seminar.]

Books and Papers

Abbott, Justin E., and N. R. Godbole, *Stories of Indian Saints: Translation of Mahipati's Marathi Bhaktavijaya*. Delhi: Motilal Banarsidass, 2014. Seventh reprint. First published 1934.

Acworth, Harry Arbuthnot. *Ballads of Marathas*. London: Longmans, Green, and Co., 1894.

Acworth, Harry Arbuthnot, and S. T. Shaligram. *Itihasaprasiddha Purushamce va Striyamce Povade* [Povadas of historically famous men and women]. Bombay: Nirnayasagar, 1891. Second edition, Pune: Aryabhushan Press, 1911.

Ahmad, Aziz. "The Role of Ulema in Indo-Muslim History." *Studia Islamica* 31 (1970): 1–13.

Ahmed, Faiz. *Afghanistan Rising: Islamic Law and Statecraft between the Ottoman and British Empires*. Cambridge: Harvard University Press, 2017.

Ahmed, Faiz. "In the Name of a Law: Islamic Legal Modernism and the Making of Afghanistan's 1923 Constitution." *International Journal of Middle East Studies* 48, no. 4 (2017): 655–77.

Akbar, Mubashar J. *Nehru: The Making of India*. London: Viking, 1988.

Aklujkar, Vidyut. "Battle as Banquet: A Metaphor in Suradasa." *Journal of the American Oriental Society* 111, no. 2, (April–June 1991): 353–61.

———. "Sharing the Divine Feast: Evolution of Food Metaphor in Marathi Sant Poetry." In *The Eternal Food: Gastronomic Ideas and Experiences of Hindus and Buddhists*, edited by R. S. Khare, 95–116. Albany: SUNY Press, 1992.

Ali, Shamshad. "The Ottoman Caliphate and British Imperialism in India." *Proceedings of the Indian History Congress* 54 (1993), 739–47.

Ambedkar, B. R. *Beef, Brahmins and Broken Men: An Annotated Critical Selection from "The Untouchables."* Edited and annotated by Alex George and S. Anand. New York: Columbia University Press, 2020.

———. "Caste in India: Their Mechanism, Genesis and Development." In *Dr. Babasaheb Ambedkar: Writings and Speeches*, compiled by Vasant Moon, vol. 1, 6–8. Bombay: The Education Department, Government of Maharashtra, 1987.

———. (1919). "Evidence before the Southborough Committee on franchise" In *Dr. Babasaheb Ambedkar: Writings and Speeches*, compiled by Vasant Moon, vol. 1, 247. Bombay: The Education Department, Government of Maharashtra, 1987.

———. *Gandhi and Gandhism*. Jullundur: Bheem Patrika Publications, 1970.

Andurkar, V. G. *Shatruchya Gotat Savarkar* [Savarkar in the enemy camp]. Solapur: Suras Granthamala, 1970.

Ansari, K. H. "Pan-Islam and the Making of the Early Indian Muslim Socialists." *Modern Asian Studies* 20, no. 3 (1986): 509–37. http://www.jstor.org/stable/312535.

Aphle, Govindswami. *Sāvarakara Gāthā* [Story of Savarkar]. Pune: A Vi Gruh Prakashan, 1967.

Apte, Mahadev L. "Lokahitavadi and V. K. Chiplunkar: Spokesmen of Change in Nineteenth-Century Maharashtra." *Modern Asian Studies* 7, no. 2 (1973): 193–208.

Arnold, David. *Gandhi: Profiles in Power*. Harlow, UK: Longman, 2001.

Ashe, Geoffrey. *Gandhi*. New York: Stein and Day, 1968.

Astourian, Stephan. "The Armenian Genocide: An Interpretation." *The History Teacher* 23, no. 2 (1990): 111–60. https://doi.org/10.2307/494919.

Athavale, S. C. *Barrister Vinayak Damodar Savarkar: Shalaka Parichay* [Barrister Vinayak Damodar Savarkar: a quick introduction]. Thane: R. M. Athavale Prakashan, 1937.

Athavale, Shriram. *Kavyamay Savarkar Darshan* [Poetic meeting with Savarkar]. Pune: Gaurav Prakashan, 1968.

Auerbach, Erich. *Mimesis: The Representation of Reality in Western Literature.* Translated by Willard Trask. Princeton, NJ: Princeton University Press, 2003.

Bahuguna, Rameshwar Prasad. "The Ideological Political Role of Brahmans in Later Medieval India." *Proceedings of the Indian History Congress* 72 (2011): 353–59.

Bakhle, Janaki. "Country First? Vinayak Damodar Savarkar (1883–1966) and the Writing of *Essentials of Hindutva.*" *Public Culture* 22, no. 1 (2010): 149–86.

———. "Savarkar (1883–1966), Sedition and Surveillance: The Rule of Law in a Colonial Situation." *Social History* 35, no. 1 (2010): 51–75.

Bapat, Govind Pandurang. *Atmakatha* [Autobiography]. Pune: Kaal Prakashan, 1972.

Bapat, N. S. *Smrutipushpe: Svatantryaveer Vinayakarav Savarkaranchya Sahavasachya Athvani* [Flowers of memories: remembrances of time spent with freedom fighter Vinayakrao Savarkar]. Pune: Charuchandra Prakashan, 1979.

Barfield, Thomas. *Afghanistan: A Cultural and Political History.* Princeton, NJ: Princeton University Press, 2010.

Barwe, S. N. *Swatantryaveer: Barrister Savarkar yanchya charitrateel kahi padyamaya prasanga* [Freedom fighter: some memorable events in the life of Barrister Savarkar]. Pune: Vishnu C. Chitale, 1947.

Berlant, Lauren. *The Anatomy of National Fantasy: Hawthorne, Utopia, and Everyday Life.* Chicago: University of Chicago Press, 1991.

Beverley, Eric Lewis. *Hyderabad, British India, and the World: Muslim Networks and Minor Sovereignty, c. 1850–1950*, Cambridge: Cambridge University Press, 2015.

Bhadru, G. "Contribution of Satyashodhak Samaj to the Low Caste Protest Movement in 19th Century." *Proceedings of the Indian History Congress* 63 (2002): 845–54.

Bhagat, R. B. "Fact and Fiction." *Economic and Political Weekly* 39, no. 39 (September 25), 2004.

Bhagwat, Vidyut. "Marathi Literature as a Source for Contemporary Feminism." *Economic and Political Weekly* 30, no. 17 (1995): WS 24–29.

———. "Shri Shripad Mahadeva Mate: 1886–1957." In *Maharashtrateel Jaatisansthavishayak Vicar* [Thoughts on the caste system in Maharashtra], edited by Yashwant Sumant and Dattatreya Punde, 219–30. Pune: Pratima Prakashan, 1988.

Bhalerao, Sudhakar. *Swatantryaveer Savarkar Vicarmanthan* [Savarkar's thought]. Nagpur: Swatantryaveer Savarkar Putala Nagarik Samiti, 1984.

Bhat, V. M. *Abhinava Bharat athava Krantikarakanchi Krantikarak Gupta Sanstha* [Abhinav Bharat or the revolutionary secret society of revolutionaries]. Mumbai: Ga Pa Parchure Prakashan, 1950.

Bhat, R. S. *Mi Pahilele Savarkar: Jyani Savarkarana pahile aahe asa namvant Savarkar-bhaktancya Athavani* [The Savarkar that I saw: recollections of Savarkar-devotees who had seen Savarkar]. Pune: R. S. Bhat, Veer Gaurav Samiti, 1990.

Bhate, S. *Subhāṣitaśatakam: A Collection of Subhāṣitas with Translation in Marathi and English.* Vol. 1–3. Pune: Publications of the Centre of Advanced Study in Sanskrit, The Poona University Press, 1991.

Bhavare, N. G. "Review of *Social Life in Maharashtra under the Peshwas.*" *India Quarterly* 39, no. 3 (1983): 359–62.

Bhole, Bhaskar Laksmana. *Ekonisavya Shatakatil Marathi Gadya, Khanda 2* [Nineteenth-century Marathi prose, volume 2]. New Delhi: Sahitya Akademi, 2006.

———. "Prastavana" [Preface]. In *Visavya Shatakatil Marathi Gadya, Khanda 1* [Twentieth-century Marathi prose, volume 1]. New Delhi: Sahitya Akademi, 2010.

Bhope, R. G. *Swatantryaveer Barrister Vinayakrao Savarkar Yanche Jeevan-Charitra* [Freedom fighter Barrister Vinayakrao Savarkar, a biography]. Ahmednagar/Pune: printed by the author, 1938.

Bickers, Robert. *Britain in China: Community, Culture and Colonialism, 1900–1949*. Manchester: Manchester University Press, 2017.

Blecher, Joel. *Said the Prophet of God: Hadith Commentary across a Millennium*. Berkeley: University of California Press, 2018.

Blinkhorn, Martin. *Fascism and the Right in Europe 1919–1945*. Harlow, UK: Pearson Education, 2000.

Bodas, Captain Anand Jayram. *Savarkaranchi Teesri Janmathep* [Savarkar's third life sentence]. Bombay: Manorama Prakashan, 2007.

Boehmer, Elleke. "The Hero's Story: The Male Leader's Autobiography and the Syntax of Postcolonial Nationalism." In *Stories of Women: Gender and Narrative in the Postcolonial Nation*, 66–87. Manchester: Manchester University Press, 2005. https://doi.org/10.2307/j.ctt155j4ws.8.

Borayin Larios. *Embodying the Vedas: Traditional Vedic Schools of Contemporary Maharashtra*. Poland: De Gruyter Open, 2017.

Bronkhorst, Johannes. *Buddhism in the Shadow of Brahminism*. Leiden: Brill, 2011.

———. *Greater Magadha: Studies in the Cultures of Early India*. New Delhi: Motilal Banarsidas, 2013.

———. *How the Brahmins Won: From Alexander to the Guptas*. Leiden: Brill, 2016.

Brough, John. "The Early History of the Gotras." *The Journal of the Royal Asiatic Society of Great Britain and Ireland*, no. 1 (1946): 32–45. http://www.jstor.org/stable/25222063.

Bryant, Edwin. *The Quest for the Origins of Vedic Culture: The Indo-Aryan Migration Debate*. Oxford: Oxford University Press, 2001.

Buzpinar, S. Tufan. "The Question of Caliphate under the Last Ottoman Sultans." In *Ottoman Reform and Muslim Regeneration: Studies in Honour of Butrus Abu-Manneh*, edited by Itzchak Weismann and Fruma Zachs, 17–36. London: IB Tauris, 2005.

Camp, Elisabeth. "Sarcasm, Pretence, and The Semantics/Pragmatics Distinction." *Noûs* 46, no. 4 (2012): 587–634. http://www.jstor.org/stable/41682690.

Chakrabarty, Dipesh. *The Calling of History: Sir Jadunath Sarkar and His Empire of Truth*. Chicago: University of Chicago Press, 2015.

Chakravarti, Uma. *Rewriting History: The Life and Times of Pandita Ramabai*. New Delhi: Zubaan, 2013.

Chaturvedi, Vinayak. *Hindutva and Violence: V. D. Savarkar and the Politics of History*, Albany: SUNY Press, 2022.

———. "A Revolutionary's Biography: The Case of VD Savarkar." *Postcolonial Studies* 16, no. 2 (2013): 124–39.

Chatterji, Jogesh Chandra. *Indian Revolutionaries in Conference*. India: Firma K. L. Mukhopadhyay, 1961.

Chatterjee, Partha. *Lineages of Political Society: Studies in Postcolonial Democracy*. New York: Columbia University Press, 2011.

Chatterji, Rakhahari, *Gandhi and the Ali Brothers: Biography of a Friendship*. New Delhi: SAGE Publications, 2013.

Chiplunkar, Vishnushastri. *Nibandhamala* [Collection of essays]. Pune: Chitrashala, 1917.

Chirol, Valentine. *Indian Unrest*. London: Macmillan and Co, 1910.

Chitragupta. *Life of Barrister Savarkar*. Madras: B.G. Paul and Co. Publishers, 1926.

Chitrav, Siddheshwarshastri. *Bharatvarshiya Prachin Charitrakosh* [Compilation of ancient Indian biographies], vol. 1. Poona: Bharatvarshiya Charitrakosh Mandal, 1854. (Digitized by the Government of Maharashtra, for the Asiatic Society of Mumbai)

Clifford, Nicholas Rowland. *Shanghai, 1925: Urban Nationalism and the Defense of Foreign Privilege*. Ann Arbor: University of Michigan Press, Center for Chinese Studies, 1979.

Cohn, Bernard S. "The Pasts of an Indian Village." *Comparative Studies in Society and History* 3, no. 3 (1961): 241–49.

Constable, Philip. "Early Dalit Literature and Culture in Late Nineteenth- and Early Twentieth-Century Western India." *Modern Asian Studies* 31, no. 2 (1997): 317–38.

Copland, Ian. "The Maharaja of Kolhapur and the Non-Brahmin Movement 1902–10." *Modern Asian Studies* 7, no. 2 (1973): 209–25.

Dace, Wallace. "The Concept of 'Rasa' in Sanskrit Dramatic Theory." *Educational Theatre Journal* 15, no. 3 (1963): 249–54. https://doi.org/10.2307/3204783.

Dacosta, John. *Remarks on the Vernacular Press Law of India, or Act IX of 1878*. Pamphlets. W.H. Allen and Co., 1878. https://jstor.org/stable/10.2307/60246900.

Dahiwale, S. M. "Consolidation of Maratha Dominance in Maharashtra." *Economic and Political Weekly* 30, no. 6 (1995), 336–42.

Damle, Keshav Bhikaji. *Savarkaranchi Kavita* [Savarkar's poems]. Mumbai: Shrisamartha Sadan, 1943.

Damle, M. V. *Savarkar Smruti* [Memories of Savarkar]. Ratnagiri: Sou. Saroj Desai, 1982.

Damle, Y. B. "A Note on Harikatha." *Bulletin of the Deccan College Research Institute* 17, no. 1 (1955): 15–19. http://www.jstor.org/stable/42929619.

Daniel, E. Valentine. *Fluid Signs: Being a Person the Tamil Way*. Berkeley: University of California Press, 1984.

Dandekar, R. N., ed. *Sanskrit and Maharashtra: A Symposium*. Poona: Bhandarkar Institute Press, 1972.

Danzig, Richard. "The Announcement of August 20th, 1917." *The Journal of Asian Studies* 28, no. 1 (1968): 19–37.

Das, Veena. "The Figure of the Abducted Woman: The Citizen as Sexed." In *Political Theologies: Public Religions in a Post-Secular World*, edited by Hent De Vries and Lawrence E. Sullivan, New York: Fordham University Press, 2006.

Dasgupta, Alokeranjan. "Biography: A Māyā? The Indian Point of Departure." *Indian Literature* 48, no. 1 (219) (2004): 156–64. http://www.jstor.org/stable/23341435.

Date, S. R. *Bharatiya Swatantryache Ranazhunzhaar* [Warriors of Indian freedom struggle]. Pune: Abhinava Bharat Smarak Chitraprabodhini, 1970.

Datta, Pradip Kumar. *Carving Blocs: Communal Ideology in Early Twentieth-Century Bengal*. New York: Oxford University Press, 1999.

———. "'Dying Hindus': Production of Hindu Communal Common Sense in Early 20th Century Bengal." *Economic and Political Weekly* 28, no. 25 (1993): 1305–19.

Desai, Dhananjay. *Hindurashtracha Jwalamukhi* [Volcano of the Hindu nation]. Mumbai: Dhananjay Desai, 2000.

Desai, Sudha Vishwanath. *Social Life in Maharashtra under the Peshwas*. Bombay: Popular Prakashan, 1980.

Deshpande, B. G. *Geet Savarkar* [Poems]. Aurangabad: Dr. Satish Bhaskarrao Deshpande, 1983.

Deshpande, Govind Purushottam. *The World of Ideas in Modern Marathi: Phule, Vinoba, Savarkar*. New Delhi: Tulika, 2009.

Deshpande, Kusumavati, and Mangesh Vitthal Rajadhyaksha. *A History of Marathi Literature*. New Delhi: Sahitya Akademi, 1988.

Deshpande, Madhav M. "'The Arctic Home in the Vedas': Religion, Politics and the Colonial Context," In *Political Hinduism: The Religious Imagination in Public Spheres*, edited by Vinay Lal, New Delhi: Oxford University Press, 2009.

———. "Aryan Origins: Arguments from the Nineteenth-Century Maharashtra." In *The Indo-Aryan Controversy*, edited by Edwin Bryant and Laurie Patton, 419–45. London: Routledge, 2004.

———. "Ksatriyas in the Kali Age? Gagabhatta & His Opponents." *Indo-Iranian Journal* 53, no. 2 (2010): 95–120.

———. "Pandit and Professor: Transformations in the 19th Century Maharashtra." In *The Pandit: Traditional Scholarship in India*, edited by Aithal K. Parameswara and Axel Michaels, New Delhi: Manohar, 2021.

———. "Pune: An Emerging Center of Education in Early Modern Maharashtra." *International Journal of Hindu Studies* 19, no. 1/2 (2015): 59–96.

Deshpande, Prachi. *Creative Pasts: Historical Memory and Identity in Western India, 1700–1960*. New York: Columbia University Press, 2007.

———. *Scripts of Power: Writing, Language Practices, and Cultural History in Western India*. Ranikhet: Permanent Black, 2022.

———. "Shuddhalekhan: Orthography, Community and the Marathi Public Sphere." *Economic and Political Weekly* 51, no. 6 (2016): 72–82.

Deshpande, S. H. *Savarkar te Bha Ja Pa: Hindutva-Vicharacha Chikitsak Aalekh* [From Savarkar to BJP: an analytical study of Hindutva ideas]. Pune: Rajhans Prakashan, 1992.

Deshpande, Sunita, ed. *Encyclopaedic Dictionary of Marathi Literature*. Vol. 1 and 2. New Delhi: Global Vision Publishing House, 2020.

Devanesan, Chandran. *The Making of the Mahatma*. Madras: Orient Longman, 1969.

Devare, Aparna. *History and the Making of a Modern Hindu Self*. New Delhi: Routledge, 2013.

Devdhar, S. K. *Swatantryaveer Savarkar* [Freedom fighter Savarkar]. Bombay: Jyotsna Prakashan, 1966.

Devji, Faisal. *The Impossible Indian: Gandhi and the Temptation of Violence*, Cambridge, Massachusetts: Harvard University Press, 2012.

Dharwadker, Vinay. "Some Contexts of Modern Indian Poetry." *Chicago Review* 38, no. 1/2 (1992): 219. https://doi.org/10.2307/25305599.

Dharup, G. G. *Hutatma Anant Laxman Kanhere yanche charitra* [Martyr Anant Laxman Kanhere, a biography]. Nasik: Gopal Govind Dharup, 1947.

Dharup, V. G. *Vinayaki hi katha krantichi* [Revolutionary story of Savarkar]. Pune: Arunodaya Raste Prakashan, 1992.

Dhawale, V. R., and V. D. Kulkarni, eds. *Marathi Kavita: Prachin Kalakhanda, 1150–1840* [Marathi poetry: early period, 1150–1840]. Bombay: Mumbai Marathi Sahitya Sangh, 1969.

Dhere, Ramchandra Chintaman. "The Gondhali: Singers for the Devi," trans. Anne Feldhaus. In *The Experience of Hinduism: Essays on Religion in Maharashtra*, edited by Eleanor Zelliot and Maxine Berntsen, 174–89. Albany: SUNY Press, 1988.

Dighe, Prabhakar. *Svadesha Krantiche Pranete Vasudev Balvanta Phadke* [Revolutionary pioneer for independence]. Dombivli: Arti Prakashan, 1992.

Dirks, Nicholas. *Autobiography of an Archive*. New York: Columbia University Press, 2015.

———. *Castes of Mind: Colonialism and the Making of Modern India*. Princeton, NJ: Princeton University Press, 2001.

Divekar, V. D. "Survey of Material in Marathi on the Economic and Social History of India—1" in *Indian Economic and Social History Review* 15, no. 1 (1978): 81–117.

Dixit, Raja, ed. *Nivadaka Sejavalakara* [selection of writings of T. S. Shejwalkar]. New Delhi: Sahitya Akademi, 2007.

Doniger, Wendy. *The Rig Veda: An Anthology: One Hundred and Eight Hymns*. London: Penguin Books, 1981.

Dugal, N. D. *Deshprema tujhe nav Savarkar* [Patriotism thy name is Savarkar]. Kolhapur: Anilkumar Mehta Ajab Pustakalaya, 1983.

Edgerton, Franklin. "The History of Caste in India. Volume I. Evidence of the Laws of Manu on the Social Conditions in India during the Third Century A.D., Interpreted and Examined; with an Appendix on Radical Defects in Ethnology. By Shridhar V. Ketkar. (Ithaca: Taylor and Carpenter, 1909.)." *The American Political Science Review* 4, no. 3 (1910): 446–48. https://doi.org/10.2307/1945888.

Edwardes, S. M. *The Bombay City Police: A Historical Sketch, 1672–1916*. London: Oxford University, 1923.

Engblom, Philip C. "Keshavsut and Early Modernist Strategies for Indigenizing the Sonnet in Marathi: A Western Form in Indian Garb." *Journal of South Asian Literature* 23, no. 1 (1988): 42–66.

———. "Marathi Poetry in English Translation." *Journal of South Asian Literature* 17, no. 1 (1982): 115–32.

———. "Vishnu Moreshwar Mahajani and Nineteenth-Century Antecedents." In *Writers, Editors, and Reformers: Social and Political Transformations of Maharashtra*, edited by N. K. Wagle, 143. New Delhi: Manohar, 1999.

Faruqui, Munis D. "At Empire's End: The Nizam, Hyderabad and Eighteenth-Century India," *Modern Asian Studies* 43, no. 1 (2009): 5–43.

Feldhaus, Anne. *Connected Places: Region, Pilgrimage and Geographical Imagination in India*. New York: Palgrave Macmillan, 2003.

Ferrar, M. L. "The New Penal System in the Andamans." *Journal of the Royal Society of Arts* 80, no. 4123 (1931): 48–61. http://www.jstor.org/stable/41358921.

Fischer, Louis. *Life of Mahatma Gandhi*. New York: Harper & Row, 1951.

Fitzgerald, Timothy. "Politics and Ambedkar Buddhism in Maharashtra." In *Buddhism and Politics in Twentieth-Century Asia*, edited by Ian Harris, 79–104. London: A&C Black, 2001.

Flatt, Emma. *The Courts of the Deccan Sultanates: Living Well in the Persian Cosmopolis*. Cambridge: Cambridge University Press, 2019.

Forjett, Charles. *Our Real Danger in India*. New Delhi: Isha Books, 2013. First published 1877.

Fulzele, A. D., and S. Meshram. "V. R. Shinde: An Analysis of Social and Political Alterations among Untouchables." *Vidyabharati International Interdisciplinary Research Journal* 11, no. 10 (September 2022): 116–126.

Gadkari, Ram Ganesh. *Vagvaijayanti*. Pune: Ramyakatha Prakashan, 1970.

Ganachari, Arvind. "British Official View of 'Bhagwat Gita' as 'Text-Book for the Mental Training of Revolutionary Recruits.'" *Proceedings of the Indian History Congress* 56 (1995): 601–10. http://www.jstor.org/stable/44158678.

———. *Gopal Ganesh Agarkar: The Secular Rationalist Reformer*. Mumbai: Popular Prakashan, 2005.

Gandhi, Mohandas K. *Gandhi and Communal Problems*. Compiled by Centre for Study of Society and Secularism. Mumbai: Centre for Study of Society and Secularism, 1994.

———. "The Hindu Caste System." In *The Collected Works of Mahatma Gandhi*, vol. 15, 258–60. New Delhi: Publications Division, Ministry of Information and Broadcasting, Government of India, 2000.

Garnett, David, *The Golden Echo*. London: Chatto and Windus, 1953.

Garud, Sushma. *Geet Vinayak* [Songs]. Dombivli: Moraya Prakashan, 2003.

Gawade, P. L. *Savarkar: Ek Chikitsak Abhyas* [Savarkar: a critical study]. Pune: Swadhyaya Mahavidyalaya Prakashan, 1984.

Gerow, Edwin. *A Glossary of Indian Figures of Speech*. Vol. 16. Berlin: Walter de Gruyter Mouton: 1971.

Ghai, R. K. "Hindu-Muslim Relations during the 1920s with Special Reference to Shuddhi and Tabligh." *Proceedings of the Indian History Congress* 46 (1985): 526–34.

Ghosh, Durba. *Gentlemanly Terrorists: Political Violence and the Colonial State in India, 1919–1947*. Cambridge: Cambridge University Press, 2017.

Ghurye, G. S. "Social change in Maharashtra (I)." *Sociological Bulletin* 1, no. 1 (1952): 71–88.

Gladstone, William Ewart. *Bulgarian Horrors and the Question of the East*. London: John Murray, 1876.

Godbole, Arvind. *Ase Ahet Savarkar* [Such is Savarkar]. Pune: Bharatiya Vicar Sadhana Pune Prakashan, 2005.

Gokhale, Balkrishna Govind. "The Religious Complex in Eighteenth-Century Poona." *Journal of the American Oriental Society* 105, no. 4 (1985): 719–24.

Gokhale, D. N. *Svatantryaveer Savarkar: Ek Rahasya* [Freedom fighter Savarkar: a mystery]. Mumbai: Mauj Prakashan Griha, 1989.

Gokhale, M. S. *Veer Savarkar*. Bombay: Hind Prakashan Sanstha, 1940.

Gokhale, S. P. *Ashi Garajli Virvani* [Thus roared the warrior]. Pune: Lokmanya Prakashan, 1969.

———. *Jhep ani Jhunzha* [Leap and struggle.]. Pune: n.p., 1984.

———. *Savarakaransi Sukhasanvada* [Conversations with Savarkar]. Mumbai: Majestic Book Stall, 1969.

Gokhale, Vidyadhar. *Jhanjavata: Hinduhrudaysamrat Tatyarao Savarkar Yanchya Ajaramar Jivanachi Yashogatha* [A hurricane: beloved of Hindus Tatyarao Savarkar's immortal life epic]. Bombay: Manorama Prakashan, 2005.

Gold, Daniel. "Organized Hinduisms: From Vedic Truth to Hindu Nation." In *Fundamentalisms Observed* 1, edited by Martin E. Marty and R. Scott Appleby, 531–93. Chicago: University of Chicago Press, 1991.

Gopal, Sarvepalli. *Jawaharlal Nehru: A Biography*. New Delhi: Oxford University Press, 1989.

Gordon, Leonard A. *Brothers against the Raj: A Biography of Indian Nationalists Sarat and Subhas Chandra Bose*. New York: Columbia University Press, 1990.

Gore, M. S. *Vitthal Ramji Shinde, an Assessment of His Contributions*. Vol. 64. Bombay: Tata Institute of Social Sciences, 1990.

Grew, Joseph Clark. "The Lausanne Peace Conference of 1922–1923." *Proceedings of the Massachusetts Historical Society* 69 (1947): 348–67.

Griffin, Roger, ed. *Fascism*. Oxford: Oxford University Press, 1995.

Griffiths, Percival Joseph. *To Guard My People: The History of the Indian Police*. London: Ernest Benn, 1971.

Güçlü, Yücel. "The Struggle for Mastery in Cilicia: Turkey, France, and the Ankara Agreement of 1921." *The International History Review* 23, no. 3 (2001): 580–603.

Guha, Sumit. "The Maratha Empire." In *Oxford Research Encyclopedia of Asian History*, edited by David Ludden. Oxford: Oxford University Press, 2019. https://doi.org/10.1093/acrefore/9780190277727.013.356.

Guida, Michelangelo. "Seyyid Bey and the Abolition of the Caliphate." *Middle Eastern Studies* 44, no. 2 (2008): 275–89.

Gupta, Charu. "Articulating Hindu Masculinity and Femininity: 'Shuddhi' and 'Sangathan' Movements in United Provinces in the 1920s." *Economic and Political Weekly* 33, no. 13 (1998): 727–35.

———. *Sexuality, Obscenity, Community: Women, Muslims, and the Hindu Public in Colonial India*. New Delhi: Orient Blackswan, 2005.

Haddad, Mahmoud. "Arab Religious Nationalism in the Colonial Era: Rereading Rashīd Riḍā's Ideas on the Caliphate." *Journal of the American Oriental Society* 117, no. 2 (1997): 253–77.

Hardiman, David. *Gandhi in His Time and Ours: The Global Legacy of His Ideas*. New York: Columbia University Press, 2003.

Hardy, Peter. *Partners in Freedom and True Muslims: The Political Thought of Some Muslim Scholars in British India 1912–1947*. Vol. 5. Lund: Studentlitteratur, 1971.

Harshe, D. S. *Savarkar Darshan: Rajkaranache Hindukaran ni Hindunche Sainikikaran Kara* [Meeting Savarkar: Hinduize politics and militarize Hindus]. Satara: printed by the author, 1990.

Hasan, Mona. *Longing for the Lost Caliphate: A Transregional History*. Princeton, NJ: Princeton University Press, 2016.

Hasan, Mushirul. "Communalism in the Provinces: A Case Study of Bengal and the Punjab, 1922–26." *Economic and Political Weekly* 15, no. 33 (1980): 1395–406.

———, ed. *Islam and Indian nationalism: Reflections on Abul Kalam Azad*. New Delhi: Manohar Publications, 1992.

Hendrix, Burke A., and Deborah Baumgold, eds. *Colonial Exchanges: Political Theory and the Agency of the Colonized*. Manchester: Manchester University Press, 2017.

Hermansen, Marcia. "Rewriting Sufi Identity in the 20th Century: The Biographical Approaches of Maulānā Ashraf 'Alī Ṯẖānvī and Khwājah Ḥasan Niẓāmī." *Islamic Studies* 46, no. 1 (2007): 15–39. http://www.jstor.org/stable/20839053.

Hofmann, Reto. *The Fascist Effect: Japan and Italy, 1915–1952*. New York: Cornell University Press, 2015.

Husain, Iqbal. "Barkatullah—A Half-Forgotten Revolutionary." *Proceedings of the Indian History Congress* 66 (2005): 1061–72. http://www.jstor.org/stable/44145919.

Hutton, John Henry. "Census of India, 1931. Vol. I: India. Part I: Report." Delhi: Government of India Publications Department, 1933.

Ilbert, Courtenay. "British India." *Journal of the Society of Comparative Legislation* 6, no. 2 (1905): 336–41. http://www.jstor.org/stable/752051.

Irschick, Eugene F. *Politics and Social Conflict in South India*. Berkeley: University of California Press, 1969.

Jadhav, Gangadhar. *Jay Jay Mrutyunjay Savarkar* [Hail hail Immortal Savarkar]. Nagpur: Sha La Abhyankar, 1983.

Jaffrelot, Christophe. *The Hindu Nationalist Movement and Indian Politics: 1925 to the 1990s: Strategies of Identity-Building, Implantation and Mobilisation (with Special Reference to Central India)*. New Delhi: Penguin Books India, 1999.

Jagadeesan, P. "Secularising the Institution of Marriage with Particular Reference to Tamil Nadu." *Proceedings of the Indian History Congress* 52 (1991): 771–77. http://www.jstor.org/stable/44142700.

Jasper, Daniel. "Commemorating the 'Golden Age' Of Shivaji in Maharashtra, India and the Development of Maharashtrian Public Politics." *Journal of Political & Military Sociology* 31, no. 2 (2003): 215–30.

Javalkar, Dinkarrao. *Dēśācē Duśmana* [Enemies of the nation]. Pune: Sumedh Prakashan, 2005.

Joglekar, J. D. *Dnyanayukta Krantiyoddha* [Intellectual revolutionary warrior]. Mumbai: Manorama Prakashan, 2002.

———. *Svatantryaveer Savarkar- Vadali Jeevan* [Freedom fighter Savarkar: a tempestuous life]. Pune: Utkarsha Prakashan, 1983.

Jordens, Joseph Teresa Florent. *Swami Shraddhananda: His Life and Causes*. Delhi: Oxford University Press, 1981.

Joshi, Mahadevshastri. *Bharatiya Sanskritikosha*. Vol. 5. Pune: Shaniwar Peth, 1974.

Joshi, V. S. *Adya Krantikarak: Vasudev Balwant Phadke* [First revolutionary: Vasudev Balwant Phadke]. Bombay: Raja Prakashan, 1947.

———. *Krantikallo̤la: Svatantryavira Ba. Savarakara Yancya Krantikaraka Jivanacya Kalakhandaca Cittavedhaka Citrapata* [A captivating film about the revolutionary life of Savarkar]. Mumbai: Manorama Prakashan, 1985.

Joshi, Mrinalini. *Avadhya mi! Ajinkya mi!* [Indestructible me! Unconquerable me!]. Pune: n.p., 1983.

Kallis, Aristotle A., ed. *The Fascism Reader*. London: Routledge, 2003.

Kallol, Anant. *Swatantryaveer Savarkar*. Nagpur: n.p., 1980.

Kaloudis, George. "Ethnic Cleansing in Asia Minor and the Treaty of Lausanne." *International Journal on World Peace* 31, no. 1 (2014): 59–88.

Kamble, R. H. *Swatantryavira Savarkaranche Ratnagiritil Samajik Karya* [The social work of freedom fighter Savarkar in Ratnagiri]. Pune: Diamond Publications, 2016.

Kanhere, S. G. "Waman Pandit—Scholar and Marathi Poet." *Bulletin of the School of Oriental Studies, University of London* 4, no. 2 (1926): 305–14. http://www.jstor.org/stable/606845.

Kantak, Madhav. Biographical essay in T. S. Shejwalkar, *Panipat: 1761* (Marathi). Poona: Deccan College Post Graduate and Research Institute, 1946.

Kayali, Hasan. *Arabs and Young Turks: Ottomanism, Arabism, and Islamism in the Ottoman Empire, 1908–1918*. Berkeley: University of California Press, 1997.

Kapila, Shruti. *Violent Fraternity: Indian Political Thought in the Global Age*. Princeton, NJ: Princeton University Press. 2021.

Karandikar, S. L. *Ase Hote Veer Savarkar* [Such was Savarkar]. Pune: Sitabai Karandikar, 1966.

———. *Savarkaranche Sahakari* [Comrades of Savarkar]. Pune: Ga Pa Parchure Prakashan, 1947.

———. *Savarkar Charitra (kathan)* [Narrating the biography of Savarkar]. Pune: Varada Prakashan Mumbai, 1943.

Karandikar, V. R., ed. *Samartha Ramdas: Vivekdarshan* [Samartha Ramdas's wisdom]. New Delhi: Sahitya Akademi, 2008.

Kasbe, Raosaheb. *Hindurashtravad: Svatantryaveer Savarkarancha ani Rashtriya Svayansevak Sanghacha* [Hindu nationalism: that of Savarkar and that of RSS]. Pune: Manovikas Prakashan, 2018.

Kedar, Kavi, and Ga Vi Thekedar, *Swatantryaveergatha* [Story]. Pune: n.p., 1992.

Kelkar, N. C. *Lokamanya Tilak Yanche Charitra* [Biography of Lokmanya Tilak]. 3 vols., Pune: printed by the author, 1923–28.

Kelkar, Y. N. *Aitihasik Powade: Marathyancha Kavyamaya Itihas* [Historical ballads: poetic history of Marathas]. Pune: Bharat Itihas Sanshodhan Mandal, 1928.

Kelly, Saul. "'Crazy in the Extreme'? The Silk Letters Conspiracy." *Middle Eastern Studies* 49, no. 2 (2013): 162–78.

Keer, Dhananjay. *Lokamanya Tilak: Father of the Indian Freedom Struggle*. Bombay: SB Kangutkar, 1959.

———. *Veer Savarkar*. Bombay: Popular Prakashan, 1966.

Keune, Jon. *Shared Devotion, Shared Food: Equality and the Bhakti-Caste Question in Western India*. New York: Oxford University Press, 2021.

Kevles, Daniel J. *In the Name of Eugenics: Genetics and the Uses of Human Heredity*. Cambridge: Harvard University Press, 2004.

Kévorkian, Raymond. *The Armenian Genocide: A Complete History*. London: I.B. Tauris, 2011.

Khadilkar, P. D. *Swa Savarkar yancha Powada* [*Povāḍā* of freedom fighter Savarkar]. Bombay: Pa Da Khadilkar, 1939.

Khobrekar, V. G. *Hutatma Damodar Hari Chaphekar yanche atmavrut* [Autobiography of martyr Damodar Hari Chaphekar]. Bombay: Sahitya Sanskriti Mandal, 1974.

Klein, Ira. "Plague, Policy and Popular Unrest in British India." *Modern Asian Studies* 22, no. 4 (1988): 723–55. http://www.jstor.org/stable/312523.

Kidambi, Prashant. *The Making of an Indian Metropolis: Colonial Governance and Public Culture in Bombay, 1890–1920*. London: Routledge, 2016.

Kirloskar, S. N. *Shanavakiya*. Pune: Sadhna Prakashan, 1974.

Kolff, D. H. A. *Naukar, Rajput, and Sepoy: The Ethnohistory of the Military Labour Market in Hindustan, 1450–1850*, Cambridge: Cambridge University Press, 1990.

Kolte, V. B. "Preface." In *Mhaimbhat Sankalit Lilacharita* [Lilacharita compiled by Mhaimbhat]. Bombay: Maharashtra Rajya Sahitya Sanskriti Mandal, 1978.

Kosambi, Meera. "Indian Response to Christianity, Church and Colonialism: Case of Pandita Ramabai." *Economic and Political Weekly* 27, no. 43/44 (1992): WS61–71.

———. "Women, Emancipation and Equality: Pandita Ramabai's Contribution to Women's Cause." *Economic and Political Weekly* 23, no. 44 (1988): WS38–49.

Koselleck, Reinhart. *Futures Past: On the Semantics of Historical Time*. New York: Columbia University Press, 2004.

Krishna, Gangadhar. *Samayocitapadyamālikā* [Collection of memorable verses]. Bombay: Nirnaya-sagar Press, n.d.

Kulkarni, A. R. "Maratha Swarajya: Its Extent and Income." *Proceedings of the Indian History Congress* 51 (1990): 321–25.

Kulkarni, Kedar. *World Literature and the Question of Genre in Colonial India: Poetry, Drama, and Print Culture, 1790–1890*. New Delhi: Bloomsbury India, 2022.

Kulkarni, S. V. *Vasa Vadalacha* [Poems]. Meraj: Sharad Kulkarni, 1983.

Kumaraswamy, P. R. "The Jews: Revisiting Mahatma Gandhi's November 1938 Article." *International Studies* 55, no. 2 (2018): 146–66.

Kunte, Mahadev Moreshwar. *The Vicissitudes of Åryan Civilization in India: An Essay, which Treats of the History of the Vedic and Buddhistic Polities, Explaining Their Origin, Prosperity, and Decline*. Bombay: Oriental Printing Press, 1880.

Lad, Purushottam Mangesh, ed. *Shri Tukarambawancya Abhanganci Gatha* [Collected poems of Shri Tukarambua]. Mumbai: Maharashtra Rajya Sahitya and Sanskriti Mandal, 1950.

Latter, Edwin. "The Indian Army in Mesopotamia 1914–1918." *Journal of the Society for Army Historical Research* 72, no. 290 (1994): 92–102.

Laine, James W. *Shivaji: Hindu King in Islamic India*. Oxford: Oxford University Press, 2003.

Larios, Borayin. *Embodying the Vedas: Traditional Vedic Schools of Contemporary Maharashtra*. Warsaw: De Gruyter Open Limited, 2017.

Laurence, Jonathan. *Coping with Defeat: Sunni Islam, Roman Catholicism and the Modern State*. Princeton, NJ: Princeton University Press: 2021

Lele, R. K. *Marathi Vruttapatrancha Itihas* [History of Marathi newspapers]. Pune: Continental Press, 2009.

Lelyveld, David. *Aligarh's First Generation: Muslim Solidarity in British India*. Princeton, NJ: Princeton University Press, 1978.

MacFie, A. L. "British Intelligence and the Turkish National Movement, 1919–22." *Middle Eastern Studies* 37, no. 1 (2001): 1–16.

Madan, T. N. "Is the Brahmanic Gotra a Grouping of Kin?" *Southwestern Journal of Anthropology* 18, no. 1 (1962): 59–77. http://www.jstor.org/stable/3629124.

Mahabala, Krantigeeta. *Vaineteyachi Gaganbharari: Arthat Mahakavi Savarkaranchi Kavya Pratibha* [Garuda soaring in the sky: meaning the poetic talent of the great poet Savarkar]. Bombay: Swatantryaveer Savarkar Rashtriya Smarak, 2010.

Mamdani, Mahmood. *Good Muslim, Bad Muslim: America, the Cold War, and the Roots of Terror*. New York: Pantheon, 2004.

Mandal, Saptarshi. "Ambedkar's Illegal Marriage: Hindu Nation, Hindu Modernity and the Legalization of Intercaste Marriage in India." *Indian Law Review* 6, no. 2 (2021): 1–23

Mangrulkar, A. G., Leela Arjunwadkar, and K. S. Arjunwadkar. "Influence of Sanskrit on the Language, Literature, and Thought of Maharashtra." In *Sanskrit and Maharashtra: A Symposium*, edited by R. N. Dandekar, 91–104. Poona: Bhandarkar Institute Press, 1972.

Marsden, Magnus, and Benjamin D. Hopkins. *Fragments of the Afghan Frontier*. New York: Columbia University Press: 2011.

Marwah, Inder S. "Darwin in India: Anticolonial Evolutionism at the Dawn of the Twentieth Century." In *Perspectives on Politics*, edited by Michael Bernhard and Daniel I. O'Neill, 1–16. Cambridge: Cambridge University Press, 2023. doi:10.1017/S1537592722004133.

———. "Rethinking Resistance: Spencer, Krishnavarma, and *The Indian Sociologist*." In *Colonial Exchanges: Political Theory and the Agency of the Colonized*, edited by Burke A. Hendrix and Deborah Baumgold, 57–65. Manchester: Manchester University Press, 2017.

———. "The View from the Future: Aurobindo Ghose's Anticolonial Darwinism." *American Political Science Review*, forthcoming 2023. https://doi.org/10.1017/S0003055423000576.

Mate, M. S. "Downfall of the Marathas." *Bulletin of the Deccan College Research Institute* 24 (1963): 31–35.

Mate, S. M. *Asprushya Vichar* [Thoughts on untouchables]. Pune: Sadashiv Krishnarao Shindkar, 1922.

Maydev, Vasudeo, ed. *Savarkaranchi Kavita* [Savarkar's poetry]. Mumbai: Keshav Bhikaji Dhavle, 1943.

McCrea, Lawrence. "Poetry beyond Good and Evil: Bilhana and the Tradition of Patron-Centered Court Epic." *Journal of Indian Philosophy* 38, no. 5 (2010): 503–18.

McMeekin, Sean. *The Berlin Baghdad Express: The Ottoman Empire and Germany's Bid for World Power*. Cambridge: Belknap Press, 2010.

Mehra, Rachna. "A Nation Partitioned or Homes Divided? The Severed Relationship between the State, Community and Abducted Women in the Post Partition Period." In *Proceedings of the Indian History Congress*, vol. 73, 1391–97. Indian History Congress, 2012.

Mehrunkar, Prabhakar. *Tejonidhi Savarkar* [Effulgent Savarkar]. Dombivli: Moriya Prakashan, 1993.

Metcalf, Barbara D. "Nationalist Muslims in British India: The Case of Hakim Ajmal Khan." *Modern Asian Studies* 19, no. 1 (1985): 1–28.

Michaels, Axel, ed. *The Pandit: Traditional Scholarship in India*. New Delhi: Manohar, 2001.

Miller, Maureen C. *Clothing the Clergy: Virtue and Power in Medieval Europe, c. 800–1200*. New York: Cornell University Press, 2014.

Minault, Gail. *The Khilafat Movement: Religious Symbolism and Political Mobilization in India*. New York: Columbia University Press, 1982.

Modak, S. V. *Savarkar Yanchya Athvani* [Memories of Savarkar]. Pune: Adhikari Prakashan, 1962.

More, Sheshrao. *Savarkarance Samajkarana: Satya ani Viparyasa* [Savarkar's social work: truth and falsehood]. Pune: Rajhans Prakashan, 1992.

———. *Savarkarancha Buddhivad: Ek Chikitsak Abhyasa* [Savarkar's thought: a critical study]. Nanded: Nirmala Prakashan, 1988.

Mukharji, Projit Bihari. *Brown Skins, White Coats: Race Science in India, 1920–66*. Chicago: University of Chicago Press, 2022.

Mukhopadhyaya, Sujitkumar. "The Vajrasūci of Aśvaghoṣa: A Study of the Sanskrit Text and Chinese Version." In *Visva-Bharati Annals*, vol. 2. Santiniketan: Santiniketan Press, 1949. [Reprinted in 1950; reprinted and revised in 1960.]

Nagaraj, D. R., and Prithvi Datta Chandra Shobhi, *The Flaming Feet and Other Essays: The Dalit Movement in India*. Delhi: Seagull Books, 2011.

Nair, Neeti. "Beyond the 'Communal' 1920s: The Problem of Intention, Legislative Pragmatism, and the Making of Section 295A of the Indian Penal Code." *The Indian Economic and Social History Review* 50, no. 3 (2013): 317–40.

———. *Changing Homelands: Hindu Politics and the Partition of India.* Boston: Harvard University Press, 2011.

Naipaul, V. S. *India: A Wounded Civilization.* New York: Knopf, 1977.

Nanda, Bal Ram, ed. *Indian Foreign Policy: The Nehru Years.* Delhi: Vikas Publishing House, 1976.

Nandy, Ashis. "A Disowned Father of the Nation in India: Vinayak Damodar Savarkar and the Demonic and the Seductive in Indian Nationalism." *Inter-Asia Cultural Studies* 15, no. 1 (2014): 91–112.

Naregal, Veena. *Language, Hierarchy and Identity: Emergence of the Public Sphere in Colonial Western India.* New Delhi: Oxford University Press, 2001.

———. *Language Politics, Elites and the Public Sphere: Western India under Colonialism.* New Delhi: Permanent Black, 2001.

Natke, Arvind. *Yugapravartak Savarkar* [Epoch-making Savarkar]. Bombay: Veer Savarkar Sahitya Abhyas Mandal, 1973.

Navalgundkar, S. N. "Sva. Vinayak Damodar Savarkar: (1883–1966)." In *Maharashtrateel Jaatisansthavishayak Vicar* [Thoughts on the caste system in Maharashtra], edited by Yashwant Sumant and Dattatreya Punde, 168–74. Pune: Pratima Prakashan, 1988.

———. *Swatantryaveer Savarkar Vicharvishwa* [The intellectual world of freedom fighter Savarkar]. Pune: Anmol Prakashan, 1999.

Nehru, Jawaharlal. "The Proscription and Censorship of Books." In *Selected Works of Jawaharlal Nehru*, edited by Sarvepalli Gopal and Jawaharlal Nehru, vol. 3, 394–95. New Delhi: Orient Longman, 1972.

Nemade, Bhalchandra. *The Influence of English on Marathi: A Sociolinguistic and Stylistic Study.* Bombay: Popular Prakashan, 2014.

———. *Nativism (Desivaad).* Shimla: Indian Institute of Advanced Study, 2009.

———. "Towards a Definition of Modernity in Modern Marathi Poetry." *Mahfil* 6, no. 2/3 (1970): 71–82. http://www.jstor.org/stable/40874340.

Nora, Pierre. *Realms of Memory: Rethinking the French Past, Volume 1: Conflicts and Divisions.* New York: Columbia University Press, 1996.

Novetzke, Christian Lee. *The Quotidian Revolution.* New York: Columbia University Press, 2016.

———. *Religion and Public Memory: A Cultural History of Saint Namdev in India.* New York: Columbia University Press, 2008.

Numani, Shibli. *Turkey, Egypt, and Syria: A Travelogue.* New York: Syracuse University Press, 2020.

Nuriddin, Ayah. "Engineering Uplift: Black Eugenics as Black Liberation." In *Nature Remade: Engineering Life, Envisioning Worlds*, edited by Luis A. Campos, Michael Dietrich, Tiago Saraiva, and Christian C. Young, 186–202. Chicago: University of Chicago Press, 2021

Oak, Alok. "What Does the Shastra Have to Say: The Age of Consent Bill Controversy and the Reimagination of Hinduism in Modern Western India." In *Gender and Authority across Disciplines, Space and Time*, edited by Adele Bardazzi and Alberica Bazzoni, 171–94. Cham: Palgrave Macmillan, 2020. https://doi.org/10.1007/978-3-030-45160-8_9.

Omvedt, Gail. *Buddhism in India: Challenging Brahmanism and Caste.* New Delhi: Sage Publications India, 2003.

———. *Cultural Revolt in a Colonial Society: The Non-Brahman Movement in Western India: 1873–1930.* Bombay: Scientific Socialist Education Trust, 1976.

———. "Non-Brahmans and Nationalists in Poona." *Economic and Political Weekly* 9, no. 6/8 (1974): 201–16. http://www.jstor.org/stable/4363419.

O'Hanlon, Rosalind. *Caste, Conflict and Ideology: Mahatma Jotirao Phule and Low Caste Protest in Nineteenth-Century Western India*, Cambridge: Cambridge University Press: 1985.

———. *A Comparison between Women and Men: Tarabai Shinde and the Critique of Gender Relations in Colonial India*. New York: Oxford University Press, 1994.

———. "Maratha History as Polemic: Low Caste Ideology and Political Debate in Late Nineteenth-Century Western India." *Modern Asian Studies* 17, no. 1 (1983): 1–33.

Padhye, Sadashiv Krishna. *Savarkar Vividh Darshan* [Varied views of Savarkar]. Pune: Venus Prakashan, 1958.

Padmanabhan, R. A. *V. V. S. Aiyar*. New Delhi: National Book Trust, 1980.

Palshikar, Vasant. "'Jaatyuchedak nibandh' va Savarkarance Asprushyta-Nivarak karya" ["Essays on destroying caste or Savarkar's work in ending untouchability"]. In *Maharastrateel Jaatisansthavishayak Vicar*, edited by Yashwant Sumant and Dattatreya Punde, 176–78. Pune: Pratima Prakashan, 1988.

Palsule, G. B. *Dhanyoham Dhanyoham* [Be blessed]. Pune: n.p., 1935.

Pandey, B. N. *The Indian Nationalist Movement, 1885–1947*. London: Palgrave Macmillan, 1979.

Pandey, Gyanendra. *The Ascendancy of the Congress in Uttar Pradesh*. London: Anthem Press, 2002.

———. "Which of Us Are Hindus?" In *Hindus and Others: The Question of Identity in India Today*, edited by G. Pandey, 238–71. New Delhi: Viking, 1993.

Pandit, B. "Savarkaranchi Kavyasrushti" [Savarkar's world of poetry]. In *Savarkar Vividh Darshan*, by Sadashiv Krishna Padhye. Pune: Venus Publications, 1958.

Pangarkar, L. R. *Moropanti Vence* [Poems of Moropant]. Pune: La Ra Pangarkar Prakashan, 1921.

Pant, Vijay Prakash. "Maulana Abul Kalam Azad: A Critical Analysis Life and Work." *The Indian Journal of Political Science* 71, no. 4 (2010): 1311–23.

Paradkar, Ramkrisha Dattatreya. *Astottarshata Ramayane* [One hundred and eight Rāmāyaṇas]. Pune: Yashwant Publishing, 1961.

Parchure, G. P. *Mulanche Tatyarao Savarkar* [Tatyarao Savarkar for children]. Bombay: printed by the author, 1941.

Parchure, Dr. Shri D. *Natak-kar Savarkar: Ek Chikitsa* [Playwright Savarkar: a critical study]. Bombay: Veer Savarkar Prakashan, 1966.

Pasha, Talaat. "Posthumous Memoirs of Talaat Pasha." *Current History (1916–1940)* 15, no. 2 (1921): 287–95.

Pawar, G. M. *Vitthal Ramji Shinde*. Delhi: National Book Trust, 1992.

Pavgi, N. *Saptasindhuca Pranta Athva Aryavartatil Amchii Janmabhumi va Uttar Dhruvakadil Amchya Vasahati* [The Aryavartic home and the Aryan cradle in the Sapta Sindhus or from Aryavarta to the Arctic and from the cradle to the colony]. Poona: Arya Bhushan Press, 1915. [Reprinted in 1920.]

Paxton, Robert O. *The Anatomy of Fascism*. New York: Vintage, 2007.

Payne, Stanley G. *A History of Fascism, 1914–1945*. Madison: University of Wisconsin Pres, 1996.

Pethe, M. K. *Savarkar Gaurav Gaan* [Poems]. Bombay: n.p., 1984.

Phadke, Y. D. *Shahu Chhatrapati ani Lokmanya*. [Shahu Chhatrapati and Lokmanya (Tilak)]. Pune: Shrividya Prakashan, 1986.

_______. *Śōdha Sāvarakarāñcā* [Searching for Savarkar]. Pune: Shrividya Prakashan, 1984.

———, ed. *Tatvadnya Savarkar Nivdak Vichar* [Philosopher Savarkar, selected thoughts]. Pune: Continental, 1986.

———. *Vyakti ani Vichar* [The individual and his thoughts]. Pune: Shrividya Prakashan, 1979

Phadakule, Nirmalkumar. *Kahi Ranga Kahi Resa* [A few colors, a few rasas]. Pune: Mehta Publishing House, 1986.

Phatak, N. R. *Eknath: Vangmaya ani Karya* [Shri Eknath: literature and work]. Bombay: Mauj Prakashan, 1950.

———. *Lokmanya*. Mumbai: Mauj Prakashan. 2006.

———. *Ramdas: Vangmaya ani Karya* [Ramdas: literature and work]. Bombay: Mauj Prakashan, 1953.

Philliou, Christine M. *Turkey: A Past against History*. Berkeley: University of California Press, 2021.

"The Plague in India." *The British Medical Journal* 1, no. 1934 (1898): 238–39. http://www.jstor.org/stable/20253203.

Provence, Michael. *The Last Ottoman Generation and the Making of the Modern Middle East*. Cambridge: Cambridge University Press, 2017.

Qureshi, M. Naeem. *Ottoman Turkey, Atatürk, and Muslim South Asia: Perspectives, Perceptions, and Responses*. Oxford: Oxford University Press, 2014.

———. *Pan-Islam in British Indian Politics: A Study of the Khilafat Movement, 1918–1924*. Leiden: Brill, 1999.

Raeside, Ian. "Early Prose Fiction in Marathi, 1828–1885." *The Journal of Asian Studies* 27, no. 4 (1968): 791–808. https://doi.org/10.2307/2051580.

Rahurkar, V. G. "The Origin of the Gotra-System in the Ṛgveda." *Annals of the Bhandarkar Oriental Research Institute* 53, no. 1/4 (1972): 93–99. http://www.jstor.org/stable/41688765.

Ramaswamy, Sumathi. *The Goddess and the Nation: Mapping Mother India*. Durham, NC: Duke University Press, 2010.

Ranade, Ashok. "Performing Arts and Narrative," *Sangeet-Natak*, no. 95 (January–March 1990).

———. "The Povada." In *Lesser-Known Forms of Performing Arts in India*, edited by Durgadas Mukhopadhyay, 58–64. New Delhi: Sterling Publishers, 1978.

Ranade, S. R. *Swatantryaveer Barrister Vinayakrao Savarkar yanche Sankshipt Charitra* [A concise biography of the freedom fighter Barrister Vinayakrao Savarkar]. Makhjan, Ratnagiri: printed by the author, 1924.

Rao, Anupama. *The Caste Question: Dalits and the Politics of Modern India*. Berkeley: University of California Press, 2009.

———. "Sexuality and the Family Form." *Economic and Political Weekly* 40, no. 8 (2005): 715–18. http://www.jstor.org/stable/4416226.

Rao, Parimala V. *A Century of Consolidation and Resistance: Caste and Education in Maharashtra, 1818–1918*. New Delhi: Nehru Memorial Museum and Library, 2014.

———. "Educating Women and Non-Brahmins as 'Loss of Nationality': Bal Gangadhar Tilak and the Nationalist Agenda in Maharashtra." New Delhi: Centre for Women's Development Studies, 2008.

———. *Foundations of Tilak's Nationalism: Discrimination, Education and Hindutva*. New Delhi: Orient Blackswan, 2011.

Rao, P. Hari. *The Indian Police Act (Act V of 1861): And the Indian Police Act (III of 1888) and the Police (incitement to Disaffection) Act (XXII of 1922): with Commentaries and Notes of Case-law Thereon*. printed by the author, 1927.

Rao, Vasanta Dinanath, "Side-Light on the Maratha Life from the Bardic (Śāhiri) Literature of the 18th Century," *Proceedings of the Indian History Congress* 3 (1939): 1194–212.

Raykar, G. K. *Swatantryaveer Savarkar*. Bombay: Jay Hind Prakashan, 1966.

Reetz, Dietrich. *Hijrat: The Flight of the Faithful: A British File on the Exodus of Muslim Peasants from North India to Afghanistan in 1920*. Berlin: Verlag Das Arabische Buch, 1995.

Rege, Sharmila. "Conceptualising Popular Culture: 'Lavani' and 'Powada' in Maharashtra." *Economic and Political Weekly* 37, no. 11 (2002): 1038–47.

Rocher, Ludo. *The Puranas. (A History of Indian Literature, Vol. II, fasc. 3)*. Wiesbaden: Harrassowitz, 1986.

Rustow, Dankwart A. "The Army and the Founding of the Turkish Republic." *World Politics* 11, no. 4 (1959): 513–52.

Sahasrabuddhe, Pra Ga. *Swatantryaveer Savarkar*. Bombay: Jyotsna Prakashan, 1966.

Salahudheen, O. P. "Political Ferment in Malabar." *Social Scientist* 35, no. 11/12 (2007): 29–38.

Salvi, A. G. *Savarkar Yancya Athvani: Swatantryaveer Savarkarancya Sahavasat* [Memories of Savarkar: in Savarkar's company]. Parts 1 and 2. Ratnagiri: printed by the author, 1976.

Sampath, Vikram. *Echoes from a Forgotten Past, 1883–1924*. New Delhi: Viking, 2019.

———. *Savarkar (Part 2): A Contested Legacy, 1924–1966*. New Delhi: Viking, 2021.

Sane, Chandrashekhar. "Lekhak Savarkar ani Savarkarance Lekhak," *Tarun Bharat*, January 4, 2020. https://www.mahamtb.com/Encyc/2020/1/4/Article-on-Veer-Savakar-as-a-writer-and-literature-on-Savarkar-.amp.html.

Sanyal, Usha. *Ahmad Riza Khan: In the Path of the Prophet*. Oxford: One World Publications, 2005.

Sarkar, Sumit. "Intimations of Hindutva: Ideologies, Caste, and Class in Post-Swadeshi Bengal." In *Proceedings of the Indian History Congress* 60 (1999), 655–66.

Sarkar, Jadunath. *Fall of the Mughal Empire, Vol II, 1754–1771*. Calcutta: M C Sarkar, 1934.

———. *History of Aurangzeb*. 3 vols. Calcutta: M.C. Sarkar, 1928.

Savarkar, Vinayak. *The Indian War of Independence of 1857*. n.p,, 1909.

———. *Hindu Pad-Padashahi or A Review of the Hindu Empire of Maharashtra*. Madras: B G Paul and Co, 1925.

———. "Letters from Andaman" (PDF). Published and compiled by Savarkar.org. Accessed May 3, 2023. https://savarkar.org/en/pdfs/letters_from_Andamans.v001.pdf.

_______. *Malā kāya tyācē? (Arthāta Mōpalyāñcē Baṇḍa)* [How does it matter to me? (Meaning the Mappillah Rebellion)]. Mumbai: Veer Savarkar Prakashan, 1982.

_______. *Pracin Arvacin Mahila* [Ancient and modern woman]. Mumbai: Veer Savarkar Prakashan, 1982

———. *Samagra Savarkar Vangmaya*. 8 vols. Pune: Samagra Savarkar Vangmay Prakashan, Maharashtra Prantik Hindusabha Samiti [MPHS], 1963–65.

———. *Samagra Savarkar Vangmaya*. 9 vols. Mumbai: Svatantryaveer Savarkar Rashtriya Smarak Prakashan [SSRSP], Mumbai: 2000–2001.

———. *Saṅgīta San'yasta Khaḍga*. Mumbai: Veer Savarkar Prakashan, 1982.

———. *Saṅgīta Uḥśāpa*. Mumbai: Veer Savarkar Prakashan, 1982.

———. *Saṅgīta Uttarakriya*. Mumbai: Veer Savarkar Prakashan, 1982.

———. *Savarkar Atmacharitra Arthat Majhya Athvani: Bhag Pahila* [Autobiography meaning my memories: first volume]. Pune: Venus Book Stall, 1949.

———. *Selected Works of Veer Savarkar*. 4 vols. Chandigarh: Bharat Bhushan Abhishek Publications, 2007.

———. *Six Glorious Epochs of Indian History*. Edited and translated by S. T. Godbole. Bombay: Bal Savarkar, 1971.

———. *Sphut Lekh* [Selected essays]. Mumbai: Svatantryaveer Savarkar Rashtriya Smarak Prakashan, 1982.

Savarkar, Balarao. *Hindusamaj Sanrakshak Sva. Veer. Vi. Da. Savarkar Ratnagiri Parva, San 1924 te 1937* [Protector of Hindu Society Swatantryaveer V. D. Savarkar, Ratnagiri section, circa 1924–1937]. Mumbai: Veer Savarkar Prakashan, 1972.

———. *Mahayogi Vira Savarkar* [The great seer Veer Savarkar]. Mumbai: Veer Savarkar Prakashan, 1983.

———. *Savarkar ani Bhagur* [Savarkar and Bhagur]. Mumbai: Savarkar Janmabhumi Pratishthan, 1994.

———. *Veer Savarkar Darshan* [Meeting Veer Savarkar]. Mumbai: Veer Savarkar Prakashan, 1983.

———. *Yogi Yoddha Vidasa* [Seer, warrior, vi da sa(varkar)]. Mumbai: Veer Savarkar Prakashan, 1996.

Savarkar, Ganesh Damodar. *Khristaparicaya arthat Khristacce Hindutva* [The Hindutva of the Christians]. Pune: Dr. Padmakar Vishnu Vartak, 1942.

Savarkar, Vishwas. *Athavani Angaracya* [Memories of embers]. Pune: Snehal Prakashan, 1986.

———. *Parisparsha Swatantryaveeranca* [Immortal touch of Swatantryaveer Savarkar]. Pune: Snehal Prakashan, 2008.

Sawant, Akshay. "Marathas, Brahmin and Non-Brahmin Contestations: Press and Public Sphere in Early 20th Century." In *Caste, Communication and Power*, edited by Biswajit Das and Debendra Prasad Majhi, 341–56. New Delhi: Sage Publications India, 2021.

Schultz, Anna. "Cosmaharaja: Popular Songs of Socialist Cosmpolitanism in Cold War India." In *Sound Alignments: Popular Music in Asia's Cold Wars*, edited by Michael K. Bourdaghs, Paola Iovene, and Kaley Mason, 201–30. Durham, NC: Duke University Press, 2021. https://doi.org/10.2307/j.ctv1n6pvn4.11.

———. *Singing a Hindu Nation: Marathi Devotional Performance and Nationalism*. New York: Oxford University Press, 2013.

Sen, Amiya P. "A Hindu Conservative Negotiates Modernity: Chandranath Basu (1844–1910) and Reflections on the Self and Culture in Colonial Bengal." In *HerStory: Historical Scholarship between South Asia and Europe: Festschrift in Honour of Gita Dharampal-Frick*, edited by Rafael Klöber and Manju Ludwig, 175–88. Heidelberg: Heidelberg University Library, 2018.

Sen, Satadru. *Disciplining Punishment: Colonialism and Convict Society in the Andaman Islands*. New Delhi: Oxford University Press, 2000.

———. *Savagery and Colonialism in the Indian Ocean: Power, Pleasure and the Andaman Islanders*. London: Routledge, 2010.

Sen, Shila. "Khilafat Non-Cooperation Movement in Bengal and Hindu-Muslim Relation: An Outline." *Proceedings of the Indian History Congress* 51 (1990): 465–68.

Sethi, Devika. *War over Words: Censorship in India, 1930–1960*. New Delhi: Cambridge University Press, 2019.

Shahasne, Chandrakant. *Ase Ahet Savarkar* [Such is Savarkar]. Bombay: Karnala Charitable Trust, 2004.

Sharma, Arvind. "The Puruṣasūkta: Its Relation to the Caste System." *Journal of the Economic and Social History of the Orient* 21, no. 3 (1978): 294–303. https://doi.org/10.2307/3632200.

Sharma, R. K. "A Study of the Gotras and Pravaras in the Kalachuri Inscriptions." *Proceedings of the Indian History Congress* 27 (1965): 92–98. http://www.jstor.org/stable/44140596.

Shejwalkar, T. S. "A Ballad on Bhau and the Panipat in Hindustani." *Bulletin of the Deccan College Post-Graduate and Research Institute* 4, no. 3 (March 1943): 161–85.

———. *Panipat: 1761*. Poona: Deccan College Post Graduate and Research Institute, 1946. [Marathi and English editions.]

Shelar, Sanjay Tulshiram. "The Role of Dinkarrao Javalkar Non-Brahmin Movement in Maharashtra (Special Reference to 'Deshache Dushaman')." *Proceedings of the Indian History Congress* 79 (2018): 598–602.

Shidore, P. G. *Swatantryaveer Savarkar* [Freedom fighter Savarkar]. Bombay: N. V. Sane, 1983.

Shikhare, D. N. *Swatantryaveer Savarkar* [Freedom fighter Savarkar]. Bombay: Keshav Bhikaji Dhawale Prakashan, 1958.

Shinde, Tarabai. "Stripurushtulana" [A comparison between man and woman]. In *Ekonisavya Shatakatil Marathi Gadya* [Marathi prose of the nineteenth century], edited by Bhaskara Lakshmana Bhole, vol. 2, 92–106. New Delhi: Sahitya Akademi, 2006.

Shirer, William L. *Gandhi: A Memoir*. New York: Simon and Schuster, 2012.

Siddiqui, Samee. "Coupled Internationalisms: Charting Muhammad Barkatullah's Anti-Colonialism and Pan-Islamism." *ReOrient* 5, no. 1 (2019): 25–46. https://doi.org/10.13169/reorient.5.1.0025.

Sikand, Yoginder. "Sikh-Muslim Harmony: Contributions of Khwaja Hasan Nizami." *Economic and Political Weekly* 39, no. 11 (2004): 1113–16. http://www.jstor.org/stable/4414757.

Singh, Kunwar Na Pra. *Poorna Savarkar Charitam*. Gorakhpur: Vishwa Sanskrit Pratisthan Uttar Pradesh, 1993.

Singh, Parminder. "Trial and Martyrdom of Dhingra: Reaction of Press." *Proceedings of the Indian History Congress* 72 (2011): 728–39. http://www.jstor.org/stable/44146765.

Soitkar, Anjali. "Emergence of Nomenclature: Sinnar." *Proceedings of the Indian History Congress* 77 (2016): 115–19.

Solomon, Rakesh H. "Culture, Imperialism, and Nationalist Resistance: Performance in Colonial India." *Theatre Journal* 46, no. 3 (1994): 323–47. https://doi.org/10.2307/3208610.

Sowani, M. V. *Savarkar Chitramay Charitra "Mrutyunjay"* ["Immortal," a pictorial biography of Savarkar]. Pune: Chitrasadhan Prakashan, 1967.

Sreenivasan, Ramya. *The Many Lives of a Rajput Queen: Heroic Pasts in India, c. 1500–1900*. Seattle: University of Washington Press, 2017.

Sternbach, Ludwik. "Subhasita, Gnomic and Didactic Literature." In *A History of Indian Literature*, edited by Jan Gonda, vol. 4, fasc. 1, Wiesbaden: Otto Harrassowitz Verlag, 1974.

Stolte, Carolien. "'Enough of the Great Napoleons!' Raja Mahendra Pratap's Pan-Asian Projects (1929–1939)." *Modern Asian Studies* 46, no. 2 (2012): 403–23.

Subrahmanyam, Sanjay. "Inventing a 'Genocide'": The Political Abuses of a Powerful Concept in Contemporary India." *The Journal of Holocaust Research* 37, no. 1 (2023): 102–7.

Sulṭān-I-Rome. "The Role of the North-West Frontier Province in the Khilafat and Hijrat Movements." *Islamic Studies* 43, no. 1 (2004): 51–78.

Tegart, Charles. *Terrorism in India*. Calcutta: New Age Publishers, 1983.

Teitelbaum, Joshua. "Sharif Husayn ibn Ali and the Hashemite Vision of the Post-Ottoman Order: From Chieftaincy to Suzerainty." *Middle Eastern Studies* 34, no. 1 (1998): 103–22.

———. "'Taking Back' the Caliphate: Sharīf Ḥusayn Ibn ʿAlī, Mustafa Kemal and the Ottoman Caliphate." *Die Welt Des Islams* 40, no. 3 (2000): 412–24.

Teltumbde, Anand. *Dalits: Past, Present and Future*. New York: Routledge, 2020.

Temple, Sir Richard. *Men and Events of My Time in India*. London: John Murray, 1882.

Thakare, Keshav Seetaram. *Majhi Jeevangatha* [The story of my life]. Mumbai: Navataa Book World: 2016.

Tikekar, S. R. *Lokahitvadinchi Shatpatren* [Hundred letters by Lokahitvadi]. Edited by Usha Prakashan. Pune: Oundh, 1940.

Tilak, B. G. *The Arctic Home in the Vedas: Being Also a New Key to the Interpretation of Many Vedic Texts and Legends*. Poona: Kesari, 1903. [Second reprint in 1956.]

———. "Hindutva ani Sudharna" [Hindutva and reform]. In *Samagra Lokmanya Tilak*, vol. 5 (*Samaj va Sanskruti*) [Society and culture], 294–98. Pune: Kesari Prakashan, 1976. [Originally published in *Kesari* on January 12, 1904]

Tinker, Hugh. "India in the First World War and After." *Journal of Contemporary History* 3, no. 4 (1968): 89–107.

Treanor, Tom. *One Damn Thing after Another: The Adventures of an Innocent Man Trapped between Public Relations and the Axis*. New York: Doubleday, Doran & Company, Inc., 1944.

Trivedi, Raj Kumar. "Turco-German Intrigue in India during the World War I." *Proceedings of the Indian History Congress* 43 (1982): 653–65.

Tucker, Richard. "Hindu Traditionalism and Nationalist Ideologies in Nineteenth-Century Maharashtra." *Modern Asian Studies* 10, no. 3 (1976): 321–48.

"Turkey under Kemal" in *Advocate of Peace through Justice* 87, no. 12 (1925): 662–64. http://www.jstor.org/stable/20661091.

Utpat, V. N. *Savarkar: Aakshep ani Khandan* [Savarkar: arguments and clarifications]. Pandharpur: printed by the author, 2004.

Valimbe, V. S. *Swatantryavira Savarkar* [Freedom fighter Savarkar]. Pune: Kesari Publications, 1963.

Varhadpande, V. K, V. S. Jog, and Shrimati M. Pande, eds. *Garudjhepa: Savarkar Gaurava Grantha* [Eagles' flight: essays in praise of Savarkar]. Nagpur: Vijay Prakashan, 1983.

Vartak, Shridhar Raghunath. *Bharatiya Svatantryache Ranajhunjar: Abhinav Bharat Smarak Chitraprabodhini* [Warriors of Indian freedom struggle: Abhinava Bharat Smarak Chitraprabodhini]. Pune: Kal Prakashan, 1970.

———. *Svatantryaveer Savarkaranci Prabhaval* [People associated with freedom fighter Savarkar]. Nashik: printed by the author, 1972.

Velkar, Pratap. *Tisara Savarakara arthata viragrani Dr Narayaṇa Damodara Savarakara* [The third Savarkar meaning the brave Dr. Narayana Damodar Savarkar]. Pune: Manorama Prakashan, 2002.

Visana, Vikram. "Savarkar before Hindutva: Sovereignty, Republicanism, and Populism in India, c. 1900–1920." *Modern Intellectual History* 18, no. 4 (2021): 1106–29.

Vohra, Rajendra ed. *Adhunikata ani parampara: Ekonisavya satakatila Maharastra: Pra Ya Di Phadake Gaurava Grantha* [Modernity and tradition: nineteenth-century Maharastra: festschrift for Professor Y. D. Phaadke]. Pune: Pratima Prakashan,: 2000.

Vyas, V. D. *Swatantryaveer Vinayak Damodar Savarkar Yanchya Jeevanavar Khand Kavya* [A long poem on the life of Savarkar]. Solapur: printed by the author, 1983.

Wagle, N. K. *Writers, Editors and Reformers: Social and Political Transformations of Maharashtra 1830–1930*. New Delhi: Manohar, 1999.

Wagle, Narendra K. "Ritual and Change in Early Nineteenth-Century Society in Maharashtra: Vedokta Disputes in Baroda, Pune and Satara, 1824–1838." In *Religion and Society in Maharashtra*, edited by N. K. Wagle and Milton Israel. Toronto: The Centre for South Asian Studies, 1987.

Wagner, Kim A. *Amritsar 1919: An Empire of Fear and the Making of a Massacre*. New Haven, CT: Yale University Press, 2019.

Walinjkar, Atmaram. *Uttar Konkan Dalitmukti calwal parivartanace sandarbha: 1900–1960* [The progressive context of North Konkan Dalit emancipation movement]. Thane: Dimple Publications, 2007.

Wasti, Syed Tanvir. "Sir Syed Ahmad Khan and the Turks." *Middle Eastern Studies* 46, no. 4 (2010): 529–42.

Weismann, Itzchak, and Fruma Zachs, eds. *Ottoman Reform and Muslim Regeneration: Studies in Honour of Butrus Abu-Manneh*. London: I.B. Tauris, 2005.

Willis, John. "Debating the Caliphate: Islam and Nation in the Work of Rashid Rida and Abul Kalam Azad." *The International History Review* 32, no. 4 (2010): 711–32.

Wolf, Siegfried O. "Vinayak Damodar Savarkar's 'Strategic Agnosticism': Compilation of His Socio-political Philosophy and Worldview." *Heidelberg Papers in South Asian and Comparative Politics* 51 (2010).

Zachariah, Benjamin. "A Voluntary Gleichschaltung? Indian Perspectives towards a Non-Eurocentric Understanding of Fascism." *The Journal of Transcultural Studies* 5 no. 2 (2014): 63–100. https://doi.org/10.11588/ts.2014.2.15554.

Zaman, Muhammad Qasim. *Ashraf Ali Thanawi: Islam in Modern South Asia*. New York: Simon and Schuster, 2012.

———. "Evolving Conceptions of Ijtihād in Modern South Asia." *Islamic Studies* 49, no. 1 (2010): 5–36.

———. *Modern Islamic Thought in a Radical Age: Religious Authority and Internal Criticism*. New York: Cambridge University Press, 2012.

Zekeria, M. "The New Turkish Caliph." *Current History (1916–1940)* 17, no. 4 (1923): 669–71.

Zelliott, Eleanor. "Experiments in Dalit Education: Maharashtra, 1850–1947." In *Education and the Deprivileged: Nineteenth and Twentieth Century India*, edited by Sabyasachi Bhattacharya, 35–49. Hyderabad: Orient Longman, 2002.

———. "A Medieval Encounter between Hindu and Muslim: Eknath's Drama-Poem *Hindu-Turk Samvad*." In *India's Islamic Traditions, 711–1750*, edited by Richard M. Eaton, 64–83. New Delhi: Oxford University Press, 2003.

Zürcher, Erik Jan. *Political Opposition in the Early Turkish Republic: The Progressive Republican Party 1924–1925*. Leiden: E. J. Brill, 1991.

INDEX

A NOTE ON THE TYPE

This book has been composed in Arno, an Old-style serif typeface in the classic Venetian tradition, designed by Robert Slimbach at Adobe.